Frommer's®

Portugal

D1117955

Other Great Guides for Your Trip:

Frommer's Europe

Frommer's Europe from $50 a Day

Frommer's France

Frommer's Spain

Frommer's®

16th
Edition

Portugal

by Darwin Porter and Danforth Prince

IDG Books Worldwide, Inc.
An International Data Group Company
Foster City, CA • Chicago, IL • Indianapolis, IN • New York, NY

ABOUT THE AUTHORS

A native of North Carolina, **Darwin Porter** was bureau chief for the *Miami Herald* when he was 21 and was assigned to write the very first edition of a Frommer's guide devoted solely to one European country. Since then he has written numerous best-selling Frommer guides. He is joined by **Danforth Prince,** formerly of the Paris bureau of *The New York Times,* who has lived and traveled in Italy extensively. This team writes a number of best-selling Frommer's guides, notably England, France, Germany, and the Caribbean.

IDG BOOKS WORLDWIDE, INC.

An International Data Group Company
919 E. Hillsdale Blvd.
Suite 400
Foster City, CA 94404

Find us online at **www.frommers.com**

ISBN 0-02-863601-5
ISSN 1042-8399

Editor: Marie Morris
Production Editor: Jenaffer Brandt
Page Creation by Heather Pope, Angel Perez, and David Faust
Design by Michele Laseau
Digital Carography by Hans Anderson
Staff Cartographers: John Decamillis, Roberta Stockwell

SPECIAL SALES

For general information on IDG Books Worldwide's books in the U.S., please call our Consumer Customer Service department at 1-800-762-2974. For reseller information, including discounts, bulk sales, customized editions, and premium sales, please call our Reseller Customer Service department at 1-800-434-3422.

Manufactured in the United States of America

5 4 3 2 1

Contents

List of Maps

An Invitation to the Reader

In researching this book, we discovered many wonderful places—hotels, restaurants, shops, and more. We're sure you'll find others. Please tell us about them, so we can share the information with your fellow travelers in upcoming editions. If you were disappointed with a recommendation, we'd love to know that, too. Please write to:

Frommer's Portugal 16th Edition
IDG Travel
1633 Broadway
New York, NY 10019

An Additional Note

Please be advised that travel information is subject to change at any time—and this is especially true of prices. We therefore suggest that you write or call ahead for confirmation when making your travel plans. The authors, editors, and publisher cannot be held responsible for the experiences of readers while traveling. Your safety is important to us, however, so we encourage you to stay alert and be aware of your surroundings. Keep a close eye on cameras, purses, and wallets, all favorite targets of thieves and pickpockets.

What the Symbols Mean

✪ Frommer's Favorites

Our favorite places and experiences—outstanding for quality, value, or both.

The following abbreviations are used for credit cards:

AE	American Express	EURO	Eurocard
CB	Carte Blanche	JCB	Japan Credit Bank
DC	Diners Club	MC	MasterCard
DISC	Discover	V	Visa
ER	EnRoute		

Find Frommer's Online

Arthur Frommer's Budget Travel Online (**www.frommers.com**) offers more than 6,000 pages of up-to-the-minute travel information—including the latest bargains and candid, personal articles updated daily by Arthur Frommer himself. No other Web site offers such comprehensive and timely coverage of the world of travel.

The Best of Portugal

Centuries ago, Portugal was a pioneer of worldwide exploration. Until recently, however, it was never as successful in attracting visitors to its own shores. Outside of greater Lisbon, the Algarve, and the island of Madeira, Portugal remained unknown and undiscovered by the mainstream visitor for many decades.

Today's travelers are beginning to realize that Portugal was unjustly overlooked. It offers sandy beaches, art treasures, flavorful cuisine, a unique form of architecture (*Manueline*), charming handcrafts, a mild climate, relatively moderate hotel rates, and polite and friendly people. Only two million annual visitors came to Portugal in the late 1970s. The number swelled to 20 million in the mid-1990s, and an explosion of hotel and resort building has kept pace.

Despite its small size—it's 140 miles wide and 380 miles long—Portugal is one of the most rewarding travel destinations in Europe. Exploring its towns, cities, villages, and countryside will likely take far longer than expected, because there is so much richness and variety along the way.

The people, whose warmth is legendary, inhabit a majestic land of extraordinary variety. You'll see almond trees in the African-looking Algarve; cork forests and fields of golden wheat in Alentejo; ranches in Ribatejo; narrow, winding streets in the Alfama in Lisbon; ox-drawn carts crossing the plains of Minho; and vineyards in the Douro. Azaleas, rhododendrons, and canna grow for miles on end; the sound of *fado* music drifts out of small cafes; windmills clack in the Atlantic breezes; sardine boats bob in the bays; and gleaming whitewashed houses glisten in the sun. The sea is never far away.

This list is an embarkation point for the discoveries, like those by the mariners of old, that you'll eventually make on your own.

1 The Best Travel Experiences

- **Hiking in the Algarve:** Portugal's incredible physical beauty makes it a spectacular place for outdoor activities. In the southern Algarve region's low-lying lagoons and rocky highlands, the panoramas extend for miles over the nearby ocean. Especially rewarding is trekking through the territory near Sagres, which has retained its mystical hold on journeyers since it was known as "the end of the world." Other worthwhile hikes include the footpaths around the villages of Silves and Monchique, where eroded river valleys have changed little since the Moorish occupation.

- *Pousada*-**Hopping:** After World War II, the Portuguese government recognized that the patrimony of its great past was desperately in need of renovation. It transformed dozens of monasteries, palaces, and convents into hotels, honoring the historical authenticity of their architectural cores. Today's travelers can intimately experience some of Portugal's greatest architecture by staying in a *pousada*, part of a chain of state-owned and -operated hotels. The rooms might not be as opulent as you'd hoped, and the government-appointed staffs will probably be more bureaucratic than you'd care to encounter. Nonetheless, pousada-hopping rewards the visitor with insights into the Portugal of long ago.

- **Playing Golf by the Sea:** British merchants trading in Portugal's excellent wines imported the sport around 1890. Until the 1960s, it remained a diversion only for the very wealthy. Then an explosion of interest from abroad—coupled with reasonably priced land, a climate similar to California's, and topography loaded with the surprises that golf enthusiasts love—led to the creation of at least 30 major courses. Today, Portugal is a prime golf vacation site. Many courses lie near Estoril and in the southern Algarve. The combination of great weather, verdant fairways, and azure seas and skies is almost addictive (as if golf fanatics needed additional motivation). And there's never a shortage of terraces on which to enjoy Portuguese wine after the game is over.

- **Swooning to *Fado*:** After soccer, *fado* (which translates as "fate") music is the national obsession. A lyrical homage to the bruised or broken heart, fado assumes forms that are as old as the troubadours. Its four-line stanzas of unrhymed verse, performed by such legendary stars as Amália Rodrigues, capture the nation's collective unconscious. Hearing the lament of the *fadistas* in clubs is the best way to appreciate the melancholy dignity of Iberia's western edge.

- **Finding a Solitary Beach:** Portugal has long been famous for the glamour and style of the beaches near Estoril, Cascais, Setúbal, and Sesimbra. More recently, the Algarve, with its 125 miles of tawny sands, gorgeous blue-green waters, and rocky coves, has captivated the imagination of northern Europeans. While the most famous beaches are likely to be very crowded, you can find solitude on the sands if you stop beside lonely expanses of any coastal road in northern Portugal.

- **Fishing in Rich Coastal Waters:** Portugal's position on the Atlantic, its unpolluted waters, and its flowing rivers encourage concentrations of fish. You won't be the first to plumb these waters—Portugal fed itself for hundreds of generations using nets and lines, and its maritime and fishing traditions are among the most entrenched in Europe. The mild weather allows fishing year-round for more than 200 species, including varieties not seen anywhere else (such as the 6-foot-long scabbard). The country's rivers and lakes produce three species of trout, black bass, and salmon; the cold Atlantic abounds in sea bass, shark, tope, grouper, skate, and swordfish.

- **Trekking to the End of the World:** For medieval Europeans, the southwestern tip of Portugal represented the final frontier of human security and power. Beyond that point, the oceans were dark and fearful, filled with demons waiting to devour the bodies and souls of mariners foolhardy enough to sail upon them. Adding Sagres and its peninsula to the Portuguese nation cost thousands of lives in battle against the Moors, and getting there required weeks of travel over rocky deserts. Making a pilgrimage to this outpost is one of the loneliest and most majestic experiences in Portugal. Come here to pay your respects to the navigators who embarked from Sagres on journeys to death or glory. Half a millennium later, the excitement of those long-ago voyages still permeates this lonely corner. See chapter 8.

Portugal

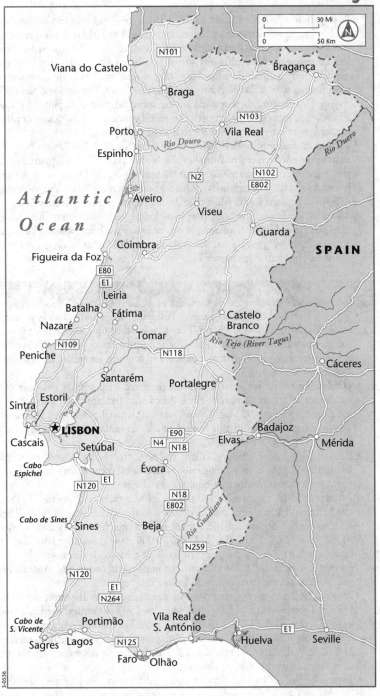

- **Losing It at a Spa:** Compared to the sybaritic luxury of spas in Germany and France, Portuguese spas are underaccessorized, and by California's frenetic standards they're positively sleepy. Still, central and northern Portugal share about half a dozen spas whose sulfur-rich waters have been considered therapeutic since the days of the ancient Romans. Luso, Monte Real, and Curia are the country's most famous spas, followed closely by Caldas do Gerês, Vimeiro, and São Pedro do Sul. Don't expect the latest in choreographed aerobics and spinning classes; instead, sink into communion with nature, rid your body of the toxins of urban life, and retire early every night for recuperative sleep.
- **Tasting & Touring in Port Wine Country:** Across the Rio Douro from the heart of the northern city of Porto lies Vila Nova de Gaia, the headquarters of the port-wine trade since the 1600s. From vineyards along the Douro, wine is transported to "lodges" (warehouses), where it is matured, bottled, and eventually shipped around the world. More than 25 companies, including such well-known names as Sandeman, maintain port-wine lodges here. Each offers free guided tours, always ending with a tasting of one or two of the house wines. The tourist office in Porto will provide you with a map if you'd like to drive along the Douro to see the vineyards. See chapter 11.

2　The Best Towns to Visit

- **Sintra:** Since the Moorish occupation, Portuguese kings and nobles have recognized this town's irresistible charm. They have lavished time and money to create a denser concentration of beautiful villas and gardens than you'll find anywhere else in Portugal. At least five major palaces and convents are tucked amid the lush vegetation. See chapter 5.
- **Óbidos:** This town is the most perfectly preserved 13th-century village in central Portugal. Its historic authenticity is the primary concern of the population of less than 5,000. For 600 years Óbidos was the personal property of Portuguese queens, a symbolic love offering from their adoring husbands. Óbidos has always breathed romance. See chapter 7.
- **Nazaré:** This folkloric fishing village in central Portugal produces wonderful handcrafts. The town has a strong sense of traditional culture that's distinctly different from that of nearby communities. See chapter 7.
- **Fátima:** In 1913, an apparition of the Virgin Mary appeared to three shepherd children from Fátima, who were called upon to spread a message of peace. Their story was at first discounted, then embraced by a church hierarchy under assault by the ravages of World War I. Later, 70,000 people assembled on the site claimed to have seen a similar apparition. Today, Fátima is the most-visited pilgrimage site in Iberia, home to dozens of imposing churches and monuments, vital elements in the town's religious fervor. See chapter 7.
- **Évora:** A well-preserved ancient Roman temple rises across the street from convents and monasteries that flourished when the kings of Portugal used this town as their capital in the 12th century. These buildings combine with remnants of the Moorish occupation to form one of the most alluring architectural medleys in Europe. Although not large, Évora is one of the country's most perfectly preserved architectural gems. See chapter 9.
- **Tomar:** Beginning in the 12th century, the Knights Templar and later the Knights of Christ (two warlike and semimonastic sects) designated Tomar as their Portuguese headquarters. They lavished the town with adornments over the

centuries until it looked, as it does today, like a living monument to the architecture of medieval Portugal. See chapter 9.

- **Coimbra:** The country's academic center, this town boasts a university with roots in the Middle Ages, a rich historic core, and a tradition of troubadour-style singing that's one of the most vital in Iberia. See chapter 10.
- **Porto:** The second city of Portugal, Porto has rich associations with the port-wine trade. The town is often overlooked in favor of Lisbon. Entrepreneurs who returned home after making their fortunes in Brazil built some of the town's most imposing villas in the late 19th century. See chapter 11.
- **Guimarães:** The birthplace of the country's first king, Afonso Henríques, and the core from which the country expanded, Guimarães is the cradle of Portugal. The town suffers from a benign malady that the French call *un embarras de richesses.* Its medieval core is one of the most authentic anywhere. The town was also the birthplace of Gil Vicente (1470?–1536?), a playwright who has been referred to as the "Shakespeare of Portugal." See chapter 12.
- **Viana do Castelo:** This town, the northern city with the strongest folkloric traditions, is noted for pottery, women's regional dresses, abundant rainfall, and a collection of distinctive and dignified public buildings. Its heyday was in the 1500s, when fleets departed from here to fish for cod as far away as Newfoundland. Profits from their activities helped pay for the town's handsome collection of Manueline buildings. See chapter 12.

3 The Best Beaches

- **Costa do Sol:** Sometimes called the Estoril Coast, this stretch of seafront extends 20 miles west of Lisbon. Its two major resorts are Estoril and Cascais. Once the playground of the wintering wealthy, including exiled royalty, the area now attracts throngs of tourists, mainly from northern Europe. See chapter 5.
- **The Algarve:** This region at the southern tip of Portugal gained its place on world tourist maps because of its string of beautiful, clean, sandy beaches. Tawny cliffs and surf border miles of unspoiled seashore. Lovely coves, caves, and grottos—some accessible only by boat—add to the region's allure. There are hundreds of beaches to choose from. Albufeira and Praia da Rocha are set against a backdrop of towering rock formations; the best cove beach is at Lagos, a former Moorish town with a deep-water harbor and wide bay. Once here, head for Praia do Camilo, one of the beaches on the promontory south of Lagos. See chapter 8.
- **Alentejo:** The country's largest and most sparsely populated province is associated with dusty fields of cork and olive trees. But savvy travelers know that it has some of the best and least crowded beaches in Portugal. They stretch from the southern extremity of the province at Odeceize north to the tip of the Tróia Peninsula (see chapter 6). Even in July and August, when most European beaches barely allow you to spread out a towel, these beaches seem isolated. The best include Praia Grande and Praia do Carvalhal at Almograve. The beaches at Porto Covo and Vila Nova de Milfontes offer the standard beach amenities and a few restaurants; elsewhere, don't expect much in the way of facilities. See chapter 9.
- **The Beiras:** In central Portugal, north of Lisbon, some of the finest beaches in Europe open onto the Atlantic. Like gems in a necklace, good, sandy beaches stretch from Praia de Leirosa north to Praia de Espinho. The surf can be heavy and the undertow strong. Major resorts include Figueira da Foz and Buarcos. The beaches between Praia de Mira and Costa Nova are more secluded. See chapter 10.

- **Costa Verde:** As the northern coastline approaches Galicia in Spain, the Atlantic waters grow colder, and even in summer they're likely to be windswept. But on certain days they're among the most dramatic in Europe. We like the wide, sandy beach at Ponte de Lima, but there are many others. Notable destinations are the resort of Espinho, south of Porto, and other beach meccas, including Póvoa de Varzim and Ofir, which have some of the best hotels, restaurants, and water-sports equipment in the country. See chapter 11.

4 The Best Hotels

- **Four Seasons Hotel The Ritz Lisbon** (Lisbon; ☎ 800/332-3442 in the U.S., or 21/383-20-20): Built in the 1950s and host to a roster that reads like a who's who of international glamour, the Ritz is one of Portugal's legendary hotels. Hallways and lobbies are appropriately expansive; everywhere in the hotel, you'll get the impression that a swanky reception is about to begin. See chapter 3.
- **York House** (Lisbon; ☎ 21/396-24-35): A former 17th-century convent and private home, York House is *the* place to stay in Lisbon. It abounds with climbing vines, antiques, four-poster beds, and Oriental carpeting—fittings and furnishings that maintain the building's historic character without flattening your wallet. See chapter 3.
- **Hotel Albatroz** (Cascais; ☎ 21/483-28-21): In a garden overlooking the Atlantic, this inn was originally built as the summer residence of the dukes of Loulé. Since its transformation into a stylish hotel, its aristocratic elegance has drawn guests from throughout Europe. Service, as you'd expect, is impeccable. See chapter 5.
- **Palácio Hotel** (Estoril; ☎ 21/464-80-00): The Palácio enjoyed its heyday during the 1950s and 1960s, when every deposed monarch of Europe seemed to disappear, with an entourage, into the art deco hotel's sumptuous suites. The result: the curious survival in Estoril of the royal ambience of a Europe gone by. Today, "the Palace" maintains a staff whose old-timers are among the best in Europe at offering royal treatment to guests. See chapter 5.
- **Hotel Palácio de Seteais** (Sintra; ☎ 21/923-32-00): One of the most elegant hotels in Portugal bears one of the country's most ironic names. In 1807, a treaty ending the Napoleonic campaign in Portugal was signed here, with terms so humiliating to the Portuguese that they labeled the building the "Palace of the Seven Sighs." Any sighing you're likely to do today will be from pleasure—at the setting, the lavish gardens, and the reminders of an old-world way of life. See chapter 5.
- **Hotel de Lagos** (Lagos; ☎ 282/76-99-67): This hotel is a 20th-century castle on 3 acres of hilltop above one of the largest towns in the Algarve. Some visitors compare the hotel to the elegant haciendas of Latin America; everyone calls it luxurious. See chapter 8.
- **Le Méridien Dona Filipa** (Vale de Lobo, Almancil; ☎ 289/39-41-41): Rising above the sea, this hotel is comfortable, modern, well designed, and sophisticated, but the most stunning feature is the 450 acres surrounding it. Part of the land is devoted to a superb golf course. Don't let the severe exterior fool you—the inside is richly appointed with Chinese and Portuguese accessories, many of them antique. See chapter 8.
- **Palace Hotel do Buçaco** (Buçaco; ☎ 231/93-01-01): This palace, built between 1888 and 1907 as a sylvan refuge for the royal family, saw tragedy early. A year after its completion, the king and his oldest son were assassinated, leaving

Queen Amélia to grieve within its *azulejo*-sheathed walls. In 1910, the palace's enterprising Swiss chef persuaded the government to allow him to transform the place into an upscale hotel. Bittersweet memories of its royal past still seem to linger within the thick walls. See chapter 10.

- **Infante de Sagres** (Porto; ☎ 22/200-81-01): A textile magnate built this hotel in 1951 in the style of a Portuguese manor house. Its elegant detailing makes it appear much older than it is. It's the most nostalgic, elegant, and ornate hotel in Porto. The managers began their careers here as teenage bellboys, and the staff members have obvious pride in their hotel. See chapter 11.

- **Reid's Palace** (Funchal, Madeira; ☎ 800/223-6800 in the U.S., or 291/71-71-71): For more than a century, Reid's has fulfilled the colonial fantasies of every British imperialist abroad. Set on a rocky promontory, it serves tea promptly at 4pm, contains English antiques that the Portuguese staff waxes once a week, and plays chimes to announce the beginning of the dinner service. Founded in 1891 and enlarged in 1968, it features terraced gardens spilling down to the sea and a very correct clientele that once included Winston Churchill. See chapter 13.

5 The Best Pousadas

Pousadas are government-run accommodations, most of which occupy historically important buildings, including monasteries, convents, and palaces. Emblematic of the Portuguese aesthetic, they afford a glimpse into the country's storied past. Here are five of the most intriguing.

- **Pousada de São Filipe** (Setúbal; ☎ 265/52-38-44): During the 1500s, the structure served as a defensive link in a chain of fortresses surrounding Lisbon. Today, it boasts antique *azulejos* (glazed earthenware tiles), panoramic views of the town, and a keen sense of Portuguese history. The rooms are simple (some might say monastic), but comfortable and tidy. See chapter 6.

- **Pousada do Castelo** (Óbidos; ☎ 262/95-91-05): This pousada lies in a wing of the castle that protects one of the most perfectly preserved medieval towns in Portugal. In 1285 King Dinis offered the castle—along with the entire village—to his beloved Queen Isabel. Inside, the medieval aesthetic coexists with improved plumbing, electricity, and unobtrusive contemporary comforts. See chapter 7.

- **Pousada de Santa Luzia** (Elvas; ☎ 268/62-21-94): It opened in 1942 during the most horrible days of World War II, near the strategic border crossing between neutral Portugal and Fascist Spain. Vaguely Moorish in design, with two low-slung stories, it was most recently renovated in 1992. It offers comfortable, colorful lodgings. See chapter 9.

- **Pousada da Rainha Santa Isabel** (Estremoz; ☎ 268/33-20-75): Housed in a structure originally built during the Middle Ages to protect the Portuguese interior against invasions from nearby Spain, the Santa Isabel is the most lavish pousada in Portugal. Reproductions of 17th-century antiques, about an acre of gleaming marble, and elaborately detailed tapestries create one of the most authentic old-fashioned decors in the region. Guests have included Vasco da Gama, who was received here by Dom Manuel before the explorer's departure for India. See chapter 9.

- **Pousada dos Lóios** (Évora; ☎ 266/70-40-51): This pousada was conceived as a monastery and rebuilt in 1485 adjacent to the town's ancient Roman temple. The purity of its design and the absence of encroachments from the modern world contribute to one of the most aesthetically thrilling experiences in Portugal. Inside there are no traces left of its original austerity—everything is luxurious and comfortable. See chapter 9.

6 The Best Restaurants

- **Gambrinus** (Lisbon; ☎ 21/342-14-66): It isn't as upscale as some of its competitors, or the preferred rendezvous of the country's most distinguished aristocrats. Nonetheless, this is one of the hippest, best-managed seafood restaurants in Lisbon; the stand-up bar proffers an astonishing array of shellfish. Enjoy a glass of dry white port accompanied by some of the most exotic seafood in the Atlantic. See chapter 3.
- **Tágide** (Lisbon; ☎ 21/342-07-20): The ambience is Old Portugal, with French overtones in the cuisine and decor. The setting, an antique manor house overlooking the Tagus, is suitably noble. The food represents the city's most refined versions of Portuguese regional dishes, particularly such fresh fish courses as scallops of salted cod and baby octopus in red-wine sauce. International dishes—mainly French—are no less succulent, especially when accompanied by a selection of one of the 200 or so bottles of Portuguese and French wine in the cellar. See chapter 3.
- **Casa da Comida** (Lisbon; ☎ 21/388-53-76): This place is probably at its best on foggy evenings, when roaring fireplaces remove the damp chill from the air. Don't let the prosaic name fool you—some visitors prefer its Portuguese-French cuisine over the food at any other restaurant in Lisbon. Portions are ample, and the ambience is bracing and healthful. See chapter 3.
- **Conventual** (Lisbon; ☎ 21/390-91-96): The facade that shields this restaurant from the medieval square is as severe as that of a convent—which in fact the Conventual used to be. Inside, you're likely to find the prime minister of Portugal dining with assorted ministers. You'll always find a collection of panels from antique churches, and rich but refined cuisine based on the bourgeois traditions of Old Portugal. See chapter 3.
- **Cozinha Velha** (Queluz; ☎ 21/435-02-32): During the 1700s, food for the monarchy's most lavish banquets was prepared here (the name means "old kitchen"). Today, the high-ceilinged kitchens serve an unusual restaurant whose cuisine reflects the old days of Portuguese royalty. The Portuguese dishes include *cataplana,* a savory fish stew with clams, shrimp, and monkfish. Equally outstanding is soufflélike *bacalhau espiritual* (codfish), which takes 45 minutes to prepare and should be ordered when you make your reservation. The restaurant is celebrated for its desserts, many of which are based on ancient convent recipes. See chapter 5.
- **Reijos Restaurant** (Cascais; ☎ 21/483-03-11): Founded by a Portuguese-American partnership, this unpretentious place is convivial, bustling, and international. The result is a pleasing mixture of culinary inspirations from both sides of the Atlantic. The menu also features many Portuguese regional dishes, including *bacalhau à Reijos* (dry codfish baked with cheese sauce). If you're homesick for such delights as roast beef, lobster Thermidor, pepper steak, or even baked Virginia ham, you'll find these dishes on the menu as well. See chapter 5.
- **Restaurante Porto de Santa Maria** (Praia do Guincho; ☎ 21/487-02-40 or 21/487-10-36): The understated beige-and-white decor highlights the restaurant's bubbling aquarium and sea view. The menu lists every conceivable kind of

shellfish, served in the freshest possible combinations in a justifiably popular dining room. See chapter 5.

- **Four Seasons** (in the Palácio Hotel, Estoril; ☎ **21/464-80-00**): This tranquil restaurant, with its rich colors and artful accents, has been a fixture in Estoril since the days when deposed European monarchs assembled here with their entourages. High glamour, old-world service, impeccably prepared international cuisine, and towering expense are this place's hallmarks. See chapter 5.
- **Hotel La Réserve** (Santa Bárbara de Nexe; ☎ **289/99-94-74**): The finest dining room on the Algarve (which bristles with less qualified competitors), this restaurant serves international cuisine. Elegant but not stuffy, the place is eminently familiar with the dining rituals of customers from virtually everywhere in Europe. See chapter 8.
- **Casa Velha** (Quinta do Lago, near Almancil; ☎ **289/39-49-83**): On a rocky hilltop above the modern resort of Quinta do Lago (with which it is not associated), this restaurant occupies a century-old farmhouse. The kitchens have been modernized for the preparation of gourmet food. The sophisticated cuisine derives from preparations of upscale French and Portuguese recipes. See chapter 8.

7 The Best Romantic Getaways

If Iberia inspires you with thoughts of love (or merely escape), here are five of the country's most romantic getaways.

- **Guincho:** On the Estoril Coast, 5½ miles northwest of Cascais, this is the westernmost point in continental Europe. It's a dramatic, spectacular site where waves crash against three sides of a restored 17th-century fortress (now the Hotel do Guincho, one of the most unusual, luxurious hotels in Europe). Balconies—perhaps best shared with a loved one—overlook the panoramic scene, with beaches on both sides. The crashing surf makes good background music for a torrid affair straight out of a romance novel. See chapter 5.
- **Sintra:** Since the time of the Moorish occupation, Sintra has been considered one of the most beautiful and desirable sites in Portugal. The Moors began the tradition by erecting a pair of fortresses; since then, Sintra has been favored by Catholic monarchs, industry moguls, and members of the Portuguese gentry. See chapter 5.
- **Serra da Arrábida:** This whale-shaped ridge never exceeds 500 feet in height. The masses of wildflowers that flank its sides are among the most colorful and varied in Iberia. The serra lies between Sesimbra and Setúbal, across the estuary of the Tagus from Lisbon. En route from Lisbon, you'll find crowded and secluded beaches, a medieval Capuchin monastery (the Convento Novo), and a smattering of good restaurants. The town of Sesimbra, with its historic, sleepy main square and ruined fortresses, offers bars, restaurants, and insight into the Iberia of a bygone era. See chapter 6.
- **Óbidos:** After Dom Afonso Henríques wrenched the village from the Moors, he offered Óbidos as a wedding gift to his betrothed, his beloved Isabel. (The village remained the personal property of the queens of Portugal until 1834.) Today, the town's ramparts, its quintet of cobblestone streets, and its 14th-century facades make Óbidos the most romantic spot in Portugal. See chapter 7.
- **Buçaco:** This forest figures more prominently in the national psyche than any other in Portugal, partly because of its association with the doomed royal family. In the 7th century, Benedictine and Capuchin monks labored to diversify the

number of exotic trees that flourish in the forest. Around 1900, the Portuguese royal family built a palace here—but spent only a few summers before assassinations and revolutions changed the role of the monarchy forever. Today, the palace functions as a supremely romantic hotel. See chapter 10.

8 The Best Palaces & Castles

Whether designed for defense or for grandeur, Portuguese castles are among the most romantic buildings in Europe. Here are five of the most interesting.

- **Castelo São Jorge,** the Alfama, Lisbon: Before the Romans' occupation of Iberia and during every regime since their departure, this hilltop has been valued as a fortification to protect settlements along the Tagus. Today the bulky castle crowns one of the most densely populated medieval neighborhoods of Lisbon, the Alfama. It encompasses a nostalgic collection of thick stone walls, medieval battlements, Catholic and feudal iconography, verdant landscaping, and sweeping views of one of Europe's greatest harbors. See chapter 4.

- **Palácio Nacional de Queluz,** near Lisbon: Designed for the presentation of music and royal receptions in the 1700s, this castle was modeled as a more intimate version of Versailles. It's a symmetrical building ringed with gardens, fountains, and sculptures of mythical heroes and maidens. Although gilt, crystal, and frescoes fill its interior, most Portuguese are proudest of the *azulejos* room, where hand-painted blue-and-white tiles depict day-to-day life in the Portuguese colonies of Macao and Brazil. See chapter 5.

- **Palácio Nacional de Pena,** Sintra: Only a cosmopolitan 19th-century courtier could have produced this eclectic, expensive melange of architectural styles. Set in a 500-acre walled park, it was commissioned by the German-born consort of the Portuguese queen; the pastiche of styles reminds some visitors of the Bavarian castles of Mad King Ludwig. Appointed with heavy furnishings and rich ornamentation, it's a symbol of the Portuguese monarchs in their most aesthetically decadent stages. See chapter 5.

- **Castelo dos Mouros,** Sintra: In the 19th century the monarchs ordered that this castle, evocative of the Moorish occupation of Portugal, remain as a ruined ornament to embellish their sprawling parks and gardens. Set near the much larger, much more ornate Pena palace (see above), the squat, thick-walled fortress was begun around A.D. 750 by the Moors and captured with the help of Scandinavian Crusaders in 1147. It retains its jagged battlements, a quartet of eroded towers, and a ruined Romanesque chapel erected by the Portuguese as a symbol of their newfound domination of former Moorish territories. See chapter 5.

- **Palace Hotel do Buçaco,** in the Forest of Buçaco: Of all the buildings in this list, the Palace of Buçaco is the most important national icon. Completed in 1907, it's also the only one that operates as a hotel, allowing visitors to sleep within the walls of a former royal palace permeated with Portuguese *saudade* (best translated as "longing" or "nostalgia"). Constructed from marble, bronze, stained glass, and exotic hardwoods and inspired by the greatest buildings in the empire, it represents, more poignantly than any other Portuguese palace, the final days of the doomed aristocracy. See chapter 10.

9 The Best Museums

- **Museu da Fundação Calouste Gulbenkian,** Lisbon: Its namesake was an Armenian oil czar, Calouste Gulbenkian (1869–1955), whose fortune derived from a 5% royalty on most of the oil pumped out of Iraq. His eclectic collections of Asian and European sculpture, paintings, antique coins, carpets, and furniture are on display in a modern compound in a lush garden. Easily the most famous museum in the country, it operates as a private charitable foundation in Portugal, Britain, and France. See chapter 4.

- **National Coach Museum (Museu Nacional dos Coches),** Lisbon: Founded by Queen Amélia in 1904, when the horse-drawn buggy was becoming obsolete, this museum is on the premises of the riding school of the Palácio do Belém (the official home of the Portuguese president). It contains dozens of magnificent state carriages, some decorated with depictions of Portugal's maritime discoveries. See chapter 4.
- **National Museum of Medieval Art (Museu Nacional de Arte Antiga),** Lisbon: In the 1830s, the power of many of Portugal's fabulously wealthy monasteries was violently curbed. Many of the monasteries' art treasures, including the country's best collection of Portuguese primitives, as well as gold and silver plate crafted from raw materials mined in India, are displayed at the 17th-century palace of the counts of Alvor. See chapter 4.
- **Maritime Museum (Museu de Marinha),** Lisbon: The most important maritime museum in the world—a rich tribute to Portugal's Age of Exploration—is in the west wing of the Jerónimos Monastery. The thousands of displays include royal galleons dripping with gilt and ringed with depictions of saltwater dragons and sea serpents. See chapter 4.
- **Museu Machado de Castro,** Coimbra: In the cradle of Portuguese scholarship, the ancient university town of Coimbra, this museum has the world's largest inventory of sculpture by the 18th-century master Machado de Castro. It also houses a worthy collection of religious sculpture crafted between 1300 and 1790. The setting was originally conceived as an archbishop's palace in 1592. See chapter 10.

10 The Best Churches & Abbeys

- **Jerónimos Monastery (Mosteiro dos Jerónimos),** Belém: More than any other ecclesiastical building in Portugal, this complex represents the wealth that poured into Lisbon from the colonies during the Age of Discovery. Begun in 1502 in Belém, the seaport near the gates of Lisbon, it's the world's most distinctive Manueline church. Richly ornate and unlike any other building in Europe, it has, among other features, columns carved in patterns inspired by the rigging of Portuguese caravels laden with riches from Brazil and India. See chapter 4.
- **Convento de Mafra (Palácio Nacional de Mafra):** The convent was originally intended to house only about a dozen monks, but after the king of Portugal was blessed with an heir, he became obsessed with its architecture and vastly augmented its scale. Construction began in 1717, and funding came from gold imported from Portuguese settlements in Brazil. Some 50,000 laborers toiled more than 13 years to complete the convent. Today, the buildings alone cover 10 acres, contain more than 4,500 windows and doors, and include a royal palace as well as accommodations for 300 monks. A park whose outer wall measures more than 12 miles surrounds the complex. See chapter 5.
- **Monastery of St. Mary (Mosteiro de Santa Maria),** Alcobaça: More closely associated with the Portuguese wars against the Moors than almost any other site in Iberia, this monastery was a gift from the first Portuguese king (Afonso Henríques) to the Cistercians in 1153. As part of one of the most dramatic land-improvement

projects in Portuguese history, a community of ascetic monks cleared the surrounding forests, planted crops, dug irrigation ditches, and built a soaring church (completed in 1253) that critics cite as one of the purest and most artfully simple in Europe. See chapter 7.

- **Monastery of Santa Maria da Vitória (Mosteiro de Santa Maria da Vitória),** Batalha: In 1385, the Castilian Spaniards and the Portuguese, led by a youth who had been crowned king only a week before, fought one of the most crucial battles in Iberian history. The outcome ensured Portugal's continued independence for another 200 years. It was celebrated with the construction of the monastery at Batalha, whose style is a triumph of the Manueline and Flamboyant Gothic styles. See chapter 7.

- **Convento da Ordem de Cristo,** Tomar: Built in 1160 along the most hotly contested Muslim-Christian border in Iberia, this convent was originally intended as a monastic fortress. Successive building programs lasted half a millennium, ultimately creating a museum of diverse architectural styles. Some of the interior windows, adorned with stone carvings of ropes, coral, frigate masts, seaweed, cables, and cork trees, are the most splendid examples of Manueline decoration in the world. See chapter 9.

11 The Best Wines

For generations, much of what the English-speaking world knew about Portugal came from the reports that wine merchants brought back to Britain from the wineries of the Douro Valley. Today Portugal is famous throughout the world for its port wines, and many parts of central and northern Portugal are covered with well-tended vines sprouting from intricately laid-out terraces that descend verdant hillsides.

- **Port:** Known for decades as the "Englishman's wine," port was once the drink uncorked for toasting in England. In gentlemen's clubs, vintage port (only 1% of all port made) was dispensed from a crystal decanter. Later, when the English working classes started drinking less superior port in Midland mill towns, they often spiked it with lemon. Today, the French consume almost three times the amount of port that the British do.

   Some 40 varieties of grape go into making port. Made from grapes grown in rich lava soil, port today is either vintage or blended, and ranges from whites to full-bodied tawnies and reds. The latter is often consumed at the end of a meal with cheese, fruit, or nuts. You can visit a port-wine lodge to learn more about port—and, more important, to taste it. The best lodges to visit are concentrated in Vila Nova de Gaia, a suburb of Porto across the Douro from Porto's commercial center.

- **Vinhos Verdes** (pronounced "*veen*-yosh *vair*-desh"): These "green wines" are more lemony in color. Many come from the Minho district in northwest Portugal, which, like Galicia in the north of Spain, gets an abundance of rain. Cultivated in a humid atmosphere, the grapes are picked while young. Some wine aficionados don't consider this wine serious, finding it too light. With its fruity flavor, it's said to suggest the cool breezes of summer. It's often served with fish, and many Portuguese use it as a thirst quencher in the way an American might consume a soft drink. The finest vinhos verdes are from Monção, just south of the river Minho. Those from Amarante are also praised.

- **Dão**: Dão is produced from grapes grown just south of the Douro in the north's mountainous heartland. "Our vines have tender grapes" goes the saying throughout the valleys of Mondego and Dão, each split by a river. Summers are fiery hot and winters wet, cold, and often bitter. A lot of Dão wine is red, notably the *vinhos maduros,* matured in oak casks for nearly 2 years before being bottled. The wine is velvety in texture and often accompanies roasts. At almost every restaurant in Portugal, you'll encounter either *branco* (white) or Dão *tinto* (red). The best bottles of red Dão wine are the reserve ("RESERVA" is printed on the label). Other names to look for include Porta dos Cavaleiros and Terras Altas. (No one seems to agree on how to pronounce the name—*daw-ng, da-ow,* or, least flattering, *dung.*)

- **Madeira:** Grown from grapes rooted in the island's volcanic soil, this wine traces its origins to 1419. Its history is similar to that of port, in that it was highly prized by aristocratic British families. George Washington was among the wine's early admirers, although the Madeira he consumed little resembled the product bottled today. Modern Madeira wines are lighter and drier than the thick, sweet kinds favored by generations past.

  The wine, which is fortified and blended, includes such varieties as Malmsey, Malvasia, and Boal—sweet, heavy wines usually served with dessert or at the end of a meal. The less sweet Verdelho is often consumed as a light drink between meals, in much the same way that a Spaniard downs a glass of sherry. Dry and light, Sercial is best as an apéritif and is often served in Portugal with toasted and salted almonds. None of these wines are likely to be consumed with the main dish at dinner.

12 The Best Offbeat Trips

- **Horseback Riding Along the Coast:** The Atlantic Ocean is the livelihood of many Portuguese, and the inspiration for a number of rides along its beaches. An American company, Equitour, offers these treks. (For more details, refer to "The Active Vacation Planner" in chapter 2.) In addition to beach riding, there is also trekking through olive groves, vineyards, pine forests, and lagoons. Seeing this beautiful country from the back of a well-trained, even-tempered Lusitano is a rewarding and unusual travel experience.

- **Appreciating Manueline Architecture:** *Manuelino*—as it's known in Portuguese—marked a dramatic artistic shift from the late gothic style prevalent during the reign of King Dom Manuel. It mixes Christian motifs with shells, ropes, and strange aquatic shapes and is usually crowned with heraldic or religious symbols. The best example is the grand Monastery of Jerónimos in Belém, outside Lisbon, dating from the 16th century. Another towering example is the mysterious and astrologic visions of the famous window of the Convent of Christ in Tomar, the bastion of the Knights Templar in days gone by.

- **Visiting the Lost Continent of Atlantis:** One of the most offbeat travel experiences in Europe is a trip to the Azores. Mythologists believe the remote Portuguese islands in the mid-Atlantic are the only remnants of the lost continent of Atlantis. For hundreds of years they were considered the end of the earth, the outer limits of the European sphere of influence, beyond which ships could not go. Even today they're a verdant but lonely archipelago where the winds of the ocean meet, cyclones call on each other, and urbanites can lose themselves in fogbound contact with the sea. Although space limitations do not allow us to document these fascinating islands in this guide, any branch of a Portuguese national tourist office can provide you with information.

- **Paying a Call on Berlenga Island:** Berlenga is a granite island 7 miles west of the Portuguese coastline. The island has always been the first line of defense against invaders from the sea. In 1666, 28 Portuguese tried to withstand 1,500 Spaniards who bombarded the site from 15 ships. A medieval fortress demolished in the battle was rebuilt several decades later and today houses a no-frills hostel. The entire island and the rocky, uninhabited archipelago that surrounds it are a designated nature reserve whose flora and fauna—both above and below the surface of the sea—are protected from development and destruction. Boat transport departs from the Peniche Peninsula, about 57 miles north of Lisbon. See chapter 7.

- **Heading "Beyond the Mountains":** The northernmost district of Trás-os-Montes is a wild, rugged land whose name means "beyond the mountains." Exploring this region provides a glimpse into a Portugal infrequently seen by outsiders. Most of the population lives in deep valleys, often in traditional houses built of shale or granite, and speaks a dialect of Galician similar to that spoken just across the border in northwestern Spain. Much of the plateau is arid and rocky, but swift rivers and streams provide water for irrigation, and thermal springs have bubbled out of the earth since at least Roman times. You can drive through these savage landscapes, but don't expect superhighways. What you'll find are ruins of pre-Roman fortresses, dolmens, and cromlechs erected by prehistoric Celts, and decaying old churches. See chapter 12.

13 The Best Shopping

Here's a list of some of the more enchanting artifacts and handcrafts produced in Portugal:

- **Arraiolos Carpets:** The Moorish traditions that once prevailed in the town of Arraiolos, where the carpets are still manufactured, inspired their intricate stitching. Teams of embroiderers and weavers work for many days, using pure wool in combinations of petit point with more widely spaced *ponto largo* cross-stitches. The resulting depictions of garlands of fruit and flowers (a loose interpretation of French Aubusson carpets) and animals scampering around idealized gardens (a theme vaguely inspired by carpets from Persia and Turkey) are some of the most charming items for sale in Portugal. The size of the piece and the intricacy of the design determine the price, which is often less than half what you'd pay in North America. If you can't make it to Arraiolos, you'll find the carpets for sale at outlets in Lisbon.

- **Ceramics & Tiles:** Early in Portugal's history, builders learned to compensate for the lack of lumber by perfecting the arts of masonry, stuccoing, and ceramics. All were used to construct the country's sturdy, termite-proof buildings. After the ouster of the Moors, their aesthetic endured in the designs painted on tiles and ceramic plates, vessels, and jugs. Later, styles from Holland, England, and China combined to influence a rich tradition of pottery-making. The most prevalent of these appear as the blue-and-white tiles, each with an individual design, which adorn thousands of indoor and outdoor walls throughout the country. Equally charming are the thousands of plates, wine and water jugs, and vases adorned with sylvan landscapes populated with mythical creatures. New and (to a lesser extent) antique samples of any of these items can be acquired at outlets throughout Portugal.

- **Jewelry:** In Portugal, any piece of jewelry advertised as "gold" must contain at least 19.2 karats. This purity allows thousands of jewelers to spin the shining stuff into delicate filigree work with astounding detail. Whether you opt for a simple brooch or for a depiction in gold or filigreed silver of an 18th-century caravel in full four-masted sail, Portugal produces jewelry worthy of an *infanta*'s dowry at prices more reasonable than you might expect. The country abounds in jewelry stores.

- **Handcrafts:** For centuries, the design and fabrication of lace, rugs, hand-knit clothing, wood carvings, and embroidered linens have evolved in homes and workshops throughout Portugal. Although some of the cruder objects available for sale are a bit clunky, the best can be called art. From the north to the south, store after store offers regional handcrafts.
- **Leather Goods:** Iberia has always been a land of animal husbandry, bullfighting, and cattle breeding, and the Portuguese leather-making industry is known throughout the world. Its products include jackets, shoes, pocketbooks, and wallets, all of which sell for prices much more reasonable than those outside Portugal. The best stores are concentrated in Lisbon.

2 Planning a Trip to Portugal

Just getting started is the difficult part for many travelers. This chapter addresses the where, when, and how of visiting Portugal—all the logistics of putting your trip together and taking it on the road. The "Fast Facts" section at the end of the chapter provides a quick reference.

1 Regions in Brief

Portugal's coastline stretches some 500 miles. The country is bounded on the south and west by the Atlantic Ocean and on the north and east by Spain. Continental Portugal totals some 34,000 square miles; its Atlantic islands, including Madeira and the Azores, add 1,200 square miles. The Azores lie some 700 miles west of Lisbon (Lisboa), the capital of the country. Portugal's population is about 10.3 million.

Portugal has four major rivers—the Minho in the north, which separates the country from Spain; the Douro, also in the north, known for vineyards that produce port wine; the Tagus, which flows into the Atlantic at Lisbon; and the Guadiana, in the southeast. Part of the Guadiana forms an eastern frontier with Spain.

Lisbon & the Costa do Sol   Portugal's capital is on hilly terrain beside one of the finest harbors in Europe—the estuary of the Tagus (Tejo) River. Within a few miles of the city limits, the beaches of the Costa do Sol cater to residents of the capital, who easily reach them by bus and train. Until the development of beaches in the Algarve, those on the Costa do Sol were among the most crowded and glamorous in the country. The best-known resorts include Estoril and Cascais, long playgrounds of the wintering wealthy.

Estremadura   The name translates as "the extremity," but it has radically different connotations from those associated with the harsh landscapes of Estremadura in neighboring Spain. Early in the development of the Portuguese nation, rulers based in the country's north-central region coined the term to refer to the Moorish territories to the south that the Portuguese eyed enviously. Technically, those territories included Nazaré, Óbidos, and Fátima; in many cases the word is now used to include the territory around Lisbon as well. The sea is never far in Estremadura, whose coastline is flanked by some of the country's richest fishing banks.

Regions of Portugal

0 — 30 Mi
0 — 50 Km

MINHO
Viana do Castelo
Bragança
Braga
TRÁS-OS-MONTES

Porto **ALTO DOURO** Vila Real **DOURO LITORAL**
Espinho
Rio Douro
Rio Duero

Atlantic Ocean

Aveiro
BEIRA ALTA
Viseu
BEIRA LITORAL
Guarda
Coimbra

Figueira da Foz
SPAIN

Leiria
BEIRA BAIXA
Batalha Fátima
Castelo Branco
Nazaré
Tomar
Rio Tejo (River Tagus)
Peniche
RIBATEJO
Cáceres
ESTRE-MADURA Santarém
Portalegre
Sintra Estoril
ALTO ALENTEJO
★ **LISBON** Badajoz
Cascais Elvas
Mérida
Setúbal
Cabo Espichel
Évora

Cabo de Sines
Beja
Rio Guadiana
Sines
BAIXO ALENTEJO

Cabo de S. Vicente
Portimão Vila Real de
ALGARVE S. António
Sagres Lagos Huelva Seville
Faro Olhão

3-0909

17

The Algarve   Encompassing the extreme southwestern tip of Europe, the Algarve boasts a 100-mile coastline with some of the best beaches in Europe. It's permeated with memories of the long-ago Moorish occupation, when the region was called "Al-Gharb." The garden of Portugal, the naturally arid district is laced with large-scale irrigation projects. Except for the massive and sometimes chaotic development of beach resorts since the late 1960s, the landscape in many ways resembles the coast of nearby Morocco, with which it has much in common.

Alentejo & Ribatejo   East and southeast of Lisbon, these regions form the agrarian heartland of Portugal. Underpopulated but fertile, and marked mostly by fields and grasslands, this is horse- and bull-breeding territory, with some of the most idyllic landscapes in Iberia. Their medieval cities, including Évora, Tomar, Beja, Elvas, and Estremoz, contain famous examples of Roman and Manueline architecture.

Coimbra & the Beiras   Between two of the country's most vital rivers, the Beiras were incorporated into the medieval kingdom of Portugal earlier than the territories farther south, including Lisbon. Given their history, they're among the most traditional Portuguese areas in the country. The medieval university town of Coimbra is the highlight of the region; a cluster of spas (especially Luso and Curia) and the legendary forest of Buçaco also draw visitors. The region technically consists of three districts: Coastal Beira (Beira Litoral), Low Beira (Beira Baixa), and High Beira (Beira Alta). The Beiras contain the country's highest peaks—the Serra de Estrêla—and the Mondela, the only navigable river whose sources lie within the boundaries of Portugal.

Porto & the Douro   Portugal's second-largest city, Porto has thrived as a mercantile center since English traders used it as a base for the export of port, London's favorite drink during the Regency. The river that feeds it, the Douro, flows through some of the world's richest vineyards before emptying into the Atlantic in Porto's harbor. Porto abounds with the 19th-century mansions of merchants who grew wealthy from winegrowing or through investments in such colonies as Brazil. The most popular resort in the region is the once-sleepy former fishing village of Póvoa de Varzim.

The Minho   This is the northernmost region of Portugal, an isolated, idiosyncratic area with a population descended more or less directly from Celtic ancestors. The local tongue is a tricky dialect that more closely resembles that of Galicia (in northwestern Spain) than it does Portuguese. The Minho is almost a land unto itself, with most of the population centered in Viana do Castelo, Guimarães, and Braga. Ardently provincial and suspicious of outsiders, the district figured prominently in the development of medieval Portugal as a kingdom separate from Spain, producing early kings who moved south in their conquest of territories held until then by the Moors. Even Barcelos, a relatively small town, has played an important part in the Portuguese national identity by producing lore and legends and popularizing the symbol of the victoriously crowing cock, which has long been associated with Portuguese tenacity.

Trás-os-Montes   This far northeastern and least visited corner of Portugal is a wild, rugged land whose name translates literally as "beyond the mountains." Aggressively provincial, the region nevertheless has strong ties to its neighbor, the Minho. Local granite dominates the architecture. The district stretches from Lamego and the Upper Douro to the Spanish border. Vila Real is the largest town.

Madeira   Near the coast of Africa, 530 miles southwest of Portugal, Madeira is the much-eroded peak of a volcanic mass. Wintering English gentry first discovered the island's recreational charms; today it's one of the world's most famous islands, known for the abundant beauty of its gardens. Only 35 miles long and about 13 miles across at its widest point, the island is an autonomous region of Portugal and has a relatively dense year-round population of 255,000.

The Azores   The island chain is one of the most isolated in the Atlantic Ocean. It constitutes an autonomous region and has some 240,000 year-round occupants who live amid rocky, moss-covered landscapes closely tied to the sea. The archipelago spans more than 500 miles that stretch from the southeastern tip of Santa Maria to the northwestern extremity of the island of Corvo. The chain's largest island is São Miguel, which lies a third of the way across the Atlantic, about 760 miles west of Portugal and 2,110 miles east of New York. Today, the Azores are widely known within yachting circles as the final destination for annual sailboat races from Newport and Bermuda.

2 Visitor Information

Sources of Information   Before you go, contact one of the overseas branches of the **Portuguese National Tourist Office.** The main office in the **United States** is at 590 Fifth Ave., 4th Floor, New York, NY 10036-4704 (☎ **212/354-4403**). In **Canada,** the office is at 600 Bloor St. W., Suite 1005, Toronto, ON M4W 3B8 (☎ **416/921-7376**). In the **United Kingdom,** contact the Portuguese Tourist Office, 22–25A Fackville St., 2nd Floor, London W1X 1DE (☎ **0207/494-1441**). In **Australia**, information is available at the Embassy of Portugal, 6 Campion St., Deakin (Canberra) (☎ **06/285-2084**).

HELPFUL WEB SITES

- **www.portugal.org**: Investments, Trade and Tourism of Portugal (ICEP), a government agency, maintains this site. It is a general information resource, providing data about tourism and attractions, among other information.
- **www.portugal-info.net**: This site provides a number of data banks, including accommodations, gastronomy, events, entertainment, and golf (among other sports). Its focus is on Lisbon and the Algarve, and it's of special use to the visitor from the United Kingdom.
- **www.pousadas.pt/**: This site provides the best details on *pousadas* (government-sponsored inns scattered throughout the country). It offers geographic details, current rates, information on on-line bookings, and even photographs.
- **www.nervo.com/pt/**: This site is a general travel database, with a little bit of everything that can serve as planning tools for the prospective visitor. You get everything from lodging tips to weather reports, information about getting there and geography, and tips on currency, including information about ATMs and cell-phone roaming.
- **www.tap-airportugal.pt**: This site provides data about TAP's flights in Portugal and online reservations. New features include all published fares and data about how to change reservations.
- **www.madeira-island.com**: This site covers everything about the island, from finding accommodations to shopping, renting a car, and learning about Madeira wine.

3 Entry Requirements & Customs

ENTRY REQUIREMENTS   U.S., Canadian, Australian, New Zealand, and Irish citizens, and British subjects with a valid passport do not need a visa to enter Portugal if they do not plan to stay more than 90 days and do not expect to work there. If you'd like to stay more than 90 days, you can apply for an additional stay at the nearest Portuguese embassy. As a rule, the extension is granted immediately.

PASSPORT INFORMATION

Safeguard your passport in an inconspicuous, inaccessible place like a money belt. If you lose it, visit the nearest consulate of your native country as soon as possible for a replacement. Passport applications are downloadable from the Internet sites listed below.

FOR RESIDENTS OF THE UNITED STATES

If you're applying for a first-time passport, do so in person at one of 13 passport offices throughout the United States; a federal, state, or probate court; or a major post office. (Not all post offices accept applications; call the number below to find the ones that do.) You need to present a certified birth certificate as proof of citizenship, and it's wise to bring along your driver's license, state or military ID, and social security card as well. You also need two identical passport-sized (2-by-2-inch) photos—not strip photos from a vending machine.

For people over 15, a passport is valid for 10 years and costs $60 ($45 plus a $15 handling fee); for those 15 and under, it's valid for 5 years and costs $40. If you're over 15 and have a valid passport that was issued within the past 12 years, you can renew it by mail and bypass the $15 handling fee. Allow plenty of time before your trip to apply; processing normally takes 3 weeks but can take longer during busy periods (especially spring). For general information, call the **National Passport Agency** (☎ **202/647-0518**). To find your regional passport office, consult the **National Passport Information Center** (☎ **900/225-5674;** http://travel.state.gov).

FOR RESIDENTS OF CANADA

You can pick up a passport application at one of 28 regional passport offices and most travel agencies. The passport is valid for 5 years and costs $60. Children under 16 may be included on a parent's passport but need their own to travel unaccompanied by the parent. Applications must be accompanied by two identical passport-sized photographs and proof of Canadian citizenship. They're also available from the central **Passport Office**, Department of Foreign Affairs and International Trade, Ottawa, Ont. K1A 0G3 (☎ **800/567-6868;** www.dfait-maeci.gc.ca/passport). Processing takes 5 to 10 days if you apply in person, or about 3 weeks by mail.

FOR RESIDENTS OF THE UNITED KINGDOM

As a resident of a member of the European Union, you need only an identity card, not a passport, to travel to other EU countries. If you have a passport, it's always useful to carry it. To pick up an application for a regular 10-year passport (the Visitor's Passport has been abolished), visit your nearest passport office, major post office, or travel agency. You can also contact the **London Passport Office** (☎ **0171/271-3000;** www.open.gov.uk/ukpass/ukpass.htm). Passports are £21 for adults, £11 for children under 16.

FOR RESIDENTS OF IRELAND

You can apply for a 10-year passport at the Passport Office, Setanta Centre, Molesworth Street, Dublin 2 (☎ **01/671-1633;** www.irlgov.ie/iveagh/foreignaffairs/services). It costs IR£45. Those under age 18 and over 65 must apply for a 3-year passport (IR£10). You can also apply at 1A South Mall, Cork (☎ **021/272-525**), or over the counter at most main post offices.

FOR RESIDENTS OF AUSTRALIA

Apply at your local post office or passport office, or search the government Web site (www.dfat.gov.au/passports/). Passports for adults are A$126, for those under 18, A$63.

FOR RESIDENTS OF NEW ZEALAND

You can pick up a passport application at any travel agency or Link Centre. For more info, contact the Passport Office, P.O. Box 805, Wellington (☎ **0800/225-050**). Passports for adults are NZ$80, for those under 16, NZ$40.

CUSTOMS   Visitors to Portugal, age 17 and older, can bring in 200 cigarettes, 50 cigars, or 250 grams of loose tobacco; 2 liters of still table wine, 1 liter of liquor with alcohol content over 22%, or 2 liters of liquor under 22%; 2 fluid ounces of perfume; 10 rolls of film; two still cameras; one laptop or PC if it shows signs of use; plus sporting equipment for your own use in the country.

IMPORT RESTRICTIONS

Returning **U.S. citizens** who have been away for 48 hours or more are allowed to bring back, once every 30 days, $400 worth of merchandise duty-free. You'll be charged a flat rate of 10% duty on the next $1,000 worth of purchases. Be sure to have your receipts handy. On gifts, the duty-free limit is $100. You cannot bring fresh food-stuffs into the United States; tinned foods are allowed. For more information, contact the **U.S. Customs Service,** 1301 Constitution Ave. (P.O. Box 7407), Washington, DC 20044 (☎ **202/927-6724**), and request the free pamphlet *Know Before You Go.* It's also available on the Web (www.customs.ustreas.gov/travel/kbygo.htm).

Citizens of the United Kingdom who are **returning from a European Community (EC) country** go through a separate Customs exit (the "Blue Exit") especially for EC travelers. In essence, there is no limit on what you can bring back from an EC country, as long as the items are for personal use (this includes gifts), and you have already paid the necessary duty and tax. However, customs law sets out guidance levels. If you exceed those levels, you may be asked to prove that the goods are for your own use. Guidance levels on goods bought in the EC for your own use are 800 cigarettes, 200 cigars, 1 kilogram smoking tobacco, 10 liters of spirits, 90 liters of wine (of this not more than 60 liters can be sparkling wine), and 110 liters of beer. For more information, contact **HM Customs & Excise,** Passenger Enquiry Point, 2nd Floor Wayfarer House, Great South West Road, Feltham, Middlesex, TW14 8NP (☎ **0181/910-3744,** or 44/181-910-3744 from outside the U.K.; www.open.gov.uk).

For a clear summary of **Canadian** rules, write for the booklet *I Declare,* issued by **Revenue Canada,** 2265 St. Laurent Blvd., Ottawa K1G 4KE (☎ **613/993-0534**). Canada allows its citizens a $500 exemption, and you're allowed to bring back duty-free 200 cigarettes, 2.2 pounds of tobacco, 40 imperial ounces of liquor, and 50 cigars. In addition, you're allowed to mail gifts to Canada from abroad at the rate of C$60 a day, provided they're unsolicited and don't contain alcohol or tobacco (write on the package "Unsolicited gift, under $60 value"). All valuables should be declared on the Y-38 form before departure from Canada, including serial numbers of valuables you already own, such as expensive foreign cameras. Note: The $500 exemption can only be used once a year and only after an absence of 7 days.

The duty-free allowance in **Australia** is A$400 or, for those under 18, A$200. Personal property mailed back from England should be marked "Australian goods returned" to avoid payment of duty. Upon returning to Australia, citizens can bring in 250 cigarettes or 250 grams of loose tobacco, and 1,125 milliliters of alcohol. If you're returning with valuable goods you already own, such as foreign-made cameras, you should file form B263. A helpful brochure, available from Australian consulates or Customs offices, is *Know Before You Go.* For more information, contact **Australian Customs Services,** GPO Box 8, Sydney NSW 2001 (☎ **02/9213-2000**).

The duty-free allowance for **New Zealand** is NZ$700. Citizens over 17 can bring in 200 cigarettes, 50 cigars, or 250 grams of tobacco (or a mixture of all three if their combined weight doesn't exceed 250 grams); plus 4.5 liters of wine and beer, or 1.125 liters of liquor. New Zealand currency does not carry import or export restrictions. Fill out a certificate of export, listing the valuables you are taking out of the country, and you can bring them back without paying duty. *New Zealand Customs Guide for Travellers, Notice no. 4*, a free pamphlet available at New Zealand consulates and Customs offices, answers most questions. For more information, contact **New Zealand Customs,** 50 Anzac Ave., P.O. Box 29, Auckland (☎ **09/359-6655**).

4 Money

There are no limits on foreign currency brought into Portugal, but visitors are advised to declare the amount carried. That proves to the Portuguese Customs Office that the currency came from outside the country, and allows you to take out the same amount or less.

CURRENCY/CASH   The basic unit of Portuguese currency is the **escudo** (plural: escudos), which is divided into 100 **centavos.** A *conto* is 1,000 escudos. Check a newspaper or bank for the latest exchange rate before departing.

   Portugal is a reasonably priced travel destination, though prices rose dramatically in the late 1990s. Naturally, you get far better values in the countryside than you do in high-priced cities (such as Lisbon) or such chic resorts as Madeira and the Algarve. Americans visiting Portugal for the first time often panic at price quotations. The Portuguese escudo is written as 1$00, with the dollar sign between the escudo and the centavo. Bank notes are issued in denominations of 100, 500, 1,000, 2,000, 5,000, and 10,000 escudos. In coins of silver and copper, the denominations are 1, 2½, 5, 10, 20, 25, 50, 100, and 200 escudos.

EURO CURRENCY   The **euro,** the new single European currency, became the official currency of Portugal and 10 other countries on January 1, 1999, but not in the form of cash. On January 1, 2002, euro bank notes and coins will be introduced. During a 6-month transition period, escudo notes and coins will be withdrawn from circulation, and starting July 1, 2002, only the euro will be accepted.

   The symbol of the euro is €; its official abbreviation is EUR.

   No euro bank notes or coins are currently in circulation. Payment in euros can be made only by check, credit card, or another bank-related system. Although at this time very few, if any, Portuguese hotel and restaurant bills are paid in euros, the new pan-European currency will become increasingly widespread during the lifetime of this edition.

TRAVELER'S CHECKS

Traveler's checks are something of an anachronism from the days before the ATM (automated-teller machine) made cash accessible at any time. The only sound alternative to traveling with dangerously large amounts of cash, traveler's checks were as reliable as currency, unlike personal checks, but could be replaced if lost or stolen, unlike cash.

   These days, traveler's checks seem less necessary because most cities have 24-hour ATMs that allow travelers to withdraw small amounts of cash as needed, and avoid the risk of carrying a fortune around an unfamiliar environment. Many banks, however, impose a fee every time a card is used at an ATM in a different city or bank. If you're withdrawing money every day, you might be better off with traveler's checks—provided that you don't mind showing identification every time you want to cash a check.

You can get traveler's checks at almost any bank. **American Express** offers denominations of $10, $20, $50, $100, $500, and $1,000. You'll pay a service charge ranging from 1% to 4%. You can also get American Express traveler's checks over the phone by calling ☎ 800/221-7282; by using this number, Amex gold and platinum cardholders are exempt from the 1% fee. AAA members can obtain checks without a fee at most AAA offices.

Visa offers traveler's checks at Citibank locations nationwide, as well as several other banks. The service charge is 1.5% to 2%; checks come in denominations of $20, $50, $100, $500, and $1,000. **MasterCard** also offers traveler's checks. Call ☎ **800/223-9920** for a location near you.

ATMS

ATMs are linked to a national network that most likely includes your bank at home. **Cirrus** (☎ **800/424-7787;** www.mastercard.com/atm/) and **Plus** (☎ **800/843-7587;** www.visa.com/atms) are the two most popular networks; check the back of your ATM card to see which network your bank belongs to. Use the 800 numbers to locate ATMs in your destination.

If you're traveling abroad, ask your bank for a list of overseas ATMs. Be sure to check the daily withdrawal limit before you depart, and ask whether you need a new personal identification number (PIN). If you use letters for your PIN, be warned that some keyboards have only numbers, no letters.

If you have a PIN and a Visa, MasterCard, or EuroCard, you can head for the main office of **Unicre-Unibanco,** av. Antonio Augusto de Aguiar 122, Lisbon 1070 (☎ **21/350-9500**). ATMs are in a generally secure area that's accessible 24 hours a day from the sidewalk. Some branches also have ATMs.

If you have an American Express card and a PIN, you can use almost any ATM in Portugal, including the Unicre-Unibanco location listed above. Machines are usually reliable, but it's best to have a backup system for getting cash in case the ATMs in Portugal can't decipher the numbers on your card.

If you want to get cash as a debit against your **American Express** account, consult Amex's Portuguese representative, Top Tours (see "American Express" in "Fast Facts: Portugal," later in this chapter). Bring your Amex card, a photo ID or passport, and one of your personal checks drawn on virtually any bank in the world.

CREDIT CARDS

Credit cards are invaluable when traveling. They are a safe way to carry money and provide a convenient record of all your expenses. You can also withdraw cash advances from your credit cards at any bank (though you'll start paying hefty interest on the advance the moment you receive the cash, and you won't receive frequent-flyer miles on an airline credit card). At most banks, you don't even need to go to a teller; you can get a cash advance at the ATM if you know your PIN. If you've forgotten your PIN (or didn't even know you had one), call the phone number on the back of your credit card and ask the bank to send it to you. It usually takes 5 to 7 business days, though some banks will provide the number over the phone if you tell them your mother's maiden name or pass some other security clearance.

Impressions

The Portuguese and the English have always been the best of friends because we can't get no Port Wine anywhere else.

—Capt. Frederick Marryat, *Peter Simple* (1834)

The Escudo, the U.S. Dollar, the British Pound & the Euro

At this writing, US$1 equals approximately 180 Portuguese escudos, and £1 equals approximately 312 Portuguese escudos. (In other words, 1 escudo equals about US6¢ and about ⅓ of a British pence.) Those rates were used to calculate the rounded dollar equivalents of Portuguese escudo amounts throughout this guidebook, as well as within the chart below. At press time, the euro wasn't particularly widespread within Portugal, although we expect it to gain in market share during the lifetime of this edition. Rates were permanently fixed at about 200 escudos to 1 euro.

Exchange rates affecting the values of all three of these currencies fluctuate from day to day, and may not be the same by the time of your trip. Be sure to check last-minute rates, and use this table only as an approximate indicator of relative values.

For an on-line currency converter with up-to-date quotations, check **www.oanda.com** or **www.x-rates.com**.

Escudos	US$	UK£	Euro	Escudos	US$	UK£	Euro
50	0.28	0.16	0.25	20,000	112.00	64	100
100	0.56	0.32	0.50	25,000	140.00	80.00	125.00
300	1.68	0.96	1.50	30,000	168.00	96.00	150.00
500	2.80	1.60	2.50	35,000	196.00	112.00	175.00
700	3.92	2.24	3.50	40,000	224.00	128.00	200.00
1,000	5.60	3.20	5.00	45,000	252.00	144.00	225.00
1,500	8.40	4.80	7.50	50,000	280.00	160.00	250.00
2,000	11.20	6.40	10.00	100,000	560.00	320.00	500.00
3,000	16.80	9.60	15.00	125,000	700.00	400.00	625.00
4,000	22.40	12.80	20.00	150,000	840.00	480.00	750.00
5,000	28.00	16.00	25.00	200,000	1,120.00	640.00	1,000.00
7,500	42.00	24.00	37.50	250,000	1,400.00	800.00	1,250.00
10,000	56.00	32.00	50.00	500,000	2,800.00	1,600.00	2,500.00
15,000	84.00	48.00	75.00	1,000,000	5,600.00	3,200.00	5,000.00

THEFT Almost every credit card company has a toll-free emergency number that you can call if your wallet or purse is stolen. The company may be able to wire you a cash advance against your credit card immediately, and in many places, it can deliver an emergency credit card in a day or two. The issuing bank's number is usually on the back of the credit card—though of course that doesn't help you much if the card was stolen. The toll-free information directory (☎ **800/555-1212**) will provide the number. Citicorp Visa's U.S. emergency number is ☎ **800/336-8472.** American Express cardholders and traveler's check holders should call ☎ **800/221-7282** for all money emergencies. MasterCard holders should call ☎ **800/307-7309.**

If you opt to carry traveler's checks, be sure to keep a record of their serial numbers, separately from the checks of course, so you're ensured a refund in an emergency.

Odds are that if your wallet is gone, the police won't be able to recover it for you. However, after you realize that it's gone and you cancel your credit cards, it is still

What Things Cost in Lisbon	U.S.$	U.K.£
Taxi from the airport to the city center	11.20–16.80	9.10
Average Metro ride	.45	.33
Local telephone call	.10	.05
Double room at Four Seasons Hotel The Ritz Lisbon (very expensive)	140–336	169.70
Double room at the Janelas Verdes Inn (moderate)	163.50–201.05	99.10
Double room at the Residência Nazareth (inexpensive)	44.80	27.15
Lunch for one, without wine, at Bachus (moderate)	23.80	14.40
Lunch for one, without wine, at O Funil (moderate)	12.70	7.70
Dinner for one, without wine, at Tágide (expensive)	38.50	23.35
Dinner for one, without wine, at Chester (moderate)	26.00	15.75
Dinner for one, without wine, at Sancho (inexpensive)	12.20	7.40
Glass of beer	2.80	1.70
Coca-Cola in a restaurant	1.10	.65
Cup of coffee in a cafe	.55	.35
Roll of ASA 100 color film, 24 exposures	2.25	1.35
Admission to the Museu Nacional dos Coches	2.50	1.50
Movie ticket	4.50	2.70
Theater ticket	11.20	6.80

worth informing them. Your credit card company or insurer may require a police report number.

MONEYGRAM If you find yourself out of money, a wire service provided by American Express can help you tap friends and family for emergency funds. Through MoneyGram, 6200 S. Quebec St. (P.O. Box 5118), Englewood, CO 80155 (☎ **800/926-9400**), money can be sent around the world in less than 10 minutes. Senders should call American Express to learn the address of the closest outlet that handles MoneyGrams. Cash, credit card, and sometimes personal checks (with ID) are acceptable forms of payment. Amex's fee for the service is $10 for the first $300, with a sliding scale for larger sums. The service includes a short telex message and a 3-minute phone call from sender to recipient. The recipient must present a photo ID at the outlet where the money is received.

CURRENCY EXCHANGE Many hotels in Portugal don't accept dollar- or pound-denominated checks, and if they do, they will charge for the conversion. In some cases they'll accept countersigned traveler's checks or a credit card, but if you're prepaying a deposit on hotel reservations, it's cheaper and easier to pay with a check drawn on a Portuguese bank.

This can be arranged by a large commercial bank or by a specialist like **Ruesch International,** 700 11th St. NW, Washington, DC 20001 (☎ **800/424-2923** or 202/408-1200). Ruesch performs a wide variety of conversion-related tasks, usually for only $3 U.S. per transaction.

If you need a check payable in escudos, call Ruesch's toll-free number, describe what you need, and note the transaction number given to you. Mail your dollar-denominated personal check (payable to Ruesch International) to its office. Upon receipt, the company will mail a check denominated in escudos for the financial equivalent, minus the $3 charge. The company does not sell traveler's checks denominated in escudos, but can help you with wire transfers and conversion of value-added tax (VAT) refund checks. It will mail brochures and information packets on request.

5 When to Go

CLIMATE   "We didn't know we had an April," one Lisbon resident said, "until *that* song came out." As a song and a season, "April in Portugal" is famous. Summer may be the most popular time to visit, but for the traveler who can chart his or her own course, spring and autumn are the most delectable seasons.

To use a North American analogy, the climate of Portugal most closely parallels that of California. The Portuguese consider their climate one of the most ideal in Europe, and they're right. There are only slight fluctuations in temperature between summer and winter; the overall mean ranges from 77°F in summer to about 58°F in winter. The rainy season begins in November and usually lasts through January. Because of the Gulf Stream, Portugal's northernmost area, **Minho,** enjoys mild (albeit very rainy) winters, even though it's at approximately the same latitude as New York City.

Snow brings many skiing enthusiasts to the **Serra de Estrêla** in north central Portugal. For the most part, however, winter means only some rain and lower temperatures in other regions. The **Algarve** and especially **Madeira** enjoy temperate winters. Madeira, in fact, basks in its high season in winter. The Algarve, too, is somewhat of a winter Riviera that attracts sun worshipers from North America and Europe. Summers in both tend to be long, hot, clear, and dry.

Lisbon and **Estoril** enjoy 46°F (7.7°C) to 65°F (18.3°C) temperatures in winter and temperatures between 60°F (15.5°C) and 82°F (27.7°C) in summer.

Average Daytime Temperature (°C & °F) & Monthly Rainfall (inches) in Lisbon

	Jan	Feb	Mar	Apr	May	June	July	Aug	Sept	Oct	Nov	Dec
Temp.(°C)	13.8	15	17.2	19.4	21.6	25C	27.2	27.7	26.1C	22.2	17.2	14.4
Temp.(°F)	57	59	63	67	71	77	81	82	79	72	63	58
Rainfall	4.3	3.0	4.2	2.1	1.7	0.6	0.1	0.2	1.3	2.4	3.7	4.1

HOLIDAYS   Watch for these public holidays, and adjust your banking needs accordingly: January 1 (New Year's Day and Universal Brotherhood Day); Carnaval, early March (dates vary); Good Friday, March or April (dates vary); April 25 (Liberty Day, anniversary of the revolution); May 1 (Labor Day); Corpus Christi, June (dates vary); June 10 (Portugal Day); August 15 (Feast of the Assumption); October 5 (Proclamation of the Republic); November 1 (All Saints' Day); December 1 (Restoration of Independence); December 8 (Feast of the Immaculate Conception); and December 25 (Christmas Day). June 13 (Feast Day of St. Anthony) is a public holiday in Lisbon, and June 24 (Feast Day of St. John the Baptist) is a public holiday in Porto.

Portugal Calendar of Events

We suggest that you verify dates with a tourist office, because festival dates can vary greatly from year to year. Sometimes last-minute adjustments are made because of scheduling problems.

Note that Lisbon does not merit a separate calendar. Even some small towns have more celebrations than the capital. The high point of Lisboans' festival revelry is in June (see "Festas dos Santos Populares," below).

January

- **Festa de São Gonçalo e São Cristovão,** Vila Nova de Gaia, across the river from Porto. These resemble fertility rites and are two of the most attended religious festivals in Portugal. An image of São Gonçalo is paraded through the narrow streets as merrymakers beat drums. Boatmen along the Douro ferry a figure of São Cristovão with a huge head down the river. Much port wine is drunk, and cakes baked into phallic shapes are consumed by all. Early January. Call ☎ 22/205-27-40 for more information.

March

- **Carnaval** (Mardi Gras), throughout the country, notably in Nazaré, Ovar, Loulé, and Funchal (Madeira). Each town has its unique way of celebrating. Masked marchers, flower-bedecked floats, and satirically decorated vehicles mark the occasion. Food and wine are consumed in abundance. This is the final festival before Lent. For more details, check with a Portuguese national tourist office (see "Visitor Information," above). Early March.

April

- **Easter,** all over Portugal. Some of the most noteworthy festivities take place at Póvoa de Varzim, Ovar, and especially the town of Braga, whose Holy Week processions feature masked marchers and bejeweled floats along with fireworks, folk dancing, and torch parades. The faithful—often colorfully dressed—march in parades. For more details, check with a Portuguese national tourist office (see "Visitor Information," above).

May

- **Festas das Cruzes,** Barcelos on the river Cávado, near Braga. Since 1504 this festival has been celebrated with a "Miracle of the Cross" procession centered around a carpet made of millions of flower petals. Women in colorful regional dress adorn themselves with large gold chains. A giant fireworks display on the river signals the festival's end. Call ☎ 253/81-18-82 for more information. Early May.
- ○ **First pilgrimage of the year to Fátima.** In 1930 the bishop of Leiria authorized pilgrimages to this site. Today, people from all over the world flock here to commemorate the first apparition of the Virgin to the little shepherd children in 1917. The year's last pilgrimage is in October (see below). Make hotel reservations months in advance, or plan to stay in a neighboring town. For more information, call the Fátima tourist office (☎ 249/53-11-39). May 13.

June

- **Feira Nacional da Agricultura** (also known as the Feira do Ribatejo), Santarém, north of Lisbon on the river Tagus. This is the most important agricultural fair in Portugal. The best horses and cattle from all provinces are on display, and horse shows and bullfights enliven the festival. Food pavilions feature various regional cuisines. For more information, call ☎ 243/33-33-18. June 5 to 13.
- **Feast of St. John,** Porto, home of the famous port wine. Honoring St. John (São João in Portuguese), this colorful festival features bonfires, all-night singing and dancing, and processions of locals in colorful costumes. Call ☎ 22/323-303 for more information. June 23 and 24.

○ **Festas dos Santos Populares,** throughout Lisbon. Celebrations begin on June 13 and 14 in the Alfama, with feasts honoring Saint Anthony. Parades commemorating the city's patron saint feature *marchas* (parading groups of singers and musicians) along avenida da Liberdade, singing, dancing, drinking wine, and eating grilled sardines. Vendors peddle pots of sweet basil. On June 23 and 24, for the Feast of St. John the Baptist, bonfires brighten the night and participants jump over them. The night of the final celebration is the Feast of St. Peter on June 29. The Lisbon tourist office (☎ **21/346-63-07**) supplies details about where some of the events are staged, although much of the action is spontaneous. June 12 to 29.

• **Festas do São Pedro,** Mintijo, near Lisbon. This festival honoring St. Peter has been held since medieval times. On the final day there's a blessing of the boats and a colorful procession. Grilled sardines are the main item on the menu. Bull breeders bring their beasts into town and release them through the streets to chase foolish young men, who are often permanently injured or killed. There are also bullfights. On the final night, participants observe the pagan rite of setting a skiff afire and offering it as a sacrifice to the Tagus. Call ☎ **21/346-63-07** for more information. June 28 and 29.

July

• **Colete Encarnado** ("Red Waistcoat"), Vila Franca de Xira, north of Lisbon on the river Tagus. Like the more famous *feria* in Pamplona, Spain, this festival involves bulls running through narrow streets, followed by sensational bullfights in what aficionados consider the best bullring in Portugal. Fandango dancing and rodeo-style competition among the Ribatejo *campinos* (cowboys) mark the event. For more information, call ☎ **252/64-27-00.** First or second Sunday in July.

• **Estoril Festival.** Outside Lisbon at the seaside resort of Estoril, this festival of classical music occupies two concert halls that were built for the 500th anniversary of Columbus's first voyage to the New World. For information, write Associação International de Música da Costa do Estoril, Casa dos Arcos, Estrada Marginal, P-2775 Parede, Portugal, or call ☎ **21/466-38-13.** Mid-July to first week in August (dates vary).

August

• **Feast of Our Lady of Monte,** Madeira. On Assumption Eve and Day (August 14 and 15), the island's most important religious festival begins with devout worship and climaxes in an outburst of fun. There's music, dancing, eating, and general drinking and carousing until dawn. For more information, call ☎ **291/22-90-57.**

○ **Festas da Senhora da Agonia,** Viana do Castelo, at the mouth of the river Lima, north of Porto. The most spectacular festival in the north honors "Our Lady of Suffering." A replica of the Virgin is carried through the streets over carpets of flowers. The bishop directs a procession of fishers to the sea to bless the boats. Float-filled parades mark the 3-day-and-night event as a time of revelry and celebration. A blaze of fireworks ends the festival. Call the tourist office (☎ **258/82-26-20**) for exact dates, which vary from year to year. Reserve hotel rooms well in advance or be prepared to stay in a neighboring town. Late August.

September

• **Romaria da Nossa Senhora de Nazaré,** Nazaré, Portugal's most famed fishing village. The event ("Our Lady of Nazaré Festival") includes folk dancing, singing, and bullfights. The big attraction is the procession carrying the image of Nossa Senhora de Nazaré down to the sea. For more information, call ☎ **262/56-11-94.** Early to mid-September.

- **Folk Music and Dance Festival,** Algarve region, southern Portugal. In early September, many of the big towns of the Algarve—including Faro, Lagos, Silves, and Albufeira—stage a weekend of celebration and fun. It ends with a big "blowout" at Praia da Rocha on Sunday night, with music, drinking, eating, and fireworks. Call ☎ **289/80-36-04** in Faro for more information.

October
- **Last Pilgrimage of the Year to Fátima.** Thousands of pilgrims from all over the world descend on Fátima to mark the occasion of the last apparition of the Virgin, which is said to have occurred on October 12, 1917. Call ☎ **249/53-11-39** for more information. October 12.

6 The Active Vacation Planner

BULLFIGHTS   No discussion of Portuguese recreation would be complete without a reference to bullfighting (*la tourada*). Unlike the rituals in Spain and parts of South America, in Portuguese bullfighting the bull is not killed at the end of the event, but is released to a life of grazing and stud duties. The *cavaleiros* (horsemen) dress in 18th-century costumes, which include silk jackets, tricornered hats, and tan riding breeches. Bullfights are held regularly in Lisbon's campo Pequeno area, across the Tagus in the working-class city of Santarém, throughout the south-central plains, and in the Azores.

FISHING   The north of Portugal receives abundant rainfall and contains rugged hills and some of the best-stocked streams in Iberia. Most noteworthy are the Rio Minho, the Ria Vouga, the Ria Lima, and the creeks and lakes of the Serra de Estrêla. For fishing in the area in and around Lisbon, contact the **Clube dos Amadores de Pesca de Lisboa,** travessa do Adro 12, 1100 Lisbon (☎ **21/314-01-77**), or the **Clube dos Amadores de Pesca da Costa do Sol,** rua dos Fontainhos 16, 2750 Cascais (☎ **21/484-16-91**). For information about fishing elsewhere in the country, contact regional tourist offices.

Fishing in inland waters is limited compared to fishing along the 500 miles of coastline. Deep-sea fishing, in waters richly stocked with fish swept toward Europe on northeast-flowing ocean currents, yields abundant catches. Fishing boats can be rented, with and sometimes without a crew, all along the Algarve as well.

FOOTBALL   True football—called soccer in the United States—is the most popular sport in Portugal. It's taken so seriously that on Sunday afternoons during important matches (with Spain or Brazil, for example) the country seems to come almost to a standstill. Notices about the venues of upcoming matches are prominently posted with hotel concierges, in newspapers, and on bulletin boards throughout various cities. One of the most-watched teams is that of Porto, which won the European Cup in 1987. The loyalty of Lisbon fans seems equally divided between the two hometown teams, Benfica and Sporting Club.

GOLF   With its sun-flooded expanses of underused land and its cultural links to Britain, Portugal has developed a passion for golf. Most of the nation's finest courses date from the late 1970s. The most important ones are in the Algarve; many are world-class. Others have been developed near Lisbon and Estoril, near Porto, and even on Madeira and the Azores. Usually within sight of the sea, most courses incorporate dramatic topography, and most were conceived by such famed golf-course designers as Robert Trent Jones, Henry Cotton, and Frank Pennink. For more information and an overview, contact the **Federação Portuguesa de Golf** (Portuguese Golf Federation), rua Almeida Brandão 39, 1200 Lisboa (☎ **21/412-37-80**).

HORSEBACK RIDING The Portuguese have prided themselves on their equestrian skills since their earliest battles against Roman invaders. Some of the last of the world's horses bred solely from European stock are the Alter horses, which live for the most part in the Royal Stables at Alter do Chão, on the Portuguese plains. Most of the resorts along the Algarve, plus a few in Cascais, maintain stables stocked with horses for long trail rides over hills, along beaches, and through ancient sun-baked villages. For more information, contact the **Federação Equestre Portuguesa** (Portuguese Equestrian Federation), av. Duque d'Ávila 9, 1000 Lisboa (☎ **21/847-87-74**).

The best offering available from **Equitour**, P.O. Box 807, Dubois, WY 82513 (☎ **800/545-00-19**, or 307/455-33-63; e-mail: equitour@wyoming.com), is a program of 8 days and 7 nights with Lisbon as a meeting point. The price is $890 per person, and the weight limit is 175 pounds. Accommodations and special transfers are included in this tour, "the Blue Coast Ride." The rides go across some of the most scenic parts of Portugal, through valleys, along passes, and past waterfalls.

NATURE WATCHING Hiking in Portugal is great for bird-watchers. The westernmost tip of continental Europe lies along the main migration routes between the warm wetlands of Africa and the cooler breeding grounds of northern Europe. The moist, rugged terrain of northern Portugal is especially suited for nature watching, particularly around Peneda-Gerês, where wild boar, wild horses, and wolves still roam through hills and forests.

WATER SPORTS With much of its national identity connected to the sea, Portugal offers a variety of water sports. Outside the Algarve, few activities are highly organized, although the country's 500 miles of Atlantic coastline are richly peppered with secluded beaches and fishing hamlets. A recent development, especially in the Algarve, is the construction of a series of **water parks,** with large swimming pools, wave-making machines, water slides, and fun fountains.

Sailing on well-designed oceangoing craft can be arranged at the Cascais Yacht Club, at any of the marinas in the Tagus, near Lisbon, or along the Algarve—particularly near the marina at Vilamoura. The **surfing** along the sun-blasted, windswept coast at Guincho has attracted fans from throughout Europe. For information about sailing and water events, contact the **Associação Naval de Lisboa,** Doca de Belém, 1300 Lisboa (☎ **21/363-72-38**); the **Federação Portuguesa de Vela** (Portuguese Sailing Federation), Doca de Belém, 1300 Lisboa (☎ **21/364-73-24**); or the **Federação Portuguesa de Actividades Subaquáticas** (Portuguese Underwater Sports Federation), rua Almeida Brandão 39, 1200 Lisboa (☎ **21/846-01-74**).

7 Educational Vacations

CULTURAL EXCHANGES **Servas** ("to serve" in Esperanto), 11 John St., Room 407, New York, NY 10038 (☎ **212/267-0252;** fax 212/267-0292), is a nonprofit, nongovernmental, international, interfaith network of travelers and hosts. Its goal is to help build world peace, goodwill, and understanding by providing opportunities for deeper, more personal contacts among people of diverse cultural and political backgrounds. Servas travelers share living space, without charge, with members of communities worldwide. Visits last a maximum of 2 nights. Visitors pay a $65 annual fee, plus a $25 deposit for access to lists of international hosts. Visitors fill out an application and are interviewed for suitability by one of more than 200 Servas interviewers throughout the country. They then receive a directory listing the names and addresses of prospective hosts.

Friendship Force, 34 Peachtree St., Suite 900, Atlanta, GA 30303 (☎ **404/522-9490**), is a nonprofit organization intended to foster friendships among disparate peoples around the world. Dozens of branch offices throughout North America arrange en masse visits, usually once a year. Because of these group bookings, the price of air transportation is usually less than what volunteers would pay if they bought APEX tickets individually. Each participant is required to spend 2 weeks in the host country (in Europe and throughout the world). One stringent requirement is that a participant must spend 1 full week in the home of a family as a guest. Most volunteers spend the second week traveling.

HOME EXCHANGES   The **Invented City,** 41 Sutter St., Suite 1090, San Francisco, CA 94104 (☎ **800/788-CITY** or 415/252-1141; www.invented-city.com), is an international home-exchange agency. Listings are published in February, May, and November. A membership fee of $75 to $125 allows you to list your home, and you can give your preferred time to travel, your occupation, and your hobbies.

   Intervac U.S., P.O. Box 590504, San Francisco, CA 94159 (☎ **800/756-HOME** or 415/435-3497; www.interval.com), is part of the largest worldwide exchange network. It publishes four catalogs a year, containing some 10,000 homes in more than 36 countries. Members contact one another directly. The $65 fee, plus postage, includes the purchase of all three of the company's catalogs and the inclusion of your own listing in the catalog you choose. A fourth catalog costs an extra $25.

LEARNING THE LANGUAGE   The **National Registration Center for Study Abroad (NRCSA),** P.O. Box 1393, Milwaukee, WI 53201 (☎ **414/278-0631**), allows you to experience Portugal by living and learning the language. The NRCSA has helped people of all ages and backgrounds participate in foreign travel and cultural programs since 1968. Contact the NRCSA for details about the courses and their costs.

8 Health & Insurance

Portugal does not offer free medical treatment to visitors, except for citizens of certain countries, such as Great Britain, which have reciprocal health agreements. Nationals from such countries as Canada and the United States have to pay for medical services rendered.

   You will encounter few health problems traveling in Portugal. The tap water is generally safe to drink, the milk is pasteurized, and health services are good. Occasionally the change in diet may cause some minor diarrhea, so you may want to take some antidiarrhea medicine along.

   Limit your exposure to the sun, especially during the first few days of your trip and, thereafter, from 11am to 2pm. Use a sunscreen with a high protection factor and apply it liberally. Remember that children need more protection than adults do.

WHAT TO DO IF YOU GET SICK AWAY FROM HOME

It can be hard to find a doctor you can trust when you're in an unfamiliar place. Try to take proper precautions the week before you depart, to avoid falling ill while you're away from home. Amid the frenzy that often precedes a vacation break, make an extra effort to eat and sleep well—especially if you feel an illness coming on.

   If you worry about getting sick away from home, you may want to consider **medical travel insurance** (see the section on travel insurance later in this chapter). In most cases, however, your existing health plan will provide all the coverage you need. Be sure to carry your identification card in your wallet.

   If you suffer from a chronic illness, consult your doctor before your departure. For conditions like epilepsy, diabetes, or heart problems, wear a **Medic Alert Identification Tag** (☎ **800/825-3785;** www.medicalert.org), which will immediately alert doctors to your condition and give them access to your records through Medic Alert's 24-hour hot line. Membership is $35, plus a $15 annual fee.

Pack prescription medications in your carry-on luggage. Carry written prescriptions in generic, not brand-name form, and dispense all prescription medications from their original labeled vials. Also bring along copies of your prescriptions in case you lose your pills or run out.

If you wear contact lenses, pack an extra pair in case you lose one.

Contact the **International Association for Medical Assistance to Travelers (IAMAT)** (☎ **716/754-4883** or 416/652-0137; www.sentex.net/~iamat). This organization offers tips on international travel and health concerns, and lists many local English-speaking doctors. The United States **Centers for Disease Control and Prevention** (☎ **404/332-4559;** www.cdc.gov) provides up-to-date information on necessary vaccines and health hazards by region or country. By mail, its booklet is $20; on the Internet, it's free. When you're abroad, any local consulate can provide a list of area doctors who speak English. If you do get sick, you may want to ask the concierge at your hotel to recommend a local doctor—even his or her own. This will probably yield a better recommendation than any referral service.

If you can't find a doctor who can help you right away, try the emergency room at the local hospital. Many emergency rooms have walk-in clinics for emergency cases that are not life-threatening. You may not get immediate attention, but you won't pay the high price of an emergency room visit (usually a minimum of $300 just for signing your name, on top of whatever treatment you receive).

INSURANCE

Remember that Medicare covers only U.S. citizens traveling in Mexico and Canada. It does not include Portugal. Also note that to submit any claim you must always have thorough documentation, including all receipts, police reports, medical records, and the like.

There are three kinds of travel insurance: trip cancellation, medical, and lost luggage coverage. **Trip cancellation insurance** is a good idea if you have paid a large portion of your vacation expenses up front. The other two types of insurance, however, don't make sense for most travelers. Rule number one: check your existing policies before you buy any additional coverage.

Your existing **health insurance** should cover you if you get sick while on vacation (though if you belong to an HMO, you should check to see whether you are fully covered when away from home). If you need hospital treatment, most health insurance plans and HMOs will cover out-of-country hospital visits and procedures, at least to some extent. However, most make you pay the bills up front at the time of care, and you'll get a refund after you've returned and filed all the paperwork. Members of **Blue Cross/Blue Shield** can now use their cards at select hospitals in most major cities worldwide. Call (☎ **800/810-BLUE;** www.bluecares.com/blue/bluecard/wwn) or check the Web site for a list of hospitals. For independent travel health-insurance providers, see below.

Your homeowner's insurance should cover **stolen luggage.** The airlines are responsible for $1,250 on international flights if they lose your luggage; if you plan to carry anything more valuable than that, keep it in your carry-on bag.

The differences between travel assistance and insurance are often blurred. In general, the former offers on-the-spot assistance and 24-hour hot lines (mostly oriented toward medical problems), while the latter reimburses you for travel problems (medical, travel, or otherwise) after you have filed the paperwork. The coverage you should consider will depend on how much protection your existing health insurance or other policies already offer. Some credit- and charge-card companies may insure you against travel accidents if you buy plane, train, or bus tickets with their cards. Before buying additional insurance, read your policies and agreements carefully. Call your insurers or credit- or charge-card companies if you have questions.

Some credit cards (American Express and certain gold and platinum Visa and MasterCards, for example) offer automatic flight insurance against death or dismemberment in case of an airplane crash.

If you do require additional insurance, try one of the companies listed below. But don't pay for more than you need. For example, if you need only trip cancellation insurance, don't purchase coverage for lost or stolen property. Trip cancellation insurance costs approximately 6% to 8% of the total value of your vacation.

Among the reputable issuers of travel insurance are:

Access America, 6600 W. Broad St., Richmond, VA 23230 (☎ 800/284-8300)

Travel Guard International, 1145 Clark St., Stevens Point, WI 54481 (☎ 800/826-1300)

Travel Insured International, Inc., P.O. Box 280568, East Hartford, CT 06128 (☎ 800/243-3174)

Columbus Travel Insurance, 279 High St., Croydon CR0 1QH (☎ 0171/375-0011 in London; www2.columbusdirect.com/columbusdirect)

International SOS Assistance, P.O. Box 11568, Philadelphia PA 11916 (☎ 800/523-8930 or 215/244-1500), strictly an assistance company

Travelex Insurance Services, P.O. Box 9408, Garden City, NY 11530-9408 (☎ 800/228-9792)

For Blue Cross/Blue Shield coverage abroad, see "Health" above. Companies specializing in accident and medical care include:

MEDEX International, P.O. Box 5375, Timonium, MD 21094-5375 (☎ 888/MEDEX-00 or 410/453-6300; fax 410/453-6301; www.medexassist.com)

Travel Assistance International (Worldwide Assistance Services, Inc.), 1133 15th St. NW, Suite 400, Washington, DC 20005 (☎ 800/821-2828 or 202/828-5894; fax 202/828-5896)

CAR RENTER'S INSURANCE

For information on car renter's insurance, see "Getting Around by Car," below.

9 Tips for Travelers with Special Needs

FOR TRAVELERS WITH DISABILITIES

Travelers with disabilities have more resources than ever before. *A World of Options,* a 658-page book of resources, covers everything from biking trips to scuba outfitters. It costs $35 ($30 for members) and is available from **Mobility International USA,** P.O. Box 10767, Eugene, OR 97440 (☎ **541/343-1284,** voice and TDD; www.miusa.org). Annual membership is $35, which includes the quarterly newsletter, *Over the Rainbow.* **Twin Peaks Press,** P.O. Box 129, Vancouver, WA 98666 (☎ 360/694-2462), publishes travel-related books for people with disabilities.

The Moss Rehab Hospital (☎ 215/456-9600) has been providing friendly, helpful phone advice and referrals for years through its **Travel Information Service** (☎ 215/456-9603; www.mossresourcenet.org).

You can join the **Society for the Advancement of Travel for the Handicapped** **(SATH),** 347 Fifth Ave. Suite 610, New York, NY 10016 (☎ **212/447-7284;** fax

212/725-8253; www.sath.org). Membership ($45 annually, $30 for seniors and students) includes access to a vast network of connections in the travel industry. The society provides information sheets on travel destinations, and referrals to tour operators that specialize in traveling with disabilities. The quarterly magazine, *Open World for Disability and Mature Travel,* is full of good information and resources. A year's subscription is $13 ($21 outside the U.S.).

Travelers with disabilities may also want to consider joining a tour that caters specifically to them. One of the best operators is **Flying Wheels Travel,** 143 West Bridge (P.O. Box 382), Owatonna, MN 55060 (☎ **800/535-6790;** www.flyingwheels.com). It offers escorted tours, with an emphasis on sports, as well as private tours in minivans with lifts. Other reputable specialized tour operators include **Access Adventures** (☎ **716/889-9096**), which offers sports-related vacations; **Accessible Journeys** (☎ **800/TINGLES** or 610/521-0339), for slow walkers and wheelchair travelers; the **Guided Tour, Inc.** (☎ **215/782-1370**); and **Directions Unlimited** (☎ **800/ 533-5343**).

You can obtain a copy of *Air Transportation of Handicapped Persons* by writing to Free Advisory Circular No. AC12032, Distribution Unit, U.S. Department of Transportation, Publications Division, M-4332, Washington, DC 20590.

Vision-impaired travelers should contact the **American Foundation for the Blind,** 11 Penn Plaza, Suite 300, New York, NY 10001 (☎ **800/232-5463**), for information on traveling with seeing-eye dogs.

In the United Kingdom, **British Rail** offers discounts of up to 50% on some fares to anyone using a wheelchair and traveling with one companion. The **Royal Association for Disability and Rehabilitation (RADAR),** Unit 12, City Forum, 250 City Rd., London EC1V 8AF (☎ **0207/250-3222**), publishes two annual holiday guides for travelers with disabilities: *Holidays and Travel Abroad* and *Holidays in the British Isles.* It also acts as a clearinghouse for information about travel for and with people with disabilities, and provides a number of holiday fact sheets and pamphlets. There's a nominal charge for all publications.

Another unusual clearinghouse of data of interest to elderly travelers or travelers with disabilities is **Holiday Care Service,** 2 Old Bank Chambers, Station Rd., Horley, Surrey, England RH6 9HW (☎ **01293/774-535;** fax 01293/784-647).

FOR GAY & LESBIAN TRAVELERS

The **International Gay & Lesbian Travel Association,** or IGLTA (☎ **800/ 448-8550** or 954/776-2626; fax 954/776-3303; www.iglta.org), links travelers with the appropriate gay-friendly service organization or tour specialist. With around 1,200 members, it offers quarterly newsletters, marketing mailings, and a membership directory that's updated quarterly. Membership often includes gay or lesbian businesses but is open to individuals for $150 yearly, plus a $100 administration fee for new members. Members are kept informed of gay and gay-friendly hoteliers, tour operators, and airline and cruise-line representatives. Contact the IGLTA for a list of its member agencies, who will be tied into IGLTA's information resources.

General gay and lesbian travel agencies include **Family Abroad** (☎ **800/999-5500** or 212/459-1800; gay and lesbian); **Above and Beyond Tours** (☎ **800/397-2681;** mainly gay men); and **Yellowbrick Road** (☎ **800/642-2488**; gay and lesbian).

There are also two good, biannual English-language gay guidebooks. Both focus on gay men and include information for lesbians. You can get the *Spartacus International Gay Guide* or *Odysseus* from most gay and lesbian bookstores, or order them from Giovanni's Room (☎ **215/923-2960**) or A Different Light Bookstore (☎ **800/343-4002** or 212/989-4850). Both lesbians and gays might want to pick up a copy of *Gay Travel A to Z* ($16). *The Ferrari Guides* (www.q-net.com) is another very good series of gay and lesbian guidebooks.

Out and About, 8 W. 19th St. no. 401, New York, NY 10011 (☎ **800/929-2268** or 212/645-6922), offers guidebooks and a monthly newsletter packed with good information on the global gay and lesbian scene. A year's subscription to the newsletter costs $49. *Our World,* 1104 North Nova Rd., Suite 251, Daytona Beach, FL 32117 (☎ **904/441-5367**), is a slicker monthly magazine promoting and highlighting travel bargains and opportunities. Annual subscription rates are $35 in the United States, $45 outside the United States.

FOR SENIORS

Members of the **American Association of Retired Persons (AARP)**, 601 E St. NW, Washington, DC 20049 (☎ **800/424-3410** or 202/434-2277; www.aarp.org), get discounts on hotels, airfares, and car rentals. AARP offers members a wide range of special benefits, including *Modern Maturity* magazine and a monthly newsletter.

The **National Council of Senior Citizens,** 8403 Colesville Rd., Suite 1200, Silver Spring, MD 20910 (☎ **301/578-8800**), a nonprofit organization, offers a newsletter six times a year (partly devoted to travel tips) and discounts on hotel and auto rentals. Annual dues are $13 per person or couple.

Mature Outlook, P.O. Box 9390, Des Moines, IA 50306 (☎ **800/336-6330**), began as a travel organization for people over 50, though it now caters to people of all ages. Members receive discounts on hotels and receive a bimonthly magazine. Annual membership is $19.95, which entitles members to discounts and, often, free coupons for discounted merchandise from Sears.

The Mature Traveler, a monthly 12-page newsletter on senior citizen travel, is a valuable resource. It is available by subscription ($30 a year) from GEM Publishing Group, Box 50400, Reno, NV 89513-0400 (☎ **800/460-6676**). GEM also publishes *The Book of Deals* ($9.95), a collection of more than 1,000 senior discounts on airlines, lodging, tours, and attractions around the country. Another helpful publication is *101 Tips for the Mature Traveler,* available from Grand Circle Travel, 347 Congress St., Suite 3A, Boston, MA 02210 (☎ **800/221-2610** or 617/350-7500; fax 617/346-6700; www.gct.com).

Grand Circle Travel is also one of the hundreds of travel agencies specializing in vacations for seniors. Many of these packages, however, are of the tour-bus variety, with free trips thrown in for those who organize groups of 10 or more. Seniors seeking more independent travel should probably consult a regular travel agent. **SAGA International Holidays,** 222 Berkeley St., Boston, MA 02116 (☎ **800/343-0273;** www.sagaholidays.com), offers inclusive tours and cruises for those 50 and older. SAGA also sponsors the more substantial "**Road Scholar Tours**" (☎ **800/621-2151**), which are fun-loving but with an educational bent.

If you want something more than the average vacation or guided tour, try **Elderhostel,** 75 Federal St., Boston, MA 02110-1941 (☎ **877/426-8056**; www.elderhostel.org), or the University of New Hampshire's **Interhostel** (☎ **800/733-9753;** www.learn.unh.edu). They're variations on the same theme: educational travel for senior citizens. On these escorted tours, the days are packed with seminars, lectures, and field trips. Academic experts lead the sightseeing. Elderhostel arranges study programs for those aged 55 and over (and a spouse or companion of any age) in the United States and in 77 countries. Most courses last about 3 weeks and many include airfare, accommodations in student dormitories or modest inns, meals, and tuition. Write or call for a free catalog, which lists upcoming courses and destinations. Interhostel takes travelers 50 and over (with companions over 40), and offers 2- and

3-week trips, mostly international. The courses in both programs are ungraded, involve no homework, and often focus on the liberal arts. They're not luxury vacations, but they're fun and fulfilling.

FOR FAMILIES

If you're flying with kids, don't forget a deck of cards, toys, extra bottles, pacifiers, diapers, and chewing gum to help them relieve ear pressure buildup during ascent and descent.

Family Travel Times is published six times a year by Travel with Your Children, or TWYCH, 40 Fifth Ave., 7th floor, New York, NY 10011 (☎ **888/822-4388** or 212/477-5524), and includes a weekly call-in service for subscribers. Subscriptions are $40 a year. A free publication list and a sample issue are available by calling or sending a request to the above address.

Families Welcome!, 92 N. Main, Ashland, OR 97520 (☎ **800/326-0724** or 541/482-6121), a travel company specializing in worry-free vacations for families, offers "City Kids" packages to certain European cities.

The University of New Hampshire runs **Familyhostel** (☎ **800/733-9753**), an intergenerational alternative to standard guided tours. You live on a European college campus for the 2- or 3-week program, attend lectures and seminars, go on lots of field trips, and sightsee—all guided by a team of experts and academics. It's designed for children 8 to 15, parents, and grandparents.

The best deals for British families are often package tours put together by some travel-industry giants. Foremost among these is **Thomsons Tour Operators.** Through its subsidiary, **Skytours** (☎ **0207/387-9321**), it offers dozens of air-land packages to Portugal (mostly the Algarve). A designated number of airline seats are reserved for the free use of youths under 18 accompanying their parents. To qualify, parents must book airfare and hotel accommodations for 2 weeks or more as far in advance as possible. Savings for families with children can be substantial.

FOR STUDENTS

The best resource for students is the **Council on International Educational Exchange,** or CIEE. It can set you up with an ID card (see below), and its travel branch, **Council Travel Service** (☎ **800/226-8624;** www.ciee.com), is the biggest student travel agency operation in the world. It can get you discounts on plane tickets, rail passes, and the like. Ask for a list of CTS offices in major cities so you can keep the discounts flowing (and aid lines open) as you travel.

From CIEE you can obtain the student traveler's best friend, the $18 **International Student Identity Card** (ISIC). It's the only officially acceptable form of student identification, good for cut rates on rail passes and plane tickets, and other discounts. It also provides you with basic health and life insurance and a 24-hour help line. If you're no longer a student but are under 26 you can get a GO 25 card from the same organization. It will get you the insurance and some of the discounts, but not student admission prices at museums.

In Canada, **Travel CUTS,** 200 Ronson St., Suite 320, Toronto, ONT M9W 5Z9 (☎ **800/667-2887** or 416/614-2887; www.travelcuts.com), offers similar services. **Campus Travel,** 52 Grosvenor Gardens, London SW1W 0AG (☎ **0171/730-3402;** www.campustravel.co.uk), opposite Victoria Station, is Britain's leading specialist in student and youth travel.

FOR SINGLE TRAVELERS

Many people prefer traveling alone—save for the relatively steep cost of booking a single room, which is usually well over half the price of a double. **Travel Companion**

(☎ 516/454-0880) is one of the nation's oldest roommate finders for single travelers. Register to find a trustworthy travel mate who will split the cost of the room and be around as little, or as often, as you like during the day.

Several tour organizers cater to solo travelers. **Experience Plus** (☎ **800/685-4565;** fax 907/484-8489) offers an interesting selection of single-only trips.

Travel Buddies (☎ **800/998-9099** or 604/533-2483) runs single-friendly tours with no singles supplement. **The Single Gourmet Club,** 133 E. 58th St., New York, NY 10022 (☎ **212/980-8788;** fax 212/980-3138), is an international social, dining, and travel club for singles. It has offices in 21 American and Canadian cities, and in London.

You may also want to research the **Outdoor Singles Network,** P.O. Box 781, Haines, AK 99827. An established (since 1989) quarterly newsletter for outdoor-loving singles, ages 19 to 90, the network will help you find a travel companion, pen pal, or soul mate within its pages. A one-year subscription costs $45, and your personal ad is printed free in the next issue. Current issues are $15. Write for free information or check out www.kcd.com/bearstar/osn.html.

Many British agents are keenly aware of the needs of the single traveler. One tour operator whose groups are usually at least half singles is **Explore Worldwide Ltd.,** 1 Frederick St., Aldershot, Hampshire, England GU11 1LQ (☎ **01252/344-161**). It has a well-justified reputation for offering offbeat tours, including 14-day expeditions to five islands of the Azores, and motor coach tours through the highlights of "Unknown Spain and Portugal." Groups rarely include more than 16 participants; children under 14 are not allowed.

10 Getting There

BY PLANE

Flying from New York to Lisbon typically costs less than from New York to Paris, Amsterdam, or Frankfurt.

In today's marketplace, one airline proposes a fare structure, and another airline follows with a competing and perhaps different fare structure. The competition may or may not result in uniform prices for all airlines flying to that particular country. It all adds up to chaos—but often *beneficial* chaos for the alert traveler willing to study and consider all the fares available. The key to bargain airfares is to shop around.

Flying time from New York to Lisbon is about 6½ hours; from Atlanta to Lisbon (with a stopover), 12 hours; from Los Angeles to Lisbon (with a stopover), 15 hours; from Montréal or Toronto, 8 hours.

Major Airlines When it was established in 1946, **TAP** (☎ **800/221-7370;** www.tap-airportugal.pt), the national airline of Portugal, flew only between Lisbon and Angola and Mozambique (then Portuguese colonies). Today TAP flies to four continents and has one of the youngest fleets in the airline industry—its aircraft have an average age of only 4 years. Its U.S. gateways include JFK, in New York City, and Newark, in New Jersey. In Portugal, it flies to nine destinations, the most popular of which are Lisbon, Porto, Faro, Funchal (Madeira), and Terceira (the Azores).

Delta (☎ **800/241-4141;** www.delta-air.com) and **TWA** (☎ **800/221-2000;** www.twa.com) also offer daily nonstop service from JFK to Lisbon. Connections can be made from most major points throughout North America on TWA's or Delta's network, but if you live outside New York, you must change planes at JFK.

In 1997 **Continental Airlines** (☎ **800/231-0856;** www.flycontinental.com) began flying to Lisbon from Newark International Airport. The increased capacity comes as a welcome addition to existing air service, particularly during heavy travel periods in summer.

Air Canada (☎ 800/776-3000; www.aircanada.ca) no longer offers direct flights to Lisbon, but it does offer daily flights from Toronto and Montréal to Paris, where you can transfer to another carrier to reach Lisbon.

For flights from the U.K., contact **British Airways** (☎ 0208/897-4000, or 0345/222-111 outside London; www.british-airways.com)) or **TAP,** Gillingham House, 38–44 Gillingham St., London SW1V 1JW (☎ 0207/828-0262).

TAP also has frequent flights on popular routes from major cities in western Europe. Its flights to Lisbon from London are an especially good deal; sometimes they're priced so attractively that one might combine a sojourn in England with an inexpensive side excursion to Portugal. TAP gives passengers the option of stopping midway across the Atlantic in the Azores, and makes baggage transfers and seat reservations on connecting flights within Portugal much easier.

Regular Fares   All airlines divide their calendar year into three seasons—basic, shoulder, and peak—whose dates might vary slightly from airline to airline. TAP's basic season is November 1 to December 14 and December 25 to March 31. The most expensive season, when passengers tend to book most transatlantic flights solidly, is June 1 to September 15. Other dates are shoulder season.

Discounted Fares   All the major carriers offer an **APEX** ticket, generally the cheapest transatlantic option. Usually such a ticket must be purchased 14 to 21 days in advance, and a stay in Europe must last at least 7 days but not more than 30. Changing the date of departure from North America within 21 days of departure will sometimes entail a penalty of around $150; with some tickets, no changes of any kind are permitted.

A more flexible (but more expensive) option is the **regular economy fare.** This ticket offers the same seating and services as the APEX ticket for a shorter stay than the 7-day APEX minimum requirement. One of the most attractive side benefits of an economy-class ticket is the absolute freedom to make last-minute changes in flight dates, and unrestricted stopovers.

For families, one strong attraction of TAP is that **infants under 2 years** pay 10% of the adult fare. (About a half-dozen bassinets are available on transatlantic flights, allowing parents to lift infants off their laps onto specially designed brackets during certain segments of the flight.) **Children under 12** pay 75% of the adult price for most categories of tickets.

TAP offers a **winter senior citizen fare** from its three U.S. gateways to anywhere in Portugal. The discount is 10% off published fares. The discount applies for senior citizens (travelers 62 years of age or older) plus a companion of any age (spouse, grandchild, friend). The maximum stay abroad with this type of ticket is 2 months. Tickets must be purchased at least 14 days before departure.

Subject to change, TAP offers a one-way **youth fare.** It's 50% off the regular fare, depending on the season, between New York or Boston and Lisbon. Tickets of this type can only be purchased at the last minute, because they can be booked only within 72 hours of departure. Youth fares are offered only to travelers aged 12 to 24, and only if space is available. They cannot be mailed and must be purchased in person at a travel agent or any TAP counter.

None of the above options take into account **promotional fares** airlines might initiate while you're planning your trip. These are usually particularly attractive during the basic season.

Clients who prefer not to specify when they'll return home, or who can't purchase their tickets within 21 days before takeoff, usually opt for TAP's **excursion fare.** It costs more than either APEX option, but has no restrictions on advance purchases or time of travel. You're allowed one stopover free, and an additional one for $50.

The airline's most exclusive, and most expensive, class of service is named after the seafaring pioneers who spread Portugal's empire throughout the world. **Navigator Class** passengers benefit from better service and upgraded food and drink. This is TAP's version of business class, comparable to first class on other major carriers.

BY TRAIN

Thousands of holiday-making Brits (and foreigners visiting the U.K.) cross France and Spain by rail to begin their Portuguese holiday. If you opt for this, expect lots of worthwhile scenery, and be aware that you'll have to change trains in Paris.

Trains from London originate in Waterloo Station, pass through the Channel Tunnel, and arrive in Paris at Gare du Nord. Don't expect to merely cross over a railway platform to change trains: You'll have to traverse urban Paris, moving from Gare du Nord to Gare Montparnasse. You can do this for the cost of a Métro ticket, but if you have luggage, hiring a taxi makes the transit a lot easier. (Taxis line up in long queues near your point of arrival.) From Gare Montparnasse, the train continues through France, but requires a change of equipment in Hendaye, on the Spanish-French border. It continues to Lisbon's St. Apolonia station. Total travel time for this itinerary is 22 hours, so we strongly recommend reserving a couchette (sleeping car). Budgeteers can save about 10% off fares by taking a slower, less convenient ferry across the English Channel. However, this option adds at least 5 hours, additional transfers, and many hassles at the docks on either side of the water, and will involve you in imbroglios that probably aren't worth the savings.

An especially convenient outlet in London for buying railway tickets lies opposite Platform 2 in Victoria Station, London SW1V 1JY. **Wasteels Ltd.** (☎ **0207/ 834-7066**) will provide railway-related services and discuss fares and rail passes and their various drawbacks, and its staff will probably spend a bit more time with a client during the planning of an itinerary. Depending on circumstances, Wasteels sometimes charges a £5 fee for its services, but for the information it has available, this can be money well spent.

From Paris, the most luxurious way to reach Portugal is by the overnight Paris–Madrid *TALGO* express train. It leaves from Gare d'Austerlitz and arrives in Madrid's Chamartín Station, where you transfer to the *Lisboa Express*.

In Madrid the *Lusitania Express* leaves the Atocha Station at 10:35pm and arrives in Lisbon at 9:10am; the 11pm train arrives in Lisbon at 8:40am. For more complete information about rail connections, contact **Caminhos de Ferro Portuguêses,** Calçada do Duque 20, 1200 Lisboa (☎ **21/888-40-25** in Lisbon).

If you plan to travel a lot on European railroads, secure the latest copy of the *Thomas Cook European Timetable of Railroads.* This comprehensive 500-plus-page timetable documents all of Europe's main-line passenger rail services with detail and accuracy. It's available exclusively in North America from the **Forsyth Travel Library,** P.O. Box 480800, Kansas City, MO 64148 (☎ **800/367-7984**). It costs $27.95, plus $4.50 postage for priority airmail to the United States and US$6.50 for shipments to Canada. You can buy rail passes (see below) from Forsyth.

RAIL PASSES For years, many travelers to Europe have been taking advantage of one of its greatest travel bargains, the **EurailPass.** It permits unlimited first-class rail travel in any country in western Europe (except the British Isles) and Hungary. Passes are available for periods as short as 15 days and as long as 3 months.

The pass cannot be purchased in Europe, so you must secure one before leaving home. Passes cost $554 for 15 days, $718 for 21 days, $890 for 1 month, $1,260 for

Flying for Less: Tips for Getting the Best Airfares

Passengers within the same airplane cabin rarely pay the same fare for their seats. Business travelers who need to purchase tickets at the last minute, change their itinerary at a moment's notice, or get home before the weekend pay the premium rate, known as the full fare. Passengers who can book far in advance, who don't mind staying over Saturday night, or who are willing to travel on Tuesday, Wednesday, or Thursday after 7pm pay a fraction of the full fare. On most flights, even the shortest hops, the full fare is close to $1,000 or more, but a 7- or 14-day advance purchase ticket is closer to $200 to $300. Here are a few other easy ways to save.

1. Airlines periodically lower prices on their most popular routes. Check your newspaper for advertised discounts or call the airlines directly and ask if any **promotional rates** or special fares are available. You'll almost never see a sale during the peak summer vacation months of July and August, or during the Thanksgiving or Christmas seasons. In periods of low-volume travel, you should pay no more than $400 for a cross-country flight. If your schedule is flexible, ask if you can secure a cheaper fare by staying an extra day or by flying midweek. (Many airlines won't volunteer this information.) If you already hold a ticket when a sale breaks, it may even pay to exchange your ticket, which usually incurs a $50 to $75 charge.

   Note, however, that the lowest-priced fares are often nonrefundable, require advance purchase of 1 to 3 weeks and a certain length of stay, and carry penalties for changing dates of travel.

2. **Consolidators,** also known as "bucket shops," are a good place to find low fares. Consolidators buy seats in bulk from the airlines and sell them back to the public at prices below even the airlines' discounted rates. Their small, boxed ads usually run in the Sunday travel section at the bottom of the page. Before you pay a consolidator, however, ask for a record locator number and confirm your seat with the airline itself. Be prepared to book your ticket with a different consolidator—there are many to choose from—if the airline can't confirm your reservation. Also be aware that bucket shop tickets are usually nonrefundable or carry stiff cancellation penalties, often as high as 50% to 75% of the ticket price.

   Council Travel (☎ **800/226-8624;** www.counciltravel.com) and **STA Travel** (☎ **800/781-4040;** www.sta.travel.com) cater especially to young travelers, but their bargain-basement prices are available to people of all ages. **Travel Bargains** (☎ **800/AIR-FARE;** www.1800airfare.com) was formerly owned by TWA but now offers the deepest discounts on many other airlines, with a 4-day advance purchase. Other reliable consolidators include **1-800-FLY-CHEAP** (www.1800flycheap.com) and **TFI Tours International** (☎ **800-745-8000** or 212/736-1140), which serves as a clearinghouse for unused seats. "Rebaters" such as **Travel Avenue** (☎ **800/333-3335** or 312/876-1116) and the **Smart Traveller** (☎ **800/448-3338** in the U.S., or 305/448-3338) rebate part of their commissions to you.

3. Search the **Internet** for cheap fares—though it's still best to compare your findings with the research of a dedicated travel agent, if you're lucky enough to have one, especially when you're booking more than just a flight. Two respected virtual travel agents are **Travelocity** (www.travelocity.com) and **Microsoft Expedia** (www.expedia.com). Each has quirks—Expedia, for example, requires you to register—but they all provide variations of the same service. Just enter the dates you want to fly and the cities you want to visit, and the computer roots out the lowest fares. Expedia's site will e-mail you the best airfare deal once a week on request. Travelocity uses the SABRE computer reservations system that most travel agents use, and has a "Last Minute Deals" database that advertises really cheap fares for those who can get away at a moment's notice.

4. Great last-minute deals are also available through a free e-mail service, provided directly by the airlines, called **E-savers.** Each week, the airline sends you a list of discounted flights, usually leaving the upcoming Friday or Saturday, and returning the following Monday or Tuesday. You can sign up for all the major airlines at once by logging on to **Smarter Living** (www.smarterliving. com), or go to each individual airline's web site.

5. Book a seat on a **charter flight.** Discounted fares have pared the number available, but they can still be found. Most charter operators advertise and sell their seats through travel agents, making these local professionals your best source of information for available flights. Before deciding to take a charter flight, however, check the restrictions on the ticket. You may be asked to purchase a tour package, to pay in advance, to be amenable if the day of departure is changed, to pay a service charge, to fly on an airline you're not familiar with (this usually is not the case), and to pay harsh penalties if you cancel—but be understanding if the charter doesn't fill up and is canceled up to 10 days before departure. Summer charters fill more quickly than others and are almost sure to fly, but if you decide on a charter flight, seriously consider cancellation and baggage insurance.

6. Look into **courier flights.** Companies that hire couriers use your luggage allowance for their business baggage; in return, you get a deeply discounted ticket. Flights are often offered at the last minute, and you may have to arrange a pretrip interview to make sure you're right for the job. **Now Voyager,** open Monday to Friday 10am to 5:30pm, Saturday noon to 4:30pm (☎ **212/ 431-1616;** www.nowvoyagertravel.com), flies from New York and also offers noncourier discounted fares.

7. Join a travel club such as **Moment's Notice** (☎ **718/234-6295**) or **Sears Discount Travel Club** (☎ **800/433-9383**, or 800/255-1487 to join), which supply unsold tickets at discounted prices. You pay an annual membership fee to get the club's hotline number. Of course, you're limited to what's available, so you have to be flexible.

2 months, and $1,558 for 3 months. Children under 4 travel free if they don't occupy a seat (otherwise, they're charged half fare); children under 12 are charged half fare.

A **Eurail Flexipass** offers the same privileges as the EurailPass but allows passengers to visit Europe in first class. It provides a number of individual travel days that can be used over a much longer period of consecutive days. That makes it possible to stay in one city and not lose a single day of discounted travel. There are two passes: $654 for 10 days of travel within 2 months, $862 for 15 days of travel within 2 months.

If you're under 26, you can buy a **Eurail Youthpass**, good for unlimited second-class travel wherever EurailPass is honored. It costs $623 for 1 month, $882 for 2 months. A **Eurail Youth Flexipass** is also good for travelers under 26. Two passes are available: $458 for 10 days of travel within 2 months, $599 for 15 days of travel within 2 months.

The **Eurail Saverpass** offers discounted 15-day travel, but only if a group of three people travels constantly and continuously together between April and September, or if two people travel constantly and continuously together between October and March. The price of a Saverpass, valid all over Europe and good for first class only, is $470 for 15 days, $610 for 21 days, and $756 for 1 month.

The advantages are tempting: There are no tickets and no supplements—simply show the pass to the ticket collector, then settle back to enjoy the scenery. Seat reservations are required on some trains. Many trains have couchettes (sleeping cars), which cost extra. Obviously, the 2- or 3-month traveler gets the greatest economic advantages; the EurailPass is ideal for such extensive trips. Pass holders can visit all of Portugal's major sights, then end their vacation in Norway, for example.

Voyagers with 14 days or 1 month have to estimate rail distance before determining if a pass works to their benefit. To obtain full advantage of the ticket for 15 days or 1 month, you'd have to spend a great deal of time on the train.

Travel agents in all towns and railway agents in such major cities as New York, Montréal, and Los Angeles sell passes. One of the most cooperative (and easy to reach) agencies is **Rail Europe,** 226–230 Westchester Ave., White Plains, NY 10604 (☎ **800/438-7245** or 914/681-3232), or 2087 Dundas St. E., Suite 105, Mississauga, ON L4X 1M2 (☎ **800/361-7245**).

VIA THE CHANNEL TUNNEL

The *Eurostar Express* began twice-daily passenger service between London and both Paris and Brussels in 1994. The $15 billion Channel Tunnel, one of the great engineering feats of all time, is the first link between Britain and the Continent since the Ice Age. The 31-mile journey between France and Great Britain takes 35 minutes, although actual Chunnel time is only 19 minutes.

Rail Europe (☎ **800/94-CHUNNEL** for information; for reservations, 0990/186-186 from the U.K., 800/387-6782 from the U.S.; www.raileurope.com) sells tickets on the *Eurostar* with direct service between Paris or Brussels and London. Your best deal is to book with the 0990 number in England. If you reserve at least 7 days in advance, you get a £159 ($262.35) round-trip in first class, including a three-course dinner with wine. The bargain is the £89 ($146.85) second-class fare, which does not include dinner. Through the 800 number in the United States, fares range from $358 (nonrefundable) to $438 (refundable). Second-class fares run $218 (nonrefundable) to $298 (refundable).

BY BUS

There is no convenient bus service from other parts of Europe to Portugal. Flying, driving, or traveling by rail are the preferred methods. However, the buses that do make

Portuguese Rail System

To Tuy & Vigo

Caminha
Valença
do Minho
Viana do Castelo
Barcelos
Braga
Chaves
Bragança
Guimarães
Baulhe
Vila
Real
Mirandela
Póvoa de Varzim
Porto
Armarante
Regua
Pocinho
Espinho
Sernada
Aveiro
Viseu
Guarda
Vila Formoso
Nelas
To Salamanca
& Paris
Cantanhede
Sta. Comba Dão
Pampilhosa
Figueira da Foz
Coimbra
Covilhã
Fundão
Pombal
Tomar
Castelo Branco
Batalha
Fátima
Leiria
Alcobaça
Abrantes
Caldas da
Rainha
Castelo de Vide
Óbidos
Santarém
To Madrid
Setil
Mafra
Mora
Portalegre
Queluz
Sintra
Estremoz
Elvas
Cascais
Arraiolos
Estoril
LISBON
Palmela
Badajoz
Casa Branca
Évora
Setúbal
Alcárcer do Sal
Reguengos
Moura
Sines
Beja

Atlantic
Ocean

SPAIN

Tãmega Line ❶
Corgo Line ❷
Tua Line ❸
Douro Line ❹
Vouga Line ❺

Silves
Lagos
Tunes
To Huelva & Sevilla
Sagres
Tavira
Albufeira
Faro
Vila Real
de Santo António

0   30 Mi
0   50 Km

the trip—say, from London or France—offer somewhat lower prices (and significantly less comfort) than equivalent journeys by rail.

The largest bus line in Europe, **Eurolines Ltd.,** 52 Grosvenor Gardens, London SW1W OUA (☎ **0207/730-8235**), operates bus routes to Portugal that stop at several places in France (including Paris) and Spain along the way. Buses leave from London's Victoria Coach Station every Saturday at 10pm, travel by ferry across the English Channel, and arrive in Lisbon 24 hours later. The bus stops every 4 hours for 30 to 45 minutes, adding considerably to the transit time. Tickets from London to Lisbon cost £101 ($166.65) one way, £169 ($278.85) round-trip.

The same company offers service from London's Victoria Coach Station to Faro, in southern Portugal, every Monday and Friday at 10pm. Arrival is 2 days later, after multiple stops and delays. The cost is £107 ($176.55) one way, £177 ($292.05) round-trip. For more detailed information, call Eurolines (☎ **01582/404-511**) in the London suburb of Luton.

BY BOAT

BY FERRY **Brittany Ferries** operates from Plymouth, England, to Santander, Spain. From March through November, crossing time is 23 to 24 hours. Between October and April, the trip takes 30 to 33 hours. Contact **Brittany Ferries,** Millbay Docks, Plymouth, England PL1 3EW (☎ **0870/90-12-400** or 0990/143-537), for exact schedules and more information. From Santander you can drive west to Galicia, in Spain, then head south toward Portugal, entering through the Minho district.

BY SEACAT Traveling by SeaCat (a form of high-speed catamaran) cuts your journey time from the United Kingdom to the Continent. A SeaCat trip can be a fun adventure, especially for first-timers or children, because the vessel is technically "flying" above the surface of the water. A SeaCat crossing from Folkestone to Boulogne is longer in miles but takes less time than the Dover–Calais route used by conventional ferries. For reservations and information, call **HoverSpeed** (☎ **01304/240-241**).

BY PACKAGE TOUR

There are many advantages to organized tours. You need not be afraid of traveling alone or with timid companions. Everything is arranged for you—transportation in the countries you visit, hotels, service, sightseeing trips, excursions, luggage handling, tips, taxes, and many meals. You're given time to go shopping or to nose around on your own.

Many people book packages through their preferred airline. Delta offers some of the best as part of its **Delta Dream Vacations** (☎ **800/872-7786**).

TWA Getaway Tours (☎ **800/438-2929**) are popular. The 12-day "Highlights of Spain and Portugal" visits many destinations in Spain, but also takes in such Portuguese cities as Lisbon, Coimbra, and Fátima.

Trafalgar Tours, 11 E. 26th St., Suite 1300, New York, NY 10010-1402 (☎ **800/854-0103** or 212/689-8977), has an exceptional schedule of moderately priced 14- to 17-day tours to Spain and Portugal. (Two go to Morocco as well.) Ask about CostSaver tours, which book you in tourist-class hotels.

Other leading tour operators to Portugal include **Spain Tours and Beyond,** 261 W. 70th St., New York, NY 10023 (☎ **212/595-2400**); **Jet Vacations,** 1775 Broadway, New York, NY 10019 (☎ **800/538-2762** or 212/474-8740); and **DER Tours,** 9501 W. Devon Ave., Rosemont, IL 60018 (☎ **800/937-1235**).

Miami is an increasingly popular launching pad for Iberia. The best tours in Florida are offered by **4th Dimension Tours,** 7101 SW 99th Ave., Suite 105, Miami, FL 33173 (☎ **800/644-0438** or 305/279-0014).

In the United Kingdom organized tours operators include **Magic of Portugal,** Shepherds Bush Road, London W6 7AS (☎ **0208/741-1181**), and **Mundo Color,** 276 Vauxhall Bridge Rd., London SW1V 1BE (☎ **0207/828-6021**).

THEME TOURS   Cycling tours are a good way to see the back roads of a country and stretch your limbs. Although dozens of companies in Britain offer guided cycling tours on foreign turf, only a handful offer itineraries through Portugal. One is the **Cyclists' Tourist Club,** 69 Meadrow, Godalming, Surrey GU7 3HS (☎ **01483/ 417-217**). It charges £25 ($41.25) a year for membership, which includes information and suggested cycling routes through Portugal and dozens of other countries.

In the United States, bicyclists can contact **Backroads,** 1516 5th St., Berkeley, CA 94710 (☎ **800/462-2848** or 510/527-1555). Another outfitter arranging bike tours is **Uniquely Europe,** 2819 First Ave., Seattle, WA 98121 (☎ **800/426-3615** or 206/441-8682). In Canada, contact **Butterfield & Robinson,** 70 Bond St., Toronto, ON M5B 1X3 (☎ **800/678-1147** or 416/864-1354).

The best golf tours (usually in the Algarve) are arranged by **Golf International,** 275 Madison Ave., New York, NY 10016 (☎ **800/833-1389** or 212/986-9176). West Coast residents can contact **ITC Golf Tours,** 4134 Atlantic Ave., Suite 205, Long Beach, CA 90807 (☎ **800/257-4981** or 562/595-6905).

Coopersmith's England, P.O. Box 900, Inverness, CA 94937 (☎ **415/669-1914**), offers tours exploring the art, architecture, and most beautiful gardens of Lisbon and Madeira.

Tours on the best hiking and walking trails are available through **Adventure Center,** 1311 63rd St., Emeryville, CA 94608 (☎ **800/227-8747** or 510/654-1879). For kayaking, contact **Mountain Travel–Sobek,** 6420 Fairmount Ave., El Cerrito, CA 94530 (☎ **800/227-2384** or 510/527-8100). It leads kayakers through the Douro River valley outside Porto.

Portugal, with its historic sights and beautiful country, is an appealing place for hill climbing and hiking. In the United Kingdom, **Waymark Holidays,** 44 Windsor Rd., Slough, Berkshire SL1 2EJ (☎ **01753/516-477**), offers 7-day walking tours through the verdant hills of Main Lands about four times a year. **Sherpa Expeditions,** 131a Heston Rd., Hounslow, Middlesex TW5 0RD (☎ **0208/577-7187**), offers trips through off-the-beaten-track regions of the world, which sometimes (but rarely) include the hills and mountains of Iberia.

You may have read about archaeology tours, but most permit you only to look at the sites, not actually dig. A notable and much-respected exception is **Earthwatch Europe,** 57 Woodstock Rd., Oxford, England OX2 6HU (☎ **01865/311-600**). It offers more than 150 programs designed and supervised by well-qualified academic and ecological authorities. At any time, at least 50 programs welcome participants for hands-on experience in preserving or documenting historical, archaeological, or ecological phenomena of interest to the global community. Projects in Portugal have included digs that uncovered a string of ancient and medieval hill forts across the country.

In the United Kingdom, for the best sampling of possibilities, contact the **Association of Independent Tour Operators** (☎ **0208/744-9280**). The staff can provide names and addresses of tour operators that specialize in travel relating to your particular interest.

11 Getting Around

BY CAR

Many scenic parts of Portugal are isolated from train or bus stations, so it's necessary to have a private car to do serious touring. That way, you're on your own, unhindered by the somewhat fickle train and bus timetables, which often limit your excursions to places close to the beaten track.

There are few superhighways in Portugal, and they're often interrupted by lengthy stretches of traffic-clogged single-lane thoroughfares. The roads, however, provide access to hard-to-reach gems and undiscovered villages.

RENTALS   Most visitors opt for a plan that provides weekly rentals with unlimited mileage included in the overall price. Three of North America's major car-rental companies maintain dozens of branches at each of Portugal's most popular commercial and tourist centers, at rates that are usually competitive.

Budget Rent-a-Car (☎ **800/472-3325** in the U.S.) has offices in more than a dozen locations in Portugal. The most central and most used are in Lisbon, Faro (the heart of the Algarve), Porto, Praia da Rocha (also a popular Algarve destination), and Madeira. Its least expensive car is a two-door Opel Corsa, which costs about 42,000$ ($235.20) per week, plus the mandatory 17½% VAT. An optional (but highly recommended) additional insurance policy, the CDW (collision-damage waiver), costs around $9 per day, depending on the value of the car. If you decline this option, you'll be responsible for the first 800,000$ ($4,480) worth of vehicle damage if you have an accident. Because Portugal has one of the highest accident rates in Europe, it's an excellent idea to buy this extra insurance.

Note that some North American credit- and charge-card issuers, especially American Express, sometimes agree to pay any financial obligations incurred after an accident involving a client's rented car, but only if the imprint of the card is on the original rental contract. Because of this agreement, some clients opt to decline the extra insurance coverage offered by the car-rental company. To be sure that you qualify for this free insurance, check in advance with your card issuer. Know that even though the card's issuer may eventually reimburse you, you'll still have to fill out some complicated paperwork and usually advance either cash or a credit- or charge-card deposit to cover the repair cost.

Avis (☎ **800/331-1084** in the U.S.) maintains offices in downtown Lisbon and at the airport, and at 17 other locations throughout Portugal. The main office is at av. Praia da Vitória 12-C, Lisbon (☎ **21/754-78-39**). Prices start at around 60,250$ ($337.40) per week for its cheapest car, an Opel Corsa. At the opposite end of the spectrum, a Mercedes 250 goes for a year-round rental rate of around 283,000$ ($1,584.80) per week, with unlimited mileage. The 17½% VAT is extra.

Hertz (☎ **800/654-3001** in the U.S.) has about two dozen locations in Portugal and requires a 3-day advance booking for its lowest rates. Hertz's main office is at av. 5 de Outubro 10, Lisbon (☎ **21/849-27-22**). A Peugeot 106 (or a similar car) with manual transmission and no air-conditioning costs around 49,700$ ($278.30) per week, with unlimited mileage, including the 17½% VAT. Hertz's most expensive car, a Mercedes 180C, rents for 211,000$ ($1,181.60) per week. Prices include insurance.

Kemwel Holiday Autos, 106 Calvert St., Harrison, NY 10528 (☎ **800/678-0678**), sometimes offers a viable alternative to more traditional car rental companies. Kemwel leases entire blocks of cars a year in advance at locations throughout Portugal, then rents them to qualified customers who pay the entire price in advance. In Portugal, cars can be retrieved at Lisbon. Kemwel, along with its competitor, **Auto**

Europe (see below), issues vouchers in advance of your departure. The price includes taxes, airport surcharges, unlimited mileage and, on request, insurance premiums. The result is a cost-effective car rental with few, if any, bill-related surprises when you return the car.

Auto Europe, 39 Commercial St., Portland, ME 04101 (☎ 800/223-5555), leases cars, on an as-needed basis, from larger car-rental companies throughout Europe. Its rates sometimes are less than those at Hertz and Avis. In a system that's equivalent to the one used by Kemwel (see above), vouchers are issued in advance for car rentals, with most or all incidentals included. Prepayment of 20% to 60%, depending on the value of the car, is required.

GASOLINE   Unlike the situation only a few years ago, gasoline ("petrol," to the British) stations are now plentiful throughout Portugal. However, should you wander far off the beaten track, it's always wise to have a full tank and to get a refill whenever it's available, even if your tank is still more than half full. The government clamps price controls on gas, and it should cost the same everywhere. Credit and charge cards are frequently accepted at gas stations, at least along the principal express routes. You should note that ever-changing gas prices are much higher than you're probably used to paying, and gas is measured in liters.

DRIVER'S LICENSES   U.S. and Canadian driver's licenses are valid in Portugal. If you're at least 18 and touring Europe by car, you should probably invest in an international driver's license. In the United States, apply through any local branch of the American Automobile Association (AAA); for a list of local branches, contact the national headquarters, 1000 AAA Dr., Heathrow, FL 32746-5063 (☎ 800/AAA-HELP). Include two 2-by-2-inch photographs, a $10 fee, and a photocopy of your state driver's license. In Canada, you pay C$10 and apply to the Canadian Automobile Association (CAA), 2 Carlton St., Toronto, ON M5B 153 (☎ 613/247-0117).

Note that your international driver's license is valid only if it's accompanied by an authorized license from your home state or province.

In Portugal, as elsewhere in Europe, to drive a car legally you must have in your possession an international insurance certificate, known as a Green Card (Carte Verte or Carte Verde). The car-rental agency will provide you with one as part of your rental contract.

DRIVING RULES   Continental driving rules apply in Portugal, and international road symbols and signs are used. Wearing safety belts is compulsory. Speed limits are 90 kilometers per hour (55 m.p.h.) on main roads, 60 kmph (37 m.p.h.) in heavily populated or built-up sections. On the limited number of express highways, the speed limit is 120 kmph (75 m.p.h.).

ROAD MAPS   Michelin publishes the best road maps, available at many stores and map shops throughout Europe and in the United States and Canada. If you can't find them, you can order them from Michelin Guides and Maps, P.O. Box 19008, Greenville, SC 29602-9008 (☎ 800/423-0485, or 864/458-5619 in South Carolina). The maps are updated every year; always try to obtain the latest copy, because Portugal's roads are undergoing tremendous change. One of the best Michelin maps to Portugal is no. 440 (on a scale of 1:400,000, or 1 inch = 6 miles). Scenic routes are outlined in green, and major sights and national parks along the way are indicated.

BREAKDOWNS   If you rent your car from one of the large companies, such as Avis or Hertz, 24-hour breakdown service is available in Portugal. If you're a member of a major automobile club, such as AA, CAA, or AAA, you can get aid from the ACP—Automovel Clube de Portugal, Amoreiva Shopping Center, 1070 Lisboa

(☎ **21/387-18-80**). In the north, the branch office of the club is at rua Gonçalo Cristovão 2–6, 4000 Porto (☎ **22/31-67-32**).

Demystifying Renter's Insurance   Before you drive off in a rental car, be sure you're insured. Hasty assumptions about your personal auto insurance or a rental agency's additional coverage could end up costing you tens of thousands of dollars—even if you are involved in an accident that was clearly the fault of another driver.

If you hold a **private auto insurance** policy, coverage probably doesn't extend outside the United States, however. Be sure to find out whether you are covered in the area you are visiting, whether your policy extends to all persons who will be driving the rental car, how much liability is covered in case an outside party is injured in an accident, and whether the type of vehicle you are renting is included under your contract. (Rental trucks, sport-utility vehicles, and luxury vehicles may not be covered.)

Most **major credit cards** provide some degree of coverage as well—provided they were used to pay for the rental. Terms vary widely, however, so be sure to call your credit card company directly before you rent.

If you are **uninsured or driving abroad,** your credit card provides primary coverage as long as you decline the rental agency's insurance. This means that the credit card will cover damage or theft of a rental car for the full cost of the vehicle. If you already have insurance, your credit card will provide secondary coverage—which basically covers your deductible.

Credit cards **will not cover liability**, or the cost of injury to an outside party, damage to an outside party's vehicle, or both. If you do not hold an insurance policy, or if you are driving outside the United States, you may seriously want to consider purchasing additional liability insurance from your rental company. Be sure to check the terms, however: some rental agencies cover liability only if the renter is not at fault; even then, the rental company's obligation varies from state to state.

Bear in mind that each credit card company has its own peculiarities. Most American Express Optima cards, for instance, do not provide any insurance. American Express does not cover vehicles valued at over $50,000 when new, luxury vehicles, or vehicles built on a truck chassis. MasterCard does not provide coverage for loss, theft, or fire damage, and covers collision only if the rental period does not exceed 15 days. Call your own credit card company for details.

The basic insurance coverage offered by most car rental companies, known as the **Loss/Damage Waiver (LDW)** or **Collision Damage Waiver (CDW),** can cost as much as $20 a day. It usually covers the full value of the vehicle with no deductible if an outside party causes an accident or other damage to the rental car. In all states but California, you will probably be covered in case of theft as well. Liability coverage varies according to the company policy and state law, but the minimum is usually at least $15,000. If you are at fault in an accident, however, you will be covered for the full replacement value of the car but not for liability. Some states allow you to buy additional liability coverage for such cases. Most rental companies will require a police report in order to process any claims you file, but your private insurer will not be notified of the accident.

Package Deals   Many packages are available that include airfare, accommodations, and a rental car with unlimited mileage. Compare these prices with the cost of booking airline tickets and renting a car separately to see if these offers are good deals.

Arranging Car Rentals on the Web   Internet resources can make comparison shopping easier. **Microsoft Expedia** (www.expedia.com) and **Travelocity** (www.travelocity.com) help you compare prices and locate car-rental bargains from various companies nationwide. They will even make your reservation for you once you've found the best deal.

HITCHHIKING

There's no law against hitchhiking, but it isn't commonly practiced. If you decide to hitchhike, do so with discretion. Usually, Portuguese auto insurance doesn't cover hitchhikers. Considering the potential danger to both the passenger and the driver, hitchhiking is *not* recommended by *Frommer's Portugal*. Certainly no woman alone should attempt to hitchhike in Portugal, and even two women traveling together take great risks. Men, of course, are also at risk.

BY PLANE

Portugal is a small country, and flying from one place to another is relatively easy. Train is the usual method of public transportation (see below). Nevertheless, **TAP Air Portugal** flies four times a day to Faro, in the Algarve, and Porto, the main city of the north. Service to Faro is likely to be more frequent in July and August. There are also four flights a day to Funchal, capital of Madeira, plus limited service to the Azores. The planes are usually Boeing 727s.

For ticket sales, flight reservations, and information about the city and the country, you can get in touch with the polite personnel of TAP Air Portugal, praça Marquês de Pombal 3A, 1200 Lisboa (☎ **21/841-69-90**).

BY TRAIN

The Portuguese railway system is underdeveloped compared to those of the more industrialized nations of western Europe. Still, there are connections (mainly electric and diesel) between the capital and more than 20 major towns. Express trains run from Lisbon, Coimbra (the university city), and Porto. Electric trains, which leave from the Lisbon waterfront, travel along the Costa do Sol (Estoril and Cascais) and on to Queluz and Sintra.

At Lisbon's **Santa Apolónia Station,** you can make connections for international service and the Northern and Eastern lines. The **Rossio Station** serves Sintra and the Western Lines; the **Cais do Sodré Station** handles service for the Costa do Sol resorts of Estoril and Cascais. Finally, trains leave from the **Sul e Sueste Station** for the Alentejo and the Algarve. In addition, express trains connect Lisbon to all the major capitals of Western Europe, and there's a direct link with Seville.

In summer, express trains depart Lisbon for the Algarve Monday to Saturday. They leave from the **Barreiro Station** (across the Tagus—take one of the frequently departing ferries). Off-season service runs four times weekly. For **information about rail travel in Portugal,** phone ☎ **21/888-40-25** in Lisbon.

Railroad information and tickets for travel between almost any two stations in Europe, including stations throughout Portugal, is available from the representatives of the Portuguese National Railway, **Rail Europe, Inc.,** 226–230 Westchester Ave., White Plains, NY 10604 (☎ **800/848-7245** or 914/681-3232). The telephone representatives sell one-way and round-trip tickets into or out of Portugal, tickets for travel within Portugal, and rail passes for travel within Portugal and the rest of Europe. Couchettes (sleeping cars) can be arranged. See "Getting There," above, for information on rail passes.

SENIOR DISCOUNTS   The Portuguese National Railway's 50% discount policy applies for people 65 and older. These tickets are good all year.

BY BUS

This is a cheap means of transportation in Portugal. A network of buses links almost all the major towns and cities. Many routes originate in Lisbon. The former national bus company, **Rodoviária** (☎ 21/354-57-75), has been privatized but essentially offers the same service as before. In addition, there are local and private regional bus links.

Express coaches between major cities are called *expressos*. Once in most cities and towns, you can take cheap bus rides to nearby villages or sights. Of course, in many towns and all cities you can take buses to get around within the city.

12　Tips on Accommodations

When you check into a hotel, you'll see the official rates posted in the main lobby and somewhere in your room, perhaps at the bottom of the closet. These rates, dictated by the Directorate of Tourism, are regulated and really are a form of rent control. They include the 13.1% service charge and 17½% value-added tax (VAT).

Should an infraction such as overcharging occur, you may demand to be given the Official Complaints Book, in which you can write your allegations. The hotel manager is obligated to turn your comments over to the Directorate of Tourism. The directorate staff reviews them to see if punitive action should be taken.

Hotels in Portugal are rated from five stars to one. The difference between a five-star hotel and a four-star hotel will not always be apparent to the casual visitor. Often the distinction is based on square footage of bathrooms and other technicalities. When you go below this level, you enter the realm of the second- and third-class hotel. Some (primarily three-star hotels) can be decent and even excellent places to stay. Third-class hotels are bare-bones accommodations in Portugal.

Coastal hotels, especially those in the Algarve, are required to grant off-season (November to February) visitors a 15% discount. To attract more off-season business, a number of establishments offer this discount from mid-October and through March.

BUDGET TIPS

Try a reservations bureau such as **Accommodations Express** (☎ 800/950-4685; www.accommodationsxpress.com); **Hotel Reservations Network** (☎ 800/96-HOTEL; www.180096HOTEL.com); **Quikbook** (☎ 800/789-9887, includes fax-on-demand service; www.quikbook.com); or **Room Exchange** (☎ 800/846-7000 in the U.S., 800/486-7000 in Canada).

At the inexpensive end, **Hostelling International/American Youth Hostels,** 733 15th St. NW, Suite 840, Washington, DC 20005 (☎ 800/444-6111 or 202/783-6161), offers a directory of low-cost accommodations.

On-line, try booking your hotel through **Arthur Frommer's Budget Travel** (www.frommers.com), and save up to 50% on the cost of your room. **Microsoft Expedia** (www.expedia.com) features a "Travel Agent" that will also direct you to affordable lodgings.

Prices & Ratings in This Guide　Unless otherwise indicated, prices in this guide include service and taxes. Breakfast may or may not be included; individual write-ups reflect various hotel policies about breakfast. All references in Portugal to "including breakfast" refer to continental breakfast of juice, coffee or tea, croissants, butter, and jam. If you stay at a hotel and order bacon and eggs or other extras, you'll likely be billed for them as à la carte items. Parking rates are per day.

POUSADAS   When traveling through the countryside, plot your trips so you'll stop over at the government-owned *pousadas* (tourist inns). They range from restored Atlantic coast castles to mountain chalets. The Portuguese government has established these inns in historic buildings, such as convents, palaces, and castles. Often they occupy beautiful physical settings. Generally (but not always) the pousadas are in regions that don't have many suitable hotels—everywhere from Henry the Navigator's Sagres to a feudal castle in the walled city of Óbidos. The rates are not low but, for the quality and services offered, are moderate. A guest can't stay more than 5 days, because there's usually a waiting list. Special terms are granted to honeymoon couples. For our recommendations, see "The Best Pousadas" in chapter 1.

Travel agents can make reservations at pousadas, or you can contact **Enatur-Pousadas of Portugal,** av. Sta. Joana Princesa 10, 1700 Lisboa (☎ **21/844-20-01**).

COUNTRY HOMES   Far more exciting—at least to us—than the pousadas is the chain of farm estates, country homes, and restored manor houses that have opened to the public. These properties are the most highly recommended in this guide, and they offer grand comfort and lots of charm, often in a historic setting.

The best and most extensive network is in the region of Viana do Castelo, where you can sometimes board with the poor but proud Portuguese aristocracy. Many of these manors and farms are called *quintas.* An association, **Turismo de Habitação** (Country House Tourism), which mostly operates in the north, has been formed to publicize and link these unique accommodations. In recent years areas such as the Beiras and Alentejo have been included. Local tourist offices provide directories that include color photographs and maps with directions. All of these properties are privately run, and breakfast is always included. Contact the association at av. Antonio Augusto de Aguiar, 1099 Lisboa (☎ **21/286-79-58**), or Praça da República, 4990 Ponte de Lima (☎ **258/74-28-27**).

OTHER SPECIAL ACCOMMODATIONS   Tourist inns not run by the government are known as *estalagems.* Often these offer some of the finest accommodations in Portugal; many are decorated in the traditional Portuguese, or *típico,* style and represent top-notch bargains.

The *residência* is a form of boardinghouse, without board. These establishments offer a room and breakfast only. The *pensão* is a boardinghouse that charges the lowest rates in the country. The "deluxe" *pensão* is a misnomer; the term simply means that the *pensão* enjoys the highest rating in its category. The accommodation is decidedly not luxurious. A "luxury" *pensão* is generally the equivalent of a second-class hotel. The boardinghouses are finds for the budget hunter. Many prepare generous portions of good local cuisine. There are both first- and second-class boardinghouses.

A more recent addition to the accommodations scene are the *solares.* Most are spacious country manor houses, formerly property of the Portuguese aristocracy, that are now being restored and opened as guest houses. Many date from the Age of Exploration, when navigators brought riches back from all over the world and established lavish homes that have been passed down to their heirs. The inns are all over the country, but most are along the Costa Verde, between Ponte de Lima and Viana do Castelo.

Information on the solares program is available from the **Portuguese National Tourist Office,** 590 Fifth Ave., 4th Floor, New York, NY 10036 (☎ **212/354-4403;** fax 212/764-6137).

If you prefer to stay on the Costa Verde, you can receive information and assistance from Central Reservations for the houses of the **Delegação de Turismo de Ponte de Lima,** praça da República, 4990 Ponte de Lima (☎ **258/74-28-27**). You can arrange to go from one solar to the next through this office.

One of the best associations for arranging stays in private homes is **Privetur,** largo das Pereiras, 4990 Ponte de Lima (☎ **258/74-14-93**). It represents manor houses and country homes in all the major tourist districts. Privetur can arrange accommodations in circumstances that are sometimes more personalized than stays in large hotels.

CAMPING & TRAILERS   Portugal provides parks for campers and house trailers (caravans) near beaches and in wooded areas all over the country. Some have pools, athletic fields, markets, and restaurants, among other facilities. Many others are simply convenient sites with water and toilets away from the hustle and bustle of cities and towns. For a list of campgrounds throughout the country, contact the **Federação Portuguesa de Campismo e Caravanismo** (Portuguese Camping and Caravanning Federation), av. 5 de Outubro 15, 1000 Lisbon (☎ **21/812-68-90**).

RESERVATIONS   Reservations are essential for peak-season summer travel in Portugal, when many hotels fill with vacationing Europeans. Unless you're incurably spontaneous, you'll probably be better off with some idea of where you'll spend each night, even in low season.

Most hotels require at least a day's deposit before they'll reserve a room. This can be accomplished with an international money order, or, if agreed in advance, with a personal check. You can usually cancel a room reservation 1 week ahead of time and get a full refund. A few hotel managers will return your money 3 days before the reservation date, but some will take your deposit and never return it, even if you cancel far in advance. Many budget-hotel owners operate on such a narrow margin of profit that they find just buying stamps for airmail replies too expensive. Therefore, it's important that you enclose a prepaid International Reply Coupon with your payment, especially if you're writing to a budget hotel. Better yet, call and speak to a staff member, or send a fax.

If you're booking into a chain hotel, such as Sheraton or Méridien, you can call in North America and easily make reservations over the phone. Toll-free numbers, when available, are included in hotel reviews in this guide.

Suggested Itineraries

If You Have 1 Week

Days 1–3   Head for **Lisbon,** the gateway to Portugal. Count on using the 1st day for rest time. On the 2nd day, see the highlights of the capital, including **St. George's Castle** and the major attractions of **Belém,** such as Jerónimos Monastery. On the 3rd day, while still based in Lisbon, explore the environs. Head first to **Quelez Palace,** 9½ miles from Lisbon, then to **Sintra,** 18 miles from Lisbon.

Days 4–5   Head to a resort along the Costa do Sol, principally **Cascais** or **Estoril.** This sun coast, also called "coast of kings," is easy to reach from Lisbon. You can relax in the sun or continue to explore. The most interesting sights are at **Guincho,** near the westernmost point in continental Europe, and **Mafra,** which is Portugal's version of Spain's El Escorial.

Day 6   Head south from Lisbon across the Tagus (see chapter 6) to **Setúbal,** 31 miles from Lisbon. After exploring the area and visiting **Palmela Castle,** seek accommodations in and around Setúbal.

Day 7   Time your return to Lisbon to match your flight schedule home.

If You Have 2 Weeks

Spend the first week as outlined above.

Days 8–10   Journey to the **Algarve** (see chapter 8), settle in to a village, town, or resort, and explore the full length of the coast. Allow a minimum of 3 days and nights. If you stay at **Faro,** you'll be roughly in the center of the Algarve and can branch out east or west. The coastline stretches 100 miles, but it will be slow moving, regardless of which direction you select.

Day 11   On the 11th day, if you must leave, we recommend that you return to Lisbon by a different route, heading first for **Beja,** the capital of Baixo Alentejo, 96 miles north of Faro. After a stopover, you might continue north to **Évora,** 90 miles east of Lisbon, where you may want to spend the night. After exploring Évora the next morning, you can drive west to Lisbon.

Days 12–14   From Lisbon, fly to **Madeira** for a minimum of 3 days to spend time in the sun. Allow a full day for exploring the island, one of the most beautiful in the world. If you prefer to remain on the mainland, you can knock 3 days off the itinerary by skipping Madeira and heading north of Lisbon toward Óbidos.

Fast Facts: Portugal

American Express   The entity representing American Express throughout Portugal is **Top Tours.** Its headquarters are in **Lisbon** at av. Duque de Loulé 108, 1000 Lisboa (☎ **21/315-58-85**). Branch offices are at rua Alferes Malheiro 96, 4000 Porto (☎ **22/208-27-85**); estrada da Rocha, Praia de Rocha, 8500 Portimão (☎ **282/41-75-52**); and av. Infante de Sagres 73, 8125 Quarteira (☎ **289/30-27-26**).

Baby-Sitters   Check with your hotel's staff for arrangements. Most first-class hotels can provide baby-sitters from lists that the concierge keeps. At smaller establishments, the baby-sitter is likely to be the daughter of the proprietor. Rates are low. Remember to request a baby-sitter no later than the morning if you're going out that evening. Also request one with at least a minimum knowledge of English, if you and your children do not speak Portuguese.

Business Hours   Hours vary not throughout the country, but there is a set pattern. **Banks** generally are open Monday to Friday from 8:30am to 3pm. **Currency-exchange offices** at airports and rail terminals are open longer hours, and the office at Portela airport outside Lisbon is open 24 hours a day. Most **museums** open at 10am, close at 5pm, and often close for lunch between 12:30 and 2pm. Larger museums with bigger staffs can remain open at midday. **Shops** are open, in general, Monday to Friday 9am to 1pm and 3 to 7pm, Saturday 9am to 1pm. Most **restaurants** serve lunch from noon until 3pm and dinner from 7:30 to 11pm; many close on Sunday. Many **nightclubs** open at 10pm, but the action doesn't really begin until after midnight, and often lasts until 3 or 5am.

Crime   See "Safety," below.

Currency   See "Money," earlier in this chapter.

Drugs   Illegal drugs are plentiful, although penalties may be severe if you're caught possessing or selling illegal narcotics. Judges tend to throw the book at foreigners caught selling illegal narcotics. Bail for foreigners is rare, and local prosecutors have a high conviction rate. All the U.S., British, and Canadian consulates might do is provide you with a list of local attorneys.

Drugstores   The Portuguese government requires selected pharmacies to stay open at all times of the day and night. They do so under a rotation system. Check with your concierge for the locations and hours of the nearest drugstores, called *farmácias de serviço.* In general, pharmacies in Portugal are open Monday to Friday 9am to 1pm and 3 to 7pm, Saturday 9am to 1pm.

Electricity   Voltage is 200 volts AC (50 cycles). Many hardware stores in North America sell the appropriate transformers. The concierge desks of most hotels will lend you a transformer and plug adapters, or tell you where you can buy them nearby. If you have any doubt about whether you have the appropriate transformer, ask at your hotel desk before you try to plug in anything.

Embassies/Consulates   If you lose your passport or have some other pressing problem, you'll need to get in touch with your embassy.

The Embassy of the **United States,** on avenida das Forças Armadas (Sete Rios), 1600 Lisboa (☎ 21/727-33-00), is open Monday to Friday 8am to 12:30pm and 1:30 to 5pm. If you've lost a passport, the embassy can take photographs for you and help you to obtain the proof of citizenship needed to get a replacement.

The Embassy of **Canada** is at av. da Liberdade 144, 4th Floor, 1250 Lisboa (☎ 21/347-48-92). It's open Monday to Friday 8:30am to 12:30pm and 1:30 to 5pm (in July and August, the embassy closes at 1pm on Friday).

The Embassy of the **United Kingdom,** rua São Bernardo, 1200 Lisboa (☎ 21/392-40-00), is open Monday to Friday 10am to 12:30pm and 3 to 4:30pm.

The Embassy of the **Republic of Ireland,** rua de Imprensa à Estrêla 1, 1200 Lisboa (☎ 21/396-15-69), is open Monday to Friday 9:30am to noon and 2:30 to 4:30pm.

Australians and **New Zealanders** should go to the British Embassy (see above).

Emergencies   For the **police** (or an ambulance) in Lisbon, telephone ☎ **115.** In case of **fire,** call ☎ **32-22-22** or 60-60-60. For the **Portuguese Red Cross,** call ☎ **61-77-77.** The national **emergency** number in Portugal is ☎ **115.**

Language   English is often spoken in the major resorts and at first-class and deluxe hotels; in smaller places you'll often need the help of a phrase book or dictionary. One of the most helpful is the *Portuguese Phrase Book* (Berlitz). Another option is the *Useful Common Dictionary: Portuguese-English/English-Portuguese* (Crown).

Legal Aid   If you're a foreigner in Portugal, all your consulate can do is advise you of your rights if you run into trouble with the law. The consulate staff will also provide a list of English-speaking lawyers, but after that, you're at the mercy of the local courts.

Liquor Laws   You have to be 18 to drink. Liquor is sold mostly in markets, not package stores as in most of the United States. In Lisbon you can drink until dawn. There's always an open bar or fado club serving alcoholic beverages.

Mail   While in Portugal, you may have your mail directed to your hotel (or hotels), to the American Express representative, or to General Delivery (*Poste Restante*) in Lisbon. You must present your passport to pick up mail. The **general post office** in Lisbon is on praça do Comércio, 1100 Lisbon (☎ 21/346-32-31); it's open daily 8am to 10pm.

Maps   If you'd like a map before your trip to plan your itinerary, you can obtain one from Rand McNally, Michelin, or the AAA. These are sold at bookstores all over the United States. **Rand McNally** has retail stores in large cities, including 150 E. 52nd St., New York, NY 10022 (☎ **212/758-7488**); 444 N. Michigan Ave., Chicago, IL 60611 (☎ **312/321-1751**); and 595 Market St., San Francisco, CA 94105 (☎ **415/777-3131**). The U.S. headquarters of **Michelin** is at P.O. Box 19008, Greenville, SC 29602-9008 (☎ **800/423-0485,** or 864/458-5619 in South Carolina).

Newspapers/Magazines   The *International Herald Tribune* and *USA Today* are sold at most Lisbon newsstands and in major hotels or along the street in most big cities and resorts. If you read Portuguese, the most popular centrist newspaper is the influential *Diário de Notícias.* To the right of center is *O Dia;* to the left is *O'Diário.* Most major newsstands sell the European editions of *Time* and *Newsweek.*

Pets   Pets brought into Portugal must have the approval of the local veterinarian and a health certificate from your home country.

Safety   Portugal remains one of the safest countries in Western Europe, but crime rose dramatically in the 1990s, sparked by the flood of homeless and penniless immigrants from the faraway countries of the former Portuguese empire. Lisbon is the most dangerous city, followed by the tourist-infested Algarve, where many hustlers prey on unsuspecting travelers. Pickpocketing remains the major crime against tourists; violent attacks are relatively rare. Petty criminals stalk overnight trains and crowded buses. Take special care, and leave your valuables at your hotel.

Taxes   Since Portugal and neighboring Spain simultaneously joined the Common Market (now the European Union) on January 1, 1986, Portugal has imposed a value-added tax (VAT) on most purchases made within its borders. It ranges from 8% to 30%. Known in Portugal as the IVA, the amount is almost always written into the bottom line of the bill for any purchase a foreign visitor makes. Hotel and restaurant bills are taxed at 17½%. Car rentals are subject to an additional 17½% tax (less than in some other European countries).

Such deluxe goods as jewelry, furs, and expensive imported liquors include a 30% built-in tax. Because a scotch and soda in a Portuguese bar carries this high tax, many people have changed their choice of alcohol from scotch to Portuguese brandy and soda or, more prosaically, beer.

To get a VAT refund on purchases that qualify (ask the shopkeeper), present your passport to the salesperson and ask for the special stamped form. Present the form with your purchases at the booth marked for IVA tax refunds at the airport. You'll get your money refunded right at the booth.

Telegram/Telex/Fax   At most hotels, the receptionist will help you send one of these messages. Otherwise, go to the nearest post office for assistance.

Telephone   Old-fashioned coin-drop pay phones are disappearing and being replaced by new white Portugal Telecom phones that accept coins or a prepaid phone card (see below). Calling from a booth with the right change or card allows you to avoid high hotel surcharges. Booths take 10$, 20$, 50$, and 100$ coins. Put the coins in a slot at the top of the box while you hold the receiver, then dial your number after hearing the dial tone. Once a connection is made, the necessary coins will automatically drop. If enough coins are not available, your connection will be broken. A warning tone will sound and a light over the dial will go on if more coins are needed. For long-distance (trunk) calls within the country, dial the city code, followed by the local number. *Note:* The telephone numbers in this book reflect changes made to the Portuguese phone system (effective October 31, 1999). If you see a city code that begins with a zero, drop this initial zero and substitute a "2".

At "CrediFone" locations and at post offices, special phones take prepaid cards in denominations of 50, 100, and 150 units. Sold at post offices, the cards cost 555$ ($3.10), 1,011$ ($5.65), and 1,624$ ($9.10), respectively.

Telephone calls can also be made at all post offices, which also send telegrams. International calls are made by dialing 00 (double zero), followed by the country code, the area code (not prefaced by 0), then the local phone number. The country code for the United States and Canada is 1. The country code for Portugal is 351. For further information, see "Telephone Tips" on the back cover.

Television/Radio   Lisbon has two major TV channels—Channel 1 (VHF) and Channel 11 (UHF)—and two minor (private) channels. Many foreign films are shown, often in English with Portuguese subtitles. Many hotels have cable reception. It brings in such networks as CNN from the United States, MTV and Skychannel from Britain, and, depending on the hotel, broadcasts from Spain, Italy, and France. For radio, see "Radio" under "Fast Facts: Lisbon" in chapter 3.

Time   Portugal is 6 hours ahead of the eastern time zone in the United States. Like most European countries, Portugal has daylight saving time. It moves its clocks ahead an hour in late spring and an hour back in the fall, corresponding roughly to daylight saving time in the United States; exact dates vary.

Tipping   Portugal has now caught up with the rest of western Europe. Most service personnel expect a good tip rather than a small one, as in the past.

Hotels add a **service charge** (known as *serviço*), which is divided among the entire staff, but individual tipping is also the rule. Tip 100$ (55¢) to the bellhop for running an errand; 100$ (55¢) to the doorman who hails you a cab; 100$ to 200$ (55¢ to $1.10) to the porter for each piece of luggage carried; 500$ ($2.80) to the wine steward if you've dined often at your hotel; and 300$ ($1.70) to the chambermaid.

In first-class or deluxe hotels, the concierge will present you with a separate bill for extras, such as charges for bullfight tickets. A gratuity is expected in addition to the charge. The amount will depend on the number of requests you've made.

Figure on tipping about 20% of your **taxi** fare for short runs. For longer treks—for example, from the airport to Cascais—15% is adequate.

Restaurants and **nightclubs** include a service charge and government taxes of 17½%. As in hotels, this money is distributed among the entire staff, including the waiter's mistress and the owner's grandfather—so extra tipping is customary. Add about 5% to the bill in a moderately priced restaurant, up to 10% in a deluxe or first-class establishment. For hatcheck in fado houses, restaurants, and nightclubs, tip at least 100$ (55¢). Washroom attendants also get 100$ (55¢).

Water   Tap water is generally potable throughout Portugal, but bottled water is always safer. Even if the water in Portugal isn't bad, you won't be used to the microbes and can become ill. In rural areas, the water supply may not be purified. Under no circumstances should you swim in or drink from freshwater rivers or streams.

Settling into Lisbon 3

In its golden age, Lisbon gained a reputation as the eighth wonder of the world. Travelers returning from the city boasted that its riches rivaled those of Venice.

As one of the greatest maritime centers in history, the Portuguese capital imported exotic wares from the far-flung corners of its empire. In addition to gaining the wealth of foreign cultures, it established essential footholds in trade routes. Lisbon stockpiled goods, beginning with its earliest contacts with the Calicut and Malabar coasts. Treasures from Asia—including porcelain, luxurious silks, rubies, pearls, and other rare gems—arrived at Indian seaports on Chinese junks and eventually found their way to Lisbon. The abundance and variety of spices from the East, such as turmeric, ginger, pepper, cumin, and betel, rivaled even Keats's vision of "silken Samarkand."

From the Americas came red dye-wood (brazilwood), coffee, gold (discovered in 1698), diamonds (first unearthed in 1729), and other gemstones. The extensive contact signaled a new era in world trade, and Lisbon sat at the center of a great maritime empire, a hub of commerce for Europe, Africa, and Asia.

Today, after a decades-long slumber, there is excitement again in this luminous city. Not since the earthquake of 1755 has there been a building boom like the one in the late 1990s. Construction went on around the clock as Lisbon prepared for EXPO '98, which marked the 500th anniversary of Vasco da Gama's journey to India. Lisbon welcomed the world to its doorstep, and the visitors found a brighter, restored, fresher city.

The most dramatic change of all was the opening of the Vasco da Gama bridge spanning the Tagus. Ponte Vasco da Gama speeds access to other areas of Portugal, including Alentejo province, with links to Spain. An entire new suburb being created along the east bank of the Tagus has brought Lisbon a new railway hub, Gare de Oriente. Brash postmodern office buildings and restored medieval facades are just some of the changes that have altered the skyline. Still in place is the Lisbon of old, with its great art and architecture—which is what probably brought you here in the first place.

A BIT OF BACKGROUND Many Lisboans claim unabashedly that Ulysses founded their city. Others, with perhaps a more scholarly bent, maintain that the Phoenicians or the Carthaginians were the original settlers. The body of the country's patron saint, Vincent, is

The Marquês de Pombal:
Builder & Rebuilder of Portugal

An aristocrat and politician, Sebastião José de Carvalho e Mello (1699–1782) was one of the most effective envoys Portugal ever sent to the courts of Europe. Better known as the marquês de Pombal, he was the Portuguese ambassador first to London and then to Vienna. Pombal strengthened Portugal's legendary friendship with Britain, encouraging a wine trade that continues to this day. Famous for his almost unchallenged influence over the benevolent but indolent Joseph Emanuel (who reigned from 1750 to 1777), he served as Portuguese minister of foreign affairs and eventually conducted much of the country's day-to-day administration. He liberated the slaves in Brazil and reduced the power of the Jesuits, who had spearheaded many of the torments of the Portuguese Inquisition. Above all else, Pombal is remembered for brilliantly organizing the rebuilding of Lisbon after the 1755 earthquake reduced much of the capital to rubble.

said to have arrived in Portugal on an abandoned boat, with two ravens to guide it. According to legend, the two birds lived in the cathedral tower as late as the 19th century.

The Romans settled in Lisbon in about 205 B.C., later building a fortification on the site of what is now St. George's Castle. The Visigoths captured the city in the 5th century A.D.; in 714, centuries of Moorish domination began. The first king of Portugal, Afonso Henríques, captured Lisbon from the Moors in 1147. But it wasn't until 1256 that Afonso III moved the capital here, deserting Coimbra, now the country's major university city.

The Great Earthquake occurred at 9:40am on All Saints' Day, November 1, 1755. "From Scotland to Asia Minor, people ran out of doors and looked at the sky, and fearfully waited. It was, of course, an earthquake," chronicled *Holiday* magazine. Tidal waves 50 feet high swept over Algeciras, Spain. The capitals of Europe shook. Churches were packed to overflowing; smoky tapers and incense burned on altars. Some 22 aftershocks followed. Roofs caved in; hospitals (with more than 1,000 patients), prisons, public buildings, royal palaces, aristocratic town houses, fishers' cottages, churches, and houses of prostitution all were toppled. Overturned candles helped ignite a fire that consumed the once-proud capital in just 6 days, leaving it in gutted, charred shambles. Voltaire described the destruction in *Candide:* "The sea boiled up in the harbor and smashed the vessels lying at anchor. Whirlwinds of flame and ashes covered the streets and squares, houses collapsed, roofs were thrown onto foundations and the foundations crumbled." All told, 30,000 inhabitants were crushed beneath the tumbling debris.

When the survivors of the initial shocks ran from their burning homes toward the mighty Tagus, they were met with walls of water 40 feet high. Estimates vary, but approximately 60,000 drowned or died in the 6-day holocaust.

Voltaire cynically commented on the aftermath of the disaster: "It was decided by the University of Coimbra that the sight of several people being slowly burned with great ceremony was an infallible means of preventing the earth from quaking."

After the ashes had settled, the marquês de Pombal, the prime minister, ordered that the dead be buried and the city rebuilt at once. To accomplish that ambitious plan, the king gave him virtually dictatorial powers.

Lisbon

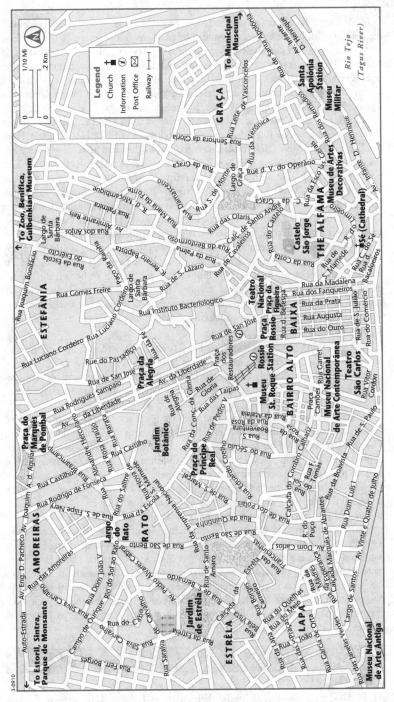

Legend
- Church
- Information
- Post Office
- Railway

0   1/10 Mi
0   .2 Km

To Municipal Museum↑

Rio Tejo
(Tagus River)

Santa Apolónia Station

Museu Militar

GRAÇA

Av. Infante D. Henrique

Rua de Santa Apolónia

Av. Infante D. Henrique

Rua Leite de Vasconcelos

Rua dos Remédios

Rua Senhora da Glória

Rua da Graça

Rue d. V. do Operário

Rua de Benformoso

Rua das Olaris

Calç. de Santo André

Museu de Artes Decorativas

← To Zoo, Benfica, Gulbenkian Museum

To Estoril, Sintra, Parque de Monsanto →

Auto-Estrada

Av. Eng. D. Pacheco

Largo de Santa Bárbara

Av. Almirante Reis

Rua Palmira

R. d. Moçambique

Rua Maria da Fonte

Rua Damasceno

Largo de Graça

Largo de Santa Bárbara

THE ALFAMA

Castelo São Jorge

Rua do Costa

Rua de S. Mamede

Rua C. do Sé

Sé (Cathedral)

Rua do Limoeiro

Rua da Madalena

Rua dos Fanqueiros

Rua da Prata

Rua Augusta

Rua do Ouro

Rua de S. Julião

Rua do Comércio

BAIXA

Teatro Nacional

Praça da Figueira

Praça Rossio

Rua d. Betesga

Rossio Station

St. Roque Station

Museu

BAIRRO ALTO

Teatro São Carlos

Museu Nacional de Arte Contemporânea

Rua Garret

Praça Camões

Rua da Atalaia

Rua da Rosa

Rua de S. Paulo

ESTEFÂNIA

Rua Joaquim Bonifácio

Rua Gomes Freire

Rua Luciano Cordeiro

Rue do Passadiço

Rua de San José

Rua de S. Lázaro

Rua Instituto Bacteriologico

Praça da Alegria

Rua da Fé

Av. da Liberdade

Praça dos Restauradores

Rua de San José

Rua de Conc. da Glória

Rua de Gloria

Rua das Taipas

Jardim Botânico

Praça do Príncipe Real

AMOREIRAS

Praça do Marquês de Pombal

Av. Joaquim A. d'Aguiar

Rua Castilho

Rua Rosa Araújo

Rua Alexandre Herculano

Rua Castilho

Av. da Liberdade

Rua Rodrigues Sampaio

Rua Rodrigo de Fonseca

RATO

Largo do Rato

Rua das Amoreiras

Rua das Amoreiras

Rua Silva Carvalho

Campo de Ourique

Rio do Sol ao Rato

Av. Pedro Alvares Cabral

Rua de São Bento

Rua da Quintinha

Rua da Imprensa Nacional

Rua de S. Marçal

Rua do Salitre

Rua S. Filipe Néri

Rua Nova

Rua S. Mamede

Rua Eduardo Coelho

ESTRÊLA

Jardim de Estrêla

Calçada da Estrêla

Rua Saraiva

Rua Ferr. Borges

Campo de Ourique

LAPA

Rua Dom Luís I

Av. Dom Carlos I

Rua das Francesinhas

Av. Vinte e Quatro de Julho

Museu Nacional de Arte Antiga

Largo de Santos

59

What Pombal ordered constructed was a city of wide, symmetrical boulevards leading into handsome squares dominated by fountains and statuary. Bordering these wide avenues would be black-and-white mosaic sidewalks, the most celebrated in Europe. The mixture of old and "new" (postearthquake) is so harmonious that travelers today consider Lisbon one of the most beautiful cities on earth. Under a stark blue sky, the medley of pastel-washed houses dazzles the eyes, like a city in North Africa. The Tagus, the river flowing through Lisbon, has been called the city's "eternal lover."

Seagulls take flight from the harbor, where trawlers from Africa unload their freight. Pigeons sweep down on praça do Comércio, also known as Black Horse Square. From the Bairro Alto (Upper City), cable cars run down to the waterfront. Streets bear colorful names or designations, such as rua do Açúcar (Street of Sugar). Fountains abound; one, the Samaritan, dates from the 16th century. The boulevards flank new high-rise apartment houses, while in other quarters laundry hanging from 18th-century houses flaps in the wind. It's a city that gives nicknames to everything, from its districts (the Chiado, named after a poet) to its kings. Fernando, who built one of the most characteristic walls around Lisbon, was honored with the appellation "the Beautiful."

Many who have never been to Lisbon know it well from watching World War II spy movies on TV. It seems natural to expect to see Hedy Lamarr slinking around the corner at any moment. In the classic film *Casablanca*, Lisbon embodied the passage point to the Americas for refugees stranded in northern Africa. During the war, Lisbon, officially neutral, was a hotbed of intrigue and espionage. It was also a haven for thousands of refugees. Many, including deposed royalty, remained, settling into villas in Estoril and Sintra.

LISBON TODAY   No longer the provincial town it was in the 1970s, Lisbon today has blossomed into a cosmopolitan city often beset with construction pains. Many of its old structures are simply falling apart, and must be either restored or replaced. Some of the formerly clogged streets of the Baixa have been closed to traffic, and cobblestone pedestrian malls have been created.

Lisbon is growing and evolving, and the city is considerably more sophisticated than it once was, no doubt due in part to Portugal's joining the European Union (EU). The smallest capital of Europe is no longer a backwater at the far corner of Iberia. Some 1.6 million people now live in Lisbon, and many of its citizens, having drifted in from the far corners of the world, don't even speak Portuguese. Lisbon presides over a country with one of the fastest-growing economies in Europe, much of it fueled by investments that have poured in since Portugal joined the EU. Textiles, shoes, clothing, china, and earthenware are among its leading industries.

Sections along avenida da Liberdade, the main street of Lisbon, at times evoke Paris. As in Paris, sidewalk portrait painters will sketch your likeness, and artisans will offer you jewelry claiming that it's gold (when you both know it isn't). Handcrafts, from embroidery to leatherwork, are peddled right on the streets as they are in New York.

Consider an off-season visit, especially in the spring or fall when the city enjoys glorious weather, before the hot, humid days of July and August descend. The city isn't overrun with visitors then, and you can wander about and take in its attractions without fear of being trampled.

1 Essentials

ARRIVING

BY PLANE   Foreign and domestic flights land at Lisbon's **Aeroporto de Lisboa** (☎ **21/840-20-60**), about 4 miles from the heart of the city. For airport information, telephone ☎ **21/841-35-00** or 21/840-22-62.

An **AERO-BUS** runs between the airport and the Cais do Sodré train station every 20 minutes from 7am to 9pm. The fare is 430$ ($2.40). It makes 10 intermediate stops, including praça dos Restauradores and praça do Comércio. There's no charge for luggage. **Taxi** passengers line up, British style, in a usually well-organized queue at the sidewalk in front of the airport. The average taxi fare from the airport to central Lisbon is 2,000$ to 3,000$ ($11.20 to $16.80). Each piece of luggage is 300$ ($1.70) extra.

For ticket sales, flight reservations, and information about the city and the country, you can get in touch with the Lisboa personnel of **TAP Air Portugal,** praça do Marquês de Pombal 3A (☎ **21/841-69-90** for reservations).

BY TRAIN   Most international rail passengers from Madrid and Paris arrive at the **Estação da Santa Apolónia,** avenida Infante Dom Henrique, the major terminal. It's by the Tagus near the Alfama district. Two daily trains make the 10-hour run from Madrid to Lisbon. Rail lines from northern and eastern Portugal also arrive at this station. EXPO '98 brought a new, modern terminal to Lisbon. **Gare de Oriente** at Expo Urbe—connected to the metro system—opened in 1998 and is the hub for some long-distance and suburban trains, including service to such destinations as Porto, Sintra, the Beiras, Minho, and the Douro. At the **Estação do Rossio,** between praça dos Restauradores and praça de Dom Pedro IV, you can get trains to Sintra. The **Estação do Cais do Sodré,** just beyond the south end of rua Alecrim, east of praça do Comércio, handles trains to Cascais and Estoril on the Costa do Sol. Finally, you can catch a ferry at Sul e Sueste, next to the praça do Comércio. It runs across the Tagus to the suburb of Barreiro; at the station there, **Estação do Barreiro,** you can catch a train for the Algarve and Alentejo. For all **rail information,** at any of the terminals above, call ☎ **21/888-40-25.**

BY BUS   Buses from all over Portugal, including the Algarve, arrive at the **Rodoviária da Estremadura,** av. Casal Ribeiro 18B (☎ **21/357-77-15**), which lies near praça Saldanha, about a 30-minute walk from the praça dos Restauradores. Buses no. 1, 21, and 32 will deliver you to the Rossio. Bus no. 1 goes on to the Cais do Sodré, if your hotel is in Estoril or Cascais. At least 10 buses a day leave for Lagos, a gateway to the Algarve, and 15 buses head north every day to Porto. There are eight daily buses to Coimbra, the university city to the north.

BY CAR   International motorists must arrive through Spain, the only nation connected to Portugal by road. You'll have to cross Spanish border points, which usually pose no great difficulty. The roads are moderately well maintained. From Madrid, if you head west, the main road (N620) from Tordesillas goes southwest by way of Salamanca and Ciudad Rodrigo and reaches the Portuguese frontier at Fuentes de Onoro.

If you have a rented car, make sure that your insurance covers Portugal. Drive on the right side of the road; international signs and symbols are used. Most of the 15 border crossings are open daily from 7am to midnight.

VISITOR INFORMATION

The main tourist office in Lisbon is at the **Palácio da Foz,** praça dos Restauradores (☎ **21/346-63-07**), at the Baixa end of avenida da Liberdade. The office is devoted to Portugal in general. It's open Monday to Saturday 9am to 8pm, Sunday 10am to 6pm. Metro: Restauradores.

Lisboa Turismo, rua do Jardim do Reqedor 50 (☎ **21/343-36-72**), dispenses information about the city. It is open daily from 9am to 6pm. It sells the Lisbon Card, an "open sesame" for visitors and an inexpensive and convenient way to see the town. The card provides free city transportation and entrance fees to museums and other attractions, plus discounts on admission to events. For adults, a 1-day pass costs

1,900$ ($10.65); 2 days, 3,100$ ($17.35), 3 days, 4,000$ ($22.40). Children 5 to 11 pay 750$ ($4.20), 1,100$ ($6.15), and 1,500$ ($8.40), respectively.

CITY LAYOUT

MAIN STREETS & SQUARES   Now in its seventh century as the center of the Portuguese nation, Lisbon is the westernmost capital of continental Europe. According to legend, it spreads across seven hills, like Rome. That statement, though perhaps once true, has long been outdated—Lisbon now sprawls across more hills than that. Most of the city lies on the right (north) bank of the Tagus.

No one ever claimed that getting around Lisbon was a breeze. Streets rise and fall across the hills, at times dwindling into mere alleyways. Exploring the city, however, is well worth the effort.

Lisbon is best approached through its gateway, **praça do Comércio** (Commerce Square), bordering the Tagus. Like a formal parlor, it's one of the most perfectly planned squares in Europe, rivaled only by the piazza dell'Unità d'Italia in Trieste, Italy. Before the 1755 earthquake, praça do Comércio was known as terreiro do Paço, the Palace Grounds, because the king and his court lived in now-destroyed buildings on that site. To confuse matters further, English-speaking residents often refer to it as "Black Horse Square" because of its statue (actually a bronze-green color) of José I.

Today, the square is the site of the Stock Exchange and various government ministries. Its center is used as a parking lot, which destroys some of its harmony. In 1908, an event here echoed around the world: Carlos I and his elder son, Luís Filipe, were fatally shot by an assassin. The monarchy held on for another 2 years under the rule of a younger prince, but the House of Bragança effectively came to an end that day.

Directly west of the square stands the City Hall, fronting **praça do Município.** The building, erected in the late 19th century, was designed by the architect Domingos Parente.

Heading north from Black Horse or Commerce Square, you enter the hustle and bustle of **praça de Dom Pedro IV,** popularly known as the **Rossio.** The "drunken" undulation of the sidewalks, with their arabesques of black and white, have led to the appellation, used mainly by tourists, of "the dizzy praça." Here you can sit sipping strong unblended coffee from the former Portuguese provinces in Africa. The statue on the square is that of the Portuguese-born emperor of Brazil.

Opening onto the Rossio is the Teatro Nacional de Dona Maria II, a freestanding building whose facade has been preserved. From 1967 to 1970 workers gutted the interior to rebuild it completely. If you arrive by train, you'll enter the Estação do Rossio, whose exuberant Manueline architecture is worth seeing.

Separating the Rossio from avenida da Liberdade is **praça dos Restauradores,** named in honor of the Restoration, when the Portuguese chose their own king and freed themselves from 60 years of Spanish rule. An obelisk commemorates the event.

Lisbon's main avenue is **avenida da Liberdade** (Avenue of Liberty). The handsomely laid-out street dates from 1880 and was once called the "antechamber of Lisbon." Avenida da Liberdade is like a mile-long park, with shade trees, gardens, and center walks for the promenading crowds. Flanking it are fine shops, the headquarters of many major airlines, travel agents, coffeehouses with sidewalk tables, and hotels, including the Tivoli. The comparable street in Paris would be the Champs-Elysées; in Rome, via Vittorio Veneto.

At the top of the avenue is **praça do Marquês de Pombal,** with a statue erected in honor of the 18th-century prime minister credited with Lisbon's reconstruction in the aftermath of the earthquake.

Proceeding north, you'll enter **Parque Eduardo VII,** named in honor of the son of Queen Victoria, who paid a state visit to Lisbon. In the park is the Estufa Fria, a greenhouse well worth a visit.

FINDING AN ADDRESS   Finding an address in the old quarters of Lisbon is difficult, because street numbering at times follows no predictable pattern. When trying to locate an address, always ask for the nearest cross street before setting out. Addresses consist of a street name followed by a number. Sometimes the floor of the building is given as well. For example, av. Casal Ribeiro 18 3° means that the building is at number 18 and the address is on the third floor. In Lisbon, the ground floor is not called the first floor as in the United States; what Americans would call the fourth floor is actually the third floor in Portugal. "ESP" after a floor number indicates that you should go left, and "DIR" means turn right.

STREET MAPS   Arm yourself with a good city map before setting out. Maps with complete indexes of streets are available at most newsstands and kiosks. Those given away by tourist offices and hotels aren't adequate, because they don't show the maze of little streets.

Neighborhoods in Brief

Baixa   The business district of Lisbon, Baixa contains much Pombaline-style architecture. (The term refers to the 18th-century prime minister who rebuilt Lisbon following the earthquake.) Many major Portuguese banks are headquartered here. Running south, the main street of Baixa separates praça do Comércio from the Rossio. In fact, a triumphal arch leads from the square to **rua Augusta,** where there are many clothing stores. The two most important streets of Baixa are **rua da Prata** ("Street of Silver") and **rua Aurea,** formerly called rua do Oro ("Street of Gold"). Silversmiths and goldsmiths are located on these streets.

Chiado   If you head west from Baixa, you'll enter this shopping district. From its perch on a hill, it's traversed by **rua Garrett,** named for the noted romantic writer João Batista de Almeida Garrett (1799–1854). Many of the finest shops in the city, such as the **Vista Alegre,** a china and porcelain house, are here. One coffeehouse in particular, **A Brasileira,** has been a traditional gathering spot for the Portuguese literati.

Bairro Alto   Continuing your ascent, you'll arrive at the Bairro Alto (Upper City). This sector, reached by trolley car, occupies one of the legendary seven hills of Lisbon. Many of its buildings were left fairly intact by the 1755 earthquake. Containing much of the charm and color of the Alfama, it's the location of some of the finest **fado clubs** in Lisbon, as well as excellent restaurants and unpretentious bars. Several of Lisbon's new **nightspots** are here. There are also antique shops.

The Alfama   East of praça do Comércio lies the oldest district, the Alfama. Saved only in part from the devastation of the 1755 earthquake, the Alfama was the Moorish section of the capital. Centuries later, before the earthquake struck, it was the aristocratic residential district. Nowadays it's home in some parts to stevedores, fishermen, and *varinas* (fishwives). Overlooking the Alfama is **Castelo São Jorge,** or St. George's Castle, a Visigothic fortification that was later used by the Romans. On the way to the Alfama, on rua dos Bacalheiros, stands another landmark, the **Casa dos Bicos** (House of the Pointed Stones)—an early 16th-century town house whose facade is studded with diamond-shaped stones. Be careful in parts of the Alfama at night.

Belém   In the west, on the coastal road to Estoril, is the suburb of Belém. It contains some of the finest monuments in Portugal, several built during the Age of Discovery, near the point where the caravels set out to conquer new worlds (at Belém, the Tagus reaches the sea). At one time, before the earthquake, Belém was an aristocratic sector filled with elegant town houses.

Two of the country's principal attractions stand here: the **Mosteiro dos Jerónimos,** a Manueline structure erected in the 16th century, and the **Museu Nacional dos Coches,** the National Coach Museum, the finest of its kind in the world. Belém is Lisbon's land of museums—it also contains the **Museu de Arte Popular** and the **Museu de Marinha.**

Cacilhas   On the south side of the Tagus, where puce-colored smoke billows from factory stacks, is the left-bank settlement of Cacilhas. Inhabited mainly by the working class, it's often visited by right-bank residents who come here for the **seafood restaurants.** You can reach the settlement by way of a bridge or a ferryboat from praça do Comércio.

The most dramatic way to cross the Tagus is on the **Ponte do 25 de Abril,** the longest suspension bridge in Europe. Completed in 1966, the bridge helped open Portugal south of the Tagus. The bridge is 7,473 feet long, and its towers are 625 feet high. In 1998, the longest suspension bridge in Europe, **Ponte Vasco da Gama,** opened in time for the EXPO '98. Spanning the Tagus, it stretches for 10 miles and relieves overcrowding on the April 25 bridge. It opens areas to the north of the country and the southern Algarve, and east across the Alentejo plain to southern Spain—all of which are now more accessible. Standing guard on the left bank is a monumental **statue of Jesus** with arms outstretched.

2 Getting Around

Public transportation is inexpensive but inadequate at times. Yet, considering the hilly terrain and that many of the streets were designed for donkey carts, the system works well. Even the most skilled chauffeurs, however, have been known to scrape the fenders of their clients' rented limousines while maneuvering through the narrow alleyways.

A lot of the city can be covered on foot, especially by those adept at hill climbing. However, to get from one point to another—say, from the Alfama to the suburb of Belém—you'll need to use public transport or your own car.

As Evamarie Doering of Belmont, California, wrote, "In the 15 years since my last visit there, Lisbon has become one of the noisiest cities I've ever visited. Traffic is outrageous; driving is difficult because of the speed and the tendency of the natives to ride 6 inches from your rear bumper. The buses, of which there are a great many, are very noisy, and produce volumes of smoke. Honking of car horns seems to be a national pastime." Her description is, unfortunately, apt.

BY PUBLIC TRANSPORTATION

CARRIS (☎ **21/363-20-44** or 21/363-93-43) operates the network of funiculars, trains, subways, and buses in Lisbon. The company sells a "bilhete de assinatura turístico" that's good for 4 days of unlimited travel on its network. It costs 1,600$ ($8.95). A 1-day pass goes for 430$ ($2.40), a 7-day pass for 2,265$ ($12.70). Passes are sold in CARRIS booths, open from 8am to 8pm daily, in most Metro stations and network train stations. You must show a passport to buy a pass.

METRO   Lisbon's Metro stations are designated by large M signs, and the subway system has more than 24 stations. A single ticket costs 80$ (45¢); 10 tickets at one time cost 550$ ($3.10). One of the most popular trips—and likely to be jam-packed on *corrida* (bullfight) days—is from avenida da Liberdade to campo Pequeno, the brick building away from the center of the city. Service runs daily from 6am to 1am. For more information, call ☎ **21/355-84-57.**

Surprisingly, riding the Lisbon Metro is like visiting an impressive art collection. Paintings, glazed tiles, and sculptures make for a real museum in the underground. You'll see interesting collections of contemporary art, including some works by famous Portuguese artists such as Maria Keil and Maria Helena Vieira da Silva. Stations that display some of the finest art include Cais do Sodré, Baixa/Chiado, Campo Grande, and Marquês de Pombal.

BUS & TRAM   These are among the cheapest in Europe. The trolley cars (trams)— *eléctricos*—make the steep run up to the Bairro Alto. The **double-decker buses** come from London and look as if they need Big Ben in the background to complete the picture. If you're trying to stand on the platform at the back of a jammed bus, you'll need both hands free to hold on.

The basic fare on a bus or eléctrico is 160$ (90¢) if you buy the ticket from the driver. The transportation system within the city limits is divided into zones ranging from one to five. The fare depends on how many zones you traverse. Buses and eléctricos run daily from 6am to 1am.

At the foot of the Santa Justa Elevator, on rua Aurea, there's a stand with schedules pinpointing the zigzagging tram and bus routes. Your hotel concierge should have information.

The antediluvian eléctricos, much like San Francisco's cable cars, have become a major tourist attraction. Instead of phasing them out, Lisbon authorities sent them to Germany to be overhauled and refurbished, then shipped back to Portugal. Beginning in 1903, the eléctricos replaced horse-drawn trams. The most interesting ride for sightseers is on **eléctrico no. 28,** which takes you on a fascinating trip through the most history-rich part of Lisbon.

ELECTRIC TRAIN   A smooth-running, modern electric train system connects Lisbon to all the towns and villages along the Portuguese Riviera. There's only one class of seat, and the rides are cheap and generally comfortable. You can board the train at the waterfront **Cais do Sodré Station** in Lisbon and head up the coast all the way to Cascais.

The electric train does not run to Sintra. For Sintra, you must go to the **Estação do Rossio** station, opening onto praça de Dom Pedro IV, or the Rossio, where frequent connections can be made. The one-way fare from Lisbon to Cascais, Estoril, or Sintra is 180$ ($1) per person.

FUNICULARS   Lisbon has a trio of **funiculars: the Glória,** which goes from praça dos Restauradores to rua São Pedro de Alcântara; the **Bica,** from the calçada do Combro to rua do Boavista; and the **Lavra,** from the eastern side of avenida da Liberdade to campo Martires da Pátria. A one-way ticket on any of these costs 60$ to 180$ (35¢ to $1).

FERRY   Long before the bridges across the Tagus were built, reliable ferryboats chugged across the Tagus, connecting the left bank with the right. They still do, and have been rebuilt and remotorized so they're no longer noisy. Many Portuguese who live on the bank opposite Lisbon take the ferry to avoid the heavy bridge traffic during rush hour.

Most boats leave from Cais de Alfândega (praça do Comércio) and Cais do Sodré, heading for Cacilhas. The trip is worth it for the scenic views alone. Arrivals are at the Estação do Barreiro, where trains leave about every 30 minutes for the Costa Azul and the Algarve. Ferries depart Lisbon throughout the day about every 30 minutes; trip time across the Tagus is 30 minutes. The cost of the continuing train ticket includes the ferry. The separate ferry fare from the center of Lisbon to Cacilhas is 95$ (55¢).

BY TAXI

Taxis in Lisbon tend to be inexpensive and are a popular means of transport for all but the most economy-minded tourists. They usually are diesel-engine Mercedes. The basic fare is 250$ ($1.40) for the first 480 yards, 10$ (5¢) for each extra 162 meters, plus 20% from 10pm to 6am. The law allows drivers to tack on another 50% to your bill if your luggage weighs more than 66 pounds. Portuguese tip about 20% of the modest fare. For a **Radio Taxi,** call ☎ **21/811-90-00** or 21/793-27-56.

Many visitors stay at a Costa do Sol resort hotel, such as the Palácio in Estoril or the Cidadela in Cascais. If you stay there, then you'll probably find taxi connections from Lisbon prohibitively expensive. Far preferable for Costa do Sol visitors is the electric train system (see above).

BY CAR

In congested Lisbon, driving is extremely difficult and potentially dangerous—the city has an alarmingly high accident rate. It always feels like rush hour in Lisbon (theoretically, rush hours are Monday to Saturday from 8am to 10am, 1 to 2pm, and 4 to 6pm). **Parking** is seemingly impossible. Wait to rent a car until you're making excursions from the capital. If you drive into Lisbon from another town or city, call ahead and ask at your hotel for the nearest garage or other place to park. Leave your vehicle there until you're ready to depart.

CAR RENTALS The major international car-rental companies are represented in Lisbon. There are kiosks at the airport and offices in the center. They include **Avis,** av. Praia da Vitória 12C (☎ **21/356-11-76**), open daily 8am to 7pm; and **Hertz,** Qto. Frangelha Baixio (☎ **21/849-27-22**), open Monday to Friday 8am to 7pm, Saturday and Sunday 9am to 1pm and 2 to 7pm. **Budget,** av. Visconte Valmar 36 (☎ **21/ 994-04-43**), is open Monday to Saturday 8am to 8pm, Sunday 8am to 6:30pm.

GASOLINE Lisbon has many garages and gasoline pumps; some are open around the clock.

THE TAGUS BRIDGES The suspension bridge Ponte do 25 de Abril, one of the longest in Europe, connects Lisbon with the district south of the Tagus. The 10-mile Ponte Vasco da Gama, which opened in 1998, is the longest suspension bridge in Europe. It has greatly relieved overcrowding on the April bridge. Tolls are based on the size of the car. You take these bridges to reach Cacilhas and such cities as Setúbal, in the south, and Évora, the old Roman city in the east.

ON FOOT

Central Lisbon is relatively compact, and because of heavy traffic it's best explored by foot. That's virtually the only way to see such districts as the Alfama. However, when you venture farther afield, such as to Belém, you'll need to depend on public transportation (see above).

Fast Facts: Lisbon

Your hotel's concierge usually is a reliable source of information. See also "Fast Facts: Portugal" in chapter 2.

Baby-Sitters Most first-class hotels can provide baby-sitters from lists the concierge keeps. At small establishments, the sitter is likely to be a relative of the proprietor. Rates are low. Remember to request a baby-sitter early—no later than the morning if you're planning on going out that evening. Also request a sitter with at least a minimum knowledge of English. If your sitter is fluent in English, count yourself lucky.

Currency Exchange See "American Express" in "Fast Facts: Portugal" in chapter 2. There are currency-exchange booths at Santa Apolónia station and at the airport, both open 24 hours a day. ATMs offer the best exchange rates. They pepper the streets of the central Baixa district, and are also found less frequently in other parts of the city. The post office (see "Mail," below) will also exchange money.

Dentist The reception staffs at most hotels maintain lists of local, usually English-speaking dentists who are available for dental emergencies. Some of them will contact a well-recommended dental clinic, **Clinica Medical da Praça d'Espanha,** rua Dom Luís de Narona 32 (☎ **21/796-74-57**). Some of the staff members speak English.

Doctor See "Hospitals," below.

Drugstores **Farmácia Vall,** av. Visconde Valmor 60A (☎ **21/797-30-43**), is centrally located and well stocked.

Emergencies To call the **police** or an **ambulance**, telephone ☎ **112.** In case of **fire,** call ☎ **21/342-22-22.**

Eyeglasses One of the city's best-recommended eyeglass shops is **Oculista das Avenidas,** av. do Marquês de Tomar 71A (☎ **21/796-42-97**), which seems to be the favorite of many residents in its downtown neighborhood. The staff is skilled at crafting both eyeglasses and contact lenses.

Hairdressers/Barbers A recommended hairdresser for women is **Hair,** rua Castilho 77 (☎ **21/387-78-55**). A sophisticated counterpart for men is **Bengto,** in the Amoreiras shopping center, travesso das Amoreiras (☎ **21/383-29-29**).

Hospitals In case of a medical emergency, ask at your hotel or call your embassy and ask the staff there to recommend an English-speaking physician. Or try the **British Hospital,** rua Saraiva de Carvalho 49 (☎ **21/395-50-67**), where the telephone operator, staff, and doctors speak English.

Hot Lines The **drug abuse hot line** is ☎ 21/726-77-66.

Laundry Keeping your clothes clean can be a problem if you're not staying long in Lisbon. For a self-service laundry, try **Lavatax,** rua Francisco Sanches 65A (☎ **21/812-33-92**). It's part of a chain that has four branches in Lisbon, one in Estoril, and one in Cascais.

Lost Property Go in person to the municipal **Governo Civil,** next to the São Carlos Opera House. Office hours are Monday to Saturday 9am to noon and 2 to 6pm. For items lost on public transportation, inquire at **Secção de Achados da PSP,** Olivais Sul, praça da Cidade Salazar Lote 180 (☎ **21/853-54-03**), which is open Monday to Friday 9am to noon and 1:30 to 5pm.

Luggage Storage/Lockers These can be found at the **Estação da Santa Apolónia,** by the river near the Alfama. Lockers cost 450$ to 600$ ($2.50 to $3.35) for up to 48 hours.

Mail While in Portugal you may have your mail directed to your hotel (or hotels), to the American Express representative, or to General Delivery (*Poste Restante*) in Lisbon. You must present your passport to pick up mail. The **main**

post office (Correio Geral) in Lisbon is at praça do Comércio, 1100 Lisboa
(☎ **21/346-32-31**). It's open Monday to Friday 8:30am to 6:30pm.

Photographic Needs   One of the best places to go for your film needs,
including processing, is **Fotosport,** Centro Comercial Amoreiras, Shop no. 1080
(☎ **01/383-21-01**). It's open daily 10am to midnight.

Police   Call ☎ **115.**

Radio   English-speaking listeners in Lisbon can pick up the BBC World Service
and Voice of America. Hourly news is broadcast on 648 KHz medium wave and
15.07 MHz short wave. Between 8:30 and 10am daily, Portuguese radio presents
English-language programs for tourists—between 558 and 720 KHz (87.9 and
95.7 FM), depending on where you are in the city.

Safety   Lisbon used to be one of the safest capitals of Europe, but that hasn't
been true for a long time. It's now quite dangerous to walk around at night.
Many travelers report being held up at knifepoint. Some bandits operate in pairs
or in trios. Not only do they take your money, they demand your ATM code.
One of the robbers holds a victim captive while another withdraws money. (If the
number proves fake, the robber might return and harm the victim.) During the
day, pickpockets galore prey on tourists, aiming for wallets, purses, and such possessions as cameras. Congested areas are particularly hazardous. Avoid walking at
night, especially if you're alone.

Taxes   Lisbon imposes no city taxes. However, the national value-added tax
(VAT) applies purchases and services (see "Taxes" under "Fast Facts: Portugal" in
chapter 2).

Telegrams/Telex/Fax   At most hotels the receptionist will help you send a
telegram. If not, there's a cable dispatch service, open 24 hours a day, at **Marconi**
(the Portuguese Radio Communications Office), rua de São Julião 131. To send
telegrams from any telephone to points outside Portugal, dial ☎ **182** to reach
Marconi. To send telegrams within Portugal (your Portuguese-language skills had
better be good), dial ☎ **183** from any telephone. Most foreign visitors leave the
logistics to the hotel concierge. Telexes and faxes can be sent from most hotels,
or you can go to the general post office (see "Mail," above).

Telephone   You can make a local call in Lisbon in one of the many telephone
booths. For most long-distance telephone calls, particularly transatlantic calls, go
to the central post office (see "Mail," above). Give an assistant the number, and
he or she will make the call for you, billing you at the end. Some phones are
equipped for using calling cards, including American Express and Visa. You can
also purchase phone cards. See "Telephone" under "Fast Facts: Portugal" in
chapter 2. In hotels, local calls are billed directly to your room. Phone debit cards
can be used only in public phones in public places. The debit cards are either
T.L.P. or CrediFone. Both are sold at the cashier's desks of most hotels and at post
offices throughout the country.

Television   Lisbon has two government-controlled TV stations (Channels 1
and 2) and two privately operated TV stations (SIC, on Channel 3, and TVY, on
Channel 4). Many hotels throughout the country have cable reception. It brings
in such foreign broadcasting networks as CNN from the United States; MTV
and Skychannel from Britain; and, depending on the hotel, broadcasts from
Spain, Italy, and France.

Time   For the local time in Lisbon, phone ☎ **15.**

Transit Information For **airport information,** call ☎ **21/841-35-00.** For **train information,** dial ☎ **21/888-40-25. TAP Air Portugal** is at praça do Marquês de Pombal 3A (☎ **21/841-69-90**).

Weather To find out about the weather, if you don't speak Portuguese, ask someone at your hotel desk to translate one of the weather reports that appear daily in the leading newspapers. Or call ☎ **150** (available only in Portuguese).

3 Where to Stay

Lisbon has a much wider range of accommodations than ever before. But here's the rub: Lisbon's hotels, especially the first-class and deluxe places, are no longer the bargains they once were. They once were so cheap that they were reason alone to travel to Lisbon. Today, hotels such as the Four Seasons Hotel The Ritz Lisbon and the Hotel Tivoli charge virtually the same prices as first-class hotels in other high-priced European capitals.

Some of the newer hotels appear to have been hastily erected to benefit from the tourist boom in Portugal. They seem more intent on courting tour groups from Japan and elsewhere than they do in catering to the individual. Of course, we don't include such establishments in our recommendations.

Most visitors in Lisbon have to make a major decision, usually before they arrive: whether to stay in a hotel in the city proper or at a resort in the neighboring towns of Estoril and Cascais (see chapter 5). Much will depend on their interests. If it's summer and you'd like to have a sea-resort vacation while experiencing Lisbon's cultural attractions, then a beach resort might be ideal, even though you'd have to commute into Lisbon. Electric trains run about every 20 minutes, so it's entirely possible to stay on the Costa do Sol and still go sightseeing in Lisbon.

If you're primarily interested in seeing Lisbon's attractions and are pressed for time, perhaps having no more than 2 days, then you'll probably opt to stay in the city. Also, the off-season (November to March) is not ideal for a sea-resort vacation.

If you can't afford to stay in Lisbon's world-class hotels, you'll find reasonably priced guest houses—called *pensãos*—in Portugal. Most of these are no-frills accommodations. Often you'll have to share a bathroom, although many have hot and cold running water in a sink in your room. Sometimes there's a shower. In many cases, the toilet is across the hall. Some of the pensions in Lisbon are centrally located and are a good way to see the sights day and night without shelling out a lot of money for accommodations.

If you arrive without a reservation, begin your search for a room as early in the day as possible. If you arrive late at night, you may have to take what you can get, often at a much higher price than you would have paid otherwise.

IN THE CENTER
VERY EXPENSIVE

✪ **Da Lapa.** Rua do Pau de Bandeira 4, 1200 Lisboa. ☎ **21/395-00-05.** Fax 21/395-06-65. www.orient-expresshotels.com. E-mail: reservas@hotelapa.com. 102 units. A/C MINIBAR TV TEL. 55,000$–100,000$ ($308–$560) double; from 90,000$ ($504) suite. Rates include breakfast. AE, DC, MC, V. Free parking. Bus: 13 or 27.

In a palace built for the count of Valença in 1870, this five-star hotel, purchased by Orient Express in 1998, is the most talked-about accommodation in Lisbon. We never thought we'd see a hotel replace the Four Seasons Hotel The Ritz as the city's premier address, but Da Lapa has done just that. In 1910, the de Valença family sold the villa and its enormous gardens to a wealthy, untitled family that retained it until 1988. After more than 4 years of renovation, it opened in 1992 amid a flurry of publicity. Its lushly manicured gardens (huge by urban standards) lie close to the Tagus, south of the city center; most of Portugal's foreign embassies are in the Lapa district.

All but about 20 of the rooms are in a modern six-story wing. The spacious guest rooms in both sections contain amply proportioned marble surfaces, reproductions of French and English furniture, and a classic design inspired by a late 18th-century model. The marble bathrooms are among the city's most elegant, often adorned with bas-relief and containing hair dryers, robes, and in some cases whirlpool baths. Each unit opens onto a balcony. The older rooms have more charm and grace; many of the newer ones open onto panoramic vistas of Lisbon. The public areas have multicolored ceiling frescoes and richly patterned marble floors laid out in sometimes startling geometric patterns.

Dining/Diversions: The Embaixada restaurant (see "Where to Dine," later in this chapter) is one of the most popular in the neighborhood, although prohibitively expensive for most people. Sun-flooded lunches and candlelit dinners are served beside the pool in the Pavilhão. The bar is sumptuous.

Amenities: Concierge, 24-hour room service, laundry, dry cleaning, outdoor pool, business center with translation services and secretarial services.

✪ **Four Seasons Hotel The Ritz Lisbon.** Rua Rodrigo de Fonseca 88, 1200 Lisboa. ☎ **800/332-3442** in the U.S., or 21/383-20-20. Fax 21/383-17-83. www.fourseasons.com. 284 units. A/C MINIBAR TV TEL. 25,000$–60,000$ ($140–$336) double; from 65,000$ ($364) suite. AE, DC, MC, V. Free parking. Metro: Rotunda. Bus: 1, 2, 9, or 32.

The Ritz, built by the dictator Salazar in the late 1950s, is now operated by Four Seasons. There's so much marble here that entire quarries must have been denuded for its creation. Its suites boast the finest decoration you'll see in any major Portuguese hotel: slender mahogany canopied beds with fringed swags, marquetry desks, satinwood dressing tables, and plush carpeting—no wonder this has traditionally been the preferred choice of celebrated guests. Some of the soundproofed, spacious, modern rooms have terraces opening onto Edward VII Park; each boasts a marble bathroom with double basin, local and satellite TV, and a hair dryer. One floor is reserved for nonsmokers. The least desirable rooms are the even-numbered ones facing the street. The odd-numbered accommodations, opening onto views of the park, are the best. Some studios with double beds are rented as singles, attracting business travelers.

Dining/Diversions: The main dining room, Veranda, is highly acclaimed. The breakfast and luncheon buffets are renowned for variety; the dinner menu features delectable Portuguese flavors and fresh seafood. From May to October you can take meals out onto the attractive Veranda Terrace. The staff is cited for its impeccable service—although few must be happy when the check is presented. The Ritz Bar is a major rendezvous point. Lodged in a corner of the hotel, overlooking the terrace and park, it offers everything from a Pimm's No. 1 Cup to a mint julep.

Amenities: 24-hour room service, baby-sitting, laundry and valet, coffee shop, tearoom, fitness center, beauty parlor.

✪ **Hotel Dom Pedro.** Av. Engenheiro Duarte Pacheco, 1070 Lisboa. ☎ **21/389-66-00.** Fax 21/389-66-01. www.dompedro-hotels.com. E-mail: dp.lisboa@mail.telepac.pt. 262 units. A/C MINIBAR TV TEL. 40,000$–60,000$ ($224–$336) double; from 70,000$ ($392) suite. Suite rates include breakfast. AE, DC, MC, V. Free parking. Metro: Marquês de Pombal.

Lisbon's newest major hotel opened in the spring of 1998 and quickly showed signs of surpassing its older and more staid rivals. Rated five stars by the Portuguese government, and associated with some of the most glamorous hotels of the Algarve and

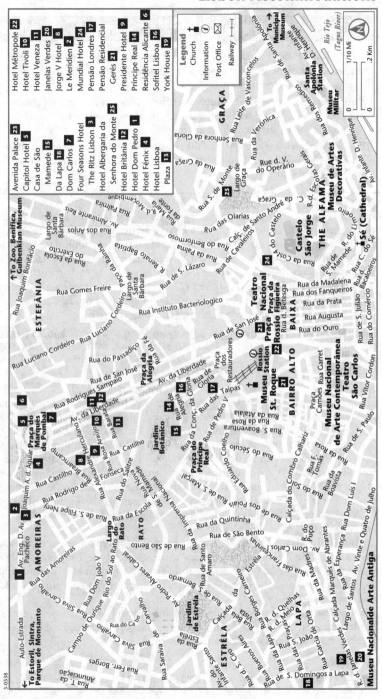

Lisbon Accommodations

Legend
- ✚ Church
- ℹ Information
- ⊠ Post Office
- Railway

Avenida Palace 23
Capitol Hotel 5
Casa de São Mamede 15
Da Lapa 18
Dom Carlos 7
Four Seasons Hotel
The Ritz Lisbon 3
Hotel Albergaria da Senhora do Monte 25
Hotel Britânia 12
Hotel Dom Pedro 4
Hotel Fénix 13
Hotel Lisboa Plaza 13

Hotel Métropole 22
Hotel Tivoli 10
Hotel Veneza 11
Janelas Verdes 20
Jorge V Hotel 8
Le Meridien 2
Mundial Hotel 24
Pensão Londres 17
Pensão Residencial Gerés 21
Presidente Hotel 9
Príncipe Real 14
Residência Alicante 6
Sofitel Lisboa 16
York House 19

71

ⓘ Family-Friendly Hotels

Hotel Lisboa Plaza *(see page 73)*   In the heart of Lisbon, this family owned and operated hotel offers spacious rooms where children 11 and under stay free if sharing a room with their parents.

Hotel Príncipe *(see page 78)*   Kind to families with children, the staff charges half-price for kids 5 to 7 staying in their parents' room; those under 5 stay free. Baby-sitting can be arranged. Prices are reasonable.

Presidente Hotel *(see page 79)*   In the center, near avenida da Liberdade, this hotel is recommended for families because it adds an extra bed to any room and can arrange baby-sitting.

Madeira, it's in the central Amoreiras district, across from one of the city's biggest shopping centers. A hypermodern sheathing of reflective glass covers its 21 stories. The interior is as conservative and rich-looking as the exterior is futuristic. The good-sized guest rooms are richly furnished, usually with heraldic symbols or medallions (or both) woven subtly through the fabrics and wallpapers.

Dining: Il Gatto Pardo (see "Where to Dine," later in this chapter) is an Italian restaurant with a leopard-skin theme. There's also an upscale bistro, Le Café.

Amenities: 24-hour room service, laundry and valet, concierge.

Lisboa Sheraton Hotel & Towers. Rua Latino Coelho 1, 1097 Lisboa. ☎ **800/325-3535** in the U.S., or 21/357-57-57. Fax 21/314-22-92. 388 units. A/C MINIBAR TV TEL. 44,000$ ($246.40) double; from 90,000$ ($504) suite. AE, DC, MC, V. Parking 1,900$ ($10.65). Bus: 1, 2, 9, or 32.

Built in 1972, this five-star hotel was completely renovated in 1993. The 25-floor sky-scraper lies at a traffic-clogged intersection a bit removed from the center of the action, a few blocks north of praça do Marquês de Pombal. Most of the guests are business travelers. The impressive pink marble lobby features chandeliers and fancy carpeting. The guest rooms don't match the grandeur of the public spaces, but they're generally spacious. The understated decor includes thick wool carpeting, print fabrics, traditional (if a bit chunky) wood furniture, and excellent beds. The marble bathrooms are a highlight, with such amenities as hair dryers. The most desirable rooms are in the tower, opening onto views of the longest bridge in Europe, the Tagus, or the city. There's also a private lounge and bar. Executive-suite guests have separate check-in. The "soundproof" rooms don't live up to their name.

Dining/Diversions: The richly decorated cocktail bar has live music at night. You can also enjoy drinks throughout the day and evening on the 26th floor, with a panoramic view of Lisbon and dancing to live music nightly. The à la carte grill, known for its fine cuisine and impeccable service, offers a selection of Portuguese and continental dishes.

Amenities: Concierge (who's a wealth of information), 24-hour room service, laundry and valet, baby-sitting, hairdresser, barber, massage, sauna and solarium, car-rental facilities, boutiques, health club, outdoor pool.

EXPENSIVE

Avenida Palace. Rua 1er Dezembro 123, 1200 Lisboa. ☎ **21/346-01-51.** Fax 21/342-28-84. E-mail: hotel.av.palace@mail.telepac.pt. 96 units. A/C MINIBAR TV TEL. 27,000$–36,000$ ($151.20–$201.60) double; 55,000$ ($308) junior suite; 75,000$ ($420) suite. Rates include breakfast. AE, DC, MC, V. Free parking. Metro: Restauradores. Tram: 35.

Built in 1892, Avenida Palace is the grandest old-fashioned hotel in Lisbon, an antique-filled link to the past. Its location right at the Rossio is terribly convenient and terribly noisy, but once inside it is another world entirely. It closed in the late 1990s for a massive overhaul. Still the grand dame of Lisbon hotels, it retains its 19th-century aura and elegance, with polished wood, a marble staircase, beautiful salons, and silk brocades. The belle epoque–style Palace offers all the modern comforts, especially in its restored guest rooms. They're soundproofed and elegantly furnished, often in the 17th- or 18th-century style. Mattresses are deluxe, and bathrooms adorned with the finest Portuguese marble.

Dining/Diversions: The hotel has one of the most elegant, fashionable bars in midcity. There's no restaurant, but dozens of good restaurants are nearby.

Amenities: TV salon, business rooms, room service (7:30am to midnight), laundry and valet, concierge.

✪ **Hotel Tivoli.** Av. da Liberdade 185, 1298 Lisboa Codex. ☎ **21/319-89-00.** Fax 21/319-89-50. E-mail: htllisboa@mail.telepac.pt. 357 units. A/C MINIBAR TV TEL. 26,000$–34,000$ ($145.60–$190.40) double; from 50,000$ ($280) suite. Rates include continental breakfast. AE, DC, MC, V. Parking 1,600$ ($8.95). Metro: Avenida. Bus: 1, 2, 9, or 32.

Hotel Tivoli has enticing features, including the only hotel pool in central Lisbon. A much-needed renovation in 1992 made the hotel sparkle. Right on the main boulevard, and large enough to accommodate more than 600 guests, it has extensive facilities. Best of all, its prices are not extravagant, considering the amenities. The two-story reception lobby has an encircling mezzanine lounge that's almost arena-size, with comfortable islands of furniture arranged on Oriental rugs. Adjoining the O Terraço restaurant is a homey salon with a wood-burning fireplace.

The guest rooms contain a mixture of modern and traditional furniture. The larger and best rooms face the front, although those in the rear are quieter. For some reason, rooms ending in the number "50" have the most spacious bathrooms. Not all the units are standard: Some are better appointed and roomier than others. Unlike the climate control in many Lisbon hotels, the air-conditioning here really seems to work. The Tivoli Jardim, next door, is under the same ownership as but inferior to the Hotel Tivoli.

Dining: The wood-paneled O Zodíaco restaurant serves a buffet at lunch and dinner. The top-floor O Terraço offers a view of Lisbon and à la carte meals. The emphasis is on steaks and chops that you select, cooked on a tile charcoal grill. Although in general the hotel offers good value in its category, meals seem a little overpriced.

Amenities: 24-hour room service, concierge, baby-sitting, laundry, business center, boutiques. Guests have access to the Tivoli Club, which has a lovely garden, a pool that can be heated when necessary, tennis court, solarium, bar, and a restaurant that serves light snacks.

Hotel Lisboa Plaza. Travessa do Salitre 7, av. da Liberdade, 1269 Lisboa. ☎ **21/346-39-22.** Fax 21/347-16-30. www.heritage.pt. E-mail: plaza.hotels@heritage.pt. 112 units. A/C MINIBAR TV TEL. 23,500$–34,600$ ($131.60–$193.75) double; 35,000$–48,000$ ($196–$268.80) suite. Rates include buffet breakfast. Children under 13 free in parents' room. AE, DC, MC, V. Parking 2,300$ ($12.90) nearby. Metro: Avenida. Bus: 1, 2, 36, or 44.

Hotel Lisboa Plaza, in the heart of the city, is a charmer. A family owned and operated four-star hotel, it has many appealing art nouveau touches, including the facade. The turn-of-the-century–style bar has soothing colors and tufted leather chairs. The hotel was built in 1953 and completely overhauled and modernized in 1988. A well-known Portuguese designer, G. Viterbo, decorated it in contemporary classic style.

The midsize guest rooms—with well-stocked marble bathrooms, hair dryers, and in-house videos—are well styled and comfortable. Renovation is an ongoing program. Seek a unit in the rear, looking out over the botanical gardens. No-smoking rooms are available, and windows are double-glazed.

Dining: The Quinta d'Avenida Restaurant specializes in a traditional Portuguese cuisine.

Amenities: 24-hour room service, baby-sitting, same-day laundry, car-rental desks, business services.

Hotel Real Parque. Av. Luís Bivar 67, 1050 Bivar. ☎ **21/357-01-01.** Fax 21/357-07-50. E-mail: realparque@mail.telepac.pt. 155 units. A/C MINIBAR TV TEL. 19,000$–23,000$ ($106.40–$128.80) double; 35,000$–45,000$ ($196–$252) suite. Rates include breakfast. AE, DC, MC, V. Parking 1,200$ ($6.70). Metro: Picoas, São Sebastião, or Parque.

This 10-story modern building, near the Sheraton and the Parque Eduardo VII, opened as a four-star hotel in 1995. Stylish and modern, it offers excellent service in an uncontroversial, blandly international decor that nonetheless offers real comforts. The rooms aren't overly large, but do have all the conveniences you'd expect, and views out over neighborhoods where old-fashioned and modern mingle.

Dining/Diversions: The Cozinha do Real restaurant, open daily for lunch and dinner has a reputation for well-prepared Portuguese and international food. There's also a coffee shop and a bright, cosmopolitan bar.

Amenities: Concierge, 24-hour room service, laundry service, convention facilities.

Le Méridien. Rua Castilho 149, 1070 Lisboa. ☎ **21/383-04-00.** Fax 21/387-04-72. E-mail: reservas.lisboa@lemeridien.pt. 347 units. A/C MINIBAR TV TEL. 32,500$–38,000$ ($182–$212.80) double; from 65,000$ ($364) suite. AE, DC, MC, V. Parking 2,400$ ($13.45). Metro: Rotunda. Bus: 1, 2, 9, or 32.

One of the most dramatic major hotels in Lisbon, Le Méridien opened in 1985 in an 18-floor tower of concrete and mirrored glass. It's across the street from the superior Four Seasons Hotel The Ritz Lisbon. The air-conditioned lobby has lost some of its early glitter, but it's still impressive, with white marble, polished chromium, and mirrors. A symmetrical entrance frames the tile-bottomed fountains, whose splashing water rises to the top of the sunlit atrium. Reached by speedy elevators, the small guestrooms are soundproof and rather plainly decorated with business travelers in mind. They have thermostats and queen- or king-size beds. The marble bathrooms have robes, hair dryers, and toilet kits.

Dining/Diversions: There's a tearoom with Portuguese tiles; Le Ganesh, with a view of the park and the adjacent boulevard, on the ground floor; and the formal, glamorous Restaurant L'Appart upstairs. Le Nautique piano bar is elegantly decorated, and there's disco action.

Amenities: 24-hour room service, laundry and valet, baby-sitting, health club with sauna and massage, car-rental kiosk, business center.

Sofitel Lisboa. Av. da Liberdade 123, 1250 Lisboa. ☎ **21/342-92-02.** Fax 21/342-92-22. 168 units. A/C MINIBAR TV TEL. 35,000$ ($196) double; 55,000$ ($308) suite. AE, DC, MC, V. Metro: Avenida.

In the center of one of Lisbon's showcase boulevards, this member of a French-based chain is one of the capital's newest deluxe hotels. With a high-tech edge to its design, the hotel features touches of intimacy. Guests are often conventioneers. The comfortably appointed and good-sized guest rooms offer the standard amenities, and accommodations on each of the building's nine floors are outfitted with a different color scheme. Special rooms for business travelers offer extra amenities. The better units face the front, and some are for nonsmokers. The rooms are well insulated and soundproofed, and the air-conditioning is reliable. Other than Portuguese, French is the most common language here, although many staff members speak passably good English.

Dining/Diversions: Local businesspeople patronize the main restaurant, Cais d'Avenida, which has street and lobby entrances. Its mainly French menu is reasonably priced. The richly paneled bar, Molière, three steps up from the lobby, is popular with the locals.

Amenities: 24-hour room service, concierge, laundry and valet, business services.

MODERATE

Capitol Hotel. Rua Eça de Queiroz 24, 1000 Lisboa. ☎ **21/353-68-11.** Fax 21/352-61-65. www.rex.pt. E-mail: rex.hotel@mail.telepac.pt. 58 units. A/C MINIBAR TV TEL. 19,000$–22,300$ ($106.40–$124.90) double; from 24,000$ ($134.40) suite. Rates include buffet breakfast. AE, DC, MC, V. Bus: 1, 2, 9, or 32. Metro: Rotunda.

This fine little hostelry, last renovated in 1994, is minutes from the top of avenida da Liberdade and 2 blocks east of praça do Marquês de Pombal. It's away from the busy boulevards and opens onto a wedge-shaped park with weeping willows and oaks. The simply furnished midsized rooms have light-wood furnishings, comfortable beds, and such amenities as safes. They're inviting, although a bit sparse. The rooms in the front open onto balconies—and the city's notorious street noise. Some of the units at the rear and side also have balconies, but don't expect panoramas. Try to avoid staying here when a tour group arrives from Madrid. On the premises are a bar, a snack bar, and a restaurant with tired decor but consistently good regional and continental cuisine.

Dom Carlos. Av. Duque de Loulé 121, 1050 Lisboa. ☎ **21/351-25-90.** Fax 21/352-07-28. E-mail: hdcarlos@mail.telepac.pt. 76 units. A/C MINIBAR TV TEL. 20,800$ ($116.50) double; 24,000$ ($134.40) triple. Rates include buffet breakfast. AE, DC, MC, V. Metro: Marquês de Pombal. Bus: 1, 36, 44, or 45.

Just off praça do Marquês de Pombal, this hotel was completely renovated in early 1995. The reason to stay here is economy: The Dom Carlos charges only a fraction of what its rivals in the neighborhood get. The curvy facade is all glass, lending an out-doorsy feeling reinforced by trees and beds of orange and red canna. The good-sized guest rooms are paneled in reddish Portuguese wood; even so, they're rather unin-spired and functional. An occasional hand-carved cherub softens the Nordic-inspired furnishings. The hotel faces a triangular park dedicated to the partially blind Camilo Castelo Branco, a 19th-century "eternity poet." The lobby lounge is satisfactory; more inviting is the mezzanine salon, where sofas and chairs face the park. Breakfast is the only meal served. The miniature bar, with leather chairs, is ideal for a tête-à-tête. The hotel has laundry service, baby-sitting, and a car-rental desk.

Hotel Britânia. Rua Rodrigues Sampaio 17. ☎ **21/315-50-16.** Fax 21/315-50-21. www.heritage.pt. E-mail: britania.hotel@heritage.pt. 30 units. A/C MINIBAR TV TEL. 19,500$–30,600$ ($109.20–$171.35) double. Rates include buffet breakfast. AE, DC, MC, V. Metro: Avenida. Bus: 1, 2, 11, or 21.

In its own way, the Britânia is one of the most traditional and refreshingly conserva-tive hotels in Lisbon. The well-known Portuguese architect Cassiano Branco designed the art deco building in 1944. Located about a block from the capital's Champs-Elysées, avenida da Liberdade, it boasts a distinguished, loyal clientele and an old-fashioned, almost courtly, staff. In 1995, the five-story hotel was refurbished, making the exceedingly spacious rooms more comfortable. Each has an excellent mattress and renewed plumbing. There's a bar on the premises. The only meal served is breakfast, but the facilities of the much larger Lisboa Plaza Hotel (with which the Britânia is affiliated) lie just across the busy avenue.

Hotel Fénix. Praça do Marquês de Pombal 8, 1200 Lisboa. ☎ **800/44-UTELL** in the U.S., or 21/386-21-21. Fax 21/386-01-31. 123 units. A/C MINIBAR TV TEL. 20,500$ ($114.80) double; 40,000$ ($224) suite. Rates include continental breakfast. AE, DC, MC, V. Metro: Marquês de Pombal.

The once-tired Fénix is more comfortable and brighter than ever. A good value for the area, the hotel was greatly improved during recent renovations. It enjoys a front-row position on the circular plaza dedicated to the 18th-century prime minister, which is both a blessing and a curse. The location is convenient, but the noise overpowers the double-glazing on the windows. From most of the guest rooms, you can view the trees on the avenue and in Edward VII Park. All are handsomely decorated; some are quite spacious, while others are too small. Those facing the side street running along the park are your best bets. There are no balconies in front, and rooms on the lower floors have no views. The hotel draws many repeat guests. The public rooms are air-conditioned, and there is a lobby bar. The basement restaurant, El Bodegón (see "Where to Dine," later in this chapter), serves Spanish and Portuguese food.

Hotel Metropole. Rossio 30, 1100 Lisboa. ☎ **21/346-91-64.** Fax 21/346-91-66. 36 units. A/C TV TEL. 23,200$–27,000$ ($129.90–$151.20) double. Rates include buffet breakfast. AE, DC, MC, V. Metro: Rossio.

This hotel, originally built around 1900, has a symmetrical formality in keeping with the other stately buildings that line Lisbon's central square, the Rossio. It's the most centrally located hotel in town, ideal for theater, sightseeing, dining, or business. In 1993, it was elaborately renovated into one of the most comfortable middle-bracket (three-star) hotels in town. A narrow flight of marble stairs runs to the lobby. Many art deco appointments adorn the public rooms. The cozy guest rooms, which vary greatly in size, are freshly painted. They contain reproductions of traditional furniture, and have firm beds. Those in front overlook the noisy, animated square; the rooms in back overlook the congestion of the Barrio Alto. There's no restaurant on the premises, and few amenities other than a tactful, hardworking staff, but throughout, there's a sense of small-scale, carefully orchestrated charm. Room service is available daily from 7am to midnight.

Hotel Veneza. Av. da Liberdade 189, 1200 Lisboa. ☎ **21/352-26-18.** Fax 21/352-66-78. E-mail: 3k.hotels@mail.telepac.pt. 36 units. A/C MINIBAR TV TEL. 18,000$ ($100.80) double. Rates include continental breakfast. AE, DC, MC, V. Parking 1,400$ ($7.85). Metro: Avenida.

The Veneza, which opened in 1990, occupies one of the few remaining turn-of-the-century palaces that once lined avenida da Liberdade. A grand staircase leads to the three upper floors. The well-appointed, midsized guest rooms are furnished in soothing modern style, and have firm mattresses. The staff is pleasant. The Veneza has a bar and serves only breakfast. Guests have access to the facilities at the better-equipped Hotel Tivoli (see above), including several restaurants, a bar, a health club, and a pool.

✪ **Janelas Verdes Inn.** Rua das Janelas Verdes 47, 1200 Lisboa. ☎ **21/396-81-43.** Fax 21/396-81-44. www.heritage.pt. E-mail: jverdes@heritage.pt. 17 units. A/C TV TEL. 29,200$–35,900$ ($163.50–$201.05) double; 39,000$–45,300$ ($218.40–$253.70) triple. Rates include continental breakfast. AE, DC, MC, V. Bus: 27, 40, 49, or 60.

Owned by the proprietors of the Hotel Lisboa Plaza (see above), this aristocratic 18th-century mansion near the Museum of Ancient Art was the home of the late Portuguese novelist Eça de Queiroz. It was an annex to York House before becoming a historic hotel. The large, luxurious, marvelously restored rooms have abundant closet space, excellent beds, and generous tile bathrooms. The predominantly red lounge evokes turn-of-the-century Lisbon. Breakfast is served on a tray in your room, in the lounge, or on the rear terrace.

Lisboa Penta Hotel. Av. dos Combatentes, 1070 Lisboa. ☎ **21/723-54-00.** Fax 21/726-42-81. E-mail: pentahotel@mail.telepac.pt. 592 units. A/C MINIBAR TV TEL. 18,200$–26,000$ ($101.90–$145.60) double; 40,000$ ($224) suite. Rates include buffet breakfast. Parking 1,250$ ($7). Metro: Cidade Universitária.

A 10-minute ride north of the center and convenient to the airport, this member of the worldwide Penta chain occupies a panoramic site atop a hill overlooking the city. Many guests attend the conferences held in the public areas. Visitors traveling for pleasure can expect modern comfort, tile bathrooms with touches of Portuguese marble, and uncontroversial monochromatic styling. Most of the firm beds are twins. There's a standard restaurant and bar, plus Grill Passarola, a more expensive choice. The hotel has a pool, gym, squash courts, sauna, and massage facilities.

Mundial Hotel. Rua Dom Duarte 4, 1100 Lisboa. ☎ **21/884-20-00.** Fax 21/884-21-10. 250 units. A/C MINIBAR TV TEL. 19,600$ ($109.75) double; 29,000$ ($162.40) suite. Rates include buffet breakfast. AE, DC, MC, V. Metro: Rossio or Martimonis.

One block from the Rossio, the recently expanded Mundial is in the heart of everything. The hotel is high on the list of many European business travelers. The location is both good and bad—the colorful street out front is a bit sleazy, especially at night, but theaters and shops are nearby. The staff is efficient, and everything is properly manicured and polished. The rooms are comfortable, spacious, and restrained in decor. Units in the rear are much quieter than the front rooms, which can be noisy. The tiled bathrooms have bidets, shower/tub combinations, and plenty of mirrors and shelf space.

The top-floor Varanda de Lisboa restaurant overlooks St. George's Castle and the Alfama. It features French and Portuguese cuisine but is known for regional dishes. Service is professional, and the cookery is competent, if at times in need of a little more zest. A pianist entertains at dinner, and the hotel also has a bar. Laundry, concierge, baby-sitting, 24-hour room service, and car rental are available.

Príncipe Real. Rua de Alegria 53, 1200 Lisboa. ☎ **21/346-01-16.** Fax 21/342-21-04. E-mail: hbelver@mail.telepac.pt. 24 units. A/C MINIBAR TV TEL. 25,500$–29,000$ ($142.80–$162.40) double. Rates include buffet breakfast. AE, DC, MC, V. Metro: Avenida or Rotunda. Bus: 2.

This modern five-story hotel near the botanical gardens houses the overflow from the Four Seasons Hotel The Ritz Lisbon (see above). It's a long, steep climb from avenida da Liberdade. The carefully appointed guest rooms are small but tasteful. The beds, reproductions of fine antiques, have excellent mattresses. The hotel restaurant opens onto panoramic views of Lisbon and serves excellent Portuguese cuisine. There's also a cozy bar downstairs, with a cafe and snack bar. Laundry, 24-hour room service, and car-rental facilities are available.

✪ York House. Rua das Janelas Verdes 32, 1200 Lisboa. ☎ **21/396-24-35.** Fax 21/397-27-93. E-mail: yorkhouse@telepac.pt. 34 units. TV TEL. 30,000$–41,000$ ($168–$229.60) double. Rates include buffet breakfast. AE, DC, MC, V. Free parking on street. Bus: 27, 40, 49, 54, or 60.

York House mixes the drama of the past with modern convenience. Once a 16th-century convent, it lies outside the center of traffic-filled Lisbon, attracting those who desire peace and tranquility. It has long been known to the English and to diplomats, artists, writers, poets, and professors. Book well in advance. Near the National Art Gallery, it sits high on a hillside overlooking the Tagus and surrounded by a garden. A distinguished Lisbon designer selected the tasteful furnishings. Guest rooms vary in size; all have antique beds, soft mattresses, and 18th- and 19th-century bric-a-brac. The lack of air-conditioning can be a problem in summer. The public rooms boast inlaid chests, coats of armor, carved ecclesiastical figures, and ornate ceramics. The former monks' dining hall has deep-set windows, large niches for antiques, and—best of all—French-Portuguese cuisine. Guests gather in the two-level lounge for drinks before and after dinner. Street parking, though free, is rarely available.

INEXPENSIVE

Casa de São Mamede. Rua da Escola Politécnica 159, 1250 Lisboa. ☎ **21/396-31-66.** Fax 21/395-18-96. 28 units. TV TEL. 12,500$ ($70) double; 15,000$ ($84) triple. Rates include continental breakfast. No credit cards. Tram: 24. Bus: 22, 49, or 58.

Built in the 1800s as a private villa for the count of Coruche, this building behind the botanical gardens became a hotel in 1945. The Marquês family manages the hotel. Although renovated, the high-ceilinged rooms retain an aura of their original slightly dowdy, somewhat frayed charm. The hotel lies between avenida da Liberdade and the Amoreiras shopping center. Breakfast is served in a sunny second-floor dining room decorated with antique tiles.

Hotel Príncipe. Av. Duque d'Ávila 201, 1000 Lisboa. ☎ **21/356-15-94.** Fax 21/353-43-14. E-mail: confortprincipe@mail.telepac.pt. 67 units. A/C TV TEL. 13,000$ ($72.80) double. Children 5–7 half-price, children under 5 free, in parents' room. Rates include continental breakfast. AE, DC, MC, V. Metro: São Sebastião. Tram: 20. Bus: 41 or 46.

More than a quarter of a century old, this nondescript place is a favorite with visiting Spanish and Portuguese matadors. Most guest rooms are spacious, and most open onto their own balconies. The hotel recently finished adding air-conditioning to all of them. The matadors seem to like the Príncipe's dining room and bar. Don't confuse this hotel with the first-class Príncipe Real (see above). Laundry service is available; there's room service until midnight. The hotel's eight floors are accessible by two elevators.

Jorge V Hotel. Rua Mouzinho da Silveira 3, 1200 Lisboa. ☎ **21/356-25-25.** Fax 21/315-03-19. 49 units. A/C TV TEL. 14,000$ ($78.40) double; 18,000$ ($100.80) suite. Rates include continental breakfast. AE, DC, MC, V. Parking 1,500$ ($8.40). Metro: Avenida or Marquês de Pombal.

The Jorge V is a neat little hotel with a 1960s design. It boasts a choice location a block off the noisy avenida da Liberdade. Its facade contains rows of balconies, roomy enough for guests to have breakfast or afternoon "coolers." A tiny elevator runs to a variety of aging rooms, which aren't generous in size but are comfortable; all have small tile bathrooms. Room service is provided until midnight. The reception lounge shares space with a bar. Guests particularly enjoy the regional-style combination bar and breakfast room.

Miraparque. Av. Sidónio Pais 12, 1000 Lisboa. ☎ **21/352-42-86.** Fax 21/357-89-20. E-mail: miraparque@esoterica.pt. 108 units. A/C MINIBAR TV TEL. 14,500$ ($81.20) double. Rates include buffet breakfast. AE, DC, MC, V. Bus: 91. Metro: Parque.

Miraparque lies on a secluded, quiet street opposite Edward VII Park. The small guest rooms haven't been called modern since the 1960s, but they're well maintained. The hotel is a little worn but still recommendable because of its central location and low prices. The wood-paneled lounges are furnished in simulated brown leather. The tiny bar, with stools and lounge chairs, has a comfortable ambience. The paneled dining room has a wall-wide mural.

Pensão Residencial Gerês. Calçada do Garcia 6, 1150 Lisboa. ☎ **21/881-04-97.** Fax 21/888-20-06. 20 units, 16 with bathroom. TV TEL. 6,500$–8,000$ ($36.40–$44.80) double without bathroom, 10,000$ ($56) double with bathroom. Rates include continental breakfast. AE, DC, MC, V. Metro: Rossio.

Just a 2-block walk west of praça do Rossio and convenient to the railway station, this simple pension occupies two floors of a four-story building erected as an apartment house in the 1860s. The small rooms are high-ceilinged and completely unpretentious. Pensão Residencial Gerês has recently enjoyed a flood of North American business, thanks to publicity in the American media.

Presidente Hotel. Rua Alexandre Herculano 13, 1150 Lisboa. ☎ **21/353-95-01.** Fax 21/352-02-72. 59 units. A/C MINIBAR TV TEL. 13,000$–17,100$ ($72.80–$95.75) double. Rates include buffet breakfast. AE, DC, MC, V. Metro: Marquês de Pombal. Bus: 1, 36, 44, or 45.

This small-scale establishment lies near avenida da Liberdade on a busy corner. It doesn't deserve a spectacular rating, but it's a decent place to spend the night. Built in the late 1960s, it was renovated in 1992. It's recommended for families because the management will add an extra bed to any room for 3,000$ ($16.80), and baby-sitting can be arranged. On the premises are a laundry and medical service. The guest rooms are small and nicely laid out, each with a built-in chestnut headboard, bed lights, double-view windows, a small entry with two closets, a bathroom tiled in bright colors, and even a valet stand. The modest-size reception lounges are on three levels, connected by wide marble steps. There's room service until midnight. Breakfast, lunch, and dinner are served in the wood-paneled mezzanine lounge, featuring light fare—burgers, omelettes, and sandwiches.

Residência Alicante. Av. Duque de Loulé 20, 1000 Lisboa. ☎ **21/353-05-14.** Fax 21/352-02-50. 36 units. TV TEL. 8,900$ ($49.85) double. Rates include buffet breakfast. AE, DC, MC, V. Metro: Picoas or Marquês de Pombal. Bus: 1, 2, 9, 32, 36, or 45.

This hotel's burnt-orange postwar facade curves around a quiet residential corner in an undistinguished neighborhood. The Alicante is welcoming and safe. You register on the street level, with kindly staff members who speak little or no English; a small elevator runs to the four upper floors. Furnishings and room size vary, but most budget-minded visitors find the Alicante an acceptable place to stay. The quieter rooms overlook an interior courtyard. Fourteen units are air-conditioned.

Residência Imperador. Av. do 5 de Outubro 55, 1050 Lisboa. ☎ **21/352-48-84.** Fax 21/352-65-37. 43 units. A/C TV TEL. 8,000$ ($44.80) double. Rates include continental breakfast. AE, DC, MC, V. Metro: Saldanha. Bus: 44, 45, or 90.

The Portuguese-pinewood entrance of the Residência Imperador is small, even claustrophobic. However, the rooms and the upper lounge are adequate in size. The units are neatly planned, with comfortable beds and simple lines. The decor, however, is dowdy. On the top floor are a public room and terrace with a glass front, where breakfast is served. The hotel is not far from the center.

Residência Nazareth. Av. António Augusto de Aguiar 25, 1000 Lisboa. ☎ **21/354-20-16.** Fax 21/356-08-36. 32 units. A/C MINIBAR TV TEL. 8,000$ ($44.80) double. Rates include continental breakfast. AE, DC, MC, V. Metro: São Sebastião or Parque. Bus: 31, 41, or 46.

You'll recognize this establishment by its dusty-pink facade and its windows, some of which are beneath decorative arches raised in low relief. An elevator runs to the fourth-floor landing, where, far from the beauticians, hair stylists, and offices below, there's a medieval vaulting. The distressed plaster and wrought-iron lanterns are obvious facsimiles. Even the spacious bar and TV lounge looks like a vaulted cellar. Some of the basic guest rooms contain platforms, requiring guests to step up or down to the bathroom or to the comfortable bed. A little refurbishing is in order here.

IN THE BAIRRO ALTO

Pensão Londres. Rua Dom Pedro V 53, 1200 Lisboa. ☎ **21/346-22-03.** Fax 21/346-56-82. 39 units, 15 with bathroom (some with tub, some with shower), 8 with shower and sink only. TEL. 7,000$ ($39.20) double with sink only, 9,000$ ($50.40) double with sink and shower only, 11,000$ ($61.60) double with bathroom. Rates include continental breakfast. DC, MC, V. Tram: 20 or 24. Bus: 58 or 100.

Originally a dignified mansion, with high ceilings and ornate moldings, this establishment now functions as a slightly battered, unpretentious hotel. Take the elevator to the second-floor reception area, where the helpful staff will assist you. The small guest rooms contain simple furniture; some (especially on the third and fourth floors) have views of the city. The pension is accessible by taking the funicular by the Palácio da Foz in praça dos Restauradores. Many inexpensive restaurants and bars, including fado clubs, lie just down the hill in the winding streets of the Bairro Alto. The hotel is near the belvedere São Pedro de Alcântara.

IN THE GRAÇA DISTRICT

Hotel Albergaria da Senhora do Monte. Calçada do Monte 39, 1100 Lisboa. ☎ **21/886-60-02.** Fax 21/887-77-83. 32 units. A/C TV TEL. 17,500$ ($98) double; 27,500$ ($154) suite. Rates include continental breakfast. AE, DC, MC, V. Metro: Socorro. Tram: 28. Bus: 12, 17, or 35.

This unique little hilltop hotel is perched near a belvedere, the Miradouro Senhora do Monte. There's a memorable nighttime view of the city, the Castle of St. George, and the Tagus. Built as an apartment house, the hotel has been converted into a clublike establishment. The intimate living room features large tufted sofas and oversize tables and lamps. Multilevel corridors lead to the excellent guest rooms, all of which have verandas. The rooms reveal a decorator's touch, especially the gilt-edged door panels, the grass-cloth walls, and the tile bathrooms with bronze fixtures. Room service and laundry and valet service are available. Breakfast is the only meal served. The location is far from the center, and there's no restaurant.

IN THE CAMPO GRANDE DISTRICT

Radisson SAS Lisboa. Av. Marechal Craveiro Lopes, 1700 Lisboa. ☎ **800/333-3333** in the U.S., or 21/759-96-39. Fax 21/758-69-49. 236 units. A/C MINIBAR TV TEL. 36,000$ ($201.60) double; from 45,000$ ($252) suite. Rates include breakfast. AE, DC, MC, V. Parking: 1,200$ ($6.70). Metro: Campo Grande.

One of the city's most visible hotels—formerly the Holiday Inn Crowne Plaza—was built in the early 1990s. The Radisson/SAS group took it over in 1996, and it appeals mostly to business travelers. Sheathed in pink stone, it rises 12 floors above the Campo Grande residential district, 2 miles north of the Rossio. The stylish but conservative lobby contains hundreds of slabs of gray-and-white marble. The midsized guest rooms have excellent beds, hair dryers, and big windows. They're decorated in bland international style, with comfortable, durable furnishings.

Dining: The restaurant, Bordal Pinheiro, serves international cuisine, including luncheon buffets.

Amenities: Health club, 24-hour room service, laundry and valet, concierge.

4 Where to Dine

The explosion of restaurants in Lisbon in the late 1990s indicates that the Portuguese regard dining just as seriously as Spaniards. High prices have not suppressed their appetites, and residents of the capital are dining out more frequently than in the past.

You no longer have to go to one of the classic restaurants, such as Gambrinus or António Clara, for good food. Even at modest places, the fare is top-rate. Plenty of restaurants serve the usual fish and shellfish, and many erstwhile Portuguese colonials from Brazil, and even Mozambique and Goa, have opened restaurants in the capital. The menus in the top establishments remain on a par with those of Europe's leading restaurants. In Lisbon, you'll encounter the best of Portuguese cooking mixed with continental classics.

You needn't pay exorbitant prices for top-quality food. Restaurants featuring Portuguese and foreign fare—from beer-and-steak taverns to formal town house dining rooms to cliff-side restaurants with panoramic views—suit all budgets. You may also want to consider an evening meal at a fado cafe (see chapter 4). Lisboans tend to eat much later than most American, Canadian, and British visitors, though not as late as their Spanish neighbors. Some restaurants (including Gambrinus, Bachus, and Cervejaria Trindade) stay open very late.

Lisbon also has many "green lungs" (public parks) where you can go with picnic fixings. Of these, the finest is **Parque Eduardo VII,** at the top of avenida da Liberdade, which has picnic tables. A good place to stock up is **Celeiro,** rua do 1 de Dezembro 65 (☎ 21/342-74-95). To accompany your sandwiches, you'll find a wide selection of cheeses and wines, along with fresh fruits and breads. You can also order a roast chicken for 1,100$ ($6.15) per kilo (2.2 lb.). It's open Monday to Friday 8:30am to 8pm, Saturday 9am to 7pm. Metro: Rossio.

IN THE CENTER
VERY EXPENSIVE

✪ **Gambrinus.** Rua das Portas de Santo Antão 25. ☎ **21/342-14-66.** Reservations required. Main courses 6,000$–13,000$ ($33.60–$72.80). AE, MC, V. Daily noon–1:30am. Metro: Rossio. SEAFOOD.

One of the city's premier restaurants, Gambrinus is the top choice for fish and shellfish. It's in the congested heart of the city, off the Rossio near the rail station on a little square behind the National Theater. You can enjoy an apéritif at the bar in front while downing seafood delicacies. The dining room is resolutely macho, with leather chairs under a beamed cathedral ceiling, but you can also select a little table beside a fireplace on the raised end of the room.

Gambrinus offers a diverse à la carte menu and specialties of the day. The shades and nuances of the cuisine definitely appeal to the cultivated palate, focused as they are on exciting flavor harmonies. The soups are good, especially the shellfish bisque. The most expensive items, logically, are shrimp and lobster dishes. However, you might try conch with shellfish thermidor, or sea bass *minhota*. If you don't fancy fish but do like your dishes *hot*, ask for chicken piri-piri. Desserts are elaborate. Coffee with a 30-year-old brandy is the perfect end to a sumptuous meal here.

EXPENSIVE

✪ **António Clara.** Av. da República 38. ☎ **21/799-42-80.** Reservations required. Main courses 2,500$–3,500$ ($14–$19.60). AE, DC, MC, V. Mon–Sat noon–3pm and 7–10:30pm. Metro: Saldainha. PORTUGUESE/INTERNATIONAL.

Even if it weren't one of the capital's best restaurants, this exquisite turn-of-the-century art nouveau villa would be famous as the former home of one of Portugal's most revered architects. Miguel Ventura Terra (1866–1918), whose photograph hangs amid polished antiques and gilded mirrors, built it in 1890. The soaring height of the curved staircase and elegant moldings are attractive backdrops for 17th-century wood carvings and belle epoque porcelain. You might enjoy a before-dinner drink in the

19th-century salon, where griffins snarl from the pink-shaded chandelier. Even the service areas of this house, rarely seen by visitors, display ceiling frescoes. The dining room is one of the loveliest in Lisbon.

The updated classic cooking is guaranteed to please. Most of the flavors are sublime. Meals include such specialties as smoked swordfish, paella for two, chateaubriand béarnaise, monkfish rice, codfish Margarida da Praça, and beef Wellington. The dishes may be familiar, but only the highest-quality ingredients are used. Seafood dishes change often, to reflect the best of market offerings. A well-coordinated group of wine stewards, headwaiters, and attendants make wine tasting a veritable ceremony. The ground-floor bar, accessible through its own entrance, is perfect for an after-dinner drink. The bar contains an art gallery with frequent shows.

✪ **Casa da Comida.** Travessa de Amoreiras 1 (off rua Alexandre Herculano). ☎ **21/388-53-76.** Reservations required. Main courses 3,200$–5,000$ ($17.90–$28). AE, DC, MC, V. Mon–Fri 1–3pm; Mon–Sat 8pm–midnight. Metro: Rato. PORTUGUESE/FRENCH.

Local gourmets tout Casa da Comida as offering some of the finest food in Lisbon. If you're in the city on a wintry day, a roaring fire greets you. At any time of year, you'll find the food good and the atmosphere pleasant. The dining room is handsomely decorated, the bar is done in period style, and there's a charming walled garden. Specialties include lobster with vegetables, roast kid with herbs, a medley of shellfish Casa da Comida, and *faisoa à convento de Alcântara* (stewed pheasant marinated in port wine for a day). The cellar contains an excellent selection of wines. The food is often more imaginative here than at some of the other top-rated choices. The chef is extraordinarily attentive to the quality of his ingredients, and the menu never fails to deliver some delightful surprises.

Clara. Campo dos Mártires da Pátria 49. ☎ **21/885-30-53.** Reservations required. Main courses 2,900$–4,000$ ($16.25–$22.40). AE, DC, MC, V. Mon–Sat noon–3:30pm and 7pm–midnight. Closed Aug 1–15. Metro: Avenida. PORTUGUESE/INTERNATIONAL.

On a hillside, amid decaying villas and city squares, this green-tile house owned by Zelia Pimpista contains an elegant restaurant. You can enjoy a drink under the ornate ceiling of the bar, which at various times has functioned as an antique store, the living room of a private apartment, and the foyer of a palatial house. Soft piano music accompanies dinner. At night, an indoor seat—perhaps near the large marble fireplace—is especially appealing. During lunch, however, you might prefer a seat near the garden terrace's plants and fountain. Specialties include tournedos Clara, stuffed rabbit with red-wine sauce, four kinds of pasta, codfish Clara, fillet of sole with orange, pheasant with grapes, and Valencian paella. Again, as in too many of Lisbon's top-rated restaurants, these dishes aren't creative and innovative in any way, but they're often prepared flawlessly. As one of the staff told us, "When a dish has stood the test of time, why change it?" Perhaps you'll agree.

Embaixada. In the Da Lapa hotel, rua do Pau de Bandeira 4. ☎ **21/395-00-05.** Reservations recommended. Main courses 2,700$–6,000$ ($15.10–$33.60); fixed-price luncheon buffet 4,800$ ($26.90); tasting menu 8,700$ ($48.70). AE, DC, MC, V. Daily 12:30–3:30pm and 7:30–10:30pm. Tram: 25 or 28. Bus: 13 or 27. INTERNATIONAL/PORTUGUESE.

This is the most upscale and most highly recommended restaurant in Lisbon's major five-star hotel (see above). The dignified, elegant dining room has a view of one of the most lavish gardens in this exclusive neighborhood. Embaixada is a favorite with diplomats from the many embassies and consulates nearby—no surprise, given its name. Especially popular is the fixed-price luncheon buffet, which offers an array of international food. À la carte items available at lunch and dinner vary with the season.

Lisbon Dining

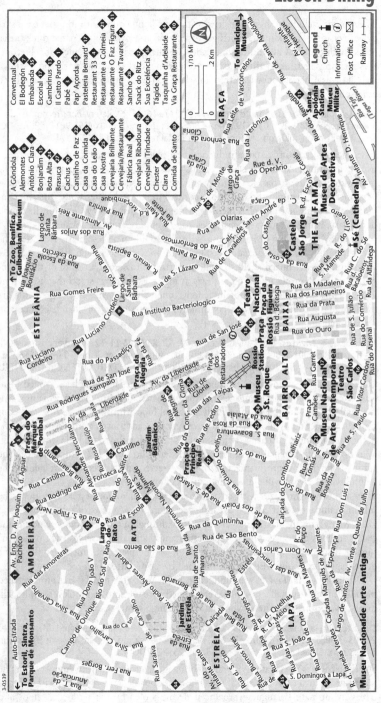

A Góndola **5**
Alemontes **7**
António Clara **14**
Bonjardim **40**
Bota Alta **20**
Brasuca **16**
Cachus **28**
Cantinho de Paz **22**
Casa da Comida **3**
Casa do Leão **35**
Casa Nostra **18**
Cervejaria Brilhante **49**
Cervejaria/Restaurante Fábrica Real **45**
Cervejaria Ribadouro **13**
Cervejaria Trindade **26**
Chester **2**
Clara **6**
Comida de Santo **10**

Conventual **25**
El Bodegón **7**
Embaixada **8**
Escorial **24**
Gambrinus **11**
Il Gatto Pardo **4**
Pabé **1**
Pap' Açorda **23**
Pasteleria Bernard' **12**
Restaurant 33 **17**
Restaurante a Colmeia **19**
Restaurante O Faz Figura **41**
Restaurante Tavares **15**
Sancho **21**
Snack do Ritz **9**
Sua Excelência **33**
Tágide **42**
Tasquinha d'Adelaide **35**
Via Graça Restaurante **40**

GRAÇA

To Municipal Museum

THE ALFAMA

BAIXA

BAIRRO ALTO

ESTEFÂNIA

AMOREIRAS

RATO

ESTRÊLA

LAPA

83

They might include fresh salmon fried with sage, lamb chops with mint sauce, a succulent version of a traditional Portuguese *feijoada,* and perfectly prepared duck breast baked with pears. While diners may not have the gourmet experience of a lifetime, they're amply rewarded with deluxe ingredients perfectly handled by the professional staff. This is a perfect spot to retreat to when you want an elegant meal in a refined atmosphere.

Escorial. Rua das Portas de Santo Antão 47. ☎ **21/346-44-29.** Reservations recommended. Main courses 3,500$–8,000$ ($19.60–$44.80); tasting menu 9,800$ ($54.90) for 2. AE, DC, MC, V. Daily noon–midnight. Metro: Rossio or Restauradores. INTERNATIONAL.

In the heart of Lisbon's restaurant district, near praça dos Restauradores, this Spanish-owned restaurant combines classic Spanish dishes with an inviting ambience. The dining-room walls are paneled in rosewood, with frosted-globe lighting. You can have a before-dinner drink in the Art Room cocktail lounge, which exhibits work by contemporary Portuguese artists. A menu is printed in English (always look for the course of the day). you're the most expensive selection would be from the lobster tank, or you might enjoy a sampling of Portuguese oysters or squid on a skewer. A selection of the chef's carefully crafted specialties is likely to include barbecued baby goat, beef Stroganoff, paella, mixed shellfish grill, or partridge casserole. In spite of the neighborhood, which grows increasingly sleazy at night, Escorial has stood the test of time and remains an enduring if not incredibly innovative favorite. The ingredients are fresh, and the food and service continue to be remarkable for their elegance and professionalism.

Restaurante Tavares. Rua da Misericórdia 37. ☎ **21/342-11-12.** Reservations required. Main courses 6,000$–8,000$ ($33.60–$44.80); fixed-price lunch or dinner 10,000$ ($56). AE, DC, MC, V. Mon–Fri 12:30–3pm; Sun–Fri 8–10:30pm. Bus: 15. PORTUGUESE/CONTINENTAL.

Once known for serving the best food in Lisbon, Tavares has long been rivaled by at least five other major competitors. Still, the oldest restaurant in Lisbon remains a sentimental favorite. It serves competently prepared food with flawless service, and continues to attract many diplomats and government heads as well as the literati. It's one of the capital's more glittering settings, but it's beginning to show a little wear and tear. White- and gold-paneled walls, three chandeliers, and Louis XV armchairs keep the spirit of the 18th century intact. Drinks are served in the petite front salon. The helpful wine steward will aid you in your selection.

Your meal might begin with crepes *de marisco.* A main-course selection might be sole in champagne, stuffed crab Tavares style, clams *Bulhão Pato,* or tournedos Grand Duc. Many continental dishes are scattered throughout the menu, including the classic scallops of veal viennoise. The restaurant nearly always serves such basic Portuguese dishes as sardines and salted codfish. To complete your meal, try the chef's dessert specialty, a high-rise soufflé, followed by a café filtro.

Originally a cafe, Tavares was founded in 1784. When the two Tavares brothers died in the 19th century, half a dozen waiters formed a partnership and took it over; it's still owned by a group of waiters, who maintain its high standards.

Sua Excelência. Rua do Conde 34. ☎ **21/390-36-14.** Reservations required. Main courses 2,500$–3,000$ ($14–$16.80). AE, MC, V. Mon–Tues and Thurs–Fri 1–3pm; Thurs–Sun 8–10:30pm. Closed Sept. Bus: 27 or 49. Tram: 25. PORTUGUESE.

Sua Excelência is the creation of Francisco Queiroz, a travel agent in Angola before he settled in Portugal. His restaurant feels like a fashionable drawing room, with colorful tables in intimate Portuguese provincial decor, cooled by the terra-cotta floor and high, painted ceiling. Some dishes served are uncommon in Portugal, such as Angolan chicken Moamba. Sure-to-please specialties include prawns piri-piri (not unreasonably

---

ⓘ Family-Friendly Restaurants

The Big Apple *(see page 89)*   Your kids will feel right at home at this tongue-in-cheek version of an American eatery. They can select one of 18 kinds of burgers (each a meal in itself) and finish their meal with a dessert crepe.

Bonjardim *(see page 89)*   Nearly all kids love chicken, and the best roasted ones are found at this inexpensive place in the center of Lisbon, near praça dos Restauradores. Ask for *frango no espeto,* chicken roasted golden brown on the spit and served with french fries.

Snack do Ritz *(see page 91)*   Located in Lisbon's most prestigious hotel, this moderately priced restaurant is a good place to introduce your kids to regional Portuguese cuisine. They can always find familiar fare on the English menu, too.

---

hot), *lulas à moda da casa* (squid stewed in white wine, crème fraîche, and cognac), rollmop sardines, the self-proclaimed "best smoked swordfish in Portugal," and clams prepared five different ways. One unusual specialty is "little jacks," a small fish eaten whole, served with a well-flavored paste made from 2-day-old bread. The restaurant is just a block up the hill from the entrance to the National Art Gallery; it could be part of a museum-luncheon adventure, though its ambience is more charming in the evening. Over the years it has remained popular with our readers. We were the first guidebook to discover it, although today it seems to be on everybody's list.

MODERATE

A Gôndola. Av. de Berna 64. ☎ **21/797-04-26.** Reservations required. Main courses 3,500$–4,000$ ($19.60–$22.40). AE, DC, MC, V. Mon–Fri 12:30–3pm and 7:30–10pm. Metro: Praça de Espanha. Bus: 16, 26, 31, or 46. ITALIAN/PORTUGUESE.

A Gôndola—Lisbon's "Little Italy"—serves some of the finest Italian specialties in town. The restaurant offers seating indoors and in the courtyard. Although the decor isn't particularly inspired, the good food makes the restaurant worth the trip out of the city center. The price makes a full dinner quite a buy, considering what you get. A first-course selection might be Chaves ham with melon and figs, followed by fillet of sole meunière or grilled sardines with pimientos. Yet another course—ravioli or cannelloni Roman style or veal cutlet Milanese—follows. The banquet might conclude with fruit or dessert. The Italian dishes don't compare with the best in Italy, but they're competent and professionally served, and this is a safe choice if you're yearning for Italian food. The restaurant is convenient to the Gulbenkian Museum.

Alemontes. Traversa da Santa Marta 4A. ☎ **21/315-77-93.** Reservations recommended. Main courses 2,500$–4,000$ ($14–$22.40). AE, MC, V. Daily 12:30–5pm and 7:30pm–midnight. Metro: Marquês de Pombal. PORTUGUESE.

Owners of inexpensive hotels in Lisbon often send their guests to this little bistro, as if it were a special secret. They're justified—the place offers excellent food with good, well-chosen ingredients, all at a fair price. "We don't get movie stars around here," said one of the waiters, "just people wanting a honest and decent meal." Fadistas entertain nightly, and the place has a cozy atmosphere, with simple decor of hand-crafted rugs and decorative dishes. Many menu items are based on recipes from the Portuguese provinces of Trás-os-Montes. Try such delights as tender loin of veal grilled perfectly and served with fresh potatoes and vegetables. Another excellent dish is grilled pork. The excellently prepared regional dishes include hare with white beans and roasted suckling pig on the spit.

Bachus. Largo da Trindade 9. ☎ **21/342-28-28.** Reservations recommended. Main courses 1,600$–3,500$ ($8.95–$19.60). AE, DC, MC, V. Mon–Fri noon–3pm, Sat 7pm–midnight. Metro: Chiado. Bus: 58. INTERNATIONAL.

Amusing murals cover the wood-paneled facade of this deluxe restaurant; inside, the decor is elaborate and sophisticated. The ambience is a mixture of a private salon in a Russian palace, a turn-of-the-century English club, and a stylized Manhattan bistro. A brass staircase winds around a column of illuminated glass to the dining room. Menu specialties change frequently, depending on what ingredients are available. Full meals might include mixed grill Bachus, chateaubriand with béarnaise, mountain goat, beef Stroganoff, shrimp Bachus, or other daily specials. The chef has a conservative approach, and perhaps because of this, he reportedly rarely gets complaints. The wine list is extensive.

Chester. Rua Rodrigo de Fonseca 87D. ☎ **21/388-78-11.** Reservations recommended. Regular main courses 2,000$–3,200$ ($11.20–$17.90); seafood main courses 5,800$–12,000$ ($32.50–$67.20). AE, DC, MC, V. Mon–Fri 12:30–3pm; Mon–Sat 7:30–10:30pm. Metro: Rotunda. STEAKS/CONTINENTAL.

Chester, near the Four Seasons Hotel The Ritz Lisbon, is an attractive restaurant and bar, with a good cellar and efficient service. Its specialties are grilled steaks and continental dishes. A range of tasty dishes might include *camarão tigre à Chester* (giant prawns Chester style), *lombo Bárbaro* (steak Barbarian style), *lagosta à Cardinal* (lobster Cardinal style), *salmão grelhado com molho béarnaise* (grilled salmon with béarnaise), *Cataplana rica de peixes* (stewed fish Cataplana style), *costeletas de cordeiro com molho polã* (lamb chops with mint sauce), or *costeletas de javali* (sautéed wild boar chops). In the words of one habitué, "Always reliable, always dependable, and nothing to get you too excited about—but isn't that what you want sometimes?" The restaurant is upstairs; the cozy bar lies below.

✪ Conventual. Praça das Flores 45. ☎ **21/390-91-96.** Reservations required. Main courses 2,300$–3,500$ ($12.90–$19.60). AE, DC, MC, V. Mon–Fri 12:30–3:30pm and 7:30–11:30pm, Sat 7:30–11:30pm. Metro: Avenida. Bus: 100. PORTUGUESE.

Many admirers (who include the prime minister of Portugal) rank Conventual as the single finest place to dine out in Lisbon today—even though its prices are about a quarter less than those at many of its towering competitors. Conventual is on one of the loveliest residential squares in town, behind a plain wooden door. Inside, you'll see a display of old panels from baroque churches, religious statues, and bric-a-brac. The owner invented many of the delectably flavored recipes: creamy coriander soup, stewed partridge in port, duck in rich champagne sauce, grilled monkfish in herb-flavored cream sauce, osso buco, frogs' legs in buttery garlic, and—one of our favorites—stewed clams in a sauce of red peppers, onions, and cream.

El Bodegón. In the Hotel Fénix, praça do Marquês de Pombal 8. ☎ **21/386-31-55.** Reservations required. Main courses 1,800$–3,600$ ($10.10–$20.15). AE, DC, MC, V. Daily 12:30–3pm and 7:30–10:30pm. Metro: Rotunda. PORTUGUESE/SPANISH/INTERNATIONAL.

El Bodegón is a first-class restaurant in a recommended hotel. After stopping for an apéritif in the bar, you'll dine in a tavern setting, with a beamed ceiling, tile floors, and wood-paneled pillars. You might enjoy delectable quail, partridge, or fresh salmon from the north of Portugal, depending on what's available. You can also order cultivated oysters, which are at their best after October. The specials menu features a different Portuguese dish daily. Among the à la carte selections are perfectly prepared fried squid, Valencian paella, and some Italian dishes. For dessert, try the succulent fresh strawberries from Sintra, if they're featured. We've found the fare here reliable and professionally served over the years, but some of our readers find the Iberian dishes too heavy in a hot climate, or "too intimidating," according to one reader from California.

Frei Papinhas. Rua Dom Francisco Manuel de Melo 32A (just off rua Castilho, near Edward VII Park). ☎ **21/385-87-57.** Reservations required. Regular main courses 2,600$–6,500$ ($14.55–$36.40); seafood main courses 5,200$–12,000$ ($29.10–$67.20). AE, DC, MC, V. Daily 12:30–3pm and 7pm–midnight. Metro: São Sebastião. INTERNATIONAL.

Frei Papinhas is an easy walk from the Four Seasons Hotel The Ritz and Le Méridien (see "Where to Stay," earlier in this chapter). A group of writers and intellectuals created it because they wanted a place where they could meet for good food and enjoy vigorous conversation at their leisure. The attractive, cozy eating place offers excellent service. The interior is done in sophisticated country style, relying on such natural elements as a wall of exposed stone, old brick behind the front bar, heavy black beams, and whitewashed walls. In air-conditioned comfort, you can enjoy an array of international cookery, including fresh fish and game dishes. The fare is creative, refined, and balanced. You might begin with one of the chef's cold soups, such as vichyssoise or gazpacho, followed by fillet of swordfish or pork Alentejo. The best Portuguese wines are available.

Il Gatto Pardo. In the Hotel Dom Pedro, av. Engenheiro, Duarte Pacheco. ☎ **21/389-66-00.** Reservations recommended. Main courses 2,200$–3,200$ ($12.30–$17.90); set-price menus 6,000$–8,000$ ($33.60–$44.80). AE, DC, MC, V. Daily 12:30–3:30pm and 8–11pm. Metro: Marquês de Pombal. ITALIAN.

The most appealing and stylish Italian restaurant in Lisbon is distinctly different from the pasta and pizza joints that have filled that niche until now. On the third floor of the hotel (see "Where to Stay," above), it has a soothing color scheme of beiges, browns, exposed hardwoods, and leopard skin. Virtually everything was imported from Italy, including many staff members, who prepare ultrafresh seafood and pastas, among other dishes. We're mad for pappardelle seasoned with cubed zucchini and saffron, and pasta with succulent clams. Risotto with cuttlefish is another winner, as are sea wolf coated with bread crumbs and sautéed, delectable grilled swordfish steak in parsley sauce, and roasted veal cooked in heady Barolo wine. The chef is adept at preparing tender duck breast flavored with honey and vinegar sauce. An outdoor terrace ringed with potted shrubs and vines provides sweeping views over the surrounding district.

O Funil. Av. Elias Garcia 82A. ☎ **21/796-60-07.** Reservations recommended. Main courses 1,450$–2,950$ ($8.10–$16.50). MC, V. Tues–Sun noon–3:30pm; Tues–Sat 7–10:30pm. Metro: Campo Pequeno. Bus: 1, 32, 36, 38, 44, or 45. PORTUGUESE.

O Funil (The Funnel) does *cozinha Portuguesa* (Portuguese cuisine) so well and so inexpensively that a line forms at the door; it's often hard to get a table. The owners serve their own *vinho da casa* (house wine)—try the red Alijo. The kitchen buys good-quality meats and fish fresh daily. The menu offers an array of excellent choices, including fillet of fresh fish with rice, strips of cooked codfish flavored with herbs, roast goat with vegetables and roast potatoes, tiger shrimp in a picante sauce, and clams in wine sauce.

Pabe. Rua Duque de Palmela 27A. ☎ **21/353-74-84.** Reservations required. Main courses 2,300$–4,000$ ($12.90–$22.40). AE, DC, MC, V. Daily noon–1am. Metro: Rotunda. PORTUGUESE/INTERNATIONAL.

Convenient to praça do Marquês de Pombal, this cozy pub (*pabé* is Portuguese for pub) has done its best to emulate English establishments. There's soft carpeting, mugs hanging over the long bar, a beamed ceiling, coats of arms, and engravings of hunting scenes around the walls. Two saloon-type doors lead into a wood-paneled dining room, where you can dine on meat specially imported—not from England, but the United States. Chateaubriand for two is among the fanciest dishes. If you prefer local fare, start with shrimp cocktail, then try Portuguese veal liver or *supremo de galinha* (chicken breast with mushrooms). Finish with sorbet. The crowd tends to be a well-groomed Portuguese set, as well as resident Americans and Brits. The fare, although decent, seems to have no clear sense of direction. Service can be spasmodic, and the staff speaks broken English at best.

✪ **Restaurant 33.** Rua Alexandre Herculano 33A. ☎ **21/354-60-79.** Reservations recommended. Main courses 2,500$–3,600$ ($14–$20.15). AE, DC, MC, V. Mon–Fri noon–3:30pm; Mon–Sat 8–10:30pm. Metro: Rotunda. Bus: 6 or 9. PORTUGUESE/INTERNATIONAL.

Restaurant 33 is a treasure. Decorated in a style evocative of an English hunting lodge, it lies near many recommended hotels, including the Four Seasons Hotel The Ritz Lisbon. It specializes in succulent seafood dishes, including shellfish rice served in a crab shell, smoked salmon, and lobster Tour d'Argent; it also features tender, well-flavored pepper steak. One reader from New Rochelle, New York, found her meal here "flawless." Large portions, tasty stews, and strong-flavored ingredients characterize this place. A pianist performs during dinner. You can enjoy a glass of port in the small bar at the entrance.

Telheiro. Rua Latino Coelho 10A. ☎ **21/353-40-07.** Reservations recommended. Main courses 1,000$–3,000$ ($5.60–$16.80). AE, DC, MC, V. Daily noon–3pm and 7–10:30pm. Metro: Picoas. Bus: 30. PORTUGUESE.

Telheiro (Portuguese for "the roof") is a bistrolike place not far from the Sheraton Hotel. Under beamed ceilings, you sit on wooden chairs with heart shapes carved out of their backs. Many staff members are from the former Portuguese colony of Angola. Different robust, hearty specialties are featured every day, including gazpacho, cabbage-and-potato soup, mussels, suckling pig, grilled fresh sea bass or sole, and seafood with rice in a casserole. For dessert, try fresh Portuguese fruit. Note that the kitchen makes little concession to "lily-livered" foreign tastes.

Tía Matilde. Rua da Beneficência 77. ☎ **21/797-21-72.** Main courses 1,000$–3,400$ ($5.60–$19.05). AE, DC, MC, V. Mon–Sat noon–4pm; Mon–Fri 7–10:30pm. Closed Aug 9–23. Metro: Praça d'Espanha or Palhavã. Bus: 31. PORTUGUESE.

Tía Matilde is a large, busy place in the praça de Espanha area. The atmosphere is often hectic, but the Portuguese love this restaurant—foreign visitors are rare. You can sample the savory specialties of Ribatejo, including *cabrito assado* (roast mountain goat), *arroz de frango* (chicken with rice), *bacalhau* (codfish) à Tía Matilde, and pungent *caldeirada* (fish stew). As one Portuguese father here told his son, "Food like this will make a man out of you." Let it do the same to you.

INEXPENSIVE

António Oliveira. Rua Tomás Ribeiro 63. ☎ **21/353-87-80.** Main courses 790$–1,500$ ($4.40–$8.40). MC, V. Mon–Sat 7:30am–10:30pm. Metro: Picoas. Bus: 44, 55, 94, 101. PORTUGUESE/INTERNATIONAL.

This place was created especially for Portuguese businesspeople who want relaxing ambience and good food. A bit removed from the din of central traffic, it's a refreshing oasis of blue-and-white glazed earthenware tiles, a free-form blue ceiling, and white tablecloths topped with blue linen. The menu is printed in English. You can start with excellent shellfish soup. Fish dishes garnished with vegetables include fillets with tomato sauce, and baked sole. *Polvo à lagareira* (octopus with broiled potatoes, olive oil, and garlic) is a justifiably popular specialty. If you prefer fowl or meat, try *frango na prata* (chicken broiled in foil with potatoes) or pork with clams Alentejana style. The owner-manager recommends *açorda de marisco,* and the stewlike breaded shell-fish-and-egg dish is a treat. The dessert list is extensive, even listing a banana split. The chefs still cook exactly as their mothers and fathers did—perhaps as their grandparents did—and that seems to please the mainly local clientele.

The Big Apple. Av. Elias Garcia 19B. ☎ **21/797-55-75.** Burgers 850$–1,200$ ($4.75–$6.70); steaks 1,200$–2,200$ ($6.70–$12.30). AE, DC, MC, V. Daily noon–3pm and 7–11pm. Metro: Campo Pequeno. AMERICAN.

Dozens of tongue-in-cheek accessories adorn the walls and menu of this American-style eatery on a tree-lined boulevard in a residential neighborhood. You'll find a true Texan's map of the United States (Amarillo appears just south of the Canadian border) and a red-white-and-blue checkerboard awning out front. It's simple and pleasant. Many of the 18 variations of hamburgers constitute a meal in themselves. You can also select from five kinds of dinner crepes and five varieties of temptingly sweet dessert crepes.

Bonjardim. Travessa de Santo Antão 10. ☎ **21/342-74-24.** Main courses 1,100$–2,900$ ($6.15–$16.25). AE, DC, MC, V. Daily noon–11pm. Metro: Restauradores. PORTUGUESE.

Bonjardim rightly deserves this enthusiastic endorsement of a traveler from Boston: "I was given the names of eight inexpensive restaurants to try in Lisbon during my 5-day stay. I ended up trying only two, as I took the rest of my meals at Bonjardim, sampling a different dish for lunch and dinner every day." The restaurant caters mostly to families, providing wholesome meals that fit most budgets. The operation has been so successful that it has taken over a building across the street, where the same menu is offered. The restaurant, one of the most popular in Lisbon, is just east of avenida da Liberdade near the grimy praça dos Restauradores.

In the main restaurant, the air-conditioned, sun-flooded second-floor dining room is designed in rustic Portuguese style, with a beamed ceiling and a tile mural depicting farm creatures. The street-floor dining room, with an adjoining bar for before-meal drinks, has walls of decorative tiles. During dinner, the aroma of plump chickens roasting on the charcoal spit is likely to prompt you to try one. An order of this house specialty, *frango no espeto,* is adequate for two, with a side dish of french fries. The cook also bakes hake in the Portuguese style; or try pork fried with clams. For dessert, you can order a cassate. If you want to be daring, order chicken with piri-piri, a fiery chile sauce from the former Portuguese colonies in Africa.

Bonjardim also has a self-service cafeteria nearby, at travessa de Santo Antão II (☎ **21/342-43-89**). It serves Portuguese dishes, including seafood soup; half a roast chicken with trimmings; garoupa fish à Bretone, the chef's specialty; and velvety chocolate mousse. A meal begins at 1,800$ ($10.10), excluding beverages. The decor is simple, plastic, and efficient.

Cervejaria Brilhante. Rua das Portas de Santo Antão 105 (opposite the Coliseu). ☎ **21/346-14-07.** Main courses 1,600$–3,400$ ($8.95–$19.05); tourist menu 1,800$ ($10.10). AE, DC, MC, V. Daily noon–midnight. Metro: Rossio. Bus: 1, 2, 36, 44, or 45. SEAFOOD/PORTUGUESE.

Lisboans from every walk of life stop here for a stein of beer and *mariscos* (seafood). The tavern is decorated with stone arches, wood-paneled walls, and pictorial tiles of sea life. You can dine at the bar or a marble table. The front window is packed with an appetizing array of king crabs, oysters, lobsters, baby clams, shrimp, even barnacles. The price changes every day, depending on the market, and you pay by the kilo. This is hearty, robust eating, although attracting a waiter's attention is a challenge.

Cervejaria Ribadoura. Av. da Liberdade 155 (at rua do Salitre). ☎ **21/354-94-11.** Main courses 1,200$–3,600$ ($6.70–$20.15). AE, DC, MC, V. Daily 9am–1:30am. Metro: Avenida. Bus: 1, 2, 44, or 45. SEAFOOD.

Cervejaria Ribadoura is one of the typical shellfish-and-beer eateries in central Lisbon, located midway along the city's major boulevard. The decor in this tavern-style restaurant is simple—the emphasis is on the fish. Try the *bacalhau* (codfish) à Bras. You can dine lightly, particularly at lunch, on such plates as a shrimp omelette. Many diners follow their fish with a meat dish. However, only those raised on the most mouthwilting Indian curries should try the sautéed pork cutlets with piri-piri, made with red-hot peppers from Angola. A wedge of Portuguese cheese "from the hills" finishes the meal nicely. Although we've always found fish on our 25-odd visits here, some readers have reported that on occasion the fish market was bare, but that they found other items from the kitchen to satisfy them.

Cervejaria Trindade. Rua Nova de Trindade 20B. ☎ **21/342-35-06.** Main courses 1,500$–3,000$ ($8.40–$16.80). AE, DC, MC, V. Daily 9am–1:30am. Metro: Rossio. Bus: 15, 20, 51, or 100. PORTUGUESE.

Cervejaria Trindade is a combination German beer hall and Portuguese tavern. In operation since 1836, it's the oldest tavern in Lisbon, owned by the brewers of Sagres beer. It was built on the foundations of the 13th-century Convento dos Frades Tinos, which was destroyed by the 1755 earthquake. Surrounded by walls tiled with Portuguese scenes, you can order tasty little steaks and heaps of crisp french-fried potatoes. Many Portuguese diners prefer *bife na frigideira* (steak with mustard sauce and a fried egg, served in a clay frying pan). The tavern features shellfish, which comes from private ponds; the house specialties are *ameijoas* (clams) à Trindade and giant prawns. A small stein of beer goes nicely with the main courses. For dessert, try a slice of *queijo da serra* (cheese from the mountains) and coffee. Meals are served in the inner courtyard on sunny days.

Pastelaria Sala de Cha Versailles. Av. da República 15A. ☎ **21/354-63-40.** Sandwiches 265$ ($1.50); pastries 130$–160$ (75¢–90¢); plats du jour 1,150$–2,400$ ($6.45–$13.45). AE, MC, V. Daily 7:30am–10pm. Metro: Salvanhe. SANDWICHES/PASTRIES.

The most famous teahouse in Lisbon, this place has been declared part of the "national patrimony." Some patrons reputedly have been coming here since it opened in 1932. In older days the specialty was Licungo, the famed black tea of Mozambique; you can still order it, but nowadays many drinkers enjoy English brands. (The Portuguese claim that they, not the English, introduced the custom of tea-drinking to the English court, after Catherine of Bragança married Charles II in 1662.) The decor is rich, with chandeliers, gilt mirrors, stained-glass windows, tall stucco ceilings, and black-and-white marble floors. You can also order milkshakes, mineral water, and fresh orange juice, along with beer and liquor. The wide variety of snacks includes codfish balls and toasted ham-and-cheese sandwiches. Also available is a limited array of platters of simple but wholesome Portuguese fare.

Restaurante a Colmeia. Rua da Emenda 110. ☎ **21/347-05-00.** Main courses 600$–1,500$ ($3.35–$8.40). No credit cards. Mon–Fri noon–7pm. Metro: Baixa Chiado. Tram: 28. Bus: 58 or 100. MACROBIOTIC VEGETARIAN.

On the top floor of a corner building, this center of healthful eating and living offers vegetarian and macrobiotic cuisine. In addition, you'll find a miniature natural-foods shop. The food, although presumably healthful, is rather bland.

Sancho. Travessa da Glória 14 (just off av. da Liberdade, near praça dos Restauradores). ☎ **21/346-97-80.** Reservations recommended. Main courses 1,290$–2,100$

($7.20–$11.75). AE, DC, MC, V. Mon–Sat noon–3pm and 7–10:30pm. Metro: Avenida or Restauradores. PORTUGUESE/INTERNATIONAL.

Sancho is a cozy rustic-style restaurant with classic Iberian decor—beamed ceiling, fireplace, leather-and-wood chairs, and stucco walls. In summer there's air-conditioning. Fish gratinée soup is a classic way to begin. Shellfish, always expensive, is the specialty. Main dishes are likely to include the chef's special hake or pan-broiled Portuguese steak. If your palate is fireproof, order *churrasco de cabrito ao piri-piri* (goat with pepper sauce). For dessert, sample the crêpes Suzette or perhaps chocolate mousse. This is a longtime (since 1962) local favorite, and the recipes never change. As a waiter said, "As long as we can keep the dining room full every night, why change?"

Snack do Ritz. In the Four Seasons Hotel The Ritz Lisbon, rua Castilho 77C. ☎ **21/383-20-20.** Main courses 1,500$–2,800$ ($8.40–$15.70). AE, DC, MC, V. Mon–Sat noon–11:30pm. PORTUGUESE/INTERNATIONAL.

This is the least expensive dining choice at this legendary hotel—provided you avoid some of the shellfish main courses. It's on several levels, with its own entrance facing Edward VII Park. The polite staff wears formal uniforms. The menu (available in English) features a variety of excellent dishes, including platters of fresh grilled fish and meats, such as grilled fillet of salmon in a caper sauce and roast chicken with nuts and honey. Regional Portuguese dishes, which change daily, receive special emphasis. An assortment of tarts, cakes, ice cream "coupes," and cheeses completes your meal.

IN THE BAIRRO ALTO
EXPENSIVE

Tasquinha d'Adelaide. Rua do Patrocinio 70. ☎ **21/396-22-39.** Reservations recommended. Main courses 2,000$–4,000$ ($11.20–$22.40). AE, DC, MC, V. Mon–Sat 8:30pm–2am. Closed 15 days in Aug. Metro: Rato. Tram: 25, 28, or 30. REGIONAL PORTUGUESE.

At the western edge of the Bairro Alto, about 2 blocks northeast of the Alcântara subway station and 2 blocks west of the Basilica da Estrêla, this restaurant is cramped and convivial, with no more than 25 seats. It's known for the culinary specialties of Trás-os-Montes, a rugged province in northeast Portugal, and for its homey, unpretentious warmth. Robust specialties include *alheriras fritas com arroz de grelos* (tripe with collard greens and rice) and *lulas grelhadas* (grilled squid served in a black clay casserole). To finish, try Dona Adelaide's *charcade de ovos* (a secret recipe made with egg yolks). Although we like this hearty cooking of northeast Portugal, the flavors might be too pungent for some palates.

MODERATE

Comida de Santo. Calçado Engenheiro Miguel Pais 39. ☎ **21/396-33-39.** Reservations required. Regular main courses 1,650$–3,500$ ($9.25–$19.60); seafood main courses 1,900$–2,500$ ($10.65–$14). AE, DC, MC, V. Daily 12:30–4pm and 7:30pm–1am. Metro: Rato. Bus: 58. BRAZILIAN.

Comida de Santo, which opened in the early 1980s, was the first all-Brazilian restaurant in Lisbon. At the edge of the Barrio Alto, in a century-old former private house, it contains only 12 tables. Appreciative Lisboans usually keep it fully booked. Recorded Brazilian music plays softly from the bar, lending a New World flavor, and a quintet of oversized panels (*Amazônia*) depicts huge, idealized jungle scenes. The appropriate beginning of any meal is a deceptively potent caipirinha (aguardiente cocktail with limes and sugar) that might make you want to samba. Main courses include spicy versions of *feijoada* (meat-and-bean stew); *picanha* (boiled Brazilian beef with salt), *vatapá* (peppery shrimp), and several versions of succulent grilled fish. The place is incredibly popular; reservations are very important.

Pap' Açorda. Rua da Atalaia 57–59. ☎ **21/346-48-11.** Reservations recommended. Main courses 1,900$–4,400$ ($10.65–$24.65). AE, DC, MC, V. Tues–Sat noon–2:30pm and 7–10pm. Closed Aug. Metro: Baixa/Chiado. PORTUGUESE.

Pap' Açorda's facade was originally conceived for a bakery. Today, it welcomes one of Lisbon's most colorful collections of people (of all lifestyles and sexual persuasions) into its pink-and-white interior. Most visitors order a before-dinner drink at the long marble-topped bar, which dominates the front of the restaurant. No one will object if you never get around to actually dining; if you do, there are two dining rooms, one outfitted like a garden. Both are ornamented with Empire-style crystal chandeliers. The delectable cuisine includes Spanish-style mussels, shellfish rice, sirloin steak with mushrooms, and a wide array of fish and shellfish dishes. Be extremely careful in ordering shellfish here—it's priced by the kilogram (2.2 lb.), and costs as much as 15,000$ ($84) per kilo for prawns. The house specialty, *açorda,* is a traditional dish with coriander, bread, seafood, eggs, garlic, and olive oil.

INEXPENSIVE

Bota Alta. Travessa da Queimada 35–37. ☎ **21/342-79-59.** Reservations required. Main courses 1,300$–2,300$ ($7.30–$12.90). AE, DC, MC, V. Mon–Fri noon–2:30pm; Mon–Sat 7–10:30pm. Bus: 58 or 100. PORTUGUESE.

Bota Alta, at the top of a steep street in the Bairro Alto, boasts a faithful clientele that eagerly crams into its two dining rooms and sometimes stands at the bar waiting for a table. It contains rustic artifacts and lots of original art and photographs. Meals— some familiar to 19th-century diners—might include beefsteak Bota Alta; several preparations of codfish, including *bacalhau real* (fried codfish with port wine and cognac); and a frequently changing array of daily specials, including Hungarian goulash. We still aren't sure why bacalhau is so popular—the Portuguese claim to have as many fish off their coast as there are days on the calendar—but don't leave Portugal without sampling it at least once.

Brasuca. Rua João Pereira da Rosa 7 (off rua do Seculo). ☎ **21/322-07-40.** Reservations recommended. Main courses 1,550$–2,050$ ($8.70–$11.50). AE, DC, MC, V. Tues–Sun noon–3pm and 7–11pm. Closed for lunch in Aug. Tram: 28. BRAZILIAN.

On the edge of the Bairro Alto, near praça do Principe Real and largo de Camoes, this is Lisbon's finest Brazilian restaurant. Owner-chef Juca Oliveira presides over the former private mansion, as he has for the past 2 decades. The traditional decor incorporates 19th-century antiques and an open fireplace. The hearty food includes *feijoada,* the traditional Brazilian dish of black beans with meat, rice, and cabbage. Another favorite is *bauru a brasuca,* a tender steak in onion sauce served with cheese and ham. Beef predominates—after all, the food is Brazilian—but the lamb and pork dishes are equally good. Codfish also appears in several tempting ways. Instead of the usual wine, you might decide to try a Brazilian beer.

Cantinho da Paz. Rua da Paz 4 (off rua dos Poiais de São Bento). ☎ **21/396-96-98.** Reservations required. Main courses 1,780$–2,500$ ($9.95–$14). AE, DC, MC, V. Tues–Sun 12:30–2:30pm and 7:30–11pm. Tram: 26. Bus: 6 or 49. GOAN.

This restaurant honors the cuisine of the lost colony of Goa, which the government of India took over in 1961, chasing out the Portuguese. Many Portuguese Goans brought their spicy cuisine to Lisbon and set up dining rooms, and this is the best of the lot. The curries draw discerning diners, who are richly rewarded with spices and flavors. Our favorite is shrimp curry flavored with coconut and laced with cream. But you may opt for a fiery version made with lamb, fish, or poultry. Veal stew comes with different types and levels of hotness, and succulent medallions of pork are richly flavored with ginger and garlic. The helpful owners speak English.

Cais da Ribeira. Cais do Sodré. ☎ **21/342-36-11.** Reservations recommended. Main courses 1,500$–5,500$ ($8.40–$30.80). AE, DC, MC, V. Wed–Fri and Sun noon–3pm; Tues–Sun 7:30–11pm. Metro: Cais do Sodré. PORTUGUESE.

This superb little regional restaurant in a former fish warehouse serves some of the best charcoal-grilled fresh fish in Lisbon. It's a cozy waterfront place, with views over the Tagus, that uses generations-old recipes. *Caldeirada,* the hearty local version of fishermen's stew, will fortify you for a day. The chef also prepares a good-tasting paella for two, and tender grilled steaks, sometimes with a peppercorn sauce. Most dishes, except the expensive shellfish, are at the lower end of the price scale.

Casa Nostra. Rua de Rosa 84–90 (enter at travessa de Poco da Cidade 60). ☎ **21/342-59-31.** Reservations recommended. Regular main courses 1,000$–2,600$ ($5.60–$14.55); seafood main courses 1,900$–2,400$ ($10.65–$13.45). AE, MC, V. Tues–Fri 12:30–2:30pm, Sun 1–2:30pm; Tues–Sat 8–11pm. Metro: Chiado. Tram: 28 or 28B. ITALIAN.

Maria Paola Porru, a movie sound engineer whose travels have exposed her to cinematic circles across Europe, created this hip postmodern hideaway. Behind a century-old, deliberately understated facade, the setting is simple, stylish, and informal. All pastas are homemade on the premises. Accomplished menu items include fettuccine al mascarpone, lasagna, spaghetti with Portuguese clams, and several versions of grilled meat. A favorite dessert is Sicilian-style tiramisu, a rich dessert made with ladyfingers, coffee, and mascarpone cream.

Cervejaria/Restaurante Fábrica Real. Rua da Escola Politécnica 275–283. ☎ **21/387-29-18.** Regular main courses 1,000$–2,000$ ($5.60–$11.20); seafood main courses 1,000$–5,000$ ($5.60–$28); tourist menu 1,100$ ($6.15). AE, DC, MC, V. Mon–Sat 7am–2am. Bus: 6, 9, 36. Metro: Rato. PORTUGUESE.

On the northern edge of the Bairro Alto, between the Rossio station and the botanical gardens, this is a tastefully remodeled 18th-century silk factory. The bar is on the ground floor, the spacious restaurant one floor above street level. The food is pub style, portions are ample, and prices are relatively modest. Many patrons crowd in here just for a glass or two of beer. Worthwhile dining choices include *bife à la Real Fábrica* (steak with cream and mushrooms) and *leitão da bairrada* (crisp roast suckling pig), a regional specialty that goes especially well with beer.

IN THE CHIADO DISTRICT
EXPENSIVE

✪ **Tágide.** Largo da Academia Nacional de Belas Artes 18–20. ☎ **21/342-07-20.** Reservations required. Main courses 3,000$–5,000$ ($16.80–$28). AE, DC, MC, V. Mon–Fri 12:30–2:30pm and 7:30–10:30pm. Metro: Chiado. Tram: 20. Bus: 15. PORTUGUESE/INTERNATIONAL.

Once the town house of a diplomat, then a major nightclub, Tágide is now one of Lisbon's leading restaurants. It's up from the docks, atop a steep hill overlooking the old part of Lisbon and the Tagus. The dining room has a view of ships moored in the port; glittering above are crystal chandeliers.

The cuisine is fashionable, competent, and always tantalizing, while never going so far as to offend unadventurous palates. The Portuguese and international dishes and selections are beautifully served. For an appetizer, we suggest salmon pâté, cold stuffed crab, or smoked swordfish. Other specialties include suprême of halibut with coriander, pork with clams and coriander, and grilled baby goat with herbs. For dessert, try cold orange-and-lemon soufflé with hot chocolate sauce. Patrons from the world of Lisbon finance and government, including the president of Portugal, receive preferential seating and treatment.

INEXPENSIVE

Pastelaria Bernard'. Rua Garrett 104. ☎ **21/347-31-33.** Sandwiches 300$–400$ ($1.70–$2.25); continental breakfast 500$ ($2.80). AE, DC, MC, V. Mon–Sat 8am–midnight. Metro: Baixa Chiado. SANDWICHES/SNACKS.

Pastelaria Bernard' is the most fashionable teahouse in Lisbon. Dating from the 1800s, it lies in the heart of the Chiado. In fair weather, there's sidewalk seating. Lunch, served in a back room, is a full meal of such Portuguese specialties as codfish with almonds. Most visitors come here for tea, served with sandwiches and snacks. Desserts, including duchesses (whipped-cream cakes) are justifiably famous. Proper dress is required inside, although visitors in shorts sometimes occupy the outside tables. This is a good choice for breakfast, which includes fresh croissants.

IN THE GRAÇA DISTRICT
MODERATE

Restaurante O Faz Figura. Rua do Paraíso 15B. ☎ **21/886-89-81.** Reservations required. Main courses 2,000$–3,400$ ($11.20–$19.05). AE, DC, MC, V. Mon–Sat 12:30–3pm and 8pm–midnight. Metro: Santa Apolónia. PORTUGUESE/INTERNATIONAL.

This is one of the best and most attractively decorated dining rooms in Lisbon, and service is faultless. When reserving a table, ask to be seated on the veranda, over-looking the Tagus. You can stop for a before-dinner drink in the "international cocktail bar." Specialties include *feijoada de marisco* (shellfish stew) and *cataplana* of fish and seafood. The cuisine generally abounds in flavor and occasional fire.

Via Graça Restaurante. Rua Damasceno Monteiro 9B. ☎ **21/887-08-30.** Reservations recommended. Main courses 2,000$–3,400$ ($11.20–$19.05). AE, DC, MC, V. Mon–Fri 12:30–3:30pm; Mon–Sat 7:30–11pm. Tram: 28. PORTUGUESE.

On a hillside in the residential Graça district, a few blocks northeast of the fortifications that surround Castelo de São Jorge, this restaurant boasts a panoramic view that encompasses the castelo and the Basílica da Estrêla. Flickering candles and attentive service enhance the romantic setting. Dishes aren't inventive, but they're savory and appealing to traditionalists who opt for hearty fare. Specialties of the house include such traditional Portuguese dishes as *pato assado com moscatel* (roast duck with wine from the region of Setúbal) and *linguado com recheio de camarão* (stuffed fillet of sole served with shrimp).

INEXPENSIVE

Restaurant d'Avis. Rua de Grilo 98. ☎ **21/868-13-54.** Reservations recommended. Main courses 1,200$–2,400$ ($6.70–$13.45). DC, MC, V. Mon–Sat noon–3pm and 7:30–10pm. Closed Aug. Bus: 39 or 59. PORTUGUESE.

This simple but pleasing restaurant is not associated with the Restaurante Aviz, once an important culinary citadel on rua Serpa Pinto. This humbler, less expensive, competitor was established in the late 1980s as a purveyor of the cuisine of Alentejo to cost-conscious diners. It serves regional dishes such as roast pork with clams, roast baby goat, steaming bowls of *caldo verde* (a fortifying soup made from high-fiber greens and potatoes), and perfectly prepared fresh fish. Don't expect a luxurious setting or anything even vaguely formal—few members of the staff speak English, and the rustic venue is deliberately unpretentious.

IN THE BELÉM DISTRICT
MODERATE

São Jerónimo. Rua dos Jerónimos 12. ☎ **21/364-87-97.** Reservations recommended. Main courses 2,200$–3,500$ ($12.30–$19.60). AE, DC, MC, V. Mon–Fri 12:30–3pm; Mon–Sat 7:30–10:30pm. Bus: 15, 27, 28, or 29. PORTUGUESE/INTERNATIONAL.

You might combine a visit to this lighthearted, elegant restaurant with a trip to the famous monastery of the same name. São Jerónimo sits east of the monastery, behind a big-windowed facade that floods the interior with sunlight. It takes its inspiration from the Roaring Twenties, with French-style decoration; the chairs are by Philippe Starck, the bar's armchairs are by Le Corbusier. The food is not inspired, but it's usually created from market-fresh ingredients. This place depends on foreign visitors—not wanting to offend the international palate, it sticks to somewhat bland fare.

Vela Latina. Doca do Bom Sucesso. ☎ **21/301-71-18.** Main courses 2,200$–3,600$ ($12.30–$20.15). AE, DC, MC, V. Mon–Sat 12:30–3pm and 8–11pm. PORTUGUESE.

In a verdant park, close to the Tagus and the Tower of Belém, this inviting, high-ceilinged restaurant offers well-prepared food, lots of greenery, big windows, and peace. Many visitors opt for lunch here after a visit to the nearby Jerónimos Monastery or the Coach Museum. Specialties include a wide array of classic, well-prepared Portuguese dishes, such as lobster-filled crepes, platters of fresh fish, quail salad, lamb cutlets, and fillet of hake with rice. Dessert might be flan, fruit tart, or ice cream. The price of some shellfish dishes can soar.

IN THE ALFAMA

Casa do Leão. Castelo de São Jorge. ☎ **21/887-59-62.** Reservations recommended. Main courses 1,900$–4,600$ ($10.65–$25.75). AE, DC, MC, V. Daily 12:30–3:30pm and 8–10:30pm. Bus: 37. PORTUGUESE/INTERNATIONAL.

Stop for a midday meal at this restaurant, in a low-slung stone building inside the walls of Saint George's Castle. You'll pass between a pair of ancient cannons before entering a sun-flooded vestibule, where the splashing from a dolphin-shaped fountain and the welcoming voice of the uniformed maître d' greet you. In the spacious dining room, you'll enjoy a panoramic view of the Alfama and the legendary hills of Lisbon. Your lunch might include roast duck with oranges or grapes, pork chops Saint George style, codfish with cream, or smoked swordfish from Sesimbra. The chefs obviously cook with the international visitor in mind, but what they prepare can be very satisfying. Menus change with the season. We'd like the service to be more attentive, but the hardworking waiters may already be moving at peak capacity.

IN THE ALCÂNTARA

Café Alcântara. Rua Maria Luisa Holstein 15. ☎ **21/363-71-76.** Reservations recommended. Main courses 3,500$–7,000$ ($19.60–$39.20). AE, DC, MC, V. Daily 8pm–1am. Bar daily 9pm–3am. Bus: 57. FRENCH/PORTUGUESE.

Since its establishment in 1989, this has become one of the city's most fun dining-and-entertainment complexes. It lies within the solid walls of a 600-year-old timber warehouse. Today, the vast building has forest-green and Bordeaux walls, exposed marble, ceiling fans, plants, and simple wooden tables and chairs. The clientele is about as varied as you'll find in Portugal and includes resident Brazilian, British, and American expatriates. Chefs make the most of regional foodstuffs and prepare hearty fare that is filled with flavor and plenty of spices—maybe too much so for some palates. Menu items include rillettes of salmon, fresh fish, lacquered duck, steak tartare, and a Portuguese platter of the day, which might include fried *bacalhau* (codfish) or a hearty *feijoada,* a bean-and-meat stew inspired by the traditions of Trás-os-Montes.

4

Exploring Lisbon

Many visitors use Lisbon as a base for exploring nearby sites, but often neglect the cultural gems tucked away in the Portuguese capital. They leave Lisbon to explore Sintra, the Portuguese Riviera (Estoril and Cascais), Mafra, and even Nazaré and Fátima.

One reason Lisbon gets overlooked is that visitors don't budget enough time for it. You need at least 5 days to do justice to the city and its environs. In addition, even Lisbon's principal attractions remain relatively unknown, a blessing for travelers tired of fighting their way to overrun sights elsewhere in Europe.

This chapter will guide you to the unknown treasures of the capital. If your time is limited, explore the **National Coach Museum,** the **Jerónimos Monastery,** and the **Alfama** and the **Castle of St. George.** At least two art museums, although not of the caliber of Madrid's Prado, merit attention: the **Museu Nacional de Arte Antiga** and the **Museu da Fundação Calouste Gulbenkian.**

If you have time, visit the **Fundação Ricardo Espírito Santo** and watch reproductions of antiques being made or books being gold-leafed. You could also spend time seeing the gilded royal galleys at the **Naval Museum,** wandering through the **fish market,** visiting Lisbon's new **aquarium,** or exploring the arts and crafts of **Belém's Folk Art Museum.**

Suggested Itineraries

If You Have 1 Day

This is only enough time to take a stroll through the Alfama (see "Walking Tour 1," later in this chapter), the most interesting district of Lisbon. Visit the 12th-century **Sé** (cathedral), and take in a view of the city and the river Tagus from the **Santa Luzia Belvedere.** Climb up to the **Castelo de São Jorge** (St. George's Castle). Take a taxi or bus to Belém to see the **Mosteiro dos Jerónimos** (Jerónimos Monastery) and the **Torre de Belém.** While at Belém, explore one of the major sights of Lisbon, the **Museu Nacional dos Coches** (National Coach Museum).

If You Have 2 Days

On Day 2, head for Sintra, the single most visited sight in the environs of Lisbon—Byron called it "glorious Eden." You can spend the

Up, Up & Away

For a splendid rooftop view of Lisbon, take the **Santa Justa elevator** on rua de Santa Justa. The ornate concoction was built by a Portuguese engineer, Raoul Mesnier de Ponsard, born to French immigrants in Porto in 1849. (It's often mistakenly attributed to the French engineer Alexandre-Gustave Eiffel, who built the tower in Paris that bears his name). The elevator goes from rua Aurea, in the center of the shopping district near Rossio Square, to the panoramic viewing platform. It operates daily from 7am to 11pm. A ticket costs 160$ (90¢), and children under 4 ride free. Because of damage caused by a 1992 fire, you can no longer use the pedestrian walkway to explore the Bairro Alto, but must ride the elevator back down to the Baixa neighborhood. Metro: Rossio.

day, exploring the castle and other palaces in the stunning area. Try at least to visit the **Palácio Nacional de Sintra** and the **Palácio Nacional da Pena.** Return to Lisbon for a night at a fado cafe.

If You Have 3 Days

Spend a morning at the **Museu da Fundação Calouste Gulbenkian,** one of Europe's artistic treasure troves. Have lunch in the Bairro Alto. In the afternoon, see the **Fundação Ricardo Espírito Santo** (Museum of Decorative Art) and the **Museu Nacional de Arte Antiga** (National Museum of Ancient Art). At the day's end, wander through Parque Eduardo VII.

If You Have 4 Days

On the 4th day, take an excursion from Lisbon (for convenience, consider an organized tour—see listings later in this chapter): Visit the fishing village of **Nazaré** and the walled city of **Óbidos.** Those interested in Roman Catholic sights might also want to include a visit to the shrine at **Fátima,** although seeing this on the same day would be hectic.

If You Have 5 Days

On the final day, slow your pace a bit, with a morning at the beach at **Estoril** on Portugal's Costa do Sol. Then continue along the coast to **Cascais** for lunch. After lunch, wander around the old fishing village, now a major resort. Go to **Guincho,** 4 miles along the coast from Cascais, which is near the westernmost point on the European continent and has panoramic views.

1 The Top Attractions: The Alfama, Belém & Museums

✪ THE ALFAMA

The Lisbon of bygone days lives on in the Alfama, the most emblematic quarter of the city. The wall built by the Visigoths and incorporated into some of the old houses is a reminder of its ancient past. In east Lisbon, the Alfama was the Saracen sector centuries before its conquest by the Christians.

The devastating 1755 earthquake spared some of the buildings, and the Alfama has retained much of its original charm. You'll see narrow cobblestone streets, cages of canaries chirping in the afternoon sun, strings of garlic and pepper adorning old taverns, street markets, and charming balconies. Houses are so close together that in many places it's impossible to stretch your arms wide. The poet Frederico de Brito dramatically expressed that proximity: "Your house is so close to mine! In the starry night's bliss, to exchange a tender kiss, our lips easily meet, high across the narrow street."

Stevedores, fishmongers, and sailors still occupy the Alfama. Streamers of laundry protrude from the smallest houses, and the fishwives make early morning appearances on their iron balconies to water their pots of geraniums. In the street markets, you can wander in a maze of brightly colored vegetables from the countryside, bananas from Madeira, pineapples from the Azores, and assorted fish. Armies of cats prowl in search of rats. Occasionally, a black-shawled widow, stooping over a brazier grilling sardines in front of her house, will toss a fish head to a passing feline.

Aristocrats once lived in the Alfama; a handful still do, but their memory is perpetuated mostly by the noble coats of arms fading on the fronts of some 16th-century houses. The best-known aristocratic mansion is the one formerly occupied by the count of Arcos, the last viceroy of Brazil. Constructed in the 16th century and spared, in part, from the earthquake, it lies on largo da Salvador.

As you explore, you'll suddenly be rewarded with a perspective of the contrasting styles of the Alfama, from a simple tile-roofed fishmonger's abode to a festively decorated baroque church. One of the best views is from the belvedere of **largo das Portas do Sol,** near the Museum of Decorative Art. It's a balcony opening onto the sea, overlooking the typical houses as they sweep down to the Tagus.

One of the oldest churches in Lisbon is **Santo Estevão** (St. Stephen), on largo de Santo Estevão, originally constructed in the 13th century. The present marble structure dates from the 1700s. Also of medieval origin is the **Church of São Miguel** (St. Michael), on largo de São Miguel, deep in the Alfama on a palm tree–shaded square. Reconstructed after the 1755 earthquake, the interior is richly decorated with 18th-century gilt and trompe l'oeil walls.

Rua da Judiaria is another poignant reminder of the past. It was settled largely by Jewish refugees fleeing Spain to escape the Inquisition.

At night the neighborhood's spirit changes. Street lanterns cast patterns against medieval walls, and the plaintive voice of the *fadista* rings out until the early morning hours. Although the Bairro Alto is the city's traditional fado quarter, the cafes of the Alfama also reverberate with these nostalgic sounds. Amália and Celeste Rodrigues, two celebrated fadistas, got their start around the docks here, peddling flowers to tourists arriving on boats.

For specific routes through the Alfama, refer to the walking tour later in this chapter. The Alfama is best explored by day; it can be dangerous to wander around the area at night.

✪ **Castelo de São Jorge.** Rua da Costa do Castelo. No phone. Free admission. Apr–Sept daily 9am–9pm; Oct–Mar daily 9am–6pm. Bus: 37. Tram: 12 or 28.

Locals speak of Saint George's Castle as the cradle of their city, and it may have been where the Portuguese capital began. Its occupation is believed to have predated the Romans—the hilltop was used as a fortress to guard the Tagus and its settlement below. Beginning in the 5th century A.D., the site was a Visigothic fortification; it fell to the Saracens in the early 8th century. Many of the existing walls were erected during the centuries of Moorish domination. The Moors held power until 1147, the year Afonso Henríques, the first king of the country, chased them out and extended his kingdom south. Even before Lisbon became the capital of the newly emerging nation, the site was used as a royal palace.

For the finest view of the Tagus and the Alfama, walk the esplanades and climb the ramparts of the old castle. The castle's name (George is the patron saint of England)

> ### ⓧ Frommer's Favorite Lisbon Experiences
>
> **On the Trail of Fado in the Alfama.** *Fado,* an authentic Portuguese musical genre, means "fate" or "destiny." Its lament of lost love and glory is heard nightly in the little houses of the Alfama (and in the Bairro Alto). Twelve-string guitars accompany women swathed in black—called *fadistas,* as are male fado singers. Listening to the melancholy songs is the quintessential Lisbon experience.
>
> **Shopping for Handcrafts.** The shopping in Lisbon is irresistible. Artisans from all over the country display their finest wares: ceramics, embroidery (from the Azores and Madeira), silver, elegant porcelain, gleaming crystal, *azulejos* (glazed earthenware tiles), hand-woven rugs, and hand-knit sweaters.
>
> **An Afternoon in Sintra.** Some savvy travelers claim that after visiting Sintra, the rest of Europe seems like a footnote. Follow in the footsteps of Portuguese kings and queens of yesteryear and head for Byron's "glorious Eden." Byron was not alone in proclaiming the village of Sintra "perhaps the most delightful in Europe." Even the sometimes-skeptical Spanish proclaim: "To see the world and yet leave Sintra out/ Is, verily, to go blindfold about."

commemorates an Anglo-Portuguese pact dating from as early as 1371. (Portugal and England have been traditional allies, although their relationship was strained in 1961 when India, a member of the Commonwealth of Nations, seized the Portuguese overseas territories of Goa, Diu, and Damão.)

Huddling close to the protection of the moated castle is a sector that appears almost medieval (many houses retain their Moorish courtyards, though others have been greatly altered). At the entrance, visitors pause at the Castle Belvedere. The Portuguese refer to this spot as their "ancient window." It overlooks the Alfama, the Serras of Monsanto and Sintra, Ponte do 25 de Abril spanning the Tagus, praça do Comércio, and the tile roofs of the Portuguese capital. In the square stands a heroic statue—sword in one hand, shield in the other—of the first king, Afonso Henríques.

Inside the castle grounds you can stroll through olive, pine, and cork trees, all graced by the appearance of a flamingo. Swans with white bodies and black necks glide in a silence shattered only by the piercing scream of the rare white peacock.

Sé (Cathedral). Largo da Sé. ☎ **21/88-67-52.** Admission: Cathedral, free; cloister, 100$ (55¢). Mon–Sat 10am–5pm. Tram: 28 (Graça). Bus: 37.

Even official tourist brochures admit that this cathedral is not very rich. Characterized by twin towers flanking its entrance, it represents an architectural wedding of Romanesque and gothic style. The facade is severe enough to resemble a medieval fortress. At one point the Saracens reportedly used the site of the present Sé as a mosque. When the city was captured early in the 12th century by Christian crusaders, led by Portugal's first king, Afonso Henríques, the structure was rebuilt. The Sé then became the first church in Lisbon. The earthquakes of 1344 and 1755 damaged the structure.

Beyond the rough exterior are many treasures, including the font where St. Anthony of Padua is said to have been christened in 1195. A notable feature is the 14th-century gothic chapel of Bartholomeu Joanes. Other items of interest are a crib by Machado de Castro (the 18th-century Portuguese sculptor responsible for the equestrian statue on praça do Comércio), the 14th-century sarcophagus of Lopo Fernandes Pacheco, and the original nave and aisles.

A visit to the sacristy and cloister requires a guide. The cloister, built in the 14th century by King Dinis, is of ogival construction, with garlands, a Romanesque wrought-iron grille, and tombs with inscription stones. In the sacristy are marbles, relics, valuable images, and pieces of ecclesiastical treasure from the 15th and 16th centuries. In the morning, the stained-glass reflections on the floor evoke a Monet painting.

Santo António de Lisboa. Largo de Santo António de Sé. ☎ **21/886-91-45.** Free admission. Daily 7:30am–7:30pm. Métro: Rossio. Bus: 37.

St. Anthony of Padua, an itinerant Franciscan monk who became the patron saint of Portugal, was born in 1195 in a house that once stood here. The 1755 earthquake destroyed the original church, and Mateus Vicente designed the present building in the 18th century.

In the crypt, a guide will show you the spot where the saint was reputedly born (he's buried in Padua, Italy). The devout come to this little church to light candles under his picture. He's known as a protector of young brides, and has a special connection with the children of Lisbon. To raise money to erect the altar at the church, the children of the Alfama built miniature altars with a representation of the patron saint. June 12 is St. Anthony's Day, a time of merrymaking, heavy eating, and drinking. In the morning there are street fires and singing, followed by St. Anthony's Feast on the following day.

BELÉM

At Belém, where the Tagus (*Tejo* in Portuguese) meets the sea, the Portuguese caravels that charted the areas unknown to the Western world set out: Vasco da Gama to India, Ferdinand Magellan to circumnavigate the globe, and Bartholomeu Dias to round the Cape of Good Hope.

Belém emerged from the Restelo, the point of land from which the ships set sail across the so-called Sea of Darkness. The district flourished as riches, especially spices, poured into Portugal. Great monuments, including the **Belém Tower** and **Jerónimos Monastery,** were built and embellished in the Manueline style.

In time, the royal family established a summer palace here. Much of the district's character emerged when wealthy Lisboans began moving out of the city center and building town houses here. For many years Belém was a separate municipality. Eventually it was incorporated into Lisbon as a parish. Nowadays it's a magnet for visitors to its many museums. For most tourists, the primary sight is the Torre de Belém.

Torre de Belém. Praça do Império, av. de Brasília. ☎ **21/362-00-34.** Admission 400$ ($2.25) adults, 200$ ($1.10) children, free for seniors (65 and over). Tues–Sun 10am–5pm. Tram: 15 or 17. Bus: 27, 28, 43, 49, or 51.

The quadrangular Tower of Belém is a monument to Portugal's Age of Discovery. Erected between 1515 and 1520, the Manueline-style tower is Portugal's classic landmark, and often serves as a symbol of the country. A monument to Portugal's great military and naval past, the tower stands on or near the spot where the caravels once set out across the sea.

Its architect, Francisco de Arruda, blended Gothic and Moorish elements, using such architectural details as twisting ropes carved of stone. The coat of arms of Manuel I rests above the loggia, and balconies grace three sides of the monument. Along the balustrade of the loggias, stone crosses represent the Portuguese crusaders.

The richness of the facade fades once you cross the drawbridge and enter the Renaissance-style doorway. Gothic severity reigns. There are a few antiques, including a 16th-century throne graced with finials and an inset paneled with pierced gothic

Belém Attractions

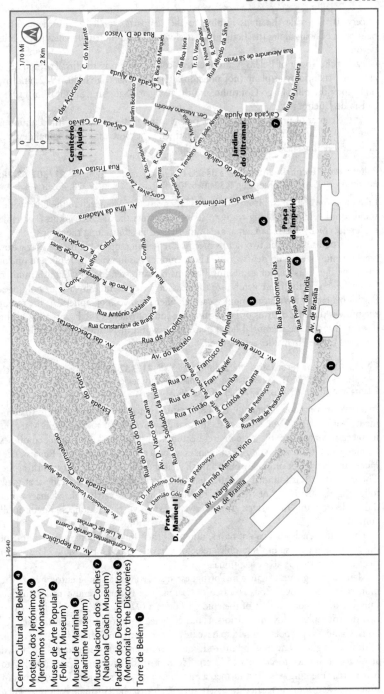

Centro Cultural de Belém 4

Mosteiro dos Jerónimos 6
(Jerónimos Monastery)

Museu de Arte Popular 2
(Folk Art Museum)

Museu de Marinha 3
(Maritime Museum)

Museu Nacional dos Coches 7
(National Coach Museum)

Padrão dos Descobrimentos 5
(Memorial to the Discoveries)

Torre de Belém 1

tracery. If you scale the steps leading to the ramparts, you'll be rewarded with a panorama of boats along the Tagus and pastel-washed, tile-roofed old villas in the hills beyond.

Facing the Tower of Belém is a monument commemorating the first Portuguese to cross the Atlantic by airplane (not nonstop). The date was March 30, 1922, and the flight took the pilot Gago Coutinho and the navigator Sacadura Cabral from Lisbon to Rio de Janeiro.

At the center of praça do Império at Belém is the Fonte Luminosa (the Luminous Fountain). The patterns of the water jets, estimated at more than 70 original designs, make an evening show lasting nearly an hour.

Padrão dos Descobrimentos. Praça da Boa Esperança, av. de Brasília. ☎ **21/301-62-28.** Admission 300$ ($1.70). Tues–Sun 9:30am–6:30pm. Tram: 15. Bus: 27, 28, 43, or 49.

Like the prow of a caravel from the Age of Discovery, the Memorial to the Discoveries stands on the Tagus, looking ready to strike out across the Sea of Darkness. Notable explorers, chiefly Vasco da Gama, are immortalized in stone along the ramps.

At the point where the two ramps meet is a representation of Henry the Navigator, whose genius opened up new worlds. The memorial was unveiled in 1960, and one of the stone figures is that of a kneeling Philippa of Lancaster, Henry's English mother. Other figures in the frieze symbolize the crusaders (represented by a man holding a flag with a cross), navigators, monks, cartographers, and cosmographers. At the top of the prow is the coat of arms of Portugal at the time of Manuel the Fortunate. On the floor in front of the memorial lies a map of the world in multicolored marble, with the dates of the discoveries set in metal.

✪ **Mosteiro dos Jerónimos.** Praça do Império. ☎ **21/362-00-34.** Admission to church free. To cloisters 500$ ($2.80); free for children and seniors (65 and over). Tues–Sun 10am–5pm. Tram: 15. Bus: 27, 28, 29, 43, or 49.

In an expansive mood, Manuel I, the Fortunate, ordered this monastery built to commemorate Vasco da Gama's voyage to India and to give thanks to the Virgin Mary for its success. Manueline, the style of architecture that bears the king's name, combines Flamboyant Gothic and Moorish influences with elements of the nascent Renaissance. Henry the Navigator originally built a small chapel dedicated to St. Mary on this spot. The monastery was founded in 1502, partially financed by the spice trade that grew following the discovery of the route to India. The 1755 earthquake damaged but didn't destroy the monastery. It underwent extensive restoration, some of it ill conceived.

The church encloses a trio of naves, noted for their fragile-looking pillars. Some of the ceilings, like those in the monks' refectory, have a ribbed barrel vault. The "palm tree" in the sacristy is also exceptional.

Many of the greatest figures in Portuguese history are said to be entombed at the monastery; the most famous is Vasco da Gama. The Portuguese also maintain that Luís Vaz de Camões, author of the epic *Os Lusíadas* (*The Lusiads*), in which he glorified the triumphs of his compatriots, is buried here. Both tombs rest on the backs of lions. Camões's epic poetry is said to have inspired a young Portuguese king, Sebastião, to dreams of glory. The foolish king—devoutly, even fanatically, religious—was killed at Alcácer-Kibir, Morocco, in a 1578 crusade against the Muslims. Those refusing to believe that the king was dead formed a cult known as Sebastianism; it rose to minor influence, and four men tried to assert their claim to the Portuguese throne. Each maintained steadfastly, even to death, that he was King Sebastião. Sebastião's remains were reputedly entombed in a 16th-century marble shrine built in the Mannerist style.

The romantic poet Herculano (1800–54) is also buried at Jerónimos, as is the famed poet Fernando Pessoa.

✪ **Museu de Marinha (Maritime Museum).** Praça do Império. ☎ **21/362-00-19.** Admission 400$ ($2.25) adults, 200$ ($1.10) students, free for children under 10 and seniors (65 and over). Tues–Sun 10am–6pm; off-season Tues–Sun 10am–5pm. Bus: 27, 28, 29, 43, 49, or 51.

The Maritime Museum, one of the most important in Europe, evokes the glory that characterized Portugal's domination of the high seas. Appropriately, it's installed in the west wing of the Mosteiro dos Jerónimos. These royal galleys re-create an age of opulence that never shied away from excess. Dragon heads drip with gilt; sea monsters coil with abandon. Assembling a large crew was no problem for kings and queens in those days. Queen Maria I ordered a magnificent galley built for the 1785 marriage of her son and successor, Crown Prince João, to the Spanish Princess Carlota Joaquina Bourbon. Eighty dummy oarsmen, elaborately attired in scarlet- and mustard-colored waistcoats, represent the crew.

The museum contains hundreds of models of 15th- to 19th-century sailing ships, 20th-century warships, merchant marine vessels, fishing boats, river craft, and pleasure boats. In a section devoted to the East is a pearl-inlaid replica of a dragon boat used in maritime and fluvial corteges. A full range of Portuguese naval uniforms is on display, from one worn at a Mozambique military outpost in 1896 to a uniform worn as recently as 1961. In a special room is a model of the queen's stateroom on the royal yacht of Carlos I, the Bragança king who was assassinated at praça do Comércio in 1908. It was on this craft that his son, Manuel II, his wife, and the queen mother, Amélia, escaped to Gibraltar following the collapse of the Portuguese monarchy in 1910. The Maritime Museum also honors some early Portuguese aviators.

✪ **Museu Nacional dos Coches (National Coach Museum).** Praça de Afonso de Albuquerque. ☎ **21/895-59-94.** Admission 450$ ($2.50) adults, 225$ ($1.25) students 14–25, free for children under 14. Tues–Sun 10am–5:30pm. Closed holidays. Tram: 15. Bus: 14, 27, 28, 29, 43, or 49.

Visited by more tourists than any other attraction in Lisbon, the National Coach Museum is the finest of its type in the world. Founded by Amélia, wife of Carlos I, it's housed in a former 18th-century riding academy connected to the Belém Royal Palace. The coaches stand in a former horse ring; most date from the 17th to the 19th century. Drawing the most interest is a trio of opulently gilded baroque carriages used by the Portuguese ambassador to the Vatican at the time of Pope Clement XI (1716). Also on display is a 17th-century coach in which the Spanish Hapsburg king, Phillip II, journeyed from Madrid to Lisbon to see his new possession.

Museu de Arte Popular. Av. de Brasília. ☎ **21/301-12-82.** Admission 300$ ($1.70), free for children under 10. Tues–Sun 10am–12:30pm and 2–5pm. Closed holidays. Tram: 15. Bus: 27, 28, 29, 43, 49, or 51.

The Folk Art Museum is the most dramatic exhibition of Portuguese folk arts and customs. Some of the best contemporary artists in Portugal—including Carlos Botelho, Eduardo Anahory, Estrêla Faria, Manuel Lapa, Paulo Ferreira, and Tomás de Melo—painted the walls. Enlarged photographs of the people of the provinces supplement the artists' work. The 1948 establishment of the Folk Art Museum was a result of a campaign for ethnic revival directed by António Ferro. The collections, including ceramics, furniture, wickerwork, clothes, farm implements, and painting, are displayed in five rooms that correspond more or less to the provinces, each of which maintains its own distinct personality. The building housed the Regional Center during the 1940 Portuguese World's Exhibition.

Centro Cultural de Belém. Praça do Império. ☎ **21/361-24-00** or 01/362-41-91. Admission to center free; varies for temporary exhibitions. Daily 11am–8pm. Tram: 15. Bus: 27, 28, 29, 43, or 49.

This center occasionally functions as a showcase for temporary exhibitions of Portuguese art. Although it is mostly devoted to conventions, the center also functions at least part of the time as a concert hall, a temporary art museum, or a catch-all venue. Events staged here, widely publicized in local newspapers, might include classical concerts and film festivals, in addition to industrial conventions. There are an inexpensive cafeteria and a handful of shops on the premises. The building was constructed in the early 1990s as a convention hall for the meetings that brought Portugal membership in the European Union.

TWO MORE TOP MUSEUMS

Most major Lisbon museums are at Belém, but two major attractions are in the city proper: the **National Art Gallery** and the **Gulbenkian Center for Arts and Culture.** For details about two additional notable museums—the **St. Roque Museum** of ecclesiastical art and the **Archaeological Museum** in the ruins of the Carmo Church— refer to "More Attractions," later in this chapter.

✪ **Museu Nacional de Arte Antiga (National Museum of Medieval Art).** Rua das Janelas Verdes 9. ☎ **21/396-41-51.** Admission 500$ ($2.80) adults, 250$ ($1.40) students, free for children under 14. Tues 2–6pm, Wed–Sun 10am–6pm. Tram: 15 or 18. Bus: 7, 40, 49, or 60.

The National Museum of Ancient Art houses the country's greatest collection of paintings. It occupies two connected buildings—a 17th-century palace and an added edifice that was built on the site of the old Carmelite Convent of Santo Alberto. The convent's chapel was preserved and is a good example of the integration of ornamental arts, with gilded carved wood, glazed tiles, and sculpture of the 17th and 18th centuries.

The museum has many notable paintings, including the famous polyptych from St. Vincent's monastery attributed to Nuno Gonçalves between 1460 and 1470. There are 60 portraits of leading figures of Portuguese history. Other outstanding works are Hieronymus Bosch's triptych *The Temptation of St. Anthony;* Hans Memling's *Mother and Child;* Albrecht Dürer's *St. Jerome;* and paintings by Velázquez, Zurbarán, Poussin, and Courbet. Paintings from the 15th through the 19th century trace the development of Portuguese art.

The museum also exhibits a remarkable collection of gold- and silversmiths' works, both Portuguese and foreign. Among these is the cross from Alcobaça and the monstrance of Belém, constructed with the first gold brought from India by Vasco da Gama. Another exceptional example is the 18th-century French silver tableware ordered by José I. Diverse objects from Benin, India, Persia, China, and Japan were culled from the proceeds of Portuguese expansion overseas. Two excellent pairs of screens depict the Portuguese relationship with Japan in the 17th century. Flemish tapestries, a rich assemblage of church vestments, Italian polychrome ceramics, and sculptures are also on display.

✪ **Museu da Fundação Calouste Gulbenkian.** Av. de Berna 45. ☎ **21/795-02-36.** Admission 500$ ($2.80), free for children under 10 and seniors (65 and over). Free to all Sun. Tues 2–6pm, Wed–Sun 10am–6pm. Metro: Sebastião. Tram: 24. Bus: 16, 26, 31, 46, or 56.

Opened in 1969, this museum, part of the Fundação Calouste Gulbenkian, houses what one critic called "one of the world's finest private art collections." It belonged to the Armenian oil tycoon Calouste Gulbenkian, who died in 1955. The modern, multimillion-dollar center is in a former private estate that belonged to the count of Vilalva.

Secrets of Lisbon

The places below provide a view of Lisbon not often seen by the casual visitors passing through the city.

The Markets   The big market of **Ribeira Nova** is as close as you can get to the heart of Lisbon. Near the Cais do Sodré (where trains leave for the Costa do Sol), an enormous roof shelters a collection of stalls offering the produce used in Lisbon's fine restaurants. Foodstuffs arrive each morning in wicker baskets bulging with oversize carrots, cabbages big enough to be shrubbery, and stalks of bananas. Some of the freshly plucked produce arrives by donkey, some by truck, some balanced on the heads of Lisboan women in the Mediterranean fashion. The rich soil produces the juiciest peaches and the most aromatic tomatoes.

At the market, women festively clad in voluminous skirts and calico aprons preside over the mounds of vegetables, fruit, and fish. On cue, the vendors begin howling about the value of their wares, stopping only to pose for an occasional snapshot.

Fishing boats dock at dawn with their catch. The fishers deposit the cod, squid, bass, hake, and swordfish on long marble counters. The *varinas* (fishwives) balance wicker baskets of the fresh catch on their heads. They climb the cobblestone streets of the Alfama or the Bairro Alto to sell fish from door to door.

Estufa Fria (The Greenhouse)   The Estufa Fria is in the handsome Parque Eduardo VII (☎ **21/388-22-78**), named after Queen Victoria's son to commemorate his three trips to Lisbon. Against a background of streams and rocks, tropical plants grow in such profusion that the place resembles a rain forest. The park lies at the top of avenida da Liberdade, crowned by a statue of the marquês de Pombal, with his "house pet," a lion. There's a 100$ (55¢) fee to enter the greenhouse, which is open daily, 9am to 6pm April to September and 9am to 5pm October to May. Metro: Rotunda. Bus: 2, 11, 12, 27, 32, 38, 44, 45, or 83.

Cemitério dos Ingleses (British Cemetery)   The British Cemetery lies up rua da Estrêla at one end of the Estrêla Gardens. It's famous as the burial place of Henry Fielding, the novelist and dramatist who's best known for *Tom Jones*. A sick man, Fielding went to Lisbon in 1754 to recover his health; his posthumous tract *Journal of a Voyage to Lisbon* tells the story of that trip. He reached Lisbon in August and died 2 months later. A monument honoring him was erected in 1830. Ring the bell for entry.

Aqueduto das Aguas Livres (Aguas Livres Aqueduct)   An outstanding baroque monument, this aqueduct runs from the Aguas Livres River in Caneças to the Casa da Agua reservoir in Amoreiras. The aqueduct, built under João V in the early 18th century, stretches for about 11 miles and is visible from the highway (N7) that leads to Sintra and Estoril. Part of it lies underground; some of the 109 stone arches are visible aboveground. The best view is of the 14 arches stretching across the valley of Alcântara from Serafina to the Campolide hills.

Jardim Botânico   Connected with the National Costume Museum is the Parque do Monteiro-Mor, largo Julio de Castilho, Lumiar. It's one of Lisbon's most beautiful botanical gardens. A **restaurant** (☎ **21/759-03-18**) lies on the park grounds. The park is open Tuesday to Sunday, 10am to 6pm June to September and 10am to 5:30pm October to May. Admission is 200$ ($1.10), free for children under 10. It's free to all Sunday morning. A combination ticket with the National Costume Museum costs 400$ ($2.25). Bus: 1, 3, 4, or 36.

The collection covers Egyptian, Greek, and Roman antiquities; a remarkable assemblage of Islamic art, including ceramics and textiles from Turkey and Persia; Syrian glass, books, bindings, and miniatures; and Chinese vases, Japanese prints, and lacquerware. The European displays include medieval illuminated manuscripts and ivories, 15th- to 19th-century painting and sculpture, Renaissance tapestries and medals, important collections of 18th-century French decorative works, French impressionist paintings, René Lalique jewelry, and glassware.

In a move requiring great skill in negotiation, Gulbenkian managed to buy art from the Hermitage in St. Petersburg. Among his most notable acquisitions are two Rembrandts: *Portrait of an Old Man* and *Alexander the Great.* Two other well-known paintings are *Portrait of Hélène Fourment* by Peter Paul Rubens and *Portrait of Madame Claude Monet* by Pierre-Auguste Renoir. In addition, we suggest that you seek out Mary Cassatt's *The Stocking.* The French sculptor Jean-Antoine Houdon is represented by a statue of *Diana.* Silver made by François-Thomas Germain, once used by Catherine the Great, is here, as well as one piece by Thomas Germain, the father.

As a cultural center, the Gulbenkian Foundation sponsors plays, films, ballet, and concerts, as well as a rotating exhibition of works by leading modern Portuguese and foreign artists.

2 More Attractions

✪ THE BAIRRO ALTO

Like the Alfama, the Bairro Alto (Upper City) preserves the characteristics of the Lisbon of yore. In location and population, it once was the heart of the city. Many of its buildings survived the 1755 earthquake. Today, it's home to some of the finest fado cafes in Lisbon, making it a center of nightlife. It's also a fascinating place to visit during the day, when its charming, narrow cobblestone streets and alleys, lined with ancient buildings, can be appreciated in the warm light coming off the sea.

Originally called Vila Nova de Andrade, the area was started in 1513 when the Andrade family bought part of the huge Santa Catarina, then sold the land as construction plots. Early buyers were carpenters, merchants, and ship caulkers. Some of them immediately resold their land to aristocrats, and little by little noble families moved to the quarter. The Jesuits followed, moving from their modest College of Mouraria to new headquarters at the Monastery of São Roque, where the Misericórdia (social assistance to the poor) of Lisbon proceeds today. The Bairro Alto gradually became a working-class section. Today, the quarter is also the domain of journalists—most of the big newspapers' plants are here. Writers and artists have been drawn here to live and work, attracted by the ambience and the good local cuisine.

The area is resoundingly colorful. From the windows and balconies, streamers of laundry hang out to dry, and there are cages of canaries, parrots, parakeets, and other birds. In the morning housewives hit the food markets, following the cries of the *varinas* (fishmongers) and other vendors. Women lounge in doorways or lean on windowsills to watch the world go by.

This area comes alive at night, luring visitors and natives with fado, food, discos, and small bars. Lisbon's budget restaurants, the *tascas,* abound, together with more deluxe eateries. Victorian lanterns light the streets, and people stroll leisurely.

CHURCHES

"If you want to see all of the churches of Lisbon, you'd better be prepared to stay here for a few months," a guide once told a tourist. True enough, the string of churches seems endless. What follows is a selection of the most interesting.

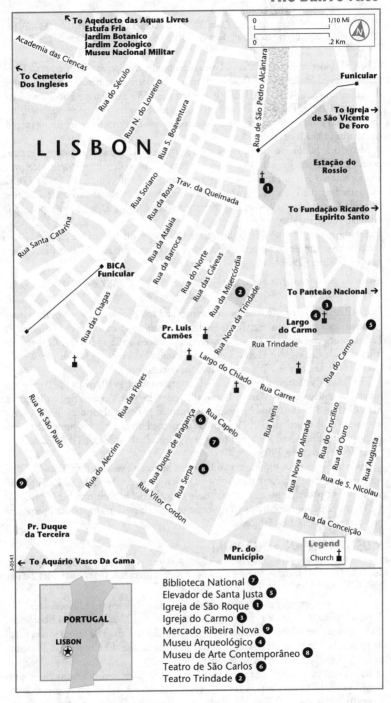

The Bairro Alto

**↖ To Aqeducto das Aquas Livres
Estufa Fria
Jardim Botanico
Jardim Zoologico
Museu Nacional Militar**

Academia das Ciencas

**← To Cemeterio
Dos Ingleses**

Funicular

**To Igreja →
de Sâo Vicente
De Foro**

**Estação do
Rossio**

LISBON

**To Fundação Ricardo →
Espirito Santo**

Rua do Século

Rua N. do Loureiro

Rua S. Boaventura

Rua de São Pedro Alcântara

Rua Soriano

Rua da Rosa

Trav. da Queimada

Rua da Atalaia

Rua da Barroca

Rua do Norte

Rua das Gáveas

Rua da Misercórdia

Rua Santa Catarina

**BICA
Funicular**

Rua das Chagas

To Panteão Nacional →

Rua Nova da Trindade

**Largo
do Carmo**

**Pr. Luis
Camões**

Rua Trindade

Rua do Carmo

Largo do Chiado

Rua Garret

Rua das Flores

Rua de São Paulo

Rua do Alecrim

Rua Capelo

Rua Duque de Bragança

Rua Serpa

Rua Vitor Cordon

Rua Ivens

Rua Nova do Almada

Rua do Crucifixo

Rua do Ouro

Rua de S. Nicolau

Rua Augusta

Rua da Conceição

**Pr. Duque
da Terceira**

← To Aquário Vasco Da Gama

**Pr. do
Município**

Legend
Church †

3-0541

PORTUGAL

LISBON ★

Biblioteca National **7**
Elevador de Santa Justa **5**
Igreja de São Roque **1**
Igreja do Carmo **3**
Mercado Ribeira Nova **9**
Museu Arqueológico **4**
Museu de Arte Contemporâneo **8**
Teatro de São Carlos **6**
Teatro Trindade **2**

Panteão Nacional. Largo de Santa Clara. ☎ **21/888-15-29.** Admission 250$ ($1.40), free for children under 10. Free to all Sun. Tues–Sun 10am–6:30pm. Closed holidays. Bus: 9 or 46. Tram: 28.

When a builder starts to work on a Portuguese house, the owner will often say, "Don't take as long as St. Engrácia." Construction on this Portuguese baroque church, Igreja de Santa Engrácia, began in 1682; it resisted the 1755 earthquake but wasn't completed until 1966. The building, with its four square towers, is pristine and cold, and the state has fittingly turned it into a neoclassic National Pantheon containing memorial tombs to heads of state.

Memorials honor Henry the Navigator; Luís Vaz de Camões, the country's greatest poet; Pedro Álvares Cabral, "discoverer" of Brazil; Afonso de Albuquerque, viceroy of India; Nuno Álvares Pereira, warrior and saint; and, of course, Vasco da Gama. Entombed in the National Pantheon are presidents of Portugal and several writers: Almeida Garrett, the 19th-century literary figure; João de Deus, a lyric poet; and Guerra Junquiero, also a poet.

Ask the guards to take you to the terrace for a beautiful view of the river. A visit to the pantheon can be combined with a shopping trip to the Flea Market (walk down campo de Santa Clara, heading toward the river).

Igreja da São Vicente de Fora. Largo de São Vicente. ☎ **21/887-64-70.** Free admission. Daily 9am–12:30pm and 3–6pm. Bus: 12 or 28. Tram: 28.

In this Renaissance church, the greatest names and some forgotten wives of the House of Bragança were laid to rest. It's more like a pantheon than a church. Originally a 12th-century convent, the church was erected between 1582 and 1627. At that time it lay outside the walls of Lisbon (hence the name, "St. Vincent Outside the Walls"). On the morning of the 1755 earthquake, the cupola fell in.

The Braganças assumed power in 1640 and ruled until 1910, when the Portuguese monarchy collapsed and Manuel II and the queen mother, Amélia, fled to England. Manuel II died in 1932, and his body was returned to Portugal for burial. Amélia, the last queen of Portugal, died in 1951 and is entombed here, as are her husband, Carlos I (the painter king), and her son, Prince Luís Felipe; both were killed by an assassin at praça do Comércio in 1908.

Aside from the royal tombs, one of the most important reasons for visiting St. Vincent is to see its spectacular tiles, some of which illustrate the fables of La Fontaine. While we suspect that no one has officially counted them, their number is placed at 1 million. Look for the curious ivory statue of Jesus, carved in the former Portuguese province of Goa in the 18th century.

MUSEUMS & AN AQUARIUM

Centro de Arte Moderna. Rua Dr. Nicolau de Bettencourt. ☎ **21/795-02-41.** Admission 500$ ($2.80), free for children under 10. Free to all Sun. Wed–Sun 10am–6pm, Tues 2–6pm. Metro: Praça d'Espagna. Bus: 16, 26, 31, 46, or 56.

Around the corner from the entrance to the Calouste Gulbenkian Museum (see "The Top Attractions," earlier in this chapter), the Center of Modern Art is Lisbon's first major permanent exhibition center of modern Portuguese art. The center shares park-like grounds with the Gulbenkian Foundation and was, like the Gulbenkian Museum, a legacy of the late Armenian oil magnate.

It's housed in a British-designed complex of clean lines and dramatically proportioned geometric forms with a Henry Moore sculpture in front. The museum owns some 10,000 items, including the works of such modern Portuguese artists as Souza-Cardoso, Almada, Paula Rego, João Cutileiro, Costa Pinheiro, and Vieira da Silva.

Fundação Ricardo Espírito Santo. Largo das Portas do Sol 2. ☎ **21/886-21-83.** Admission 800$ ($4.50), free for children under 12 and seniors. Tues–Sun 10am–5pm. Tram: 12 or 28. Bus: 37.

The Museum of Decorative Art is a foundation established in 1953 through the vision and generosity of Dr. Ricardo Espírito Santo Silva. He endowed it with items from his personal collection and set up handcraft workshops that encompass nearly all activities related to the decorative arts. The handsomely furnished museum is in one of the many aristocratic mansions that used to grace the Alfama. In the workshops you can see how perfect reproductions of furniture and other objects are made in the purest styles. The foundation also restores furniture, books, and Arraiolos rugs. The workshops may be visited on Wednesday.

The museum has been given the appearance of an inhabited palace, and visitors get a fairly accurate picture of what the interior of an upper-class Lisbon home might have been like in the 18th and 19th centuries. There are outstanding displays of furniture, Portuguese silver, and Arraiolos rugs, all from the 17th to the 19th century.

Museu do Chiado. Rua Serpa Pinto 4. ☎ **21/343-21-48.** Admission: Museum, 400$ ($2.25). Tues 2–6pm, Wed–Sun 10am–6pm. Metro: Chiado. Tram: 28. Bus: 58 or 100.

Housed in the former Convento de São Francisco, the Chiado museum was designed by the French architect Jean-Michel Wilmotte. It replaced the Museum of Contemporary Art. The permanent collection of post-1850 art and sculpture extends to 1950 and crosses the artistic bridge from romanticism to postnaturalism. Some excellent examples of modernism in Portugal are on display. The museum also houses frequently changing contemporary exhibitions devoted to art, sculpture, photography, and mixed media.

Museu Nacional Militar. Largo do Museu de Artilharia. ☎ **21/884-25-56.** Admission 300$ ($1.70) adults, 75$ (40¢) children. Tues–Sun 10am–5pm. Bus: 9, 25, 25A, 35, 39, or 46.

The National Military Museum sits in front of the Santa Apolónia Station, not far from terreiro do Paço and Castelo de São Jorge. It's on the site of a shipyard built during the reign of Manuel I (1495–1521). During the reign of João III, a new foundry for artillery was erected; it was also used for making gunpowder and storing arms to equip the Portuguese fleet. A fire damaged the buildings in 1726, and the 1755 earthquake destroyed them completely. Rebuilt on the orders of José I, the complex was designated as the Royal Army Arsenal. The museum, originally called the Artillery Museum, was created in 1851. Today, the facility exhibits not only arms but also painting, sculpture, tiles, and examples of architecture.

The museum boasts one of the world's best collections of historical artillery. Bronze cannons of various periods include one from Diu, weighing 20 tons and bearing Arabic inscriptions. Some iron pieces date from the 14th century. Light weapons, such as guns, pistols, and swords, are displayed in cases.

Museu de São Roque/Igreja de São Roque. Largo Trindade Coelho. ☎ **21/323-53-80.** Admission 150$ (85¢), free for children under 10 and seniors. Free to all Sun. Tues–Sun 10am–5pm. Metro: Chiado. Bus: 28.

The Jesuits founded St. Roque Church in the late 16th century. Beneath its painted wood ceiling, the church contains a celebrated chapel by Luigi Vanvitelli honoring John the Baptist. The chapel, ordered by the Bragança king João V in 1741, was assembled in Rome from such precious materials as alabaster and lapis lazuli, then dismantled, shipped to Lisbon, and reassembled. The marble mosaics look like a painting. You can also visit the sacristy, rich in paintings illustrating scenes from the lives of saints pertaining to the Society of Jesus. The Jesuits held great power in Portugal, at one time virtually governing the country for the king.

The St. Roque Museum inside the church merits a visit chiefly for its collection of baroque silver. A pair of bronze-and-silver torch holders, weighing about 840 pounds, is among the most elaborate in Europe. The 18th-century gold embroidery is a rare treasure, as are the vestments. The paintings, mainly from the 16th century, include one of a double-chinned Catherine of Austria and another of the wedding ceremony of Manuel I. Look for a remarkable 15th-century *Virgin (with Child) of the Plague* and a polished 18th-century conch shell that served as a baptismal font.

✪ **Oceanario de Lisboa.** Parque das Naçõas. ☎ **21/891-70-02.** Admission 1,500$ ($8.40) adults, 800$ ($4.50) students and children under 13. Daily 10am–7pm. Metro: Estação do Oriente.

This world-class aquarium is the most enduring and impressive achievement of EXPO '98. Marketed as the second-biggest aquarium in the world (the largest is in Osaka, Japan), it's in a stone-and-glass building whose centerpiece is a 1.3-million gallon (5-million liter) holding tank. Its waters consist of four distinct ecosystems that replicate the Atlantic, Pacific, Indian, and Antarctic oceans. Each is supplemented with above-ground portions on which birds, amphibians, and reptiles flourish. Look for otters in the Pacific waters, penguins in the Antarctic section, trees and flowers that might remind you of Polynesia in the Indian Ocean division, and puffins, terns, and seagulls in the Atlantic subdivision. Don't underestimate the national pride associated with this huge facility: Most Portuguese view it as a latter-day reminder of their former mastery of the seas.

3 Especially for Kids

Jardim Zoológico de Lisboa. Estada de Benfica 58. ☎ **21/726-93-49.** Zoo admission 1,950$ ($10.90) adults, 1,500$ ($8.40) children 3–8. Daily 9am–8pm. Metro: Mardim Zoologico. Bus: 15, 16, 16C, 26, 31, 46, 58, 63, or 68.

The Zoological Garden, with a collection of some 2,000 animals, occupies a flower-filled setting in the 65-acre Park of Laranjeiras. It's about a 10-minute subway ride from the Rossio. There are also a small tram and rowboats.

Planetário Calouste Gulbenkian. Praça do Império, Belém. ☎ **21/362-00-02.** Admission 500$ ($2.80) adults, 200$ ($1.10) children 10–18, free for seniors and children 6–9. Free to all Sun. Children under 6 not admitted. Bus: 29, 43, or 49.

An annex of the Maritime Museum, the Calouste Gulbenkian Planetarium is open to the public all year, with astronomical shows on Wednesday and Thursday at 11am, 3pm, and 4:15pm. On Saturday and Sunday there are sessions at 3:30pm and 5pm. On Sunday at 11am there's a special session for children. Each show lasts 50 minutes.

Aquário Vasco da Gama. Rua Direita do Dafundo. ☎ **21/419-63-37.** Admission 500$ ($2.80) adults, 200$ ($1.10) children 7–17, free for children under 7. Daily 10am–6pm. Metro: Algés. Bus: 29 or 51.

The Vasco da Gama Aquarium, on N6, near Algés on the Cascais railway line, has been in operation since 1898. Live exhibits include the eared seals pavilion and a vast number of tanks that hold fish and other sea creatures from all over the world. A large portion of the exhibits consists of zoological material brought back from oceanographic expeditions by Carlos I. They include preserved marine invertebrates, water birds, fish, and mammals, and some of the king's laboratory equipment.

4 City Strolls

Lisbon is a walker's delight; the city's principal neighborhoods abound with major sights and quiet glimpses into daily life.

Walking Tour 1—
The Alfama

Start: Take a taxi to Largo do Salvador.
Finish: Miradouro de Santa Luzia.
Time: 2 hours, or more if you add sightseeing time.
Best Times: Any sunny day.
Worst Times: Twilight or after dark.

The streets of the Alfama are best traversed on foot; at times you must walk up steep stone stairs. Once aristocratic, this fabled section has fallen into decay. Parts of it allow the visitor a rare opportunity to wander back in time. Be aware that the Alfama can be dangerous at night.

A good point to begin your tour is:

1. **Largo do Salvador.** Here you'll see a 16th-century mansion that once belonged to the count of Arcos. From here, turn down rua da Regueira to:

2. **Beco do Carneiro,** the "cul-de-sac of rams." This lane is impossibly narrow. Families live in houses that are at most just 4 feet apart. At the end of the alley, circle back using the flight of steps to your left to:

3. **Largo de Santo Estevão,** named after the church on the site. Round the church, and from the back proceed to the:

4. **Pátio das Flores,** using a flight of steps. Here you can see some of the most delightful little houses in the Alfama, adorned with characteristic Portuguese azulejos (tiles). Walk down the steps to rua dos Remédios, cutting right to:

5. **Largo do Chafariz de Dentro,** where you can see housewives drawing water from a fountain. Many apartments don't have hot and cold running water. From the square, connect with:

6. **Rua de São Pedro,** perhaps the most animated street in the Alfama. Strolling deep into the street, you'll probably attract a trail of boisterous children.

   You'll pass some local taverns; venture inside to sample a glass of *vinho verde* (green wine). Stepping out onto the narrow street again, you might cross paths with an old fisherman, saffron- and brown-colored nets draped over his shoulder, as he heads to the sea.

   Rua de São Pedro leads into:

7. **Largo de São Rafael,** which might convince you that the 17th century never ended. You pass a *leitaria* (dairy), which now sells milk by the bottle; cows used to be kept right inside. Off the square is:

8. **Rua da Judiaria,** so called because of the many Jews who settled here after escaping the Inquisition in Spain. Go back to largo de São Rafael, crossing to rejoin rua de São Pedro. Walk down the street to the intersection, forking left. You enter:

9. **Largo de São Miguel,** with its richly baroque church. From here, walk up rua de São Miguel, cutting left into:

10. **Beco de Cardosa,** where many fishermen and their wives (called *varinas*) still live. They often decorate their homes' wrought-iron balconies with flowers. At

Walking Tour—The Alfama

1. Largo do Salvador
2. Beco do Carniero
3. Largo de Santo Estevão
4. Pátio das Flores
5. Largo do Chafariz de Dentro
6. Rua de São Pedro
7. Largo de São Rafael
8. Rua da Judiaria
9. Largo de São Miguel
10. Beco de Cardosa
11. Largo das Portas do Sol
12. Miradouro Santa Luzia
    Cerca Moura

Legend
† Church
🌀 "Take a Break" stop

the end of the alley, you connect with Beco Santa Helena, which leads several flights to:

11. **Largo das Portas do Sol.** On this square is the Museum of Decorative Art (Fundação Ricardo Espírito Santo; see "More Attractions," earlier in this chapter).

☕ **TAKE A BREAK**   At the Miradouro de Santa Luzia are several tiny little **cafes** and **bars** with outside seating. Visitors from all over the world come here to order coffee and refreshments and take in the view of the shipping activity on the Tagus. These establishments are virtually all the same. We recommend **Cerca Moura,** largo das Portas do Sol 4 (☎ **21/887-48-59**), which offers the finest menu of snacks and drinks in the area, and affords a breathtaking view.

Continue south down rua Limoeiro until you reach one of the Alfama's most fabled belvederes:

12. **Miradouro de Santa Luzia,** a "balcony" with a view of the sea. The belvedere overlooks the houses of the Alfama as they sweep down in a jumbled pile to the Tagus.

Walking Tour 2— Baixa, the Center & the Chiado

Start: Praça do Comércio.
Finish: Elevador de Santa Justa.
Time: 3 hours.
Best Times: Any sunny day except Sunday.
Worst Times: Monday to Saturday from 7:30 to 9am and 5 to 7pm; Sunday, when shops are closed.

The best place to begin this tour is:

1. **Praça do Comércio** (also known as terreiro do Paço). This is at the waterfront end of Baixa. The House of Bragança ended here with the assassination of Carlos I and his elder son, Luís Filipe, in 1908. Regrettably, employees in the surrounding government buildings now use the praça as a parking lot. The marquês de Pombal designed the square when he rebuilt Lisbon following the 1755 earthquake. The equestrian statue is of Dom José, the Portuguese king at the time of the earthquake.

From the square, head west along avenida Ribeira das Naus until you reach:

2. **Cais do Sodré,** the train station. As you walk, you can enjoy views of the Tagus. At Cais do Sodré, you'll come to an open-air produce market on the waterfront behind the station. The Ribeiro fish market takes place in a domed building on the right daily (except Sunday) starting at dawn. *Varinas* (fishwives) carry away huge baskets of the catch of the day, which they deftly balance on their heads.

Return to praça do Comércio, but this time take a street away from the river, going east along rua do Arsenal until you reach the northwest corner of the square. After all that walking, especially if it's a hot day, you may need to:

☕ **TAKE A BREAK**   The **Café Martinho da Arcada,** praça do Comércio 3 (☎ **21/887-92-59**), has been the haunt of the literati since 1782, attracting such greats as the Portuguese poet Fernando Pessoa. The old restaurant has gone up-market, but it adjoins a cafe and bar, often called "the best cafe in Portugal."

If you're here for lunch, ask for a savory kettle of fish called *cataplana* or clam stew, served in the style of the Algarve.

After dining, head north along:

3. **Rua Augusta,** one of Baixa's best-known shopping streets. Leather stores and bookshops, embroidery outlets, and even home-furnishings stores line the bustling street. Many of the cross streets are closed to traffic, making window-shopping more enjoyable. The glittering jewelry stores you'll see often have some good buys in gold and silver. The many delis display vast offerings of Portuguese wine and cheese, along with endless arrays of the pastries Lisboans are so fond of.

The western part of this grid of streets is known as the **Chiado.** It's the city's most sophisticated shopping district. In 1988, a devastating fire swept the area, destroying many shops, particularly those on the periphery of rua Garrett. The area has bounced back with vigor.

Rua Augusta leads into the:

4. **Rossio,** formally called praça de Dom Pedro IV. The principal square of Baixa, it dates from the 1200s. During the Inquisition, it was the setting of many an auto-da-fé, during which Lisboans turned out to witness the torture and death of an "infidel," often a Jew. This was the heart of Pombaline Lisbon as the marquês rebuilt it following the 1755 earthquake. Neoclassical buildings from the 1700s and 1800s line the square, which has an array of cafes and souvenir shops. The 1840 Teatro Nacional de Dona Maria II sits on the north side of the square, occupying the former Palace of the Inquisition. The statue on its facade is of Gil Vicente, the "Shakespeare of Portugal," credited with the creation of the Portuguese theater.

Crowds cluster around two baroque fountains at either end of the Rossio. The bronze statue on a column is of Pedro IV, for whom the square is named. (He was also crowned king of Brazil as Pedro I.) Dozens of flower stalls soften the square's tawdry, overly commercial atmosphere.

☕ **TAKE A BREAK** The **Café Nicola,** praça de Dom Pedro IV 24–25 (☎ **21/346-05-79**), dates from 1777. It gained fame as a gathering place of the Portuguese literati in the 19th century. Though somewhat short on charm, it's the most popular cafe in Lisbon. Pastries, endless cups of coffee, and meals can be consumed indoors or out.

From the Rossio, proceed to the northwest corner of the square and walk onto the satellite square, praça da Camara. If you continue north, you'll reach the beginning of:

5. **Avenida da Liberdade,** Lisbon's main thoroughfare, laid out in 1879. More than 300 feet wide, the avenue runs north for a mile, cutting through the heart of the city. It has long been hailed as the most splendid boulevard of Lisbon, although many of the Art Deco and belle epoque mansions that once lines it are gone. Its sidewalks are tessellated in black and white. This is the heart of Lisbon's cinema district; you'll also pass airline offices, travel agencies, and other businesses. An open-air *esplanada* lies in the center. Almost immediately you come to:

6. **Praça dos Restauradores,** named for the men who, in 1640, revolted against the reign of Spain. The event led to the reestablishment of Portugal's independence. An obelisk in the center of the square commemorates the uprising. The deep-red Palácio Foz, now the Ministry of Information, is also on the square.

Walking Tour—Baixa, the Center & the Chiado

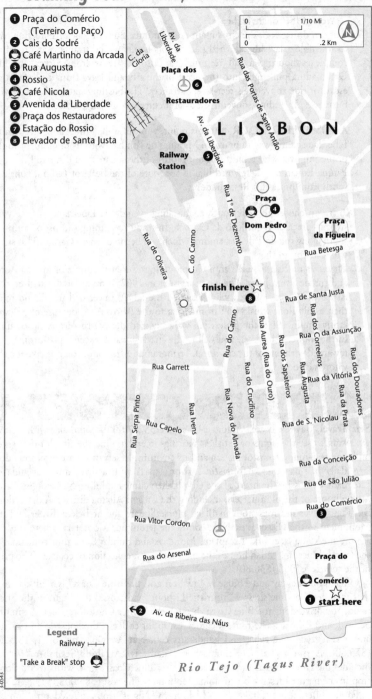

1 Praça do Comércio (Terreiro do Paço)
2 Cais do Sodré
Café Martinho da Arcada
3 Rua Augusta
4 Rossio
Café Nicola
5 Avenida da Liberdade
6 Praça dos Restauradores
7 Estação do Rossio
8 Elevador de Santa Justa

0   1/10 Mi
0   .2 Km

C. da Gloria

Av. da Liberdade

Plaça dos

Restauradores

Rua das Portas de Santo Antão

Av. da Liberdade

L I S B O N

Railway Station

Rua 1° de Dezembro

Rua de Oliveira

C. do Carmo

Praça

Dom Pedro

Praça da Figueira

Rua Betesga

finish here

Rua de Santa Justa

Rua do Carmo

Rua Nova do Almada

Rua do Crucifixo

Rua Aurea (Rua do Ouro)

Rua dos Sapateiros

Rua dos Correeiros

Rua Augusta

Rua da Vitória

Rua 1° da Assunção

Rua dos Douradores

Rua da Prata

Rua Garrett

Rua Serpa Pinto

Rua Capelo

Rua Ivens

Rua de S. Nicolau

Rua da Conceição

Rua de São Julião

Rua do Comércio

3

Rua Vitor Cordon

Rua do Arsenal

Praça do

Comércio

1 start here

2 Av. da Ribeira das Náus

Legend
Railway ⊢—⊢
"Take a Break" stop

Rio Tejo (Tagus River)

3-0543

West of the square is the:

7. Estação do Rossio, the city's main rail terminus. Built in mock Manueline style to resemble a lavishly adorned palace, this is one of the strangest architectural complexes housing a rail terminal in Europe. Trains from Sintra and the Estremadura pull right into the heart of the city and leave from a platform an escalator ride above the street-level entrances. The bustling station abounds with businesses, including souvenir shops and currency-exchange offices.

A POSSIBLE DETOUR   At this point, you can walk a mile along avenida da Liberdade all the way to praça do Marquês de Pombal, with its monument to the prime minister who rebuilt Lisbon. North of the square, you can stroll through Parque Eduardo VII. If you'd like to see more of the heart of Lisbon, continue south from praça dos Restauradores.

If you choose to walk south again along avenida da Liberdade, retrace your steps to praça de Dom João da Câmara. Instead of returning to Rossio, continue south along rua do 1 de Dezembro, which will become rua do Carmo. This street will lead you to the:

8. Elevador de Santa Justa, in a Gothic-style tower at the junction of rua Aurea and rua de Santa Justa. The elevator, built in 1902, is often falsely attributed to Alexandre-Gustave Eiffel, who designed the fabled tower of Paris. In no more than a minute it whisks you from Baixa to the Bairro Alto. Because of a devastating fire in 1992, the pedestrian walkway into the Bairro Alto is closed until further notice. However, you will find a snack bar and a scenic platform. You're rewarded with one of the city's grand panoramas. Afterward, you can take the elevator back down.

5 Organized Tours

Star Travel, travessa Escola Arauio 31 (☎ 21/352-00-00), is popular with visitors who want to see the sights or get their bearings in and around the city. It offers seven different year-round tours of Lisbon and its environs. Reservations are recommended.

A daily half-day tour, **"Touristic Lisbon"** starts with a drive down avenida da Liberdade to Rossio, the heart of the city. It then climbs uphill to St. George's Castle for a glimpse of the old quarters, including the ancient Alfama district. A drive along the Tagus River includes stops in Black Horse Square and at Belém Tower and the Monument to the Discoveries. Next comes the Jerónimos Monastery, where you can admire the stone lacework. Except on Mondays and holidays, the tour concludes at the Coach Museum, which houses the nation's largest collection of coaches. The price of the tour is 5,500$ ($30.80).

Offered on Tuesday and Thursday, **"Lisbon and the Blue Coast"** is a full-day tour that includes the same sites as "Touristic Lisbon," and crosses the Tagus in the afternoon. You drive along the Blue Coast through the "Three Castles" region of Sesimbra, Setúbal, and Palmela. The route includes a stop for coffee at the Pousada do Castelo, and a visit to a wine cellar and handcrafts center at Azeitão. The cost is 13,500$ ($75.60). A similar half-day tour, offered daily, is **"Arrábida/Sesimbra,"** which includes the same stops as the afternoon of the "Blue Coast" tour, with an additional stop in the nature preserve on Arrábida Mountain. The cost is 8,900$ ($49.85).

For a different view, take the **"Lisbon by Night"** tour, offered on Monday, Wednesday, and Friday evenings. It includes the same city stops as the other tours, then delves into the old quarter of Alcântara. The evening concludes with dinner and drinks at a restaurant featuring entertainment by a *fadista*. The price of the tour is 11,000$ ($61.60) with two drinks at the restaurant, or 13,000$ ($72.80) for dinner and drinks. A nighttime offering on Tuesday, Thursday, or Saturday, the **"Casino Estoril"** tour has the same itinerary as "Lisbon by Night," but concludes with dinner and an international show at the casino in the coastal resort of Estoril. The cost is 13,000$ ($72.80) with two drinks at the casino, or 14,500$ ($81.20) with dinner.

If you'd rather see the beaches, sign up for the **"Costa do Estoril/Sintra"** tour. It explores the coast at Estoril and Cascais, but also stops at the cliffs of Boca do Inferno, and the westernmost point in Europe, Cabo da Roca. You then cross Sintra Mountain to conclude at the Vila Palace (except on Wednesday when it's closed, and the trip ends at the Queluz Palace). It costs 8,900$ ($49.85). Another venture into Lisbon's surroundings, the **"Cascais/Mafra/Sintra/Estoril/Queluz"** tour strikes out daily for a full day that includes visiting the sumptuous 18th-century rooms of the Queluz Palace (closed on Tuesday) and the basilica in Mafra. After lunch in the seaside resort of Ericeira, it continues with the Pena palace in Sintra, and passage through the resorts of Guincho, Cascais, and Estoril. The price is 14,000$ ($78.40).

6 Outdoor & Recreational Activities

Lisbon itself has very few sports facilities. Most outdoor activities, such as water sports, fishing, and scuba diving, take place on the Costa do Sol, north of the city.

If you want to lie on the beach, you can take the train from Lisbon to the Costa do Sol; the main resorts there are Estoril and Cascais (see chapter 5).

FISHING Head for Sesimbra (see chapter 6), south of Lisbon, where local fishers take visitors out on boats looking for "the big one." Fees can be negotiated.

FITNESS CENTERS Some hotels recommended in chapter 3, including the Lisboa Sheraton, allow nonguests to use their health clubs for a fee. It's always best to call in advance.

GOLF The best courses lie along the Costa do Sol and Estoril Coast. The closest course to Lisbon (but not the best) is at the **Lisboa Sports Club,** Casal da Carregueira, near Belas (☎ **21/432-14-74**). It's about a 25-minute drive from the center; allow more time if traffic is heavy. A former playground for the Portuguese royal family, the **Penha Longa Golf Club,** Quinta da Penha Longa, is at Linhó, near Sintra (☎ **21/924-90-31**), 20 miles northwest of Lisbon. Designed by Robert Trent Jones Jr. in 1992, the resort is open to members and guests of the Caesar Park Penha Longa, Estate da Logoa Azul, Linhó, 2710 Sintra (☎ **21/924-90-11;** fax 21/924-90-07). Serious golfers should consider a stay at this 177-room Westin hotel overlooking the golf course. For 18 holes, greens fees range from 13,000$ to 17,000$ ($72.80 to $95.20).

JOGGING We used to recommend Parque Eduardo VII as the best place for jogging, but joggers there have recently been the victims of muggings. Daytime jogging in the park is risky enough, but nighttime jogging is unwise. Some joggers head for the Estádio Nacional (National Stadium), on the northern outskirts of the city on the road to Estoril. A track worn smooth by joggers winds through pine woods. It is also unsafe at night. You might prefer to jog along the Tagus between Ponte do 25 de Abril (the major suspension bridge) and Belém, heading north. Another possibility (but likely to be congested) is the median strip of the main street of Lisbon, avenida da Liberdade, from praça do Marquês de Pombal toward Baixa.

SWIMMING Options include the **Piscina do Campo Grande,** campo Grande (☎ 21/795-79-45); the **Piscina dos Olivais,** avenida Dr. Francisco Luís Gomes (☎ 21/851-46-30), 3 miles northeast of Lisbon; and the **Piscina do Areiro,** avenida de Roma (☎ 21/848-67-94). They charge 235$ ($1.30) for adults, 120$ (65¢) for children.

TENNIS Public tennis courts are available at **Campo Grande Estádio do 1 de Maio,** at Alvalade. To play, inquire at the main tourist office in Lisbon. Real tennis buffs will head for either the **Club de Tenis de Estoril** at Estoril or the **Quinta da Marinha** at Cascais.

7 Spectator Sports

The following activities are accessible from the city center.

BULLFIGHTING Bullfighting was once the sport of Portuguese noblemen. Unlike in neighboring Spain, the bull is not killed—a prohibition the marquês de Pombal instituted in the 18th century, after the son of the duke of Arcos was killed in the sport. Bullfights here differ in other respects from the Spanish version. Much ceremony and pageantry attend the drama: The major actors are elegantly costumed *cavaleiros,* who charge the bull on horseback, and *maços de forçado,* who grapple with the bull. Many find this face-to-face combat the most exciting component of the bullfight.

Warning: Bullfights are not spectacles fit for every taste. Even though the animal is not killed, many spectators find the event nauseating and object to the notion that it's a beautiful art form. The spears that jab the bull's neck draw blood, of course, making the animal visibly weaker. One reader wrote to us, "The animals are frightened, confused, and badgered before they are mercifully allowed to exit. What sport!"

The bullfighting season runs from Easter until mid-October. Lisbon's 8,500-seat **Praça de Touros,** campo Pequeno, avenida da República (☎ 21/793-24-42; Metro: Campo Pequeno), is the largest ring in the country. It usually presents fights on Thursday or Sunday afternoon. These *touradas* and the names of the stars are announced well in advance. Your hotel concierge can help you; many arrange tickets.

Another major bullring is the **Monumental de Cascais,** at Cascais (☎ 21/483-31-03), the resort west of Estoril on the Costa do Sol. The electric train from Lisbon runs to Cascais; from the station, the ring is an inexpensive taxi ride away, just outside the town center. The best place to buy tickets is the arena's ticket office. For the best seats, pay the usual 10% commission to an agency. The best is **Agência de Bilhetes para Espectáculos Públicos,** praça dos Restauradores (☎ 21/346-11-89). Tickets generally cost 2,000$ to 12,000$ ($11.20 to $67.20), depending on whether they're in the sun or shade.

SOCCER The Portuguese love football (known to Americans as soccer). Nothing—not even politics, boiled codfish, or fado—excites them more. When favorite teams are playing, soccer has a following of startling passion and hysteria. "It's better than sex," one fan told us, although his wife disagreed. It's also a way for pickpockets to earn a living. They work the intent crowds, lifting wallets during intense moments.

Lisbon has a trio of teams that play almost every Sunday, but the season stretches only from September to May. You'll miss out if you visit in the summer. Try to arrive at least an hour before the match is scheduled to begin; pregame entertainment ranges from marching bands to fireworks.

The best-known team is **Benfica,** which holds matches in northwest Lisbon at the gigantic **Estádio da Luz,** avenida General Norton Matos (☎ 21/726-61-29). One of the largest sports stadiums in Europe, it evokes memories of the legendary Eusebio,

> ## ❷ Did You Know?
>
> - Locals claim that the legendary Ulysses founded Lisbon.
> - The 1755 earthquake killed 30,000 people and left most of the city in ruins.
> - In Lisbon in 1481, Columbus proposed to João II his plan to sail west, but was turned down.
> - Henry Fielding, the great English novelist, arrived in Lisbon in 1754 to improve his health but died 2 months later; he is buried in the British cemetery in Lisbon.
> - In 1955, an Armenian oil magnate from Turkey (Calouste Gulbenkian) bequeathed to Lisbon one of the richest private art collections in the world.
> - After the Portuguese empire collapsed, refugees from the former colonies flooded Lisbon with African food and music.
> - The Igreja (church) de Santa Engrácia was begun in the 17th century but not completed until 1966.
> - Bullfights in Lisbon are called *touradas*. Unlike the Spanish, the Portuguese don't kill the bulls in the ring.
> - The Alfama was built Kasbah style, with many streets little more than 8 feet wide.
> - Guidebooks consistently credit the Frenchman Alexandre-Gustave Eiffel with the creation of Lisbon's famed Elevador de Santa Justa; actually, Raoul Mesnier de Ponsard, a Portuguese citizen (of French descent), designed it.

who led his team to five European championship finals in the 1960s. All young soccer players in Lisbon grow up with dreams of becoming the next Eusebio.

The **Sporting Clube de Portugal** plays at the **Estádio do José Alvalade** (☎ 21/759-41-61), in the north of the city, near campo Grande. The third team is Belém's **Belenenses,** who play at the **Estádio do Rastelo** (☎ 21/301-04-61). The team may not be as good or nearly as famous as Benfica, but don't tell that to a loyal fan during the heat of the game.

Tickets vary in price depending on the event but average 2,500$ ($14). You can buy them on the day of the game at all three stadiums. However, when Benfica plays Sporting, tickets usually sell out; buy them in advance at the booth in praça dos Restauradores. Tickets also go fast when FC Porto, from the northern city of Porto, Lisbon's main rival, is in town to play Benfica or Sporting.

8 Lisbon Shopping: From Antiques to Wine

Portuguese handcrafts often exhibit exotic influences, in large part because of the artisans' versatility and their skill in absorbing other styles. Portugal's vast history as a seafaring nation also surely has something to do with it. The best place to see their work is in Lisbon, where shopkeepers and their buyers hunt out unusual items from all over Portugal, including the Madeira Islands and the Azores.

SHOPPING AREAS   Shops operate all over the city, but **Baixa,** in downtown Lisbon, is the major area for browsing. **Rua Aurea** (Street of Gold, the location of the major jewelry shops), **rua da Prata** (Street of Silver), and **rua Augusta** are Lisbon's three principal shopping streets. The Baixa shopping district lies between the Rossio and the river Tagus.

Rua Garrett, in the Chiado, is where you'll find many of the more up-market shops. A major fire in 1988 destroyed many shops, but new ones have arisen.

Antique lovers gravitate to **rua Dom Pedro V** in the Bairro Alto. Other streets with antique stores include rua da Misericórdia, rua de São Pedro de Alcântara, rua da Escola Politécnica, and rua do Alecrim.

HOURS, SHIPPING & TAXES   Most stores open between 9 and 10am, close at noon for lunch, reopen at 2pm, and close for the day at 7pm. However, many shopkeepers take lunch from 1 to 3pm, so check before making the trip. On Saturday many stores open from 9 or 10am to 1pm; on Sunday, most stores in Lisbon and elsewhere in Portugal are closed. If the open hours of an individual place listed below differ from the norm, we give the specific hours.

Many establishments will **crate and ship** bulky objects. Any especially large item, such as a piece of furniture, should be sent by ship. Every antique dealer in Lisbon has lists of reputable maritime shippers. For most small and medium-size shipments, air freight isn't much more expensive than sending the items by ship. **TAP,** the Portuguese airline, has a separate toll-free U.S. number for cargo inquiries (☎ **800/221-7890**). Once in Lisbon, you can contact TAP to make air-shipping arrangements for larger purchases by calling the Lisbon cargo department offices at ☎ **21/841-54-33** or 21/841-50-01. They're open Monday to Friday from 8:30am to 7:30pm.

Remember that all your air-cargo shipments will need to clear customs in the United States, Canada, or your home country. This involves some additional paperwork and perhaps a trip to the airport near where you live. It's usually best to hire a commercial customs broker to do the work for you.

Value-added tax (called **IVA** in Portugal) ranges from 8% for basics, such as books and food, to 17% for luxury goods and for most of the things a foreign visitor would want or need during a holiday in Portugal. The tax is already factored into the sales price of virtually every good and service you're likely to come across, making payment seem relatively painless.

Foreigners traveling in Portugal with valid passports can obtain a refund for the value of the tax they pay on purchases in stores that display a government-approved tax-free logo if they spend more than 12,180$ ($68.20) in any one store. Ask before you make the purchase whether the store is equipped for the mechanics of arranging refunds on the tax (again, it's factored into the price), then ask the staff to fill out a "Tax Free Check." When you leave Portugal, you exchange the check for cash at the airport or frontier.

Note that the IVA you'll pay in the semiautonomous regions of the Azores and Madeira, ranging from 4% to 12%, is less than that on the Portuguese mainland. Other than that, tax refunds work the same.

When you leave Portugal, show your passport and purchases (which you must carry by hand, not check with your luggage) to the Portuguese Customs officials. If everything is in order, your Tax Free Checks will be stamped and you can redeem them at a Tax Refund counter for cash. Tax Refund offices are at the airport and the Lisbon harbor.

BEST BUYS   Regardless of where it's made—from the Azores to the remote northeast province of Trás-os-Montes—merchandise from all over Portugal ends up in Lisbon stores. If you're going to a particular province, try to shop locally, where prices are often about 20% less than those in Lisbon. A general exception is the fabled handmade **embroideries** from Madeira; prices there are about the same as in Lisbon.

Products made of **cork,** which range from place mats to cigarette boxes, are good buys. Collectors seek out **decorative glazed tiles.** You also might find good buys in

Lisbon in **porcelain** and **china,** in **fisher's sweaters** from the north, and in **fado recordings.**

Intricately woven lightweight **baskets** make attractive, practical gifts. It's best to shop for handmade **lace** in Vila do Conde, outside Porto, where you get a better buy; many Lisbon outlets carry the lace as well.

Pottery is one of the best buys in Portugal, and pottery covered with brightly colored roosters from Barcelos is legendary. In fact, the rooster has become the virtual symbol of Portugal. Blue-and-white pottery is made in Coimbra and often in Alcobaça. Our favorite items come from Caldas da Rainha. They include yellow-and-green dishes in the shape of vegetables (especially cabbage), fruit, animals, and even leaves. Vila Real is known for its black pottery, and Aceiro for polychrome pottery. Some red-clay pots from the Alentejo region in the southeast are based on designs that go back to the Etruscans. **Atlantis crystal** is another good buy. **Suede** and **leather,** as in Spain, are also good buys. In the Algarve, handsome **lanterns, fire screens,** and even **outdoor furniture** are constructed from metal, mainly copper, brass, and tin.

The best buy in Portugal, **gold,** is strictly regulated by the government. Jewelers must put a minimum of 19.2 karats into the jewelry they sell. **Filigree jewelry** in gold and silver is popular in Lisbon and elsewhere in Portugal. The art of ornamental open-work made of fine gold or silver wire dates to ancient times. The most expensive items—often objets d'art—are fashioned from 19¼-karat gold. Filigree is often used in depictions of caravels. Less expensive trinkets are often made of sterling silver, sometimes dipped in 24-karat gold.

Portugal is also famous for **Arraiolos carpets,** fine woolen rugs that have earned an international reputation. You can visit the little town of Arraiolos, in Alentejo. According to legend, Moorish craftsmen expelled from Lisbon in the early 16th century first made the rugs. The patterns were said to imitate Persian designs. Some Arraiolos carpets eventually find their way into museums.

SHOPPING A TO Z
ANTIQUES

Along both sides of the narrow **rua de São José** in the Graça District are treasure troves of shops packed with antiques from all over the world. Antique dealers from the United States come here to survey the wares. You'll find ornate spool and carved beds, high-back chairs, tables, wardrobes with ornate carving, brass plaques, copper pans, silver candelabra, crystal sconces, chandeliers, and a wide selection of wooden figures, silver boxes, porcelain plates, and bowls. But don't count on getting spectacular bargains.

Solar. Rua Dom Pedro V 68–70. ☎ **21/346-55-22.** Metro: Restauradores. Bus: 58 or 100.

Rua Dom Pedro V is another street lined with antique shops; this is our favorite. It's stocked with antique tiles salvaged from some of Portugal's historic buildings and manor houses. The condition of the tiles varies. Many date from the 15th century. The store also sells 18th- and 19th-century Portuguese ceramics and antique Portuguese furniture from different eras in varying price ranges.

ART GALLERIES

EuroArte. Rua Rodrigo de Fonseca 107. ☎ **21/385-40-69.** Metro: Marquês de Pombal. Bus: 2.

Many members of Iberia's emerging community of young painters hope to exhibit here. EuroArte's focus on contemporary art is roughly equivalent to that of the Galeria Yela (see below). Look for trends (often short-lived) and sometimes genuine value, should you catch artists on the road to fame.

Galeria 111. Campo Grande 113. ☎ **21/797-74-18.** Metro: Campo Grande. Tram: 36A or 57.

Operated by Manuel and Arlete de Brito since 1964, Galeria 111 is one of Lisbon's major art galleries. The wide-ranging exhibitions of sculpture, painting, and graphics include work by leading contemporary Portuguese artists. The gallery also sells drawings, etchings, silk screens, lithographs, art books, and postcards. Closed August 4 to September 4.

Galeria Sesimbra. Rua Castilho 77. ☎ **21/387-02-91.** Metro: Marquês de Pombal. Bus: 2, 11, or 58.

Near the Ritz Hotel, this is one of the city's leading art galleries, operated by one of the most distinguished art dealers in Iberia. It sells finest Portuguese painting, sculpture, and ceramics. A moderately liberal purveyor of fine contemporary artwork, the gallery avoids displaying artists who might strike some as too experimental and bizarre. The focus is on evocative pieces that appeal to the traditionally upscale clientele. The work is mainly by Portuguese artists, plus foreign artists "who have lived in Portugal long enough to get a feeling for the country." The best-known works are Agulha tapestries, whose controlled variation of stitching makes them more desirable than those made on looms. Former U.S. president Jimmy Carter owns an Agulha tapestry.

Galeria Yela. Rua Rodrigo de Fonseca 103. ☎ **21/388-03-99.** Metro: Marquês de Pombal.

This showcase near the Ritz Hotel prides itself on its cutting-edge expositions of emerging Iberian artists. The EuroArte gallery (see above) is its only rival on the contemporary-art scene. Look for acrylics, drawings, and engravings, most of them avant-garde in their focus and inspiration.

BASKETS

One of the best selections of Portuguese baskets is at the **Feira da Ladra** (see "Markets," below). Another good outlet is **Centro do Turismo e Artesanato** (see "Pottery & Ceramics," below).

BOOKS

Livraria Bertrand. Rua Garrett 73. ☎ **21/346-86-46.** Metro: Chiado.

You'll find a good selection at Livraria Bertrand, which has the latest best-sellers (Grisham and the like), along with some English-language magazines, travel guides, and maps of Lisbon and Portugal.

Livraria Britanic. Rua Luís Fernandes 14–16. ☎ **21/342-84-72.** Metro: Rato. Bus: 100.

This shop across from the British Institute in the Bairro Alto stocks the best selection of English-language books in Lisbon. Livraria Britanic has a good collection of popular novels in English, along with reprints of some classics.

Tabacaria Mónaco. Rossio 21. ☎ **21/346-81-91.** Metro: Rossio. Tram: 12, 20, or 28.

This narrow *tabacaria* (magazine and tobacco shop) opened in 1893 and has kept its original art nouveau look. Tiles from Rafael Bordalo Pinheiro and an adobe painting by Rosendo Carmalheira adorn the interior. You'll find a selection of international periodicals, guidebooks, and maps.

CARPETS

✪ **Casa Quintão.** Rua Serpa Pinto, 12-A. ☎ **21/346-58-37.** Metro: Chiado.

In Lisbon, Casa Quintão is *the* showcase for Arraiolos carpets. Rugs are priced by the square foot, according to the density of the stitching. Casa Quintão can reproduce intricate Oriental or medieval designs in rugs or tapestries, and can create customized patterns. The shop also sells materials and gives instructions on how to make your own carpets and tapestry-covered pillows. The staff is genuinely helpful.

CHINA & GLASSWARE

✪ **Vista Alegre.** Largo do Chiado 18. ☎ **21/347-54-81.** Metro: Chiado. Tram: 24.

This company, founded in 1824, turns out some of the finest porcelain dinner services in the country. It also carries objets d'art and limited editions for collectors, and a range of practical day-to-day tableware. The government presents Vista Alegre pieces to European heads of state as of their visits.

CORK PRODUCTS

Casa das Cortiças. Rua da Escola Politécnica 4–6. ☎ **21/342-58-58.** Bus: 58. Metro: Rato.

For typically Portuguese souvenirs, try Casa das Cortiças. "Mr. Cork," the original owner, became somewhat of a legend in Lisbon for offering "everything conceivable" that could be made of cork (of which Portugal controls a hefty part of the world market). He's long gone, but the store carries on. A surprising number of items are made from cork, including a chess set and a checkerboard.

CRYSTAL

Deposito da Mainha Grande. Rua de São Bento 234–242. ☎ **21/396-32-34.** Bus: 6, 49, or 100.

This unpretentious store offers glass items created in the century-old Marinha Grande factory. The merchandise includes traditional *bico de Jacpues* (thick patterned glass) service glasses, dishes, water pitchers, and salt and pepper shakers, as well as modern colored glass services. Other items include Atlantis crystal services and Vista Alegre porcelain. Atlantis crystal from Marinha Grande is renowned in Portugal, and there are some good buys here. You can purchase full services or individual pieces. Another store is down the road at rua de São Bento 418–420 (☎ **21/396-32-34**).

EMBROIDERY

Casa Bordados da Madeira. Rua do 1 de Dezembro 137. ☎ **21/342-14-47.** Metro: Restauradores. Bus: 1, 2, 36, or 44.

In the same building as the Hotel Avenida Palace, this establishment offers handmade embroideries from Madeira, Viana, and Lixa e Prado. If you wish to place an order, the staff will mail it to you. In the winter, the store sells thick fisher's sweaters from Póvoa do Varzim.

✪ **Casa Regional da Ilha Verde.** Rua Paiva de Andrade 4. ☎ **21/342-59-74.** Tram: 28. Metro: Chiado.

This shop in the Chiado specializes in handmade items, especially embroideries from the Azores—that's why it's called the "Regional House of the Green Island." Each piece carries a made-by-hand guarantee. Some of the designs on the linen place mats with napkins have been in use for centuries. You can get some good buys here.

✪ **Madeira House.** Rua Augusta 131–135. ☎ **21/342-68-13.** Metro: Chiado. Tram: 28 or 28B.

Madeira House specializes in high-quality regional cottons, linens, and gift items. Its other location in Lisbon is at av. da Liberdade 159 (☎ **21/315-15-58**).

⭐ **Príncipe Real.** Rua da Escola Politécnica 12–14. ☎ **21/346-59-45.** Bus: 58. Metro: Rato or Chiado.

Príncipe Real specializes in linens elegant enough to grace the tables of monarchs, including that of the late Princess Grace of Monaco. Owned by Cristina Castro and her son, Victor Castro, this store is one of the last that does artistic manual embroidery by order. It produces some of Europe's finest tablecloths and sheets in cotton, linen, and organdy. The owner-designer sells to famous names (the Rockefellers, Michael Douglas, the Kennedys, and many European members of royalty), but the merchandise is not beyond the means of the middle-class tourist—especially with beneficial escudo exchange rates. The shop's factory handles custom orders quickly and professionally. It employs 80 skilled workers who can execute a linen pattern to match a client's favorite porcelain or one of Cristina Castro's original designs.

Teresa Alecrim. Rua Nova do Almada 76. ☎ **21/346-30-69.** Tram: 28 or 28B. Bus: 2. Metro: Chiado.

This store bears the name of the owner, who creates refined embroideries in the style of Laura Ashley. You'll see sheets, pillowcases, towels, and bedcovers in plain and patterned cotton, plus monogrammed damask cotton hand towels.

FADO RECORDINGS

Valentim de Carvalho. Rossio 57. ☎ **21/322-44-00.** Metro: Rossio.

This large, modern store carries a comprehensive roster of recordings by the country's most popular fado artists. If you want an introduction to Portugal's most enduring musical form, names to look for include Amália Rodriguez, Nuno Câmara Pereira, Carlos Ducarmo, and Carlos Paredes. The *Fado Capital* series of CDs showcases at least three lesser-known fadistas on each recording.

Valentim de Carvalho carries books about the music world and English-language books in addition to music. On the ground floor, you'll find fado compact discs and LPs, Portuguese folk music, contemporary rock, and recordings by international artists in musical styles from classical to punk rock.

FASHION

⭐ **Ana Salazar,** an internationally known name in fashion, is the most avant-garde Portuguese designer of women's clothes. Known for her stretch fabrics, Salazar designs clothes that critics have called "body-conscious yet wearable." Her main store is at rua do Carmo 89 (☎ **21/347-22-89;** metro: Rossio; bus: 21); has another location in Lisbon at av. de Roma 16E (☎ **21/848-67-99**).

Two of Lisbon's most prominent menswear stores are **Rosa y Peixeira,** av. da Liberdade 204 (☎ **21/311-03-50;** metro: Avenida); and **Laurenço y Santos,** praça dos Restauradores 47 (☎ **21/346-25-70;** metro: Restauradores). Both are places where the concierge at a grand hotel might refer a well-dressed guest who needs to augment his wardrobe with anything from a business suit to a golf outfit.

LEATHER & SUEDE

Buckles & Company. Benovo Comercial do Vestuareo Alea Cascals, estrada nacional 9 (N9), near Estoril. ☎ **21/460-25-62.**

In a mirrored, wood-paneled setting, this store specializes in high-quality leather jackets, bags, and shoes, as well as clothing by national and foreign makers. The staff is knowledgeable. The store is accessible by train from Cais do Sodré.

MARKETS

At the **Feira da Ladra,** you can experience the fun of haggling for bargains. The open-air street market resembles the flea markets of Madrid and Paris. Nearly everything you can imagine is for sale. Vendors peddle their wares on Tuesday and Saturday; for the finest pickings, go in the morning. The market is about a 5-minute walk from the waterfront in the Alfama district. Start your browsing at campo de Santa Clara. Portable stalls and individual displays climb the hilly street.

METALS

Casa Maciel Ltda. Rua da Misericórdia 63–65. ☎ **21/342-24-51.** Metro: Rossio. Tram: 10, 24, 29, or 30.

Founded in 1810 as a specialized tinker shop that created the city's best lanterns and original cake molds, this house has distinguished itself in numerous national and international contests. You can select from the in-house patterns or have the artisans create pieces from your designs; the store will also ship items.

PORCELAIN

Many stores in Lisbon sell Portuguese porcelain—notably the landmark **Fábrica Viúva Lamego** (see "Tiles," below). **Deposito da Marinha Grande** (see "Crystal," above) carries a good selection of Vista Alegre porcelain.

POTTERY & CERAMICS

Centro do Turismo e Artesanato. Rua Castilho 61B. ☎ **21/386-38-30.** Metro: Rotunda. Tram: 25 or 26. Bus: 20, 22, or 27.

Here you'll find handcrafts, including pottery, ceramics, baskets, and embroidery. The good selection of pottery and ceramics includes items from all over Portugal. Worthwhile ceramic objects begin at around 1,500$ ($8.40) each, and some less significant objects (ashtrays, small vases, and the like) might begin at around 750$ ($4.20). The extensive clothing selection includes a Póvoa do Varzim sweater for 5,000$ to 9,000$ ($28 to $50.40) and a fisher's plaid shirt for 9,000$ ($50.40). The shop also stocks Portuguese wines and liqueurs.

SILVER, GOLD & FILIGREE

Joalharia do Carmo. Rua do Carmo 87B. ☎ **21/342-42-00.** Metro: Rossio. Bus: 21, 31, 36, or 41.

Nearly a century old, this is one of the best shops in Lisbon for filigree work. It stocks everything from simple, elegant pendants to models of fully rigged caravels fashioned entirely from thin strands of gold or silver (or both) woven together. All the silver pieces are handmade. Precious or semiprecious stones adorn some gold items. You'll also see platinum pieces, often in stunning designs. For the simplest items, such as bangles and earrings, prices start at around 3,500$ ($19.60), but most of the inventory is more valuable.

✪ W. A. Sarmento. Rua Aurea 251. ☎ **21/347-07-83.** Metro: Rossio. Tram: 28 or 28B. Bus: 11, 13, 25, or 81.

At the foot of the Santa Justa elevator, W. A. Sarmento has been in the hands of the same family for well over a century. They are the most distinguished silver- and goldsmiths in Portugal, specializing in lacy filigree jewelry, including charm bracelets. The shop has been Lisboans' favorite place to buy treasured confirmation and graduation gifts, and its clientele includes Costa do Sol aristocracy as well as movie stars and diplomats.

SWEATERS

The vendors at the **Feira da Ladra** marketplace (see "Markets," above) sell a wide selection of Portuguese sweaters. You can also check out the selection at **Centro do Turismo e Artesanato** (see "Pottery & Ceramics," above). **Casa Bordados da Madeira** (see "Embroidery," above) carries a fine selection of Nazaré-style fisher's sweaters.

Casa do Turista. Av. da Liberdade 159. ☎ **21/315-15-58.** Metro: Avenida. Bus: 41, 45, 44, or 46.

This centrally located store stocks more than 2,000 handmade items from throughout Portugal. Regional clothing and accessories include sweaters from Póvoa do Varzim and traditional scarves from Minho. (The fabled fisher's sweaters of Nazaré are much more likely to be made in Póvoa do Varzim than in Nazaré.) Other items for sale include embroidered hand towels and napkins, tablecloths, ceramics, and straw baskets.

TILES

Fábrica Viúva Lamego. Largo do Intendente 25. ☎ **21/885-24-08.** Metro: Intendente. Tram: 17, 19, or 28.

Founded in 1879, this shop offers contemporary tiles—mostly reproductions of old Portuguese motifs—and pottery, including an interesting selection of bird and animal motifs. When you reach the store, you'll know you're at the right place: Its facade is decorated with colorful glazed tiles.

✪ **Sant'Anna.** Rua do Alecrim 95–97. ☎ **21/342-25-37.** Metro: Estação do Cais do Sodré. Tram: 20, 29, or 30.

Founded in 1741 in the Chiado district, Sant'Anna is Portugal's leading ceramic center. It's famous for its glazed tiles. You can also visit the factory at calçada da Boa Hora 96 (☎ **21/363-31-17**), but you must telephone ahead for an appointment. The artisans who create some of the designs are among the finest in Europe, and many of them employ designs in use since the Middle Ages.

WINE

Mercearia Liberdade. Av. da Liberdade 207. ☎ **21/354-70-46.** Metro: Avenida. Bus: 41, 44, or 45.

Some of the best port and Madeira wines in the country line the green shelves at this charming, typically Portuguese shop. A bottle of wine costs 3,000$ to 160,000$ ($16.80 to $896). The shop also sells regional handcrafts and ceramics created by prominent artists. Portuguese wine merchants approach the question of vintage years for port wine gingerly, because quality varies even within a given year. Despite their wariness, 1994 is generally considered an excellent year.

9　Lisbon After Dark

If you have only one night in Lisbon, spend it at a fado club. The nostalgic sounds of fado, Portuguese "songs of sorrow," are at their best in Lisbon—the capital attracts the greatest fadistas (fado singers) in the world. However, don't go to hear fado—high art in Portugal—and plan to carry on a private conversation; it's bad form. (For more on fado, see the box "Fado: The Music of Longing," on page 127.) Most of the authentic fado clubs cluster in the Bairro Alto and in the Alfama, between St. George's Castle and the docks. You can "fado hop" between the two quarters. If you're visiting the

Fado: The Music of Longing

The *saudade* (Portuguese for "longing" or "nostalgia") that infuses the country's literature is most evident in *fado*. The traditional songs express Portugal's sad, romantic mood. The traditional performers are women (*fadistas*), often accompanied by a guitar and a viola.

Experiencing the nostalgic sounds of fado is essential to apprehending the Portuguese soul. Fado is Portugal's most vivid art form; no visit to the country is complete without at least one night spent in a local tavern listening to this traditional folk music.

A rough translation of *fado* is "fate," from the Latin *fatum* ("prophecy"). Fado songs usually tell of unrequited love, jealousy, or a longing for days gone by. The music, as is often said, evokes a "life commanded by the Oracle, which nothing can change."

Fado became famous in the 19th century when Maria Severa, the beautiful daughter of a gypsy, took Lisbon by storm. She sang her way into the hearts of the people of Lisbon—especially the count of Vimioso, an outstanding bullfighter. Legend has it that present-day fadistas wear a black-fringed shawl in her memory.

The most famous 20th-century exponent of fado was Amália Rodrigues, who was introduced to American audiences in the 1950s at the New York club La Vie en Rose. Born into a simple Lisbon family, she was discovered while walking barefoot and selling flowers on the Lisbon docks, near the Alfama. For many she is the most famous Portuguese figure since Vasco da Gama. Swathed in black, sparing of gestures and excess ornamentation, Rodrigues almost single-handedly executed the transformation of fado into an international form of poetic expression.

Alfama, have the taxi driver let you off at **largo do Chafariz,** a small plaza a block from the harbor; in the Bairro Alto, get off at **largo de São Roque.** Most of the places we recommend lie only a short walk away.

Fado outshines all other nighttime entertainment in Lisbon. For a change of pace and more information about nighttime attractions, go to the tourist office, which maintains a list of events. Another helpful source is the **Agência de Bilhetes para Espectáculos Públicos** in praça dos Restauradores (☎ **21/346-11-89**). It's open daily from 9am to 10pm; go in person instead of trying to call. The agency sells tickets to most theaters and cinemas, except the Teatro Nacional de São Carlos; for those tickets, go to the theater box office (see below).

Also consult a copy of ***What's On in Lisbon*** or ***Your Companion in Portugal,*** available at most newsstands. You might also consult *Sete,* a weekly magazine with entertainment listings, or the free monthly guides *Agenda Cultural* and *LISBOaem.* Your hotel concierge is also a good bet for information, because one of his or her duties is reserving seats. The local newspaper, *Diário de Notícias,* carries all cultural listings, but only in Portuguese.

By the standards of the United States and Canada, "the party" in Lisbon begins late. Many bars don't even open until 10 or 11pm, and very few savvy young Portuguese would set foot in a club before 1am. The Bairro Alto, with some 150 restaurants and bars, is the most happening place after dark.

THE PERFORMING ARTS
OPERA & BALLET

Teatro Nacional de São Carlos. Rua Serpa Pinto 9. ☎ **21/346-59-14.** Tickets 2,500$–9,600$ ($14–$53.75). Box office daily 1–7pm. Tram: 24, 28, or 28B. Bus: 15 or 100.

The Teatro Nacional de São Carlos attracts opera and ballet aficionados from all over Europe. Top companies from around the world perform at the 18th-century theater. The season begins in mid-September and extends through July. There are no special discounts.

CLASSICAL MUSIC

Museu da Fundação Calouste Gulbenkian. Av. de Berna 45. ☎ **21/793-51-31.** Metro: Sebastião. Bus: 16, 18, 26, 31, 42, 46, or 56.

From October through June, concerts, recitals, and occasionally ballet performances take place here; sometimes there are also jazz concerts.

Teatro Municipal de São Luís. Rua António Maria Cardoso 40. ☎ **21/325-08-00.** Tickets 1,000$–2,500$ ($5.60–$14). Metro: Estação Cais do Sodré. Tram: 10, 28, or 28B.

Chamber music and symphony concerts are often performed here, as well as ballet.

THEATER

Teatro Nacional de Dona Maria II. Praça de Dom Pedro IV. ☎ **21/342-22-10.** Tickets 1,500$–3,000$ ($8.40–$16.80); 50% discount for students with valid ID. Metro: Rossio. Bus: 21, 31, 36, or 41.

At the most famous theater in Portugal, the season usually begins in the autumn and lasts through spring. It presents a repertoire of both Portuguese and foreign plays, with performances strictly in Portuguese.

THE CLUB & MUSIC SCENE
FADO CLUBS

In the clubs listed below, it isn't necessary to have dinner. You can just have a drink. However, you often have to pay a minimum consumption charge. The music begins between 9 and 10pm, but it's better to arrive after 11pm. Many clubs stay open until 3am; others, until dawn.

Adega Machado. Rua do Norte 91. ☎ **21/347-05-50.** Cover (including 2 drinks) 2,500$ ($14). Bus: 58 or 100.

This spot has passed the test of time and is one of the country's favored fado clubs. Alternating with such modern-day fadistas as the critically acclaimed Marina Rosa are folk dancers whirling, clapping, and singing native songs in colorful costumes. Dinner is à la carte, and the cuisine is mostly Portuguese, with a number of regional dishes. Expect to spend 5,000$ to 6,000$ ($28 to $33.60) for a complete meal. The dinner hour starts at 8:30pm, music begins at 9:15pm, and the doors don't close until 3am. Open Tuesday to Sunday.

A Severa. Rua das Gaveas 51. ☎ **21/346-40-06.** Cover (including 2 drinks) 3,500$ ($19.60). Bus: 20 or 24.

Good food and the careful selection of fadistas make this a perennial favorite. Every night top male and female singers appear, accompanied by guitar and viola music, alternating with folk dancers. In a niche you'll spot a statue honoring the club's namesake, Maria Severa, the legendary 19th-century gypsy fadista. As difficult or as unsettling as it may be to imagine, before he became president Richard Nixon came here with his wife, Patricia, leading a congalike line between tables while warbling the refrain, "Severa . . . Severa . . . Severa." After midnight, tourists seem to recede a bit in favor of loyal habitués, who request and sometimes join in on their favorite fado number (though not usually forming Nixonian conga lines).

The kitchen turns out regional dishes based on recipes from the north of Portugal. Expect to spend at least 6,000$ ($33.60) per person for a meal with wine. Open Friday to Wednesday from 8pm to 3:30am.

Lisboa a Noite. Rua das Gaveas 69. ☎ **21/346-85-57.** Cover (including 2 drinks) 3,000$ ($16.80). Bus: 58 or 100.

"Lisbon at Night" is one of several well-recommended fado clubs that compete for the attention and business of local residents and foreign visitors. The undisputed star of the outfit is tempestuous owner Fernanda Maria. In recent years she has made room for at least four other singers, the most visible of whom is João Kuaros. Together they evoke the nostalgia of old Portugal. The setting—a former stable decorated in a style inspired by the Age of Discovery—is rustic yet luxurious. When it's cold outside, scented eucalyptus logs crackle in a high fireplace. In the rear is an open kitchen and charcoal grill. House specialties include dry codfish Fernanda Maria and steak Lisboa a Noite flambé. The price of an average meal is around 8,000$ ($44.80). Open Monday to Saturday from 8pm to 3am; shows begin at 9:30pm.

Luso. Travessa da Queimada 10. ☎ **21/342-22-81.** Cover (credited toward drinks) 3,500$ ($19.60). Bus: 58 or 100.

In a vaulted network of 17th-century stables, Luso is one of the most famous and enduring fado clubs of the Bairro Alto. Despite a recent trend toward the touristy, it still exerts a folkloric appeal, as it has since it was transformed into a restaurant with music in the 1930s. The entertainment and regional food are presented most nights to some 160 patrons. Full dinners are served, costing 6,000$ ($33.60). Open Monday to Saturday 8pm to 3am; the show runs from 9:30 to 11pm.

Parreirinha da Alfama. Beco do Espírito Santo 1. ☎ **21/886-82-09.** Cover (credited toward drinks) 2,000$ ($11.20). Bus: 39 or 46.

Every fadista worth her shawl seems to have sung at this old-time cafe, just a minute's walk from the docks of the Alfama. It's fado and fado only here, not folk dancing, and the place has survived more or less unchanged since its establishment in the early 1950s. In the first part of the program fadistas get the popular songs out of the way, then settle in to their more classic favorites. You can order a good regional dinner for around 5,000$ ($28), although many visitors opt to come here just to drink. Open daily from 8:30pm to 2:30am; music begins at 9:30pm. The atmosphere is a lot more convivial after around 10:30pm, when local stars (who include such luminaries and divas as Lina Maria) have warmed up the crowd a bit.

COFFEEHOUSES

To the Portuguese, the coffeehouse is an institution, a democratic parlor where they can drop in for their favorite libation, abandon their worries, relax, smoke, read the paper, write a letter, or chat with friends about tomorrow's football match.

The coffeehouse in Portugal, however, is now but a shade of its former self. The older and more colorful places, filled with turn-of-the-century charm, are rapidly yielding to chrome and plastic.

One of the oldest surviving coffeehouses in Lisbon, **A Brasileira,** rua Garrett 120 (☎ **21/346-95-41;** metro: Rossio), lies in the Chiado district. It has done virtually nothing to change the opulent but faded art nouveau decor that has prevailed since it became a fashionable rendezvous in 1905. Once a gathering place of Lisbon's literati, it was the favored social spot of the Portuguese poet Bocage of Setúbal, whose works are read by high school students throughout Portugal. He was involved in an incident that has since been elevated into Lisbon legend: When accosted by a bandit who asked him where he was going, he is said to have replied, "I am going to the Brasileira, but if you shoot me I am going to another world." Patrons sit at small tables on chairs made of tooled leather, amid mirrored walls and marble pilasters. A statue of the great Portuguese poet Fernando Pessoa sits on a chair amid the customers. At a table, sandwiches run 260$ to 550$ ($1.45 to $3.10), pastries are 150$ to 300$ (85¢ to $1.70), a demitasse costs 150$ (85¢), and bottled beer goes for 200$ ($1.10). Prices are a bit lower at the bar, but you'll probably want to linger awhile—we recommend sitting down to recover from the congestion and heat. It's open daily from 7:30am to 2pm; cash only.

Although lacking A Brasileira's tradition and style, the **Pastelaria Suiça,** on the south corner of praça de Dom Pedro IV in the Baixa (☎ 21/321-40-90), is a sprawling cafe-pastelaria. It stretches all the way back to the adjoining praça da Figueira. This house draws more visitors than any other cafe in Lisbon. The outdoor tables fill first, especially in fair weather. In addition to serving an array of coffee and tea, the pastelaria is also known for its tempting pastries baked on-site. The atmosphere is boisterous and the place generally mobbed. Open daily 7am to 10pm.

Another possibility is **Versailles,** av. da República 15 (☎ 21/354-63-40), long known as the grande dame of Lisbon coffeehouses. It's also an ideal place for afternoon tea, in a faded but elegant 60-year-old setting of chandeliers, gilt mirrors, and high ceilings. As an old-fashioned and formal touch, immaculately attired waiters serve customers from silver-plated tea services. In addition to coffee and tea, the house specialty is hot chocolate. The homemade cakes and pastries are delectable (they're baked on site). Open daily 7am to 10pm.

PORT-WINE TASTING

Solar do Vinho do Porto. Rua de São Pedro de Alcântara 45. ☎ **21/347-57-07.** Bus: 58 or 100.

Solar is devoted exclusively to the drinking and enjoyment of port in all its glory and varieties. A quasi-governmental arm of the Port Wine Institute established the bar a few years after World War II as a low-key merchandizing tool. In a 300-year-old setting near the Bairro Alto and its fado clubs, about 50 yards from the upper terminus of the Glória funicular, it exudes Iberian atmosphere. The *lista de vinhos* includes more than 200 types of port wine, in an amazing variety of sweet, dry, red, and white. A glass of wine costs 200$ to 4,210$ ($1.10 to $23.60). Open Monday to Saturday 2pm to midnight.

DANCE CLUBS & LIVE MUSIC

The Bar of the Café Alcântara. Rua Maria Luisa Holstein 15. ☎ **21/363-71-76.** No cover. Bus: 12 or 18.

Although this establishment draws most of its business from its sophisticated restaurant (see the Café Alcântara in "Where to Dine" in chapter 3), many club-hoppers come here only for the bar. It's in a former factory and warehouse beside the river, decorated with accessories that evoke a railway car in turn-of-the-century Paris. The patrons—Americans, Portuguese, English, Germans, and Brazilians—aren't shy about striking up dialogues with attractive newcomers. Draft beer in the bar begins at 550$ ($3.10); imported whisky sells for 1,000$ ($5.60) and up. Expect lots of deliberately provocative outrageousness, gay customers mingling with straights, and, sometimes, one of the highest percentages of flamboyant drag queens in Lisbon. Open nightly from 8pm to 3am.

Blues Café. Rua Cintura do Armazan 3. ☎ **21/395-70-85.** Cover 10,000$ ($56) if full; otherwise free. Tram: 15.

You'll probably like this place (as we do), even though it has very little to do with blues music and doesn't even remotely resemble a cafe. It's in a publike space on the river; an eagle's-nest balcony rings one floor, Docks (see below) is next door, and there's a restaurant that serves late-night platters of uncomplicated Portuguese food. The patrons, usually in their 20s to early 30s, are well versed in the nuances of the latest hip-hop and garage music. Beer costs 600$ to 900$ ($3.35 to $5.05) a bottle, depending on the brand. Open Monday to Thursday 8:30pm to 4am, Friday to Sunday 8:30pm to 6am.

Docks. Av. do 24 de Julio, at Centro Mare. ☎ **21/395-08-56.** Cover 10,000$ ($56) if full; otherwise free. Tram: 15.

As its name implies, this place is on the Tagus, with windows overlooking the river. Sophisticated and stylish, with one of the most beautiful interiors in the neighborhood, it attracts a 30-something clientele. The club has vaguely nautical decor and one busy floor that's ringed, amphitheater-style, with a circular mezzanine overlooking the action below. Beer costs around 600$ ($3.35) a bottle, and recorded music plays in ways that sometimes gets people up and dancing. Open Tuesday to Saturday 11:30pm to 6am.

Model's. Travessa Teixeira Junior 6. ☎ **21/363-39-59**. Cover 1,200$ ($6.70). Bus: 4, 27, 28, 32. Tram: 15, 18.

If you're up for late-night, high-energy partying with student-aged hipsters who like to dance, this is the place to go. The large, echoing space contains virtually indestructible bar tops and dance floors. The music changes every night, according to the preferences of management and the DJs—tribal underground, techno, garage, house, and sometimes a scattering of salsa and merengue. Opens Tuesday to Sunday 11:30pm to 4am .

Kapital. Av. do 24 de Julio 68. ☎ **21/395-71-01.** Cover 1,000$–4,500$ ($5.60–$25.20). Tram: 15.

Next to the docks of the Tagus, this disco and bar appeals to one of the widest socioeconomic ranges of Portuguese society. You're likely to find surprisingly elite patrons rubbing elbows with regular folks who have managed to overlook the fact that the late hour might not be conducive to work the following day. Detractors claim that Kapital is for people with money or for rich wannabes; still, it can be a whole lot of fun, especially if you limit your visit to a single night so that the novelty doesn't wear off. In the animated disco on the ground floor, the music is loud, sometimes experimental, danceable, and up-to-date. The second floor contains a central bar surrounded by rows of comfortable chairs and sofas; the third floor has a disco with predominantly 1980s dance music. The cover charge varies widely depending on whether the doorman thinks you're cool, well-dressed, or rich-looking enough. Open nightly 11:30pm till dawn; Sunday, Monday, and Tuesday are least crowded.

Kremlin. Escadinhas da Praia 5. ☎ **21/390-87-60.** Cover from 1,000$ ($5.60). Bus: 32 or 37.

This cellar-level establishment, a former stable, attracts a hip crowd of late-night revelers, both hetero and homo. The entertainment ranges from heavy metal to techno, and management seems to change the decor almost as frequently as it does the DJs. The cover charge is usually around 1,000$ ($5.60), but can sometimes go higher, depending on the whim of the doorman. The club is less prestigious and crowded than in the past, so the entrance policy is less restrictive than it used to be. Beer costs 600$

($3.35); a whisky with soda goes for 1,000$ ($5.60). Open Tuesday to Sunday 11am to 5am.

Plateau. Escadinhas da Praia 3. ☎ **21/396-51-16.** Cover 1,000$ ($5.60). Tram: 15.

Near the Kapital and Kremlin clubs (see above), this is a one-story nightclub with a confetti-colored decor and a mixed clientele. The elite mingle with everyday folk who are just looking for love and good music. What you see is what you get—comfortable seating, cooperative bartenders skilled at mixing anything you can think of, and an appealing mixture of rock 'n' roll, garage, hip-hop, and, on rare occasions, even reggae. Surprisingly, the place is less dance oriented than you might think—many patrons come to watch and listen, not to boogie. Open Tuesday to Saturday midnight to 4:30am.

Rock City. Rua Cintura do Porto de Lisboa, Armazém (Warehouse) 225. ☎ **21/342-86-36.** Cover (credited toward drinks) 1,000$ ($5.60) Fri–Sat. Tram: 15.

This funky spot is one of the few venues in Lisbon devoted to live music—a welcome interlude from clubs that feature only recorded tunes by overseas artists. Guitars hang from the walls, and an airplane is suspended from the ceiling. Night owls come to hear live rock performing on a stage near a bar that can get very busy. There are only a few tables, usually occupied by customers who order a simple platter of food from the short menu. Regrettably, this place seems to focus on performances by a limited number of bands who appear again and again, usually emulating the hits of such 1970s and 1980s greats as Bruce Springsteen and Queen. Beer prices begin at 600$ ($3.35) a bottle. Open daily 2am to 7am.

THE BAR SCENE
Bachus. Largo da Trindade 9. ☎ **21/342-28-28.** Bus: 58 or 100.

This restaurant offers one of the capital's most convivial watering spots. Surrounded by Oriental carpets, bronze statues, intimate lighting, and polite uniformed waiters, you can hobnob with some of the most glamorous people in Lisbon. Late-night candlelit suppers are served in the bar. The array of drinks is international; prices start at 600$ ($3.35). Open daily noon to midnight.

Bar Nova. Rua da Rosa 261. ☎ **21/346-28-34.** Bus: 58 or 100.

This battered Bairro Alto meeting place is for the true night owl who wants to enjoy a last drink before hitting the clubs. The bar contains three dark low-ceilinged rooms where you can get a beer for 500$ ($2.80) or a mixed drink for about 600$ ($3.35). Open daily from 10pm to 2am.

Bora-Bora. Rua da Madalena 201. ☎ **21/887-20-43.** Metro: Rossio. Tram: 12 or 28.

A Polynesian bar might seem out of place in Lisbon, but the theme draws packs of locals who are tired of a constant diet of Iberian folklore. As you might expect from an urban bar with a Hawaiian theme, Bora-Bora specializes in imaginative variations on fruited, flaming, and rum-laced drinks. The couches are comfortable and inviting, angled for views of the Polynesian art that lines the walls. Beer costs 650$ ($3.65); mixed drinks are 1,100$ ($6.15) and up. Open Sunday to Thursday 9pm to 2am, Friday and Saturday 9pm to 3am.

Café Bar Tagus. Rua Diário de Noticias 40B. ☎ **21/347-64-03.** Bus: 58 or 100. Metro: Chiado.

At 10pm this bar turns into a hot nightspot where fashionable people meet for an after-dinner drink at the black-lacquer-and-mahogany bar. On weekends, the crowd spills into the street of an otherwise relatively quiet neighborhood in the Bairro Alto. It's a mellow and dialogue-inducing bar favored by journalists, artists, and notables from some of Lisbon's biggest newspapers and TV stations. Beer costs 600$ ($3.35); whisky and soda goes for 850$ ($4.75) and up. Open daily until 3am.

Indochina. Rua Cintura Armazém (Warehouse) H, Apt. Nave C. ☎ **21/395-58-75.** No cover. Tram: 15.

Best defined as a "night bar," Indochina doesn't try to compete with other clubs that emphasize danceable, recently released music. The comfortable seats invariably encourage conversation among patrons both gay and straight. The atmosphere is generally calmer, gentler, and softer than the hard-edged danceteria modes of some nearby competitors. There's an Asian restaurant on the premises, but most people come here just to drink and judge who's looking the most chic. Open daily 11:30pm till dawn.

Os Três Pastorinhos. Rua da Barroca 111–113. ☎ **21/346-43-01.** Bus: 58 or 100.

This late-night bar ("The Three Shepherds") emphasizes drinking much more than dancing. The late-night crowds appreciate the relaxed mood of the two-room interior. Students, models, and film-industry figures often turn up. There's a small dance floor that seems to be mostly ignored. Video screens broadcast international hip-hop and funk band clips. Beer costs 600$ ($3.35), and whisky starts at 900$ ($5.05). Open Tuesday to Sunday midnight to 2am.

The Panorama Bar. In the Lisboa Sheraton Hotel, rua Latino Coelho 1. ☎ **21/357-57-57.** Bus: 1, 2, 9, or 32. Metro: Picoas.

The Panorama Bar occupies the top floor of one of Portugal's tallest buildings, the 30-story Lisboa Sheraton. The view (day or night) is of the old and new cities of Lisbon, the mighty Tagus, and many of the towns on the river's far bank. The cosmopolitan decor incorporates chiseled stone and stained glass. You'll pay 1,400$ to 1,800$ ($7.85 to $10.10) for a whisky and soda. Open daily from 6pm to 2am.

Portas Largas Bar. Rua da Atalaia 105. ☎ **21/346-63-79.** Bus: 58 or 100.

This cosmopolitan watering hole in the Bairro Alto, with its worn-out marble counter and hardwood chairs, is an example of an old Portuguese *tasca*. The clientele, however, is as varied and contemporary as you'll see anywhere else in town—a comforting mixture of "gay, straight, black, yellow, white, and Portuguese people." Early on, the music tends toward recorded fado by such divas as Amália Rodrigues. After midnight, it switches to Portuguese and international rock groups. On weekends the crowd overflows into the street, and patrons mingle with the crowd from the mostly gay Frágil (see below), across the street. Beer runs about 400$ ($2.25); the price of whisky starts at 600$ ($3.35). Open daily from 8pm to 3am.

Procópio Bar. Alto de São Francisco 21A. ☎ **21/385-28-51.** Closed Aug 1–15. Bus: 9.

A longtime favorite of journalists, politicians, and foreign actors, the once-innovative Procópio has become a tried-and-true staple among Lisbon's watering holes. Guests sit on tufted red velvet, surrounded by stained and painted glass and ornate brass hardware. Mixed drinks cost 850$ ($4.75) and up, beer 600$ ($3.35) and up. Procópio might easily become your favorite bar, if you can find it. It lies just off rua de João Penha, which is off the landmark praça das Amoreiras. Open Monday to Saturday from 6pm to 3am.

GAY & LESBIAN BARS & CLUBS

Although this ultra-Catholic country remains one of the most closeted in Western Europe, at least eight gay nightspots have sprung up in the district known as Príncipe Real. With each passing year, the gay presence in Lisbon becomes more visible. You might begin your night crawl at either of the first two establishments listed below.

Agua no Bico. Rua de São Marçal 170. ☎ **21/347-28-30**. No cover. Bus: 15, 58, 100.

At the eastern edge of the Bairro Alto, this bar and dance club combines aspects of an English pub with the futuristic trappings of a gay club. It's marked by a discreet brass plaque on a steeply sloping street lined with 18th-century villas. The young crowd sometimes remains after the "official" 2am closing for all-male porn flicks. Beer prices start at 400$ ($2.25); whisky and soda goes for 600$ ($3.35) or more. We recommend that you take a taxi here, because public transport in this neighborhood is difficult at night. A medieval folk tale inspired the name ("Water in the Beak"). If you're curious, ask one of the handsome bartenders to recite the original folk tale. Open nightly from 9pm to 2am.

Frágil. Rua da Atalia 126–128. ☎ **21/346-95-78**. Cover 1,000$ ($5.60). Tram: 28. Bus: 15 or 100.

Nearly 2 decades old, this dance bar and music joint features DJs who play the latest in underground music. The chic crowd includes many professional and attractive gay men—Lisbon's core of gay journalists, designers, painters, and financiers. There's a large dance floor. The owner changes the decor every 6 months, and often throws a dance party for the occasion. You'll pay 600$ ($3.35) for a beer; the price for a whisky starts at 900$ ($5.05). Open Monday to Saturday from 11:30pm to 4am.

Memorial Bar. Rua Gustavo de Matos Sequeira 42A. ☎ **21/396-88-91**. Cover 1,000$ ($5.60). Bus: 58 or 100.

In the narrow streets of the Bairro Alto, the Memorial Bar is a household word (or phrase) in the city's lesbian community. Around 60% of its patrons are women—the remainder are gay men, whose numbers seem to diminish every year. Most of the staff members speak Spanish, French, and English, and newcomers will usually be able to strike up a conversation with one of the regulars. Twice a week (days vary), the joint features live entertainment—including comedy, cross-dressing shticks, or live Portuguese musicians. A beer costs 600$ ($3.50). Open Tuesday to Saturday from 10pm to 4am (disco music begins at midnight), Sunday 4 to 8pm.

Queens. Rua de Cintura do Porto de Lisboa, Armazém (Warehouse) 8, Naves A&B, Doca de Alcântara Norte. ☎ **21/395-58-70**. Cover 1,000$ ($5.60). Tram: 15.

This nightclub, in a cavernous, industrial-looking building near the Tagus, is larger than any of its nearby competitors. The sophisticated sound system floods the enormous dance floor with late-breaking music. Most of the crowd is male and under 35. Open Monday to Saturday from 10pm till 6am.

Trumps. Rua da Imprensa Nacionale 104B. ☎ **21/397-10-59**. Cover (credited toward drinks) 1,000$ ($5.60). Bus: 58.

Popular with the expatriate community, Trumps is the most sophisticated gay bar in Lisbon, and one of the most up-to-date. Positioned near (but not in) the Bairro Alto, it has several bars scattered throughout its two levels, an active dance floor, and lots of cruising options in its shadowy corners. The management estimates that 70% of the patrons are gay men, in a mix of ages and orientations that seems to include every subculture except leather. Gay women make up about one-quarter of the crowd, and the remaining 5% are heterosexual (or asexual, one supposes) friends of the majority. There's a coffee bar near the entrance. A beer runs 600$ ($3.35), and at least some members of the staff speak French, Spanish, and English. Open daily from 10pm to 4am, and sometimes as late as 6am.

Estoril, Cascais & Sintra

5

Lured by Guincho (near the westernmost point in continental Europe), the Boca do Inferno (Mouth of Hell), and Lord Byron's "glorious Eden" at Sintra, many travelers spend much of their time in the area around Lisbon. You could spend a day drinking in the wonders of the library at the monastery-palace of Mafra (Portugal's El Escorial), dining in the pretty pink rococo palace at Queluz, or enjoying seafood at the Atlantic beach resort of Ericeira.

The main draw in the area is the Costa do Sol. The string of beach resorts, including Estoril and Cascais, forms the Portuguese Riviera on the northern bank of the mouth of the Tagus. If you arrive in Lisbon when the sun is shining and the air is balmy, consider heading straight for the shore. Estoril is so near that darting in and out of the capital to see the sights or visit the fado clubs is easy. An inexpensive electric train leaves from the Cais do Sodré station in Lisbon frequently throughout the day and evening; its run ends in Cascais.

Although the beachfront strip of the Costa do Sol is justifiably famous, it's generally recommended that you swim in the pools (indoor or outdoor) at the resort hotels. The waters along the coast are, for the most part, polluted. They're not recommended for swimming, although the beaches are still great for getting a suntan.

The sun coast is sometimes known as A Costa dos Reis, "the Coast of Kings," because it's a magnet for deposed royalty—exiled kings, pretenders, marquesses from Italy, princesses from Russia, and baronesses from Germany. Some live simply, as did the late Princess Elena of Romania (Magda Lupescu), a virtual recluse in an unpretentious villa. Others insist on a rigid court atmosphere, as did Umberto, who was king of Italy for 1 month in 1946, then forced into exile. Other nobles who settled here included Don Juan, the count of Barcelona, who lost the Spanish throne in 1969 when his son, Don Juan Carlos, was named successor by Generalissimo Franco; Joanna, the former queen of Bulgaria; and the Infanta Dona Maria Adelaide de Bragança, sister of the pretender to the Portuguese throne.

Despite the heavy concentration of royals, the Riviera is a microcosm of Portugal. Take a ride out on the train, even if you don't plan to stay here. You'll pass pastel-washed houses with red-tile roofs and facades of antique blue-and-white tiles; miles of modern apartment dwellings; rows of canna, pine, mimosa, and eucalyptus; swimming pools; and, in the background, green hills studded with villas, chalets, and new homes.

Lisbon is the aerial gateway for the Costa do Sol and Sintra. Once in Lisbon, you can drive or take public transportation.

Exploring the Region by Car

Regrettably, the coast, like all major beach resorts in Europe, has become overdeveloped, which detracts greatly from its charm. It has less traffic on weekdays than it does on Saturday and Sunday, when people from Lisbon flock there. If you have a choice, try to avoid weekends, especially from June to September.

The environs of Lisbon can be explored by car while you're based at a hotel in the city, or you can seek lodgings en route. Estoril, Cascais, and Sintra are the most popular places to stay. The palace at Queluz is a popular day trip from Lisbon.

Day 1   Spend the day driving along and exploring the **Estoril Coast,** which extends for 20 miles west of Lisbon. Leave Lisbon on A7, and proceed 15 miles to Estoril. You can spend the day enjoying the beaches at Estoril, and perhaps visiting the **casino.** If you plan to continue your journey the next day, it's best to spend the night here instead of returning to traffic-clogged Lisbon.

Day 2   In the morning, follow signs west for 4 miles to the resort of **Cascais,** a former fishing village that's now one of Portugal's major beach resorts. If you don't want to go to the beach, Cascais is home to a few monuments. A good place to stop for lunch in Cascais is Dom Manolo (see below). After lunch, continue along the coast highway for 1¼ miles to the best-known sight in the area, the **Boca do Inferno** or "Mouth of Hell." Here, the sea pounds an impressive natural grotto. After viewing the turbulent natural formation, you can take a scenic 5½-mile ride along the coast to the surfing beach at **Guincho,** site of some of the best seafood in the Lisbon area. If you decide to swim, beware—the undertow is dangerous. Spend the night in Guincho or the Cascais area.

Day 3   From Guincho, you can backtrack along the coast road to Cascais or Estoril, or you can turn inland and head north on national highway N247 to **Cabo da Roca,** the westernmost point on the European continent. Then follow signs east to **Sintra,** where you'll definitely want to spend most of the day (and longer, if possible) to explore the castles and churches.

Day 4   Continue to **Mafra,** site of the fabled monastery palace, one of the largest historic monuments in Europe. After a visit, head 7 miles northwest on N116 to **Ericeira,** where there's a small beach with colorful fishing boats. Have lunch at a seafood restaurant.

1 Estoril: Playground of Royalty

8 miles S of Sintra, 15 miles W of Lisbon

This chic resort with its beautiful beaches along the Portuguese Riviera has long basked in its reputation as a playground of monarchs. Fading countesses arrive at the railway station, monarchs in exile drop in at the Palácio Hotel for dinner, and the sons of deposed dictators sunbathe by the pool. Today's Estoril was the creation of Fausto Figueiredo, who built the deluxe Palácio in 1930. The casino opened in the late 1960s. During World War II, as Nazi troops advanced across Europe, many collapsed courts fled to Estoril to wait out the war in a neutral country.

Estoril & Environs

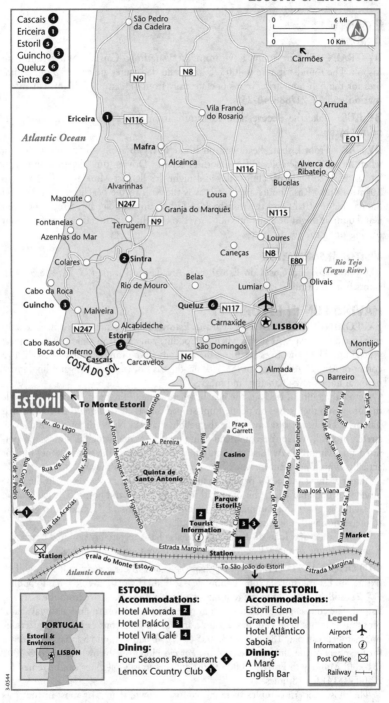

Cascais **4**
Ericeira **1**
Estoril **5**
Guincho **3**
Queluz **6**
Sintra **2**

0   6 Mi
0   10 Km

São Pedro
da Cadeira

Carmões

N9   N8

Arruda

Ericeira **1**   N116

Vila Franca
do Rosario

EO1

Atlantic Ocean

Mafra

Alcainca

N116

Alverca do
Ribatejo

Bucelas

Alvarinhas

Magoute

N247

Lousa

N115

Fontanelas

Granja do Marquês

Azenhas do Mar

Terrugem   N9

Loures

2 Sintra

Caneças   N8

E80

*Rio Tejo
(Tagus River)*

Colares

Rio de Mouro

Belas

Lumiar

Olivais

Cabo da Roca

Queluz **6** N117

Guincho 3   Malveira

LISBON

Alcabideche

Carnaxide

N247

Estoril

5

Cabo Raso

Boca do Inferno **4**

Cascais

São Domingos

Montijo

Carcavelos   N6

COSTA DO SOL

Almada

Barreiro

Estoril

To Monte Estoril

Av. do Lago

Rua Afonso Henriques Fausto Figueiredo

Rua Alentejo

Praça
a Garrett

Rua da Holanda

Av. da Suiça

Rua de Nice

Av. Saboia

Av. A. Pereira

Rua Melo e Sousa

Av. Aida

Casino

Av. dos Bombeiros

Rua Vale de Stat. Rita

Av. de S. Pedro

Rua Conde Moser

**Quinta de
Santo Antonio**

Rua das Acacias

**Parque
Estoril**

Av. de Portugal

Rua do Porto

Rua José Viana

Rua Vale de Stat. Rita

1

2
**Tourist
Information**
ⓘ

Av. Clotilde

3 **3**

4

Market

Estrada Marginal

✉
Station

Praia do Monte Estoril

Station

To São João do Estoril

Estrada Marginal

Atlantic Ocean

PORTUGAL

**Estoril &
Environs**

★ LISBON

**ESTORIL
Accommodations:**
Hotel Alvorada **2**
Hotel Palácio **3**
Hotel Vila Galé **4**
Dining:
Four Seasons Restauarant **3**
Lennox Country Club **1**

**MONTE ESTORIL
Accommodations:**
Estoril Eden
Grande Hotel
Hotel Atlântico
Saboia
Dining:
A Maré
English Bar

Legend
Airport ✈
Information ⓘ
Post Office ✉
Railway ⊢——⊣

3-0544

137

ESSENTIALS
ARRIVING

BY TRAIN Electric trains leave from the waterfront Cais do Sodré station in Lisbon. The round-trip fare is 400$ ($2.25), and departures are every 12 to 30 minutes for the half-hour trip. Trains operate daily from 5:30am to 2:30am. For **information,** call ☎ **21/888-40-25.**

BY BUS Take the electric train to Estoril; from there, you can visit Sintra (see below) by bus.

BY CAR From Lisbon, head west on Route 6; try to avoid driving on weekends, when there's considerable traffic in both directions. Driving time depends on traffic, which tends to be heavy almost day and night. It's lightest Monday to Friday from 10am to 4pm. Rush hours are brutal, as is the rush to the beach on Saturday and Sunday before 10am and the rush back to Lisbon on Saturday and Sunday between 4 and 6pm. It might be easier on your nerves to take the electric train and forget about driving along the coast.

VISITOR INFORMATION

The **Junta Turismo Costa do Estoril** is at Arcadas do Parque (☎ **21/466-38-13**), across from the train station.

HAVING FUN IN ESTORIL

EXPLORING THE RESORT **Parque Estoril,** in the center of town, is a well-manicured landscape. At night, when it's floodlit, you can stroll amid the subtropical vegetation. The palm trees studding the grounds have prompted many to call it "a corner of Africa." At the top of the park sits the **casino,** which offers gambling, international floor shows, dancing, and movies.

Across the railroad tracks is the **beach,** where some of the most fashionable people in Europe sun themselves on peppermint-striped canvas chairs along the **Praia Estoril Tamariz.** The beach is sandy, unlike the pebbly strand at Nice. Although it is a lovely stretch of sand, we don't recommend going into the water, which is almost too polluted for swimming. At least you can enjoy the sands and the beach scene, but for actually swimming, head for one of the many hotel pools in the area.

Tamariz draws more gay patrons than any other beach in Portugal, although the beach in general has a little bit of everything, both hetero and homo. The gay section is easy to discern. How, you might ask. As one beach buff said, "It's easy. Just gravitate to the section with the most pumped-up bodies."

To the east is **São João do Estoril,** which also has a regrettably polluted beach and many handsome private villas. Most visitors go there to dine and dance.

OUTDOOR ACTIVITIES Other than the beach, the big activity here is golf. A fixture in Estoril since 1940, **Clube de Golf do Estoril,** avenida da República (☎ **21/468-01-76**), lies in the foothills of Sintra, a 3-minute drive from the casino at Estoril. The course, one of the finest in Europe, has played host to international championship matches. The club has a 9-hole and an 18-hole course. Monday to Friday nonmembers can play 18 holes for 8,600$ ($48.15). Saturday and Sunday are reserved for members of the club or guests of the Palácio Hotel (see below), who pay 3,000$ ($16.80) Monday to Friday, 5,000$ ($28) on weekends. Golf clubs can be rented for 2,500$ ($14) for 18 holes.

The most modern complex of tennis courts in town, shared by most of the city's major resorts, is the **Clube de Tenis do Estoril,** Avenida Conte de Barcelona (☎ **21/466-2770**). It offers more than 20 tennis courts, including most of the newest in town, and charges 1,000$ ($5.60) per person per hour for play. Within a short walk of the Palácio Hotel, it's open daily from 7:30am till dusk.

SHOPPING   Other than the upscale hotel boutiques that sell scarves and poolside accessories, Estoril does not abound with shopping options. Most dedicated consumers head for the markets of Lisbon, or for the large-scale shopping center in Cascais (see "Cascais," later in this chapter), a 10-minute drive from Estoril.

In July and August, the resort sponsors an open-air handcrafts fair, the **Feira do Artesanato,** near the casino. It's worth a visit even if you're staying in Cascais. The fair runs nightly from around 5pm until midnight. In addition to good regional specialties, the stalls sell handcrafts and art, including ceramics, from all parts of Portugal. You can also drive 4 miles southeast of Estoril to the town of **Carcavelos,** which has a busy market on Thursday from 7am to 5pm. You'll see local arts and crafts along with more mundane items such as food and clothing. You can also reach Carcavelos by train from Estoril; it's best to go in the morning.

WHERE TO STAY
EXPENSIVE

✪ **Palácio Hotel.** Rua do Parque, 2765 Estoril. ☎ **21/464-80-00.** Fax 21/464-81-59. 162 units. A/C MINIBAR TV TEL. 30,000$–35,000$ ($168–$196) double; from 45,000$ ($252) suite. Rates include breakfast. AE, DC, MC, V. Free parking.

The Palácio Hotel is legendary as a retreat for exiled royalty and a center of espionage during World War II. At its 1930 debut, the Palácio received the honeymooning Japanese crown prince and his bride. Umberto, the deposed king of Italy, and Don Juan, the count of Barcelona, followed. During World War II, when people escaped from Nazi-occupied Europe with little more than a case of jewels and the clothes on their back, the hotel accepted diamonds, rubies, and gold instead of money.

The reception rooms are Pompeiian, with sienna-colored marble pillars, bold bands of orange, and handmade carpets. The intimate salons are ideal for a tête-à-tête. The large guest rooms are traditional, with fine Regency-style furnishings, walk-in closets, and luxurious bathrooms with bidets and heated towel racks. Refurbishment was begun in 1990 and still not completed at the millennium. Single rooms facing the rear are the smallest, but also the quietest. The hotel opens onto the side of Estoril Park, which is capped by the casino. The beach is a short walk away.

Dining: A major asset of the Palácio is the restaurant-grill Four Seasons (see "Where to Dine," below). The Atlântico Restaurant serves breakfast; the Bar Estoril features piano entertainment. After-dinner coffee is served in the classic central drawing room.

Amenities: 24-hour room service, baby-sitting, hairdresser, laundry and valet, pool, special privileges at the hotel's nearby championship golf course.

MODERATE

Hotel Alvorada. Rua de Lisboa 3, 2765 Estoril. ☎ **21/468-00-70.** Fax 21/468-72-50. E-mail: hotelavorada@ip.pt. 53 units. A/C TV TEL. 10,000$–17,000$ ($56–$95.20) double; 12,000$–22,000$ ($67.20–$123.20) triple. Rates include continental breakfast. AE, DC, MC, V. Free parking.

The fully renovated but still merely functional Hotel Alvorada opened its doors in 1969. It provides pousada-style accommodations on a small scale. The hotel stands opposite the casino and the Parque Estoril, just a 3-minute walk from the beach. It's recommended for its well-maintained but unstylish midsize guest rooms, each of which has a balcony. The hotel was completely renovated in the mid-1990s, with special attention paid to the bathrooms. The inviting public rooms include the lobby, decorated with modern Portuguese paintings and provincial-style furnishings. The top-floor solarium offers a panoramic view of the sea. Only breakfast is served.

Hotel Vila Galé. Estrada Marginal, 2765 Estoril. ☎ **21/468-18-11.** Fax 21/468-18-15. www.vilagale.pt. E-mail: galeestoril@vilagale.pt. 126 units. A/C MINIBAR TV TEL. 15,000$– 30,000$ ($84–$168) double. Rates include breakfast. AE, DC, DISC, MC, V. Parking 760$ ($4.25).

Built in the late 1950s next door to the far more glamorous Palácio (see above), this hotel has seven floors with walls of soaring glass. About half the rooms boast good-size balconies overlooking the water and the casino. Only a minute or so from the sea and the electric train station, it's in the center of Estoril's boutique district.

Expansion of the hotel and much-needed guest-room renovations were completed in 1996. The room count has nearly tripled since 1995. New rooms and old feature stylish modern stained-wood furniture, including twin beds, a wardrobe, and a safe-deposit box. The renovations have taken their toll on the low room rates that were once the hotel's hallmark, but some inexpensive rooms are still available.

The lobby-level dining room, which serves Portuguese cuisine, provides unobstructed vistas of the sea and the nearby hills studded with villas. In the marble-floored lounge and bar, contemporary design prevails. The hotel has laundry service, babysitting, 24-hour room service, and Budget car-rental facilities.

Lennox Country Club. Rua Eng. Álvaro Pedro Sousa 5, 2765 Estoril. ☎ **21/468-04-51.** Fax 21/467-08-59. 32 units. A/C MINIBAR TEL. 20,000$–23,400$ ($112–$131.05) double; 25,000$–35,000$ ($145–$203) suite. Rates include buffet breakfast. AE, DC, MC, V. Free parking.

Partially because of its emphasis on golf, this hillside hotel, renovated in 1993, seems a lot like a corner of Scotland. Near the bar there's even a map of the golf course at St. Andrews, close to autographed photos of the many championship golfers who have stayed here. The gardens make this place one of the town's prime attractions.

The midsize accommodations are comfortable and attractive. Some are scattered in a collection of buildings a short walk from the reception area. The most desirable and spacious are in the main building, a former private home. Suites are equipped with kitchenettes. The restaurant serves English cuisine, including steak-and-kidney pie, along with regional Portuguese dishes. The hotel has room service, baby-sitting, laundry service, and a heated pool.

NEARBY PLACES TO STAY

A satellite of Estoril, **Monte Estoril** is half a mile west, on the road to Cascais. Built across the slope of a hill, it opens onto a vista of Cascais Bay and the Atlantic beyond.

EXPENSIVE

Estoril Eden. Av. Sabóia 209, Monte Estoril, 2765 Estoril. ☎ **21/467-05-73.** Fax 21/466-76-01. www.maisturism.pt. E-mail: eden@mail.telepac.pt. 162 apts. A/C TV TEL. 14,700$–21,000$ ($82.30–$117.60) apt for 2. Rates include breakfast. AE, DC, MC, V. Parking 1,300$ ($7.30).

The four-star Estoril Eden is a great place for families. Built in 1985, the white-walled tower sits on a rocky knoll above the road paralleling the edge of the sea. The sound-proof, moderately sized apartments are decently decorated. Each has a kitchenette, firm beds, in-house video, and a balcony with a sea view. In the studio apartments, the beds are in the wall, providing more living space. The decor is a bit worn.

Dining/Diversions: The Garden Patio offers regional and international cuisine served à la carte or buffet. There's a poolside cafe-bar, Le Bistrot. You can stock up on food supplies in a minimarket. A pianist plays at dinner, and there's a disco in the evenings.

Amenities: Laundry service (but a slow-moving staff), outdoor and indoor pools, sauna, health club, solarium, 24-hour concierge, free summer entertainment program for kids, baby-sitting.

Grande Hotel. Av. Sabóia 488, Monte Estoril, 2765 Estoril. ☎ **21/464-97-00.** Fax 21/468-48-34. E-mail: grandehotel@ip.pt. 73 units. A/C TV TEL. 10,000$–20,000$ ($56–$112) double. Children under 8 half-price in parents' room. Rates include buffet breakfast. AE, DC, MC, V. Free parking.

A grand hotel has stood on this site since 1895; the present building is a reconstruction. Just a few minutes up from the beach, it offers seven floors of spacious, well-furnished rooms, about half of which have balconies large enough for breakfast or sunbathing. Totally renovated in 1996, it's welcoming and comfortable. The public rooms are inviting, with a fireplace and groupings of casual furnishings. The guest rooms are furnished in contemporary style, with modern headboards and Nordic-style chairs. Both business travelers and beach buffs frequent this hotel, which has a good restaurant and a cozy bar. There's also a swimming pool with lounge chairs and parasols. Laundry and room service (7am to 10pm) are available, as is baby-sitting.

Hotel Atlântico. Estrada Marginal 7, Monte Estoril, 2765 Estoril. ☎ **21/468-02-70.** Fax 21/468-36-19. E-mail: hotel.atlantico@telepac.pt. 175 units. TV TEL. Mid-May to Sept 25,000$–30,000$ ($140–$168) double; Apr to mid-May and Oct 20,000$–25,000$ ($112–$140) double; Nov–Mar 15,000$–18,000$ ($84–$100.80) double. Rates include breakfast. AE, DC, MC, V. Free parking.

The six-story Hotel Atlântico is a self-contained playground, almost directly on the sandy beach but separated from the shore by the electric train tracks. Its disadvantages are the whizzing coastal-road traffic in front and the train clatter in the rear. However, if you get a room high enough up facing the sea, you can be assured of quiet. The guest rooms are medium-size and moderately well furnished, with built-in headboards, firm beds, reading lights, Swedish-style desks and armchairs, and excellent tile bathrooms and showers. In 1996, the fourth and fifth floors were renovated with new bedding and modern wooden furnishings. More than 80 rooms are air-conditioned and have minibars. The dining room, built like a cave under the hotel, has a view through an all-glass wall overlooking the pool and sea. One TV lounge has video; another lounge offers live music in the evening. The hotel has 24-hour room service, laundry, baby-sitting, a wide sun terrace, and an outdoor saltwater pool.

INEXPENSIVE

Saboia Hotel. Rua Belmonte 1, Monte Estoril, 2765 Estoril. ☎ **21/468-11-22.** Fax 21/468-11-17. www.hotelabroad.co.uk/b1552.htm. 48 units. TV TEL. 12,000$–14,000$ ($67.20–$78.40) double. Rates include buffet breakfast. MC, V. Free parking.

You'll find comfortable 1970s-style accommodations in this white-and-cream-colored tower jutting skyward from a neighborhood of 19th-century villas above town. In the late 1990s the three-star hotel got a completely new look following renovations. Each small to midsize guest room contains a firm bed as well as access to the rectangular pool. Non-smoking rooms are available. The ground-floor bar has air-conditioning and large windows. There's a basement-level snack bar and restaurant. The hotel has a pool, and the beach is a 10-minute walk away.

WHERE TO DINE
EXPENSIVE

English Bar. Av. Sabóia 9, Monte Estoril. ☎ **21/468-04-13.** Reservations recommended. Main courses 4,500$–6,000$ ($25.20–$33.60). AE, DC, MC, V. Mon–Sat 12:30–4pm and 7:30pm–midnight. Closed 2nd and 3rd week in Aug. PORTUGUESE.

Many couples come to this popular establishment—which is neither English nor a bar—just to watch the sunset over the Bay of Cascais. Despite the mock-Elizabethan facade, the well-prepared food is essentially Portuguese. Many international dishes are also served. Try for a window seat in the handsome dining room, with wide-plank floors and comfortable leather-backed wood chairs. From the à la carte menu, you can sample such highly recommended dishes as a savory *crème de mariscos* (cream of shell-fish soup), sea bass with clams, or fillet steak. The chef's specialty is *cherne na canoa*, turbot served with baby clams and a succulent sauce. In season, you can order *perdiz Serra Morena* (roast partridge). An excellent dessert is mousse made with nuts.

✪ **Four Seasons.** In the Palácio Hotel, rua do Parque. ☎ **21/464-80-00.** Reservations required. Regular main courses 2,000$–2,700$ ($11.20–$15.10); seafood main courses 2,500$–13,000$ ($14–$72.80); fixed-price menu 5,500$ ($30.80). AE, DC, MC, V. Daily 1–3pm and 7:30–10:30pm. INTERNATIONAL.

For fine food, go to the Four Seasons, whose connection with one of Portugal's most famous hotels gives it immediate cachet. Even if it were independently operated, it would be one of the finest—and one of the most expensive—restaurants in Estoril.

The menus and the service at the Four Seasons actually reflect the seasons: The dishes, uniforms, linen, china, and glasses change four times a year. Other than the handful of intimate tables set imperially on the upper mezzanine, the elaborately decorated tables cluster around a beautiful but purely decorative Iberian kitchen. The quiet, the candles, and the rich colors invite comparison to an elegant 19th-century Russian home. However, the discreet charm and polite manners of the well-trained staff are distinctively Portuguese.

The international cuisine is superb. For an appetizer, you might select three-cheese crepes, lobster bisque, or chilled mussel soup. To follow, try sole meunière, medallions of grouper with seaweed and salmon roe, flamed shrimp amira, or a parrillada of lobster, shrimp, mussels, and clams for two. Meat dishes include beef and veal stuffed with shrimp, medallions of venison with chestnuts, and wild boar cutlets with pineapple. The fixed-price menu includes soup or appetizer, a main course, dessert, mineral water, and coffee. Wine can be added for a supplement of 1,000$ ($5.60). You can enter directly from the street or from the hotel lobby.

MODERATE

A Choupana. Estrada Marginal, São João do Estoril. ☎ **21/468-3099.** Main courses 2,000$–5,000$ ($11.20–$28). AE, DC, MC, V. Daily 9am–2am. PORTUGUESE/INTERNATIONAL.

Just east of Estoril, this restaurant can be your destination for the evening—there is dancing nightly until 2am. Opening onto panoramic views of the Bay of Cascais, it also serves great food—its savory *cataplana*, for example, is a combination of chicken and clams (you heard that right). Other tasty dishes include seafood curry, baked grouper, and the best paella along the coast. You can always count on finding the freshest seafood here.

A Maré. Alameda Columbano 6, Monte Estoril. ☎ **21/468-55-70.** Reservations recommended. Main courses 1,500$–3,200$ ($8.40–$17.90); fixed-price menus (groups of 10 or more) 3,000$–5,000$ ($16.80–$28) per person. AE, DC, MC, V. Daily noon–3pm and 7–11pm. PORTUGUESE.

This is one of the most reliable and best-managed restaurants in Estoril, with a loyal local following. In an old-fashioned villa previously inhabited by a mysteriously deposed countess, it's romantically decorated. The menu almost always contains at least seven types of fresh fish, prepared in many delectable styles. Many diners prefer fillets prepared simply, fried with parsley or herbs and garlic. Also available is an assortment of fresh shellfish. There are seven succulent fixed-price menus, the most expensive of which includes shellfish dishes. All include an appetizer, main course, wine, and coffee.

ESTORIL AFTER DARK

GAMBLING   An alcohol-stoked crawl through the upscale bars of such hotels as the Palácio might provide insights into the glamour of this pocket of Portugal. If you're looking for something more formal, check out the **Estoril Casino,** in the Parque Estoril, praça José Teodoro dos Santos (☎ **21/468-45-21**). There's a cover charge of 500$ ($2.80) for entrance into the section with the gaming tables (roulette, French banque, chemin de fer, blackjack, and craps), you can gamble to your heart's content every day between 3pm and 3am. You must present a passport, driver's license, or other form of photo ID, and you must be 18 or over. Entrance to the separate slot-machine room is free and requires no ID. Built in the late 1950s, the casino rises from a formally landscaped garden on a hilltop near the town center. Glass walls simulate a museum of modern art, and enclose an inner courtyard with fountains and tiled paths.

CLUBS & BARS   The casino is the venue for the region's splashiest and most colorful cabaret act, **Salão Preto e Prata,** in the Estoril Casino, Parque Estoril, praça José Teodoro dos Santos (☎ **21/468-45-21**). We usually skip the dinner offered here and pay a cover charge of 5,000$ ($28), which includes the first two drinks. Shows begin at 11pm, and most spectators who aren't dining show up at around 10:30pm for views of leggy, feathered, and bejeweled dancers strutting around in billowing trains and bespangled bras. Food is served in the 700-seat theater or in a 150-seat satellite restaurant, Wunderbar. Dinner, including access to the show, costs 9,000$ to 14,000$ ($50.40 to $78.40) per person.

The most popular and impressive disco is **Frolic,** in the Parque do Estoril (☎ **21/468-12-19**). Adjacent to the Hotel Palácio and close to the casino, it caters to a well-heeled clientele over 25. The cover charge is 3,000$ ($16.80), which includes the first drink. Glossy, urbane, and reminiscent of big-city discos in Madrid or Lisbon, it's open every night from 11pm to dawn.

You might opt for a more regional, less dynamic watering hole. Try a fast pick-me-up at a raffish-looking bar in Estoril's **Forte Velho (Old Fort),** Estrada Marginal, São João do Estoril (☎ **21/468-13-37**). It isn't the most fashionable club in the region (contenders in Lisbon long ago took over that title), but its location within the 500-year-old walls of a once-powerful fort adds an undeniable allure. Look for a much-used bar area, a roster of recorded disco hits, a high-energy crowd of under-30s on weekends, and a more varied age range on weeknights. There's no cover charge; a beer costs around 600$ ($3.35).

Looking to rub elbows with some of the Costa do Sol's corps of English-speaking expatriates enjoying their gin and tonics? Head for the long-established premises of **Ray's Cocktail Bar & Lounge,** av. Sabóia 425, Monte Estoril (☎ **21/468-01-06**). The eclectic, kitschy colonial decor seems to celebrate English-speaking, hard-drinking communities throughout the world. Mixed drink prices start at 600$ ($3.35), beer costs at least 425$ ($2.40). Open daily from 1pm to 2am.

2 Cascais

4 miles W of Estoril, 19 miles W of Lisbon

In the 1930s, Cascais was a tiny fishing village that attracted artists and writers to its little cottages. But its history as a resort is old. In fact, it was once known as a royal village because it enjoyed the patronage of Portugal's ruling family. When the monarchy died, the military replaced it. Gen. António de Fragoso Carmona, president of Portugal until 1951 (and responsible for naming Dr. Salazar minister of finance), once occupied the 17th-century fort guarding the Portuguese Riviera.

To say Cascais is growing would be an understatement: It's exploding! Apartment houses, new hotels, and the finest restaurants along the Costa do Sol draw a never-ending stream of visitors every year.

However, the life of the simple fisher folk goes on. Auctions, called *lotas,* of the latest catch take place on the main square—with a modern hotel in the background. In the small harbor, rainbow-colored fishing boats share space with pleasure craft owned by an international set that flocks to Cascais from early spring until autumn.

The town's tie with the sea is old. If you speak Portuguese, chat up any of the local fishers, with their weather-beaten faces. You'll hear that one of their own, Afonso Sanches, discovered America in 1482. Legend has it that Columbus learned of his accidental find, stole the secret, and enjoyed the subsequent acclaim.

ESSENTIALS
ARRIVING
BY TRAIN   The electric train from Lisbon's waterfront Cais do Sodré station ends its run at the center of Cascais. Trains arrive from (and return to) Lisbon every 15 to 30 minutes. Service is daily from 5:30am to 2:30am. The round-trip fare is 400$ ($2.25). For **information,** call ☎ **21/888-40-25.**

BY BUS   Take the electric train from Lisbon to Cascais, unless you're coming from Sintra. Eleven buses a day make the 1-hour run to Cascais. The round-trip fare is 300$ ($1.70).

BY CAR   From Estoril (see "Estoril," earlier in this chapter), continue west along Route 6 for another 4 miles.

VISITOR INFORMATION
The **Cascais Tourist Office** is at av. Combatentes da Grande Guerra 25 (☎ **21/486-82-04**).

HAVING FUN IN CASCAIS
EXPLORING THE TOWN   Many visitors, both foreign and domestic, clog the roads to Cascais on summer Sundays when there are bullfights at the **Monumental de Cascais,** a ring outside the "city" center (see "Spectator Sports" in chapter 4).

When you're not at the beach, a good place to relax is the sprawling **Parque do Marechal Carmona,** open daily from 9am to 8pm. It lies at the southern tip of the resort, near the water. Here you'll find a shallow lake, a cafe, and a small zoo. Chairs and tables are set out under shade trees if you'd like to picnic.

The most important church is the **Igreja de Nossa Senhora da Assunção** (Church of Our Lady of the Assumption), on largo da Assunção (☎ **21/483-04-77**), a leafy square toward the western edge of town. It's open daily from 9am to 1pm and 5 to 8pm. Paintings by Josefa de Óbidos, a 17th-century artist, fill the nave. They're unusual because women rarely attained such artistic posts in those days. The hand-painted *azulejos* (tiles) date from 1720 and 1748. The beautiful altar dates from the end of the 16th century.

Cascais also has some minor museums, including the **Museu do Mar** (Museum of the Sea), avenida da República (☎ **21/486-13-77**). The museum displays fishing arti-facts, including equipment and model boats. Also on exhibit is folkloric apparel worn by residents in the 1800s. Old photographs and paintings re-create the Cascais of long ago. The museum is open Tuesday to Sunday from 10am to 5pm; admission is 200$ ($1.10).

Another museum is the **Museu do Conde de Castro Guimarães,** estrada da Boca do Inferno (☎ 21/482-06-56). On the grounds of the Parque do Marechal Carmona, it occupies the former 19th-century home of a family whose last surviving member died in 1927. The museum offers a rare glimpse into life in the 18th and 19th centuries, with ceramics, antiques, artwork, silver ewers, samovars, and Indo-Portuguese embroidered shawls—you name it. It's open Tuesday to Sunday from 10am to 12:30pm and 2 to 5pm; admission is 250$ ($1.40).

The most popular excursion outside Cascais is to ✪ **Boca do Inferno** (Mouth of Hell). The formation deserves its ferocious reputation. Thundering waves sweep in with such power and fury that they long ago carved a wide hole, or *boca,* into the cliffs. However, if you should arrive when the sea is calm, you'll wonder why it's called a cauldron. The Mouth of Hell can be a windswept roar if you don't stumble over too many souvenir hawkers. Take the highway toward Guincho, then turn left toward the sea.

OUTDOOR ACTIVITIES   Most visitors are content with the trio of fair beaches here. Lying on the lovely, sandy beach here is fine, but swimming is another matter entirely. Unless signs direct you otherwise, stay out of the water, which is likely to be too polluted for swimming. Should you want more activity, **Equinócio,** Verandas de Cascais 3 (☎ 21/483-53-54), rents surfing equipment.

To go fishing, contact the **Clube Naval de Cascais,** Esp. Príncipe Luís Filipe, in front of the Hotel Baia (☎ 21/483-01-25). It organizes trips to nearby spots in the Atlantic.

The best year-round center for horseback riding is **Quinta da Marinha** (☎ 21/486-90-84), 2½ miles west of Cascais. Call for directions and information.

The best golf course at Cascais is at the **Clube de Golfe da Marinha,** Quinta da Marinha (☎ 21/486-98-81), which was carved out of a sprawling woodland of umbrella pines. The master himself, Robert Trent Jones Sr., designed the 18-hole course, the showcase of an upscale residential resort complex that stretches over some 325 acres. Windblown dunes and sea-lashed outcroppings are part of the backdrop along its 6,685 yards. The 14th hole, facing a deep rocky gorge, is the most challenging. Weekday greens fees are 7,900$ ($44.25), or 4,200$ ($23.50) after 4pm; on weekends the fees are 9,500$ ($53.20) until 4pm, then 5,200$ ($29.10).

SHOPPING   As a prominent beachfront resort, Cascais offers lots of simple kiosks selling sunglasses and beachwear. The region's densest concentration of stores catering to united Europe's definition of the good life is nearby. The sprawling shopping center **Shopping Cascais,** Estrada de Sintra (☎ 21/460-00-53 for information), is beside highway 5A, the road between Cascais and Sintra. Some locals refer to it as "Shopping Center of Cascais," dropping the English-language term easily. It contains two floors and more than 100 boutiques, with special emphasis on housewares, home furnishings and accessories, and clothing. There's also a **movie theater** (☎ 21/460-04-20), which shows films in their original language with Portuguese subtitles.

If you're in the mood for more folkloric, less overtly commercial settings, you might want to ignore the megamall. Wander instead through the warren of small ceramics shops that surround Cascais's church, or walk along the town's most commercialized street, **rua da Raita,** an all-pedestrian walkway in the town center.

The most intriguing shopping possibilities are at the **markets.** Head north of the center along rua Mercado, off avenida do 25 be Abril, on Wednesday or Saturday morning and you'll find a fruit and vegetable market (along with a lot of other items). Another sprawling market operates at the bullring, Praça de Touros, on avenida Pedro Álvares, west of the center, on the first and third Sunday of each month.

WHERE TO STAY

Advance reservations are necessary in July and August.

EXPENSIVE

✪ **Cascais Vila Dom Pedro.** Rua Fernandes Tomaz 1, 2750 Cascais. ☎ **21/486-3410.** Fax 21/484-46-80. 10 units. A/C MINIBAR TV TEL. 35,000$–41,000$ ($196–$229.60) double. Rates include breakfast. AE, DC, MC, V. Free parking.

In the center of Cascais, near the rail station, this former private home has been tastefully converted into a choice five-star hotel. It opens onto the Bay of Cascais. The gracious inn offers beautifully furnished, spacious rooms, with deluxe mattresses and state-of-the-art plumbing. The hotel's fourth floor is a roof terrace.

Dining: The dining room serves top-rate Portuguese and international cuisine. A gourmet menu costs 7,000$ ($39.20). Even if you're not a guest, consider calling for a dinner reservation.

Amenities: 24-hour room service, laundry, valet, concierge, Jacuzzi.

✪ **Estalagem Senhora da Guia.** Estrada do Guincho, 2750 Cascais. ☎ **21/486-92-39.** Fax 21/486-92-27. E-mail: senhora.da.guia@mail.telepac.pt. 42 units. A/C MINIBAR TV TEL. 19,000$–35,000$ ($106.40–$196) double; from 48,000$ ($268.80) suite. Rates include buffet breakfast. Children 2–12 4,000$ ($22.40) in parents' room. AE, DC, MC, V. Free parking.

The Ornelas family returned to its native Portugal after a sojourn in Brazil and opened this hotel. It has turned the former country villa of the Sagres brewery family into one of the loveliest hotels in the region. The 1970 house has thick walls, high ceilings, and elaborately crafted moldings that give the impression of a much older building.

A trio of multilingual siblings restored the house to its former glory. The elegant midsize guest rooms and suites contain reproductions of 18th-century Portuguese antiques, thick carpets, louvered shutters, spacious modern bathrooms, and many amenities such as deluxe mattresses. Because the villa sits on a bluff above the sea, the views are excellent.

Dining/Diversions: The sun-washed bar is one of the more alluring rooms in the house. It's filled with family antiques, many of them English pieces acquired during the Ornelases's years in Madeira, and has a fireplace. Breakfast is served under parasols at the edge of the pool. The formal dining room, where lunch and dinner are served, remains cool even on the hottest days.

Amenities: Concierge, room service, 15% discount at nearby golf club.

Estoril Sol. Parque Palmela, 2750 Cascais. ☎ **21/483-90-00.** Fax 21/483-22-80. 309 units. A/C MINIBAR TV TEL. 30,000$ ($168) double; 47,000$–56,000$ ($263.20–$313.60) suite. Rates include buffet breakfast. AE, DC, MC, V. Parking 1,200$ ($6.70).

The Estoril Sol is a luxury high-rise holiday world, perched on a ledge with the coastal highway and electric train tracks separating it from the beach. It represents a dream come true for its late owner, José Teodoro dos Santos, a self-made man who arrived in Lisbon with less than a dollar in his pocket. He created a modern land of resort living, with public rooms large enough for a great invasion of sun-seeking visitors.

The Estoril Sol is one of the largest hotels in Portugal. Its guest rooms and suites overlook the sea or the hills beyond. Rooms, small to midsize, have rather dull commercial furnishings but comfortable beds. The marble bathrooms that are even better than the sleeping units, with hair dryers, deluxe toiletries, dual basins, and robes. It boasts a spacious main lounge (a traffic cop would be helpful here), the most expansive veranda on the peninsula, and a beach reached by an underground passageway.

Dining: Options include the Ain Restaurant and the Grill; both serve Portuguese and French cuisine. A piano player entertains in the Grill at dinner.

Amenities: 24-hour room service, laundry and valet, baby-sitting, gymnasium, Olympic-size pool for adults, smaller pool for children, sauna, solarium, health club with squash courts, facilities for horseback riding and water-skiing, shopping arcade, service station.

✪ **Hotel Albatroz.** Rua Frederico Arouca 100, 2750 Cascais. ☎ **21/483-28-21.** Fax 21/484-48-27. www.albatrozhotel.pt. E-mail: albatroz@mail.telpac.pt. 40 units. A/C MINIBAR TV TEL. Nov–Mar 28,000$–38,500$ ($156.80–$215.60) double; 46,000$ ($257.60) suite. Apr–Oct 39,500$–55,000$ ($221.20–$308) double; 75,000$ ($420) suite. AE, DC, MC, V. Free parking.

Whether you're seeking rooms or food, this hotel ("the Albatross") is your best choice on the Costa do Sol. On a rock ledge just above the ocean, it centers around a neo-classic villa built as a luxurious holiday retreat for the duke of Loulé. The count and countess de Foz acquired it in the 19th century. In the 20th century it became an inn.

Today, the hotel has undergone a tastefully elegant refurbishing. The understated decor incorporates lavish use of intricately painted tiles, acres of white latticework, and sweeping expanses of glass. The stone-trimmed 19th-century core has been expanded with a series of terraced additions that contain guest rooms. Units vary in size, and all are luxuriously comfortable. The rooms facing the street can be noisy at times.

Steeped in history, the Albatroz has received such famous guests as Anthony Eden, Cary Grant, U.S. Chief Justice Warren Burger, the duke and duchess of Bedford, Claudette Colbert, William Holden, Amy Vanderbilt, and the former queen of Bulgaria. Prince Rainier and the late Princess Grace visited more than once.

Dining: The à la carte restaurant is one of the finest along the coast (see "Where to Dine," below).

Amenities: 24-hour room service, baby-sitting, laundry and valet, pool, sun terrace.

MODERATE

Estalagem Farol. Estrada da Boca do Inferno 7, 2750 Cascais. ☎ **21/483-01-73.** Fax 21/484-14-47. 14 units. MINIBAR TV TEL. 12,500$–14,000$ ($70–$78.40) double. Rates include buffet breakfast. AE, DC, MC, V. Free parking.

When the Estalagem Farol was built in the late 19th century, its stone walls housed the entourage of the count of Cabral. In 1988, it became an inn. The owners have transformed the back gardens into a stone-ringed concrete slab with a small swimming pool in the center, a few steps from the sea.

The small guest rooms are tastefully furnished and comfortable, with firm beds. One of our favorite places here is the richly decorated bar area; a water view and hand-crafted paneling create an elegant rendezvous. The restaurant, Santa Marta, exudes Iberian charm. Laundry and baby-sitting can be arranged. The disco next door may be too loud for some guests.

INEXPENSIVE

Albergaria Valbom. Av. Valbom 14, 2750 Cascais. ☎ **21/486-58-01.** Fax 21/486-58-05. 40 units. A/C TEL. 6,000$–12,500$ ($33.60–$70) double. Rates include breakfast. AE, DC, MC, V. Free parking.

Built in 1973, this hotel has an indistinct white-concrete facade with evenly spaced rows of recessed balconies. The interior is warmly and comfortably decorated, and the staff helpful and polite. Conservatively decorated guest rooms, each with firm mattresses, surround the sun-washed TV lounge. The quieter accommodations look out over the back. There's a spacious sienna-colored bar on the premises. The Valbom lies on a drab commercial-residential street close to the center of Cascais, near the rail station.

✪ **Casa Pérgola.** Av. Valbom 13, 2750 Cascais. ☎ **21/484-00-40.** Fax 21/483-47-91. E-mail: pergolahouse@mail.telpac.pt. 11 units. A/C. 14,000$–20,000$ ($78.40–$112) double. Rates include breakfast. No credit cards. Closed Nov–Feb.

Built in the 18th century, this elegant villa behind a garden offers one of the most charming, tranquil interiors in Cascais. In the center of town, it stands in a neighborhood filled with restaurants and shops. This is the domain of Maria de Luz. Her genteel staff proudly displays a collection of antique furniture and blue-glazed tiles that surround the elegant second-floor sitting room. Each small accommodation is well furnished, with excellent beds. Reserve in advance. Although it's technically closed from November through February, the hotel will open during that time for any party that reserves five or more rooms.

Solar Dom Carlos. Rua Latina Coelho, 2750 Cascais. ☎ **21/482-8115.** Fax 21/486-5155. www.portugalinfo.net-d-carlos. E-mail: solardcarlos@mailtelepac.pt. 18 units. TV TEL. 8,000$–10,000$ ($44.80–$56). Rates include breakfast. AE, DC, MC, V. Free parking.

If you're saving money and your expectations aren't too high, this little back-street inn is most inviting. Once the mansion of a local aristocrat, it dates from the 1500s. An original chapel from the nobleman's home remains intact. The place is immaculately kept and makes heavy use of tiled floors. The comfortably furnished rooms are often large and have good beds, but not a lot of other amenities. Many families stay here because a third bed can easily be added. The inn also has a private garden. Breakfast is the only meal served.

WHERE TO DINE

After Lisbon, sprawling Cascais offers the second-highest concentration of quality restaurants. Even if you're based in the capital, consider a trip to Cascais for seafood.

EXPENSIVE

✪ **Restaurant Albatroz.** In the Hotel Albatroz, rua Frederico Arouca 100. ☎ **21/483-28-21.** Reservations required. Main courses 3,200$–4,500$ ($17.90–$25.20). AE, DC, MC, V. Daily 12:30–3pm and 7:30–10pm. PORTUGUESE/INTERNATIONAL.

One of the finest places to dine along the Costa do Sol, this elegantly decorated restaurant is part of the most famous hotel on the coast (see "Where to Stay," above). Its summer-style decor is inviting year-round. The room is not grand or stuffy, but the service is rather formal—diners' attire is probably best described as "neat casual."

Begin with an apéritif on the covered terrace high above the sea. Afterward, you'll be ushered into a glistening dining room that serves some of the finest Portuguese and international cuisine in Cascais. Your excellent options might include poached salmon, partridge stew, chateaubriand, or a savory version of stuffed sole with shellfish. There are also daily fresh fish specials; one especially succulent offering is monkfish with sea clams. For dessert, choices range from crêpes Suzette to iced soufflé. There's a wide selection of Portuguese and international wines.

Visconde da Luz. In the Jardim Visconde da Luz. ☎ **21/486-68-48.** Reservations required. Main courses 2,000$–6,000$ ($11.20–$33.60). AE, DC, MC, V. Tues–Sun noon–4pm and 7pm–midnight. PORTUGUESE/SEAFOOD.

The location of this well-known restaurant is one of its most appealing features: It sits in a low-slung bungalow at the edge of a park in the center of Cascais. The view encompasses rows of lime trees and towering sycamores where flocks of birds congregate at dusk (be warned if you're walking underneath). The decor is modernized art nouveau. The uniformed staff is polite and eager. Before you enter, you might be interested in looking at the blue-and-white-tile kitchen. The Portuguese food is well prepared with fresh ingredients. A meal might include fried sole, shellfish, pork with clams, seafood curry, or clams in garlic sauce, finished off with almond cake. Many seafood choices are sold by the kilogram (2.2 lb.), a generous portion that can easily feed two.

MODERATE

Beira Mar. Rua das Flores 6. ☎ **21/483-73-80.** Reservations recommended. Main courses 2,800$–4,200$ ($15.70–$23.50). AE, DC, MC, V. Wed–Mon noon–3pm and 7–11pm. PORTUGUESE.

Across from the Cascais fish market, this popular little restaurant specializes in the fruits of the sea, and does so exceedingly well. As you enter, you're greeted with an old cart showing the rich bounty of produce from Estremadura. The hearty fare is meant to be accompanied by the region's fine wines. You're seated at immaculate tables, where the service is both considerate and efficient. Begin with savory littleneck clams or another kind of shellfish, such as *sopa marisco* (shellfish soup). Your main course might be whitefish crowned with a banana. Grilled sole and many other dishes round out the menu. For dessert, one reader savored "a crown of freshly picked forest raspberries drizzled with cream" followed by a "tiny crystal of aged port."

Eduardo. Largo das Grutas 3. ☎ **21/483-19-01.** Reservations recommended. Main courses 1,700$–3,200$ ($9.50–$17.90); fixed-price menu 3,800$ ($21.30). AE, DC, MC, V. Thurs–Tues noon–3pm and 7–11pm. PORTUGUESE/FRENCH.

Rustically decorated with regional artifacts, this provincial restaurant occupies the street level of a postwar apartment building in the center of Cascais. It's named after its Belgian-born owner, Edouard de Beukelaer, who turns out savory Portuguese and French meals. The well-prepared food might include fillet steaks, braised fillet of turbot, crayfish in butter sauce with capers, and veal liver. Nothing very imaginative is served, but everything is decently prepared.

O Pipas. Rua das Flores 18. ☎ **21/486-45-01.** Reservations recommended. Main courses 2,000$–3,000$ ($11.20–$16.80). AE, DC, MC, V. Daily noon–3:30pm and 7–11:30pm. PORTUGUESE/INTERNATIONAL.

If you order shellfish, a meal here can be very expensive; otherwise, this popular restaurant offers well-prepared food at affordable prices. Many diners consider it the resort's finest independent (nonhotel) restaurant. The two-level space resembles a Portuguese bistro, with racks of exposed wine bottles and big picture windows letting in sunlight and views of the busy street outside. The menu includes lobster, clams, shellfish of all kinds (including oysters), several preparations of sole, squid, and a mixed shellfish grill. The shellfish meal for two runs 14,000$ ($78.40).

✪ **Reijos Restaurant.** Rua Frederico Arouca 35. ☎ **21/483-03-11.** Reservations required for dinner. Main courses 3,000$–5,000$ ($16.80–$28). AE, DC, MC, V. Mon–Sat 12:30–3:30pm and 7–11pm. Closed Dec 20–Jan 20. AMERICAN/PORTUGUESE.

This place is likely to be crowded, so in high season you'll have to wait for a table or abandon all hope—the intimate, informal bistro is that good. The menu combines fine American and Portuguese foods, with pleasing results. Ray Ettinger, a U.S. citizen, long ago teamed with Portuguese Tony Brito to create this successful enterprise.

To the homesick Mr. Ettinger, at times nothing is more delectable than roast beef à l'inglese or Salisbury steak with mushroom sauce. Other justifiably popular items include lobster Thermidor, pepper steak, shrimp curry, and filet mignon. Two dishes from Macau are prepared at your table: beef with garden peppers, and shrimp and cucumbers. Fresh seafood includes sole, sea bass, garoupa, and fresh salmon, as well as the famous bacalhau a Reijos (oven-baked dry codfish with cheese sauce). Unlike many European restaurants, Reijos serves fresh vegetables with its main dishes at no extra cost. In addition, Mr. Ettinger makes the outstanding selection of desserts on the premises from fresh seasonal ingredients. The service is excellent.

Restaurante o Batel. Travessa das Flores 4. ☎ **21/483-02-15.** Reservations required. Main courses 1,500$–5,000$ ($8.40–$28); fixed-price menu 3,200$ ($17.90). AE, DC, MC, V. Tues–Sun noon–4pm and 6:30pm–midnight. PORTUGUESE/INTERNATIONAL.

O Batel fronts the fish market. Styled as a country inn, it's semirustic, with rough white walls and beamed ceilings. The reasonable prices and hearty regional cuisine explain why the tiny tables are usually filled at every meal. A typically good value is a fixed-price menu that includes soup, a main course, dessert, and your choice of mineral water, coffee, or half a bottle of wine. Lobster Thermidor and lobster stewed in cognac (both priced daily) are the house specialties. For something less expensive, we recommend succulent Cascais sole with banana, clams with cream, or savory mixed shellfish with rice. For an appetizer, try the prawn cocktail. Desserts include pineapple with Madeira wine. A Casal Mendes rosé is a cool wine choice.

INEXPENSIVE

Dom Manolo. Av. Marginal 13. ☎ **21/483-1126.** Main courses 1,000$–2,000$ ($5.60–$11.20). No credit cards. Daily 10am–11:30pm. Closed Jan. PORTUGUESE.

In the center of Cascais—in fact, on its main street—this Spanish-operated restaurant and grill looks like a Spanish tavern. The kitchen dishes out reasonably priced, tasty, uncomplicated regional fare. It attracts more local residents than fancy foreign visitors. Many diners come here at least once a week to dig into the perfectly cooked spit-roasted chicken. It comes with freshly made french fries or a salad. Try the savory grilled sardines, any shrimp dish, and most definitely the fresh catch of the day. The waiters will advise you. For dessert, there's velvety flan.

John Bull/Britannia Restaurant. Largo Luís de Camões 4A. ☎ **21/483-33-19.** Main courses 1,500$–2,300$ ($8.40–$12.90); fixed-price menu 3,500$ ($19.60). AE, DC, MC, V. Daily 12:30–3:30pm and 7:30–11:30pm. ENGLISH/PORTUGUESE/AMERICAN.

This centrally located pub and restaurant shows its English roots in both the black-and-white timbered Elizabethan facade and the John Bull Pub. The street-level room has dark wooden paneling, oak beams, fireplace, rough-hewn stools and tables, and pewter pots. Pints of hand-pumped ales and lagers are popular with those who want only to drink and talk. Hungry customers head upstairs to the Britannia Restaurant, where the menu features English, American, and Portuguese dishes. Popular items include cottage pie, Southern fried chicken, T-bone steaks, and local seafood. The food is solid and reliable—nothing more.

CASCAIS AFTER DARK

Nightlife in this burgeoning resort incorporates old-fashioned fado and glittery urban-style discos.

FADO CLUBS   The most popular and critically acclaimed fado emporium in Cascais is the legendary **Rodrigo,** rua de Birre 961, Forte Dom Rodrigo, estrada de Birre (☎ 21/487-13-73). It presents well-orchestrated versions of traditional fado Tuesday to Sunday from 10pm till 2am. Full meals cost 5,000$ to 8,000$ ($28 to $44.80). We prefer to drop in only for drinks; the cover charge of around 3,000$ ($16.80) includes the first two drinks. The club's owner and namesake, Rodrigo Inaçio, has attracted many Lisbon socialites with his vast repertoire of fado songs and soulful performances.

DISCOS & DANCE CLUBS   Cascais nightspots come and go as quickly as summer visitors, but the most popular in town with both straights and gays is **Coconuts,** in the Estalagem Farol, estrada do Guincho (☎ **21/483-01-73**). In an annex of the hotel, it contains two dance floors, six bars, a separate karaoke space, and a view over the sea. Between April and September, it's open nightly from 11pm to dawn; the rest of the year it's open the same hours, but only on Wednesday, Friday, and Saturday. Entrance costs 2,000$ ($11.20) and includes the first drink. For part of 2000, this club will be closed for renovations—check its status before heading there.

Entertainment with a calmer, and cornier, motif is available at the **Palm Beach Karaoke Bar,** Alameda Duguesa de Palmela (☎ **21/483-08-51**). The most consistent aspect of the place is the pub-style bar, where anyone can be a star for a few moments at the mike. The format of the associated restaurant changes frequently according to the seasons and the clientele. Beer prices start at 600$ ($3.35). Open Tuesday to Sunday from 7pm to 2am.

3 Guincho

4 miles N of Cascais, 6 miles N of Estoril

Guincho is best translated as "caterwaul"—the cry that swallows make while darting along the air currents over the wild sea. The swallows stay at Guincho year-round. Sometimes at night the sea, driven into a frenzy, howls like a wailing banshee, and that, too, is *guincho*.

The town lies near the westernmost point on the European continent, known to the Portuguese as **Cabo da Roca.** The beaches are spacious and sandy, the sunshine incandescent, and the nearby promontories, jutting into white-tipped Atlantic waves, spectacular. Wooded hills back the windswept dunes, and to the east the Serra de Sintra is silhouetted on the distant horizon.

ESSENTIALS
ARRIVING
BY BUS   From the train station at Cascais, buses leave for the Praia do Guincho every hour. The trip takes 20 minutes.

BY CAR   From Cascais, continue west along Route 247.

VISITOR INFORMATION
The nearest tourist office is in Cascais (see above).

TREACHEROUS BEACHES & SEAFOOD FEASTS
The **Praia do Guincho** draws large beach crowds. The undertow is treacherous, so it's wise to keep in mind the advice of Jennings Parrott, writing in the *International Herald Tribune:* "If you are caught up by the current, don't fight it. Don't panic. The wind forces it to circle, so you will be brought back to shore." A local fisherman, however, advises that you take a box lunch along. According to him, "Sometimes it takes several days to make the circle."

One of the primary reasons for coming to Guincho is to sample its **seafood restaurants** (see "Where to Dine," below). You can try the crayfish-size, box-jaw lobsters known as *bruxas,* which in Portuguese means "sorcerer," "wizard," "witch doctor," and even "nocturnal moth." To eat like the Portuguese, you must also sample the barnacles, called *percêbes.* (Many foreign visitors fail to comprehend their popularity with the Portuguese.) The fresh lobsters and crabs are cultivated in nearby shellfish beds, fascinating sights in themselves.

A Toast to Colares

At the end of the Serra de Sintra toward the sea is Colares, a small town with winding streets, old *quintas* (manor houses), bright flowers, and vineyards. The town is known for its white and red wines produced from grapes grown on the surrounding sandy soil. The good land and sea breezes are the foundation for some of the best wine in the country.

Colares lies 22 miles west of Lisbon and 5 miles west of Sintra. Many visitors drive here just to visit the wineries. Others prefer the quiet town to more crowded Sintra as a place to spend the night.

The Portuguese winemaking industry has dramatically raised its international profile since the 1980s, thanks partly to the promotional skills of such districts as Colares. A sophisticated core of entrepreneurial grape producers has accessorized the village to welcome wine lovers in the style they want and need.

The first stop on your exploration should be the headquarters of the region's largest cooperative, **Adega de Colares,** rua Alameda Coronel Linhares de Lima (☎ **21/929-12-10**). This is the premier wine-tasting and wine-buying venue in Colares, in a century-old former manor house. Beneath intricately crafted wooden ceilings, you can taste the wine that's blended, selected, and bottled from grapes brought in by more than a hundred local growers. You can also visit the labyrinth of cellars, which radiate, in the form of tunnels, out from beneath the house. Bottles are for sale, and there's always a sample available to help you distinguish the commonplace from the extraordinary. Open daily 9am to noon and 3 to 5pm.

Another option lies 3 miles to the north in the hamlet of Azenhas do Mar. **Adegas Beira-Mar (Soc. Chitas),** Azenhas do Mar (☎ **21/929-20-36**), is the region's biggest individual producer of reds and whites. It maintains an intricate combination of old and new cellars and processing plants—less charming than you might expect, but they turn out some superb, internationally renowned wines. There's someone on hand to guide you through the premises, and bottles are available for sale. Open daily 9am to noon and 3 to 5pm.

Should you wish to spend the night, the most appealing choice is the **Estalagem de Colares,** estrada nacional 247, 2710 Colares (☎ **21/928-29-42;** fax 21/928-29-83). It offers 12 handsomely furnished rooms, all with bathroom, air-conditioning, TV, and phone. Portuguese entrepreneur Cristina Sousa, a resident of Cascais, restored the building with painstaking devotion and opened for business

WHERE TO STAY
EXPENSIVE

✪ **Hotel do Guincho.** Praia do Guincho, 2750 Cascais. ☎ **21/487-04-91.** Fax 21/487-04-31. www.guinchotel.pt. E-mail: reservation@guinchotel.pt. 29 units. A/C MINIBAR TV TEL. 23,000$–38,000$ ($128.80–$212.80) double; 43,000$ ($240.80) suite. Rates include buffet breakfast. AE, DC, MC, V. Free parking.

Hotel do Guincho is a fine place to spend the night. In the 17th century, within a few hundred feet of the westernmost point in Europe, an army of local masons built one of the most forbidding fortresses along the coast. The twin towers that flank the vaguely Moorish facade still stand sentinel over the sun-bleached terrain of sand and rock.

You enter the hotel through an enclosed courtyard, where there's a well that used to provide water for the garrison. The public rooms contain all the antique trappings of in 1996. She transformed a run-down restaurant that had thrived here since around the turn of the century into a sophisticated small hotel with a fine dining room. The beautifully maintained and inviting rooms are done in traditional Portuguese style. A double goes for 14,000$ to 18,000$ ($78.40 to $100.80), including breakfast. Parking is free.

The establishment sits close to the center of Colares, in a 2-acre garden where chaise longues flank flowering shrubs beside the banks of the local river, Ribeira de Colares. Main courses in the restaurant cost 1,500$ to 2,800$ ($8.40 to $15.70). Open hours are 12:30 to 3pm and 7:30 to 10:30pm daily. The ambience is sophisticated and continental, evocative of an upscale country home. The hotel accepts major credit cards.

The most likable restaurant in the district, **Refúgio da Roca,** estrada de Cabo de Roca (☎ 21/929-08-98), is on the main street of the hamlet of Azoya, 5 miles south of Colares. It specializes in ultrafresh fish (especially sea bass, sea bream, and sole) grilled over charcoal. The gratifyingly simple fare is a good match for a dining room sheathed with folkloric accessories from the region's agrarian and wine trade. Expect to spend 4,500$ to 5,000$ ($25.20 to $28) for an excellent regional dinner accompanied by one of the local wines. Open Wednesday to Monday 12:30 to 3pm and 8 to 11pm. Major credit cards are accepted.

You might also try **Da Aldeia,** estrada nacional, Azoya (☎ 21/928-00-01; fax 21/928-01-63). It's less than 100 yards from the Refúgio da Roca, with which it shares an owner. Da Aldeia is more formal, more expensive, and proud of its local shellfish. The building conveys a strong sense of the maritime traditions of this part of Portugal. Look for succulent versions of a parrillada of mariscos, laden with shellfish, clams, oysters, crayfish, and lobster. Grilled fish and a traditional version of roast pork with clams are also worthwhile. Regular main courses cost 1,950$ to 2,600$ ($10.90 to $14.55); shellfish and seafood main courses run 2,500$ to 7,000$ ($14 to $39.20). Open Thursday to Tuesday 12:30 to 3:30pm and 7:30 to 10:30pm. Major credit cards are accepted.

Da Aldeia rents 14 well-furnished rooms with TV, phone, air-conditioning, and minibar. A double costs 12,000$ to 16,000$ ($67.20 to $89.60). Rates include breakfast, and parking is free. There's 24-hour room service, a concierge, a swimming pool, and tennis courts.

an aristocratic private home. In cold weather, a fire might blaze in a granite-framed fireplace, illuminating the thick carpets and the century-old furniture.

Each small but luxuriously furnished guest room is behind a thick pine door heavily banded with iron and under a vaulted stone ceiling. Most rooms overlook the water and have a medieval and Portuguese provincial décor. Some beds are set in alcoves. The marble bathrooms are supplied with robes and hair dryers. There are also three small but elegant suites, some with their own fireplaces.

Past guests have included Orson Welles, who reportedly was fascinated by the mist and waves. Princess Grace and prime ministers of both Italy and Portugal also found the place intriguing.

Dining: The newly renovated restaurant is one of the most superb in the area. The cuisine is mostly French; fixed-price dinners cost 6,500$ to 9,500$ ($36.40 to

$53.20). The chefs coax every nuance of flavor from the fine regional ingredients. There's also a fashionable bar.

Amenities: Concierge, 24-hour room service, laundry, baby-sitting, solarium, swimming pool.

INEXPENSIVE

Estalagem do Forte Muchaxo. Praia do Guincho, 2750 Cascais. ☎ **21/487-02-21.** Fax 21/487-04-44. 60 units. TEL. 10,000$–26,000$ ($56–$145.60) double. Rates include breakfast. AE, DC, MC, V. Free parking.

Four decades ago the proprietor, the senior Muchaxo, sold brandy and coffee to fishers from a simple straw hut on wave-dashed rocks. Gradually he started to cook for them, and in time, beach-loving Europeans discovered the place. Eventually even royalty arrived, wanting to be fed.

The Muchaxo family still operates this overblown hacienda, and has preserved the original straw hut. The best guest rooms overlook the sea. Each unit is unique; most have stark white walls with beamed ceilings. At one side, thrust out onto rock walls, is a pool with terraces and diving boards. In cooler weather, guests gather in the chalet living room to warm themselves at the huge raised-stone fireplace.

There's a choice of two dining rooms. One is modern, and the other has a bamboo ceiling and hand-painted provincial furniture. People drive from miles around just to sample the Portuguese and French cuisine, highly praised by such discriminating travelers as the author James Michener. The adventurous begin with barnacles. The house specialty is lobster Barraca style.

WHERE TO DINE

✪ **Restaurante Porto de Santa Maria.** Estrada do Guincho. ☎ **21/487-10-36** or 21/487-02-40. Regular main courses 2,000$–10,000$ ($11.20–$56); seafood main courses 4,500$–9,000$ ($25.20–$50.40). AE, DC, MC, V. Tues–Sun 12:15–3:30pm and 7–10:30pm. PORTUGUESE.

If you drive to this isolated stretch of roadside, you won't be alone. Hundreds of discerning Europeans and Portuguese vacationers might join you, especially in summer. This restaurant is one of the most appealing of its type along the coast. It serves some of the best seafood in the area, worth the ride out from Lisbon. A doorman ushers you into the low-lying seafront building whose large windows take in views of the occasionally treacherous surf.

An enormous aquarium made from white marble and thick sheets of glass brightens the stark decor. The polite staff serves every conceivable form of succulent shellfish, priced by the gram, as well as such house specialties as grilled sole. Shellfish rice, or *arroz de mariscos,* is the most popular specialty—and justifiably so. Try the rondelles of pungent sheep's-milk cheese that await you on the table.

4 Queluz

9 miles NW of Lisbon

Queluz, only 20 minutes from Lisbon, makes a great excursion from the capital or en route to Sintra. The Queluz Palace (see "Exploring the Palace," below), in its pink rococo glory, offers storybook Portuguese charm.

ESSENTIALS

ARRIVING

BY TRAIN   From the Estação do Rossio in Lisbon, take the Sintra line to Queluz. Departures during the day are every 15 minutes. The trip takes 30 minutes. A one-way ticket costs 155$ (85¢). Call ☎ **21/888-40-25** for schedules. At Queluz, turn left and follow the signs for half a mile to the palace.

BY CAR   From Lisbon, head west along the express highway (A1), which becomes Route 249. Turn off at the exit for Queluz. It usually takes 20 minutes.

VISITOR INFORMATION
You can ask for information at the tourist office in Sintra (see below).

EXPLORING THE PALACE
On the highway from Lisbon to Sintra, the ✪ **Palácio Nacional de Queluz,** largo do Palácio, 2745 Lisboa (☎ **21/435-00-39**), shimmers in the sunlight. It's a brilliant example of the rococo in Portugal. Pedro III ordered its construction in 1747, and the work dragged on until 1787. The architect Mateus Vicente de Oliveira was later joined by the French decorator-designer Jean-Baptiste Robillion, who was largely responsible for planning the garden and lakeside setting.

Pedro III had adapted an old hunting pavilion that once belonged to the Marquis Castelo Rodrigo. Later, the pavilion came into the possession of the Portuguese royal family. Pedro III liked it so much that he decided to make it his summer residence. What you'll see today is not what the palace was like in the 18th century. Queluz suffered greatly during the French invasions, and almost all of its belongings were transported to Brazil with the royal family. A 1934 fire destroyed a great deal of Queluz, but tasteful and sensitive reconstruction restored the lighthearted aura of the 18th century.

Blossoming mauve petunias and red geraniums highlight the topiary effects, with closely trimmed vines and sculptured box hedges. Fountain pools on which lilies float are lined with blue tiles and reflect the muted facade, the statuary, and the finely cut balustrades.

Inside, you can wander through the queen's dressing room, lined with painted panels depicting a children's romp; the Don Quixote Chamber (Dom Pedro was born here and returned from Brazil to die in the same bed); the Music Room, complete with a French grande pianoforte and an 18th-century English harpsichord; and the mirrored throne room adorned with crystal chandeliers. The Portuguese still hold state banquets here.

Festooning the palace are all the eclectic props of the rococo era. You'll see the inevitable chinoiserie panels (from Macau), Florentine marbles from quarries once worked by Michelangelo, Iberian and Flemish tapestries, Empire antiques, Delft indigo-blue ceramics, 18th-century Hepplewhite armchairs, Austrian porcelains, Rabat carpets, Portuguese Chippendale furnishings, and Brazilian jacaranda wood pieces—all of exquisite quality. When they visited Portugal, Presidents Eisenhower, Carter, and Reagan stayed in the 30-chambered Pavilion of Dona Maria I, as did Elizabeth II (on two occasions) and the prince and princess of Wales. These fabled chambers, refurbished by the Portuguese government, are said to have reverberated with the rantings of the grief-stricken monarch Maria I, who reputedly had to be strapped to her bed at times. Before becoming mentally ill, she was an intelligent, brave woman who did a great job as ruler of her country in a troubled time.

The palace is open Wednesday to Monday from 10am to 1pm and 2 to 5pm; it's closed on holidays. Admission is 500$ ($2.80), free for children under 14. Admission is free to everyone on Sunday morning.

WHERE TO STAY
✪ **Pousada Dona Maria I.** Largo do Palácio, 2745 Queluz. ☎ **800/223-1356** for reservations in the U.S., or 21/435-61-58. Fax 21/435-61-89. 26 units. A/C MINIBAR TV TEL.

20,300$–31,000$ ($113.70–$173.60) double; 24,000$–38,000$ ($134.40–$212.80) suite. Rates include breakfast. AE, DC, MC, V. From Sintra, take highway IC-19 and follow signs to Queluz. Free parking.

This building's function during the 17th century was to house the staff that maintained the Palace of Queluz, which rises in stately majesty across the road. The pousada—named after one of Portugal's most revered queens—is graced with an ornate clock tower that evokes an oversized ornament in the garden of a stately English home. In addition to the pousada's comfortable midsize guest rooms and well-managed dining room, the premises contain touches of complicated Manueline stonework. The 17th-century theater holds occasional concerts. The rooms are severely dignified, high-ceilinged, and equipped with firm mattresses. The pousada's restaurant, the Cozinha Velha, which has flourished since the 1950s, is considerably older than the pousada, which opened in 1995.

WHERE TO DINE

✪ **Cozinha Velha (The Old Kitchen).** Palácio Nacional de Queluz, largo do Palácio. ☎ **21/435-02-32.** Reservations required. Main courses 2,500$–7,950$ ($14–$44.50). AE, DC, MC, V. Daily 12:30–3pm and 7:30–10pm. PORTUGUESE/INTERNATIONAL.

If you have only two or three meals in the Lisbon area, take one at the Cozinha Velha. Once it was the kitchen of the palace, built in the grand style; it has since been converted into a colorful dining room favored by both royalty and visitors who seek a gourmet dinner in a romantic setting.

You enter the restaurant through a garden patio. The dining room is like a small chapel, with high stone arches, a freestanding fireplace, marble columns, and the original spits. Along one side is a 20-foot marble table laden with baskets of fruit and vases of flowers. You sit on ladder-back chairs surrounded by shiny copper, oil paintings, and torchières. The innovative handling of regional ingredients pleases most diners, and the cooking uses spices, herbs, and textures well. We recommend the hors d'oeuvres for two, followed by a main course such as black grouper medallions with prawn béchamel, poached sole Cozinha Velha, fried goat with mashed turnip sprouts, or pepper steak with spinach mousse. For dessert, try the crepes Cozinha Velha with champagne sorbet.

5 Sintra: Byron's "Glorious Eden"

18 miles NW of Lisbon

Writers have sung Sintra's praises ever since Portugal's national poet, Luís Vaz de Camões, proclaimed its glory in *Os Lusíadas* (*The Lusiads*). Lord Byron called it "glorious Eden" when he and John Cam Hobhouse included Sintra in their 1809 grand tour. English romantics thrilled to its description in Byron's autobiographical *Childe Harold's Pilgrimage*, which otherwise took a dim view of Portugal.

Picture a town on a hillside, with decaying birthday-cake villas covered with tiles coming loose in the damp mist. Luxuriant vegetation covers the town: camellias for melancholic romantics, ferns behind which lizards dart, pink and purple bougainvillea over garden trelliswork, red geraniums on wrought-iron balconies, eucalyptus branches fluttering in the wind, lemon trees in groves, and honey-sweet mimosa scenting the air. Be warned: Some people visit Sintra, fall under its spell, and stay forever.

Sintra is one of the oldest towns in the country. When the crusaders captured it in 1147, they fought bitterly against the Moors firmly entrenched in their hilltop castle, the ruins of which remain today.

Sintra

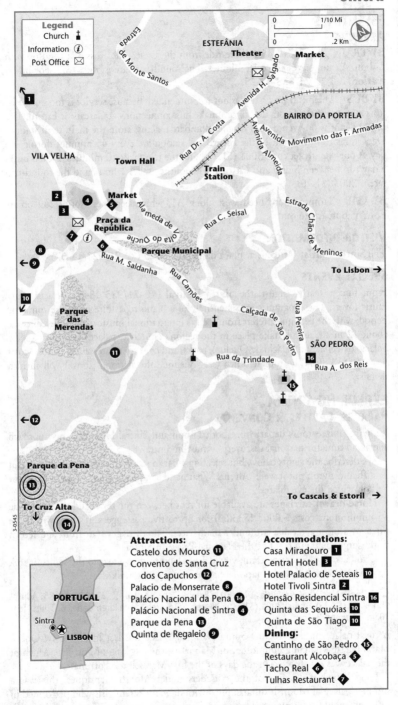

Legend
- Church ✝
- Information ⓘ
- Post Office ✉

ESTEFÂNIA
Theater   Market

Estrada de Monte Santos

BAIRRO DA PORTELA

Avenida H. Salgado
Avenida Movimento das F. Armadas
Avenida Almeida

Rua Dr. A. Costa

VILA VELHA   Town Hall   Train Station

Market
Praça da República
Parque Municipal

Alameda de V
Volta do Duche
Rua C. Seisal

Estrada Chão de Meninos

Rua M. Saldanha
Rua Camões

To Lisbon →

Parque das Merendas

Calçada de São Pedro

Rua Pereira

SÃO PEDRO

Rua da Trindade
Rua A. dos Reis

Parque da Pena

To Cruz Alta ↓

To Cascais & Estoril →

0   1/10 Mi
0   .2 Km

Attractions:
Castelo dos Mouros ⑪
Convento de Santa Cruz dos Capuchos ⑫
Palacio de Monserrate ⑧
Palácio Nacional da Pena ⑭
Palácio Nacional de Sintra ④
Parque da Pena ⑬
Quinta de Regaleio ⑨

Accommodations:
Casa Miradouro ❶
Central Hotel ❸
Hotel Palacio de Seteais ❿
Hotel Tivoli Sintra ❷
Pensão Residencial Sintra ⑯
Quinta das Sequóias ❿
Quinta de São Tiago ❿

Dining:
Cantinho de São Pedro ⑮
Restaurant Alcobaça ❺
Tacho Real ❻
Tulhas Restaurant ❼

PORTUGAL
Sintra ★
LISBON

3-0545

157

ESSENTIALS
ARRIVING

BY TRAIN   Sintra is a 45-minute ride from the Estação do Rossio at the Rossio in Lisbon. A train leaves every 15 minutes. The round-trip fare is 360$ ($2). For **information,** call ☎ **21/888-40-25.**

BY BUS   The bus from Lisbon is not recommended, because service is too slow. Visitors staying on the Costa do Sol can make bus connections at Cascais or Estoril. The Sintra depot is on avenida Dr. Miguel Bombarda, across from the main train station. Departures from in front of the **Estoril** rail station are every 45 minutes during the day. A one-way ticket costs 300$ ($1.70), and the trip takes 40 minutes. Eleven buses a day run between Sintra and **Cascais.** The journey takes 1 hour, and the round-trip fare is 300$ ($1.70).

BY CAR   From Lisbon, head west along A1, which becomes Route 249 on its eastern approach to Sintra.

VISITOR INFORMATION

The **Sintra Tourist Office** is at praça da República 23 (☎ **21/923-11-57**).

SPECIAL EVENTS

From June to early August, the **Sintra Festival** (☎ **21/923-4845**) attracts many music lovers. The program consists entirely of a piano repertoire from the romantic period, with the best interpreters from today's international music scene. The concerts, about 12 in all, usually take place in the region's churches, palaces (Palácio da Vila, Palácio da Pena, and Palácio de Queluz), parks, and country estates. Each concert costs 3,000$ ($16.80). The tourist office (see "Visitor Information," above) will furnish details.

EXPLORING SINTRA
PALACES, CASTLES & CONVENTS

Many organized tours depart from both Lisbon and Sintra. However, this approach allows no time for personal discovery, a must in Sintra.

We describe the sights below, but selecting what to see from the many treasures can be difficult. Byron put it well: "Ah me! What hand can pencil guide, or pen, to follow half on which the eye dilates?"

Horse-drawn carriages are available for rent between the town and the *serra.* The 45-minute tour costs 6,000$ ($33.60) for up to five passengers. It's well worth the price for a most agreeable trip under shady trees. The carriages start from and return to the large square in front of the National Palace of Sintra.

If you arrive in Sintra by train, you'll either have to take a taxi to the sights or trek up the long, lush hill to the national palace—a very long walk.

✪ **Palácio Nacional de Sintra.** Largo da Rainha Dona Amélia. ☎ **21/923-00-85.** Admission 400$ ($2.25) adults, 200$ ($1.10) children 6–16, free for children under 6. Thurs–Tues 10am–1pm and 2–5pm.

A royal palace until 1910, the Sintra National Palace was last inhabited by Queen Maria Pía, the Italian grandmother of Manuel II, the last king of Portugal. Much of the palace was constructed in the days of the first Manuel, the Fortunate.

Long before the arrival of the crusaders under Afonso Henríques, this was a summer palace of Moorish sultans, filled with dancing harem girls who performed in front of bubbling fountains. The original palace was torn down, and the Moorish style of architecture was incorporated into latter-day versions. The structure is now a

Crime Watch

Warning: Don't leave valuables in unguarded cars in Sintra, and beware of pickpockets and purse snatchers. Not only does the town attract virtually every tourist who sets foot on Portuguese soil, but it also attracts those who prey on them. While violence is not generally a problem, theft is.

conglomeration of styles, with Gothic and Manueline predominant. The glazed earthenware tiles lining many of the chambers are among the most beautiful in Portugal.

The Swan Room was a favorite of João I, one of the founding kings of Portugal, father of Henry the Navigator and husband of Philippa of Lancaster. It's said that one day the English queen came upon her king embracing one of the ladies of the court. Apparently she didn't hold a grudge, but the situation grew into a court scandal of which the king became painfully aware. Hoping to end speculation and save his wife further embarrassment, he called his decorators into a room, locked the door, and gave them a secret mission. When the doors finally opened, the ladies of the court discovered that the ceiling was covered with magpies. The symbol of the chattering birds scored a point and a new subject of gossip was discovered. Guides now call the salon the Chamber of the Magpies.

The Room of the Sirens or Mermaids is one of the most elegant in the palace. The Heraldic or Stag Room holds coats of arms of aristocratic Portuguese families, and hunting scenes. In most of the rooms, wide windows look out onto attractive views of the Sintra mountain range. Tile-fronted stoves are in the Old Kitchen, where feasts were held in bygone days. The best-known were game banquets during the reign of Carlos I, who was assassinated in 1908. The palace is rich in paintings and Iberian and Flemish tapestries, but perhaps you can best appreciate the place as you wander into a tree- and plant-shaded patio and listen to the water gurgling in a fountain.

As you approach the palace, you can buy a ticket at the kiosk on your left. The palace opens onto the central town square. Outside, two conical chimney towers form the most distinctive landmark on the Sintra skyline.

✪ **Palácio Nacional de Pena.** Estrada de Pena. ☎ **21/910-53-40.** Admission 475$ ($2.65), free for children under 15. Oct–May Tues–Sun 10am–1pm and 2–5pm; June–Sept Tues–Sun 10am–1pm and 2–6:30pm. Last admission half hour before closing.

On a plateau about 1,500 feet above sea level, Pena perches above Sintra like a medieval fortress. Part of the fun of visiting the castle is the ride up the verdant, winding road through the Parque das Merendas.

The inspiration behind this castle in the sky was Ferdinand of Saxe-Coburg-Gotha, the husband of Maria II. Ferdinand called on a fellow German, Baron Eschwege, to help him build his fantasy. You can see a sculpture of the baron if you look out from the Pena toward a huge rock across the way.

In the early 16th century, Manuel the Fortunate ordered a monastery for the Jerónimos monks built on these lofty grounds. Today, you can visit a preserved cloister and small ogival chapel.

Crossing over a drawbridge, you'll enter the palace proper. Its last royal occupant was Queen Amélia. One morning in 1910 she clearly saw that the monarchy in Portugal was ending. Having lost her husband and her soldier-son to an assassin 2 years before, she was determined not to lose her second son, Manuel II. Gathering her most precious possessions and small family heirlooms that could be packed quickly, she fled to Mafra, where her son waited. She did not see the Pena palace again until 1945, when she returned to Portugal under much more favorable conditions. Pena has remained much as Amélia left it, which is part of its fascination; it's a rare record of European royal life in the halcyon days preceding World War I.

Pena Park was designed and planted for more than 4 years, beginning in 1846. Ferdinand was the force behind the landscaping. He built one of the most spectacular parks in Portugal, known for the scope of its shrub and tree life. For an eye-opening vista of the park and the palace, you can make the ascent to **Cruz Alta.** Admission is free.

GETTING TO THE PALACE   If you're not driving, you can take a 20-minute taxi or bus ride; the bus departs from Sintra's main square from May to September. Many visitors have a taxi wait for them. If you walk, be warned that the arduous 1½-mile climb from the square takes about 2 hours even if you're in good shape.

✪ **Castelo dos Mouros.** Calçada dos Clérigos. ☎ **21/923-15-56.** Free admission. Daily June–Sept 10am–6pm; Oct–May 9am–5pm. From Pena palace (10-min. walk), follow signs to the castelo.

The Castle of the Moors was built sometime between the 8th and 9th century in a position 1,350 feet above sea level. In 1147 Scandinavian crusaders besieged and captured it from its Moorish occupants. Ferdinand of Saxe-Coburg-Gotha, the royal consort responsible for Pena palace (see above), attempted to restore the castle in the 19th century. He was relatively unsuccessful.

From the parking area, a guide will send you in the right direction. From the royal tower, the view of Sintra, its palace and castle, and the Atlantic coast is panoramic.

Palácio de Monserrate. Estrada de Monserrate. ☎ **21/923-01-37.** Admission 200$ ($1.10). Daily June–Sept 10am–6pm; Oct–May 10am–5pm. From Sintra, take Route EN375 and follow signs.

The Englishman Sir Francis Cook set out between 1846 and 1850 to make Lord Byron's dream of a "glorious Eden" a reality. Bringing in landscape artists and flora from Africa, Norway, and places in between, he planned a botanical garden unrivaled in Iberia. The garden scales the slope of a hill, and exploring it takes the better part of a morning or afternoon. Walking back is rough for all but seasoned trekkers, but the vista merits the descent.

At the bottom of the hill, Cook built his palácio. For his Eden, only a Moorish temple would do, but when Cook died, Monserrate faced a troubled future. An English manufacturer purchased the property and nearly destroyed Cook's dreams. He began by selling the palace antiques. He reportedly made so much money on the sale that he recovered all the cash he sank into Monserrate, but he still wasn't satisfied. When his plans to subdivide the park and turn it into a development of villas became public, the government belatedly intervened. You'll be glad it did—lilies float on cool fountains, flowers scent the air, ferns mount the hillside, northern spruces soar upward, and flora from Africa thrives as if it were in its native habitat.

Convento de Santa Cruz dos Capuchos. Estrada de Pena. ☎ **21/923-15-56.** Admission 200$ ($1.10). Daily June–Sept 9am–6pm; Oct–May 9am–5pm.

In 1560 Dom Álvaro de Castro ordered that this unusually structured convent be built for the Capuchins. The construction used cork so extensively that the building is sometimes known as the "cork monastery."

The convent is in a secluded area 4½ miles from Sintra. You walk up a moss-covered path, like a wayfarer of old approaching for his dole. Ring the bell and a guide (not a monk) will appear to show you around the miniature cells. Today, the convent seems forlorn and forgotten. Even when it was in use, it probably wasn't noted for its liveliness. The Capuchins who lived here, perhaps eight in all, had a penchant for the most painstakingly detailed work. For example, they lined the monastery walls with cork-bark tiles and seashells. They also carved a chapel out of rock, using cork for insulation. Outside, one of them found time to do an altar fresco in honor of St. Francis of Assisi. In 1834, the monks suddenly abandoned the convent.

There's no bus service; if you're not driving, take a taxi from Sintra's main square.

Quinta de Regaleioa. Rua Visconde de Monserrate. ☎ **21/910-66-50.** Admission 2,000$ ($11.20) adults, 1,000$ ($5.60) children 8–16, free for children under 8. Daily 10am–6pm.

Classified as a World Heritage Site by UNESCO, this *quinta* (manor house) in the old quarter was built at the turn of the 20th century. It incorporates architectural elements of the Gothic, Manueline, and Renaissance styles. You can take a tour of the property, which is filled with antiques and artifacts of a vanished age. The building's turrets afford panoramic views of the countryside. After touring the house, visitors can stroll through the surrounding park.

OUTDOOR ACTIVITIES

The best golf course is the **Estoril-Sol Golf Club,** estrada da Lagoa Azul, outside Sintra (☎ **21/923-24-61**). At the foot of the Sintra mountain range, the course lies some 20 miles from Lisbon. The Palácio Nacional da Pena looms overhead, and the course occupies a forest setting with acacias and pines. It's fairly short, stretching 4,644 yards and offering only 9 holes with 18 tees. A 9-hole round costs 3,700$ ($20.70) Monday to Friday, 4,200$ ($23.50) on Saturday and Sunday. Open 8am to 7pm Monday to Friday, 8am to 8pm Saturday and Sunday.

In Sintra, you can play **tennis** at the court in Parque Liberdade (☎ **21/924-11-39**). The club is open daily 9am to 7pm. It charges 500$ ($2.80) per player per hour.

SHOPPING

Folkloric, history-rich Sintra has been a repository of salable Portuguese charm since the dawn of modern tourism. As you wander through its cobblestone streets and alleyways, you'll find many intriguing outlets for handmade folk art from the region and the rest of Portugal.

The best shops include the **Sintra Bazar,** praça da República 37 (☎ **21/923-05-14**), where seven or eight different merchants maintain individual boutiques selling creative handcrafts. On the same street is **A Esquina,** praça da República 20 (☎ **21/923-34-27**). It carries many hand-painted ceramics, some of which are reproductions of designs that originated between the 15th and 18th centuries. **Almorábida,** rua Visconde de Monserrate 12–24 (☎ **21/924-05-39**), in front of Sintra Palace, sells Arraiolos carpets, lace, and intricately hammered copperware. A worthy antique shop close to the town center, is **Henríque Peixera,** rua Consigliere de Proso 2 (☎ **21/923-10-43**). It carries sometimes dauntingly expensive furniture and accessories.

Two final contenders are emphatically aware of the desirability of handcrafts in the industrialized world. **Loja Branca,** rua Consigliere de Proso 2 (☎ **21/923-23-75**), sells roughly textured, often intriguing fabrics. **Violeta,** rua das Padarias 19 (☎ **21/923-40-95**), stocks hand-embroidered linen tablecloths, towels, sheets, and bedspreads.

WHERE TO STAY
VERY EXPENSIVE

✪ **Hotel Palácio de Seteais.** Rua Barbosa do Bocage 8, Seteais, 2710 Sintra. ☎ **21/923-32-00.** Fax 21/923-42-77. E-mail: hpseteais@mail.telepac.pt. 30 units. MINIBAR TV TEL. 35,000$–46,000$ ($196–$257.60) double; 46,000$–55,000$ ($257.60–$308) suite. Rates include breakfast. AE, DC, MC, V.

Lord Byron worked on *Childe Harold's Pilgrimage* in the front garden of this palace, which later became a hotel. Seteais looks older than it is—a Dutch Gildmeester built it in the late 18th century. The fifth marquês de Marialva, who sponsored many receptions and galas for the aristocrats of his day, later took over and restored the palace.

The hotel lies at the end of a long driveway. An arched entryway dominates the formal stone architecture. The palácio is on the crest of a hill; most of its drawing rooms, galleries, and chambers overlook the formal terraces, flower garden, and vista toward the sea. A long, galleried hall and a staircase with white-and-gilt balustrades and columns lead to the lower-level dining room, drinking lounge, and garden terraces. The library and adjoining music room are furnished with period pieces. The main drawing room contains antiques and a fine mural extending around the cove and onto the ceiling. The guest book reads like a who's who.

There are only 30 units, so advance reservations are necessary. The beautiful, spacious rooms are furnished with antiques or tasteful reproductions.

Dining/Diversions: Nonguests can have lunch or dinner if they make reservations. The fixed-price meal consists of four courses of continental and regional dishes. After-dinner coffee is taken on the adjoining terrace and loggia or in the dining room. Food is served daily from 12:30 to 2:30pm and 7:30 to 9:30pm. A pianist, harpist, and violinist often entertain.

Amenities: Room service (8am to midnight), laundry, baby-sitting, pool, two tennis courts, horseback riding.

MODERATE

Hotel Tivoli Sintra. Praça da República, 2710 Sintra. ☎ **21/923-35-05.** Fax 221/923-15-72. 75 units. A/C MINIBAR TV TEL. 21,300$ ($119.30) double. Rates include breakfast. AE, DC, MC, V. Free parking.

The finest hotel in the center of Sintra, and a favorite with groups, the modern, airy Tivoli Sintra opened in 1981. It lies only a few doors from the Central Hotel (see below) and the National Palace, and offers an abundance of modern conveniences, including a garage. The combination of amenities with traditional Portuguese decor is successful. The cavernous lobby has marble floors. The spacious guest rooms are comfortably furnished, with firm mattresses, large beds, and big easy chairs. The balconies and the public rooms look out onto a wooded hill with views of Sintra's *quintas* (manor houses). The sight, according to a reader from Berkeley, California, "could have inspired mad Ludwig of Bavaria or at least Walt Disney." The hotel has a restaurant with panoramic views of Monserrate, a bar, and a beauty parlor. Room service is available until midnight, and laundry and baby-sitting can be arranged.

✪ **Quinta das Sequóias.** Apdo. 4, 2710 Sintra. ☎ and fax **21/924-38-21.** www. portugalvirtual.pt/quinta.das.sequoias. 6 units. 17,000$–25,000$ ($95.20–$140) double. Rates include buffet breakfast. AE, DC, MC, V. Closed 2 weeks in Jan. Free parking. From Sintra, take the road signposted for Montserrate, then fork left at signpost for hotel.

About a mile south of town, this 19th-century manor house was originally built as a rural annex of a much larger palace (the Palácio do Relogio) in Sintra's center. It's a 5-minute drive from the Palácio de Seteais. Some 40 acres of land surround the *quinta*. The generally spacious rooms have high ceilings and formal 19th-century furniture. On the premises are a swimming pool, a Jacuzzi, a sauna, and a verdant English-style garden. Within a 10-mile walk from the main house are an archaeological dig, where Roman coins and artifacts from the Bronze Age have been unearthed, and bubbling springs whose pure waters were noted by historians during the 15th century. If you give notice at breakfast, dinner can be prepared.

Quinta de São Tiago. Estrada de Monserrate, 2710 Sintra. ☎ **21/923-29-23.** Fax 21/923-43-29. 13 units. 21,000$ ($117.60) double; 30,000$ ($168) suite. Rates include buffet breakfast. No credit cards. Free parking.

Visited by Lord Byron in 1809, Quinta de São Tiago is one of the most desirable places to stay in the Sintra area. Reached on a rough road, it edges up the side of a mountain in a woodland setting. Its origins as a *quinta* (manor house) go back to the 1500s. It's been refurbished and handsomely furnished with antiques. Many of the units open onto views of the Valley of Colares and the water beyond. The pool offers views of Monserrate and the Atlantic coastline.

In the finest British tradition, tea is offered in the parlor, which was transformed from the original kitchen. Dances are held in summer in the music room, and summertime buffets are true occasions. The quinta serves regional and continental cuisine; be sure to book ahead if you want to eat here. The midsize guest rooms are comfortably furnished and attractively decorated, with firm mattresses and modern plumbing.

INEXPENSIVE

✪ **Casa Miradouro.** Rua Sotto Mayor 55 (Apdo. 1027), 2710 Sintra. ☎ **21/923-59-00.** Fax 21/924-18-36. 6 units. 16,000$–21,000$ ($89.60–$117.60) double. Rates include breakfast. DC, MC, V. Closed Dec 30–Feb 19. From the Hotel Tivoli Sintra (see above), take rua Sotto Mayor for ¼ mi.

From the year of its construction (1894) until 1987, this cozy Iberian villa belonged to several generations of a family that included important figures in the Portuguese army. In 1993, Swiss-born Frederic Kneubühl bought it, renovated it, and filled it with a practical mixture of modern and late 19th-century furniture. It's now an amusing, well-managed, attractively indulgent B&B. About a quarter mile north of Sintra, it boasts a small garden, very few amenities other than the owner's genteel goodwill, and a facade that art historians have defined as Iberian chalet style. Because the B&B has no pool or other notable facilities, most guests spend their days touring Lisbon or the surrounding district. The excellently maintained rooms are most inviting, with provincial carpets, tile floors, wrought-iron bedsteads, and firm mattresses. Views from upper-floor rooms include the Pena Palace and, on clear days, the faraway Atlantic.

Central Hotel. Praça da República, 2710 Sintra. ☎ **21/923-00-63.** 10 units. TEL. 15,000$ ($84) double; 20,000$ ($112) triple. Rates include breakfast. AE, DC, MC, V.

This charming but slightly tarnished family owned and operated village inn offers personalized accommodations and good food. The hotel opens onto the main square, facing the National Palace; accommodations fronting the square are noisy. The facade is inviting, with decorative blue-and-white tiles and an awning-covered front veranda with dining tables. The interior, especially the small guest rooms, is English in style. Each room is furnished individually with such fine pieces as polished wood and inlaid desks. Nearly all the tiled bathrooms are well designed and decorated in cheerful colors.

The Central's restaurant offers seating on the veranda overlooking the village or in one of the large interior rooms. The fare is primarily Portuguese, with such main courses as escalopes of veal in Madeira sauce, veal cutlet Milanese, beef Portuguese, and chateaubriand for two. Homemade caramel pudding makes a smooth finish. Food is served daily from 12:30 to 3pm and 8 to 9pm.

Pensão Residencial Sintra (Quinta Visconde de Tojal). Travessa dos Avelares 12, 2710 Sintra. ☎ and fax **21/923-07-38.** 10 units. TEL. 12,500$–15,000$ ($70–$84) double. Rates include buffet breakfast. MC, V. Free parking. From Sintra, take a bus marked SÃO PEDRO or MIRASINTRA.

The Viscount Tojal commissioned the construction of this dignified stone house around 1850. It's in São Pedro, a verdant suburb of Sintra about half a mile east of the center. Shortly after World War II, the German-born parents of the present owner, Susana Rosner Fragoso, bought the house, added a coat of white paint, and transformed it into a dignified pensão. Surrounded by a spacious garden with venerable trees, the establishment was tastefully renovated in 1994. The pastel-colored midsize rooms contain simple but comfortable furniture from the 1950s and '60s. Breakfast is the only meal served, but bar service is available in the public areas throughout the day and evening.

WHERE TO DINE
MODERATE

Cantinho de São Pedro. Praça Dom Fernando II 18 (at Lojas do Picadeiro). ☎ **21/923-067.** Reservations recommended. Main courses 2,000$–5,000$ ($11.20–$28). AE, DC, MC, V. Daily noon–3pm and 7:30–10pm. PORTUGUESE/INTERNATIONAL.

Less than a mile southeast of Sintra, in São Pedro de Sintra, this is one of the hillside village's finest dining choices. It's right off the main square, Praça Dom Fernando II, where the Feira da Sintra (Sintra Fair) is staged every second and fourth Sunday of the month. Dating from the time of the Christian Reconquest, the fair is one of the oldest in the country. The restaurant is ideal if you're attending the fair. Lojas do Picadeiro is a row of artisans' workshops. Look for the *pratos do dia* (daily specials), or save your appetite for the tasty specialties. They include velvety crepes stuffed with fresh lobster, and meltingly tender beefsteak in green pepper sauce. On a recent visit, we enjoyed salmon and shrimp au gratin. Pork with clams in the style of the province of Alentejo remains the eternal and justifiably popular favorite.

Hotel Tivoli Sintra. Praça da República. ☎ **21/923-35-05.** Reservations recommended. Main courses 2,500$–4,000$ ($14–$22.40); fixed-price menu 3,900$ ($21.85). AE, DC, MC, V. Daily 12:30–3pm and 7:30–10pm. PORTUGUESE/INTERNATIONAL.

Because this restaurant is within the concrete-and-glass walls of the town center's most desirable hotel, many visitors might overlook the Tivoli Sintra as a dining spot. That would be too bad—it serves some of the finest food in town. Staffed by a battalion of uniformed waiters, the room has a shimmering metallic ceiling, dark paneling, and floor-to-ceiling windows on one side. The daily menu is likely to include such carefully crafted dishes as tournedos Rossini, fish soup, and fillet of turbot with mushrooms and garlic.

Tacho Real. Rua da Ferraria 4. ☎ **21/923-52-77.** Reservations recommended. Main courses 1,600$–6,000$ ($8.95–$33.60); fixed-price menu 2,500$ ($14). AE, DC, MC, V. Thurs–Tues noon–3pm and 7:30–10pm. PORTUGUESE/FRENCH.

Lisboans come in from the city to enjoy the well-prepared meals at this restaurant. The kitchen deftly handles fish and meat dishes, and some succulent poultry dishes also appear on the menu. Two popular house specialties are fish fillet with shrimp sauce and rice, and fillet steak with cream sauce and mushrooms. We always like the bubbling fish stew. The fixed-price menu is a bargain that includes soup, a main course, dessert, coffee, and half a bottle of wine. Service is efficient and polite, and English is spoken.

INEXPENSIVE

Restaurant Alcobaça. Rua das Padarias 7, 9, and 11. ☎ **21/923-16-51.** Reservations recommended. Main courses 850$–2,800$ ($4.75–$15.70); fixed-price menu 1,600$ ($8.95). MC, V. Daily noon–4pm and 7–10:30pm. PORTUGUESE.

Popular with English visitors, this shop-size restaurant occupies two floors of a centrally located building on a steep, narrow pedestrian street. The place provides one of the cheapest meals in town. The Alcobaça serves typical Portuguese cuisine, including flavorful monkfish rice, tasty roast sardines, *caldo verde,* hake fillet with rice, octopus, Alcobaça chicken, and succulent pork with clams. It's the kind of robust food beloved by locals.

Tulhas Restaurant. Gil Vicente 4. ☎ **21/961-85-80.** Main courses 1,100$–2,000$ ($6.15–$11.20); fixed-price menu 3,000$ ($16.80). AE, DC, MC, V. Thurs–Tues noon–3:30pm and 7–10pm. PORTUGUESE.

The restaurant, decorated with tiles and wood, is between the tourism office and San Martin Church. Specialties of the house are codfish in cream sauce with potatoes; roasted lamb or duck with rice; steak au poivre (pepper steak with pepper sauce), and veal Madeira. Of course, you've had better, but the quality of the meat and fish is good, and the chefs present platters with perfectly balanced flavors.

SINTRA AFTER DARK

Sintra is not a party town; the Portuguese who live or vacation here realize that the most intriguing soirées are private. A worthy bar in the town center, where you might meet people from any country in Europe, is **Adega des Caves,** praça da República (☎ 21/923-08-48). In the center of town, the establishment is a restaurant that does a busy lunch trade. After dark, it mellows into a likable bar and bodega, specializing in beer and Portuguese wine. It's open every day till around 2am. A nearby competitor and friendly rival is the **Hockey Club Bar,** praça da República (☎ 21/923-57-10). At both establishments, beer prices start at 300$ ($1.70).

6 Ericeira

13 miles NW of Sintra, 31 miles NW of Lisbon

This fishing port is nestled on the Atlantic shore. Whitewashed houses accented with pastel-painted corners and window frames line its narrow streets. To the east rise the mountains of Sintra.

The sea gives life to Ericeira, as it has for some 700 years. Fishers still pluck their food from it. The beach lures streams of visitors every summer, giving a much-needed boost to the local economy. Along the coast, cliff-side nurseries called *serrações* breed lobsters (*lagostas*). Lobster is the house specialty at every restaurant in Ericeira.

In 1584, Mateus Alvares arrived in Ericeira from the Azores, claiming to be King Sebastião, who had reportedly been killed (some say he disappeared) on the battlefields of North Africa. Alvares and about two dozen of his chief supporters were executed after their defeat by the soldiers of Philip II of Spain, but today he is regarded as the king of Ericeira. In October 1910, the fleeing Manuel II and his mother, Amélia, set sail from the Ericeira harbor to a life of exile in England.

ESSENTIALS
ARRIVING

There is no direct rail service to Ericeira.

BY BUS　Mafrense buses from both Sintra and Lisbon serve Ericeira. One bus per hour leaves Lisbon's largo Martim Moniz for the 1¼-hour trip. A one-way ticket costs 300$ ($1.70). From Sintra, there's one bus per hour. The trip takes 1 hour and costs 350$ ($1.95) one way.

BY CAR　From Sintra (see above), continue northwest along Route 247.

VISITOR INFORMATION

The **Ericeira Tourist Office** is at Largo de Santa Marta (☎ **261/86-31-22**).

EXPLORING THE TOWN

For such a small place, Ericeira has quite a few sights of religious and historic interest. The **Church of São Pedro** (St. Peter) and the **Misericórdia** (charitable institution) both contain rare 17th- and 18th-century paintings. The **Hermitage of São Sebastião,** with its Moorish designs, would seem more fitting in North Africa. There's one more hermitage, honoring St. Anthony.

The crescent-shaped, sandy **Praia do Sol**, the favorite beach of Portuguese and foreign visitors, attracts many travelers. There are three other good beaches: Ribeira Beach, North Beach, and St. Sebastian Beach. All are suitable for swimming, unlike the beaches at Estoril and Cascais.

A NEARBY ATTRACTION

✪ **Palácio Nacional de Mafra.** 2640 Mafra. ☎ **261/81-75-50.** Admission 400$ ($2.25) adults, 200$ ($1.10) seniors (65 and over), students, and children under 15. Wed–Mon 10am–5pm. Bus: Mafrense bus from Lisbon.

This palace is a baroque chef d'oeuvre—a work of extraordinary discipline, grandeur, and majesty. At the peak of its 13-year construction, it reputedly employed 50,000; a small town was built just to house the workers. Its master model was El Escorial, the Daedalian maze constructed by Philip II outside Madrid. Mafra's corridors and complex immurements may not be as impressive or as labyrinthine, but the diversity of its contents is amazing. Its 880 rooms housed 300 friars who could look through 4,500 doorways and windows. Considering building methods in those days, one wonders how such a task was ever completed in so short a time.

Mafra's birth was divinely inspired. The devout king João V seemingly couldn't sire an heir, and court gossips openly speculated that he was sterile. One day he casually mentioned to a Franciscan that if he were rewarded with an heir, he would erect a monastery to the order. Apparently the Franciscans, through what the king considered "divine intervention," came through. João produced his heir and Mafra was born. Work began in 1717. Originally it was to house 13 friars, but the figure rapidly mushroomed to 300.

The summer residence of kings, Mafra, 25 miles northwest of the Lisbon, was home to the banished queen Carlota Joaquina. In addition to having a love of painting, Carlos I, the Bragança king assassinated at praça do Comércio in 1908, was also an avid hunter. In one room he had chandeliers made out of antlers and upholstery of animal skins. His son, who ruled for 2 years as Manuel II, spent his last night on Portuguese soil at Mafra before fleeing to England with his mother, Amélia.

Two towers hold more than 110 chimes, made in Antwerp, Belgium, that can be heard for 12 to 15 miles when they're played at Sunday recital. The towers flank a basilica, capped by a dome that has been compared to that of St. Paul's in London. The church contains an assortment of chapels, 11 in all, expertly crafted with detailed jasper reredos, bas-reliefs, and marble statues from Italy. The monastery holds the pride of Mafra, a 40,000-volume library with tomes 200 and 300 years old, many gold-leafed. Viewed by some more favorably than the world-famous library at Coimbra, the room is a study in gilded light. The collection of elaborately decorated vestments in the Museum of Religious Art is outstanding.

Following the omnipresent red Sintra marble, you enter the monks' pharmacy, hospital, and infirmary. Later you can explore the spacious kitchens and the penitents' cells with the flagellation devices used by the monks. You can wander through the audience room with trompe l'oeil ceilings, of Maria I's sewing room, and Carlos' music room.

WHERE TO STAY & DINE

Hotel Vilazul. Calcada da Baleia 10, 2655 Ericeira. ☎ **261/868-00-00.** Fax 21/629-27. www.i.am/hotel.vilazul. E-mail: vilazul@ip.pt. 21 units. A/C TV TEL. 13,000$ ($72.80) double. Rates include breakfast. AE, DC, MC. V. Free parking.

The town's leading hotel also serves the best cuisine in its restaurant, O Poco. Although simply furnished, its rooms offer much comfort, and some units have small private balconies. On the third floor of the hotel is a pleasant TV lounge with a panoramic view over the south side of Ericeira.

O Poco has served excellent food since 1968. It serves local specialties, including the town's best *caldeirada* (fish stew) and grilled sardines, plus regional and international dishes. The hotel also has two bars.

Pedro o Pescador. Rua Dr. Eduardo Burnay 22, 2655 Ericeira. ☎ **261/864-032.** Fax 261/862-321. E-mail: hotel.pedro@mailtelepac.pt. 25 units. TV TEL. 7,500$–11,000$ ($42–$61.60) double. Rates include buffet breakfast. AE, DC, MC, V. Free parking.

The resort's second-best choice is a relatively modest inn that attracts a devoted clientele from Lisbon. Though relatively lean on amenities, the immaculate rooms are comfortably furnished. The owners offer a friendly work add a grace note. Call ahead to see if the restaurant, once a well-known destination, is open when you visit.

6

South of the Tagus

As travelers from Victorian England crossed the Tagus by boat and headed for the left bank of Lisbon, chances are they carried a work by Robert Southey, England's poet laureate from 1813 to 1843. The well-traveled poet did more than anyone to publicize the glories on the other bank when he wrote: "I have never seen such a sublime panorama as the Arrabida Mountains afford, which, constantly changing as we go our way, offer us new beauties at every turn."

The narrow isthmus south of the Tagus is fast becoming a major attraction. Spurring the upsurge of interest is the Ponte do 25 de Abril, a long suspension bridge that has made it possible to cross the Tagus in minutes. You can then head rapidly across good roads through pine groves to the vertices of the triangle known as "The Land of the Three Castles": Sesimbra, Setúbal, and Palmela. Traditionalists prefer taking the ferry from praça do Comércio in Lisbon and docking in Cacilhas, on the other side of the Tagus.

Historically cut off from Lisbon, the isthmus is wild, rugged, and lush. In different places, this strip of land plummets toward the sea, stretches along miles of sandy beaches, and rolls through groves heavy with the odors of ripening oranges and vineyards of muscatel grapes. With craggy cliffs and coves in the background, the crystalline Atlantic is ideal for swimming, skin-diving, or fishing for tuna, sword-fish, and bass.

The land retains vivid reminders of its past, reflected in its Moorish architecture, Roman ruins and roads, Phoenician imprints, and Spanish fortresses. Its proximity to Lisbon (Setúbal is only 25 miles southeast of the capital) makes this area ideal for a 1-day excursion. The region has an extensive network of ferry connections, as well as bus service from Lisbon. Train travel, however, is very limited. Driving is the ideal way to explore the district at your leisure (see "Exploring the Region by Car," below). Otherwise, you can take a bus from Lisbon to the beaches at Caparica in about 45 minutes.

If you take a ferry from Lisbon's praça do Comércio to Cacilhas, you can catch a bus there for the beaches of Caparica. If you're visiting the peninsula by bus, use Setúbal as your hub; from there you can take local buses to Palmela and Sesimbra.

In summer, a narrow-gauge railway runs for 5 miles along the Costa da Caparica, making 20 stops at beaches along the way. If you go by rail to the peninsula, service is to Setúbal. From there, you must rely on buses to visit the fishing villages along the southern coast.

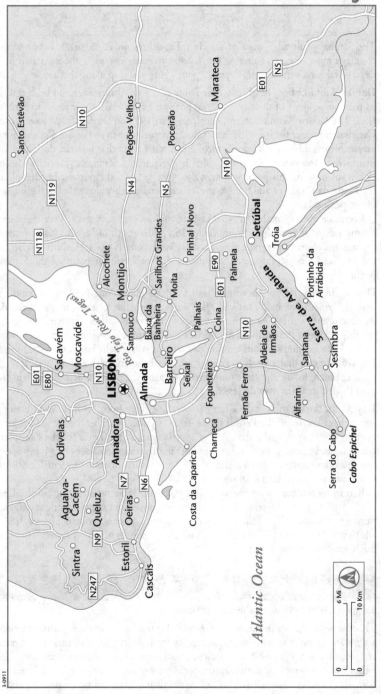

Exploring the Region by Car

The Setúbal peninsula, south of the river Tagus (*Tejo* in Portuguese), is one of the country's most rewarding driving tours. You can easily complete the excursion in 3 days, or take a lot more time, depending on where you stop along the way.

Day 1   From Lisbon, head across the Ponte do 25 de Abril suspension bridge, with its panoramic views of the city. This will put you on the main route south to Setúbal (E1). The **Cristo Rei** monument, constructed in 1959 on the left bank, towers over **Cacilhas,** a former fishing village that's now a virtual suburb of Lisbon. Cacilhas is an easy trip from Lisbon; it's known for the fish restaurants that line rua do Ginjal, its main street. You can easily visit Cacilhas by ferry from Lisbon, so you may want to skip it for now. At this point you may also want to avoid the popular beaches along the **Costa da Caparica** and head to the less crowded beaches along the southern coast of the peninsula.

Continue to the junction of N378, where you can cut south to the little resort and fishing village of **Sesimbra**. Sesimbra lies 26½ miles south of Lisbon. Plan to spend the night. Before sunset, take a 7-mile drive west along N379 to **Cabo Espichel,** at the headland. Its pilgrimage church marks the southwestern point of the Setúbal peninsula.

Day 2   In the morning, head northeast from Sesimbra along N379 on a winding, leisurely trip to Setúbal. This will take you through the foothills of the **Serra da Arrábida,** and you can have lunch at one of the little waterfront seafood eateries in the tiny village of **Portinho da Arrábida.** Lisboans frequent this place in summer for its good beaches and seafood. No single restaurant is especially better than the others. Just visit the one that appeals to you the most—or the one with an empty table.

After lunch, follow the same route east and spend the night in **Setúbal,** arriving in time to visit its **Convento de Jesús.**

Day 3   In the morning, take a ferry across the estuary from Setúbal. Visit the long spit of land known as the **Peninsula de Tróia,** studded with beaches of golden sand opening onto unpolluted waters. A large sports complex, the **Tróia Tourist Complex,** contains tennis courts, a golf course, and other attractions. Some meager ruins opposite the marina are all that remain of the 5th-century Roman town of Cetóbriga, which was destroyed by a tidal wave.

Return to Setúbal by ferry and resume your tour, this time cutting north along N252 for 5 miles to the pousada at **Palmela,** where you can spend the night (reservations are essential). The following morning, return to the national highway (E1), which will carry you back into Lisbon in plenty of time for lunch—Palmela is only 20 miles southeast of the capital.

1 Azeitão

9½ miles NW of Setúbal, 15½ miles SE of Lisbon

This sleepy village lies in the heart of *quinta* country. In its most meager incarnation, a quinta is a simple farmhouse surrounded by land. At its best, it's a mansion of great architectural style filled with art. Azeitão boasts some of the best in the country. The village makes a good base for trekkers, especially those who want to scale the limestone Serra da Arrábida. Others settle for long walks through scented pine woods or silvery olive groves. To cap your day, you can order some Azeitão cheese and a bottle of local muscatel.

ESSENTIALS
ARRIVING
BY CAR Because the village is isolated, you'll need a car. After crossing one of the bridges across the Tagus, continue south along the old road to Setúbal (Route 10) until you see the turnoff for the village of Azeitão.

VISITING THE QUINTAS
✪ **Quinta de Bacalhoa.** Vila Fresca de Azeitão. ☎ **21/218-00-11.** Admission 250$ ($1.40) adults; free for children under 13. Gardens (on request) Mon–Sat 1–5pm.

Manuel I reputedly introduced the concept of quintas in the early 16th century when he built the Quinta de Bacalhoa, where his mother once lived. In time, the son of Afonso de Albuquerque took over the building, and at one point the Braganças owned it. Eventually the quinta fell into disrepair, and vandals carted off many of its decorations, specifically the antique tiles.

An American woman bought the mansion before World War II and worked for years to restore it to its original condition. Loggias, pavilions, half-moon domes suggesting a Moorish influence, and a trio of pyramidal towers characterize the architecture. One of the panels of 16th-century *azulejos* (tiles) depicts an innocent Susanna hotly pursued by lecherous elders. Some architectural critics have suggested that the palace is the first example of the Renaissance in Portugal.

Bacalhoa is a private villa, but the gardens are open to the public on request. The quinta's farmland is devoted to vineyards owned by J. M. da Fonseca, International-Vinhos, Ltda., makers of Lancers wine. There are two J. M. da Fonseca wineries, half a mile apart: the "mother house," as it's called, and a newer plant.

The original winery and warehouses are in the center of Azeitão, as is the classic 19th-century house (also a quinta) that was the Fonseca family home. A little museum and public reception room on the ground floor of the house are open to visitors. The century-old Fonseca wineries have made their product from grapes grown on the slopes of the Arrábida Mountains since the early 19th century. The fine muscatel for which they have long been known is used in the flavoring and sweetening of white Lancers. The top product is a muscatel called Setúbal, rarely sent abroad but considered delectable by wine connoisseurs.

WHERE TO STAY & DINE
Quinta das Torres. Estrada Nacional 10, Azeitão, 2900 Setúbal. ☎ **21/218-00-01.** Fax 21/219-06-07. 10 units, 2 bungalows. 9,000$–16,000$ ($50.40–$89.60) double; 14,000$–25,000$ ($78.40–$140) bungalow. Rates include breakfast. AE, MC, V. Free parking.

A 16th-century baronial mansion of deteriorating elegance, Quinta das Torres has been kept intact for those who want to step back in time and live quietly. Owned by the same family for many generations, the estate sits behind large gates at the end of a tree-lined driveway; gradually, a pair of square peaked towers framing the entrance terrace comes into view. Each guest room is unique; they range from smaller chambers to a ballroom-size suite dominated by princess-style brass beds. Some units have high shuttered windows, time-mellowed tile floors, antique furnishings, vases of fresh flowers, oil lamps, and niches with saints or Madonnas. The bungalows, which sleep four and have kitchenettes, ensure privacy.

The dining room has a covered ceiling, a tall stone fireplace where log fires burn on chilly evenings, plus elaborate scenic tiles depicting *The Rape of the Sabine Women* and *The Siege of Troy.* The rich, heavy cuisine is well recommended; a meal costs around 4,500$ ($25.20). The bill of fare is likely to include smoked fillet of pork, steak au poivre, and giant prawns. Food is served daily from 1 to 3pm and 7 to 10pm.

2 Sesimbra

16 miles SW of Setúbal, 26½ miles S of Lisbon

Among the Portuguese, Sesimbra used to be a closely guarded secret. It was justifiably considered one of the most unspoiled fishing villages in the country. Today, signs of rapid growth are apparent in the high-rise buildings overshadowing old structures. However, the *varinas* and fishermen still go about the time-honored task of plucking their livelihood from the Atlantic. When the fleet comes in, the day's catch is auctioned at a *lota* at the harbor (Porto Abrigo). Sesimbra is also a popular sport-fishing center.

ESSENTIALS
ARRIVING
BY TRAIN   From Lisbon, the bus is a better choice. Rail passengers go to Setúbal by train, then double back on a bus to Sesimbra.

BY BUS   Buses to Setúbal leave regularly from Lisbon's praça de Espanha (Metro: Palhavã) and from Cacilhas, across the Tagus from the center of Lisbon. At Setúbal you can transfer to a local bus for the 30-minute trip southwest to Sesimbra. For **information** and schedules, call ☎ **265/52-50-51.**

BY CAR   From Lisbon, cross the Ponte do 25 de Abril bridge and continue southwest on the expressway to Setúbal. At the junction of N378, head directly south into Sesimbra.

BY FERRY   You can also get to Sesimbra by taking the ferry from the praça do Comércio wharf in Lisbon, then a bus from Cacilhas.

VISITOR INFORMATION
The **tourist office** is on largo da Marinha (☎ **21/223-57-43**).

SPECIAL EVENTS
The year's festivities begin with **Carnaval,** or Mardi Gras (Shrove Tuesday or Pancake Tuesday), when a cortege always attracts many young people. The typical **Cegadas** consist of a kind of popular burlesque theater, usually made only by men. They satirize the political, economic, or daily life events of the town, government, or country.

In April (no fixed date), Sesimbra stages the **Feira do Mare,** with live music, art exhibitions, and folkloric programs. From May 3 to 5, the **Festas em Honra do Senhor Jesús das Chagas** celebrates the patron saint of the fishers. A procession and the blessing of the sea take place on May 4. There's also an exuberant town fair. The **Festivities of the Popular Saints** run from June 23 to 30. At night, bonfires, marches, and sometimes fado create a joyful atmosphere. July 25 to 28 marks the celebration of the town's patron saint, **São Tiago.** Cultural events, including dance, are part of the festivities. On the last Sunday of September is another religious feast, **Our Lady of the Cape,** with a procession and a small fair.

EXPLORING SESIMBRA
EXPLORING THE AREA   Far down the beach, beyond the boat-clogged harbor, is the 17th-century **Fortress of St. Teodosio.** It was built to fortify the region against the pirates who plagued and plundered, carting off the most beautiful women and girls. The site is not open to the public and must be viewed from outside.

A walk along the ruined battlements of the five-towered **Castle of Sesimbra** reduces the village to a picturesque miniature. The castle was captured from the Moors in 1165 and rebuilt following the 1755 earthquake, which sent sections of its crenellated walls tumbling to the ground. It encloses a 12th-century church, the oldest monument in Sesimbra. The site is open daily from 7am to 7pm. Admission is free.

From Sesimbra, you can head west to the headland of **Cabo Espichel,** with arcaded pilgrim hospices dating from the 1700s. Often violently windswept, with seagulls circling overhead, this strip of land has been called the "Land's End of Portugal" (a reference to the far western extremity of England). A pilgrimage church, the **Santuário da Nossa Senhora do Cabo,** is in a state of disrepair, adding to the melancholy atmosphere. You can inspect its baroque interior with gilded wood and sculpture daily from 9am to 1pm and 3 to 6pm. Admission is free. Later, walk to the edge of the cliffs behind the church for a panoramic view. There's no guardrail, and it's a sheer drop of 350 feet to the ocean waters. Modern sculpture stands in the forlorn setting. At the southern end of the Arrábida chain, this pilgrimage site has been popular since the 13th century. In 1180, Fuas Roupinho routed the Moors at sea here, and his forces captured several enemy ships. From Sesimbra, six buses a day make the 30-minute journey to the southwestern cape.

OUTDOOR ACTIVITIES   Sesimbra's popularity stems from its position on a long, lovely, sandy beach. The beach is overpopulated in summer, often by Lisboans, but the unpolluted water is ideal for swimming.

Sesimbra is a center for fishing. The locals are famous for their swordfish catches. Many will take visitors out in their boats; the fee can be negotiated. Inquire at the tourist office (see "Visitor Information" under "Essentials," above) about making arrangements.

SHOPPING   Avenida da Liberdade, in the heart of town, is lined with all kinds of shops. The most impressive handcrafts outlet is **Mateus,** rua da Fortaleza (☎ 21/223-05-50). It caxies a sprawling variety of wonderful ceramic dishes and pots covered with fanciful versions of flowers, vines, trees, and animals—both biologically realistic and mythical. Anything you buy can be shipped, although (as is true anywhere else in the world) it's usually safer to haul the goods away with you physically.

Nine miles from the center of town, along the road to Setúbal, is one of the region's biggest ceramics factories. **São Simão Arte** (☎ 21/218-31-35) is the centerpiece of the hamlet of Azeitão. The factory outlet sells its products at prices that are somewhat less than in equivalent retail shops.

WHERE TO STAY

Hotel do Mar. Rua Combatentes de Ultramar 10, 2970 Sesimbra. ☎ **21/223-33-26.** Fax 21/223-38-88. 168 units. A/C TV TEL. 14,000$–24,500$ ($78.40–$137.20) double; 32,000$–62,000$ ($179.20–$347.20) suite. Children under 8 3,000$ ($17.40) in parents' room. Rates include breakfast. AE, DC, MC, V. Free parking.

One of the most unusual self-contained beach-resort hotels south of the Tagus, Hotel do Mar is a beehive construction of units spreading from a high cliff to the water below. The passageways are like art galleries, with contemporary paintings and ceramic plaques and sculpture. The main lobby houses a glassed-in tropical bird aviary. All the airy guest rooms have private terraces, with views of the ocean and gardens sweeping down the hillside; some have minibars. Some bathrooms are so small that one visitor called them "squashed." The streamlined furnishings include good beds. Suites vary widely in size, facilities, and price. Less expensive suites are comfortable standard accommodations; the more expensive deluxe units feature a pool and Jacuzzi. Breakfast is served on a flower-filled terrace.

The wood-paneled restaurant overlooks the sea. You might stop off from a day trip from Lisbon and order a meal. The before-dinner gathering point is a rustic bar; after dinner, guests congregate in the living room, which has a fireplace. The hotel offers a

The Best Beaches: Where the Locals Sun

The beaches along the **Costa da Caparica,** on the left bank of the Tagus across from the center of Lisbon, are not as polluted as those along the more fashionable Costa do Sol (Estoril and Cascais). Surprisingly, foreigners still flock to the Costa do Sol, leaving much of the Costa da Caparica to locals.

The *costa,* on the west side of the Setúbal peninsula, stretches for some 5½ miles and abounds with sandy beaches and coves. Rocky outcroppings, tiny coves, and clear, placid lagoons characterize the beaches. The farther you go from the little resort of Caparica, the better and more beautiful the beaches become.

A narrow-gauge railway serves the coast, making 20 stops. Each beach along the way has a different allure. The beaches closest to the rail terminus attract families. No. 9 is frequented by gays, and there's a nudist beach at no. 17.

To reach the beach strip by public transport, you can take a ferry from Lisbon to Cacilhas, on the other side of Tagus. They leave every 15 minutes from praça do Comércio's Terminal Fluvial. You then board a bus marked CAPARICA at the station next door to the ferry terminal. The trip to the beaches takes about 45 minutes. The narrow-gauge train runs from June to September, and the bus from Cacilhas stops at the rail terminus, where you can connect with the little train.

The Setúbal peninsula has many other wonderful beaches. There are sandy beaches at **Sesimbra** (see section 2 in this chapter), a fishing-village-turned-resort on the southern side of the Serra da Arrábida, but they are likely to be overcrowded from June to August.

The most alluring beach strip is across the mouth of the Sado at **Tróia** (see page 177), a major resort with some utterly charmless apartment complexes. Ferries leave from Setúbal harbor every 45 minutes throughout the day. Trip time is 20 minutes. The ocean side of the promontory at Tróia is less filled with beach buffs and less polluted.

Many little hidden beaches lie west of Setúbal at the foothills of the Serra da Arrábida mountain range. For example, at **Portinho do Arrábida** (see page 175), the bay makes a perfect curve, forming sand beaches and opening onto clear waters.

concierge, transfers, laundry, baby-sitting, and room service. The property contains two tennis courts, a beach, outdoor and indoor pools, a sauna, and a solarium.

Villas de Sesimbra. Altinho de São João, 2970 Sesimbra. ☎ **21/228-00-05.** Fax 21/223-15-33. E-mail: villages@oscar.pt. 207 apt. A/C TV TEL. 18,000$–25,000$ ($100.80–$140) apt for 2. AE, DC, MC, V. Free parking.

Villas de Sesimbra is currently your best bet for a holiday in Sesimbra. Challenging the Hotel do Mar's (see above) longtime monopoly on up-market tourism, it's a modern apartment-hotel complex set back in the hills, about 1¼ miles from the ocean. Its facilities are far superior to those of the Hotel do Mar. It offers all the modern resort-related activities that today's traveler seeks, including a health club complete with a gym and a sauna, heated outdoor pools, and tennis and squash courts. The family friendly resort has a children's play area.

The hotel is in a garden setting, with terraces opening onto views. As you might expect, it offers a wide range of accommodations—everything from "too small" studios to a lavish penthouse with great views. Rates are "expensive" or "moderate," depending on the accommodation. Every unit has a kitchenette and satellite TV. You can buy fish at the local market and cook your "catch" for supper. If you prefer not to cook, the on-premises restaurant serves American breakfast (7:30 to 10am) and traditional regional cuisine for lunch (12:30 to 3pm) and dinner (7:30 to 10pm).

WHERE TO DINE

Restaurante Ribamar. Av. dos Náufragos 29. ☎ **21/223-48-53.** Reservations recommended. Main courses 1,800$–2,500$ ($10.10–$14); fixed-price menu 5,000$ ($28). AE, DC, MC, V. Summer daily noon–midnight; off-season daily noon–4pm and 7–11pm. PORTUGUESE/INTERNATIONAL.

Restaurante Ribamar serves some of the best Portuguese cooking in the area. It specializes in fish and shellfish, most of it fresh from local waters. The building is in front of the sea, a short stroll from the beach, with a view of the bay. There's indoor and outdoor seating. The chef's specialty is a delectable platter of mixed fish and shellfish for two. Swordfish, caught in local waters, is another favorite. Downstairs are two large aquariums where guests can "catch" their own lobster, crayfish, or crab, but the fish don't have a sporting chance. The reasonable fixed-price menu includes soup, a main course, dessert, wine, and coffee.

SESIMBRA AFTER DARK

The town's best disco is **Belle Epoque,** in Falasia (☎ **21/223-20-01**). About a quarter-mile east of the town center, it opens nightly at 11pm and charges a 1,200$ ($6.70) cover, which includes the first drink. By almost everyone's standards it's the most important destination in the town center, and attracts virtually every night owl in town. If you're looking for a quiet hideaway for a round or two of drinks, consider either the **De Facto Bar,** avenida dos Náufragos (☎ **21/223-42-14**); or its immediate neighbor, **Bar Inglês,** avenida dos Náufragos (☎ **21/223-56-11**). Both clublike spaces are warm, safe, soothingly international, and less folkloric than you might expect.

3 Portinho da Arrábida

8 miles SW of Setúbal, 23 miles SE of Lisbon

The fishing village of Portinho da Arrábida, a favorite with Lisbon families that rent little multicolored cottages on the beach, is at the foot of the serra. If you drive here in July and August, watch out. There's virtually no parking, and the road should be one way but isn't. You can wait for hours to get back up the hill. In addition, the walk down and back could qualify you for the Olympics. Visitors in the know try to park on a wider road above the port, then negotiate the hordes of summer visitors on foot.

There's really no place to stay in Portinho; your best bet is to return to Sesimbra or to drive on to Setúbal for the night.

ESSENTIALS

ARRIVING

BY BUS Buses making the run between Sesimbra and Setúbal stop at Portinho da Arrábida.

BY CAR From Sesimbra, continue along N379 toward Setúbal, forking right at the turnoff from Portinho da Arrábida. But first see the warning about parking, above. Portinho makes a good lunch stop for motorists exploring the foothills of the Serra da Arrábida.

VISITOR INFORMATION

The nearest tourist offices are at Setúbal or Sesimbra, but offer little help to visitors to Portinho.

EXPLORING THE MOUNTAINS

The limestone, whale-backed **Serra da Arrábida** mountains stretch for about 22 miles, beginning at Palmela and rolling to a dramatic end at Cabo Espichel on the Atlantic. The Portuguese government has wisely set aside 26,688 acres between Sesimbra and Setúbal to protect the area from developers and to safeguard the local scenery and architecture.

At times, the cliffs and bluffs are so high that it seems you have to peer through clouds to see the purple waters of the Atlantic below. More than 1,000 species of plant life have been recorded, including holm oaks, sweet bay, pines, laurel, juniper, cypress, araucaria, magnolia, lavender, myrtle, and pimpernels. Our favorite time to visit is in late March or the beginning of April (around Easter), when wildflowers—everything from coral-pink peonies to Spanish bluebells—cover the mountains.

The serra abounds with caves and grottoes, the best known of which is the **Lapa de Santa Margarida.** Hans Christian Andersen wrote: "It is a veritable church hewn out of the living rock, with a fantastic vault, organ pipes, columns, and altars." Numerous sandy coves lie at the foot of limestone cliffs. Many of them open onto beaches; others are less accessible. One of the finest beaches is **Praia de Galapos.** Another popular beach is **Praia de Figuerinha,** between Portinha da Arrábida and Setúbal, and known for sport fishing, windsurfing, and sailing.

Perched on a hillside like a tiara over Portinho da Arrábida, the **Convento da Arrábida** dates from 1542. You can go to the gate and ring for the caretaker, who may or may not show you around.

WHERE TO DINE

Restaurante Beira-Mar. Portinho da Arrábida. ☎ **21/218-05-44.** Main courses 1,100$–3,200$ ($6.15–$17.90). May–Sept daily noon–9:30pm; Jan–Apr and Oct–Nov Thurs–Tues noon–9:30pm. Closed Dec. PORTUGUESE.

A meal at this airy restaurant can be your reward for the trek down the hill. The most sought-after warm-weather tables are on a concrete balcony, a few feet above the port's still waters, near the many fishing vessels. White paper usually serves as the napery for the savory but unpretentious Portuguese meals. Full meals include superb pork with clams, tender roast chicken, savory fish stew, grilled sardines, several preparations of codfish, grilled sole, shellfish rice, and several regional wines. This is hearty, robust fare. On overcrowded weekends, you may have trouble attracting the waiter's attention—if you can find a table.

4 Setúbal

25 miles SE of Lisbon

On the right bank of the Sado River lies one of Portugal's largest and oldest cities, said to have been founded by Noah's grandson. Motorists often include it on their itineraries because of the exceptional inn, the Pousada de São Filipe, in a late 16th-century fort overlooking the sea (see "Where to Stay," below).

Setúbal, the center of Portugal's sardine industry, is known for the local production of the most exquisite muscatel wine in the world. As far back as the days of the Romans and the Visigoths, connoisseurs praised the region's aromatic, hearty grapes. Orange groves (a jam is made from the fruit), orchards, vineyards, and outstanding beaches such as the popular Praia da Figuerinha lie near Setúbal. The white pyramidal mounds you see dotting the landscape are deposits of sea salt drying in the sun, another major commercial asset of this seaside community.

Many artists and writers have come from Setúbal, most notably the 18th-century Portuguese poet Manuel Maria Barbosa du Bocage, a forerunner of the Romantics. At praça do Bocage, a monument honors him.

ESSENTIALS
ARRIVING

BY TRAIN   The trip from Lisbon takes 1½ hours, and a one-way ticket costs 500$ ($2.80). For more **information** and schedules, call ☎ 21/888-40-25.

BY BUS   Buses from Lisbon arrive every hour or two, depending on the time of day. The trip takes an hour, and a one-way ticket costs 550$ ($3.10). For more **information** and schedules, call ☎ 265/52-50-51.

BY CAR   After crossing one of the Tagus bridges from Lisbon, follow the signs to Setúbal along the express highway, A2, until you see the turnoff for Setúbal. The old road (Route 10) to Setúbal is much slower.

VISITOR INFORMATION

The **Setúbal Tourist Office** is at largo do Corpo Santo (☎ 265/53-91-20).

EXPLORING SETÚBAL

✪   **Convento de Jesús.** Praça Miguel Bombarda (off avenida do 22 de Dezembro). ☎ **265/53-21-42.** Free admission. Tues–Sat 9am–1pm and 1:30–5:30pm. Bus: 1, 4, 7, 10, or 12.

The Convento de Jesús is a late 15th-century example of the Manueline style of architecture. Of particular interest are the main chapel and the ornate decorations on the main doorway and the Arrábida marble columns. Each column is actually three columns twisted together like taffy to form a cable or rootlike effect. Somehow they don't seem to hold up the vaulted ceiling, but give the illusion of appendages grown down to the floor. Hans Christian Andersen called the monument "one of the most beautiful small churches that I have ever seen." The church has been extensively restored; the latest wholesale renovation took place in 1969–70.

Museu da Setúbal. Rua Balneário Paula Borba. ☎ **265/52-47-72.** Free admission. Tues–Sat 9am–noon and 1:30–5:30pm. Bus: 1, 4, 7, 10, or 12.

Adjoining the Convento de Jesús, this unpretentious town museum houses some early 16th-century Portuguese paintings, as well as Spanish and Flemish works and contemporary art.

PENINSULA DE TRÓIA

Tróia is a long, sandy peninsula across the Sado River estuary. It's accessible by ferry from Setúbal. The pine-studded strip of land is the site of one of Portugal's largest tourist enterprises, featuring the **Tróia Tourist Complex** (☎ **265/49-90-00**), with high-rise apartment-hotels and a par-72, 6,970-yard, 18-hole golf course designed by Robert Trent Jones. The beaches are some of the best south of Lisbon, and the waters are unpolluted. Other sporting facilities include seawater swimming pools, watersports facilities, playgrounds for children, and about a dozen tennis courts. You can rent bicycles to tour the island, or go horseback riding.

You can rent an apartment on the island if you'd like a seaside holiday of a few days. Further information is available from **Torralta-CIF, S.A.,** av. Duque de Loulé 24, 1098 Lisboa Codex (☎ **21/353-87-73** or 21/355-63-10).

Cetóbriga, on the peninsula, contains ruins of a thriving Roman port. Excavations began in the mid–19th century. The city, dating from the 3rd and 4th centuries, was destroyed by the ocean, but traces have been unearthed of villas, bathing pools, a fresco-decorated temple, and a place for salt preservation of fish. There's also evidence that long-ago seafarers, the Phoenicians, inhabited the peninsula at one time. Cetóbriga's ruins are about 1½ miles from the site of the present tourist development of Tróia. The scant ruins can be seen opposite the marina.

To reach Tróia from Setúbal, buy a ticket from **Transsado,** Doca do Comércio (☎ **265/52-33-84**), off avenida Luisa Todi at the eastern sector of the waterfront. At least 36 ferries run throughout the day. The trip takes 15 minutes and costs 160$ (90¢) for adults and children. Taking a car costs 560$ ($3.15) each way. For **information,** call ☎ **265/235-101.**

OUTDOOR ACTIVITIES

The playground of Setúbal is the Peninsula of Tróia (see above), site of the best white-sand beaches. Some of the lonely, rocky stretches of land between Lisbon and Setúbal have undergone massive upgrades during the past 25 years. Some of Europe's best golf courses have emerged, emerald green, from the formerly dry terrain.

Lisbon's most acclaimed golf course is the **Aroeira Clube de Golf** (formerly Clube de Campo de Portugal), Herdade de Aroeira, Fonte da Telha, 2825 Monte de Caparica, Aroeira (☎ **21/297-13-14**). Designed as a 900-acre "golf estate" in the early 1970s by the English architect Frank Pennink, it's a par-72, 6,605-yard course. International golf magazines have hailed the layout as one of the finest in Europe. Low, rocky cliffs and a network of lakes separate the long, lush fairways and copses of pine trees from the surging Atlantic. Advance reservations are important. Greens fees for 18 holes run 9,000$ to 12,000$ ($50.40 to $67.20), depending on the time and day. Golf clubs can be rented for 3,500$ to 7,500$ ($19.60 to $42), and an electric cart costs 7,000$ ($39.20) for 18 holes. To reach the club from Lisbon, take one of the bridges over the Tagus. Drive south for 20 miles, and exit the highway at Costa da Caparica. From Setúbal, take highway N10 northwest to Lisbon and exit at Foguateiro.

If the Aroeira course is booked, you can schedule a round at another course in the region. The **Clube de Golf Perú** is near the hamlet of Negreiros (☎ **21/210-45-15**). From Setúbal, take Estrada Nacionale 10 for about 12 miles, following signs to Lisbon. Another, less prestigious option is the **Clube de Golf Montado,** in the hamlet of Montado (☎ **265/70-66-48** or 265/70-67-99). From Setúbal, drive 6 miles south along the estrada nacionale, following signs to Alentejo and Algarve. Greens fees are comparable to those at the Aroeira, but professionals don't consider either of those newcomers as exciting.

SHOPPING

Setúbal offers enough outlets for local handcrafts to keep any devoted shopper busy for at least a full afternoon. One of the most compelling targets is the shopping boutique in the **Castelo de São Filipe** (☎ **265/52-38-44**). Take the underground tunnel that leads from the castle entrance. In the town center, on the streets near the pousada and the cathedral, you'll find at least half a dozen gift shops specializing in embroideries, ceramics, wood carvings, and local leather.

Fortuna (☎ **265/287-10-68**), a ceramics factory and technical school, dominates the hamlet of Quinta do Anjo, 4 miles northeast of Setúbal. To reach it, follow signs to Palmela. A leading competitor manufactures ceramics that are glazed and painted fancifully with renditions of flowers, vines, and woodland animals, some of them mythical. **São Simão Arte** (☎ **265/208-31-35**) is the focal point of the hamlet of Vila Fresca de Azeitão, 9 miles northeast of Setúbal. Both offer factory tours and ample shopping opportunities.

WHERE TO STAY

Hotel Bonfim. Av. Alexandre Herculano 58, 2900 Setúbal. ☎ **265/53-41-11.** Fax 265/53-48-58. E-mail: hotel.bonfim@mail.telepac.pt. 100 units. A/C MINIBAR TV TEL. 17,500$ ($98) double; 25,000$ ($140) suite. Rates include breakfast. AE, DC, MC, V. Free parking.

This 10-story hotel far outranks every other hotel in the center of Setúbal. It's the most modern and international in town. It rises from the eastern edge of the inner city's largest park, a short walk inland from the sea, and offers views that its management wryly compares to those overlooking Central Park in New York. It opened in 1993, and has well-furnished midsize rooms, each with an additional phone in the bathroom. The guest rooms occupy floors 1 through 8, and conference facilities fill the 9th and 10th floors. Despite its size, it doesn't have a restaurant; breakfast is the only meal served. Many restaurants, some not especially good, lie nearby.

✪ **Pousada de São Filipe.** Castelo de São Filipe, 2900 Setúbal. ☎ **265/52-38-44.** Fax 265/53-25-38. www.pousadas.pt. 16 units. A/C TV TEL. 18,000$–30,500$ ($100.80–$170.80) double; 32,000$–38,000$ ($179.20–$212.80) suite. Rates include breakfast. AE, DC, MC, V. Free parking.

This fortress-castle, on a hilltop overlooking the town and the harbor, dates to 1590. It's the work of Italian architect Philipe Terzl, who came to Portugal during the ill-fated reign of the young King Sebastião. You wind up a curving mountain road, passing through a stone arch and past towers to the belvedere. The walls of the chapel and the public rooms contain tile dados depicting scenes from the life of São Filipe and the life of the Virgin Mary. They're dated 1736 and signed by Policarpo de Oliveira Bernardes.

Guest rooms that once housed soldiers and the governor have been tastefully furnished with antiques and reproductions of 16th- and 17th-century pieces. Guns and ammunition have given way to soft beds and ornate Portuguese-crafted headboards. Some units are air-conditioned. To reach them, you use what seems like miles of plant-filled corridors.

If you're not driving, take a taxi from Setúbal—the walk is too long for most people.

Dining: The pleasant restaurant serves traditional regional cuisine at lunch (1 to 3pm) and dinner (7:30 to 10pm). A full meal with coffee and wine runs about 5,000$ ($28). Most guests stop over on a day trip from Lisbon.

Amenities: Room service, laundry, car-rental desk.

Quinta do Patricio. Estrada do Castelo de São Filipe, 2900 Setúbal. ☎ and fax **265/338-17.** 4 units. 11,000$–13,000$ ($61.60–$72.80) double; 13,000$–15,000$ ($72.80–$84.00) apt. Rates include breakfast. MC, V. Free parking.

In the Arrábida Nature Park, this manor house offers the best quinta accommodations in the area. A member of Turismo de Habitação, the glorified B&B presents a marked contrast to the more luxurious pousada, which is nearby. The manor, a former private home, occupies a tranquil location with good views of an estuary. From the private garden, you can look out over Setúbal. There's a swimming pool. Lodging choices include rooms in the main building, a self-contained apartment, and a restored windmill with a bathroom, fireplace, and small refrigerator. Reserve as far in advance as possible, especially in summer.

Residencial Setúbalense. Rua Major Afonso Pala 17, 2900 Setúbal. ☎ and fax **265/52-57-89.** 24 units. A/C TV TEL. 5,700$–9,500$ ($31.90–$53.20) double. Rates include breakfast. AE, MC, V. Free parking.

About a minute's walk north of Setúbal's central plaza, largo da Misericórdia, this family run hotel opened in the early 1990s. The carefully restored three-story building was erected 200 years ago as a substantial private home. The midsize rooms have high ceilings and streamlined modern furniture, including firm mattresses. A cozy in-house bar area doubles as a cafe. Breakfast is the only meal served, but any of the hard-working staff members can direct you to several worthwhile restaurants nearby.

WHERE TO DINE

O Beco. Largo da Misericórdia 24 r/c. ☎ **265/52-46-17.** Main courses 1,300$–2,100$ ($7.30–$11.75). AE, DC, MC, V. Daily noon–4pm; Wed–Sun 7–10:30pm. Bus: 2, 7, 8, or 20. PORTUGUESE.

O Beco has thrived in the center of town since the 1960s. A narrow passageway leads to two dining rooms decorated with old ovens, regional artifacts, and a fireplace. The service is efficient, the food robust and full of flavor. The quantities could be smaller and still nobody would leave hungry. Shellfish soup is the classic opener. Pork chops are the acorn-sweetened variety from Alentejo; other good choices include special beefsteak, *pato com arroz a antiga* (baked duck and rice), paella, and a Portuguese stew, *cozido. Cabrito* (goat) is a Sunday special. More adventurous diners will order the grilled squid. A typical dessert is orange tart.

Restaurante Bocage. Rua da Marqueza do Faial 8–10. ☎ **265/52-25-13.** Main courses 1,000$–1,800$ ($5.60–$10.10). AE, DC, MC, V. Thurs–Tues noon–3:30pm and 7–10pm. PORTUGUESE.

Old Portugal comes alive behind the faded facade of this town house, on a corner of the traffic-free main square. You'll dine under 1950s-era ceiling fans and a coffered white ceiling. Most patrons order a fruity muscatel to accompany fresh fish. This hearty tavern is no place for those with dainty tastes. The almost exclusively local clientele comes here for regional Portuguese cookery, including *lulas de caldeirada* (squid stew). A taste of muscatel brandy traditionally tops off a meal.

SETÚBAL AFTER DARK

Hardworking Setúbal offers more options for late-night partying than you might think. The densest concentration of nightlife options lies near the western terminus of avenida Luisa Todi, the road leading west to a string of beaches. The most intriguing is **Conventual,** avenida Luisa Todi (☎ **265/53-45-29**). A series of rooms with elaborately vaulted ceilings (which long ago sheltered one of Setúbal's most visible convents) offer several bars and musical atmospheres. Although most of the place seems designed for talking and drinking, one room functions as a disco. Open daily from 10:30pm till dawn.

Another rich concentration of nightlife options is in the seafront village of Albarquel, about a mile west of Setúbal. The **Disco Albatroz** operates adjacent to its late-night eatery, **Restaurant All-Barquel,** Praia de Albarquel (☎ **265/221-191-46**). Both cater to night owls of all ages. **Alforge,** Rua Regimento Infantaria 14 (☎ **265/376-75**), is an offbeat little bar and diner near the market square. It fills with local workers during the day, but at night the crowd grows younger and more fun. Lots of vinho verde, or "green wine," is consumed. You can drop in for a full meal—try the grilled squid—perhaps a sandwich, and certainly a drink. Food is served Monday to Saturday until 2am.

5 Palmela

5 miles N of Setúbal, 20 miles SE of Lisbon

The village of Palmela lies in the heart of wine country, the foothills of the Arrábida mountains. It's famous for its fortress; from an elevation of 1,200 feet, it offers one of the best views in Portugal. Over sienna-hued valleys and vineyards flush with grapes, you can see north to the capital and south to the estuary of the Sado.

ESSENTIALS
ARRIVING
There is no bus or train service to Palmela.

BY CAR   From Lisbon, cross the Ponte do 25 de Abril bridge and head south along E1. Exit at the cutoff marked Palmela. From Setúbal, continue north along A2 to the same exit.

VISITOR INFORMATION
The local tourist office (☎ 21/233-21-22) is at the castelo de Palmela (see below).

EXPLORING THE CASTLE
Castelo de Palmela occupies a position that has long been a strategic point for securing control of the lands south of the Tagus. From Palmela, Afonso Henríques, the first king of Portugal, drove out the Moors and established his new nation's domination of the district. In its day the 12th-century fortress was a splendid example of medieval military architecture. It's believed that the Celts founded a castle on this spot in 300 B.C.

Of special interest is the Roman road that archaeologists discovered behind the castle. The only such road unearthed in Portugal, it sparked speculation about its relationship with the Roman beach colonies of Tróia, off Setúbal. You can scale the hill to the castle—now a pousada—any time of the day.

WHERE TO STAY & DINE
✪ **Pousada do Castelo de Palmela.** 2950 Palmela. ☎ **21/235-12-26.** Fax 21/233-04-40. E-mail: enatur@mail.telepac.pt. 28 units. A/C MINIBAR TV TEL. 20,300$–31,000$ ($113.70–$173.60) double; 38,000$ ($212.80) suite. Rates include breakfast. AE, DC, MC, V. Free parking.

This is one of the last remaining segments of the 12th-century castle. It was built as a monastery within the castle walls in 1482 on orders of João I and dedicated to St. James. Its use as a pousada kept it from falling into ruin. The skillful, unobtrusive conversion preserved the classic look and feel of a cloister. It's on the crest of a hill, overlooking the valley and sea in the distance. It's traditional in design; a huge square building opens onto a large courtyard, and the lower-level arches have been glassed in and furnished with lounge chairs.

Most of the guest rooms (former cells) have been opened up, enlarged, and brought glamorously up to date. They're furnished in Portuguese style, with hand-carved pieces and fine fabrics. The rooms, most of which open onto nice views, were last spruced up in 1993. Still, a few units appear stark and severe, better for devout monks than for modern travelers. Near the dining room is a comfortable drawing room with a noteworthy washbasin that the monks once used for their ablutions.

Dining: The dining room, once the monastery refectory, is stately but informal, and service is efficient. Portuguese cuisine is offered, and a meal will run between 3,700$ and 5,000$ ($20.70 and $28). Food is served daily from 8 to 10:30am, 1 to 3pm, and 7:30 to 10pm.

Amenities: Room service, laundry, concierge.

Quinta do Particio. Estrada de São Filipe, 2900 Setúbal. ☎ and fax **265/233-817.** 5 units. 9,000$–15,000$ ($50.40–$84) double. Rates include breakfast. AE, MC, V. Free parking.

The oldest part of this charming, family run bed-and-breakfast hotel is its stone-sided windmill. Built in 1798, it's now the establishment's most comfortable accommodation. Other rooms are in the main house, a short walk away through a nice garden. Don't expect a conventional, international feel: Life here is slow, revolving around the pleasant garden and tastefully decorated public areas. The simple guest rooms are small, comfortable, and well maintained, with a severe dignity that reflects the nature of the century-old house. Breakfast is the only meal served. The quinta, very popular with Portuguese and northern Europeans on holiday, lies about half a mile west of the center of town, just behind Setúbal's medieval castle.

Estremadura 7

The seeds of the Portuguese empire took root hundreds of years ago in the land north of Lisbon, whose beauty has not been diminished by time. Like the once-white limestone of Battle Abbey (Batalha), this region has been gilded in the sunlight of passing years.

Estremadura is a land of contrasts. The Atlantic crashes upon the southern coast, but farther up it can hardly muster a ripple in the snug cover of São Martinho do Porto. The coastal regions teem with seafood: nursery-bred lobster, shrimp, crabs, squid, tuna, barnacles, and albacore. The presence of the nearby sea is evident throughout Estremadura. Even in the many examples of Manueline architecture, especially at Batalha, the tie with the sea remains unbroken. Its nautical designs—ropes, cables, armillary spheres, seascape effects—reflect Portugal's essential connection to the sea.

Estremadura contains towns as old as Portuguese nationhood. Despite the name (which means "extremities"), the region is neither extremely harsh—its gardens are among the most beautiful any-where—nor especially remote. Rather, it is in many ways the spiritual heart of Portugal. Its isolation derives more from the slow, erratic, and sometimes undependable public transportation, which makes the region best suited to a driving tour.

Exploring the Region by Car

Day 1   Begin your tour near the wraparound ramparts of one of the most romantic cities in Portugal, the "museum town" of **Óbidos.** There's enough here to merit a night's stopover, especially if you've driven the 58 miles north from Lisbon.

Day 2   Depart early to visit one of the country's most prominent medieval monuments, the **Cistercian Monastery of Alcobaça.** To get there, drive northeast for 20 miles along highway N8. Experience the echoing dignity of Alcobaça's medieval stonework, then detour west for 8 miles to **Nazaré,** following N8-5. Spend the night in Nazaré, after a seafood dinner made with local ingredients caught that day.

Day 3   Visit the monastery at **Batalha,** 18 miles east of Nazaré (to reach it, drive along N242), and the world-famous pilgrimage site of **Fátima,** 12 miles east of Batalha along N356. The hotels of Fátima are less interesting than the pousada in Batalha; a half-day visit to the pil-grimage site is usually sufficient for all but the most devout travelers.

We recommend checking in to the pousada, visiting Fátima, and returning to Batalha for the night. You can visit Batalha's legendary monastery the following morning.

1 Óbidos

58 miles N of Lisbon, 4 miles S of Caldas da Rainha

Years after Afonso Henríques drove the Moors out of Óbidos, the poet king Dinis and his saintly wife, Isabella of Aragón, passed by the walls of this medieval borough and noted its beauty. The queen likened the village, with its extended walls and gleaming plaster-faced houses, to a jewel-studded crown. Eager to please, Dinis made her a present of the village. He established a tradition: Instead of precious stones, Portuguese royal bridegrooms presented Óbidos to their spouses—and it didn't cost them a penny. And what queen could complain about such a gift?

Entered through a tile-coated gatehouse, Óbidos rises on a sugarloaf hill above a valley of vineyards. Its golden towers, ramparts (rebuilt in the 12th century and subsequently restored), and crenellated battlements contrast with gleaming white houses and the rolling countryside, where windmills clack in the breeze. The town is a trip back in time.

The castle has been converted into a pousada. Its ramparts afford views of Estremadura; you can almost see Afonso Henríques's retinue marching over the hills.

ESSENTIALS
ARRIVING

BY TRAIN   From the Estação do Rossio station in Lisbon, commuter trains run to Cacém, where you change trains for Óbidos. Count on about 2 hours of travel. About eight trains a day make the run; the one-way fare is 900$ ($5.05). For **information** and schedules, call ☎ **21/888-40-25.**

BY BUS   There are bus connections from Lisbon, but the train is easier. Buses leave from avenida Casal Ribeiro in Lisbon for Caldas da Rainha, where you transfer to another bus to Óbidos. The one-way fare is 950$ ($5.30). About six buses a day make the 20-minute trip from Caldas da Rainha to Óbidos. For **information,** call ☎ **262/83-10-67.**

BY CAR   From Lisbon, N8 runs north to Óbidos via Torres Vedras.

VISITOR INFORMATION

You'll find the **Óbidos Tourist Office** on rua Direita (☎ **262/95-92-31**).

EXPLORING THE TOWN   In the Renaissance **Igreja de Santa Maria,** 10-year-old Afonso V exchanged marriage vows with his 8-year-old cousin. Blue-and-white *azulejos* (tiles) line the church's interior. Pause long enough to admire a Renaissance tomb and the paintings of Josefa of Óbidos, a 17th-century artist. The Chapel of St. Lawrence contains relics of saints' hands. The church lies to the right of the post office in the central square. It's open daily, 9:30am to 12:30pm and 4:30 to 7pm April to September, and 9:30am to 12:30pm and 2:30 to 6pm October to March. Admission is free.

The other major attraction is the *castelo* (part of which is now a tourist inn; see "Where to Stay," below). The castle suffered severe damage in the 1755 earthquake and was restored, with a multitower complex. It's one of Portugal's greatest medieval castles, with a host of Manueline architectural elements. In 1148, Dom Afonso Henríques and his troops, disguised, incredibly, as cherry trees, crept up and captured the castle from the Moors.

Estremadura

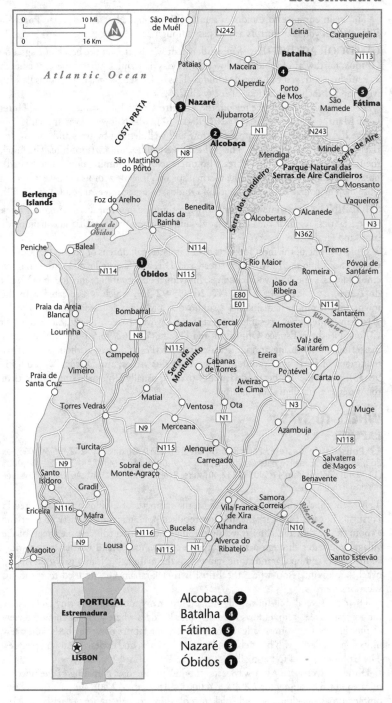

São Pedro de Muél
Leiria
Caranguejeira
N242
N113
Batalha
Pataias
Maceira
Alperdiz
Porto de Mos
São Mamede
Fátima
Nazaré
Aljubarrota
N1
N243
Alcobaça
N8
Mendiga
Minde
Serra de Aire
São Martinho do Pôrto
Parque Natural das
Serras de Aire Candieiros
Monsanto
Vaqueiros
Berlenga Islands
Foz do Arelho
Benedita
Alcobertas
Alcanede
N3
Caldas da Rainha
Serra dos Candieiro
N362
Lagoa de Óbidos
Tremes
Peniche
Baleal
N114
Río Maior
Romeira
Póvoa de Santarém
N114
Óbidos
N115
João da Ribeira
E80
E01
N114
Santarém
Praia da Areia Blanca
Bombarral
Cadaval
Cercal
Almoster
Rio Maior
Lourinha
N8
N115
Serra de Montejunto
Vale de Santarém
Campelos
Cabanas de Torres
Ereira
Vimeiro
Aveiras de Cima
Pontével
Cartaxo
Praia de Santa Cruz
Matial
Ventosa
Ota
N3
Muge
Torres Vedras
N9
Merceana
N1
Azambuja
Turcita
N115
Alenquer
N118
Carregado
Salvaterra de Magos
Santo Isidoro
Sobral de Monte-Agraço
Benavente
Gradil
Ericeira
N116
Mafra
Samora Correia
Vila Franca de Xira
Ribeira de Sorto
N116
Bucelas
Athandra
N10
Magoito
N9
Lousa
N115
N1
Alverca do Ribatejo
Santo Estêvão

Atlantic Ocean

COSTA PRATA

0   10 Mi
0   16 Km

3-0546

PORTUGAL
Estremadura
★ LISBON

Alcobaça **2**
Batalha **4**
Fátima **5**
Nazaré **3**
Óbidos **1**

The main entrance to Óbidos is a much-photographed gate, the zigzag **Porta da Villa.** Watch your car mirrors as you pass through it.

OUTDOOR ACTIVITIES   Sailboarders rent windsurfers at the beach at **Lagoa de Óbidos,** northwest of Óbidos and west of Caldas da Rainha. Surfers prefer the beach at **Peniche,** southwest of Lagoa de Óbidos. This beach stands on a high peninsula with wide sandy beaches at the foot of rocky cliffs.

The one golf course in the region, the **Vimeiro Golf Club,** is allied with the **Hotel Golf Mar,** at Torres Vedras (☎ **261/98-41-57**), which towers over the cliff. The course has nine holes, all relatively narrow and well defined by trees and shrubs; the river is an ever-present hazard. The golf club has caddies and carts for hire. The hotel, the best sports complex in the area, also offers tennis, swimming pools (one heated), horseback riding, and fishing. The thermal spa of Vimeiro, with its curative waters, is close by. The course is 21 miles south of Óbidos, and greens fees are 3,000$ ($16.80).

SHOPPING   Save some time for browsing through the **shops,** searching out thick woven fabrics, regional rugs (both hand- and machine-made), raffia and handmade bags, and local lace.

Óbidos is one of the most folkloric towns in Portugal; dozens of boutiques in thick-walled shops line the town's main street, **rua Direita.** They're loaded with ceramics, embroideries, wine, and wood carvings. Individual outlets of note include the **Oficina do Barro,** praça de Santa Maria (☎ **262/95-92-31**), which is associated with the town's tourist office. It maintains a studio that produces delicate ceramics—usually glazed in white—that resemble the texture of a woven basket. The studio is open to visitors. Nearby is **Espaço Oppidum,** rua Direita (☎ **262/95-96-53**), which does a masterful job of glazing antique terra-cotta roof tiles and etching them with artists' renditions of birds and wildlife. Finally, **Loja dos Arcos,** rua Direita (☎ **262/95-98-33**), sells wine, leather, and ceramics that are usually a bit more interesting than the wares at equivalent shops nearby.

WHERE TO STAY
EXPENSIVE

✪ **Pousada do Castelo.** Paço Real (Apdo. 18), 2510 Óbidos. ☎ **262/95-91-05.** Fax 262/95-91-48. E-mail: enatur@mail.telepac.pt. 9 units. A/C MINIBAR TV TEL. 34,000$ ($190.40) double; from 41,500$ ($232.40) suite. Rates include breakfast. AE, DC, MC, V. Free parking.

This Manueline-trimmed stone palace on the ramparts of Óbidos is firmly rooted in Portugal's history. Today, it's the most overbooked pousada in the country, so reserving a room can be difficult. After traveling through the twisting cobblestone streets of the village, you enter through a thick gothic archway. You ascend farther into a wide, sunny court, and up a grand stone stairway to the main hall. Nearby is Foz do Arelho beach, a pleasant resort where the British writer Graham Greene used to spend his vacations.

There are several well-furnished lounges, but many rooms are too tiny and austere for comfort. Deep-set windows have tiny monk ledges where you can enjoy the view of the surrounding countryside. Homelike cretonne fabrics cover the beds, and a few units contain desks with brass church lamps, armchairs, and ecclesiastical wall plaques. The bathrooms tend to be small.

Dining/Diversions: Most wayfarers stop just for the day, partaking of the uncomplicated lunch or dinner for 2,800$ to 4,000$ ($15.70 to $22.40). We particularly recommend roast suckling pig, and chicken cooked in an earthenware pot with red-wine sauce. The dining room is in the Portuguese *quinta* style. If you're not staying at the

---

The Beaches of Estremadura

Take your pick. A ribbonlike string of beaches stretches almost continuously along the coast of Estremadura. Some 150 miles of sand extend all the way to its northern edge, just south of the beach resort of **Figueira da Foz.**

There are beaches for everyone. Many are uncrowded and filled with powdery sand bordering crystal-clear waters. Others, especially those near industrial wastelands, are much less desirable and may be polluted. Look for beaches flying a blue banner, which indicates that the European Union has granted its seal of approval to the beach's hygiene and safety.

One of our favorites is the seaside village of **São Martinho do Porto,** 72 miles north of Lisbon and a short run south of overcrowded Nazaré. This resort nestles between pine-covered foothills and the ocean; the waters are calm and clear. Another good beach, north of Nazaré, is at **São Pedro de Muél,** 84 miles north of Lisbon. It has a 73-room resort hotel, **Mar e Sol,** av. da Liberdade 1 (☎ **244/59-00-00**), where you can take a room or a meal.

Another place worth seeking out is the town of **Peniche,** 57 miles north of Lisbon. The fishing port stands high on a peninsula, with wide, sandy beaches at the foot of its rocky cliffs. It doesn't always have the cleanest water (as compared to other uncrowded, remote places) but is nevertheless a family favorite. When you tire of the beach, you can explore **Cabo Carvoeiro** on the peninsula, about 3 miles east of Peniche. It offers panoramic views of the surf smashing against the wild rock formations hundreds of feet below the road.

Other less important but good beaches are at **Pedrogão, Baleal, Consolação, Porto Covo, Porto Dinheiro,** and **Santa Cruz.** All are signposted from the highway.

Many of the most popular beaches, with the most facilities, are not the cleanest. They may not have blue flags, depending on conditions when you visit. These include **Milfontes, Foz do Arelho,** and **Nazaré.**

---

pousada, call ahead for reservations in the summer. Food is served daily from 12:30 to 3pm and 7:30 to 10pm. Guests gather in the lounge or the bar for sundown drinks.

Amenities: Room service, laundry, concierge.

MODERATE

Albergaria Josefa d'Óbidos. Rua Dom João de Ornelas, 2510 Óbidos. ☎ **262/95-92-28.** Fax 262/95-95-33. 38 units. A/C MINIBAR TV TEL. 12,000$ ($67.20) double; 19,000$ ($106.40) suite. Rates include breakfast. AE, DC, MC. Free parking.

The flower-bedecked Albergaria Josefa d'Óbidos, just outside the old town's fortifications, was constructed in 1983, although it looks much older. People who can't get into the Pousada do Castelo usually end up staying here. Most of the small guest rooms contain 18th-century reproductions; some have wall-to-wall carpeting. Each unit comes with a firm mattress. Because the inn is on a hillside, there are two main doors.

There's a typical restaurant (with a private terrace), which you may want to patronize even if you're not a guest—unless it's been booked by a tour group. Service is daily from noon to 3pm and 7:30 to 10:30pm. You can have an apéritif in the bar, decorated with reproductions of artwork by Josefa d'Óbidos, the albergaria's namesake. The disco and pub are open only in winter.

Albergaria Rainha Santa Isabel. Rua Direita, 2510 Óbidos. ☎ **262/95-93-23.** Fax 262/95-91-15. 20 units. A/C TV TEL. 11,250$–12,750$ ($63–$71.40) double. Rates include breakfast. AE, DC, MC, V. Parking available on street.

Despite the necessity of negotiating a parking space on the main street, many visitors prefer this to other area hostelries. On a narrow cobblestone-covered street running through the center of town, it opened as a hotel in 1985; the building, once a private home, is many centuries old. Blue, white, and yellow tiles cover the high-ceilinged lobby. There's a comfortable bar area filled with leather-covered sofas and Victorian-style chairs. An elevator runs to the simply furnished but immaculate guest rooms, which have firm mattresses. Most guests drive through the town and deposit their luggage at the reception desk before parking free on the square in front of the village church, about 100 feet away.

Estalagem do Convento. Rua Dom João de Ornelas, 2510 Óbidos. ☎ **262/95-92-16.** Fax 262/95-91-59. E-mail: estconventhotel@mail.pt. 31 units. MINIBAR TEL. 10,000$–16,200$ ($56–$90.70) double; 14,000$–21,600$ ($78.40–$120.95) suite. Rates include breakfast. AE, MC, V. Free parking.

This former village nunnery, owned by the chemist Luís de Sousa Garcia, is outside the town walls. The reception lounge is surely the tiniest on the Iberian peninsula, with a fireplace, 17th-century chest, torchières, and a pair of gilt angels. The guest-room furniture complements the structure. The beds are old, but the mattresses, thankfully, are newer. Units open off rambling corridors with chests and benches large enough to hold the trousseaus of a dozen brides.

The public is welcome at dinner. There's a table d'hôte menu and an à la carte menu that includes such specialties as French onion soup, pepper steak, and crêpes Suzette. Under heavy black beams, the room has an open cornerstone fireplace and a brick oven. On sunny days guests dine on the rear patio, in a garden with a moldy stone wall and tangerine and orange trees. Food is served daily from 7:30 to 9:30pm. In addition to a bar with hand-hewn beams, there's a living room.

INEXPENSIVE

Pensão Martim de Freitas. Estrada Nacional 8, Arrabalde, 2510 Óbidos. ☎ **262/95-91-85.** 6 units, 4 with bathroom (tub or shower). 7,000$ ($39.20) double without bathroom, 10,000$ ($56) double with bathroom. Rates include breakfast. No credit cards. Free parking.

The pensão is outside the walls on the road that leads to Alcobaça and Caldas da Rainha. The accommodating hosts rent small, comfortable rooms, furnished in 17th-century style. Everything is spotless in this establishment, to which the tourist office directs those seeking low-cost accommodations. Breakfast is the only meal served. Absolutely no English is spoken, but the staff is kindly and helpful.

WHERE TO DINE
MODERATE

Most visitors to Óbidos like to dine at the Pousada do Castelo (see "Where to Stay," above). However, you get far better value, less formality, and more local color at one of the typical little restaurants inside or outside the walls.

Café/Restaurante 1 de Dezembro. Largo São Pedro. ☎ **262/95-92-98.** Main courses 1,400$–1,600$ ($7.85–$8.95); tourist menu 1,900$ ($10.65). V. Fri–Wed 8am–midnight. PORTUGUESE.

This snack bar and restaurant is known for its *pratos do día* (plates of the day), made with market-fresh ingredients. If you're trying to save time, skip the long, lingering lunch at the pousada (where everybody tries to get a table) and head here. You can drop in for something to eat at just about any time. The format is friendly, simple, unassuming, and convenient, and the food always reliable.

Restaurante Alcaide. Rua Direita. ☎ **262/95-92-20.** Reservations recommended. Main courses 1,600$–1,900$ ($8.95–$10.65); fixed-price menu 3,000$ ($16.80). AE, DC, MC, V. Tues–Sun 12:30–3:30pm and 7:30–10pm. Closed Nov. REGIONAL PORTUGUESE.

A family from the Azores runs our favorite restaurant inside the city walls. On a narrow street leading to the pousada, this little place is known for its tasty regional dishes and good, inexpensive wines. Decorated in the style of a Portuguese tavern, it opens onto a balcony where the lucky few land tables. Meat dishes include well-conceived versions of roast rabbit and roast goat, and a succulent stew of shredded pork and red beans. The numerous fish dishes include grilled fillets of turbot with boiled potatoes and lemon sauce, fried tuna steak with baby boiled potatoes and a medley of salads, scabbardfish, and Alcaide (house-style) codfish with rondelles of potato, olive oil, parsley, and onions.

Restaurante Dom João V. Largo da Igreja Senhor da Pedra. ☎ **262/95-91-34.** Main courses 1,300$–2,800$ ($7.30–$15.70). V. Tues–Sun noon–4pm and 7–11pm. REGIONAL PORTUGUESE.

Half a mile west of the center of Óbidos, this restaurant specializes in the regional cuisine of Estremadura, accompanied by good Portuguese wines. The dining room is spacious and the staff helpful. You're invited to look into the kitchen, so you can make your own selection if you find the menu confusing. The food is not fancy, but it's tasty and offers good value. On Sunday the special is *cabrito assado no forno* (baby goat). Parking is possible, an important plus in Óbidos.

NEARBY PLACES TO STAY & DINE

✪ **Quinta da Cortiçada.** Outeiro da Cortiçada, 2040 Riomaior. ☎ **243/47-81-82.** Fax 243/47-87-72. 9 units. 16,000$–18,000$ ($89.60–$100.80) double; 19,000$–20,000$ ($106.40–$112) suite. Rates include breakfast. AE, DC, MC, V. Free parking. From Óbidos, take N1114 24 miles southeast to the hamlet of Riomaior, then look for signs.

This is one of the most formal and elegant manor houses in the area. The Falcoa family commissioned its construction in the late 19th century. The Nobre family bought it in the 1970s, made many improvements, and turned it into a B&B. On 220 acres of field, park, and forest, it's a distinguished compound of red-walled, tile-roofed buildings surrounded by emerald lawns and a circular pool. Antiques fill the public rooms and comfortably furnished midsize guest rooms. There's a bar and a severely dignified restaurant that serves Portuguese and continental cuisine. A meal costs 3,800$ ($21.30). Rooms don't have TVs or telephones. There are tennis courts on the premises, free use of bicycles and the swimming pool, and a pond favored by birds and waterfowl.

Quinta da Ferraria. Ribeira de São João, 2040 Riomaior. ☎ **243/950-01.** Fax 243/956-96. 13 units, 2 apts. A/C TV TEL. 12,000$–15,000$ ($67.20–$84) double; 18,000$ ($100.80) suite; 23,000$ ($128.80) apt. Double and suite rates include breakfast. AE, MC, V. Free parking. From Óbidos, take N1114 24 miles southeast to the hamlet of Riomaior, then look for signs.

In 1992, a century-old, run-down compound of farm buildings was stylishly overhauled into a rustic and charming hotel. On 200 acres of rolling fields and orchards that surround it, the quinta sits behind a whitewashed wall and wrought-iron gate. Although it's less formal than the Quinta da Cortiçada (which lies in the same hamlet, about 6 miles away), some visitors appreciate this place for its authenticity and lack of pretension. There's a bar on the premises; the restaurant serves Portuguese family style meals on request for 3,800$ ($21.30) per person. Guests have the use of a swimming pool and tennis court. Bicycles are for rent, and there's horseback riding nearby.

ÓBIDOS AFTER DARK

Scattered among the many souvenir shops in the town center are about two dozen cafes and bars. In addition to beer and wine, they feature a sweet liqueur (Ginjinha) that's distilled from local cherries.

If it's winter, your evening might culminate in the town's closest approximation of a disco, called **Disco,** in the Albergaria Josefa d'Óbidos, rua Dom João de Ornelas (☎ 262/95-92-28), near the town's main entrance. In a setting best described as woodsy, patrons drink and sometimes dance. It's open Friday and Saturday only from 10:30pm until 3 or 4am. The cover charge of 500$ ($2.80) for women and 1,000$ ($5.60) for men includes the first drink.

A SIDE TRIP TO CALDAS DA RAINHA

The sister-queen of Manuel the Fortunate, after a bad night's sleep in Óbidos, set out the next day for Batalha. Passing through a small village, the rheumatic Leonor saw peasants bathing in fetid pools at the side of the road. When told of the springs' therapeutic value, she had her ladies-in-waiting clear the area (essential to protect her modesty). With a screen of fabric draped around her, she descended, partially dressed, into a foul sulfur bath.

The town has been a spa ever since. So great was Leonor's relief from her ailment that she returned to Caldas da Rainha again and again—in fact, she pawned her rubies and gold jewelry to construct a hospital and an adjoining church. The chapel, **Nossa Senhora do Pópulo,** was built in the early 16th century in the Manueline style, then at its apex, and is graced with a well-executed landmark belfry. The spa, which was particularly popular in the 19th century, lies some 60 miles north of Lisbon. It's usually visited after Óbidos, 4 miles away.

Caldas da Rainha is also noted for its ceramics, especially soup tureens and accompanying bowls with cabbage-leaf designs. Inside the town and outside, along the road to Alcobaça, many roadside stands charge far lower prices than you'd pay in Lisbon. The best selections are in the showrooms of factories, notably **Armando Baiana,** rua Cascais da Ribeira 37 (☎ 262/82-43-55), and **Secla,** rua São João de Deus (☎ 262/84-21-51).

2 Alcobaça

67 miles N of Lisbon, 10 miles NE of Caldas da Rainha

The main attraction in Alcobaça is the monastery. After your visit, you can explore the nearby market, said to sell the best fruit in Portugal. The peaches, grown in surrounding orchards originally planted by the Cistercian monks, are especially succulent. Many stalls also sell the blue-and-white pottery typical of Alcobaça.

ESSENTIALS

ARRIVING

BY TRAIN   Trains depart from Lisbon's Estação do Rossio station. The nearest rail connection is at Valado dos Frades, 3 miles away, between Nazaré and Alcobaça. For **information** and schedules, call ☎ 21/888-40-25. About 14 buses per day make the short run from the train station at Valado dos Frades to Alcobaça; a one-way ticket is 155$ (85¢).

BY BUS   About 15 buses a day connect Nazaré with Alcobaça; a one-way ticket costs 210$ ($1.20). For **information,** call ☎ **262/55-11-72.** From Lisbon, there are three *expressos* a day. The trip takes 2½ hours and costs 1,200$ ($6.70) one way.

BY CAR   From Caldas da Rainha, continue northeast along N8.

VISITOR INFORMATION

The **Alcobaça Tourist Office** is on praça do 25 de Abril (☎ **262/58-23-77**).

EXPLORING ALCOBAÇA
VISITING THE MONASTERY

✪ **Mosteiro de Santa Maria (St. Mary Monastery).** 2460 Alcobaça. ☎ **262/583-909.** Admission 400$ ($2.25). Daily Apr–Sept 9am–7pm; Oct–Mar daily 9am–5pm.

In the Middle Ages, the Cistercian Mosteiro de Santa Maria was one of the richest and most prestigious in Europe. Begun in 1178, it was founded to honor a vow made by Portugal's first king, Afonso Henríques, before he faced the Moors at Santarém. Alcobaça, at the confluence of the Alcoa and Baça Rivers, was built to show his spiritual indebtedness to St. Bernard of Clairvaux, who inspired (some say goaded) many Crusaders into battle against the infidel.

Today, the monastery, in spite of its baroque facade and latter-day overlay, is a monument to simplicity and majesty. You'll be overcome with otherworldliness as you walk down the 327-foot-long nave. Chalk-white clustered columns, like trees, support a vaulted ceiling nearly 70 feet high.

The transept shelters the Gothic tombs of two star-crossed lovers, the Romeo and Juliet of Portuguese history: Pedro the Cruel and the ill-fated Spanish beauty, Inês de Castro, his mistress and later (perhaps) his wife. Though damaged, their sarcophagi are the greatest pieces of sculpture from 14th-century Portugal. They're the work of an unknown sculptor. Hovering angels guard the oval-faced Inês, whose tomb rests on sculpted animals—with human faces said to represent the assassins who slit her throat. Inês was buried at Alcobaça following a ghoulish ceremony in which the king had her decaying body exhumed and forced his courtiers to kiss her rotted hand and honor her as queen of the realm. On a wheel of fortune at his tomb, a sculptor, following Pedro's mandate, carved the words *ate o fim do mundo* ("until the end of the world"). Guarded by angels, his feet nestled on a dog, Pedro lies in a tomb supported by lions, symbols of his timeless rage and vengeance.

There's much to see at Alcobaça. The Cloisters of Silence, with their delicate arches, were favored by Dinis, the poet king. He sparked a thriving literary colony at the monastery, where the monks were busily engaged in translating ecclesiastical writings. Aside from the tombs and cloisters, the curiosity is the kitchen, through which a branch of the Alcoa River was routed. As in most Cistercian monasteries, the flowing brook was instrumental for sanitation purposes. Chroniclers have suggested that the friars fished for their dinner in the brook and later washed their dishes in it.

Finally, in the 18th-century Salon of Kings are niches with sculptures of some Portuguese rulers. The empty niches, left waiting for the rulers who were never sculptured, lend a melancholic air. The tiles in the room depict, in part, Afonso Henríques's triumph over the Moors.

SHOPPING

Local merchants were savvy enough to congregate on the square in front of Alcobaça's famous monastery, along the perimeter of praça do 25 de Abril. A dozen or so handcraft and ceramics shops line the square. One of the best outlets is **Casa Artisate**

Off the Beaten Path: Nature in the Raw

The area around Alcobaça contains two of the least discovered but most dramatic havens for nature in Portugal: a national park, and an offshore island that's ideal for scuba diving.

The **Parque Natural das Serras de Aire e Candieiros** straddles the border between Estremadura and Ribatejo, almost halfway between Lisbon and the university city of Coimbra. The government has set aside some 75,000 acres of moors and scrubland, and the rocky landscape is sparsely settled. A center for hikers is the small hamlet of **Minde,** where women weave patchwork rugs, which are well known in the region. Take along plenty of supplies.

In this rocky landscape, farmers barely eke out a living. They gather local stones to build their shelters, and get energy from windmills. If you'd rather drive than hike through the area, take N362, which runs for some 28 miles from Batalha in the north to Santarém in the south.

The other great area of natural beauty is **Berlenga Island.** A granite rock in the Atlantic, Berlenga is an island hideaway and nature reserve. Seven miles out in the ocean west of Peniche, a medieval fortress once stood sentinel over the Portuguese coastline. The reddish granite mass of Berlenga is the largest island in a little archipelago made up of three groups of rocky rises known as the Farilhões, the Estelas, and the Forcades. Berlenga beckons skin divers and fishers, who are intrigued by the undersea fauna, the long-finned tunny (albacore), jackfish, and varieties of marine crustaceans. It has numerous coves and underwater caves.

The medieval fortress **Forte de São João Batista** was destroyed in 1666 when 28 Portuguese tried to withstand a force of 1,500 Spaniards who bombarded it from 15 ships. Rebuilt toward the end of the 17th century, it now houses a hostel. You can take a stairway from the fortress to the lighthouse, stopping along the way to look over the panorama of the archipelago. A cobblestone walk from the top of the lighthouse site takes you down to a little bay with fishers' cottages along a beach.

You can arrange a boat trip around the island at the **hostel** (☎ **262/78-25-50**). Open from June to September 21, the hostel charges 2,000$ ($11.20) per night in a double, but the facilities are raw. To stay on this islet separated from the main body of land, you should love the sea and savor the thrill of living in a converted medieval fortress. Its stone walls, towers, and turrets rise sturdily on its own rocky islet. It was built as a bulwark in the country's coastal defense.

The fortress turns its outer stone walls against the elements, opening its interior courtyards to those relaxing in the sun. Tables with umbrellas sit on stone pavements. Individual rooms are basic; some dorm accommodations are available. There is no maid service. Guests must bring in their food and linen, cook their meals, make their beds, even clean the place. Bathrooms are shared.

On the way, to the south of the hostel, you can see the **Furado Grande,** a long marine tunnel that leads to a creek walled in by the granite cliffs. Under the fortress is a cave the locals call the **blue grotto.** Its pool is closer to emerald green.

To reach the island, head first for Peniche, 57 miles north of Lisbon. A ferry makes three trips a day to the island in July and August; the first leaves at 9am. A same-day round-trip ticket costs 2,500$ ($14). From September to June there's one ferry a day, leaving at 10am and returning at 6pm. This boat ride is rough; many people get seasick.

Egarafeira (☎ 062/59-01-20), which sells antiques, ceramics, and regional wine, among other offerings.

WHERE TO STAY

Hotel Santa Maria. Rua Francisco Zagalo 20–22, 2460 Alcobaça. ☎ **262/59-73-95.** Fax 262/59-67-15. 85 units. A/C MINIBAR TV TEL. 10,000$ ($56) double. Rates include breakfast. MC, V. Free parking.

The most attractive modern hotel in town is on a sloping street just above the flower-dotted plaza in front of the monastery. It's a relatively simple place, ideally located in a quiet but central part of the historic city. Guest rooms are small and a bit cramped, but filled with polished paneling cut into geometrical shapes. They contain comfortable contemporary chairs, and some have views over the monastery. Some chambers open onto balconies looking out over the square. The combination TV salon–bar–breakfast room is on the ground floor. If parking is a problem, the hotel will open its garage free. Only breakfast is served.

WHERE TO DINE

Trindade. Praça do Dom Afonso Henríques 22. ☎ **262/582-397.** Main courses 950$–1,800$ ($5.30–$10.10). AE, MC, V. Daily noon–1am. Closed Oct. PORTUGUESE/ALENTEJO.

The most popular restaurant in town opens onto a side of the monastery, fronting a tree-shaded square. In fair weather, harried waiters rush back and forth across the street carrying cooling drinks to tables on the square. Trindade has both full restaurant service and a snack bar. Your tasty meal is likely to include shellfish soup, roast rabbit, or the fresh fish of the day. Tender roast chicken is also available. The food is hearty and full of flavor, but the place is often overrun with international religious pilgrims.

ALCOBAÇA AFTER DARK

There's more to distract you after dark in Alcobaça than you might think. A bar that doubles as a bistro is **Bar Caribas,** av. Professore Vieira Natividade 10 (☎ **262/59-86-40**). A site favored by many singles is **Cheque-Mate,** rua Eng. Bernardo Villanova (☎ **262/59-85-49**). The town's only disco, **Sunset** (☎ **262/59-70-17**), dominates the center of the nearby hamlet of Fervença, about a mile west of Alcobaça. This is where just about everyone ends up late at night before staggering off to bed. From the center of town, follow the signs to Nazaré. It's open Friday, Saturday, and Sunday from 11pm till at least 4am.

3 Nazaré

82 miles N of Lisbon, 8 miles NW of Alcobaça

The inhabitants of Portugal's most famous fishing village live in a unique, tradition-bound world that tourists threaten to engulf. Many residents have never been to Lisbon; indeed, many have never left their village, except perhaps to make the pilgrimage to nearby Fátima. The people remain insular, even as their village blossoms into a big summer resort. Writers and painters originally "discovered" Nazaré; the tourist boom began in the 1960s.

Nazaré is probably best experienced in the off-season; chances are that you won't really get to see it in summer. You'll be too busy looking for a parking place (good luck) or elbowing your way onto the beach. The hordes of tourists who come to visit what's billed as the "most picturesque fishing village in Portugal," coupled with high-rise construction on every foot of available land, have made people wonder what happened to the fishing village. Amazingly, it's still here—you just have to look for it.

ESSENTIALS
ARRIVING

BY TRAIN   There's no direct link to Lisbon. Nine trains per day run from Lisbon to Valado dos Frades; the 3-hour trip costs 1,200$ ($6.70) one way. For **information,** call ☎ 21/888-40-25. Buses (see below) run from Valado dos Frades to Nazaré.

BY BUS   About a dozen buses a day make the short run between Nazaré and Valado dos Frades (the nearest rail terminal). A one-way ticket costs 155$ (85¢). Eight express buses per day arrive from Lisbon. The trip takes 2 hours (less than the train), and costs 1,200$ ($6.70) one way. For **information,** call ☎ 262/55-11-72.

BY CAR   From Alcobaça (see above), continue northwest along N8-4.

VISITOR INFORMATION

The **Nazaré Tourist Office** is on avenida da República (☎ 262/56-11-94).

EXPLORING THE RESORT   Don't expect stunning architecture or historic sights—the big attractions are the people and their fabled boats. Many locals claim descent from Carthaginians and Phoenicians, and they have the aquiline noses and dark brows to support their belief.

The villagers' clothes are patchwork quilts of sun-faded colors. The rugged men don rough woolen shirts and trousers, patched in kaleidoscopic rainbow hues, resembling Scottish plaid. Although the origin of this apparel remains unknown, one explanation is that the fishermen picked up the designs from Wellington's troops, who passed this way during the Napoleonic wars. The men wear long woolen stocking caps, in the dangling ends of which they keep their prized possessions—a favorite pipe or a crucifix.

The women walk about mostly barefoot, wearing embroidered handmade blouses and pleated skirts of patched plaid woolens. It's customary for widows to wear black—tasseled shawls, capes, or cowls—as a sign of mourning. Unmarried girls traditionally wear seven petticoats. The tourist inclination to count the poor girls' undergarments has been squelched by the government, which made the practice illegal.

The fishing boats are Phoenician in design: slender, elongated, and boldly colored. On the high, knifelike prows, you'll often see crudely shaped eyes—eyes supposedly imbued with the magical power to search the deep for fish and to avert storms. Even so, the boats sport lanterns for the dangerous job of fishing after dark. During the gusty days of winter or at high tide, the boats are hauled into a modern harbor about 10 minutes from the center. Oxen no longer pull the boats in, having been replaced by machinery. As another sign of changing times, if you want to look at one of these boats, one of the locals will lead you—for a price.

Nazaré consists of two sections: the fishing quarter and the **Sítio,** the almost exclusively residential upper town. Near the beach you'll find handcraft shops, markets, restaurants, hotels, and boardinghouses. The main square opens directly onto the sea, and narrow streets lead to the smaller squares, evoking a medina in a Moorish village. Simple shops hang objects outside their doors to indicate what they sell (for example, a carved wooden cow head would adorn a butcher shop). At the farthest point from the cliff and square are the vegetable and fish markets, where auctions are held.

Jutting out over the sea, the promontory of the Sítio is a sheer drop to the ocean and the beach below. It's accessible by either a funicular or a goat-steep cobblestone pathway. The Virgin Mary supposedly appeared here in 1182. A young horseback-riding nobleman, Faus Roupinho, was pursuing a wild deer near the precipice, which was shrouded in mist. The fog lifted suddenly to reveal the Virgin and the chasm below. In honor of this miracle, the nobleman built the **Chapel of Memory.** Today, near the spot, you can go inside the 18th-century structure honoring the event.

SHOPPING   Few other towns in Portugal are so promising—and so disappointing. Perhaps it's the sheer volume of merchandise in the crammed boutiques, all featuring much the same wares. You'll quickly apprehend that the residents of tourist-conscious Nazaré long ago lost their enthusiasm for their ubiquitous, rough-textured fisher's sweaters, which seem to spill over shelves of virtually every boutique in town. The robust *varinas* of Nazaré gave up knitting long ago in favor of more modern commercial pursuits, such as running snack bars, souvenir shops, and postcard kiosks. Most of the knitwear you'll see here is imported from less prosperous communities in Portugal's far north.

WHERE TO STAY

Although Nazaré is one of the most popular destinations in Portugal, for some reason it has never had a first-rate hotel. Note that Beira-Mar (see "Where to Dine," below) also offers accommodations.

Albergaria Mar Bravo. Praça Sousa Oliveira 70-71, 2450 Nazaré. ☎ **262/55-11-80.** Fax 262/55-39-79. 16 units. A/C TV TEL. 14,000$–19,000$ ($78.40–$106.40) double. Rates include breakfast. AE, DC, MC, V. Parking 1,500$ ($8.40).

Once the simple Pensão Madeira, this place has been completely updated and turned into a four-star inn. The small guest rooms are comfortably furnished, and modern amenities such as private bathrooms and air-conditioning have been added. The location, on the main square in front of the beach, is ideal only if you like lots of tourists. The hotel has two restaurants and a lounge with TV and a bar. It's affiliated with the Hotel Praia (see below).

Hotel da Nazaré. Largo Afonso Zuquete, 2450 Nazaré. ☎ **262/56-90-30.** Fax 262/56-90-38. 52 units. A/C MINIBAR TV TEL. 7,200$–13,130$ ($40.30–$73.55) double; 10,870$–18,270$ ($60.85–$102.30) suite. Rates include breakfast. AE, DC, MC, V. Free parking.

Hotel da Nazaré is the runner-up to the Praia (see below). This hotel doesn't please everybody, yet many patrons count themselves lucky if they can get a room on a hot summer day. The hotel is on a busy and noisy street set back from the water, about a 3-minute walk from the promenade. It opens onto a tiny plaza, and many of the front guest rooms have private balconies. The small, simply furnished rooms have good beds. The lower rates apply in the winter. A rooftop sun terrace has views of Nazaré and the cliff-top Sítio.

The best feature of this hotel is its fourth and fifth floors, which contain a restaurant and bar. The dining room opens onto windowed walls peering out over the village housetops, the rugged cliffs, and the harbor. Specializing in fish dishes, this dining room is open to the public.

Hotel Praia. Av. Vieira Guimarães 39, 2450 Nazaré. ☎ **262/56-14-23.** Fax 262/56-14-36. 44 units. A/C TV TEL. 19,500$ ($109.20) double; 22,000$ ($123.20) suite. Rates include breakfast. AE, DC, MC, V. Parking 1,500$ ($8.40).

The leading hotel in town—where the competition is not keen—is the Praia (literally, "beach"). Built in the late 1960s, when the world's tourists were discovering Nazaré, the six-floor hotel is decorated in a modern but uninspired style. It's about a 3-minute walk from the sandy beach where the fishing boats and bathing cabins lie. Remodeled in 1993, the midsize rooms are reasonably comfortable and well maintained.

The restaurant, which is open to the public, serves regional meat and fish dishes. A typical meal averages 3,000$ ($16.80).

Pensão-Restaurante Ribamar. Rua Gomes Freire 9, 2450 Nazaré. ☎ **262/55-11-58.** Fax 262/56-22-24. 25 units. 17,300$–22,400$ ($96.90–$125.45) double; 18,800$–23,900$ ($105.30–$133.85) suite. Rates include half-board. AE, DC, MC, V. Parking 1,000$ ($5.60).

This genuine old-fashioned village inn is right on the water, and most of its small guest rooms open onto balconies. A twisting stairway in the rear leads to the old-style rooms, with rattan baskets of pine cones on each landing. Each immaculate room is individually decorated and comfortable, with good beds.

Even if you're passing through just for the day, you may want to try the regional cuisine in the traditional oak-beamed dining room. Food is served daily from 12:30 to 3pm and 7:30 to 10pm (by candlelight). Meals cost 3,500$ ($19.60) and up.

WHERE TO DINE

Beira-Mar. Av. da República 40, 2450 Nazaré. ☎ **262/56-13-58.** Main courses 980$–3,600$ ($5.50–$20.15). AE, DC, MC, V. Daily noon–3pm and 7–10pm. Closed Dec–Feb. PORTUGUESE.

Beira-Mar is one of the best restaurants in the port. In a modern building, it offers typical Portuguese dishes, including the "day's catch." Meat dishes are also available, along with regional soups, but seafood is the attraction. More than 75 diners can crowd in here on a busy day in summer. Although not imaginative, the food is tasty and uses fresh ingredients.

Opening onto the beach, this popular place also offers modest accommodations at modest prices. The 15 simply furnished, somewhat raw-boned double rooms go for 6,500$ to 14,500$ ($36.40 to $81.20). Lodging is available from March to November only.

Mar Bravo. Praça Sousa Oliveira 71. ☎ **262/55-11-80.** Reservations recommended. Regular main courses 2,500$–3,000$ ($14–$16.80); seafood main courses 4,500$–10,000$ ($25.20–$56); fixed-price menu 2,000$ ($11.20). AE, DC, MC, V. Daily noon–10pm. PORTUGUESE.

One of the busiest of the dozens of overpriced restaurants in this bustling village is Mar Bravo, on the corner of the square overlooking the ocean. The decor is tile, with a huge photo of the Nazaré beach covering the back wall. A complete and consistently pleasing meal consists of soup, followed by a fish or meat dish, and bread. An English-language menu lists à la carte specialties such as classic bass caprice, fish stew Nazaréna, lobster stew, and grilled pork. Dessert might be a soufflé, fruit salad, or pudding. Upstairs is a second dining room, with an ocean view.

NAZARÉ AFTER DARK

Many bars and bodegas line the main boulevards of Nazaré. You'll find dozens of establishments along such main arteries as avenida da República and avenida Marginale. Bar-hop as energetically as you please, but do stop at our favorite, **Bar Gaibota,** avenida Marginal (☎ **262/56-22-85**). The owners speak fluent English after a long sojourn in Canada, and no one will wince if you order a dry martini. Consider ending your pub crawl at Nazaré's most popular disco (which at press time was the only one in town), **Masartes,** avenida Marginale (☎ **262/55-14-66**). It's open on Friday, Saturday, and Sunday from 10:30pm till dawn.

4 Batalha

73 miles N of Lisbon

Batalha merits a visit for only one reason: to see the monastery. Most visitors choose to stay in Fátima or Nazaré, which have more hotels and restaurants. There are, however, places to sleep and eat in Batalha.

ESSENTIALS
ARRIVING

BY TRAIN   There's no direct rail link to Lisbon. Trains run to the junction at Valado dos Frades, and buses continue to Batalha. For rail schedules, call ☎ **21/888-40-25.**

BY BUS   From Nazaré (see above), seven buses a day make the 1-hour trip to Batalha, with a change at Alcobaça; one-way tickets cost 435$ ($2.45). From Lisbon, there are six *expresso* buses a day; the trip lasts 2 hours and costs 1,000$ ($5.60) one way.

BY CAR   From Alcobaça (see above), continue northeast along Route 8.

VISITOR INFORMATION

The **Batalha Tourist Office** is on praça Mouzinho de Albuquerque (☎ **244/76-51-80**). If you're traveling by bus, the tourist office keeps detailed schedules of the best connections to surrounding towns.

VISITING THE MONASTERY

✪ **Mosteiro de Santa Maria da Vitória.** N8. ☎ **244/765-497.** Admission 400$ ($2.25) adults; 200$ ($1.10) youths 14–25, free for children under 14. Daily Oct–Mar 9am–5pm; Apr–Sept 9am–6pm.

In 1385, João I, the founder of the House of Avíz, vowed on the plains of Aljubarrota that if his underequipped and outnumbered army defeated the invading Castilians, he would commemorate his spiritual indebtedness to the Virgin Mary. The result is the magnificent Monastery of the Virgin Mary, designed in splendid Gothic and Manueline style. Approached from the west, it's an imposing mass of steeples, buttresses, and parapets. Much restored, it's a jewel of finely cut gems in stone.

The **western porch,** ornamented by a tangled mass of Gothic sculpture of saints and other figures, sits beneath a stained-glass window of blue, mauve, and amber. The hue of the limestone has supposedly changed through the ages; today it's a light burnished beige. Napoléon's irreverent army used the stained-glass windows for target practice.

In the **Founder's Chapel,** completed in 1435, João I and his English queen, Philippa of Lancaster (daughter of John of Gaunt), lie in peaceful repose, their hands entwined. Prince Henry the Navigator's tomb is near that of his parents. His fame eclipsed theirs even though he never sat on the throne; he spent much of his life at his school of navigation at Sagres, on the southern coast of Portugal. Henry's sculpted hands are clasped in prayer. Three other princes are entombed here under a ceiling resembling snow crystals. The Royal Cloister was started by Afonso Domingues and finished by Huguet. These cloisters reveal the beginnings of the nautical-oriented Manueline architecture. (A second cloister, the King Afonso Cloister, dates from the 15th century.)

The magnum opus of the monastery is the **Chapter House,** a square chamber whose vaulting is an unparalleled example of the Gothic style, bare of supporting pillars.

Sentinels and the glow of an eternal flame guard the two tombs of Portugal's Unknown Soldiers from World War I. In one part of the quadrangle is the Unknown Soldiers Museum, which houses gifts to the fallen warriors from the people of Portugal and from other countries, including a presentation from Maréchal Joffre. Beyond the crypt are the remains of the old wine cellars.

Stunning filigree designs ornament the coral-stone entrance to the seven unfinished chapels. The capelas, under an inconstant "sky ceiling," are part of one of the finest examples of the Manueline style, a true stone extravaganza. It seems a pity that construction was abandoned so workers and architects for Manuel I could help build his monastery at Belém. Originally the chapels were ordered by Dom Duarte, the son of João I, but he died before they were completed.

Outside, in the forecourt, stands a heroic statue to Nuno Álvares, who fought with João I on the plains of Aljubarrota. It was unveiled in 1968.

WHERE TO STAY & DINE

Pousada do Mestre Afonso Domingues. Largo do Mestre Afonso Domingues, 2440 Batalha. ☎ **244/765-260.** Fax 244/765-247. 21 units. A/C MINIBAR TEL. 25,000$ ($140) double; 30,000$ ($168) suite. Rates include breakfast. AE, DC, MC, V. Free parking.

Filling a big accommodations gap in this part of the country is the Pousada do Mestre Afonso Domingues. Like a low-slung motel, it stands right across the square from the monastery. Guests can relax in well-kept modern comfort, if not great style. The good-sized rooms, soundproofed against traffic noise, are well furnished, with comfortable beds. The staff is helpful, and there's laundry service.

Even if you're not staying overnight in Batalha, you can patronize the pousada's first-class dining room. It serves typically Portuguese fare and charges 4,000$ ($22.40) for a complete meal. Food is served daily from 12:30 to 3pm and 7:30 to 10pm.

5 Fátima

88 miles N of Lisbon, 36 miles E of Nazaré

Fátima is a world-famous pilgrimage site. The terrain around the village is wild, almost primitive, with an aura of barren desolation hanging over the countryside. When religious pilgrims flock to the town, its desolation quickly turns to fervent drama.

ESSENTIALS

ARRIVING

BY TRAIN   A train runs daily from Lisbon to Chão de Maças, 12½ miles outside Fátima. For **information** and schedules, call ☎ **21/888-40-25.** Buses await passengers and run into Fátima and the pilgrimage sites.

BY BUS   On bus schedules, Fátima is often listed as "Cova da Iria," which leads to a lot of confusion. About three buses a day connect Fátima with Batalha. The trip takes 40 minutes and costs 250$ ($1.40) one way. Eight buses a day arrive from Lisbon. The 1½-hour trip costs 1,200$ ($6.70) one way. For **information** and schedules, call ☎ **249/53-16-11.**

BY CAR   From Batalha (see above), continue east along Route 356.

VISITOR INFORMATION

The **tourist office** is on avenida Dom José Alves Correia da Silva (☎ **249/53-11-39**).

A PILGRIMAGE TO FÁTIMA   On May 13 and October 13, pilgrims overrun the town. Beginning on the 12th, the roads leading to Fátima are choked with pilgrims in donkey carts, on bicycles, or in cars. Usually, however, they approach on foot; some even walk on their knees in penance. They camp out until day breaks. In the central square, which is larger than St. Peter's in Rome, a statue of the Madonna passes through the crowd. Some 75,000 handkerchiefs flutter in the breeze, like thousands of peace doves taking flight.

Then, as many as are able crowd in to visit a small slanted-roof shed known as the **Chapel of the Apparitions.** Inside stands a single white column marking the spot where a small holm oak once grew. An image of the Virgin Mary reputedly appeared over this oak on May 13, 1917, when she is said to have spoken to three shepherd children. The oak long ago disappeared, torn to pieces by souvenir collectors. The oak now standing near the chapel existed in 1917 but was not connected with the apparition. The original chapel constructed here was dynamited on the night of March 6, 1922, by skeptics who suspected the church of staging the so-called miracle.

While World War I dragged on, three devout children—Lúcia de Jesús and her cousins, Jacinta and Francisco Marto—claimed that they saw the first appearance of "a lady" on the tableland of Cova da Iria. Her coming had been foreshadowed in 1916 by what they would later cite as "an angel of peace," who is said to have appeared before them.

Attempts were made to suppress their story, but it spread quickly, eventually generating worldwide enthusiasm, disbelief, and controversy. During the July appearance, the lady was reported to have revealed three secrets to them, one of which prefigured the coming of World War II, another connected with Russia's "rejection of God." The final secret, recorded by Lúcia, was opened by church officials in 1960, but they have refused to divulge its contents.

Acting on orders from the Portuguese government, the mayor of a nearby town threw the children into jail and threatened them with torture, even death in burning oil. Still, they would not be intimidated and stuck to their story. The lady reportedly made six appearances, the final one on October 13, 1917, when the children were joined by an estimated 70,000 people who witnessed the famous "Miracle of the Sun." The day had begun with pouring rain and driving winds. Observers from all over the world testified that at noon "the sky opened up" and the sun seemed to spin out of its axis and hurtle toward the earth. Many at the site feared the Last Judgment was upon them. Others later reported that they thought the scorching sun was crashing into the earth and would consume it in flames. Many authorities, and certainly the faithful pilgrims, agreed that a major miracle of modern times had occurred. Only the children reported seeing "Our Lady," however.

Both Francisco and Jacinta died in the influenza epidemic that swept Europe after World War I. Lúcia became a Carmelite nun in a convent at the university city of Coimbra. She returned to Fátima in 1967 to mark the 50th anniversary of the apparition, and the pope flew in from Rome.

A cold, pristine white basilica in the neoclassic style was erected at one end of the wide square. If you want to go inside, you may be stopped by a guard if you're not suitably dressed. A sign posted outside reads: THE BLESSED VIRGIN MARY, MOTHER OF GOD, APPEARED IN THIS PLACE. THEREFORE, WOMEN ARE ASKED NOT TO ENTER THE SANCTUARY IN SLACKS OR OTHER MASCULINE ATTIRE. Men wearing shorts are also excluded. Outside Fátima, in the poor, simple village of **Aljustrel,** you can still see the houses of the three shepherd children.

SHOPPING   Frankly, many of the souvenirs you'll find in Fátima might be more religious in nature, and perhaps more cloying, than you feel comfortable with. If you're interested in an even-handed mixture of religious and secular objects, head for the town's biggest gift shop, **Centro Comercial,** estrada de Leira (☎ **249/53-23-75**). The staggering inventory is piled to the ceiling. If you're looking for devotional statues, or a less controversial example of regional porcelain, you'll find it here, 500 yards from the town's main religious sanctuary. There's another well-stocked gift shop in the **Pax Hotel,** rua Francisco Marto (☎ **249/53-30-10**).

WHERE TO STAY

On the days of the major pilgrimages it's just about impossible to secure a room unless you've reserved months in advance.

Estalagem Dom Gonçalo. Rua Jacinta Marto 100, 2495 Fátima. ☎ **249/53-93-30.** Fax 249/53-93-35. E-mail: hotel.d.goncalo@ip.pt. 42 units. A/C MINIBAR TV TEL. 13,550$ ($75.90) double; 16,200$ ($90.70) suite. Rates include breakfast. AE, DC, MC, V. Free parking.

This modern hotel sits in a large garden at the entrance to town. The small to midsize guest rooms are among the town's finest, although we'd give the edge to the Hotel de Fátima. All are comfortably and attractively furnished, with firm mattresses and rather uninspired decor. The bathrooms are small but well maintained, with adequate shelf space and recently renewed plumbing.

Estalagem Dom Gonçalo serves some of the best food in Fátima, with the biggest portions. The cost of a meal averages 4,200$ ($23.50). The restaurant has an à la carte menu. You can order the usual selection of fish and meat dishes, a mixed salad, or a tasty omelette. Food is served daily from noon to 3pm and 7:30 to 10pm, and the dining room is open to nonguests.

Hotel Cinquentenário. Rua Francisco Marto 175, 2495 Fátima. ☎ **249/53-34-65.** Fax 249/53-29-92. E-mail: hotel.cinquentenario@ip.pt. 146 units. A/C TV TEL. 12,500$–24,000$ ($70–$134.40) double. Rates include continental breakfast. AE, DC, MC, V. Free parking.

This balconied structure, on a corner lot a short walk east of the sanctuary, offers comfortable but small accommodations. It's heavily booked during major pilgrimages. Patterned carpets and wallpapers make the interior warmly agreeable. Each guest room has a firm mattress and well-maintained plumbing; suites contain minibars. There's a piano bar and a coffee shop on the premises, plus a dining room that serves Portuguese food.

Hotel de Fátima. Rua João Paulo II, 2495 Fátima. ☎ **249/53-33-51.** Fax 249/53-26-91. 135 units. A/C MINIBAR TV TEL. 15,000$ ($84) double; 17,600$–22,000$ ($98.55–$123.20) suite. Rates include buffet breakfast. AE, DC, MC, V. Parking 500$ ($2.80) in garage, free outside.

Rated four stars by the government, Hotel de Fátima is the leading accommodation of a dreary lot. Many of the midsize rooms overlook the sanctuary. All rooms have natural wood furnishings in the provincial Portuguese style, with colorful fabrics. The best rooms are in the newer 45-room addition. The building has three floors, serviced by two elevators.

The main floor holds a bar and a cozy reception lounge with a large sitting room. The dining room serves a standard two-course table d'hôte luncheon or dinner for 3,400$ ($19.05). The cuisine has been called "religious group fare."

Hotel Santa Maria. Rua de Santo António, 2495 Fátima. ☎ **249/53-30-15.** Fax 249/53-21-97. E-mail: santamaria.sanjose@ip.pt. 62 units. A/C TV TEL. 7,500$–9,300$ ($42–$52.10) double; from 14,000$ ($78.40) suite. Rates include continental breakfast. AE, MC, V. Free parking.

This comfortable modern hotel is on a quiet side street just a few steps east of the park surrounding the sanctuary. The lobby has a gray-and-white marble floor, lots of exposed wood, and a sunny lounge area with plants that thrive in the light streaming through stained-glass windows. Each modern room, attended by a well-trained staff, contains a balcony, firm bed, and radio. The small accommodations are plain but entirely acceptable.

Hotel São José. Av. Dom José Alves Correia da Silva, 2495 Fátima. ☎ **249/53-22-15.** Fax 249/53-32-17. 76 units. A/C TV TEL. 9,300$ ($52.10) double; 13,000$ ($72.80) suite. Rates include breakfast. AE, MC, V. Free parking.

On one of the busiest streets in Fátima, within walking distance of the sanctuary, this modern balconied hotel is large and urban. It has a uniformed staff, a marble-floored lobby, and comfortable midsize rooms. This hotel, which has two bars and a dining room, seems to have a bit more style than some of its more Spartan competitors. Each guest room has a firm bed and smoothly functioning plumbing.

Hotel Três Pastorinhos. Rua João Paulo II, 2495 Fátima. ☎ **249/53-34-29.** Fax 249/53-24-49. 92 units. A/C TEL. 10,950$ ($61.30) double; 16,000$ ($89.60) suite. Rates include continental breakfast. AE, DC, MC, V. Free parking.

This three-star establishment (the "Hotel of the Three Shepherd Children") offers modern facilities in a setting as sparse as a convent. Its newest guest rooms open onto private balconies that overlook the sanctuary. If you're just passing through, you can come in for a multicourse meal. The breakfast rooms open onto sun terraces, edged with pots of flowering plants.

WHERE TO DINE

Grelha. Rua Jacinta Marto 76. ☎ **249/53-16-33.** Main courses 1,100$–2,200$ ($6.15–$12.30); fixed-price menu 2,200$ ($12.30). AE, DC, MC, V. Fri–Wed noon–3pm and 7–10:30pm. Closed 2 weeks in Nov (dates vary). PORTUGUESE/GRILLS.

If you don't want to eat at a hotel, try Grelha, one of the best of a meager selection. It's 300 yards from the sanctuary at Fátima. It offers regional specialties but is known for its grills, especially steaks and fish. Grilled codfish is an especially good choice. In the cooler months the fireplace is an attraction, and the bar is busy year-round.

Tía Alice. Rua do Adro. ☎ **249/53-17-37.** Reservations required. Main courses 1,500$–2,800$ ($8.40–$15.70); fixed-price menu 3,700$ ($20.70). MC, V. Tues–Sun noon–3pm; Tues–Sat 7:30–10pm. Closed July. PORTUGUESE.

In a very old house in the center of town, this simple, rustic restaurant ("Aunt Alice") offers copious portions of food inspired by the rural traditions of Estremadura. It's unquestionably the finest dining choice in the area, although that's not saying a lot. The dining room, with stone walls and beamed ceilings, sits at the top of a flight of wooden stairs. The hearty specialties include broad-bean soups, roast lamb with rosemary and garlic, fried hake with green sauce, chicken, Portuguese sausages, and grilled lamb or pork chops.

FÁTIMA AFTER DARK

As you might expect of a destination for religious pilgrimages, Fátima is early to rise (in many cases, for morning mass) and early to bed. Cafes in town tend to be locked tight after around 10pm, so religion-weary residents who want to escape drive south of town for 1¼ miles along estrada de Minde. Here you'll find two music bars that are much more attuned to human frailties than the ecclesiastical monuments in the core. They are **Mario's Bar,** estrada de Minde (☎ **249/53-16-83**), and its neighbor, **Bar Truao,** estrada de Minde (☎ **249/52-15-42**).

8 The Algarve

In the ancient Moorish town of Xelb (today called Silves), a handsome and sensitive vizier once lived. During one of his sojourns into northern lands, he fell in love with a beautiful Nordic princess. After they married, he brought her back to the Algarve. Soon the young princess began to pine for the snow-covered hills and valleys of her native land. The vizier decreed that thousands of almond trees would be planted throughout his realm. Since that day, pale-white almond blossoms have blanketed the Algarve in late January and early February. The young princess lived happily ever after in her vizier's sundrenched kingdom, with its sweet-smelling artificial winters—or so the story goes.

The maritime province of the Algarve, often called the "garden of Portugal," is the southwesternmost part of Europe. Its coastline stretches 100 miles, from Henry the Navigator's Cape St. Vincent to the border town of Vila Real de Santo António, fronting once-hostile Spain. The varied coastline contains sluggish estuaries, sheltered lagoons, low-lying areas where clucking marsh hens nest, long sandy spits, and promontories jutting out into the white-capped aquamarine foam.

Called Al-Gharb by the Moors, the land south of the *serras* (hills) of Monchique and Caldeirão remains a spectacular anomaly that seems more like a transplanted section of the North African coastline than a piece of Europe. The temperature averages around 60°F in the winter, 74°F in summer. During the day the sky is pale blue, deepening in the evening to rich cerulean. The countryside abounds in vegetation: almonds, lemons, oranges, carobs, pomegranates, and figs.

Even though most of the towns and villages of the Algarve are more than 150 miles from Lisbon, the great 1755 earthquake shook this area. Entire communities were wiped out; however, many Moorish and even Roman ruins remain. In the fret-cut chimneys, mosquelike cupolas, and cubist houses, a distinct Oriental flavor prevails. Phoenicians, Greeks, Romans, Visigoths, Moors, and Christians all touched this land.

However, much of the historic flavor is gone forever, swallowed by a sea of dreary high-rise apartment blocks surrounding most towns. Years ago Portuguese officials, looking in horror at what happened to Spain's Costa del Sol, promised more limited and controlled development so that they wouldn't make "Spain's mistake." That promise, in our opinion, has not been kept.

The Algarve

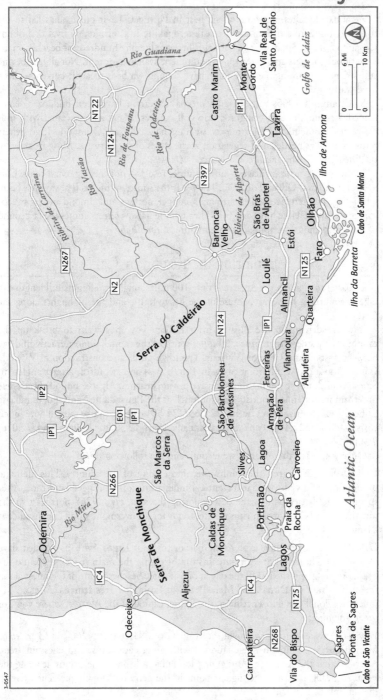

3-0547

Algarvian beaches are some of the best in Portugal. Their quality has led to the tourist boom across the southern coastline, making it a formidable rival of Lisbon's Costa do Sol and Spain's Costa del Sol. There are literally hundreds of beaches, many with public showers and water-sports equipment available for rent. Not all beaches are suitable for swimming, because some have sloping sea beds or swift currents—heed local warnings.

Since around 1965, vast stretches of coastal terrain have been bulldozed, landscaped, irrigated, and reconfigured into golf courses. Many are associated with real-estate developments or major resorts, such as the 2,000-acre Quinta do Lago, where retirement villas nestle amid vegetation at the edges of the fairways. Most are open to qualified golfers who inquire in advance.

Many former fishing villages—now summer resorts—dot the Algarvian coast: Carvoeiro, Albufeira, Olhão, Portimão. The sea is the source of life, as it always has been. The village marketplaces sell esparto mats, copper, pottery, and almond and fig sweets, sometimes shaped like birds and fish. Through the narrow streets comes the fast sound of little accordions pumping out the rhythmical *corridinho.*

Exploring the Region by Car

The coastal road along the Algarve is only 100 miles long. Traveling its full length can take several days, however, because of the heavy traffic and the highlights along the way.

If you're driving to the Algarve from Lisbon, you may want to break up the monotony by stopping in **Sines,** 99 miles south of the capital, almost exactly midway between Lisbon and Cape St. Vincent. The town holds a reconstruction of Vasco da Gama's house (he was born at Sines in 1469). Bass and swordfish attract anglers to Sines. Sand dunes rise along the extensive private beaches. Algarve-bound vacationers or returning suntanned tourists stop for lunch at the **Pousada de Santiago,** estrada de Lisboa, 7540 Santiago do Cacém (☎ **269/224-59**). A two-course table d'hôte lunch costs 4,000$ ($22.40). Food is served daily from 12:30 to 2:30pm and 7:30 to 9:30pm.

Once you reach the Algarve, we recommend the following tour:

Day 1 Start at **Sagres,** the southwesternmost point of the country. This dramatic promontory and **Cabo de São Vicente,** 4 miles away, form a rugged landscape. After spending the better part of the day exploring the area, take N268 northeast to the junction with N125, which runs east to Lagos for an overnight stop. The distance is 21 miles.

Day 2 In the morning, explore the harbor town of **Lagos,** with its arcaded slave market and Church of St. Anthony. Instead of taking the main road, N125, use the coastal road. Spend the rest of the day at one of three beaches, some of the finest along the coast: **Praia de Dona Ana, Meia Praia,** or **Praia dos Três Irmãos.** After an 11-mile drive you'll come to **Portimão,** the fishing capital of the Algarve, where you can spend the night.

Day 3 After exploring the town, head north on N124 and N266 for 13 miles to **Monchique,** a mountain range studded with pine, eucalyptus, and chestnut trees. After lunch at the Estalagem Abrigo de Montanha in Monchique, continue along the **Fóia.** At 3,000 feet, it is the highest point in the Serra de Monchique. The drive to the summit is spectacular.

After all that mountain climbing, you may be ready to hit the beaches again. Head south toward Portimão, this time stopping for the night at **Praia da Rocha.**

Day 4 After a swim in the morning, get back on the main road (N125) at Portimão and head east for 5 miles to **Lagoa,** a market town. From here, go 4 miles to **Silves**. Once the capital of the Moorish kingdom of the Algarve, Silves has a castle and a cathedral.

After lunch, return to Lagoa, where you can follow signs 3 miles south to the little fishing village of **Carvoeiro.** It's an expatriate colony, filled with sophisticated Europeans. The sandy beach nestles between two rock masses, creating a solarium. The shadows of the cliffs are cooling, the sea calm. East of the beach on a steep slope is a **belvedere,** dedicated to Our Lady of the Incarnation, that affords a commanding view of the sea and surrounding cliffs. It's worth the trip down. Accommodations are limited and tend to be heavily booked, so you may want to press on for the night.

Pick up N125 once more and drive to **Ferreiras,** where you'll turn right on N395. Proceed to Albufeira, 16 miles from Lagoa, and spend the night.

Day 5 The bustling resort town of **Albufeira** was the last Moorish stronghold in the Algarve. This former fishing village is hugely overdeveloped, and most of the remains of its history have been swept away. Nevertheless, it contains some of the best restaurants and hotels along the coast.

Day 6 Back on N125, you can drive east to **Almansil,** then follow the signposted route north to Loulé. **Loulé,** 9½ miles north of Faro, is a market town in the heart of the region's "chimney country." From many of its houses, fret-cut plaster towers rise— you may even see one on the house of a discriminating dog. They resemble fine lacework or filigree in stone; some are as delicately contrived as snow crystals blown against glass. Loulé and the villages around it are known for their handcrafts.

Return to Almancil, where you can head south to the resort and golfing complexes of the **Vila do Lobo** and the **Quinta do Lago,** two of the most fabled stops on the coast. Consider lunching in the area. After exploring a bit, you can follow the signs to **Faro** for the night.

Day 7 The modern-day capital of the Algarve, Faro merits little more than a morning sightseeing jaunt. Then head east for about 5 miles along N125 to the turnoff for **Olhão.** With its cubist-style houses—white blocks stacked one upon the other, with flat red-tile roofs and exterior stairways on the stark walls—Olhão might remind you of a Georges Braque collage.

From Olhão continue along N125, through green fields studded with almond and carob trees, to **Tavira.** A tuna-fishing center, it's cut off from the sea by an elongated spit of sand, Ilha de Tavira. This festive-looking town, with floridly decorated chimneys topping many of its houses, lies about 19 miles east of Faro. For your final night on the Algarve, continue east along N125 to the resort of **Monte Gordo,** which has many hotels. In the morning you can explore the Portuguese border town of **Vila Real de Santo António** before deciding on your next destination.

1 Sagres: "The End of the World"

174 miles S of Lisbon, 21 miles W of Lagos, 71 miles W of Faro

At the extreme southwestern corner of Europe—once called *o fim do mundo* (the end of the world)—Sagres is a rocky escarpment jutting into the Atlantic Ocean. From here, Henry the Navigator, the Infante of Sagres, launched Portugal and the rest of Europe on the seas of exploration. Here he established his school of navigation, where Magellan, Diaz, Cabral, and Vasco da Gama apprenticed. Henry died in 1460, before the great discoveries of Columbus and Vasco da Gama, but the later explorers owed him a debt. A virtual ascetic, he brought together the best navigators, cartographers, geographers, scholars, sailors, and builders, infused them with his rigorous devotion, and methodically set Portuguese caravels upon the Sea of Darkness.

ESSENTIALS
ARRIVING
BY FERRY & TRAIN   From Lisbon's praça do Comércio, you can take a ferry across the Tagus to Barreiro. From there, take the Southern Line Railway to Lagos. For **information** and schedules, call ☎ **21/888-40-25.** From Lagos, buses go to Sagres.

BY BUS   About 10 **Rodoviária** buses (☎ **282/76-29-44**) run from Lagos to Sagres each day. The trip time is 1 hour, and a one-way ticket costs 450$ ($2.50).

BY CAR   From Lagos, drive west on Route 125 to Vila do Bispo, then head south along Route 268 to Sagres.

VISITOR INFORMATION
Sagres does not have a full-time tourist office. Those functions are handled by a privately run agency, **Turifo,** praça da República (☎ **282/62-00-03**), which is also a travel agency.

WHAT TO SEE & DO IN SAGRES
EXPLORING THE AREA
Both the cape and Sagres (especially from the terrace of the pousada) offer a view of the sunset. In the ancient world, the cape was the last explored point, although in time the Phoenicians pushed beyond it. Many mariners thought that when the sun sank beyond the cape, it plunged over the edge of the world. To them, venturing around the promontory was to face the demons of the unknown.

Today, at the reconstructed site of Henry's windswept fortress on Europe's Land's End (named after the narrowing westernmost tip of Cornwall, England), you can see a huge stone compass dial. Henry supposedly used the **Venta de Rosa** in his naval studies at Sagres. Housed in the fortress is a small **museum** of minor interest that documents some of the area's history. It's open Tuesday to Sunday from 10am to noon and 2 to 6pm. Admission is 300$ ($1.70). At a simple **chapel,** restored in 1960, sailors are said to have prayed for help before setting out into uncharted waters. The chapel is closed to the public.

Three miles away is the promontory of **Cabo de São Vicente.** It got its name because, according to legend, the body of St. Vincent arrived mysteriously here on a boat guided by ravens. (Others claim that the body of the patron saint, murdered at Valencia, Spain, washed up on Lisbon's shore.) Seagulls glide on the air currents, and as you approach, you'll see goats grazing on a hill where even the trees are bent from the gusty winds. A lighthouse, the second most powerful in Europe, beams illumination 60 miles across the ocean. It's generally open daily from 8am to noon and 2 to 9pm, but you must get permission from the gatekeeper to climb it.

No buses connect the cape with Sagres. You must go by car.

OUTDOOR ACTIVITIES
BEACHES   Many beaches fringe the peninsula; some attract nude bathers. **Mareta,** at the bottom of the road leading from the center of town toward the water, is the best and most popular. East of town is **Tonel,** also a good sandy beach. The beaches west of town, **Praia de Baleeira** and **Praia de Martinhal,** are better for windsurfing than for swimming.

EXPLORING   If you'd like to rent a bike to explore the cape, go to **Turinfo,** praça da República, Sagres (☎ **282/62-00-03**). The charge is 1,200$ ($6.70) per half-day. Turinfo's Jeep tours of the natural preserve of the cape, including lunch, cost 6,900$ ($38.65).

FISHING   Between October and January you'll be assured of a prolific catch, and at times you can walk down to almost any beach and hire a local fisher to take you out for a half-day. Just about every large-scale hotel along the Algarve will arrange a fishing trip for you. At the mention of fishing, the reception staff will propose a list of local entrepreneurs who know the locations of the most abundant shoals. You can also contact **Turinfo** (see above), which offers 3-hour excursions every afternoon, weather permitting. They depart at 4:30pm from the harbor of Sagres. Prices start at 4,000$ ($22.40) per person, with equipment included. It also offers 2-hour boat rides to the tip of Cabo de São Vicente for sightseeing (no fishing) for 3,300$ ($18.50) per person, every afternoon, weather permitting, at 2pm.

WHERE TO STAY

Hotel da Baleeira. Sítio da Baleeira, Sagres, 8650 Vila do Bispo. ☎ **282/624-212.** Fax 282/624-425. E-mail: hotel.baleeira@mail.telepac.pt. 118 units. TV TEL. 18,600$ ($104.15) double. Rates include breakfast. AE, DC, MC, V. Free parking.

In a ship's-bow position, Hotel da Baleeira is a first-class whaleboat (*baleeira* in Portuguese) spread out above the fishing port. The largest hotel on this land projection, it offers guest rooms and sea-view balconies. The number of its rooms has nearly doubled in recent years; the older ones are quite small, and some have linoleum floors. The bathrooms are also tiny.

If you're exploring the Algarve and are in Sagres just for the day, you can have lunch or dinner in a dining room cantilevered toward the sea, where every seat has a view. The chef has his own lobster tanks, and the food is well prepared. Meals begin at 2,500$ ($14). There's also a cocktail lounge, an angular saltwater pool with a snack bar, a flagstone terrace, a tennis court, and a private sandy beach.

Pousada do Infante. Ponta da Atalaia, 8650 Sagres. ☎ **282/642-222.** Fax 282/642-225. www.pousadas.pt. 39 units. MINIBAR TV TEL. 16,300$–25,000$ ($91.30–$140) double; 20,800$–31,000$ ($116.50–$173.60) suite. Rates include breakfast. AE, DC, MC, V. Free parking.

The Pousada do Infante, the best address in Sagres, seems like a monastery built by ascetic monks who wanted to commune with nature. You'll be charmed by the rugged beauty of the rocky cliffs, the pounding surf, the sense of the ocean's infinity. Built in 1960, the glistening white government-owned tourist inn spreads along the edge of a cliff that projects rather daringly over the sea. It boasts a long colonnade of arches with an extended stone terrace set with garden furniture, plus a second floor of accommodations with private balconies. Each midsize guest room is furnished with traditional pieces; unfortunately, the result is rather sterile. Rooms 1 to 12 are the most desirable.

The public rooms are generously proportioned, gleaming with marble and decorated with fine tapestries depicting the exploits of Henry the Navigator. Large velvet couches flank the fireplace. *Azulejos* (tiles) line the dining-room walls, and a cone-shaped fireplace with a mounted ship model rests in the corner. Before-dinner drinks are served on the terrace. The dining room serves traditional lunches and dinners to guests. The pousada has an outdoor saltwater pool, riding stables, and a tennis court; room service is offered. An official annex, the Fortaleza do Belixe (see "Where to Dine," below), offers less luxurious rooms.

WHERE TO DINE

Fortaleza do Belixe. Fortaleza do Belixe, Vila do Bispo, 8650 Sagres. ☎ **282/62-41-24.** Main courses 980$–4,000$ ($5.50–$22.40); fixed-price menu 3,500$ ($19.60). AE, MC, V. Daily 1–3pm and 7:30–9:30pm. Closed Nov 15–Feb 15. From Sagres, drive west for 3 mi. along the coastal road, following signs to Cabo de São Vicente. PORTUGUESE/INTERNATIONAL.

This establishment occupies the much-restored remnants of a medieval fortress built around the heyday of Henry the Navigator. It's on a sandy, rocky stretch of the coastal road between Sagres and the southwesternmost tip of Portugal, Cabo de São Vicente. All four dining rooms enjoy partial, or angled, views of the nearby sea, but one offers a wider panorama—ask for it specifically if you're enamored of a sea view. The menu offerings are simple, straightforward, and flavorful. They include *caldo verde;* tasty fish soup; fried or grilled squid; grilled swordfish; well-prepared but uncomplicated versions of veal, pork, and beef; and whatever fresh fish is available from the local market.

In addition to its restaurant, the establishment maintains four guest rooms, each with TV and telephone. Doubles cost 16,000$ ($89.60), including breakfast. The place is an official annex of the more expensive, more luxurious, Pousada do Infante (see "Where to Stay," above). Parking is free.

SAGRES AFTER DARK

You'll have better luck getting a drink in Sagres than finding a worthwhile souvenir. The best of the many nightspots in the town's historic core include the **Bar Drome-dário,** rua Comandante Meteoso (☎ **282/62-42-19**), and the **A Rosa dos Ventos (Pink Wind) Bar,** praça da República (☎ **282/62-44-80**). Folks from all over Europe talk, relax, and drink beer, wine, or sangría. If you want to go dancing (only after 11pm, please), head for **Disco Tapas,** Sítio do Poço (☎ **282/62-45-48**), about half a mile east of the city's historic core.

2 Lagos

21 miles E of Sagres, 43 miles W of Faro, 164 miles S of Lisbon, 8 miles W of Portimão

Lagos, known to the Lusitanians and Romans as Locobriga and to the Moors as Zawaia, became a private, experimental shipyard of caravels during the time of Henry the Navigator. Edged by the Costa do Ouro (Golden Coast), the Bay of Sagres was at one point in its epic history big enough to allow 407 warships to maneuver with ease.

An ancient port city (one historian traced its origins to the Carthaginians, three centuries before the birth of Christ), Lagos was well known by the sailors of Admiral Nelson's fleet. From Liverpool to Manchester to Plymouth, the sailors spoke wistfully of the beautiful green-eyed, olive-skinned women of the Algarve. Eagerly they sailed into port, looking forward to carousing and drinking heady Portuguese wine.

Actually, not that much has changed since Nelson's day. Few go to Lagos wanting to know its history; rather, the mission is to drink deeply of the pleasures of table and beach. In winter, the almond blossoms match the whitecaps on the water, and the weather is often warm enough for sunbathing. In town, the flea market sprawls through narrow streets.

Less than a mile down the coast, the hustle and bustle of market day is forgotten as the rocky headland of the **Ponta da Piedade** (Point of Piety) appears. This spot is the most beautiful on the entire coast. Amid the colorful cliffs and secret grottoes carved by the waves are the most flamboyant examples of Manueline architecture.

Much of Lagos was razed in the 1755 earthquake, and it lost its position as the capital of the Algarve. Today, only the ruins of its fortifications remain. However, traces of the old linger on the back streets.

ESSENTIALS
ARRIVING

BY FERRY & TRAIN   From Lisbon, take the ferry from praça do Comércio across the Tagus to Barreiro. From there, the Southern Line Railway runs to Lagos. Three trains a day arrive from Lisbon. The trip takes 6½ hours and costs at least 1,900$ ($10.65) one way. For more **information** and schedules, call ☎ 21/888-40-25.

BY BUS   Eight buses a day make the run between Lisbon and Lagos. The trip takes 5 hours and costs 2,650$ ($14.85) each way. Call ☎ 282/76-29-44 for schedules.

BY CAR   If you're coming from Lisbon, after leaving Sines, take Route 120 southeast toward Lagos and follow the signs into the city. From Sagres, take N268 northeast to the junction with N125, which will lead you east to Lagos.

VISITOR INFORMATION

The **Lagos Tourist Office** is on largo Marquês de Pombal (☎ 282/76-30-31).

WHAT TO SEE & DO
EXPLORING THE TOWN

Igreja de Santo António. Rua General Alberto Carlos Silveira. ☎ 282/76-23-01. Admission 350$ ($1.95). Tues–Sun 9:30am–12:30pm and 2–5pm.

The 18th-century Church of St. Anthony sits just off the waterfront. Some of Portugal's most notable rococo gilt carvings, created with gold imported from Brazil, decorate the altar. Begun in the 17th century, they were damaged in the earthquake but subsequently restored. What you see today represents the work of many artisans—each, at times, apparently pursuing a different theme.

Museu Municipal Dr. José Formosinho. Rua General Alberto Carlos Silveira. ☎ 282/76-23-01. Admission 350$ ($1.95). Tues–Sun 9:30am–noon and 2–5pm. Closed holidays.

The Municipal Museum contains replicas of the fret-cut chimneys of the Algarve, three-dimensional cork carvings, 16th-century vestments, ceramics, 17th-century embroidery, ecclesiastical sculpture, a painting gallery, weapons, minerals, and a numismatic collection. An oddity is a sort of believe-it-or-not section displaying, among other things, an eight-legged calf. In the archaeological wing are Neolithic artifacts, Roman mosaics found at Boca do Rio near Budens, fragments of statuary and columns, and other remains of antiquity from excavations along the Algarve.

Antigo Mercado de Escravos. Praça do Infante Dom Henríques. Free admission. Daily 24 hours.

The Old Customs House stands as a painful reminder of the Age of Exploration. The arcaded slave market, the only one of its kind in Europe, looks peaceful today, but under its four Romanesque arches captives taken from their homelands were once sold to the highest bidders. The house opens onto the peaceful main square dominated by a statue of Henry the Navigator.

OUTDOOR ACTIVITIES

BEACHES   Some of the best beaches—including **Praia de Dona Ana,** the most appealing—are near Lagos, south of the city. Follow signs to the Hotel Golfinho. If you go all the way to the southernmost point, **Ponta da Piedade,** you'll pass some pretty cove beaches set against a backdrop of rock formations. Steps are sometimes carved into the cliffs to make for easier access. Although it's crowded in summer, another good, white-sand beach is at the 1½-mile-long **Meia Praia** ("half beach"), across the river from the center of town.

DIVING　One of the Algarve's most highly recommended outlets for scuba diving is the **Sea Sports Center,** rua Jose Daconceicon, Loja 4, Praia da Luz (☎ **282/78-95-38**). Established in 1980 by German-born Detlef Seeger, it's one of the region's few fully licensed and insured scuba outfits. It pays lots of attention to safety. Staff members focus on the coastline between Lagos and Sagres, site of numerous underwater caves and (mostly) 20th-century shipwrecks at depths between 40 and 114 feet beneath the high-tide level. Scuba outings for experienced divers cost 6,500$ ($36.40) for 2-hour (one-tank) dives, which are conducted daily at 10am and 2pm. A 5-day PADI-accredited certification course costs 55,000$ ($308). Remember that if you're already PADI-certified, European insurance regulations require that you present a letter signed by a doctor within the previous 2 years stating that your health permits you to scuba dive.

GOLF　**Palmares,** Meia Praia, 8600 Lagos (☎ **282/76-29-61**), is not a particularly prestigious or championship-level course—it's "medium" in both difficulty and desirability. Frank Pennink designed it in 1975 on land with many differences in altitude. Some fairways require driving a ball across railroad tracks, over small ravines, or around palm groves. Its landscaping suggests North Africa, partly because of its hundreds of palms and almond trees. The view from the 17th green is exceptionally dramatic. Par is 71. Greens fees are 6,000$ to 10,000$ ($33.60 to $56), depending on the season. The course lies on the eastern outskirts of Lagos, half a mile from the center. To reach it from the heart of town, follow signs toward Meia Praia.

　　Another course is **Parque da Floresta,** Budens, Vale do Poço, 8650 Vila do Bispo (☎ **282/69-00-00**). One of the few important Algarvian courses west of Lagos, it's just inland from the fishing hamlet of Salema. Designed by the Spanish architect Pepe Gancedo and built as the centerpiece of a complex of holiday villas completed in 1987, the par-72 course offers sweeping views. Some shots must be driven over vineyards, others over ravines, creeks, and gardens. Critics of the course have cited its rough grading and rocky terrain. Some of these drawbacks are offset by a clubhouse with a sweeping view over the Portuguese coast. Greens fees are 6,000$ ($33.60) for 9 holes, 10,000$ ($56) for 18. To reach the course from the center of Lagos, drive 10 miles west, following road signs toward Sagres and Parque da Floresta.

SHOPPING

Foremost among the many handcrafts dealers is **Algife,** rua Portes de Portugal 911 (☎ **282/76-14-56**), a purveyor of pottery, handblown glass and more formal leaded crystal, china, and all kinds of housewares. Even more appealing is **Casa des Verges,** rua do 25 de Abril 77 (☎ **282/76-00-28**). Endorsed by some of the most discerning homeowners and cooks in town, it sells wickerwork, leather ware, crystal, china, pottery, and kitchen accessories. Note the Algarvian blankets, woven on hand-operated looms in colorful patterns whose antecedents are as old as the country's Arab occupation.

　　Casa Papagaio, rua do 25 de Abril 27 (☎ **282/76-29-76**), carries antique furniture and art objects, including dozens of weathered hand-painted tiles. Evocatively dusty, it might remind you of a provincial museum. A jewelry shop where silver and gold filigrees seem somehow finer and more delicately wrought than anywhere else in town is **Ouraivesaria Lagos,** rua do 25 de Abril 6 (☎ **282/76-27-72**). Also look here for antique coins, silver candelabras, spoons with the royal crest of Lagos or of Portugal, and silver plates.

　　A worthy bookshop filled with books in Portuguese and English, as well as postcards and periodicals, is **Loja do Livro,** rua Dr. Joaquim Telo 3 (☎ **282/76-73-47**).

A final choice, intriguing because of its appreciation of arts and crafts from throughout the Mediterranean, is **Terra Cotta,** praça Luís de Camões (☎ **282/76-33-74**). You'll find pottery from Spain, art objects from Portugal, and inlaid wood and artfully ornate brass and copper from Morocco, Tunisia, Egypt, and Greece.

WHERE TO STAY
EXPENSIVE

✪ **Hotel de Lagos.** Rua Nova da Aldeia 1, 8600 Lagos. ☎ **282/76-99-67.** Fax 282/76-99-20. E-mail: lagos@mail.telepac.pt. 315 units. A/C TV TEL. 10,960$–27,300$ ($61.40–$152.90) double; 15,000$–30,000$ ($84–$168) suite. Rates include breakfast. AE, DC, MC, V. Free parking outside, 1,000$ ($5.60) garage.

A 20th-century castle of Moorish and Portuguese design, Hotel de Lagos has its own ramparts and moats—okay, a swimming pool and a paddling pool. It's at the eastern side of the old town, far removed from the beach. This first-class hotel spreads over 3 hilltop acres overlooking Lagos; no matter which room you're assigned, you'll have a view, even if it's of a sun-trap courtyard with semitropical greenery. The surrounding area is rather unappetizing. The main room has a hacienda atmosphere, with white-plaster walls enlivened by sunny colors. Guests, often members of tour groups, gather here. In a corner, a fireplace provides warmth in chilly weather.

Some of the midsize guest rooms have ground-level patios, but most are on the upper six floors and have a 1960s feel. Rooms are either standard or deluxe, and have stark-white walls with warm accents. Many rooms open onto a wedge-shaped balcony where you can eat breakfast. A 31-room wing, complete with pool and health club, was added in 1989.

Dining/Diversions: An expansive harbor-view room serves good meals. There's also a coffee shop, a piano bar, game rooms, a restaurant, a poolside bar, and two lounges.

Amenities: 24-hour room service, health club, gymnasium, covered pool. Hotel de Lagos owns the Duna Beach Club on Meia Praia beach, which has a saltwater pool, a restaurant, and three tennis courts; guests have free membership during their stay. A private motor coach makes regular trips to the beach club, 5 minutes from the hotel. Arrangements can be made for golf at the nearby Palmares course (where guests get a 10% to 20% discount on greens fees); skin diving and sports fishing in the waters along the coast; horseback riding; and sailing in the bay.

MODERATE

Albergaria Marina Rio. Av. dos Descobrimentos (Apdo. 388), 8600 Lagos. ☎ **282/76-98-59.** Fax 282/76-99-60. 36 units. A/C TV TEL. 7,500$–16,500$ ($42–$92.40) double. Rates include buffet breakfast. MC, V. Free parking on street, 500$ ($2.80) in garage.

The second-best place in town, this four-star hotel is in the center opposite the Lagos marina. Its small to midsize guest rooms are nicely decorated, and many open onto views of the sea. All have hair dryers and firm mattresses. On the top floor are a small pool and a sun terrace overlooking the Bay of Lagos. In summer, a courtesy bus takes guests to the beaches and golfers to the course at Palmares. The cozy bar is open all day. A major problem here is that tour agents from Germany often book the rooms en masse, shutting out the independent traveler.

Bellavista de Luz. Praia da Luz, 8600 Lagos. ☎ **282/78-86-55.** Fax 282/78-86-56. www.bellavistadaluz.com. E-mail: hoteldaluz@mail.telepac.pt. 44 units. A/C TV TEL 13,000$–18,000$ ($61.60–$100.80) double; 20,000$–27,500$ ($112–$154) suite. Rates include breakfast. AE, DC, MC, V. Free parking. Closed Jan 10–Feb 4, Nov 15–Dec 10.

This little gem is a winning choice that opens onto the bay, Praia da Luz, with an inviting sandy beach only a short walk away. The good-sized rooms are streamlined and comfortably furnished, with excellent mattresses. Each has a refrigerator, private safe, coffeemaker, and hair dryer. The beach hotel is known for its international and Portuguese cuisine, made with market-fresh, first-rate produce. The hotel has two pools, tennis facilities, a gym, and a health club. The staff can arrange sporting activities—everything from bird-watching to scuba-diving.

Hotel da Meia Praia. Meia Praia, 8600 Lagos. ☎ **282/76-20-01.** Fax 282/76-20-08. 66 units. TEL. 15,000$–18,000$ ($84–$100.80) double. Rates include breakfast. AE, DC, MC, V. Free parking. Closed Nov–Mar.

This first-class hotel, 2½ miles northeast of Lagos, is for those who want sand, sun, and good food rather than exciting decor. The hotel stands at a point where a hill begins its rise from the sea. Surrounded by private gardens, it regrettably fronts railway tracks, but also a 4-mile-long, wide, sandy beach. Guests play tennis on two professional hard courts; hit the minigolf course; linger in the informal garden, where white wrought-iron outdoor furniture sits under olive and palm trees; or loll by the large pools (one for adults, one for children). The ocean-side midsize guest rooms have balconies with partitions for sunbathing; they were recently renovated. The furnishings are uncluttered, functional, and, frankly, have known better times. Still, the place is comfortable, and the beds are firm. The best units have sea views. Across the all-glass front are the dining room, lounge, and cocktail bar.

INEXPENSIVE

✪ **Casa de São Gonçalo da Lagos.** Rua Cândido dos Reis 73, 8600 Lagos. ☎ **282/76-21-71.** Fax 282/76-39-27. 13 units. TEL. 15,000$–17,000$ ($84–$95.20) double. Rates include breakfast. AE. Closed Nov–Mar. Limited free parking on street.

This pink villa with fancy iron balconies dates to the 18th century. At the core of Lagos, close to restaurants and shops, the antique-filled home is almost an undiscovered gem. Most of the public lounges and guest rooms turn, in the Iberian fashion, to the inward peace of a sun-filled patio. Surrounded by bougainvillea climbing balconies, guests order breakfast while sitting under a fringed parasol and enjoying the splashing of the fountain. Furnishings include hand-embroidered linens, period mahogany tables, chests with brass handles, ornate beds from Angola, even crystal chandeliers. The street-level rooms can be very noisy. During the house's restoration, within the last 20 years, it gained modern amenities, including firm mattresses.

The luxury pension is in a rambling *casa.* Guests gather in the large, antique-filled living room, which has a fireplace.

WHERE TO DINE
EXPENSIVE

Alpendre. Rua António Barbosa Viana 17. ☎ **282/76-27-05.** Reservations recommended. Main courses 1,600$–3,600$ ($8.95–$20.15). AE, DC, MC, V. Daily noon–11pm. PORTUGUESE.

Gourmet magazine called the Alpendre "the most celebrated and luxurious restaurant in Lagos." That may be true, but only because the competition is so lackluster. The restaurant offers one of the region's most elaborate and sophisticated menus. The food may be tasty, but the portions aren't large. Service tends to be slow, so don't come here if you're rushed. You can start with an excellent soup, such as onion au gratin, followed by one of the house specialties. They include savory shellfish rice, steak Diane, tournedos with sautéed mushrooms, and succulent fillet of sole sautéed in butter, flambéed with cognac, and served with a sauce of cream, orange and lemon juices, vermouth, and seasonings known only to the chef. Two featured desserts are mixed fruits flambé and crepes flambés with coffee, both for two.

MODERATE

A Lagosteira. Rua do 1 de Maio 20. ☎ **282/76-24-86.** Reservations recommended. Main courses 1,200$–2,800$ ($6.70–$15.70). AE, DC, MC, V. Mon–Sat 12:30–3pm and 6:30–11pm. Closed Jan 10–Feb 10. PORTUGUESE.

A Lagosteira has long been a mecca for knowledgeable diners. Its decor is simple, and there's a small bar on one side. From the à la carte menu, the best openers for a big meal are classic Algarvian fish soup and savory clams Lagosteira style. After the fishy beginning, you might happily move on to a tender sirloin steak grilled over an open fire. Lobster is also a specialty. The selection of vintage wines complements the food.

Don Sebastião. Rua do 25 de Abril 20. ☎ **282/76-27-95.** Reservations recommended. Main courses 2,000$–4,000$ ($11.20–$22.40). Daily noon–3pm and 6:30–10pm. Closed Nov 23–Dec 26. PORTUGUESE.

This rustically decorated tavern, on the main pedestrian street, is one of the finest dining choices in Lagos. Portuguese owned and operated, it offers a varied menu of local specialties. Options include lip-smacking pork chops with figs, succulent shellfish dishes like clams and shrimp cooked with savory spices, and grills. Live lobsters are kept on the premises. One of the best selections of Portuguese vintage wines in town accompanies the filling, tasty meals. In summer, a sidewalk terrace is available for outdoor dining.

O Galeão. Rua de Laranjeira 1. ☎ **282/76-39-09.** Reservations recommended. Main courses 1,400$–3,800$ ($7.85–$21.30). AE, DC, MC, V. Mon–Sat 12:30–3pm and 7–11pm. Closed Nov 27–Dec 27. INTERNATIONAL.

Hidden on a back street, the air-conditioned Galeão offers a wide range of dishes, and you can "oversee" the action through an exposed kitchen, which gets very busy in season. Meats are savory; fish dishes are well prepared, fresh from the sea, and tasty. Seafood options include king prawns and garlic, gratinée of seafood, sole meunière with almonds, lobster Thermidor, or salmon trout in champagne sauce. You can also order meat dishes, such as savory pork medallions in curry sauce and tender sirloin steak Café de Paris.

O Trovador. Largo do Convento da Senhora de Glória 29. ☎ **282/76-31-52.** Reservations recommended. Main courses 1,700$–2,900$ ($9.50–$16.25); fixed-price dinner 3,300$ ($18.50). MC, V. Tues–Sat 7pm–midnight. Closed Dec–Jan. INTERNATIONAL.

Marion (she's German) and Dave (he's English) run O Trovador. It's especially inviting in the off-season, when comfortable chairs sit around a log-burning fireplace. But at any time of year you get a pleasant atmosphere, good service, and competently prepared food. The restaurant is up the hill behind the Hotel de Lagos (follow the signs from rua Vasco da Gama). Among the well-recommended appetizers are homemade duck-liver pâté, succulent octopus cocktail, fish pâté with a delicate salmon taste, and escargots bourguignonne. Shellfish dishes incorporate local herbs and spices. Main courses include Dave's special—beef casserole cooked in black beer. You might also enjoy Portuguese swordfish, or duck roasted with orange sauce. The desserts are all good, but we especially like homemade cheesecake, coupe Trovador (ice cream), and Marion's "world famous" lemon crunch cake.

LAGOS AFTER DARK

You'll find hints of big-city life in Lagos, and a devoted cadre of night owls. Two bars land at the top of everybody's list of favorite hangouts. The first is the **Bar Amuras,**

Marinha de Lagos (☎ 282/79-20-95), which presents live music almost nightly. Views from the nautically inspired interior take in the boats in the nearby marina. Equally popular is the unpretentious yet cosmopolitan **Bar Mullens,** rua Cândido dos Reis 86 (no phone). Its mock-medieval decor and big mirrors have witnessed the arrival of every sociable bar-hopper in town. The most popular and best-known disco inside the city limits is **Phoenix,** rua do 5 de Outubro 11 (no phone). Filled with energetic dancers in their 20s and 30s, it's open every night from 11pm till around 4am.

3 Portimão

11 miles E of Lagos, 38 miles W of Faro, 180 miles SE of Lisbon

Portimão is perfect if you want to stay in a bustling fishing port rather than a hotel perched right on the beach. Since the 1930s, **Praia da Rocha,** 2 miles away, has snared sun-loving traffic. Today, it's challenged by **Praia dos Três Irmãos,** but tourists still flock to Portimão in the summer.

The aroma of the noble Portuguese sardine permeates every street. Portimão is the leading fish-canning center in the Algarve, although it doesn't outpace Setúbal in production. For a change of pace, this town, on an arm of the Arcade River, makes a good stopover for its fine dining. Stroll through its gardens and its shops (especially noted for their pottery), drink wine in the cafes, and roam down to the quays to see sardines roasting on braziers. The routine activity of the Algarvians is what gives the town its charm.

ESSENTIALS
ARRIVING
BY TRAIN   From Lagos (see above), trains on the Algarve Line run frequently throughout the day to Portimão. The trip takes 40 minutes. For **information** and schedules, phone ☎ **21/888-40-25.**

BY BUS   An express bus from Lisbon makes the 4½-hour trip, and a bus runs from the beach at Praia da Rocha, 2 miles away. For **information** and schedules, call ☎ **21/314-77-10.**

BY CAR   The main highway across the southern coast (Route 125) makes a wide arch north on its eastern run to Portimão.

VISITOR INFORMATION
The **Portimão Tourist Office** is at largo do 1 de Dezembro (☎ **282/41-91-31**). At **Praia da Rocha,** the tourist office is on avenida Tomás Cabreiro (☎ **282/41-91-32**).

WHAT TO SEE & DO
EXPLORING THE TOWN
Although it lacks great monuments and museums, Portimão is worth exploring. Just wander through its colorful streets, stopping at any sight that interests you. The once-colorful fishing boats used to unload their catch here at the port, but have moved to a terminal across the river. High-rise buildings ring the area, but the core of the old town is still intact.

Try to be in Portimão for lunch. Of course, you can dine at a restaurant, but it's even more fun to walk down to the harborside, where you can find a table at one of the low-cost eateries. The specialty is charcoal-grilled sardines, which taste like nothing you get from a can. They make an inexpensive meal accompanied by chewy, freshly baked bread, a salad, and a carafe of regional wine. Our pick is **Flor da**

Portimao

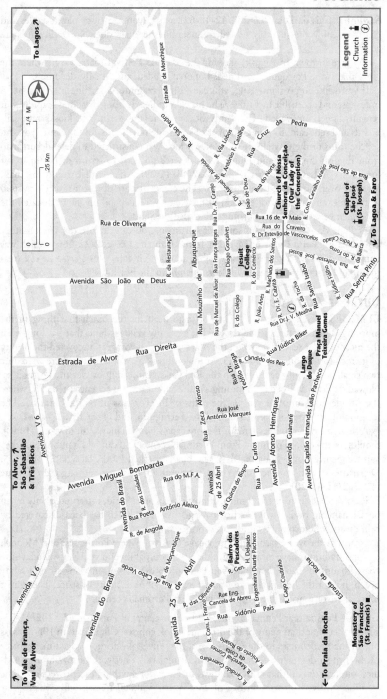

Legend
Church
Information

To Lagos ↗

To Alvor, ↗
São Sebastião
& Três Bicos

To Vale de França, ↗
Vau & Alvor

1/4 Mi
.25 Km

N

Estrada de Monchique

R. de São Pedro

Cruz da Pedra

R. Vila Lobos
R. Antônio F. Castilho
Rua de São José

R. Com. Carvalho Araújo

Rua do Norte

R. Manuel de Almeida

Rua Dr. A. Granjo

Rua França Borges

Rua Diogo Gonçalves

R. João de Deus

Rua 16 de Maio

Rua do Craveiro

R. Dr. Estevão de Vasconcelos

Church of Nossa
Senhora da Conceição
(Our Lady of
the Conception)

Chapel of
São José
(St. Joseph)

↙ To Lagoa & Faro

Rua de Olivença

R. da Restauração

Avenida São João de Deus

Rua Mouzinho de Albuquerque

Rua de Manuel de Alvor

R. do Colégio

Jesuit
College

R. do Comércio

R. Machado dos Santos

R. João Ares

R. da Tocha

R. Dr. E. Cabrita

Rua Dr. J. V. Mealha

Rua Santa Isabel

Rua Professor José Bussel

R. do Forno

R. da Barca

R. Pedro Calado

R. Júdice Fialho

Rua Serpa Pinto

Estrada de Alvor

Rua Direita

Rua Dr. Teófilo Braga

R. Cândido dos Reis

Rua Júdice Biker

Largo
do Duque

Praça Manuel
Teixeira Gomes

Rua Zeca Afonso

Rua José
António Marques

Avenida Miguel Bombarda

Rua do M.F.A.

Avenida
de 25 Abril

R. da Quinta do Bispo

Rua D. Carlos

Avenida Afonso Henriques

Avenida Guanaré

Avenida Capitão Fernandes Leão Pacheco

Avenida do Brasil

Rua dos Lusíadas

Rua Poeta António Aleixo

R. de Angola

Avenida V 6

Avenida V 6

Avenida 25 de Abril

Rua de Moçambique

Rua de Cabo Verde

Avenida do Brasil

Bairro dos
Pescadores

R. Gen. H. Delgado

R. das Oliveiras

R. Cons. J. Franco Oliveira

Rue Eng.
Cancela de Abreu

Rua Sidónio Pais

R. Engenheiro Duarte Pacheco

R. Cândido Guerreiro

R. Marechal Gomes da Costa

R. Aniceto do Rosário

R. Gago Coutinho

Estrada da Rocha

Monastery of
São Francisco
(St. Francis)

← To Praia da Rocha

Sardinha, Cais da Lota (☎ **282/42-48-62**), where you can sit at plastic tables and chairs to enjoy the superbly grilled fresh sardines at quay-side. No credit cards are accepted.

If you're in town in August, stay for the **Sardine Festival** (dates vary), where the glory that is the Portuguese sardine is honored, lauded, and, finally, devoured.

If you'd like to go sightseeing, you can visit **Ferragudo,** a satellite of Portimão, 3 miles east and accessible by bridge. The beach area here is being developed rapidly, but remains largely unspoiled. The sandy beach lies to the south, and kiosks rent sailboards and sell seafood from a number of waterside restaurants. In the center you can see the ruins of the **Castelo de São João,** which was constructed to defend Portimão from English, Spanish, and Dutch raids. There's no need to return to Portimão for lunch. Try **A Lanterna,** Parchal (☎ **282/41-44-29**), which you'll see on the main highway over the bridge from Portimão. The cooks prepare the most savory fish soup in the area, and an array of seafood dishes that always depend on the fresh catch the fishermen brought in that morning. It's closed on Sunday.

At Praia da Rocha, 2 miles south of Portimão, you can explore the 16th-century **Fortaleza de Santa Catarina,** avenida Tomás Cabreira (☎ **282/22-066**), which was constructed for defensive purposes. It has an open-air cafe, plus a *salão de cha* (tearoom) and restaurant. Picture windows open onto the beach.

OUTDOOR ACTIVITIES

BEACHES   Even those staying in Portimão head for the beach first thing in the morning. The favorite is **Praia da Rocha,** a creamy yellow strand that has long been the most popular seaside resort on the Algarve. English voyagers discovered the beauty of its rock formations around 1935. At the outbreak of World War II there were only two small hotels and a few villas on the Red Coast, most built by wealthy Portuguese. Nowadays Praia da Rocha is booming. At the end of the mussel-encrusted cliff, where the Arcade flows into the sea, lie the ruins of the **Fortress of Santa Catarina.** The location offers views of Portimão's satellite, **Ferragudo,** and of the bay.

Although **Praia dos Três Irmãos** is more expensive, you may want to visit its beach, 3 miles southwest of Portimão. From Portimão's center you can take a public bus; they run frequently throughout the day. The bus is marked PRAIA DOS TRÊS IRMÃOS. Departures are from the main **bus terminal** in Portimão at largo do Duque (☎ **282/41-81-20**).

Praia dos Três Irmãos has 9 miles of burnished golden sand, interrupted only by an occasional crag riddled with arched passageways. This beach has been discovered by skin divers, who explore its undersea grottoes and caves.

Nearby is the whitewashed fishing village of **Alvor,** where Portuguese and Moorish arts and traditions have mingled since the Arab occupation ended. Alvor was a favorite coastal haunt of João II, and now summer hordes descend on the long strip of sandy beach. It's not the best in the area, but at least you'll have plenty of space. The tourist office at Alvor is accessible by public bus from Portimão's center.

GOLF—Penina is at Penina, 3 miles west of the center of Portimão (☎ **282/41-54-15**), farther west than many of the other great golf courses. Completed in 1966, it was one of the first courses in the Algarve, and the universally acknowledged masterpiece of the British designer Sir Henry Cotton. It replaced a network of marshy rice paddies, on level terrain that critics said was unsuited for anything except wetlands. The solution involved planting groves of eucalyptus (350,000 trees in all), which grew quickly in the muddy soil. Eventually they dried it out enough for the designer to bulldoze dozens of water traps and a labyrinth of fairways and greens. The course wraps around a luxury hotel (Le Méridien Penina). You can play the main championship course (18 holes, par 73), and two 9-hole satellite courses, Academy and Resort. Greens fees for the 18-hole course are 13,500$ ($75.60); for either of the 9-hole courses, 3,000$ to 4,000$ ($16.80 to $22.40). To reach it from the center of Portimão, follow signs to Lagos, turning off at the signpost for Le Méridien Penina.

Amid tawny-colored rocks and arid hillocks, the **Vale de Pinta** (Pestana Golf) course, Praia do Carvoeiro (☎ 282/34-09-00), sends players through groves of twisted olive, almond, carob, and fig trees. Views from the fairways, designed in 1992 by Californian Ronald Fream, sweep over the low masses of the Monchique mountains, close to the beach resort of Carvoeiro. Experts say it offers one of the most varied sets of challenges in Portuguese golf. Clusters of "voracious" bunkers, barrier walls of beige-colored rocks assembled without mortar, and abrupt changes in elevation complicate the course. Oar is 72. Greens fees are 8,500$ to 12,000$ ($47.60 to $67.20). From Portimão, drive 8½ miles east on N125, following signs to Lagoa and Vale de Pinta/Pestana Golf.

WINDSURFING & WATER-SKIING—There are fewer reputable schools along the Algarve than you might imagine. The one that's always recommended for both professionalism and longevity (it was established in 1981) is the **Algarve Windsurfing School,** Praia Grande, Ferragudo (☎ 282/46-11-15). It's on the beach, 2 miles east of Portimão, in a compound that contains a tropical-style bar and lots of rental chaises. You can windsurf to your heart's content, thanks to gusts blowing up from the Sahara. A day-long communal lesson costs 10,000$ ($56), and a 1-hour private lesson is 3,500$ ($19.60). Windsurfers rent for 1,750$ to 2,500$ ($9.80 to $14) per hour. The staff also offers waterskiing, for 3,500$ ($19.60) per 12- to 15-minute ride. The entire outfit shuts down between late October and mid-March.

SHOPPING

The fishers unload their boats by tossing up wicker baskets full of freshly caught fish Monday to Saturday between 9:30 and 10:30am. **Fish, fruit, and vegetable markets** are held every morning (except Sunday) until 2pm in the market building and open square. On the first Monday of every month, a gigantic day-long regional market sells local artifacts, pottery, wicker, and even snake oil. **Boutiques** offering the Algarve's best selection of sweaters, porcelain, and pottery abound.

You'll find a veneer of modern, pan-European commercialism in this once-sleepy fishing village—most noticeably on such busy shopping streets as **rua Comerciale** and **rua Vasco da Gama.** Goods include hand-knit sweaters, hand-painted porcelains, and tons of pottery from factories and individual artisans throughout Portugal. Some of the best of it is available from a trio of connected stores, **Aquarius I, II, and II.** Begin at the headquarters (Aquarius I and II, 10 rua Direita; ☎ 282/42-66-73), and eventually head for Aquarius III, rua Vasco da Gama 41 (☎ 282/42-66-73). Look for knit ware, ceramics, pottery, leather ware, and wood carvings. **Gaby's,** rua Direita 5 (☎ 282/41-41-95), specializes in leather items, such as suitcases, handbags, briefcases, and wallets.

WHERE TO STAY

Hotels are limited in the center of Portimão, but Praia da Rocha has one of the largest concentrations on the Algarve. Praia dos Três Irmãos, though less developed, is the challenger to Praia da Rocha. In summer, don't even try to arrive at one of these beachfront establishments without a reservation.

CENTRAL PORTIMÃO
Inexpensive
Albergaria Miradouro. Rua Machado Santos 13, 8500 Portimão. ☎ and fax **282/42-30-11.** 32 units. TV TEL. 11,000$ ($61.60) double. Rates include breakfast. No credit cards. Free parking.

Albergaria Miradouro benefits from a central location on a quiet square opposite an ornate Manueline church. Its modern facade is banded with concrete balconies. A few of the no-frills guest rooms, which are rather small, contain terraces. Furnishings are meager but the beds are reasonably comfortable, and the plumbing works. Here you're likely to meet an array of European backpackers eager to converse and share travelers' tales. Motorists can usually find a parking space in the square just opposite.

Hotel Globo. Rua do 5 de Outubro 26, 8500 Portimão. ☎ **282/41-63-50.** Fax 282/48-31-42. 75 units. TEL. 14,000$–20,000$ ($78.40–$112) double; 30,000$ ($168) suite. Rates include breakfast. AE, DC, MC, V. Limited free parking in front of hotel.

Despite its location in the heart of the old town, the Globo is contemporary. A first-class hotel, it's recommended for its good design. Snug modern balconies overlook the tile rooftops crusted with moss. In 1967, the owner and manager imported an architect to turn his inn into a top-notch hotel. Each midsize guest room exhibits good taste in layout and furnishings: matching ebony panels on the wardrobes, built-in headboards, firm mattresses, and marble desks.

On the ground floor is an uncluttered, attractive lounge with an adjoining bar. Crowning the top floor is a dining room, the Aquarium, that's open for breakfast only. Its four glass walls permit unblocked views of the harbor, ocean, or mountains. Guests can also enjoy the seventh-floor cocktail bar-lounge, Al-Kantor, and a billiard table room.

PRAIA DA ROCHA
Expensive
Algarve Hotel Casino. Av. Tomás Cabreira, Praia da Rocha, 8500 Portimão. ☎ **282/41-50-01.** Fax 282/41-59-99. E-mail: h.algarve@mail.telepac.pt. 217 units. A/C MINIBAR TV TEL. 22,000$–43,000$ ($123.20–$240.80) double; 33,000$–89,000$ ($184.80–$498.40) suite. Rates include breakfast. AE, DC, MC, V. Free parking on street, 1,000$ ($5.60) in garage.

The leading hotel at the resort is strictly for those who love glitter and glamour and don't object to the prices. With a vast staff at your beck and call, you'll be well provided for in this elongated block of rooms poised securely on the top ledge of a cliff.

The midsize to spacious guest rooms have white walls, colored ceilings, intricate tile floors, mirrored entryways, indirect lighting, balconies with garden furniture, and bathrooms with separate showers. Many are vaguely Moorish in design, and many have terraces opening onto the sea. All have excellent mattresses, private safes, robes, and hair dryers. The Yachting, Oriental, Presidential, and Miradouro suites are decorative tours de force.

Dining/Diversions: Portuguese chefs with French backgrounds prepare gourmet meals for the à la carte menus in the Zodíaco and Das Amendoeiras. In season, buffet luncheons are served by the pool. The hotel's casino (see below) is the area's glittering nightlife choice. Aladino is the casino restaurant.

Amenities: 24-hour room service, laundry and dry cleaning, baby-sitting, hairdresser, barbershop, manicurist. Huge heated kidney-shaped pool, children's pool, two tennis courts at the beach, cliff-top sundeck, sauna, boutiques. The social director plans personalized activities, such as fishing parties on the hotel boat (with seafood stews), horseback riding, bridge games, barbecues on the beach, minigolf, volleyball, tennis competitions, waterskiing, and deep-sea fishing.

✪ **Bela Vista.** Av. Tomás Cabreira, Praia da Rocha, 8500 Portimão. ☎ **282/450-480.** Fax 282/41-53-69. 14 units. MINIBAR TV TEL. 23,000$ ($128.80) double; 34,000$ ($190.40) suite. Rates include breakfast. AE, DC, MC, V. Free parking.

Bela Vista is an old Moorish-style mansion built during the last century as a wealthy family's summer home. It has a minaret-type tower at one end, and a statue of the Virgin set into one of the building's corners. Since 1934 it's been a special kind of hotel, ideal for those who respond to the architecture of the past—and make a reservation way in advance. The guest rooms facing the sea, the former master bedrooms, are the most desirable, though all rooms have character. Decorations vary—from crystal sconces to an inset tile shrine to the Virgin Mary. Rated first class, the hotel is on the ocean, atop its own palisade, with access to a sandy cove where you can swim. The villa is white, with a terra-cotta tile roof, a landmark for fishers bringing in their boats at sundown. It's flanked by the owner's home and a simple cliff-edge annex shaded by palm trees.

The attractive structure and its decorations have been preserved, but the public lounges contain plastic furniture. The entry hallway has a winding staircase and an abundance of 19th-century blue-and-white tiles depicting allegorical scenes from Portuguese history. Guests gather around a baronial fireplace.

Dining/Diversions: Breakfast is the only meal served. The bar has a terrace where you can enjoy a drink while watching the sunset over the sea.

Amenities: Room service (breakfast only), laundry, concierge.

Moderate

Júpiter. Av. Tomás Cabreira, Praia da Rocha, 8500 Portimão. ☎ **282/41-50-41.** Fax 282/41-53-19. E-mail: hoteljupiter@mail.telepac.pt. 180 units. A/C TV TEL. 12,000$–20,500$ ($67.20–$114.80) double; 19,000$–26,000$ ($106.40–$145.60) suite. AE, DC, MC, V.

Júpiter occupies perhaps the most prominent street corner in this bustling summer resort. Boutiques fill the wraparound arcade, and in the spacious lobby guests relax, sometimes with drinks, on comfortable couches. The midsize guest rooms are comfortably modern but uninspired. They have firm beds and balconies, with views of the river or the sea. The hotel is just across from a wide beach, and has a covered and heated pool. The Blexus disco provides late-night diversion beneath a metallic ceiling. There's a semiformal restaurant, Barrote, and a cocktail bar. Snacks and light lunches are served poolside during summer.

Inexpensive

Pensão Tursol. Rua Eng. Francisco River, Praia da Rocha, 8500 Portimão. ☎ **282/42-40-46.** 22 units. 4,000$–9,000$ ($22.40–$50.40) double. Rates include breakfast. No credit cards. Closed Dec–Feb. Free parking.

This simple but charming hotel lies behind a garden rich with flowering vines and shrubs. You'll find it on a street running parallel to the main road beside the beach, in a quiet part of the resort not far from the center. There's a cool ground-floor TV room filled with leatherette chairs, and a breakfast lounge. Guest rooms are small but offer reasonable comfort and firm mattresses. The staff is helpful. When the weather is fair, the windows are thrown open for a view of the surrounding landscape.

Residencial Sol. Av. Tomás Cabreira 10, Praia da Rocha, 8500 Portimão. ☎ **282/42-40-71.** Fax 282/41-71-99. 22 units. TEL. 8,000$–8,500$ ($44.80–$47.60) double; 9,500$ ($53.20) suite. Rates include breakfast. AE, DC, MC, V. Free parking.

Partly because of its location near the noisy main street, the painted concrete facade of this establishment appears somewhat bleak. In this case, however, appearances are deceiving. The small to midsize guest rooms offer some of the tidiest, least pretentious, most attractive accommodations in town. Each unit is designed for two and contains a firm bed and exposed wood. The accommodations in back are quieter, but the terrace-dotted front units look across the traffic toward a bougainvillea-filled park. The breakfast lounge doubles as a TV room. Laundry and room service are provided.

PRAIA DOS TRÊS IRMÃOS
Expensive
✪ **Carlton Alvor Hotel.** Praia dos Três Irmãos, Alvor, 8500 Portimão. ☎ **282/45-89-00.** Fax 282/45-89-99. www.pestana.com. E-mail: pestana.hotel@mail.telepac.pt. 216 units. A/C MINIBAR TV TEL. 35,000$–49,300$ ($196–$276.10) double; from 40,000$ ($224) suite. Rates include buffet breakfast. AE, DC, MC, V. Free parking.

"You'll feel as if you're loved the moment you walk in the door," said a visitor from the Midwest. This citadel of hedonism, built in 1968 and constantly renewed, has more joie de vivre than any other hotel on the Algarve. Its location, building, good-sized guest rooms, decor, service, and food are ideal. The luxury hotel on a landscaped crest is so well appointed that you may never stray from the premises. Many of the guest and public rooms face the ocean, the gardens, and the free-form Olympic-size pool. Gentle walks and an elevator lead down the palisade to the sandy beach and the rugged rocks that rise out of the water. Inside, a wide domed airborne staircase leads to a lower level, which encircles a Japanese garden and lily pond.

Accommodations vary from a cowhide-decorated room evoking Arizona's Valley of the Sun to typical Portuguese-style rooms with rustic furnishings. Most contain oversize beds, plenty of storage space, long desk-and-chest combinations, and well-designed bathrooms with double basins and lots of towels. Many rooms have private balconies where guests can have breakfast facing the Bay of Lagos. Avoid rooms in the rear with so-so views, small balconies, and Murphy beds.

Dining/Diversions: The specialty dining rooms include Harrira (Moroccan), O Almofariz (Portuguese), and Sale & Pepe (Italian). Algarve folk dances and fado songs are often presented. Like an exclusive club, the main lounge has deep leather chairs and a cubistic modern ceiling. There's a restaurant at the pool, and a snack bar.

Amenities: 24-hour room service, baby-sitting, laundry, hairdresser, health club, outdoor pool, solarium, Finnish sauna, boutiques, newsstand, horseback riding, waterskiing, tennis. Greens fees discount at nearby 18-hole golf course.

Pestana Delfim Hotel. Praia dos Três Irmãos, 8501 Alvor. ☎ **282/45-89-01.** Fax 282/45-89-70. www.pestana.com. 312 units. A/C TV TEL. 18,000$–28,000$ ($100.80–$156.80) double; 40,100$ ($224.55) suite. Rates include buffet breakfast. AE, DC, MC, V. Free parking.

The developers of this tour-group haven chose their site wisely; it's near the beach, on a scrub-covered hillside whose sands offer a sweeping view of the coastline and its dozens of high-rises. With a central tower and identical wings splayed like a boomerang in flight, the hotel is one of the region's most dramatic modern buildings. In spite of the proximity of the beach, many guests prefer the parasol-ringed pool, which encloses a swim-up bar. Each well-furnished, midsize guest room has a private terrace and firm mattress. Only the suites have air-conditioning and minibars. If you're part of a tour group, you may feel a little left out here.

Dining: The Atlantic Gardens Restaurant is one of the busiest at the resort. It features Portuguese and international buffets. The Bistro serves savory international and Portuguese cuisine à la carte.

Amenities: 24-hour room service, laundry, baby-sitting, sauna, Jacuzzi, small gymnasium.

Expensive

✪ **Le Méridien Penina Golf Hotel.** Estrada Naticional 125, 8502 Portimão. ☎ **800/225-5843** in the U.S., or 282/41-54-15. Fax 282/41-50-00. E-mail: meridienalg.sm@mail. telepac.pt. 213 units. A/C MINIBAR TV TEL. 42,000$–50,000$ ($235.20–$280) double; 70,000$–130,000$ ($392–$728) suite. Children 3–11 free in parents' room. Rates include breakfast. AE, DC, MC, V. Closed Sept 3–Dec 20. Free parking.

The first deluxe hotel on the Algarve was the Penina Golf, located between Portimão and Lagos. It's now a Le Méridien property, and has serious competition from the other luxury hotels. Fans of golf (see "Outdoor Activities," above) remain loyal to the Penina, however. It's a major sporting mecca, and stands next to the Algarve's major casino. Besides the golf courses, the hotel has a private beach with its own snack bar and changing cabins, reached by a shuttle bus.

Most of the guest rooms contain picture windows and honeycomb balconies with views of the course and pool, or vistas of the Monchique hills. The standard rooms are furnished pleasantly, combining traditional pieces with Portuguese provincial spool beds. All rooms are spacious and contain good-sized beds. The so-called attic rooms have the most charm, with French doors opening onto terraces. On the fourth floor are some duplexes, often preferred by families.

Dining: There are five restaurants, and a coffee shop for light snacks. We prefer the paneled Portuguese Grill and the Terrace (for summer dining), which specializes in charcoal-grilled fish.

Amenities: 24-hour room service, laundry, baby-sitting. Three championship golf courses (see "Outdoor Activities," above), private beach, swimming pool, horseback riding and lessons, windsurfing, waterskiing. Changing rooms, lockers, golf school and shops, sauna, snooker room, beauty parlor, barbershop, six floodlit hard tennis courts, Penguin Village (nursery for children 3 to 13).

WHERE TO DINE

If you're sightseeing in Portimão, you may want to seek out a restaurant here; otherwise, most people dine along the beaches, especially those at Praia da Rocha and Praia dos Três Irmãos. All the major hotels have at least one deluxe or first-class restaurant. There's a wide selection catering to a range of budgets.

CENTRAL PORTIMÃO

Mariners. Rua Santa Isabel 28. ☎ **282/42-58-48.** Main courses 950$–2,000$ ($5.30–$11.20) at lunch, 1,200$–2,000$ ($6.70–$11.20) at dinner; Sun roasted platters 1,200$–2,300$ ($6.70–$12.90). No credit cards. Daily noon–3pm and 7–10:30pm. INTERNATIONAL.

In its way, Mariners is one of the most cosmopolitan restaurants in Portimão, combining distinctive elements from Scotland (owners James and Pamela Harley are from north of the Tweed) and Portugal. In a 400-year-old stone-sided house whose patio and garden are draped with lavish strands of bougainvillea, the restaurant is a 5-minute walk uphill from Portimão's harbor front. Lunches, served on the patio or in the bar, are relatively simple—homemade pies (chicken and mushroom or steak and kidney, for example), spaghetti Bolognese, or grilled fish. Dinners are more elaborate and formal, served on fine china and crystal in a tile-lined, candlelit dining room with vaulted ceilings. The cooking seems to derive from many different culinary traditions, perhaps to appeal to the diverse clientele. Tartan curtains and a short list of single-malt whiskies reveal the restaurant's Scottish ties. Menu items include prawns piri-piri (with hot peppers), Indian chutneys, lemon chicken, chicken teriyaki, and a wide choice of tasty casseroles that vary according to the inspiration of the chefs. The establishment remains open throughout the afternoon for beer, drinks, and wine—a Scottish version of a Portuguese *adega*.

O Bicho Restaurant. Largo Gil Eanes 12. ☎ **282/42-29-77.** Reservations recommended. Main courses 2,000$–3,000$ ($11.20–$16.80). AE, DC, MC, V. Mon–Sat noon–3pm and 7–11pm. ALGARVIAN.

O Bicho is one of the best places in the Algarve to order *cataplana*, a typical regional dish of clams, pork, green peppers, tomatoes, and spices, including hot pepper, garlic, and bay leaf. It's cooked in a special copper pot, also called cataplana, that steams the mixture under a tight lid. Other inviting choices include oysters and grilled seafood, but they don't seem to equal the cataplana. This simple place is popular with both locals and discerning visitors.

Praia da Rocha

Bamboo Garden. Edifício Lamego, Loja 1, av. Tomás Cabreira. ☎ **282/48-30-83.** Reservations recommended. Main courses 1,000$–2,000$ ($5.60–$11.20). AE, DC, MC, V. Daily 12:30–3pm and 6–11:30pm. CHINESE.

Bamboo Garden, which has a classic Asian decor, serves some of the best Chinese food on the coast. The large menu includes everything from squid chop suey to prawns with hot sauce. After deciding on a soup or an appetizer (try the spring roll), guests can select from various categories, including chicken, beef, squid, and prawns. You might, for example, try fried duck with soybean sauce or chicken with almonds from the Algarve. Peking duck is the chef's specialty. This air-conditioned spot is a safe haven for reliable food when you've overdosed on Portuguese codfish.

Safari. Rua António Feu. ☎ **282/42-35-40.** Reservations recommended. Main courses 1,500$–3,000$ ($8.40–$16.80); fixed-price menus 2,150$–3,250$ ($12.05–$18.20). AE, DC, MC, V. Daily noon–midnight. Closed Dec–Feb 15. PORTUGUESE/ANGOLAN.

Safari is a Portuguese-run restaurant with a "taste of Africa" in its cuisine; the former Portuguese colony of Angola inspired many of its savory specialties. The name also suggests a faux-African tourist trap, but this place isn't. Safari offers good value and is known for its commendable fresh fish and seafood. Many guests in neighboring hotels escape their board requirements just to sample the good home-cooked meals. On summer weekends you might hear live Brazilian or African music. The fare includes such delectable dishes as curry Safari, steak Safari, swordfish steak in pepper sauce, shrimp Safari, charcoal-grilled fresh fish, and bacalhau a Safari (fried codfish with olive oil, garlic, and peppers, served with homemade potato chips). It's customary to begin with a bowl of savory fish soup. The building stands on a cliff overlooking the beach, and has a glass-enclosed terrace.

Titanic. In the Edifício Colúmbia, rua Eng. Francisco Bivar. ☎ **282/42-23-71.** Reservations recommended, especially in summer. Main courses 1,600$–2,800$ ($8.95–$15.70). AE, DC, MC, V. Daily 7–11pm. Closed Nov 27–Dec 27. INTERNATIONAL.

Complete with gilt and crystal, the 100-seat air-conditioned Titanic is the most elegant restaurant in town. Its open kitchen serves the best food, including shellfish and flambé dishes. Despite the name, it's not on the water, but in a modern residential complex. You can dine very well here on such appealing dishes as the fish of the day, pork fillet with mushrooms, prawns *à la plancha* (grilled), Chinese fondue, or excellent sole Algarve. Service is among the best at the resort.

Praia dos Três Irmãos

Harira/O Almofariz/Sale & Pepe. In the Alvor Praia Hotel, Praia dos Três Irmãos. ☎ **282/45-89-00.** Reservations required. Main courses 2,000$–3,500$ ($11.20–$19.60).

AE, DC, MC, V. Harira Tues–Sat 7–11pm; O Almofariz Fri–Wed 7–9:30pm; Sale & Pepe Tues–Sat 7–9:30pm. Closed Thurs in summer. MOROCCAN/PORTUGUESE/ITALIAN.

To satisfy changing modern tastes, this hotel has broken up its fabled grill room into restaurants featuring three different cuisines. The menu changes every day, so we can't list specialties, but the chefs in each restaurant feature some of their particular country's finest dishes. All rely on first-rate, market-fresh ingredients.

The Moroccan restaurant, Harira, is known for its couscous and lamb dishes. Sale & Pepe, the Italian option, presents succulent pastas and flavorful meat dishes. The Portuguese restaurant, O Almofariz, serves dishes from around the country; its Algarvian specialties shine. The first-rate service and the prices are the same in all three restaurants.

Restaurante O Búzio. Aldeamento da Prainha, Praia dos Três Irmãos. ☎ **282/45-87-72.** Reservations recommended. Main courses 2,500$–4,000$ ($14–$22.40). AE, DC, MC, V. Daily 7–10:30pm. Closed Nov–Dec. INTERNATIONAL.

Restaurante O Búzio stands at the end of a road encircling a resort development dotted with private condos and exotic shrubbery. In summer so many cars line the narrow blacktop road that you'll probably need to park near the resort's entrance, then walk downhill to the restaurant.

Dinner is served in a room whose blue curtains reflect the shimmering ocean at the bottom of the cliffs. Your meal might include excellent prepared fish soup, refreshing gazpacho, or *carre de borrego Serra de Estrêla* (gratinée of roast rack of lamb with garlic, butter, and mustard). Other good choices are Italian pasta dishes, boiled or grilled fish of the day, flavorful pepper steak, and lamb kebabs with saffron-flavored rice. There's seating for 50 inside, and for almost as many on the sea-view terrace. There's an extensive wine cellar.

ESTRADA DE ALVOR

O Gato. Urbanização da Quintinha, Lote 10-RC, estrada de Alvor. ☎ **282/42-76-74.** Reservations recommended. Main courses 900$–2,000$ ($5.05–$11.20). AE, DC, MC, V. Tues–Sun 7–10pm. Take main road to Praia da Rocha; about 100 yards after first traffic circle, turn right toward Alvor. PORTUGUESE/INTERNATIONAL.

Outside Portimão, this is one of the best places to dine. The skilled chefs turn out a selection of dishes that are first-rate in both preparation and ingredients. Menu selections include such classic main dishes as pork with clams, grilled lamb chops, and sautéed swordfish meunière. Also popular are the numerous fresh fish and shellfish dishes. The attractive dining room has white walls and mahogany-beam trim. Although the kitchen sometimes falls short of its ambition, this has been a consistent winner, and we remain amazed that it's not better known.

PORCHES

O Leão de Porches. N25. ☎ **282/38-13-84.** Reservations required. Main courses 1,700$–2,900$ ($9.50–$16.25). MC, V. Thurs–Tues 6:30–10pm. Closed Jan. From Lagoa, take N25 toward Faro. INTERNATIONAL.

O Leão de Porches lies in a small village, a 3-minute drive from Lagoa. Its owner and manager, John Forbes, ran a restaurant in London that enjoyed a worldwide reputation, and he brought his expertise here. The winning cuisine includes such dishes as cataplana, roast duck with orange-and-Cointreau sauce, and fresh fish. Another good dish is pork sautéed in butter with red currants and apples, finished with cider and cream. Or try lamb sautéed with garlic and parsley, baked with tomatoes and red wine, then topped with mint leaves. You might finish with Irish coffee or homemade ice cream. The food is simple and straightforward, well balanced, and made with fresh ingredients.

Monchique: Escape to the Cool Mountains

The Monchique range of hills is the Algarve at its coolest and highest. The rocky peak of the range, some 3,000 feet high, looks down on forested slopes and green valleys, burgeoning with orange groves, Indian corn, heather, mimosa, rosemary, oleander bushes, and cork-oak, chestnut, pine, and eucalyptus trees. Icy water springs from the volcanic rock that makes up the range, flowing down to the foothills.

The towns of Monchique produce many wood handcrafts, including chairs, benches, decorated canes, and carved spoons. Local artisans also create wicker baskets, wool sweaters and stockings, and macramé lace made with linen. A typical industry of people of the Monchique is the making of charcoal, although the activity is slowly disappearing.

The largest town in the borough, also named **Monchique,** lies on the east side of Mount Fóia, 16 miles north of Portimão. The town was once engaged in the manufacture of wooden casks and barrels and the making of oakum and rough cloth. The Manueline-style parish church, with its interesting radiated door facing, dates from the 16th century. Colorful decorated tiles and carved woodwork grace the interior, along with a statue of Our Lady of the Immaculate Conception, an 18th-century work attributed to Machado de Castro. The convent of Nossa Senhora do Desterro is in ruins, but you can look at the curious tiled fountain and the impressive old magnolia tree on its grounds.

Caldas de Monchique was discovered in Roman days and turned into a spa. The waters, from springs in volcanic rock, are still considered good treatment for respiratory disorders, accompanied as they are by the clear air of the highlands.

Nearly 8 miles from the town of Monchique, **Alferce,** nestled among trees and mountains, has traces of an ancient fortification. There's also an important handicraft center here. In the opposite direction, about 8 miles west of Monchique, is Fóia, the highest point in the Algarve at almost 3,000 feet. From here you have splendid views of the hills and the sea; Cabo de São Vicente and Sagres are visible on clear days.

A small inn in the town of Monchique, the **Estalagem Abrigo de Montanha,** 8550 Monchique (☎ **282/91-21-31,** fax 282/91-36-60), is in a botanical garden. With all the blooming camellias, rhododendrons, mimosa, banana palms, and arbutus, plus the tinkling waterfalls, you'd never believe the hot Algarve coast was in the same province. The inn has 13 units, all doubles, with two suites. They have bathrooms and two beds, and are furnished in typical Portuguese style. Rates are 17,000$ ($95.20) a night for a suite or 14,000$ ($78.40) for a double, including breakfast. On chilly evenings, guests gather before a fireplace in the lounge. The attractive restaurant serves good food daily from 12:30 to 3pm and 7:30 to 9:30pm. Meal prices begin at 3,000$ ($16.80). Reservations aren't needed. American Express, Diners Club, MasterCard, and Visa are accepted.

PORTIMÃO AFTER DARK

The town center has about a dozen tascas and bodegas, but you might be happier with the glossier after-dark venues in internationally minded Praia da Rocha. Many bars and pubs, as well as the resort's casino (see below) line avenida Tomás Cabreira. Depending on your mood, you might enjoy popping in and out of several of them—a ritual akin to a London pub crawl. The most active and intriguing hangouts include **Disco Cathedral,** avenida Tomás Cabreira (☎ **282/41-45-57**), and **Farmer's Bar,** rua do Mar (☎ **282/42-57-20**), both of which serve wine, beer, and cocktails. Dance-aholics and devoted night owls appreciate the shenanigans (which change according to which northern European nationalities predominate) at **Disco Babylonia,** avenida Tomás Cabreira (☎ **282/41-68-38**), and its nearby competitor, **Disco Horago,** avenida Tomás Cabreira (☎ **282/42-63-77**). Both get going after 11pm, every night in high season, and remain open till the last person staggers off the next morning.

The **Casino Praia da Rocha** is on the glittering premises of the five-star Hotel Algarve Casino, avenida Tomás Cabreira (☎ **282/41-50-01**). Its gaming tables and slot machines open every night at 4pm and shut down at 3am, or later if business warrants. Its entertainment highlight is the cabaret show, featuring lots of dancers in spangles and feathers, magicians, and a master of ceremonies telling not-very-subtle jokes geared to the diverse international audience. Dinner, served beginning at 8pm, precedes the show, and costs 6,000$ ($33.60). If you skip dinner, the entrance fee of 2,000$ ($11.20) includes the first drink. Show time is 10pm. Also look for other forms of entertainment—live concerts or fado—interspersed with the otherwise constant diet of show-biz-style cabaret.

4 Silves

4 miles N of Lagoa, 7 miles NE of Carvoeiro

When you pass through this hillside town's Moorish-inspired entrance, you'll quickly realize that Silves is unlike other towns and villages of the Algarve. It lives in the past, recalling its heyday, when it was known as Xelb. It was the seat of Muslim culture in the south before it fell to the Crusaders. Christian warriors and earthquakes have been rough on Silves.

The Castle of Silves, crowning the hilltop, has held on, although it's seen better days. Once the blood of the Muslims, staging their last stand in Silves, "flowed like red wine," as one Portuguese historian wrote. The cries and screams of women and children resounded over the walls. Nowadays the only sound you're likely to hear is the loud rock music coming from the gatekeeper's house. Silves is most often visited on a day trip from one of the beach towns to the south.

ESSENTIALS
ARRIVING
BY TRAIN Trains from Faro serve the Silves train station, 1 mile from the center of the town. For **information,** call ☎ **089/80-17-26.**

BY BUS The bus station is on rua da Cruz de Palmeira; eight buses a day arrive from Portimão. Trip time is 45 minutes.

BY CAR Coming east or west along Route 125, the main road traversing the Algarve, you arrive at the town of Lagoa (not to be confused with Lagos). From there, head north to Silves along Route 124.

EXPLORING THE TOWN
The red-sandstone **Castelo dos Mouros** may date from the 9th century. From its ramparts you can look out on the saffron-mossed tile roofs of the village houses, down the narrow cobblestone streets where roosters strut and scrappy dogs sleep peacefully in the doorways. Inside the walls, the government has planted a flower garden with golden chrysanthemums and scarlet poinsettias. In the fortress, water rushes through

a huge cistern and a deep well made of sandstone. Below are dungeon chambers and labyrinthine tunnels where the last of the Moors hid out before the Crusaders found them and sent them to their deaths. The site is open daily from 9am to 8pm. Admission is free.

The 13th-century former **cathedral of Silves,** or Sé (now a church), on rua de Sé, was built in the Gothic style. It is one of the most outstanding religious monuments in the Algarve. You can wander through its aisles and nave, noting the beauty in their simplicity. The flamboyant Gothic style of both the chancel and the transept dates from a later period. The Christian architects who originally constructed the cathedral may have torn down an old mosque to do so. Many of the tombs here are believed to be the graves of Crusaders who took the town in 1244. It's open daily from 8:30am to 1pm and 2:30 to 5:30pm, until 6pm from June to September. Admission is free, but donations are welcome.

The best artifacts found in the area are on display at the **Museu Arqueologia,** rua das Portas de Loulé (☎ 282/44-48-32), a short walk from the Sé. The museum's major sight is an ancient Arab water cistern preserved as part of a 30-foot-deep well. Admission is 300$ ($1.70). It's open Tuesday to Sunday 10am to 7pm.

Outside the main part of town, on the road to Enxerim, near an orange grove (one of the local boys will serve as your inexpensive guide), a lonely open-air pavilion shelters a 15th-century stone lacework cross. This ecclesiastical artwork, **Cruz de Portugal,** is two-faced, depicting a pietà (the face of Christ is destroyed) on one side, the crucifixion on the other. It has been declared a national monument of incalculable value. A guide isn't really necessary.

WHERE TO DINE

Ladeira. Ladeira de São Pedro. ☎ **282/44-28-70.** Main courses 1,200$–1,800$ ($6.70–$10.10); tourist menu 1,600$ ($8.95). AE, MC, V. Mon–Sat noon–3pm and 7–10pm. PORTUGUESE.

This small, rustic restaurant is known to almost everyone in its neighborhood on the western outskirts of Silves. Steak Ladeira and mixed-fish cataplana are the two best specialties; also featured are grilled fish and regional dishes. If you call in advance, someone will explain the restaurant's location, often in great detail. In season, game such as succulent partridge or rabbit is likely to be on the menu.

Rui I. Rua Comendador Vilarim 27. ☎ **282/44-26-82.** Main courses 1,000$–5,000$ ($5.60–$28); tourist menu 3,000$ ($16.80). MC, V. Wed–Mon noon–2am. PORTUGUESE.

Rui I prides itself on seating more customers than any other restaurant in town. The availability of certain dishes varies according to what fish is fresh. The house specialty is shellfish rice, a highly recommended herb-laden stew. Other palate-pleasing choices include grilled fillet of beef, savory rack of lamb, swordfish, and a choice of traditional desserts. This is competent, hearty cooking—nothing more.

5 Albufeira

23 miles W of Faro, 202 miles SE of Lisbon

This cliff-side town, formerly a fishing village, is the St. Tropez of the Algarve. The lazy life, sunshine, and beaches make it a haven for young people and artists, although the old-timers still regard the invasion that began in the late 1960s with some ambivalence. That development turned Albufeira into the largest resort in the region. Some residents open the doors of their cottages to those seeking a place to stay. Travelers with less money often sleep in tents on the cliff or under the sky.

ESSENTIALS
ARRIVING
BY TRAIN   Trains run between Albufeira and Faro (see below), which has good connections to Lisbon. For schedule **information,** call ☎ **289/80-17-26.** The train station lies 4 miles from the center. Buses from the station to the resort run every 30 minutes; the fare is 175$ ($1) one way.

BY BUS   Buses run between Albufeira and Faro every hour. Trip time is 1 hour, and a one-way ticket costs 570$ ($3.20). Seven buses per day make the 1-hour trip from Portimão to Albufeira. It costs 700$ ($4.05) one way. For **information** and schedules, call ☎ **289/58-97-55.**

BY CAR   From east or west, take the main coastal route, N125. Albufeira also lies near the point where the express highway from the north, 264, feeds into the Algarve. The town is well signposted in all directions. Take Route 595 to reach Albufeira and the water.

VISITOR INFORMATION
The **Tourist Information Office** is at rua do 5 de Outubro (☎ **289/58-52-79**).

WHAT TO SEE & DO
EXPLORING THE TOWN
With steep streets and villas staggered up and down the hillside, Albufeira resembles a North African seaside community. The big, bustling resort town rises above a sickle-shaped beach that shines in the bright sunlight. A rocky, grottoed bluff separates the strip used by sunbathers from the working beach, where brightly painted fishing boats are drawn up on the sand. Access to the beach is through a tunneled rock passageway.

After walking Albufeira's often hot but intriguing streets, you can escape and cool off at **Zoo Marine,** N125, Guia (☎ **289/56-11-04**), 4 miles northwest. It's a popular water park, with rides, swimming pools, gardens, and even sea lion and dolphin shows. Open daily 10am to 8pm.

OUTDOOR ACTIVITIES
BEACHES   Some of the best beaches—but also the most crowded—are near Albufeira. They include **Falesia, Olhos d'Agua,** and **Praia da Oura.** Albufeira, originally discovered by the British, is now the busiest resort on the Algarve. To avoid the crowds on Albufeira's main beaches, head west for 2½ miles on a local road to **São Rafael** and **Praia da Galé.** You might also go east to the beach at **Olhos d'Agua.**

GOLF   Many pros consider the extremely well-maintained **Pine Cliffs** course, Pinhal do Concelho, 8200 Albufeira (☎ **289/50-01-00**), relaxing but not boring. It has only nine holes scattered over a relatively compact area. The course's main allure is its association with the Sheraton Algarve. Opened in 1990, its fairways meander beside copper-colored cliffs that drop 250 feet down to a sandy beach. Par is 33. Greens fees are 6,000$ ($33.60) for Sheraton guests, 7,000$ ($39.20) for nonguests. The course lies 4 miles west of Vilamoura and 3 miles east of Albufeira. To reach it from Albufeira, follow signs to the hamlet of Olhof Agua, where more signs direct you to the Sheraton and Pine Cliffs.

SHOPPING
One of the busiest resorts along the Algarve, Albufeira maintains an almost alarming roster of seafront kiosks, many selling fun-in-the-sun products of dubious (or, at best, transient) value. The main shopping areas are along **rua do 5 de Outubro** and **praça**

Duarte de Pacheco. An even denser collection of merchandise is on display in the town's largest shopping plaza, **Modelo Shopping Center,** rua de Munícipio, about a quarter-mile north of the town center. Most of the independently operated shops inside are open daily from 10am to 10pm. Although Albufeira produces limited amounts of ceramics, you'll find a wide selection of pottery and glazed terra-cotta from throughout Portugal at the **Infante Dom Henrique House,** rua Cândido do Reis 30 (☎ 289/51-32-67). Also look for woven baskets and wood carvings.

WHERE TO STAY

The town has many accommodations. However, many establishments charge rates more suited to the middle-of-the-road traveler than to the young people who favor the place.

EXPENSIVE

Clube Mediterraneo de Balaia. Praia Maria Luisa, 8200 Albufeira. ☎ **800/CLUB-MED** in the U.S., or 289/51-05-00. Fax 289/58-71-79. 412 units. A/C TV TEL. 12,200$–29,700$ ($68.30–$166.30) double per night per room. 85,400$–210,000$ ($478.25–$1,176) per person double per week. Rates include full board and use of most sports facilities. Children under 13 17,800$ ($99.70) in parents' room. AE, DC, MC, V.

On 40 acres of sun-drenched scrubland about 4 miles east of Albufeira, this all-inclusive high-rise resort is one of the most stable in the Club Med empire. Favored by vacationers from northern Europe, it encompasses a shoreline of rugged rock formations indented with a series of coves for surf swimming. The small accommodations have twin beds, two safes, and piped-in music. They're decorated in understated, uncluttered style, with private balconies or terraces. Many vacationers here appreciate the nearby golf course; others opt to participate in semiorganized sports. Meals are usually consumed at communal tables; there are many lunchtime buffets and copious amounts of local wine.

Dining/Diversions: The resort has five restaurants, several bars, a late-night disco, and occasional live entertainment by the staff or visiting groups of fado or folk singers.

Amenities: Laundry, baby-sitting, 9-hole golf course, nearby 18-hole golf course, private beach, health club, sauna, heated pool. The sports shop arranges social and sporting activities (waterskiing, clay-pigeon shooting, windsurfing, archery).

Hotel Montechoro. Rua Alexandre O'Neill (Apdo. 928), 8200 Albufeira. ☎ **089/58-94-23.** Fax 289/58-99-47. E-mail: reservas@grupomontechoro.com. 362 units. A/C TV TEL. 14,600$–29,800$ ($81.75–$166.90) double; 21,800$–44,500$ ($122.10–$249.20) suite. Rates include buffet breakfast. AE, DC, MC, V. Parking 250$ ($1.40).

The leading choice at Montechoro, 2 miles northeast of the center of Albufeira, looks like a hotel you might encounter in North Africa. It's a fully equipped, self-contained four-star resort complex, with such ample facilities that you might get lost—which is just as well, because the one thing it lacks is a beach. The spacious rooms afford views of the countryside and are generally done in modern style, with excellent beds.

Dining/Diversions: Options include the Restaurant Montechoro and the rooftop Grill das Amendoeiras. Guests gather in the evening in the Almohade piano bar.

Amenities: 24-hour room service, laundry, dry cleaning, two pools, professional tennis courts, two squash courts, sauna, gymnasium.

INEXPENSIVE

Apartamentos Albufeira Jardim. Cerro da Piedade, 8200 Albufeira. ☎ **289/58-69-78.** Fax 289/58-69-77. 460 apts. TEL. 28,000$ ($156.80) 1-bedroom apt for 4; 40,000$ ($224) 2-bedroom apt for 6. AE, DC, MC, V. Free parking.

This establishment is especially popular with northern Europeans, Spaniards, and North Americans who want to linger awhile before resuming their tour of the Algarve.

On a hill high above Albufeira, it opened in the 1970s as Jardim I. In the late 1980s it gained another section, Jardim II, a 5-minute walk away. The older section is larger and has gardens that are a bit more mature. Scattered around both sections are two restaurants, two coffee shops, three tennis courts, and five pools (including two for children). Laundry service and baby-sitting are available.

A minibus makes frequent runs from the apartments to the beach, a 10-minute drive away. The attractively furnished, good-sized units are in four- and five-story buildings. Each apartment has a balcony with a view of the faraway ocean and the town. Guests usually prepare breakfast (which is not included in the rates) in their rooms.

Aparthotel Auramar. Praia dos Aveiros, Areias de São Albufeira, 8200 Albufeira. ☎ **289/58-76-07.** Fax 289/51-33-27. 287 units. A/C TEL. 12,000$–18,000$ ($67.20–$100.80) double. Extra bed 3,000$ ($16.80). Rates include breakfast. AE, DC, MC, V. Free parking.

One of the resort's largest hotels sits about a mile east of the center, in large gardens on a low cliff overlooking a sandy beach. Built in 1974, it resembles a series of fortresses facing the ocean. The complex consists of a quartet of three-, four-, and five-story buildings separated by wide stretches of greenery. Self-contained kitchenettes make the guest rooms suitable for vacationers who prefer to eat in occasionally. Each unit has living-room furnishings, a terrace or balcony, and an excellent bed.

Close to the sea cliff is an outstanding recreation area, with the finest pool around. Other facilities include two tennis courts, a pool reserved for children, and a bookshop. Car-rental service is available.

Live entertainment is presented nightly. There's an informal snack bar and a bar-lounge. The restaurant in the main building serves Portuguese and international cuisine buffet-style.

Estalagem do Cerro. Rua Samora Barros, 8200 Albufeira. ☎ and fax **089/58-61-91.** 95 units. A/C TV TEL. 12,000$–16,000$ ($67.20–$89.60) double. AE, DC, MC, V. Limited free parking on street.

Estalagem do Cerro, built in 1964, captures Algarvian charm without neglecting modern amenities. This "Inn of the Craggy Hill" is at the top of a hill overlooking Albufeira's bay, about a 10-minute walk from the beach. A similar Moorish style unites an older, regional-style building and a more modern structure. The tastefully furnished midsize guest rooms have verandas overlooking the sea, pool, or garden.

An air-conditioned panoramic dining room serves good regional dishes and international specialties. Before and after dinner, guests gather in a modern bar or on its patio. On most nights guests can dance to disco music; fado and folkloric shows are also presented.

The inn has an outdoor heated pool, with its own bar, in a garden setting. On the premises are a hairdresser, sauna, massage facilities, solarium, coffee shop, Jacuzzi, and Turkish bath. There's also a fully equipped gym. Laundry, baby-sitting, and room service are provided.

Hotel Boa-Vista. Rua Samora Barros 6, 8200 Albufeira. ☎ **289/58-91-75.** Fax 289/58-91-80. E-mail: hbelver@mail.telepac.pt. 89 units. A/C TV TEL. 17,500$–28,000$ ($98–$156.80) double. Rates include breakfast. AE, DC, MC, V. Limited free parking on street.

Built in the Algarvian style, the "Residence of the Good View" sits high above the sea outside the center. It offers two styles of accommodations: in the amenity-loaded main building, and in a block of furnished but somewhat austere efficiencies across the street. The units open onto balconies, which afford views over orange-tile-roofed whitewashed cottages to the bay below. Traditional wicker-wood decor matches the carpets and ceramics, and bathrooms are gray and white with marble accents. The hotel has 24-hour room service, laundry service, a sauna, and an outdoor pool.

International cuisine is served in two restaurants. We prefer the more formal Restaurante Panorámico, a restaurant-grill-bar with a view of the bay. A small band plays 3 nights a week.

Hotel Rocamar. Largo Jacinto d'Ayet, 8200 Albufeira. ☎ **089/58-69-90.** Fax 089/58-69-98. 91 units. A/C TEL. 8,500$–17,000$ ($49.30–$98.60) double. Rates include breakfast. AE, DC, MC, V. Limited free parking on street.

You might think that this cubistic hotel looks like an updated version of a Moorish castle, a well-ordered assemblage of building blocks, or the partially excavated side of a stone quarry. Built in 1974, it was enlarged in 1991. It rises six stories above the tawny cliffs that slope down to one of the most inviting beaches on the Algarve. Many of its windows, and all of its balconies, benefit from the view. The hotel is a 5-minute walk from the town's attractions. Rooms are simple and sun-washed yet comfortable, with firm mattresses on good beds. An Iberian-style dining room serves conservative, well-prepared meals, and there's a congenial contemporary bar. Laundry, baby-sitting, and room service are available.

Hotel Sol e Mar. Rua Bernardino de Sousa, 8200 Albufeira. ☎ **289/58-00-80.** Fax 289/58-70-36. 74 units. A/C MINIBAR TV TEL. 18,000$ ($100.80) double. AE, DC, MC, V.

Hotel Sol e Mar occupies a prime location in the heart of Albufeira above the beach. It dates from 1969 and was enlarged in 1975. The two-story entrance on the upper palisade can be deceiving—when you walk across the spacious sun-filled lounges to the picture windows and look down, you'll see a six-story drop. Hugging the cliff are midsize guest rooms and a wide stone terrace with garden furniture and parasols. On a lower level is a sandy beach. There's also an indoor heated swimming pool. The guests are a continental crowd with a sprinkling of Americans. All units have private balconies, wooden headboards, locally painted seascapes, slim-line armchairs, and plenty of wardrobe space. Laundry, baby-sitting, and room service are provided.

Diners take their meals in a two-level room. Opposite the restaurant is a lounge that serves drinks, a room for card players, and a TV room. After-dinner concerts are played on the electric organ until long past midnight. During the day guests take the elevator to the lower sun terrace for swimming, sunbathing. The Esplanade Café, designed as a Portuguese tavern, is also on the lower terrace.

Mar a Vista. Cerro da Piedade, 8200 Albufeira. ☎ **289/58-63-54.** Fax 289/58-63-55. 42 units. MINIBAR TV TEL. 9,500$ ($53.20) double. Rates include breakfast. AE, DC, MC, V. Closed Nov–Apr. Free parking.

From this crow's-nest vantage point, you can gaze out over the rooftops of the resort below. The principal building of this first-class inn, built in sterile 1960s style, has guest rooms, a bar, and the breakfast room. A second building contains four guest rooms. Most units have private balconies. Interesting prints adorn the walls; the furnishings, although not sumptuous, are standard and comfortable, with firm mattresses. The rooftop breakfast room, decorated in provincial style with blond paneling, takes advantage of the view. There's a well-tended walled garden and plenty of parking space. Laundry, baby-sitting, and room service are available.

Villa Recife. Rua Miguel Bombarda 6, 8200 Albufeira. ☎ **289/58-67-47.** Fax 289/58-71-82. 92 units. 12,000$ ($67.20) double. Rates include breakfast. AE, DC, MC, V. Free parking on street.

In the heart of town, Villa Recife is a self-catering hotel reached through the cafe and open-air bar that fills its front garden. All but 14 of its rooms contain kitchenettes. The establishment was originally built as a private villa around 1920. The original building holds about 20 rooms; the rest are in a modern rear wing. The palms and bougainvillea planted by the original owners tower over the entranceway, whose walls are covered with blue, white, and yellow tiles. All the studio apartments have tiny terraces. Once a week (usually on Friday) a live band entertains on a wooden platform in the front garden. There's an outdoor pool and a terraced bar that's open from 3pm to midnight. Laundry service is available.

WHERE TO STAY NEARBY
PRAIA DA FALÉSIA

✪ **Sheraton Algarve.** Praia da Falésia, Pilhal do Concelho, 8200 Albufeira. ☎ **800/325-3535** in the U.S., or 289/50-01-00. Fax 289/50-19-50. www.luxurycollection.com. E-mail: sheraton_algarve@sheraton.com. 215 units. A/C MINIBAR TV TEL. 40,000$–68,000$ ($224–$380.80) double; 85,000$–140,000$ ($476–$784) suite. Rates include breakfast. AE, DC, MC, V. Free parking.

Opened in 1992, this five-star hotel is laid out like an Algarve village, with no building rising higher than three floors. About 5 miles east of Albufeira, the Sheraton was designed to blend tastefully into its oceanfront location. Its wings ramble through a subtropical garden dotted with copses of the site's original pine trees. Conceived as a complete resort incorporating a nine-hole golf course, the hotel caters to a European and international clientele. Accommodations range from midsize to spacious, and open onto land, garden, or sea views. Each is traditionally furnished with luxurious pieces, including quality mattresses and state-of-the-art plumbing.

Dining/Diversions: The main restaurant is the Alem Mar, specializing in recipes from Portugal and seafood. There's also a beach club that serves sandwiches, salads, and platters of food throughout the day. A trio plays live music on many evenings in the Jardim Colonial, one of the hotel's handful of hideaway bars. The hotel recently transformed its formal restaurant into the Nightclub Portulano, where there's live music on most nights.

Amenities: Concierge, 24-hour room service, massage, laundry, hairdresser and barber, postal service, indoor and outdoor pools, direct access to sandy beach, in-house health club, nine-hole golf course (the Pine Cliffs; see "Outdoor Activities," above), three floodlit tennis courts.

PRAIA DA GALÉ

✪ **Hotel Villa Joya.** Praia da Galé (Apdo. Postal 120), 8200 Albufeira. ☎ **289/59-17-95.** Fax 289/59-12-01. 17 units. MINIBAR TEL. 66,000$–80,000$ ($369.60–$448) double; from 150,000$ ($840) suite. Rates include half-board. AE, DC, MC, V. Closed Jan 5–Mar 1, Nov 10–Dec 20. Free parking.

The most luxurious and intimate inn in the Algarve, the Hotel Villa Joya is especially favored by Germans (ex-chancellor Willy Brandt came here just before his death). The establishment lies 9 miles west of Albufeira in a residential neighborhood dotted with other dwellings, but within the confines of its large gardens visitors can easily imagine themselves in the open countryside. A footpath leads down to the beach. Every midsize accommodation has a view of the sea and a private CD player (TVs are available on request). In the 1980s, the hotel was converted from a Morocco-inspired private villa built during the 1970s.

Dining/Diversions: The restaurant serves elegant preparations of recipes inspired mostly by France, Germany, and Portugal. Nonguests are welcome if space is available (call ahead to check). Meals are served daily from 1 to 3pm and 7:30 to 9pm (last order). There's also a bar.

Amenities: Concierge, room service, laundry, heated outdoor pool, nearby tennis courts.

WHERE TO DINE
EXPENSIVE

O Cabaz da Praia. Praça Miguel Bombarda 7. ☎ **289/51-21-37.** Reservations recommended. Main courses 2,400$–5,800$ ($13.45–$32.50). AE, MC, V. Fri–Wed noon–2pm and 7–10:30pm. FRENCH/PORTUGUESE.

Now in its third decade, the "Beach Basket," near the Hotel Sol e Mar, sits on a colorful little square near the Church of São Sebastião. In a former fisher's cottage, the restaurant has an inviting ambience and good food. It has a large, sheltered terrace and a view over the main Albufeira beach. Main courses, including such justifiable favorites as cassoulet of seafood, *salade océane,* monkfish with mango sauce, and beef fillet with garlic and white-wine sauce, are served with a selection of fresh vegetables. The restaurant is renowned for its lemon meringue pie and soufflés.

MODERATE

A Ruína. Cais Herculano. ☎ **289/51-20-94.** Reservations recommended. Main courses 2,000$–5,000$ ($11.20–$28). AE, DC, MC, V. Daily 12:30–3pm and 7–11pm. PORTUGUESE.

A Ruína sits opposite the fish market, overlooking the main beach. From the arcaded dining room, with its long candlelit wooden tables, you can watch the fishers mending their nets. Another cavelike room has more tables and a bar. The decor is unpretentious, and the reasonably priced seafood is fresh. A bowl of flavorful soup will get you going, then it's on to one of the fish specialties, such as grilled fresh tuna. The fish stew, *caldeirada,* is the chef's specialty, and our favorite dish. Desserts are usually custard and mousse.

Alfredo. Rua do 5 de Outubro 9–11. ☎ **289/51-20-59.** Reservations required. Main courses 1,000$–2,200$ ($5.60–$12.30). AE, DC, MC, V. Daily noon–10:30pm. PORTUGUESE/ITALIAN.

Just a minute's stroll from the market square, Alfredo is in a century-old building that looks as if it's always been an inn. It's full of atmosphere, with crude wooden tables and chairs made for leisurely drinking. The second-floor restaurant is a heavily beamed room with a marble slab floor and simple wooden tables. Ceiling fans create a cooling breeze, and the partially visible kitchen provides all the entertainment many diners require. Your meal of regional specialties might include tuna salad, cataplana clams, bream, or swordfish, as well as tournedos with mushrooms or Portuguese-style steak. The house wine, Portas do Sado, is available by the glass.

Café Doris. Av. Dr. Francisco Sá Carneiro, Areias de São João. ☎ **289/51-24-55.** Reservations required in summer. Main courses 1,000$–2,200$ ($5.60–$12.30). MC, V. Jan–Apr, Fri–Wed noon–3pm and 6–10pm; May–Oct, Fri–Wed noon–1:30am. Closed Nov–Dec. GERMAN/PORTUGUESE.

Café Doris is a German-operated rôtisserie-crêperie-restaurant. It turns out well-prepared crepes, home-baked cakes, and ice creams, as well as heartier fare. The ice cream comes in many flavors. Rich-tasting goulash-meat soup is always offered as an appetizer, as is savory goat stew. You might move on to roast pork with onion sauce, monkfish with rice curry, or a good steak, with cream sauce, herbs, lyonnaise potatoes, and a salad. Doris has an unusual selection of hot drinks, including coffee Algarve (with Medronho).

La Cigale. Olhos d'Agua. ☎ **289/50-16-37.** Reservations required. Main courses 1,600$–3,000$ ($8.95–$16.80); lunch 1,200$ ($6.70) and up. AE, MC, V. Daily noon–3pm and 7–11pm. PORTUGUESE/FRENCH.

La Cigale stands right on the beach, 4½ miles from Albufeira; its terrace makes it a romantic choice at night. It's a cliché of the sunny southern coast of Europe—and fortunately, the food matches the atmosphere. The wine list is fairly distinguished, in keeping with the impressive menu. The amiable management works efficiently. Specialties include clams à la Cigale, shellfish rice, steak with pepper sauce, sea bass, and a daily selection of fresh-caught fish.

O Montinho do Campo. Estrada dos Caliços, Montechoro. ☎ **289/54-19-59.** Reservations recommended in Aug. Fixed-price all-you-can-eat menu 3,300$ ($18.50). MC, V. Tues–Sat 8pm–4am. BRAZILIAN.

Two miles north of the town's commercial center O Montinho do Campo occupies a white-walled *quinta* (manor house) that was originally built a century ago as a farmhouse. It's one of the hippest, most exotic, and most popular restaurants in Albufeira. You can dine in the "upscale rustic" interior, but most visitors gravitate toward an outdoor terrace with a view down over bougainvillea-draped rose gardens to the sea. A meal here represents a break from standard Portuguese fare. The only offering is a Brazilian *rodizio:* A platter of 10 to 12 types of meats is placed on the table, accompanied by fried rice and fried bananas. A salad buffet features 10 to 15 selections. You can eat as much as you like, and the price of the meal includes beverages.

Don't overlook this place for a night out with an international crowd. Meals are deliberately scheduled late enough to allow diners to catch the live music offered Thursday, Friday, and Saturday from 11pm to 4am. Favorite drinks include margaritas, Brazilian-style caipirinhas, and beer.

INEXPENSIVE

Fernando. In the Hotel Sol e Mar, rua Bernardino de Sousa. ☎ **289/51-21-16.** Main courses 1,200$–1,800$ ($6.70–$10.10). AE, DC, MC, V. Daily noon–midnight. PORTUGUESE.

Fernando, with its large terrace and pleasant indoor dining room, serves tempting, economical fare. We always go here for the fish of the day. You can count on good soup, usually fish based. If you're tired of fish, the chef will fix you a simple steak or a Portuguese specialty such as clams with pork. Several varieties of tempting kebabs are also available. Desserts aren't special, but they're still very fattening.

ALBUFEIRA AFTER DARK

You can have a lot of fun in this hard-drinking, fun-in-the-sun town, discovering your own favorite tucked-away bar. To get rolling, you might begin at the **Falan Bar,** rua São Gonçalo de Lagos (no phone), or the nearby **Fastnet Bar,** rua Cândido dos Reis 5 (☎ **289/58-91-16**), where no one will object if you jump to your feet and begin to dance. A few storefronts away is the **Classic Bar,** rua Cândido dos Reis 8 (☎ **289/51-20-73**), a folksy, comfortably battered place that's almost completely devoid of pretension. Disco, anyone? The hottest in town are **Kiss,** Montechoro (☎ **289/51-56-39**), which draws the most energetic dance enthusiasts in town every night from 11pm to 6am, and **Silvia's Disco,** rua São Gonçalo de Lagos (☎ **289/58-85-74**).

6 Quarteira

14 miles W of Faro, 191 miles SE of Lisbon

This once-sleepy fishing village between Albufeira and Faro used to be known only to a handful of artists who amused the local fisherfolk. Now, with the invasion of outsiders, the traditional way of life has been upset. A sea of high-rise buildings has swallowed Quarteira, and the place is now a bustling, overgrown resort. The big attraction is one of the Algarve's longest beaches. In summer it's filled with vacationing Portuguese and other Europeans who supply a much-needed boost to the local economy.

Golfers who don't want to pay the high rates at Vale do Lobo or Vilamoura (both of which have 18-hole courses) can stay inexpensively in Quarteira (see "Where to Stay," below). The courses are only a 10-minute drive away, and Quarteira lies about 7 miles from the Faro airport.

The largest concentration of quality hotels and restaurants is not in Quarteira or even Praia de Quarteira, but in the satellite of Vilamoura, west of Quarteira. Buses run between Quarteira and Vilamoura frequently throughout the day. Tourist information is available in Quarteira.

At a central point on the Algarve coast, only 11 miles west of Faro airport, **Vilamoura** is an expansive land-development project, the largest private tourist "urbanization" in Europe. Although the remains of a Roman villa were discovered when builders were working on the local marina, the history of Vilamoura is yet to be written. Plans call for a city larger than Faro and an interior lake linked with the bay and ocean by two canals. There's already a marina that can hold 1,000 pleasure boats. Vilamoura is now filled with "holiday villages" and apartment complexes.

ESSENTIALS
ARRIVING
BY BUS If you're dependent on public transportation, take a plane, bus, or train from Lisbon to Faro (see "Faro," later in this chapter), then catch one of the buses that runs frequently between Faro and Quarteira.

BY CAR From Albufeira, head east along Route 125; from Faro, go west on Route 125. Signposts point to the little secondary road that runs south to Quarteira, which is the center for exploring the more extensive tourist developments along Praia de Quarteira and Vilamoura.

VISITOR INFORMATION
The **tourist information office** is at Edifício Boa Vista, Loja C, avenida Mota Pinto (☎ 289/38-92-09).

WHAT TO SEE & DO IN QUARTEIRA
OUTDOOR ACTIVITIES
Sports are a main attraction here. There are 18-hole golf courses, water sports, tennis courts, a riding center, and yachting. Shops and other tourist facilities, including restaurants and bars, also provide pleasant diversions.

BOATING Marinas have been tucked into virtually every navigable cove along the Algarve, and most contain a handful of sailboats or motorboats that can be rented, with or without a skipper, to qualified sailors. Before you can rent, you must present accreditation or some certificate from a yacht club proving your seaworthiness.

Algariate operates a boat-charter business from the 100-berth Marina de Vilamoura, 8125 Quarteira (☎ 289/38-99-33). Algariate was established in 1993 and is one of the largest yacht and motorboat charterers in the Algarve. Boats up to 40 feet in length are available, with or without a skipper. Available sailboats are up to 44 feet. Without a crew, they rent for 350,000$ to 950,000$ ($1,960 to $5,320) per week, depending on size and season. Motorboats are up to 45 feet. They rent for 600,000$ to 1,000,000$ ($3,360 to $5,600) per week, without a crew. Clients often use Vilamoura as a point of origin for visits to Madeira, North Africa, or the southern coast of Spain. If you prefer to have someone else worry about navigation, you can sail on the *Condor de Vilamoura,* which departs from the Vilamoura Marina at least once a day, depending on business, for 3-hour cruises toward Albufeira and Portimão. The cost is 6,000$ ($33.60) per person.

GOLF   Vila Sol, Alto do Semino, Vilamoura, 8125 Quarteira (☎ **289/30-05-05**), has the best fairways and the boldest and most inventive contours of any golf course in the Algarve. Designed by the English architect Donald Steel, it opened in 1991 as part of a 362-acre residential estate. Steele took great care in allowing the terrain's natural contours to determine the layout of the fairways and the impeccable greens. Although it hasn't been around long, Vila Sol has twice played host to the Portuguese Open (in 1992 and 1993). Golfers especially praise the configuration of holes 6, 8, and 14, which incorporate ponds, creek beds, and pine groves in nerve-racking order. Par is 72. Greens fees are 9,000$ to 15,000$ ($50.40 to $84). From Quarteira, drive east for 3 miles, following signs to Estrada Nacional 125, and turn off where signs point to Vila Sol.

Vilamoura has three famous courses, each with its own clubhouse and managed and owned by the same investors. They're 2½ miles east of Quarteira, and carefully signposted from the center of town. Discounts on greens fees are offered to the residents of five nearby hotels, according to a complicated, frequently changing system of hierarchies and commercial agreements.

The most famous and most sought-after of Vilamoura's trio of golf courses is the **Vilamoura Old Course,** sometimes referred to as Vilamoura I (☎ **289/31-03-43** for information). Noted English architect Frank Pennink laid out the course in 1969, long before American tastes in golf influenced Portugal. In design, texture, and conception, it's the most English of southern Portugal's golf courses, and it's invariably cited for its beauty, its lushness, and the maturity of its trees and shrubbery. Although some holes are almost annoyingly difficult (four of them are par 5), the course is among the most consistently crowded on the Algarve. Par is 73. Greens fees are 18,000$ ($100.80).

Adjacent to the Old Course are a pair of newer, less popular par-72 courses that nonetheless provide challenging golf for those who prefer different terrain. The first is the **Pinhal Golf Course,** also known as Vilamoura II (☎ **289/32-15-62**), which opened in the early 1970s. It's noted for the challenging placement of its many copses of pine trees. Greens fees run 5,250$ to 10,500$ ($29.40 to $58.80), depending on the season and the time of day. Nearby is the newest of the three courses, the **Laguna Golf Course,** or Vilamoura III (☎ **289/31-01-80**). Known for its labyrinth of water traps and lakes, it opened in the late 1980s. Greens fees run 5,250$ to 8,500$ ($29.40 to $47.60), depending on the season and the time of day. Tee times during the midday heat are less expensive than those in the early morning.

TENNIS   The English influence in southern Portugal is so strong that no self-respecting resort would be built without at least one tennis court. The **Vilamoura Tennis Centre** (☎ **289/31-21-25**) has 12. They're open to suitably dressed players for 1,200$ ($6.70) per hour.

WHERE TO STAY

Vilamoura is a better place to use as a base than Praia de Quarteira, whose less attractive accommodations are often filled with tour groups.

PRAIA DE QUARTEIRA

Atis Hotel. Av. Francisco Sá Carneiro, 8125 Quarteria. ☎ **289/38-97-71.** Fax 289/38-97-74. 98 units. A/C TV TEL. 14,100$ ($78.95) double; 17,000$ ($95.20) suite. Rates include breakfast. AE, DC, MC, V.

High-rise apartment blocks line this street so completely that it resembles the canyons of Wall Street. Fortunately, many of the Atis Hotel's balconied, basic rooms look out over the beach, a short walk away. Though small, rooms are comfortable, with standard furnishings and firm beds. A fence separates the tiny outdoor pool from the sidewalk; many guests prefer to swim at the beach. There are a cafeteria and a restaurant, a darkly paneled bar, and a bar and TV room on the ground floor. Laundry, baby-sitting, and room service are offered.

Hotel Dom José. Av. Infante do Sagres, 8125 Quarteira. ☎ **289/30-27-50.** Fax 289/30-27-55. E-mail: hoteldomjose@mail.telepac.pt. 146 units. A/C TV TEL. 8,650$–17,350$ ($48.45–$97.15) double. Rates include breakfast. AE, DC, MC, V. Parking 1,000$ ($5.60).

Hotel Dom José is sometimes completely booked, often by vacationers from Britain, who consider its amenities considerably better than its three-star status dictates. At its tallest point, the hotel has eight balconied stories; the outlying wings are shorter. The double rooms are small and plain, but comfortably furnished, with firm mattresses. A low wall separates the pool from the town's port-side promenade. The public rooms fill every evening as guests enjoy drinks, live music, and the air-conditioned sea view. In another corner of the ground floor, a lattice-covered room contains a wide-screen TV and serves salads and sandwiches. There's a sea-view restaurant as well.

VILAMOURA
Expensive
Hotel Atlantis Vilamoura. Apdo. 210, Vilamoura, 8125 Quarteira. ☎ **089/38-99-37.** Fax 089/38-99-62. 310 units. A/C MINIBAR TV TEL. 17,000$–33,000$ ($95.20–$184.80) double; 44,000$ ($246.40) suite. Rates include buffet breakfast. AE, DC, MC, V. Free parking.

This is one of the most stylish hostelries in town. Pointed arches accent the facade, adding Moorish flair. Removed from the congested section of Vilamoura, the contemporary building boasts gleaming marble, coffered wooden ceilings, and polished mirrors. The good-sized guest rooms are well furnished, often with silk wall coverings and bright fabrics. Each has a sea-view veranda. The bathrooms tend to be small, but the beds are excellent.

Dining: In the sophisticated bar, a piano provides evening music. The Grill Amendoeira serves regional cuisine, and Madeira serves Portuguese cuisine. Both are open Monday to Saturday 7:30 to 11pm. The coffee shop is open all day.

Amenities: Room service, laundry, baby-sitting, health club, three tennis courts, large terrace filled with plants, four pools, 20% discount at nearby golf course.

Vilamoura Marinotel. Vilamoura, 8126 Quarteira Codex. ☎ **289/38-99-88.** Fax 289/38-98-69. www.nexus-pt.com/marinotel. E-mail: marnotel@mail.telepac.pt. 389 units. A/C MINIBAR TV TEL. 29,400$–53,500$ ($163.30–$297.20) double; 37,400$–319,300$ ($209.45–$1,788.10) suite. Rates include buffet breakfast. AE, DC, MC, V. Free parking.

The five-star Marinotel is one of the finest deluxe hotels on the Algarve, with some 324 employees. The hotel is popular with well-heeled Portuguese and international visitors. During the slower winter months it accommodates conventions.

The massive, rectangular hotel sits next to the Vilamoura marina. Each well-furnished, good-sized guest room has a view of the marina or the ocean. Floors 8 and 9 are the most desirable. The high-ceilinged interior, with lounge space for 500, is decorated in traditional and modern designs, although the lobby is brassy and garish.

Dining/Diversions: The hotel's dining facilities are among the best at Vilamoura. The premier restaurant is Grill Sirius (see "Where to Dine," below). The large, airy Aries dining room occupies two levels and opens onto the pool and ocean. It has one of the finest young staffs on the Algarve. A fixed-price menu changes daily, and à la carte selections are available. Traditional and Iberian regional specialties are the main fare. Meal service is daily from 12:30 to 2:30pm and 7:30 to 10pm. The coffee shop by the pool serves lunch. The hotel also offers fado, folk dancing, fashion shows, and occasional barbecues.

Amenities: 24-hour room service, baby-sitting, laundry, health club with Jacuzzi and sauna, one indoor pool and two outdoor pools (one for children), two tennis courts, direct beach access.

MODERATE

Dom Pedro Golf Hotel. Vilamoura, 8125 Quarteira. ☎ **289/30-07-00.** Fax 289/30-07-01. 263 units. A/C MINIBAR TV TEL. 17,300$–28,000$ ($96.90–$156.80) double; 21,600$–41,000$ ($120.95–$229.60) suite. Rates include breakfast. AE, DC, MC, V. Free parking.

This 10-story hotel offers first-class comfort in the tourist whirl of Vilamoura. It's close to the casino and a short walk from the sands. The public rooms are sleekly styled. The midsize guests rooms are pleasantly furnished and carpeted, with private terraces and good beds, but the overall effect is uninspired. The hotel is a favorite with touring groups from England and Scandinavia.

The house band provides nightly entertainment, and there's a casino in front of the hotel. The restaurant Mimosa serves Portuguese and international specialties. There are three pools (including one for children), three tennis courts, a sauna, massage, and a hairdresser. Deep-sea fishing and horseback riding can be arranged, and guests receive a 15% to 20% discount on greens fees at various area golf courses. Laundry, baby-sitting, and room service are also available.

INEXPENSIVE

Estalagem da Cegonha. Centro Hipico de Vilamoura, 8125 Quarteira. ☎ **289/30-25-77.** Fax 289/32-26-75. 9 units. TV TEL. 14,900$ ($83.45) double. Rates include breakfast. AE, DC, MC, V. Free parking.

Estalagem da Cegonha, a 400-year-old farmhouse, is at Poço de Boliqueime, Vilamoura, on the national road between Portimão and Faro. It's about 4½ miles from the golf course, casino, marina, and beach. The best value in Vilamoura, this ancient inn occupies a peaceful setting that adjoins riding stables. In 1536 the woman who stole the heart of Portugal's greatest poet, Camões, was born here. A horse-jumping contest is held every September. The rooms are large and cozily decorated in typical Portuguese style, and have firm mattresses. The inn's chef has won an award for regional food. Before or after dinner, you can enjoy drinks in one of the comfortable bars. Room service is provided.

WHERE TO DINE
PRAIA DE QUARTEIRA

Restaurante Atlântico. Av. Infante do Sagres 91. ☎ **289/31-51-42.** Reservations recommended. Main courses 900$–2,200$ ($5.05–$12.30). DC, MC, V. Fri–Wed noon–3:30pm and 6:30–11pm. PORTUGUESE.

You'll find the protective awning of this port-side restaurant on the town's main promenade, near a cluster of other restaurants that look very much alike. The place is crowded—often when the others are empty—and it's patronized by an array of international (and often scantily clad) diners. The traditional regional cuisine uses fine local products, and the flavors are robust. The many tasty options include fish soup Algarve style, king prawns Atlântico, *pescadas a Algarvia* (hake cooked with almonds), pepper steak, chicken piri-piri (with hot peppers), clams in their shells, and other regional dishes.

Restaurante O Pescador. Largo das Cortés Reais. ☎ **289/31-47-55.** Main courses 1,200$–2,800$ ($6.70–$15.70). MC, V. Fri–Wed 1–3pm and 7–10pm. Closed Dec 16–Jan 15. ALGARVIAN/INTERNATIONAL.

O Pescador ("The Fisherman") is an unpretentious spot across the parking lot from the fish market, just west of the straw market. Although it's low-key, it serves some of the best seafood in the area. Beneath a lattice-accented wooden ceiling, diners enjoy polite service and fresh fish and vegetables. A display case contains some of the ingredients that go into the meals. The simple fare is typically Portuguese; options include fresh squid, grilled gray mullet, grilled prawns, fresh hake, steak, and grilled fillet of pork. The fish dishes are far better than the meat selections.

VILAMOURA

The Vilamoura Marinotel (see "Where to Stay," above) consistently serves the best food in town.

Grill Sirius. In the Vilamoura Marinotel. ☎ **289/38-99-88.** Reservations recommended. Main courses 2,800$–5,000$ ($15.70–$28). AE, DC, MC, V. Daily 7:30–11:30pm. POR-TUGUESE/INTERNATIONAL.

The most exclusive and expensive dining spot in this hotel is the Grill Sirius, on the main floor. It's the most elegant drinking and dining establishment in Vilamoura. A grand piano on a dais separates the restaurant from the chic Bar Castor. Live music filters into both areas. The stylish bar offers a large variety of drinks daily from 10:30am to 1am.

Overlooking the marina under high ceilings, Grill Sirius sophisticated but not fussy. The chefs prepare splendid Portuguese and international dishes, and the service is formal. You might begin with assorted smoked fish and follow with a seafood specialty, such as divinely smooth lobster cassoulet, turbot in seafood sauce, sea bass flambé with fennel, stuffed trout, or excellent fillet of sole. Meat dishes use only the finest cuts—rack of lamb, T-bone steak, and tournedos stuffed with shrimp and scallops and served with béarnaise.

QUARTEIRA AFTER DARK

Much of the tourist expansion in this region has occurred outside the immediate confines of Quarteira, so you're likely to find only a handful of sleepy bodegas and tascas inside the city limits. Most cater to locals and serve beer and wine. One of the more internationally conscious is the **Jazz Bar,** av. Infante do Sagres 133 (☎ **289/38-88-64**). It occasionally presents live entertainment by Portuguese and northern European musicians beginning around 10:30pm. Don't expect big-city gloss; the ambience is small-scale and folksy.

Glossier diversions are the norm in the massive marina and tourist developments of nearby Vilamoura. Foremost among these is the **Casino de Vilamoura** (☎ **289/30-29-96**), one of the finest and most razzmatazz nightspots in the Algarve. Its most appealing aspect is a gambling salon that offers roulette, blackjack, French banque, and baccarat. It's open every day from 7pm to 3am. To enter, you must present a passport or photo ID and pay 500$ ($2.80). A separate, less glamorous slot-machine salon, open daily from 4pm to 4am, doesn't charge admission.

The casino's 600-seat supper club serves meals nightly starting at 8:30pm; one of the Algarve's splashiest floor shows and cabaret revues begins at 10:30pm. A fixed-price meal costs 6,500$ ($36.40), including the show. The show alone costs 2,000$ ($11.20), which includes one drink. Physically part of the casino, but with a separate entrance and separate staff, is Vilamoura's most action-oriented disco, **Black Jack** (☎ **289/30-29-96**). Every dance-aholic in the region comes to get down and boogie. It's open nightly 11:30pm to 6am. The cover charge is 1,000$ ($5.60), including the first drink. The casino and its facilities are open every night except December 24 and 25.

7 Almancil

8 miles W of Faro, 190 miles SE of Lisbon

Almancil is a small market town of little tourist interest, but it's a center for two of the most exclusive tourist developments along the Algarve. Vale do Lobo lies 4 miles southeast of Almancil, and Quinta do Lago is 6 miles southeast of town.

The name Vale do Lobo ("Valley of the Wolf") suggests a forlorn spot, but in reality the *vale* is the site of a golf course designed by Henry Cotton, the British champion. It's west of Faro, about a 20-minute drive from the Faro airport. Some holes are by the sea, which results in many an anxious moment as shots hook out over the water. The property includes a nine-hole course, a nine-hole par-3 course, a putting green, and a driving range. The tennis center is among the best in Europe.

Quinta do Lago, one of the most elegant "tourist estates" on the Algarve, also has superb facilities. The pine-covered beachfront property has been a favored retreat of movie stars and European presidents. The resort's 27 superb holes of golf are also a potent lure. This is true luxury—at a price.

ESSENTIALS
ARRIVING

BY TRAIN   Faro, the gateway to the eastern Algarve, makes the best transportation hub for Almancil and its resorts. Go to Faro by train (see section 8, "Faro"), then take a bus the rest of the way.

BY BUS   Almancil is a major stop for buses to the western Algarve. About 14 a day run from Faro to Albufeira, with a stop at Almancil. For more information, call ☎ 289/80-37-92.

BY CAR   From Faro, head west along Route 125; from Albufeira or Portimão, continue east along Route 125.

VISITOR INFORMATION

There is no tourist office. Some information is available in Loulé at the Edifício do Castelo (☎ 289/46-39-00).

OUTDOOR ACTIVITIES

GOLF   One of the most deceptive golf courses on the Algarve, **Pinheiros Altos,** Quinta do Lago, 8135 Almancil (☎ 289/35-99-10), has contours that even professionals say are far more difficult than they appear at first glance. American architect Ronald Fream designed the 250 acres, which abut the wetland refuge of the Rio Formosa National Park. Umbrella pines and dozens of small lakes dot the course. Par is 73. Greens fees are 7,500$ ($42) for 9 holes, 15,000$ ($84) for 18 holes. Pinheiros Altos lies 3 miles south of Almancil. From Almancil, follow the signs to Quinta do Lago and Pinheiros Altos.

The namesake course of the massive development, Quinta do Lago, Quinta do Lago, 8135 Almancil (☎ 289/39-07-00), consists of two 18-hole golf courses, **Quinta do Lago** and **Rio Formosa.** Together they cover more than 600 acres of sandy terrain that abuts the Rio Formosa Wildlife Sanctuary. Very few long drives here are over open water; instead, the fairways undulate through cork forests and groves of pine trees, sometimes with abrupt changes in elevation. Greens fees are 7,500$ ($42) for 9 holes, 15,000$ ($84) for 18 holes. The courses are 3½ miles south of Almancil. From Almancil, follow signs to Quinta do Lago.

Of the four golf courses at the massive Quinta do Lago development, the par-72 **San Lorenzo** (São Lourenço) course, Quinta do Lago, Almancil, 8100 Loulé

(☎ **289/39-65-22**), is the most interesting and challenging. San Lorenzo opened in 1988 at the edge of the grassy wetlands of the Rio Formosa Nature Reserve. American golf designers William (Rocky) Roquemore and Joe Lee created it. The most panoramic hole is the 6th; the most frustrating, the 8th. Many long drives, especially those aimed at the 17th and 18th holes, soar over a saltwater lagoon. Priority tee times go to guests of the Granada organization's Dona Filipa and Penina Hotel, but others may play when the course is not too busy. Greens fees are 12,500$ ($70) for 9 holes, 24,000$ ($134.40) for 18 holes. From Almancil, drive 5 miles south, following signs to Quinta do Lago.

The **Vale do Lobo** course, Vale do Lobo, 8135 Almancil (☎ **289/39-39-39**), technically isn't part of the Quinta do Lago complex. Because it was established in 1968, before any of its nearby competitors, it played an important role in launching southern Portugal's image as a golfer's mecca. Designed by the British golfer Henry Cotton, it contains four distinct 9-hole segments. In order of age, they are the Green, the Orange, the Yellow, and the Blue Course, which opened with lots of international publicity in 1997. The Green and Orange courses make up the 18-hole Oceanfront Course, and the Yellow and Blue courses are the 18-hole Royal Course. All four include runs that stretch over rocks and arid hills, often within view of olive and almond groves, the Atlantic, and the high-rise hotels of nearby Vilamoura and Quarteira. Some long shots require driving golf balls over two ravines, where variable winds and bunkers that have been called "ravenous" make things particularly difficult. Greens fees, depending on the day of the week and other factors, range from 8,000$ to 11,000$ ($44.80 to $61.60) for 9 holes, 13,500$ to 18,000$ ($75.60 to $100.80) for 18 holes. From Almancil, drive 2½ miles south of town, following signs to Vale do Lobo.

HORSEBACK RIDING   One of the oldest and best-established riding stables is **Horses Paradise,** at the Oceanos, rua Cristovão Piers Norte, 8135 Almancil (☎ **289/39-41-89,** or 289/97-13-559 when the owners are out on horseback). Established in 1980, it's between Almancil, Quinta do Lago, and Vale do Lobo. Advance reservations are important for rides that go through forests, beside the fairways of golf courses, and (in some cases) beside the beach. Rides cost 4,000$ ($22.40) for 1 hour, 7,500$ ($42) for 2 hours.

WHERE TO STAY
VALE DO LOBO

✪ **Le Méridien Dona Filipa.** Vale do Lobo, 8136 Almancil. ☎ **289/39-41-41.** Fax 289/39-42-88. E-mail: gm1298@fortehotel.com. 162 units. A/C MINIBAR TV TEL. 31,000$–52,000$ ($173.60–$291.20) double; 55,000$–68,500$ ($308–$383.60) junior suite; 74,000$–107,000$ ($414.40–$599.20) deluxe suite. Rates include breakfast. AE, DC, MC, V. Free parking.

A citadel of ostentatious living, Dona Filipa is a deluxe golf hotel with such touches as gold-painted palms holding up the ceiling. The grounds are impressive, embracing 450 acres of rugged coastline with steep cliffs, inlets, and sandy bays. The hotel's exterior is comparatively uninspired, but Duarte Pinto Coelho lavished the interior with green silk banquettes, marble fireplaces, Portuguese ceramic lamps, and old prints over baroque-style love seats. The midsize to spacious guest rooms are handsomely decorated with antiques, rustic accessories, and handmade rugs. Most have balconies and twin beds; all have excellent mattresses and private safes. Bathrooms have dual basins, robes, and hair dryers.

Dining: Dining is formal and gracious, under the guidance of a knowledgeable maître d'hôtel and wine steward. International meals are served. The grill restaurant serves an à la carte menu. A coffee shop by the pool offers only lunch. The Gothic Bar is the hotel's most popular meeting place.

Amenities: 24-hour room service, laundry, baby-sitting, three tennis courts, pool, hairdresser, 15% discount on greens fees at nearby golf courses.

QUINTA DO LAGO

✪ **Quinta do Lago.** Quinta do Lago, 8135 Almancil. ☎ **800/223-6800** in the U.S., or 289/39-66-66. Fax 289/39-63-93. www.quintadolagohotel.com. E-mail: info@quintadolago-hotel.com. 141 units. A/C MINIBAR TV TEL. 35,000$–72,000$ ($196–$403.20) double; from 85,000$ ($476) suite. Rates include breakfast. AE, DC, MC, V. Free parking.

A pocket of the high life since 1986, Quinta do Lago is a sprawling 1,600-acre estate that contains some private plots beside the Ria Formosa estuary. The hotel is an investment by Prince Faisal of Saudi Arabia, who has wisely turned over management to the Orient Express hotel chain. Its riding center and 27-hole golf course are among the best in Europe.

The contemporary Mediterranean-style buildings rise three to six floors. The luxurious Quinta Park Country Club Apartments overlook a saltwater lake and feature modern comforts. Decorated with thick carpeting and pastel fabrics, the guest rooms are generally spacious, with tile or marble bathrooms. Rooms are decorated with contemporary art and light-wood furniture, and the balconies open onto views of the estuary.

Dining/Diversions: The Navegadores, an informal grill room overlooking a pool, is appropriate for both adults and children. There's a modern clubhouse with a restaurant and bar close to the driving range, overlooking the Bermuda green of the B1 fairway. The Beach Pavilion offers snacks, light meals, and drinks. Cadoro serves Italian cuisine, and the Patio Club is a sophisticated disco.

Amenities: 24-hour room service, laundry, baby-sitting, riding center, 27-hole golf course, tennis courts, indoor and outdoor pools, health club, solarium.

WHERE TO DINE

✪ **Casa Velha.** Quinta do Lago. ☎ **289/39-49-83.** Reservations recommended. Main courses 3,800$–4,600$ ($21.30–$25.75); fixed-price menu 7,500$ ($42). AE, MC, V. Mon–Sat 7:30–10:30pm. FRENCH.

Casa Velha, an excellent dining choice, is not part of the nearby Quinta do Lago resort. On a hillside behind its massive neighbor, it overlooks the resort's lake from the premises of a century-old farmhouse that has functioned as a restaurant since the early 1960s. The cuisine is mainly French, with a scattering of Portuguese and international dishes. Start with foie gras or marinated lobster salad. Specialties include a salad of chicken livers and gizzards with leeks and vinaigrette, and lobster salad flavored with an infusion of vanilla. Other choices are carefully flavored preparations of sea bass, filet of sole, and breast of duck with 12 spices.

✪ **Restaurant Ermitage.** Estrada Almancil-Vale do Lobo. ☎ **289/39-43-29.** Reservations recommended. Main courses 3,200$–4,500$ ($17.90–$25.20); fixed-price menus 9,500$ ($53.20). AE, MC, V. Tues–Sun 7–10:30pm. Closed 2 weeks in Jan, 1 week in June, 3 weeks in Dec. Drive 2 mi. from Almancil, following signs to Vale do Lobo. INTERNATIONAL.

This, our favorite restaurant in the region, is a Dutch-Swiss collaboration. It occupies an 18th-century stone farmhouse (*quinta*) about 2 miles from Almancil that's surrounded by gardens and flowering vines. In the cozy dining room, fireplaces add warmth in winter; an outdoor terrace is very popular during warm weather. The restaurant attracts a cosmopolitan clientele from throughout Europe. Starters include goose-liver terrine with blackberry sauce, and shrimp and spinach-stuffed ravioli surrounded by four other homemade pastas and sauces, all artfully arranged on an oversize platter. Delightful main courses, which change with the season and the inspiration of the chef, might include grilled fish of the day with herb-flavored hollandaise sauce, or fillet of monkfish with prawn-and-curry sauce. Everybody's favorite dessert is a walnut-flavored parfait with freshly made ice cream and mocha sauce. The restaurant's manager and chef are the Dutch-born team of Willemina Gilhooley and her husband, Vincent.

8 Faro

160 miles SE of Setúbal, 192 miles SE of Lisbon

Once loved by the Romans and later by the Moors, Faro is the provincial capital of the Algarve. In this bustling little city of some 30,000 permanent residents, you can sit at a cafe, sample the wine, and watch yesterday and today collide. An old man walks along, pulling a donkey on which sits a parasol-shaded girl in a white dress. Brushing past is a German backpacker in shorts. Faro is a hodgepodge of life and activity: It's been rumbled, sacked, and "quaked" by everybody from Mother Nature to the earl of Essex (Elizabeth I's favorite).

Since Afonso III drove out the Moors for the last time in 1266, Faro has been Portuguese. On its outskirts, an international airport brings in thousands of visitors every summer. The airport has done more than anything else to speed tourism not only to Faro, but to the entire Algarve.

Many visitors use Faro only as an arrival point, rushing through en route to a beach resort. Those who stick around will enjoy the local charm and color, as exemplified by the tranquil fishing harbor. A great deal of antique charm is gone, thanks to the earl of Essex, who sacked the town, and the 1755 earthquake. Remnants of medieval walls and some historic buildings stand in the Cidade Velha, or Old Town, which can be entered through the Arco da Vila, a gate from the 18th century.

ESSENTIALS
ARRIVING

BY PLANE   Jet service makes it possible to reach Faro from Lisbon in 30 minutes. For flight information, call the Faro airport (☎ **289/80-08-01**). You can take bus no. 14 or 16 from the airport to the railway station in Faro for 175$ ($1). The bus operates every 45 minutes daily from 7:10am to 7:45pm.

BY TRAIN   Trains arrive from Lisbon six times a day. The trip takes 7 hours and costs 2,175$ ($12.20) one way. For rail information in Faro, call the train station at largo da Estação (☎ **289/80-17-26**). For information in Lisbon, dial ☎ **21/888-40-25.**

BY BUS   Buses arrive every hour from Lisbon. The journey takes 4½ hours. The bus station is on avenida da República (☎ **289/89-97-61**); a one-way ticket costs 2,300$ ($12.90).

BY CAR   From the west, Route 125 runs into Faro and beyond. From the Spanish border, pick up N125 west.

VISITOR INFORMATION

The tourist office is at rua da Misericórdia 8–12 (☎ **289/80-36-04**). At the tourist office, you can pick up a copy of *The Algarve Guide to Walks,* which will direct you on nature trails in the area.

EXPLORING THE TOWN   The most bizarre attraction in Faro is the **Capela d'Ossos** (Chapel of Bones). Enter through a courtyard from the rear of the Igreja de Nossa Senhora do Monte do Carmo do Faro, largo do Carmo (☎ **289/82-44-90**). Erected in the 19th century, the chapel is completely lined with human skulls (an estimated 1,245) and bones. It's open daily from 10am to 1pm and 3 to 5pm. Entrance is free to the church, 120$ (65¢) to the chapel.

The church, built in 1713, contains a gilded baroque altar. Its facade is also baroque, with a bell tower rising from each side. Topping the belfries are gilded, mosquelike cupolas connected by a balustraded railing. The upper-level windows are latticed and framed with gold; statues stand in niches on either side of the main portal.

Other religious monuments include the old Sé (cathedral), on largo da Sé (☎ **289/80-66-32**). Built in the Gothic and Renaissance styles, it stands on a site originally occupied by a Muslim mosque. Although the cathedral has a Gothic tower, it's better known for its tiles, which date from the 17th and 18th centuries. The highlight is the Capela do Rosário, on the right. It contains the oldest and most beautiful tiles, along with sculptures of two Nubians bearing lamps and a red chinoiserie organ. Admission is free. The cathedral is open Monday to Friday 10am to noon, Saturday at 5pm for services, and Sunday 8am to 1pm for services.

Igreja de São Francisco, largo de São Francisco (☎ **289/82-36-96**), is the other church of note. Its facade doesn't even begin to hint at the baroque richness inside. Panels of glazed earthenware tiles in milk-white and Dutch blue depict the life of the patron saint, St. Francis. One chapel is richly gilded. Open hours are Monday to Friday 8am to 10am and 2 to 8pm (but in the sleepy Algarve, you may sometimes find it closed).

If it's a rainy day, three minor museums might hold some interest. The municipal museum, or **Museu Municipal,** praça Afonso III 14 (☎ **289/89-74-00**), is in a former 16th-century convent, the **Convento de Nossa Senhora da Assunção.** Even if you aren't particularly interested in the exhibits, the two-story cloister is worth a visit. Many artifacts dating from the Roman settlement of the area are on display. Some of the Roman statues are from excavations at Milreu. The museum is open Monday to Friday from 9am to 6:30pm. Admission is free.

The dockside **Museu Maritimo,** rua Communidade Luisada (☎ 289/80-36-01) displays models of local fishing craft and of the boats that carried Vasco da Gama and his men to India in 1497. There are replicas of a boat the Portuguese used to sail up the Congo River in 1492, and of a vessel that bested the entire Turkish navy in 1717. It's open Monday to Friday from 9am to noon and 2 to 5pm. Admission is 100$ (55¢).

Finally, the **Museu Ethnografico Regional,** rua do Pé da Cruz (☎ 289/82-76-10), is a museum devoted to the region's folkloric culture. The focus is on the fishing industry; crafts and reconstructions of regional interiors are also on display. In photographs you can see rather sad, nostalgic pictures Algarvian fishing villages before they were surrounded by high-rise developments. The museum is open Monday to Friday from 9am to 12:30pm, and 2 to 5:30pm. Admission is 300$ ($1.70).

OUTDOOR ACTIVITIES   Most visitors don't come to Faro to look at churches or museums, regardless of how interesting they are. Rather, they take the harbor ferry to the wide white-sand beaches called the **Praia de Faro,** on an islet. The ferry leaves from the jetty just below Cidade Velho; the round-trip fare is 200$ ($1.10). Three ferries depart daily from June to September. Bus no. 16 leaving from the terminal runs to Praia de Faro; the one-way fare is 150$ (85¢). A bridge also connects the mainland and the beach, about 3½ miles from the town center. At the shore, you can water-ski, fish, or just rent a deck chair and umbrella and lounge in the sun.

SHOPPING   Most of the shopping outlets in Faro are on **rua Santo António** or its neighbor, **rua Francisco Gomes,** in the heart of town. Check out **Carminho,** rua Santo António 29 (☎ 289/82-65-22), a well-recommended outlet for handcrafts and, to a lesser extent, traditional clothing. If you're interested in wandering like a local resident amid stands and booths piled high with the produce of southern Portugal, consider a trek through the **Mercado de Faro,** largo do Mercado, in the town center. It's open daily from 6:30am to 1:30pm.

WHERE TO STAY

Eva. Av. da República, 8,000 Faro. ☎ **289/80-33-54.** Fax 289/80-23-04. 148 units. A/C MINIBAR TV TEL. 16,000$–25,000$ ($89.60–$140) double; 23,500$–39,400$ ($131.60–$220.65) suite. Rates include breakfast. AE, DC, MC, V. Limited free parking available on street.

Eva dominates the harbor like a fortress. It's a modern, eight-story hotel that occupies an entire side of the yacht-clogged harbor. The hotel was beginning to look worn, but a recent rejuvenation perked it up. There are direct sea views from most of the mid-size guest rooms, which are furnished in a restrained, even austere, style. The better rooms have large balconies and open onto the water. Eva's best features are its penthouse restaurant and rooftop pool, supported on 16 posts, with sun terraces and a bar. The restaurant is open only for dinner, and there's a dinner-dance on Saturday. An informal restaurant on the ground floor serves lunch and dinner. Also on the premises are a snack bar, three cocktail bars, and a hairdresser. Laundry, room service, and baby-sitting can be arranged.

Hotel Faro. Praça D. Francisco Gomes 2, 8000 Faro. ☎ **289/80-32-76.** Fax 289/80-35-46. 52 units. A/C TEL. 15,000$ ($84) double; 18,000$ ($100.80) suite. AE, DC, MC, V.

No, it's not a drab gray office building or a factory, but a hotel with recently renovated guest rooms opening right onto the bustling harbor. The furnishings are comfortable but motel standardized. Many units have balconies that open onto the square, which tends to be noisy until late at night. Each suite has a small sitting room with a sofa bed, suitable for a third person. You can sit on the mezzanine and order drinks from the bar while surveying the scene below.

WHERE TO DINE

Dois Irmãos. Largo do Terreiro do Bispo 13–15. ☎ **289/82-33-37.** Reservations recommended. Main courses 950$–3,500$ ($5.30–$19.60); tourist menu 1,800$ ($10.10). AE, MC, V. Daily noon–11pm. PORTUGUESE.

This popular bistro, founded in 1925, has a no-nonsense atmosphere and many devotees. The menu is as modest as the establishment and its prices, but you get a good choice of fresh grilled fish and shellfish dishes. Ignore the paper napkins and concentrate on the fine kettle of fish before you. Clams in savory sauce is a justifiable favorite, and sole is regularly featured—but, of course, everything depends on the catch of the day. Service is slow and amiable.

Restaurante Cidade Velha. Rua Domingos Guieiro 19. ☎ **289/82-71-45.** Reservations recommended. Main courses 1,500$–2,500$ ($8.40–$14). AE, DC, V. Mon–Fri 12:30–2pm; Mon–Sat 7:30–10:30pm. PORTUGUESE/INTERNATIONAL.

The leading restaurant in town is the Cidade Velha, a charming hideaway in a former private home. It's in back of the cathedral, behind thick stone walls that were built at least 250 years ago. You can start with an apéritif in the tiny bar near the entrance.

Vested waiters serve meals in two rooms with vaulted brick ceilings. The cuisine has recently improved considerably. Full meals might include crab cakes or smoked swordfish with horseradish sauce, followed by roast rack of lamb with rosemary and mint sauce, roast duck with apricot sauce, or fillet of pork stuffed with walnuts and baked in port-wine sauce.

WHERE TO STAY & DINE NEARBY

✪ **Hotel La Réserve.** Estrada de Esteval, Santa Bárbara de Nexe, 8000 Faro. ☎ **289/99-94-74.** Fax 289/99-94-02. 12 studios, 8 duplexes. A/C MINIBAR TV TEL. 28,000$–40,000$ ($156.80–$224) studio; 30,000$–44,000$ ($168–$246.40) duplex. AE, DC, MC, V. Free parking. From Faro, take N125 for 4 mi.; go straight at sign for Loulé and continue 1 mi. to Esteval. Turn right at sign for Santa Bárbara de Nexe; 1 mi. later, hotel is on the right.

Hotel La Réserve, one of the two Relais & Châteaux properties in Portugal, is near a hamlet about 7 miles west of Faro. It sits on its own 6-acre parkland far from a beach. The hotel offers luxury and spacious accommodations in a modern, elegant country-estate atmosphere—all at a very high price. Two-story structures encircle the pool and sundeck, and guests are housed in studios or duplex apartments, furnished with both modern and traditional pieces. Bedside controls and thoughtful extras such as toiletries make for good R&R.

Dining/Diversions: The hotel has two bars, a snack bar, and an international restaurant. **La Réserve** restaurant, next to the hotel, is the finest dining room in the Algarve. The international dinners are carefully presented, and the owners care about the freshness of their meats, fish, and produce. A specialty is smoked swordfish. Also try the Oriental shrimp served on a bed of rice with banana croquettes. Local duckling, crisp outside and tender inside, makes a good main course. The best Portuguese vintages are on the wine list, including the well-known *vinho verde* (green wine) of the north. The restaurant is open Wednesday to Monday from 7 to 11pm. It's important to call for reservations.

Amenities: Room service, laundry, tennis courts, pool.

FARO AFTER DARK

What Bourbon Street is to New Orleans, rua do Prior is to Faro. In the heart of town, adjacent to the Faro Hotel, it's chock-a-block with dozens of night cafes, pubs (English and otherwise), and discos that rock from around 10:30pm till dawn. Head to this street anytime after noon for insights into the hard-drinking, hard-driving nature of this hot southern town, then check out the town's two most popular discos if you feel like dancing. They are **24 July,** rua do Prior (☎ 289/80-61-77), and **Millennium,** rua do Prior (☎ 289/82-36-28). Entrance to both costs around 1,000$ ($5.60) and includes the first drink.

EASY EXCURSIONS FROM FARO

Some of the most interesting towns in the Algarve surround the capital. Exploring any one takes a half day.

LOULÉ   This market town 9½ miles north of Faro lies in the heart of the Algarve's chimney district. If you think chimneys can't excite you, you haven't seen the ones here. The fret-cut plaster towers rise from many of the cottages and houses (and even the occasional dog house).

Loulé and the villages around it are known for their handcrafts. They produce work in palm fronds and esparto, such as handbags, baskets, mats, and hats. Loulé artisans also make copper articles, bright harnesses, delicate wrought-iron pieces, clogs, cloth shoes and slippers, tinware, and pottery. Products are displayed in workshops at the foot of the walls of an old fortress and in other showrooms, particularly those along rua do 9 de Abril.

In Loulé, you may want to visit the Gothic-style Igreja Matriz, or parish church, largo C. da Silva (☎ **289/46-27-92**). It was given to the town in the late 13th century. It's open Monday to Saturday from 9am to noon and 2 to 5:30pm.

The remains of the Moorish **castelo** are at largo Dom Pedro I (☎ **289/40-06-00**). The ruins house a historical museum and are open daily from 9am to 5:30pm. Admission is free.

Bus service is good during the day; about 40 buses arrive from various parts of the Algarve, mainly Faro. Five trains per day arrive from Faro at the Loulé rail station, 3 miles from the center of town. There are bus connections to the center of town from the station, or you can take a taxi.

The Loulé **Tourist Information Office** is in the Edifício do Castelo (☎ **289/46-39-00**).

For meals, try the Portuguese cuisine at **O Avenida,** av. José da Costa Mealha 13 (☎ **289/46-21-06**), on the main street close to the traffic circle. It's one of the finer restaurants in the Algarve. The specialty is shellfish cooked cataplana style. You can also order beefsteak à Avenida or sole meunière. The restaurant is open Monday to Saturday from noon to 3pm and 7 to 10pm, and closed for most of November. Meal prices start at 3,500$ ($19.60). Occasional live entertainment is featured. O Avenida accepts most major credit cards.

SÃO BRÁS DE ALPORTEL   Traveling north from Faro, you'll pass through groves of figs, almonds, and oranges, and through pine woods where resin collects in wooden cups on the tree trunks. After 12½ miles you'll come upon isolated São Brás de Alportel, one of the most charming and least-known spots on the Algarve. Far from the crowded beaches, this town attracts those in search of pure air, peace, and quiet. It's a bucolic setting filled with flowers pushing through nutmeg-colored soil. Northeast of Loulé, the whitewashed, tile-roofed town livens up only on market days. Like its neighbor, Faro, it's noted for its perforated plaster chimneys. The area at the foot of the Serra do Caldeirão has been described as one vast garden.

A change of pace from seaside accommodations is the **Pousada de São Brás,** estrada de Lisboa (N2), 8150 São Brás de Alportel (☎ **289/84-23-05**). The government-owned inn is a hilltop villa, with fret-cut limestone chimneys and a crow's-nest view of the surrounding serras. It's approached through a fig orchard in which stones have been painted with welcomes in many languages.

Many visitors come just for lunch or dinner (served daily from 12:30 to 3pm and 7:30 to 10pm), returning to the coastline at night, but a knowing few remain for the evening. In the dining room, rustic mountain-tavern chairs and tables rest on hand-woven rugs. The 3,650$ ($20.45) table d'hôte dinner offers soup, a fish course, a meat dish, vegetables, and dessert. The cuisine is plain but good. After dinner, you may want to retire to the sitting room to watch the embers of the evening's fire die down. Then trundle upstairs, past the large ornamented donkey collar. The 22 guest rooms contain private bathrooms and phones. Doubles cost 24,600$ ($137.75), including breakfast. The place has an outdoor swimming pool. Laundry service is provided, and room service is offered until 10pm. Parking is free, and most major credit cards are accepted.

OLHÃO   This is the Algarve's famous cubist town, long beloved by painters. In its heart, white blocks stacked one upon the other, with flat red-tile roofs and exterior stairways on the stark walls, evoke the Casbahs of North Africa. The cubist part is found only at the core. The rest of Olhão has almost disappeared under the onslaught of modern commercialism.

While you're here, try to attend the fish market near the waterfront when a *lota,* or auction, is under way. Olhão is also known for its "bullfights of the sea," in which fishers wrestle with struggling tuna trapped in nets and headed for the smelly warehouses along the harbor.

If you're here at lunchtime, go to one of the inexpensive markets along the waterfront. At **Casa de Pasto O Bote,** av. do 5 de Outubro 122 (☎ **289/72-11-83**), you can select your food from trays of fresh fish. Your choice is then grilled to your specifications. Meal prices start at 2,000$ ($11.20). It's open Monday to Saturday from 10am to 3pm and 7 to 11pm.

For the best view, climb **Cabeça Hill,** with grottos punctured by stalagmites and stalactites, or **St. Michael's Mount,** offering a panorama of the Casbah-like Baretta. Finally, to reach one of the most idyllic beaches on the Algarve, take a 10-minute motorboat ride to the **Ilha de Armona,** a nautical mile away. Ferries run hourly in summer; the round-trip fare is 160$ (90¢). Olhão is 5 miles east of Faro.

TAVIRA   A gem 19 miles east of Faro, Tavira is approached through green fields studded with almond and carob trees. Sometimes called the "Venice of the Algarve," Tavira lies on the banks of the Ségua and Gilão Rivers, which meet under a seven-arched Roman bridge. In the town square, palms and pepper trees rustle under the cool arches of the arcade. In spite of modern encroachments, Tavira is festive looking. Floridly decorated chimneys top many of the houses, some of which are graced with emerald-green tiles and wrought-iron balconies capped by finials. Fretwork adorns many doorways. The liveliest action centers on the fruit and vegetable market on the river esplanade.

The **Tavira Tourist Office** is on rua da Galeria (☎ 289/32-25-11). Tavira has frequent bus connections with Faro throughout the day.

At the **castelo,** reached by a stepped street off rua da Liberdade, you can explore the battlemented walls once known to the Moors. From here you'll have the best view of the town's church spires; across the river delta, you can see to the ocean. The castle is open Monday to Friday 8am to 5:30pm, Saturday and Sunday 10am to 7pm. Admission is free.

Of the churches, the **Igreja da Misericórdia,** west of the main square and just up from the tourist office, is worth a visit. It has an attractive Renaissance portal, constructed between 1541 and 1551 and dedicated to Saints Peter and Paul. It's open daily (in theory, at least) from 10am to noon and 2 to 5pm.

A tuna-fishing center, Tavira is cut off from the sea by an elongated spit of sand. The **Ilha de Tavira** begins west of Cacela and runs all the way past the fishing village of Fuzeta. On this sandbar, accessible by motorboat, are two beaches: the **Praia de Tavira** and the **Praia de Fuzeta.** Some people prefer the beach at the tiny village of **Santa Luzia,** about 2 miles from the heart of town.

If you're here for lunch, try the **Restaurante Imperial,** rua José Pires Padinha 22 (☎ 281/32-23-06). A small, air-conditioned place off the main square, it serves regional food, including shellfish, shellfish rice, garlic-flavored pork, roast chicken, fresh tuna, and other Portuguese dishes, accompanied by vegetables and good local wines. A favorite dish is pork and clams with french fries, topped off with a rich egg-and-almond dessert. Meals cost 2,500$ ($14) or more, including wine. Food is served daily from noon to 11pm. MasterCard and Visa are accepted.

ESTÓI & MILREU   A little village some 5 miles northeast of Faro, Estói is still mainly unspoiled by tourists. Buses run to the area from Faro. Visitors are objects of some curiosity, stared at by old women sheltered behind the curtains of their little houses and followed by begging children. Sometimes you may see women washing their clothing in a public trough. Garden walls are decaying here, and the cottages are worn by time and the weather.

The principal sight in Estói is the **Palácio do Visconde de Estói.** The villa, with its salmon-pink baroque facade, has been described as a cross between Versailles and the water gardens of the Villa d'Este near Rome. It was built in the late 18th century for Francisco José de Moura Coutinho; José Francisco da Silva rescued it from near ruin between 1893 and 1909. A palm-lined walk leads to terraced gardens with orange trees along the balusters.

The villa is not open to the public, but the grounds can be visited Tuesday to Saturday from 10am to 5pm. To enter, ring a bell at the iron gates outside the palm-lined walk, and a caretaker will guide you to the gardens. There's no entrance fee, but tip the caretaker.

9 Vila Real de Santo António

195 miles SE of Lisbon, 53 miles E of Faro, 31 miles W of Huelva, Spain

Twenty years after the marquês de Pombal rebuilt Lisbon, which had been destroyed in the great 1755 earthquake, he sent architects and builders to Vila Real de Santo António. They reestablished this frontier town on the bank opposite Spain in only 5 months. Pombal's motivation was jealousy of Spain. Much has changed, but praça de Pombal remains. An obelisk stands in the center of the square, which is paved with inlays of black-and-white tiles radiating like sun rays, and is filled with orange trees. Separated from its Iberian neighbor by the Guadiana River, Vila Real de Santo António has car-ferry service between Portugal and Ayamonte, Spain.

ESSENTIALS
ARRIVING
BY TRAIN   The bus (see below) is a better option for travelers from Faro. Eleven trains per day arrive from Faro. The trip takes 2½ hours and costs 500$ ($2.80) one way. Four trains make the 4½-hour trip from Lagos; a one-way ticket costs 890$ ($5). For information and schedules, call ☎ **21/888-40-25.** To make connections with trains from Spain (an hour ahead of Portuguese time in summer), take a ferry from Vila Real de Santo António to Ayamonte (for ferry information, see below). From Ayamonte, buses from the main square will deliver you to the station at Huelva or Sevilla.

BY BUS   From Faro to Vila Real, the bus is better than the train. Five *espressos* run each day. They take 1 hour and cost 710$ ($4) one way. Eight buses make the 4-hour journey from Lagos, which costs 1,100$ ($6.15) one way. For information and schedules, call ☎ **289/89-96-61**.

BY FERRY   In summer, ferries run between Ayamonte, Spain, and Vila Real daily from 8am to 7pm. The fare is 180$ ($1) per passenger or 750$ ($4.20) per car.

VISITOR INFORMATION
The **tourist office** is on avenida Infante Dom Henríque (☎ **281/54-44-95**).

EXPLORING THE TOWN
Vila Real de Santo António is a great example of 18th-century town planning. A long esplanade, **avenida da República,** follows the river, and from its northern extremity you can view the Spanish town across the way. Gaily painted horse-drawn carriages take you sightseeing past the shipyards and the lighthouse.

You can visit the **Museu de Manuel Cabanas,** praça Marquês de Pombal (tel **281/51-00-00**). On the main square of town, it contains regional ethnographical artifacts, plus some paintings and antique engravings. It's open Tuesday to Sunday from 11am to 1pm and 2 to 7pm; admission is free.

A 3-mile drive north on the road to Mertola (N122) will take you to the gull-gray castle-fortress of **Castro Marim.** This formidable structure is a legacy of the border wars between Spain and Portugal. The ramparts and walls stand watch over the territory across the river. Afonso III, who expelled the Moors from this region, founded the original fortress, which was razed by the 1755 earthquake. Inside the walls are the ruins of the **Igreja de São Tiago,** dedicated to St. James.

Southwest of Vila Real is the emerging resort of **Monte Gordo,** which has the second-greatest concentration of hotels in the eastern Algarve (after Faro). Monte Gordo, 2½ miles southwest of Vila Real the mouth of the Guadiana River, is the last in a long line of Algarvian resorts. Its wide, steep beach, Praia de Monte Gordo, is one of the finest on Portugal's southern coast. This beach, backed by pine-studded lowlands, has the highest average water temperature in Portugal.

Sadly, what was once a sleepy little fishing village has succumbed to high-rises. Nowadays the *varinas* urge their sons to work in the hotels instead of the sea, fishing for tips instead of tuna. It has many good hotels, which attract many Europeans, particularly Spaniards from across the border.

WHERE TO STAY

Although Vila Real has hotels, most visitors prefer to stay at the beach at Monte Gordo (see below).

VILA REAL

Hotel Apolo. Av. dos Bombeiros Portugueses, 8900 Vila Real de Santo António. ☎ **281/51-24-48.** Fax 081/51-24-50. 42 units. A/C TV TEL. 10,500$–20,000$ ($58.80–$112) double. Rates include breakfast. AE, DC, MC, V. Free parking.

Hotel Apolo lies on the western edge of town. Near the beach and the river, it attracts vacationers as well as travelers who don't want to cross the Spanish border at night. The hotel is a marginal choice, with a spacious marble-floored lobby leading into a large bar scattered with comfortable sofas and flooded with sunlight. Each small, simply furnished guest room has a private balcony and a firm mattress. It will not be your classiest stopover on the Algarve, but it's certainly adequate for an overnight stay.

Hotel Guadiana. Av. da República 94, 8900 Vila Real de Santo António. ☎ **281/51-14-82.** Fax 281/51-14-78. 39 units. A/C TV TEL. 15,000$ ($84) double; from 17,000$ ($95.20) suite. Rates include breakfast. AE, DC, MC, V. Free parking.

This is the best hotel in town (which isn't saying a lot), installed in a mansion classified as a national historic monument. The core was built in 1916, and after falling into disrepair, the hotel was renovated in 1992. Close to the river and the Spanish border, this is an ideal base for exploring the town, Santo António beach, and the beach attractions of Monte Gordo. Despite the renovations, the three-star hotel retains an aura of Portuguese tradition. Tiles line some walls. The small to midsize guest rooms are traditional and old-fashioned in decor, but have modern amenities, such as satellite color TVs and air-conditioning. Breakfast is the only meal served, but there's a cozy bar.

MONTE GORDO

Casablanca Inn. Rua 7, Monte Gordo, 8900 Vila Real de Santo António. ☎ **281/51-14-44.** Fax 281/51-19-99. 42 units. A/C TEL. 16,000$–18,500$ ($89.60–$103.60) double. Rates include breakfast. AE, DC, MC, V. Limited free parking on street.

Casablanca Inn is not directly on the beach, but its location on a flower-dotted downtown park makes up for it. The owner designed it to look like something you might find in a wealthy part of Morocco. There's a lush flower garden and a series of recessed arched balconies, and the design might be suitable for an updated version of *Casablanca*—in fact, the lobby bar is called Rick's and is covered with movie photos. Each midsize guest room contains a terrace and a firm mattress.

At night the bar is popular with younger people, especially on Tuesday, Friday, and Saturday, when live music begins at 10:30pm. The bar's cafe terrace serves simple lunches daily from 11am to 2pm and drinks daily from 5:30pm to 1am. Live organ music is part of the weekly entertainment. The beach is about a 10-minute stroll away.

Hotel Alcázar. Rua de Ceuta, Monte Gordo, 8900 Vila Real de Santo António. ☎ **281/51-01-40.** Fax 281/51-01-49. 97 units. 22,000$ ($123.20) double; 24,000$–29,000$ ($134.40–$162.40) suite. Rates include breakfast. AE, DC, MC, V.

Hotel Alcázar is the best in town, but don't get your hopes up too high. Curved expanses of white balconies punctuate its palm-fringed brick facade. A free-form pool is built on terraces into the retaining walls that shelter it from the wind and extend the high season far into autumn. The vaguely Arab-style interior design incorporates many arches and vaults, which create niches that are imaginatively lit at night. Each rather austere midsize room contains its own sun terrace. Beds, usually twins, are excellent. Laundry, baby-sitting, and room service are provided.

Under the restaurant's soaring ceiling, a polite staff serves formal but rather standard meals in a modern setting. Entertainment is presented at various times throughout the week. The hotel has a disco in the basement. One of the sunken living rooms off the main lobby shows recently released video movies. Near the bar, there's live music from 6pm to midnight.

Hotel dos Navegadores. Monte Gordo, 8900 Vila Real de Santo António. ☎ **281/51-08-60.** Fax 281/51-08-79. 431 units A/C TEL. 13,000$–26,000$ ($72.80–$145.60) double; 32,250$–50,000$ ($180.60–$280) suite. Rates include breakfast. AE, DC, MC, V. Free parking.

The sign in front of this large hotel is so discreet that you might mistake it for an apartment house. The establishment is popular with vacationing Portuguese and British families, who congregate under the dome covering the atrium's swimming pool, near the reception desk. You'll find a bar that serves fruit-laden drinks, and semi-tropical plants throughout the public rooms. About three-quarters of the guest rooms have private balconies. The hotel recently added 80 rooms. It remains a group tour favorite. Rooms are comfortable but standard, without any flair. The beach is a 5-minute walk away. There's an array of dull boutiques in a corridor near the pool, along with a hairdresser and a coffee shop. The hotel restaurant, open for dinner only, serves basic Portuguese and international dishes. There's a children's center for those ages 3 to 12. Baby-sitting and laundry service are provided.

Hotel Vasco da Gama. Av. Infante Dom Henríque, Monte Gordo, 8900 Vila Real de Santo António. ☎ **281/51-09-01.** Fax 281/51-09-01. E-mail: vagama@mail.telepac.pt. 172 units. A/C TV TEL. 11,500$–13,000$ ($64.40–$72.80) double; 13,500$–26,000$ ($75.60–$145.60) suite. Rates include breakfast. AE, DC, MC, V. Free parking.

The entrepreneurs here know what their northern guests seek—lots of sunbathing and swimming. Although the hotel sits on a long, wide sandy beach, it also offers an Olympic-size pool with a high-dive board and nearly an acre of flagstone sun terrace. All the Spartan, rather small guest rooms are furnished conservatively and have firm mattresses. Glass doors open onto balconies.

The sky-high oceanfront dining room had additional tables on the mezzanine, and there are several well-furnished lounges and two bars. Folk exhibitions are staged on

Monday and Saturday; there's fado music on Tuesday and Friday; and Monday and Thursday feature live piano music. Laundry service, baby-sitting, and room service are provided.

WHERE TO DINE

Edmundo. Av. da República 55. ☎ **281/54-46-89.** Reservations recommended. Main courses 1,500$–2,800$ ($8.40–$15.70). AE, DC, MC, V. Mon–Sat noon–3pm; daily 7–10pm. PORTUGUESE.

One of the most popular restaurants in Vila Real, Edmundo overlooks the river and Spain across the water—try to get a sidewalk table. It's a longtime favorite with Spaniards who visit the Algarve for the day. The people who run this place are friendly and justifiably proud of their local cuisine, especially fresh fish. You might begin with shrimp cocktail, then follow with fried sole, crayfish, or delightful sautéed red mullet. Meat dishes such as lamb cutlets and veal fillet are also available.

9

Alentejo & Ribatejo

The adjoining provinces of Alentejo and Ribatejo constitute the heartland of Portugal. Ribatejo is a land of bull-breeding pastures, Alentejo a plain of fire and ice.

Ribatejo is river country; the Tagus, coming from Spain, overflows its banks in winter. The region is famed for bluegrass, Arabian horses, and black bulls. Its most striking feature, however, is human: *campinos,* the region's sturdy horsemen. They harness the Arabian pride of their horses and discover the intangible quality of bravery in the bulls. Whether visiting the château of the Templars, which rises smack in the middle of the Tagus at Almourol, or attending an exciting *festa brava,* when horses and bulls rumble through the streets of Vila Franca de Xira, you'll marvel at the passion of the people. Ribatejo's *fadistas* have long been noted for their remarkable intensity.

The cork-producing plains of Alentejo (which means "beyond the Tagus") make up the largest province in Portugal. It's so large that the government has divided it into the northern Alto Alentejo (the capital of which is **Évora**) and southern Baixo Alentejo (whose capital is **Beja**).

Locals in Alentejo insulate themselves in tiny-windowed, white-washed houses—warm in the cold winters and cool during the scorching summers. This is the least populated of Portuguese provinces, with seemingly endless fields of wheat. It's the world's largest producer of cork, whose trees can be stripped only once every 9 years.

In winter the men make a dramatic sight, outfitted in characteristic long brown coats with two short-tiered capes, often with red-fox collars. The women are more colorful, especially when they're working in the rice paddies or wheat fields. Their short skirts and patterned undergarments allow them to wade barefooted into the paddies. On top of knitted cowls, with mere slits for the eyes, women wear brimmed felt hats usually studded with flowers.

Although dusty Alentejo is mostly a region of inland plains, it also has an Atlantic coast. It stretches from the mouth of the Sado River all the way to the border of the Algarve, just south of Zambujeira do Mar Carvalhal. This stretch of beach is the least crowded and least developed in Portugal. Towering rock cliffs punctuate much of the coastline south of Lisbon, interrupted by the occasional sandy cove and tranquil bay. Regrettably, there isn't much protection from the often-fierce

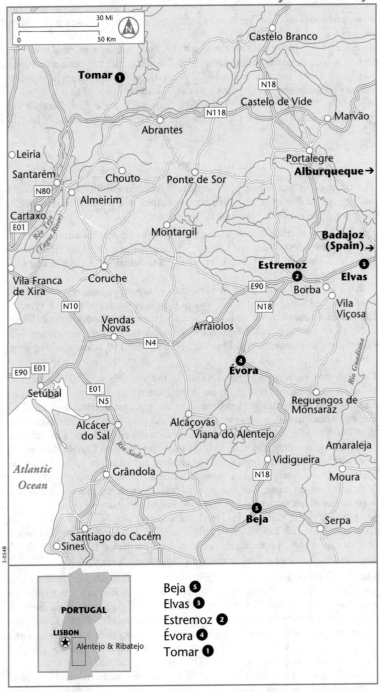

Castelo Branco

Tomar ❶

N18

Castelo de Vide

N118

Abrantes

Marvão

Leiria

Santarém

Portalegre

Alburqueque →

Chouto

Ponte de Sor

N80

Almeirim

Cartaxo

E01

Rio Tejo (Tagus River)

Montargil

Badajoz (Spain) →

Estremoz ❷

❸

Vila Franca de Xira

Coruche

E90

Borba

Elvas

N18

Vila Viçosa

N10

Vendas Novas

Arraiolos

N4

Évora ❹

E90 E01

Setúbal

E01

N5

Reguengos de Monsaraz

Alcácer do Sal

Alcáçovas

Viana do Alentejo

Amaraleja

Rio Sado

Grândola

Vidigueira

Moura

N18

Atlantic Ocean

Beja ❺

Serpa

3-0548

Santiago do Cacém

Sines

PORTUGAL

LISBON ★

Alentejo & Ribatejo

Rio Guadiana

waves and winds that rush in from the Atlantic; the waters are generally too chilly for most tastes.

Driving is the best way to see the region, because there are numerous towns to see and excursions to take from the major cities. There is public transportation, but often you'll have a long, tiresome wait between connections. Both provinces lie virtually on Lisbon's doorstep—in fact, on their edges are suburbs of the capital.

If you've just explored the Algarve (see chapter 8), you'll find Alentejo within striking distance. The best route to take into Alentejo from the south is IP-1 from Albufeira.

Exploring the Region by Car

This driving tour cuts through the provinces of Alentejo and Ribatejo. It will take you through one of Portugal's most dramatic landscapes, and some of the hottest, driest, and least densely populated regions in the country.

Day 1 In the north of Lisbon, get on the A1 toll route, near the airport. Turn off at the Vila Franca de Xira exit and take the bridge over the Tagus. Take N10 6 miles to Porto Alto. Then get on N118 heading northeast to Santarém, the administrative capital of Ribatejo.

You'll arrive at the little town of **Almeirim,** southwest of Santarém. Almeirim was once a favorite haunt of Portuguese royalty. Continue north along N118 11 miles to **Chamusca.** In the old town are houses typical of the regional architecture of Ribatejo.

North of the town, N118 becomes a secondary road. At the junction of N243, follow signs to **Tomar** (the road becomes N365 and N110 before reaching Tomar), site of your first overnight stay.

Day 2 After viewing the sights of Tomar in the morning, take N110 south for 4½ miles, turning left onto N358 and going through interesting countryside until you reach **Castelo de Bode,** Portugal's largest dam. Continue to Constância and hook up with N3 leading to **Abrantes,** 10 miles away. Consider a visit to its fortress and small museum in the Church of Santa Maria, already ancient when it was rebuilt in the 15th century.

From Abrantes, continue east along N118. Follow signs to **Castelo de Vide,** a spa town on the slopes of the Serra de São Mamede at an altitude of 1,800 feet. Inside its walls stand whitewashed houses, some on squares that have changed little since the 15th and 16th centuries. The Judiaria, or Jewish quarter, is a sector of narrow alleyways and small houses, with the richest collection of ogival doors in Portugal. You may want to spend the night at the **Hotel Sol e Serra,** estrada de São Vicente, 7320 Castelo de Vide (☎ **245/90-13-01**). Built in 1983, it offers 50 reasonably comfortable rooms, many with private balconies. A double rents for 13,500$ ($75.60). You can also dine here on regional specialties; a meal runs 2,600$ ($14.55).

Day 3 Continue on N246 for 5½ miles to the turnoff to Marvão. Follow the road another 2½ miles into the mountains until you reach **Marvão,** an ancient walled town near the Spanish border. Try to spend at least 2 hours exploring its old streets. You might stop for coffee at the **Pousada de Santa Maria** (☎ **245/99-32-01**), in the upper levels of town, sandwiched between two impossibly narrow cobblestone streets. If you'd like to spend the night, doubles cost 16,300$ to 24,600$ ($91.30 to $137.75), with meals costing 3,600$ ($20.15).

From Marvão, head south along N359 for 13 miles to **Portalegre.** Portalegre, a busy industrial city, is the capital of Alto Alentejo. Continue south along N18 through the dramatic countryside until you reach **Estremoz,** some 36 miles away. Spend the night in Estremoz.

Day 4   Take IP-7 east for 9 miles, and turn right onto N255. In **Vila Viçosa,** the seat of the dukes of Bragança, you can visit the Paço Ducal (Ducal Palace) in the morning. Retrace your steps along N255 northwest, paying a brief visit to **Borba,** the town of marble. From Borba, get on N4 (E90) heading east toward Badajoz in Spain, but stop at **Elvas** for lunch. After lunch, head back along N4 (toward Estremoz). Go southwest along N18 for 28½ miles to **Évora,** which for many will be the highlight of the driving tour. Spend the night here.

Day 5   After exploring the sights of Évora in the morning, head southeast (and at one point due south) along N18 to **Beja,** the capital of Baixo Alentejo.

1 Tomar

40 miles N of Santarém, 85 miles NE of Lisbon

Divided by the Nabão River, historic Tomar was bound to the fate of the notorious quasi-religious order of the Knights Templar. In the 12th century the powerful, wealthy monks established the beginnings of the Convento de Cristo on a tree-studded hill overlooking the town. Originally a monastery, it evolved into a kind of grand headquarters for the Templars. The knights, who swore a vow of chastity, had fought ferociously at Santarém against the Moors. As their military might grew, they built a massive walled castle at Tomar in 1160. The ruins—primarily the walls—can be seen today.

By 1314 the Templars had amassed both great riches and many enemies; the pope was urged to suppress their power. King Dinis allowed them to regroup their forces under the new aegis of the Order of Christ. Henry the Navigator became the most famous of the grand masters, using much of their money to subsidize his explorations.

ESSENTIALS
ARRIVING

BY TRAIN   The **train station** is on avenida Combatentes da Grande Guerra (☎ **249/31-28-15**), at the southern edge of town. Twelve trains arrive daily from Lisbon; the trip takes 2 hours and costs 970$ ($5.45) one way. From Porto, five trains daily make the 4-hour trip, which costs 1,500$ ($8.40) one way.

BY BUS   The **bus station** is on avenida Combatentes da Grande Guerra (☎ **249/31-27-38**), next to the train station. Six buses a day arrive from Lisbon. The 2-hour trip costs 1,500$ ($8.40) one way.

BY CAR   From Santarém, continue northeast along Route 3, then cut east at the junction of N110. When you reach Route 110, head north. To reach Santarém from Lisbon, go north on E1.

VISITOR INFORMATION

The **Tomar Tourist Office** is on avenida Dr. Cândido Madureira (☎ **249/32-24-27**).

WHAT TO SEE & DO IN TOMAR
EXPLORING THE TOWN

✪ **Convento da Ordem de Cristo.** Atop a hill overlooking the old town. ☎ **249/31-34-81.** Admission 400$ ($2.25), free for children under 15. Daily Apr–Sept 9am–6pm; Oct–Mar 9:15am–12:30pm and 2–5pm.

From its inception in 1160, the Convent of the Order of Christ monastery experienced 5 centuries of inspired builders, including Manuel I (the Fortunate). It also fell victim to destroyers, notably in 1810, when Napoléon's overzealous troops turned it into a barracks. What remains on the top of the hill is one of Portugal's most brilliant architectural accomplishments.

The portal of the Templars Church, in the Manueline style, depicts everything from leaves to chubby cherubs. Inside is an octagonal church with eight columns, said to have been modeled after the Temple of the Holy Sepulchre at Jerusalem. The mosque-like effect links Christian and Muslim cultures, as in the Mezquita in Córdoba, Spain. The author Howard La Fay called it "a muted echo of Byzantium in scarlet and dull gold." The damage the French troops inflicted is much in evidence. On the other side, the church is in the Manueline style with rosettes. Throughout, you'll see the Templars insignia.

The monastery's eight cloisters embrace a variety of styles. The most notable, a two-tiered structure dating from the 12th century, exhibits perfect symmetry, the almost severe academic use of the classical form that distinguishes the Palladian school. A guide will also take you on a brief tour of a dormitory where the monks lived in austere cells.

The monastery possesses some of the greatest Manueline stonework in Portugal. A fine example is the grotesque west window of the chapter house. At first the forms emanating from the window may confuse you, but closer inspection reveals a meticulous symbolic and literal depiction of Portugal's sea lore and power. Knots and ropes, mariners and the tools of their craft, silken sails wafting in stone and re-created coral seascapes—all are delicately interwoven in this chef d'oeuvre of the whole movement.

Capela de Nossa Senhora da Conceição. Between the old town and the Convento da Ordem de Cristo. ☎ **249/31-34-81.** Free admission. Daily 10:30am–7pm.

On the way up the hill to see the monastery, you can stop off at this chapel, crowned by small cupolas and jutting out over the town. Reached through an avenue of trees, it was built in the Renaissance style in the mid–16th century. The interior is a forest of white Corinthian pillars.

Igreja de São João Baptista. Praça da República. ☎ **249/31-26-11.** Free admission. Daily 8am–noon and 3:30–7pm.

In the heart of town is this 15th-century church, built by Manuel I. It contains black-and-white diamond mosaics and a white-and-gold baroque altar; a chapel to the right is faced with antique tiles. In and around the church are the narrow cobblestone streets of Tomar, where shops sell dried codfish and wrought-iron balconies are hung with birdcages and flowerpots.

Museu Luso-Hebraico. Rua Dr. Joaquim Jaquinto 73. ☎ **249/32-26-02.** Free admission; donations accepted. Daily 10am–1pm.

This Portuguese-Hebrew museum lies in the heart of the old Jewish ghetto. The building was the Sinogoga de Tomar—the oldest Jewish house of worship in Portugal, dating from the mid-1400s. A Jewish community worshipped here until 1496, when the Catholic hierarchy ordered its members to convert or get out of town. In time, the synagogue assumed many roles: a Christian chapel, a prison, a warehouse, even a hayloft. Today it enjoys national monument status. Samuel Schwartz, a German who devoted part of his life to restoring it, bought the building in 1923. He donated it to the Portuguese state in 1939. In return, Schwartz and his wife were awarded citizenship and protection during World War II. The museum exhibits many 15th-century tombs, with Hebrew inscriptions, along with Jewish artifacts donated from around the globe. A recent excavation unearthed a *mikvah,* or ritual purification bath.

SHOPPING

Shopkeepers in Tomar work hard to acquire premises on the town's main shopping thoroughfare, **rua Serpa Pinto,** an avenue known locally as the "Corre Doura." You'll find lots of outlets for folklore, pottery, copperware, and wrought iron. Two of the best are **Artlandica,** Convento de São Francisco, rua de São Francisco (☎ 249/32-33-55), and **Região Arte,** avenida Cândido Madureira (☎ 249/32-24-27), a recently established competitor adjacent to the tourist office that stocks hundreds of examples of rustic and charming folkloric art.

WHERE TO STAY

Hotel dos Templários. Largo Cândido dos Reis 1, 2300 Tomar. ☎ **249/32-17-30.** Fax 249/32-21-91. 177 units. A/C TV TEL. 18,100$ ($101.35) double; 29,000$ ($162.40) suite. Rates include breakfast. Children under 8 50% discount in parents' room. AE, DC, MC, V. Free parking.

This large four-star hotel on the banks of the Rio Nabão seems incongruous in such a small town—it was expanded in 1994 to make it the largest hotel in the district. Five local businessmen created the hotel in 1967, but they would hardly recognize the place today. The midsize guest rooms, although ordinary, are quite agreeable, especially those in the new wing. Many open onto views of the Convent of Christ. All are well furnished and equipped, with firm mattresses on good beds. The public areas, including the lounges and the terrace-view dining room, are spacious. The hotel offers room service, laundry, a barbershop, a beauty parlor, and baby-sitting. It has wide sun terraces, indoor and outdoor pools, a tennis court, and a greenhouse.

Guests can have breakfast in their rooms or in a sunny salon overlooking the river. If you're passing through, you can stop in for a table d'hôte luncheon or dinner for 4,850$ ($27.15). Meals are served daily from 1 to 2:30pm and 8 to 9:30pm.

Hotel Residencial Trovador. Rua 10 d'Agosto, 1385 Tomar. ☎ **249/32-25-67.** Fax 249/32-21-94. 30 units. A/C TV TEL. 7,500$–9,000$ ($42–$50.40) double. Rates include breakfast. AE, DC, MC, V. Free parking.

An inspection of the guest rooms reveals the value of a stopover here. Rooms are well scrubbed and comfortable, with conservatively patterned wallpaper and good beds. Built in 1982 by the polite family that still owns it today, the three-floor hotel contains a basement bar that plays disco music. Breakfast is the only meal served. The hotel is close to the bus station and the commercial center of town, in a drab neighborhood of apartment buildings.

A PLACE TO STAY & DINE NEARBY

✪ **Pousada de São Pedro.** Castelo de Bode, 2300 Tomar. ☎ **249/38-11-75.** Fax 249/38-11-76. www.pousadas.pt. E-mail: enatur@mail.telepac.pt. 25 units. A/C MINIBAR TV TEL. 19,500$–24,600$ ($109.20–$137.75) double; 25,000$–35,000$ ($140–$196) suite. Rates include continental breakfast. AE, DC, MC, V. Free parking.

When it was built in the 1950s, this pousada 9 miles southeast of Tomar was used to house teams of engineers working on the nearby dam at Castelo de Bode. After the dam was completed in 1970, the government converted it into one of the country's most unusual pousadas. The flagstone-covered terrace in back affords a close-up view of Portugal's version of Hoover Dam. It curves gracefully against a wall of water, upon which local residents sail, swim, and sun themselves.

The pousada has a scattering of Portuguese antiques, some of them ecclesiastical, in its stone-trimmed hallways. The tidy, unpretentious rooms are small and have good beds. Following a major fire in the early 1990s, a new annex added seven units. The public rooms are more alluring than the guest rooms.

Travel Secrets of the Portuguese Plains

Certain towns in the region—such as Évora—are on the main tourist circuit, but both Alentejo and Ribatejo abound in small towns and villages intriguing to the traveler with the time and desire to seek them out. Our favorites:

SERPA   Still languishing in the Middle Ages, Serpa is a walled town with defensive towers. It was incorporated into the kingdom of Portugal in 1295, after having belonged to the Infante of Serpa, Dom Fernando, brother of Dom Sancho II. Overlooking the vast Alentejo plain, Serpa is a town of narrow streets and latticed windows, famous for the cheese that bears its name, for pork sausage, and for sweets. Silvery olive trees surround the approaches to the town, and the whiteness of the buildings contrasts with the red-brown of the plains. The wild beauties of the river Guadiana, endless fields of grain, and cork-oak groves mark the landscape. In the town, you can see unique painted furniture, an archaeological museum, and several ancient churches. Serpa has become a lunch stop or rest stop for travelers on the way to and from Spain; many motorists spend the night at the hilltop pousada.

MONSARAZ   The old fortified town of Monsaraz lies 32 miles east of Évora en route to Spain. It's a village of antique whitewashed houses, with cobblestone lanes and many reminders of the Moors who held out here until they were conquered in 1166. Some of the women still wear traditional garb: men's hats on shawl-covered heads, and men's pants under their skirts. The custom definitely derives from a need for protection from the sun. Monsaraz overlooks the Guadiana Valley, which forms the border between Spain and Portugal.

   The walled town can easily be visited from Évora in an afternoon. As you scale the ramparts, you're rewarded with a view over what looks like a cross between a bullring and a Greek theater. The highlight of a visit is the main street, **rua**

The breezy bar near the terrace is decorated like a private living room, with well-upholstered sofas and a fireplace. The pousada serves some of the best food in the area, both international and regional specialties. Food service is daily from 12:30 to 3pm and 7:30 to 10pm. The daily menu might include such dishes as pork fillets with apples or flambéed beef fillets with peaches. The average price is 3,600$ ($20.15).

WHERE TO DINE

Bella Vista. Rua Marquês de Pombal and rua Fonte do Choupo. ☎ **249/31-28-70.** Reservations recommended. Main courses 1,000$–2,200$ ($5.60–$12.30); fixed-price menu 1,800$ ($10.10). No credit cards. Mon and Wed–Sun noon–3pm; Wed–Sun 7–9:30pm. Closed Nov. PORTUGUESE.

This restaurant, in a 150-year-old stone-sided house in the town center, has belonged to at least three generations of the Sousa family. The patriarch, Eugenio, founded it in 1975 and still operates from a perch in its busy kitchens. From your table you're likely to have a pleasant view over the old town and a small canal. There's a rustic, cozy indoor dining area, plus seating on an outdoor terrace ringed with flowering shrubs. Menu items are simple but plentiful, and prices are affordable. The cook usually makes a fresh pot of *caldo verde* every day, and shellfish soup is generally available. Main courses include several variations of Portuguese codfish, savory roast goat, grilled

Direita. It contains the most distinguished architecture, wrought-iron grilles, balconies, and outside staircases.

BORBA   On the way to Borba, you'll pass quarries filled with black, white, and multicolored deposits. In the village, marble reigns. Many cottages have marble door trimmings and facings, and the women kneel to scrub their doorways, a source of special pride. On **rua São Bartolomeu** sits a church dedicated to São Bartolomeu. It displays a groined ceiling; walls lined with blue, white, and gold *azulejos* (decorative tiles); and an altar in black-and-white marble. The richly decorated ceiling is painted with four major medallions. As Portuguese churches go, this one isn't remarkable. But there are eight nearby antiques shops (amazing for such a small town) filled with interesting items. Borba is also a big wine center, and you may want to sample the local brew at a cafe, or perhaps at the pousada at Elvas.

MARVÃO   This ancient walled hill town, close to Castelo de Vide, is well-preserved and is visited chiefly for its spectacular views. Just under 4 miles from the Spanish frontier, the once-fortified medieval stronghold retains a rich flavor of the Middle Ages. Those with limited time who can explore only one border town in Portugal should make it this one—it's that panoramic. You get to Marvão by following a road around the promontory on which the little town stands, past the Church of Our Lady of the Star, the curtain walls, watchtowers, and parapets. Arcaded passageways, balconied houses with wrought-iron grillwork and Manueline windows, and a number of churches can be seen along the hilly streets. The castle, built in the 13th century, stands at the western part of the rocky outcropping. From the parapet, you'll have a panoramic view of the surrounding country—all the way to the Spanish mountains in the east, and a vast sweep of Portuguese mountain ranges.

filet of sole, aromatic roast pork, and several versions of succulent chicken, including one with curry. Wines are unpretentious, plentiful, and inexpensive.

TOMAR AFTER DARK

Despite Tomar's small size and emphasis on folklore, there are lots of outlets for drinking and bar-hopping with gregarious locals. You'll find tascas and bars scattered throughout the town's historic core. Two of the most charming and convivial are the **Bar Akiopukas,** rua de São João (no phone), and the **Quinta Bar,** Quinta do Falcão 26 (☎ **249/38-17-67**). People between the ages of 20 and 45 hang out and listen to live music. Also worth ducking into, for at least one drink, is **Casablanca,** rua de São João (no phone), a mellow, quiet hangout with, as you might have guessed, a Sahara-Moorish theme.

2 Estremoz

28½ miles NE of Évora, 108 miles E of Lisbon, 7 miles W of Borba

Rising from the plain like a pyramid of salt set out to dry in the sun, fortified Estremoz is in the center of the marble-quarry region of Alentejo. Cottages and mansions alike use the abundant marble in their construction and trim.

ESSENTIALS
ARRIVING

There is no train service to Estremoz.

BY BUS   The **bus station** is at Rossio Marquês de Pombal (☎ **268/32-22-82**). Six buses arrive daily from Évora, 1 hour away; five buses a day arrive from Portalegre, 1½ hours away.

BY CAR   From Évora (see below), head northeast along Route 18.

VISITOR INFORMATION

The **Estremoz Tourist Office** is at Rossio Marquês de Pombal (☎ **268/33-35-41**).

WHAT TO SEE & DO IN ESTREMOZ
EXPLORING THE TOWN

With enough promenading soldiers to man a garrison, the open quadrangle in the center of the Lower Town is called the **Rossio Marquês de Pombal.** The **Town Hall,** with its twin bell towers, opens onto this square. It has a grand stairway whose walls are lined with antique blue-and-white tiles, depicting hunting, pastoral, and historical scenes.

In the 16th-century **Igreja de Santa Maria** (Church of St. Mary), you'll see pictures by Portuguese primitive painters. The church formed part of the ancient fortress. It is open Tuesday to Sunday 9:30am to noon and 3 to 5pm. Admission is free.

Another church worth a stop is about a mile south of the town on the road to Bencatel. The **Igreja de Nossa Senhora dos Mártires** (Church of Our Lady of the Martyrs) has beautiful tiles and an entrance marked by a Manueline arch. Dating from 1844, the church has a nave chevet after the French Gothic style of architecture.

Castelo da Rainha Santa Isabel. Largo de Dom Dinis. No phone.

From the ramparts of the Castle of Queen Saint Isabel, which dates from the 13th-century reign of Dinis, the plains of Alentejo spread out before you. Although one 75-year-old British lady reportedly walked it, the route to the top is best covered by car. Drive to the top of the Upper Town and stop on largo de Dom Dinis. The stones of the castle, the cradle of the town's past, were decaying so badly that the city leaders pressed for its restoration in 1970. It was turned into a luxurious pousada (see "Where to Stay," below), the best place to stay or dine.

The castle's imposing keep, attached to a palace, dominates the central plaza. Dinis's wife, Isabella, died in the castle and was unofficially proclaimed a saint by her local followers; during her reign, however, one of her detractors wrote, "Poor Dinis!" Also opening onto the marble-and-stone-paved largo are two modest chapels and a church. As in medieval days, soldiers still walk the ramparts, guarding the fortress.

Museu Rural da Casa do Povo de Santa Maria de Estremoz. Rossio Marquês de Pombal. ☎ **268/33-35-41.** Admission 130$ (75¢), free for children under 12. Tues–Sun 9–11:45am and 2–6pm.

The Rural Museum, open for guided tours, displays the life of people of the Alentejo through models and crafts. The 18th-century-style building is part of the property of the Convento das Maltezas de São João da Penitência, today the Misericórdia (national charity organization).

SHOPPING

The town's most famous product is a type of traditional earthenware **water jug.** Known as a *moringue,* it has two spouts, one handle, and sometimes a decorative crest that's stamped into the wet clay before it's fired. At least half a dozen street merchants sell the jugs in the town's main square, Rossio Marquês de Pombal. Stylish reminders of Portugal's agrarian past, they're associated with love and marriage (housewives traditionally carried water in them to workers in the fields). Some are simple, others are glazed in bright colors.

If you're looking for a traditional shop that carries another of the town's specialties, head for **Artesanato,** avenida de São António (no phone), which stocks hundreds of terra-cotta figurines. Each represents an archetype from the Alentejo workforce, and the designs include artfully naïve depictions of washerwomen, sausage makers, carpenters, priests, and broom makers. Artesanato also sells some of the region's other handcrafts, including metalwork, wood carvings, and weavings.

WHERE TO STAY
EXPENSIVE

✪ **Pousada da Rainha Santa Isabel.** Largo de Dom Dinis, 7100 Estremoz. ☎ **268/ 33-20-75.** Fax 268/33-20-79. www.pousadas.pt. 33 units. A/C MINIBAR TV TEL. 26,500$–35,000$ ($148.40–$196) double; from 42,500$–52,300$ ($238–$292.90) suite. Rates include continental breakfast. AE, DC, MC, V. Free parking.

This is one of the best of the government-owned tourist inns; reserve months in advance. In the old castle dominating the town and overlooking the battlements and the Estremoz plain, it's a deluxe establishment. Gold leaf, marble, velvet, and satin mingle with 17th- and 18th-century reproductions in the guest rooms and corridors. The accommodations range from former monks' cells to sumptuous suites with canopied beds. Ten excellent rooms are in a modern addition. Dom Manuel received Vasco da Gama in the salon of this castle before the explorer left for India. In 1698 a terrible explosion and fire destroyed the royal residence, which then underwent ostentatious alterations. It became an armory, then a barracks, then an industrial school. Its transformation into a castle pousada has restored it as a historic monument. Comfort and style fit delightfully in this historical framework.

Dining: The elegant vaulted dining room offers an international and regional menu. Try, for example, venison with wild mushrooms or vegetable-stuffed partridge. If it's featured, you might want to be daring and order the grilled wild boar with hot-pepper sauce. A meal costs 4,500$ to 4,800$ ($25.20 to $26.90). Food is served daily from 12:30 to 3pm and 7:30 to 10pm.

Amenities: 24-hour room service, laundry, outdoor pool.

INEXPENSIVE

Residência Carvalho. Largo da República 27, 7100 Estremoz. ☎ **268/33-93-70.** 18 units. 3,500$ ($19.60) double without bathroom, 5,500$ ($30.80) double with bathroom. Rates include continental breakfast. No credit cards.

Residência Carvalho is clean, simple, and inexpensive—just what you may be looking for if the pousada is full and you're tired. Rooms are small but decently furnished, with good beds and tidy maintenance. Ten units have telephones; breakfast is the only meal served. No English is spoken.

WHERE TO DINE

Águias d'Ouro. Rossio Marquês de Pombal 27. ☎ **268/33-33-26.** Reservations required. Main courses 1,400$–2,600$ ($7.85–$14.55). AE, DC, MC, V. Daily noon–3pm and 7–11pm. PORTUGUESE.

Águias d'Ouro offers good food and a pleasant ambience, but it's not as fine as dining at the pousada. The "Golden Eagle" faces the largest square in Estremoz; its mosaic-and-marble balconied facade suggests a duke's palace. On the second floor are several connecting dining rooms with heavy black-leather armchairs and white-draped tables. Your meal begins with a dish of homemade pâté with rye bread. Other offerings include a large bowl of spinach-and-bean soup with crispy croutons, and main dishes like a delectable stuffed partridge, savory pork and clams, and herb-flavored lamb. Chocolate mousse is the featured dessert.

ESTREMOZ AFTER DARK

There aren't any noteworthy discos in Estremoz, so local residents seek out centrally located pubs. Foremost among these is **Ze's Pub,** largo General Graça 78 (☎ **268/32-31-39**). Patrons aged 20 to 50 mingle gracefully over pints of beer, wine, and whisky. A slightly younger crowd congregates at the **Reguengo Bar,** rua Serpa Pinto 128 (☎ **268/33-33-78**), usually to the sound of recorded hits from throughout Europe and the Americas.

On weekends, if you're interested in hearing the sounds of fado, head for **Estamine,** rua Brito Capelo 29 (☎ **068/32-26-93**). On Friday and Saturday beginning around 11pm, fado divas from the surrounding hills and valleys usually appear to pull the audience's heartstrings. After the music begins, there's a cover charge of 1,500$ ($8.40), which includes the first drink. No food is served.

3 Elvas

7 miles W of Badajoz, Spain, 138 miles E of Lisbon

The "city of plums," Elvas is characterized by narrow cobblestone streets (pedestrians have to duck into doorways to allow automobiles to inch by) and crenellated fortifications. The Moors held the town until 1226. Later, Spanish troops frequently assaulted and besieged it. It finally fell in the 1801 War of the Oranges, which ended with a peace treaty signed at Badajoz. Elvas remained part of Portugal, but its neighbor, Olivença, became Spanish. The Elvas ramparts are an outstanding example of 17th-century fortifications, with gates, curtain walls, moats, bastions, and sloping banks (*glacis*) around them.

Lining the steep, hilly streets are tightly packed gold- and oyster-colored cottages with tile roofs. Many of the house doors are just 5 feet high. In the tiny windows are numerous canary cages and flowering geraniums. The four-tier Aqueduto da Amoreira, built between 1498 and 1622, transports water into Elvas from about 5 miles southwest of the town.

ESSENTIALS
ARRIVING

BY TRAIN   The **train station** is at Fontainhas (☎ **068/62-28-16**), 2 miles north of the city. Local buses connect the station to praça da República, in the center. Four trains a day make the 5½-hour trip from Lisbon. The one-way fare is 1,650$ ($9.25). From Évora, there's one train a day. It takes 3 hours and costs 1,100$ ($6.15) one way. From Badajoz, Spain, there are three trains per day. The trip takes 1 hour, and the fare is 620$ ($3.45) one way.

BY BUS   The **bus station** is at praça da República (☎ **268/62-87-50**). Four buses per day make the 4-hour trip from Lisbon. The one-way fare is 1,600$ ($8.95). Two buses daily make the 2-hour trip from Évora. The one-way fare is 900$ ($5.05). From Badajoz, there are frequent buses throughout the day. The ride lasts 15 minutes.

BY CAR   From Estremoz (see the preceding section), continue east toward Spain along Route 4.

Visitor Information

The **Elvas Tourist Office** is on praça da República (☎ **268/62-22-36**).

EXPLORING THE TOWN In praça Dom Sancho II, named in honor of the king who reconstructed the town, stands the **Sé** (cathedral). Under a cone-shaped dome, it's a forbidding, fortresslike building decorated with gargoyles, turrets, and a florid Manueline portal. The cathedral opens onto a black-and-white diamond square. It's open daily 9am to 12:30pm and 2 to 5pm. A short walk up the hill to the right of the cathedral leads to **largo de Santa Clara,** a small plaza that holds an odd Manueline pillory, with four wrought-iron dragon heads.

On the south side of largo de Santa Clara is the **Igreja de Nossa Senhora de Consolação** (Church of Our Lady of Consolation), a 16th-century octagonal Renaissance building with a cupola lined in 17th-century *azulejos* (tiles). It's open daily 9am to 12:30pm and 2 to 5pm.

The **castelo** (castle), praça da República, built by the Moors and strengthened by Christian rulers in the 14th and 16th centuries, offers a panoramic view of the town, its fortifications, and the surrounding countryside. It's open daily 9:30am to 1pm and 3 to 6pm (it closes at 5:30pm from October 10 to April).

SHOPPING The abundant folklore of this small town might whet your appetite for souvenirs. Take a stroll along the town's best shopping streets, **rua de Alchemin** and **rua de Olivença.** Rustic artifacts appear on all sides, allowing you to choose your favorites. If you want to target your destinations in advance, consider the handcrafts at **Alchemin,** rua de Alchemin (☎ **268/62-96-99**), or any of the merchandise at the town's leading clothier, **Rente,** rua de Alchemin (☎ **268/62-22-90**).

WHERE TO STAY
Moderate

✪ **Pousada de Santa Luzia**. Largo de Dom Diniz, av. de Badajoz-estrada N4, 7350 Elvas. ☎ **268/62-21-94.** Fax 268/62-21-27. www.pousadas.pt. 25 units. A/C MINIBAR TV TEL. 16,900$–22,500$ ($94.65–$126) double. Rates include breakfast. AE, DC, MC, V. Free parking.

A major link in the government-inn circuit is the Pousada de Santa Luzia, a hacienda-style building just outside the city walls. It sits at the edge of a busy highway (Estrada N4), about a 5-minute walk east of the town center. Fully renovated in 1994, with typical Alentejano hand-painted furniture, it was built in the 1940s as a private hotel (which failed). The bone-white stucco villa faces the fortifications. The ground floor holds a living room, an L-shaped dining salon, and a bar, all opening through thick arches onto a Moorish courtyard with a fountain, a lily pond, and orange trees.

There are some guest rooms on the upper floor, and you can also stay in the nearby annex, a villa with a two-story entrance hall and an ornate staircase. All rooms are comfortable and cozily furnished, with good beds. Laundry service and room service are provided. Because the hotel is small, getting a room without a reservation might be difficult.

The pousada's restaurant is the finest in the area. The menu is extensive. The fish dishes, including grilled red mullet and fresh oysters, are noteworthy. Food is served daily from noon to 4pm and 7:30 to 10:45pm. Meals cost 3,500$ to 4,000$ ($19.60 to $22.40).

Inexpensive

Estalagem Dom Sancho II. Praça da República 20, 7350 Elvas. ☎ **268/62-26-86.** Fax 268/62-47-17. 26 units. TEL. 5,000$–7,000$ ($28–$39.20) double. Rates include breakfast. AE, DC, MC, V. Free parking.

Running the Bulls in Ribatejo

In a land of *campinos* (Ribatejo cowboys, with their traditional stocking caps) and bullfighters, you might assume that bullfighting is all the rage. Regrettably, the great fighting bulls and leading matadors head for Lisbon, where the big money is. Bullfighting is only an occasional happening in the provinces.

Still, **Vila Franca de Xira,** 20 miles northeast of Lisbon, is known as the "Pamplona of Portugal." Twice a year it stages the frenzied community ordeal of the Colete Encarnado, the running of the bulls. The festival—the name means "Red Waistcoat"—takes place during the first week of July, and the Annual Fair is the first week of October. Bullfights go on at these events. Pasturelands in the countryside around Vila Franca are breeding grounds for the black bulls.

At the festivals, a herd of black bulls, fresh and primed for the rings of Lisbon or Cascais, is let loose in the main street of town. With the smaller side streets heavily barricaded, the *corrida* is ready to begin. When the campinos first turn the bulls loose in the streets, the animals appear bewildered and confused.

The crowds yell and shout, trying to make the massive bulls break rank. When one inevitably does, melees and frantic dashes follow, with occasional displays by young would-be matadors. Their capes are likely to be old pieces of sack cloth or quilts. The bulls are rarely intimidated by those who taunt them. Many a hopeful matador has been pulled by his arms to the safety of a spectator-filled wrought-iron balcony. Others are injured—recruits from Lisbon reinforce the hospital staff. The custom has its detractors, who consider it barbaric, but it's still practiced twice a year.

The pousada is likely to be full, so you might try the Estalagem Dom Sancho II, which sits on the main square. The location is perfect for walking around the village. Some guest rooms open onto the old square, and from your window you can look down on the former town hall and, to the north, the old cathedral. However, the rear rooms are much quieter. The hotel is furnished in period pieces. Guest rooms are small but adequate—nothing very special, although the beds are good. The mood is casual and relaxed. The excellent dining room serves Portuguese specialties every day. There's a solarium, and room service is available.

Hotel Dom Luís. Av. de Badajoz-estrada N4, 7350 Elvas. ☎ **268/62-27-56.** Fax 268/62-07-33. 90 units. A/C TV TEL. 13,000$ ($72.80) double. Rates include breakfast. AE, DC, MC, V. Free parking.

This well-run hotel—the largest in town—offers the best amenities in Elvas. Rooms have modern furnishings, and some are showing wear and tear. Laundry service and room service are offered.

The hotel also has a good air-conditioned restaurant, which offers regional wines and local dishes. Meals are served daily from 12:30 to 3:30pm and 7:30 to 10:30pm. The average price is 2,600$ ($14.55) per person. The restaurant is not an especially glamorous choice, but it is a welcome relief if you're tired and don't want to press on to the border.

WHERE TO DINE

Estalagem Don Quixote. Estrada 4, Pedras Negras. ☎ **268/62-20-14.** Reservations recommended. Main courses 1,000$–5,000$ ($5.60–$28); tourist menu 2,000$ ($11.20). AE, DC, V. Daily noon–4pm and 7pm–midnight. PORTUGUESE/FRENCH.

A more adventurous dining choice than the pousada lies about 1½ miles west of Elvas. The isolated compound is the focus of many a gastronomic pilgrimage. The place is very busy on weekends, especially with Spaniards, who create a holiday feeling with lots of convivial chatter. You can order a drink in the leather-upholstered English-style bar near the entrance, then move on to the dining room, decorated in traditional Iberian style. Rows of fresh fish arranged on ice behind glass grace the entrance to the sprawling dining room. Specialties include shellfish rice, grilled sole, grilled swordfish, roast pork, beefsteak Alentejano, and at least five kinds of shellfish. The fare is interesting and skillfully prepared, although never scaling any gastronomic peaks. Service takes a nosedive when the place is full.

ELVAS AFTER DARK

Don't expect the diversions and distractions of Lisbon—sleepy Elvas simply doesn't have them. Instead, consider a stroll through the town's historic core, looking for likable tascas (bars). Or head about a mile west of town to the **Albergaria Jardim,** estrada do Caia (☎ **268/62-10-50**). Local residents who come to drink and socialize fill the handsome pub. A generally lively place is the **Player Bar,** Barrio de Santa Onofre Alves (☎ **268/62-86-45**).

4 Évora

63 miles SW of Badajoz, Spain, 96 miles E of Lisbon

The capital of Alto Alentejo, Évora, a designated UNESCO World Heritage Site, is a historical curio. Considering its size and location, it's also something of an architectural phenomenon. Its builders freely adapted whatever they desired, from Mudejar to Manueline to Roman to rococo. Évora, once enclosed behind medieval walls, lives up to its reputation as a living museum. Sixteenth- and seventeenth-century houses, many with tile patios, fill nearly every street. Cobblestones, labyrinthine streets, arcades, squares with bubbling fountains, whitewashed houses, and a profuse display of Moorish-inspired arches characterize the town.

Many conquerors passed through Évora, and several left behind architectural remains. The Romans at the time of Julius Caesar knew the town as *Liberalitas Julia.* Its heyday was during the 16th-century reign of João III, when it became the Montmartre of Portugal; avant-garde artists, including the playwright Gil Vicente, congregated under the aegis of royalty.

Évora today is a sleepy provincial capital, perhaps rather self-consciously aware of its attractions. One local historian recommended to an American couple that they see at least 59 monuments. Rest assured that you can capture the essence of the town by seeing only a fraction of that. Évora is a popular day trip from Lisbon, but it's a long trek, and probably not enough time to enjoy the town thoroughly.

ESSENTIALS
ARRIVING

BY TRAIN   The **train station** (☎ **266/70-21-25** for information) lies a mile from the center of town. Five trains per day arrive from Lisbon; the trip takes 3 hours and costs 1,075$ ($6) one way. One train arrives from Faro, in the Algarve; the trip takes 6 hours and costs 1,650$ ($9.25) one way. There are also four trains per day from Beja (see below). The trip takes 1½ hours, and the one-way fare is 720$ ($4.05).

BY BUS   **Rodoviária Nacional,** rua da República (☎ **266/70-21-21**), provides bus service for the area. Three buses a day arrive from Lisbon; the trip takes 2½ hours and costs 1,200$ ($6.70) one way. Three daily buses make the 5-hour trip from Faro, in the Algarve. The cost is 1,570$ ($8.80) one way. Three buses a day connect Beja with Évora; the trip takes 1½ hours and costs 980$ ($5.50) one way.

BY CAR   From Beja (see below), continue north along Route 18.

VISITOR INFORMATION

The Évora **Tourist Information Office** is at praça do Giraldo 71 (☎ **266/70-26-71**).

SPECIAL EVENTS

Évora's major festival is the **Feira de São João,** a folkloric and musical extravaganza. All the handcrafts of the area, including fine ceramics, are on display, and hundreds of people from the Alentejo region come into the city. The event, which takes place over the last 10 days of June, celebrates the arrival of summer. Food stalls sell regional specialties, and regional dances are presented. The tourist office (see "Visitor Information," above) will supply more details.

WHAT TO SEE & DO IN ÉVORA
EXPLORING THE TOWN

✪ **Templo de Diana.** Largo do Conde de Vila Flor. No phone. Free admission. Daily 24 hours.

The major monument in Évora is the Temple of Diana, directly in front of the government-owned pousada (see "Where to Stay," below). Dating from the 1st or 2nd century A.D., it's a light, graceful structure with 14 granite Corinthian columns topped by marble capitals. Although no one can prove that it actually was dedicated to the goddess, that's considered a good guess. The temple withstood the 1755 earthquake, and there's evidence that it was once used as a slaughterhouse. Walk through the garden for a view of the Roman aqueduct and the surrounding countryside.

Sé (Cathedral). Largo Marquês de Mariak (largo de Sé). ☎ **266/75-93-30.** Admission to Cathedral free; to museum 450$ ($2.50) adults, free for children. Tues–Sun 9am–noon and 2–5pm.

The cathedral of Évora was built in the Roman-Gothic style between 1186 and 1204. The bulky structure was notably restored and redesigned over the centuries. Two square towers, both topped by cones, flank the stone facade; one is surrounded by satellite spires. The interior consists of a nave and two aisles. The 18th-century main altar, of pink, black, and white marble, is the finest in town. At the sculptured work *The Lady of Mothers,* young women pray for fertility.

The museum houses treasures from the church, the most notable of which is a 13th-century Virgin carved out of ivory. It opens to reveal a collection of scenes from her life. A reliquary is studded with 1,426 precious stones, including sapphires, rubies, diamonds, and emeralds. The most valuable item is a piece of wood said to have come from the True Cross.

Igreja Real de São Francisco. Rua da República. ☎ **266/70-45-21.** Admission 100$ (55¢). Daily 10am–1pm and 2:30–6pm.

The Church of Saint Francis contains a chapel that's probably unlike any you've seen: The chancel walls and central pillars of the ghoulish 16th-century Chapel of Bones (Capela dos Ossos) are lined with human skulls and other parts of skeletons. Legend has it that the bones came either from soldiers who died in a big battle or from plague victims. Over the door is a sign addressing visitors' own mortality: OUR BONES WHO STAY HERE ARE WAITING FOR YOURS! The church was built in the Gothic style with Manueline influences between 1460 and 1510.

Igreja de Nossa Senhora de Graça. Largo da Graça. Free admission. Tues–Sun 9am–noon and 2–5pm.

The Church of Our Lady of Grace is notable chiefly for its baroque facade, with huge classical nudes over the pillars. Above each group of lazing stone giants is a sphere with a flame—pieces of sculpture often compared to works by Michelangelo. The church was built in Évora's heyday, during the reign of João III. Columns and large stone rosettes flank the central window shaft, and ponderous neoclassic columns support the lower level.

Universidade de Évora. Largo do Colégio. ☎ **266/70-55-72.** Free admission. Mon–Fri 8am–7pm (with permission).

You may want to visit the ancient University of Évora. In 1559, during the town's cultural flowering, the university was constructed and placed under the tutelage of the Jesuits. It flourished until the Jesuit-hating marquês de Pombal closed it in the 18th century. The compound wasn't used as a university again until 1975.

The double-tiered baroque structure surrounds a large quadrangle. Marble pillars support the arches, and brazilwood makes up the ceilings. Blue-and-white tiles line the inner courtyard. Other azulejo representations, depicting women, wild animals, angels, cherubs, and costumed men, contrast with the austere elegance of the classrooms and the elongated refectory.

✪ **Igreja de São João Evangelista.** Largo do Conde de Vila Flor. ☎ **266/70-47-14.** Admission 500$ ($2.80). Tues–Sun 10am–noon and 2–6pm.

The Gothic-Mudejar Church of St. John the Evangelist, facing the Temple of Diana and next door to the government-owned pousada, is connected to the palace built by the dukes of Cadaval. Although one of the undisputed gems of Évora, it's seemingly little visited. It deserves to be better known: It contains a collection of 18th-century tiles, and a guide will show you a macabre sight—an old cistern filled with neatly stacked bones removed from tombs. In the chapel's sacristy are some paintings, including a ghastly rendition of Africans slaughtering a Christian missionary. A curiosity is a painting of a pope that has moving eyes and moving feet. In addition, you can see part of the wall that once encircled Évora.

✪ **Museu de Évora.** Largo do Conde de Vila Flor. ☎ **266/70-26-04.** Admission 400$ ($2.25), free for children under 15. Tues–Sun 10am–noon and 2–5pm.

The Museum of Ancient Art is in the 16th- and 18th-century episcopal palace. Roman, medieval, Manueline, and Luso-Moorish sculptures are on the ground floor. Here you'll see a remnant of a vestal virgin in marble, a 14th-century marble Annunciation, and a Holy Trinity in Anca stone, dating from the 1500s. Of major interest on the floor above is a 16th-century Flemish-school polyptych depicting the life of the Virgin, Flemish panels of an altarpiece on the subject of Christ's Passion, and pictures by Portuguese artists of the 16th and 17th centuries.

SHOPPING

Most of the interesting shops in Évora are on rua do 5 de Outubro, which leads from a point near the cathedral to the perimeter of the historic town. A particularly well-stocked shop is **Baiginho,** rua do 5 de Outubro (☎ **266/70-41-01**). Beyond that, your best bet is wandering and window-shopping in the neighborhood around the cathedral.

WHERE TO STAY
EXPENSIVE

✪ **Pousada dos Lóios.** Largo Conde de Vila Flor, 7000 Évora. ☎ **266/70-40-51.** Fax 266/70-72-48. 32 units. A/C TV TEL. 28,500$–34,000$ ($159.60–$190.40) double; 48,500$ ($271.60) suite. Rates include breakfast. AE, DC, MC, V. Free parking.

In Search of Arraiolos Carpets

Fourteen miles northwest of Évora is the hilltop village of Arraiolos. It's known for its narrow streets and whitewashed houses—and even better known for its intricately designed carpets. The industry developed in the 16th century, when Portugal had links with Persia and India. The carpets, based on old designs from the East, are still made, but aren't mass produced. They are woven in local homes using wool from Alentejo lambs. Showrooms and workshops abound in the heart of the town. The best selections are at **Condestavel,** rua Bombeiros Voluntários 7 (☎ **066/42-356**).

One of the most splendid government-owned tourist inns in Portugal is the Pousada dos Lóios, now under UNESCO protection. It occupies the Lóios Monastery, built in 1485 on the site of the old Évora Castle, which was destroyed during a riot in 1384. A powerful noble, Don Rodrigo Afonso de Melo, founded the monastery and carried on his back two baskets of soil and the first stone for the foundation ceremony. João II, IV, and V visited the monastery. Official Inquisition reports were kept in the chapter room, with 16th-century doorways in Moorish-Portuguese style. After the 1755 earthquake, extensive work was done to repair and preserve the structure. Over the years it was used as a telegraph station, a primary school, an army barracks, and offices. The 1965 opening of the pousada made possible the architectural restoration of the monastery. Its position in the museumlike center of Évora, between the cathedral and the ghostlike Roman Temple of Diana, is unrivaled.

The white-and-gold salon (once a private chapel) boasts an ornate Pompeii-style decor and frescoes and is decorated with antique furnishings, handwoven draperies, crystal chandeliers and sconces, and painted medallion portraits. All the guest rooms are furnished in traditional provincial style, with antique reproductions. As former monks' cells, however, the rooms are rather small. Make sure you duck at the doorway. Ask for a room in the interior.

Dining/Diversions: Like a pilgrim of old, stop for a regional meal of Alto Alentejo. In winter, meals are served in the main dining hall, decorated with heavy chandeliers. In fair weather most guests dine in and around the cloister, under the Manueline fan-vaulted ceiling and an ornate Moorish doorway leading to the chapter house. Meals begin at 4,000$ ($22.40). For your main course, try acorn-sweetened pork cooked with clams in the Alentejo manner. Food is served daily from 12:30 to 2:30pm and 7:30 to 10pm.

Amenities: Room service until midnight, laundry, pool.

INEXPENSIVE

Albergaria do Calvario. Traversa dos Lagares, 3700 Évora. ☎ **266/74-59-30.** Fax 266/74-59-39. www.softline.pt/calvario. 23 units. A/C TV TEL. 12,500$–15,000$ ($70–$84) double; 18,500$ ($103.60) suite. Rates include breakfast. AE, DC, MC, V. Free parking.

A former olive processing plant was renovated and turned into this well-run little hotel in 1998. It's about a 5-minute walk from the historic center. Next to the Convento do Calvario (a convent that's closed to the public), the hotel is attractively furnished, with good beds and tidy appointments, including new private bathrooms. Neoclassic and rustic reproductions of antiques are used extensively. Breakfast is served in your room or on the Esplanade Terraces. There is a TV salon, plus a bar; laundry can be arranged.

Albergaria Vitória. Rua Diana de Lis 5, 7000 Évora. ☎ **266/70-71-74.** Fax 266/70-09-74. 48 units. A/C TV TEL. 11,300$–12,000$ ($63.30–$67.20) double; from 15,500$ ($86.80) suite. Rates include breakfast. AE, DC, MC, V. Limited free parking on street.

In a somewhat inconvenient location near the beltway surrounding the old city, this modern concrete-walled hotel juts above a dusty neighborhood of villas. It's usually reached by taxi. The Albergaria sits on the southeastern edge of the city, about a mile from the cathedral, but can be a handy address in summer when all the central hotels are full. Built in 1985, it contains motel-like bedrooms, with balconies and good beds. The Restaurante Lis serves traditional Portuguese cuisine, specializing in seafood.

Residencial Riviera. Rua do 5 de Outubro 49, 7000 Évora. ☎ **266/70-33-04.** Fax 266/70-04-67. 22 units. A/C TV TEL. 10,500$–15,000$ ($58.80–$84) double. Rates include breakfast. AE, DC, MC, V. Closed Jan–Mar. Limited free parking on street.

Residencial Riviera sits beside the cobblestones of one of the most charming streets in town, about 2 blocks downhill from the cathedral. Designed as a private villa, it retains many handcrafted details from the original building, including stone window frames, ornate iron balustrades, and the blue-and-yellow tiles of its foyer. Its small guest rooms are quite comfortable, with good beds, but not very tastefully decorated.

Residencial Solar Monfalm. Largo da Misericórdia 1, 7000 Évora. ☎ **266/75-00-00.** Fax 266/74-23-67. www.monfalimtur.pt. E-mail: reservas@monfalimtur.pt. 26 units. A/C MINIBAR TV TEL. 12,500$–13,500$ ($70–$75.60) double; 16,000$ ($89.60) suite. Rates include breakfast. AE, MC, V. Free parking.

This is a delightful guest house with a touch of grandeur: A stone staircase leads up to a plant-lined entrance decorated with tiles. The hosts, the Serrabulhos, have improved the building by making the small to midsize guest rooms more comfortable but keeping the original antique atmosphere. The rooms, all in the main building, are well maintained, traditional, and quite pleasant. You can sit on the terrace nursing a drink and peering through the cloisterlike mullioned veranda. There's also a cafe on the ground floor.

WHERE TO DINE

Cozinha de São Humberto. Rua da Moeda 39. ☎ **266/70-42-51.** Reservations required. Main courses 1,600$–2,000$ ($8.95–$11.20); fixed-price menu 3,000$ ($16.80). AE, DC, MC, V. Fri–Wed noon–3pm and 7–10pm. Closed Nov. ALENTEJAN.

Évora's most atmospheric restaurant is hidden away in a narrow side street leading down from praça do Giraldo. Rustic decorations include old pots, blunderbusses, standing lamps, a grandfather clock, and kettles hanging from the ceiling. Seating is in rush chairs or on divans. In warm weather you can enjoy gazpacho Alentejana, followed by fried fish with tomato and garlic or pork Évora style (a meal in itself), topped off by regional cheese. The chefs elevate local dishes to another level with the use of seasonings and market-fresh ingredients. A bottle of Borba wine is a good complement to most meals.

✪ **Fialho.** Travessa Mascarenhas 14. ☎ **266/70-30-79.** Reservations recommended. Main courses 2,400$–2,920$ ($13.45–$16.35). AE, DC, MC, V. Tues–Sun 12:30pm–midnight. Closed Sept 1–21, Dec 24–31. ALENTEJAN.

Fialho, which has flourished on this site since the end of World War II, is Évora's most traditional restaurant. Its entrance is unprepossessing, but the interior is warmly decorated in the style of a Portuguese tavern. Although Évora is inland, Fialho serves good shellfish dishes, including sopa de Cacão (regional shark soup), along with such fare as succulent pork with baby clams in savory sauce, and partridge stew. In season, a whole partridge may be available. The air-conditioned restaurant seats 80. The staff is particularly proud of the lavish array of local wines, one of the most comprehensive cellars in the district.

Guião. Rua da República 81. ☎ **266/70-30-71.** Main courses 1,300$–2,200$ ($7.30–$12.30). AE, DC, MC, V. Tues–Sun noon–3:30pm and 7–10:30pm. Closed 2 weeks in July. REGIONAL PORTUGUESE.

Guião is a regional tavern that's widely considered one of Évora's three or four best restaurants. It lies just off the main square, praça do Giraldo. It's charmingly decorated with antique blue-and-white tiles. The family run tavern offers local wines and Portuguese specialties. The hearty, robust meals are filling, if not exceptional. A typical bill of fare includes grilled squid, grilled fish, swordfish steak, and clams with pork Alentejo style. The kitchen also prepares partridge in season.

ÉVORA AFTER DARK

The town's historic core contains a few sleepy-looking bodegas, any of which might strike your fancy as part of an after-dark pub crawl. The bar of the **Pousada dos Lóios,** largo Conde de Vila Flor (☎ 266/70-40-51), is a dignified option for a drink in a historic setting.

If you want to mingle and dance with the city's high-energy Lisbon wannabes, head for one of the town's two discos. **Discoteca Slide,** rua Serpa Pinto 135 (☎ 266/70-82-72), and **Disco Mr. Snob,** rua Valdevinos 21 (☎ 266/70-69-99), are small-scale, rustic versions of what you might find in Lisbon. They don't get going until after 10:30pm. At both, the 1,000$ ($5.60) cover charge includes the first drink. Every Wednesday and Friday night you can hear fado at **Dom Durate,** rua da Moeda 38 (☎ 266/70-78-25).

5 Beja

116 miles SE of Lisbon, 47 miles S of Évora

Julius Caesar founded Beja, which was once known as Pax Julia. The capital of Baixo Alentejo, the town rises like a pyramid above the surrounding fields of swaying wheat.

Beja's fame rests on what many authorities believe to be a literary hoax. In the mid–17th century, in the Convent of the Conceição, a young nun named Soror Mariana Alcoforado is said to have fallen in love with a French military officer. The officer, identified as the chevalier de Chamilly, reputedly seduced her, then left Beja forever.

The girl's outpouring of grief and anguish found literary release in the *Five Love Letters of a Portuguese Nun,* published in Paris in 1669. The letters created a sensation and endured as an epistolary classic. In 1926 F. C. Green wrote "Who Was the Author of the *Lettres Portugaises?*" claiming that their true writer was the comte de Guilleragues. However, a modern Portuguese study has put forth evidence that the *Lettres Portugaises* were in fact written by the nun, Sister Alcoforado.

ESSENTIALS

ARRIVING

BY TRAIN   Three trains a day make the 3-hour journey from Lisbon. The one-way fare is 1,200$ ($6.70). Six daily trains arrive from Évora. The journey takes an hour and costs 720$ ($4.05) one way. From the Algarve (see chapter 8), four trains a day leave from Faro. The trip takes 3½ hours and costs 1,200$ ($6.70) one way. For **information,** call ☎ 284/32-50-56.

BY BUS   Four *expressos* (express buses) per day make the 3-hour run between Lisbon and Beja; the one-way fare is 1,150$ ($6.45). Four buses a day come from Évora. The

2-hour trip costs 900$ ($5.05) one way. Four buses a day run from Faro; it's a 3½-hour trip and costs 1,200$ ($6.70) one way. For schedules, call ☎ 284/31-19-13.

BY CAR   From Albufeira in the Algarve, take IP-1 north to the junction with Route 263, which heads northeast into Beja.

VISITOR INFORMATION

The **Beja Tourist Office** is at rua Capitão João Francisco de Sousa 25 (☎ 284/31-19-13).

WHAT TO SEE & DO IN BEJA
EXPLORING THE TOWN

Museu Rainha Dona Leonor. Largo da Conceição. ☎ 284/32-33-51. Admission 100$ (55¢), free for children under 13. Tues–Sun 9:30am–12:30pm and 2–5:15pm.

The Queen Leonor Museum, founded in 1927–28, occupies three buildings on a broad plaza in the center of Beja: the Convento da Conceição and the Churches of Santo Amaro and São Sebastião. The main building was a convent founded in 1459 by the parents of the Portuguese king Manuel I. Favored by royal protection, it became one of the richest and most important convents of that time. The Convento da Conceição is famous throughout the world because of a single nun, Mariana Alcoforado. She is said to have written the *Lettres Portugaises,* love letters to the French chevalier de Chamilly, at the convent in the 17th century.

One of the building's most important features is the surviving pieces of the ancient convent. They are the church, with its baroque decoration, and the cloister and chapter house, which present one of the area's most impressive collections of 15th- to 18th-century Spanish and Portuguese tiles. Also on display are statuary and silverwork belonging to the convent, and a good collection of Spanish, Portuguese, and Dutch paintings from the 15th to 18th century. The *Escudela de Pero de Faria,* a piece of 1541 Chinese porcelain, is unique in the world. The first-floor permanent archaeological exhibition features artifacts from the Beja region.

The Santo Amaro church is one of the oldest churches of Beja, and rests on what may be an early Christian foundation. It houses the most important Visigothic collection (from Beja and its surroundings) in Portugal.

The Church of São Sebastião is a small temple of no great architectural interest. It houses part of the museum's collection of architectural goods from Roman to modern times. It's not open to the public; access is by special request.

Castelo de Beja. Largo Dr. Lima Faleiro. ☎ 284/31-18-00. Admission 160$ (90¢). June–Sept, Tues–Sun 10am–1pm and 2–6pm; Oct–May, Tues–Sun 9am–noon and 1–5pm. From the center, walk along rua de Aresta Branco, following signposts.

The Beja castle, which King Dinis built in the early 14th century on the ruins of a Roman fortress, crowns the town. Although some of its turreted walls have been restored, the defensive towers—save for a long marble keep—are gone. Traditionally the final stronghold in the castle's fortifications, the old keep appears to be battling the weather and gold fungi. The walls are overgrown with ivy, the final encroachment on its former glory. From the keep you can enjoy a view of the provincial capital and the outlying fields.

SHOPPING

Beja is known for handcrafts, including charming hammered copper, in the form of serving dishes and home accessories, as well as the many forms of pottery and wood carvings you might see in other parts of Ribatejo and Alentejo. **Rua Capital João Francisco de Sousa,** in the town center, is lined with all manner of shops. One of the most interesting is **Arabe,** rua de Lisboa 69 (☎ **284/32-72-08**). It specializes in handcrafts from near Beja and from virtually everywhere else in Portugal.

WHERE TO STAY
MODERATE

✪ **Pousada do Convento de São Francisco.** Largo do Nuno Álvarez Pereira, 7800 Beja. ☎ **284/32-84-41.** Fax 284/329-143. 35 units. A/C TV TEL. 29,000$–31,000$ ($162.40–$173.60) double; 51,300$ ($287.30) suite. Rates include breakfast. AE, DC, MC, V. Free parking.

In the historic heart of a town that sorely needed another hotel, this is a government-owned conversion of a 13th-century Franciscan monastery. São Francisco opened for business in 1994. From the end of World War II until the 1980s, it had functioned as an army barracks and training camp. Government architects attempted to retain some of the building's severe medieval lines, with limited success, because of serious deterioration. Rooms are generally spacious and attractively furnished, with good beds, excellent mattresses, and new plumbing. There's a garden on the premises with a modest but interesting chapel, a swimming pool, a tennis court, and a bar. The restaurant serves uncomplicated versions of Portuguese and regional cuisine.

INEXPENSIVE

Hotel Melius. Av. Fialhu Almeida, 7800 Beja. ☎ **284/32-18-22.** Fax 284/32-18-25. 60 units. A/C TV TEL. 11,000$ ($61.60) double; 14,800$–15,750$ ($82.90–$88.20) suite. Rates include breakfast. AE, DC, MC, V. Parking 300$ ($1.70).

This is the town's newest and best-recommended independent hotel, although not as good as the pousada (see above). Opened in 1995, it lies on the southern outskirts of town beside the main road to the Algarve. The three-star four-story hotel provides services that had been sorely lacking. The midsize guest rooms, though bland, are comfortable and well maintained, with good beds. The hotel has a gym and a sauna in the basement. A few steps away is the independently operated Restaurant Melius. It serves lunch and dinner Tuesday through Saturday, and lunch only on Sunday. Full meals cost 2,500$ to 3,000$ ($14 to $16.80).

Residencial Cristina. Rua de Mértola 71, 7800 Beja. ☎ **284/32-30-35.** Fax 284/32-04-60. 32 units. A/C TV TEL. 8,900$ ($49.85) double; 10,100$ ($56.55) suite. AE, DC, MC, V.

Residencial Cristina, the largest hostelry in town, is the third-best place to stay (after the Melius and the pousada). It's a five-story building on a main shopping street. The helpful management rents small, simply furnished guest rooms that, although recently restored, remain rather austere. Everything is immaculately kept. Breakfast is the only meal served.

Residência Santa Bárbara. Rua de Mértola 56, 7800 Beja. ☎ **284/32-20-28.** Fax 284/32-12-31. 26 units. A/C TV TEL. 7,000$–8,000$ ($39.20–$44.80) double. Rates include breakfast. AE, MC, V.

Santa Bárbara is a little oasis in a town that has few suitable accommodations. The residência is a shiny-clean, well-kept bandbox building. It's all small in scale, with only a whisper of a reception lobby and elevator. There are two street-level salons. The smallish guest rooms are compact but adequate, with good beds and well-maintained plumbing. Laundry service is provided. Breakfast is the only meal served.

WHERE TO DINE

Other than the hotels, Beja lacks first- or even second-class restaurants. These places are your best bets.

Esquina. Rua Infante do Henríque 26. ☎ **284/38-92-38.** Main courses 1,000$–1,500$ ($5.60–$8.40); tourist menu 2,000$ ($11.20). AE, MC, V. Mon–Sat noon–3pm and 7–10pm. PORTUGUESE.

Esquina serves well-seasoned food based on old-fashioned culinary traditions. The restaurant lies at the edge of town, a 5-minute walk from the tourist office. The setting isn't historic, but the service is warm. The fare includes soups, roast pork with clams (the chef's specialty), grilled cuts of beef, and chicken served with vegetables and savory broth. Dessert might be flan or fruit tart.

Luís da Rocha. Rua Capitão João Francisco de Sousa 63. ☎ **284/32-31-79.** Main courses 1,200$–2,200$ ($6.70–$12.30); tourist menu 1,700$ ($9.50). AE, DC, MC, V. Mon–Sat noon–3:30pm and 7–11pm. Closed May–Sept. REGIONAL PORTUGUESE.

At Luís da Rocha, on the same street as the tourist office, you can sit downstairs in the cafe or go upstairs to a spacious neon-lit dining room. Although the whole town seems to congregate for coffee and pastries here, many visitors find Esquina more appealing. You might begin with a cream soup, prepared fresh daily, then follow with boiled or fried fish, or pork with clams Alentejo style. In the words of one staff member, "It's the cooking of the people here—we don't get fancy for tourists."

BEJA AFTER DARK

The town has a worthy roster of pubs and bars. Leading destinations include **Barrote,** rua Genente Valadim (☎ 284/32-09-79), a laid-back pub. Also appealing is the **Cockpit,** rua Aferidores (no phone). It attracts music fans, mostly under 35, who congregate within earshot of live or recorded music, punk rock or otherwise. More formal and upscale is the **Bar Classico,** rua Jorge Reposo (☎ 284/32-60-00), where reminders of England sometime creep into the Portuguese setting. The **Disco República de Alcool,** rua General Teofilo de Trindade (☎ 284/32-50-00), is a young, fun cousin to larger, more richly accessorized clubs in Lisbon. It's on the edge of the city's historic core. Open nightly at 10pm.

6 Vila Nova de Milfontes

20 miles SW of Santiago do Cacém, 115 miles S of Lisbon

A good stopover in Lower Alentejo as you're heading south to the Algarve is the little beach town of Vila Nova de Milfontes. At the wide mouth of the Mira River, the sleepy resort is attracting more and more visitors because of the soft white-sand beaches that line both sides of the river. There are no other attractions, so you don't have to worry if you do nothing here but relax, or perhaps search for antiques.

The castle that once protected the area from Moroccan and Algerian pirates has been restored and is now an inn. After a day on the beach, you can head south to even more beaches.

ESSENTIALS
ARRIVING

There is no train service from Lisbon.

BY BUS   Three express buses a day make the trip from Lisbon. It takes 4 hours and costs 1,600$ ($8.95) one way. For schedules, call ☎ 21/354-58-63 in Lisbon.

BY CAR   Chances are you'll drive south from Setúbal (see chapter 6). Continue along N261 in the direction of Sines, then follow N120-1 until you see the cut-off heading west in Vila Nova de Milfontes.

VISITOR INFORMATION   The tourist office is on rua António Mantas (☎ 283/965-99).

WHERE TO STAY

Casa dos Arcos. Rua do Cais, 7645 Vila Nova de Milfontes. ☎ **283/99-71-56.** Fax 283/99-62-64. 10 units. A/C MINIBAR TV TEL. 8,000$–9,500$ ($44.80–$53.20) double. Rates include breakfast. No credit cards. Free parking. Closed Oct 15–30.

In the center of the resort, a 5-minute walk from the beach, this simple pension was renovated in 1996. The small to midsize guest rooms were modernized, with new mattresses and renewed plumbing. There is no grandeur or pretense here—the place provides an adequate stopover for the night, nothing more. The substantial continental breakfast is the only meal provided.

Castelo de Milefontes. Rua do Castelo, 7645 Vila Nova de Milfontes. ☎ **283/99-82-31.** Fax 283/99-71-22. 7 units. 26,000$ ($145.60) double. Rates include breakfast and dinner. No credit cards. Free parking.

In a castle dating from the 17th century is the area's most charming inn, which was renovated in 1998. High on a hill, "guarding" the resort, the castle has panoramic views of the sea. It's about a 3-minute walk from the center. The well-appointed midsize to spacious rooms contain old-fashioned furniture or antiques. The beds are excellent. The cuisine is well prepared with an emphasis on fresh seafood. This is one of the best stopovers on the drive from Lisbon to the Algarve.

WHERE TO DINE

Restaurante O Pescador. Largo da Praça 18. ☎ **283/99-63-38.** Reservations recommended. Main courses 1,600$–2,500$ ($8.95–$14). MC. Daily 9am–2am. Closed Oct 15–31. PORTUGUESE

"O Moura," as it's known locally, is the best *marisqueira* (seafood restaurant) at the resort. Even the town residents, who certainly know their fish, swear by it. The owners, the Moura family, serve the freshest fish in the area. Monkfish with rice is a savory offering, as is the kettle of *caldeirada,* a succulent seafood stew. The place is air-conditioned, and the welcome is friendly. Mr. and Mrs. Moura used to be fishmongers, and they know their product well. Don't expect much in the way of decor—people come here just for the fish.

10

Coimbra & the Beiras

Encompassing the university city of Coimbra, the three provinces of the Beiras are the quintessence of Portugal. *Beira* is Portuguese for "edge" or "border"; the provinces are Beira Litoral (coastal), Beira Baixa (low), and Beira Alta (high). The region embraces the Serra de Estrêla, Portugal's highest mountains—a haven for skiers in winter and a cool retreat in summer. The granite soil produced by the great range of serras blankets the rocky slopes of the Dão and Mondego river valleys and is responsible for producing the region's wine, ruby-red or lemon-yellow Dão.

The famed resort of **Figueira da Foz** draws the most beach devotees and is overcrowded in summer. However, you can take your pick of other beaches, from **Praia de Leirosa** in the south all the way to the northern tip at **Praia de Espinho.** Unlike those in the Algarve, the beaches along the Atlantic coast have powerful surf and potentially dangerous undertows, plus much cooler water. Check local conditions before going into the water. A yellow or red flag indicates that the water isn't safe for swimming (sometimes because of pollution).

Anglers from all over the world fly in to fish the waters in the **Serra de Estrêla National Park** and in the Vouga River. More casual fishing is done along the Beira Litoral beach strip, with its many rocky outcroppings. Bream, sole, and sea bass are the major catches. Ocean fishing doesn't require a permit, but local fishing (in freshwater streams and rivers) does. Regional tourist offices will give you information about permits.

Exploring the Region by Car

The Beiras lend themselves to a motor tour because many interesting villages are off the beaten track and not accessible by public transport. Traffic is generally not heavy, except in the peak of summer, when it creeps along the coastal strip.

Day 1   Some 80 miles north of Lisbon, on the road to Coimbra, **Leiria** merits at least a morning's stop. Visit its castle, take in a panoramic view, and perhaps see the 12th-century Igreja de São Pedro before going on your way. Then drive 34 miles north on N109 and A1 to **Figueira da Foz,** the most popular beach resort and fishing port on the Portuguese Atlantic coast. Spend the night.

Day 2   In the morning, head east along the clearly signposted road to Coimbra. After 16 miles you come to the small town of **Montemor-o-Velho,** dominated by one of the largest and loveliest castles in Portugal. After a brief stop, continue along N111 to complete the 18-mile journey to **Coimbra,** where you can spend the night. You'll need at least the rest of the day to take in the city's many attractions.

Day 3   Visit the Roman ruins at **Conimbriga,** 10 miles southeast of town—head south on N1 until you reach the intersection with Route 347, then go southeast. Have lunch at the pousada nearby. Return to Coimbra and drive northeast along Route 110 to Penacova; from there, continue north on a signposted secondary road to **Buçaco.** Here you can explore Portugal's most enchanting forests and visit the **Palace Hotel do Buçaco,** once a royal seat. If you can afford to spend the night there, it's ideal. Otherwise, press on to the nearby spa at **Luso,** on N255. It has far more reasonably priced hotels and restaurants.

Day 4   After a leisurely visit in Luso, drive the short distance west on N234 to the little hamlet of **Mealhada,** 12 miles north of Coimbra. Time it so that you arrive for lunch, because the town's restaurants are famous for a porcine pièce de résistance—roast suckling pig. Many restaurants specializing in roast suckling pig line the highway, but most foreign visitors seem to prefer **Pedro dos Leitões** (Peter of the Suckling Pigs), Estrada Nacionale 1 (☎ **244/82-20-62**). Pigs are spit-roasted over coals, and you can watch the process if you wish.

After lunch, continue north along A1 for a brief stop in the old spa of **Cúria** before heading to your final destination for the night: **Aveiro,** 35 miles north of Coimbra. There are many accommodations in and around Aveiro, including pousadas, so you don't have to spend the night in the city.

Day 5   Use the morning to explore Aveiro. For your final look at the Beiras, drive 60 miles east along IP-5 to **Viseu,** the capital of Beira Alta. Spend the rest of the day wandering its old streets and visiting its attractions, like the Viseu Sé (cathedral) and the Museu de Grão Vasco next door. Stay the night in Viseu.

1 Leiria

20 miles N of Alcobaça, 80 miles N of Lisbon

On the road to Coimbra, Leiria rests on the banks of the Liz and spreads over the surrounding hills. Though the modern-day town is industrial, it's still an inviting stop, with its hilltop castle, old quarter, and cathedral. Leiria is also the center of an area rich in handcrafts, like hand-blown glassware. Its folklore is comparable to that of neighboring Ribatejo. This city of 105,000 is an important transportation hub and a convenient point for exploring Nazaré or Fátima (see chapter 7), or the Atlantic coast beaches.

ESSENTIALS
ARRIVING

BY TRAIN   Leiria is 3½ hours from Lisbon. At least six trains a day make the journey; a one-way ticket is 1,000$ ($5.60). For train **information** and schedules, call ☎ **244/88-20-27** in Leiria.

BY BUS   Four express buses from Lisbon make the 2-hour run to Leiria. A one-way ticket costs 1,300$ ($7.30). You can also take one of seven daily buses from Coimbra (see section 3 in this chapter); the 1-hour trip costs 950$ ($5.30) one way. For **information** and schedules, call ☎ **244/81-15-07**.

BY CAR   Head north from Lisbon on the express highway A1.

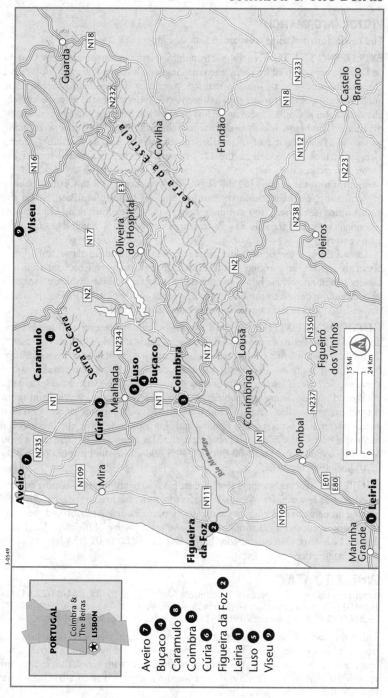

VISITOR INFORMATION

The **Leiria Tourist Office** is at Jardim Luís de Camões (☎ **244/82-37-73**).

EXPLORING THE TOWN   From any point in town you can see the great **Castelo de Leiria,** once occupied by Dinis, the poet king, and his wife, known as St. Isabella. On a summit of volcanic outcrop that was practically inaccessible to invaders, the imposing castle, with its tower top, has been extensively restored. The castle church, like the palace, is Gothic. From an arched balcony you can view the city and its surroundings. The Moors had their defense redoubt on this hill while they were taking possession of the major part of the Iberian peninsula. Portugal's first king, Afonso Henríques, took the fortress in the 12th century, and twice recovered it after the Moors had retaken it.

Admission to the fortress is 150$ (85¢). It's open daily, April to October 9am to 6:30pm, and November to March 9am to 5pm. For more information, ask at the tourist office (see above). You can drive right to the castle's front door. On the way, you might visit the **Igreja de São Pedro,** largo de São Pedro, which dates from the 12th century.

Around Leiria is one of the oldest state forests in the world. In about 1300, Dinis began the systematic planting of the **Pinhal do Rei,** with trees brought from the Landes area in France. He hoped to curb the spread of sand dunes, which ocean gusts were extending deep into the heartland. The forest, still maintained today, provided timber used to build the caravels to explore the Sea of Darkness.

OUTDOOR ACTIVITIES   If you'd like to combine sightseeing with some beach life, head to **São Pedro de Moel,** 14 miles west of Leiria and 84 miles north of Lisbon. Take N242 west of Leiria to the glass-manufacturing center of Marinha Grande, then N242 the rest of the way (6 miles) to the ocean. São Pedro de Moel, perched on a cliff above the Atlantic, is known for its bracing ocean breezes. New villas have sprung up, yet the old quarter retains its cobblestone streets. The white-sand beaches run up to the village's gray-walled ramparts, and the scattered rocks offshore create controlled conditions, rolling breakers, and rippling surf. On a palisade above the beach at the residential edge of the village is a good hotel, the **Mar e Sol,** av. da Liberdade 1, 2430 Marinha Grande (☎ **244/59-00-00;** fax 244/59-00-19). A double room is 12,500$ ($70), including breakfast.

SHOPPING   For such a small town, Leiria has a large number of shopping centers, called *centros comerciales.* We usually prefer to wander the streets of the historic core, looking for bargains and unusual handcrafts on **praça Rodrigues Lobo** and the many narrow medieval streets radiating from it. The most appealing of the many handcrafts shops is **Flabal,** av. Combatentes de Grande Guerra 54 (☎ **244/81-53-64**), noted for its reasonable prices.

WHERE TO STAY

Hotel Eurosol. Rua Dom José Alves Correia da Silva, 2410 Leiria. ☎ **244/81-22-01.** Fax 244/81-12-05. www.eurosol.pt. E-mail: eurosol@mail.telepac.pt. 142 units. A/C MINIBAR TV TEL. 14,000$ ($78.40) double; 20,000$ ($112) suite. AE, DC, MC, V. Free parking.

This is the best hotel in town, competing to dominate the skyline with the stone castle crowning the opposite hill. The midsize rooms, well liked by business travelers, are equivalent to those in any first-class hotel in the north. With views, they're all smart yet simple, with built-in headboards and wood-paneled wardrobe walls. One reader, however, found the bathrooms "pokey."

The hotel is the social hub of Leiria, attracting businesspeople to its rooftop lounge-bar and dining room. The four-course table d'hôte lunch or dinner, featuring international cuisine, is 3,500$ ($19.60). An adjoining snack bar serves lighter meals. Time your visit to enjoy a dip in the open-air polygonal pool, with its tile-covered terrace. There's also a gym, plus a lower-level boîte for after-dinner diversion.

Hotel São Francisco. Rua de São Francisco 26, 2430 Leiria. ☎ **244/82-31-10.** Fax 244/81-26-77. 18 units. A/C MINIBAR TV TEL. 8,500$ ($47.60) double. Rates include breakfast. AE, MC, V. Limited free parking on street.

São Francisco sits on the top floor of a nine-story building on the north side of town, a short walk from the river. Some of the well-maintained but small rooms offer panoramic views of Leiria. All have patterned wallpaper, functional leatherette furniture, and excellent mattresses. A cubbyhole bar in one of the public rooms serves drinks. Breakfast is the only meal served.

Hotel São Luís. Rua Henríque Sommer, 2400 Leiria. ☎ **244/81-31-97.** Fax 244/81-38-97. 48 units. A/C TV TEL. 8,500$ ($47.60) double; 11,000$ ($61.60) suite. Rates include breakfast. AE, DC, MC, V. Limited free parking on street.

The São Luís is one of the best budget hotels in Leiria. Ranked two stars by the government, it's spotless, and some of the rooms are very spacious; all have firm beds. You don't get a lot of frills, but you do get comfort and convenience at a good price. The hotel serves a good breakfast (the only meal available), including ham, fresh fruit, juice, and freshly baked bread. Laundry service is provided, and there's a bar.

WHERE TO DINE

Reis. Rua Wenceslau de Morais 17. ☎ **244/248-34.** Main courses 950$–1,500$ ($5.30–$8.40); tourist menu 1,800$ ($10.10). AE, DC, MC, V. Mon–Sat noon–3pm and 7–10pm. PORTUGUESE/SEAFOOD.

In spite of its simplicity, this is the best independent restaurant in Leiria. Reis is fairly large, seating 70. Its faithful devotees like its basic but good food and reasonable prices. The chef specializes in grills, along with such regional fare as hearty soups, excellent fresh fish, and well-seasoned meats. Portions are large. In winter, a fireplace makes the Reis more inviting.

LEIRIA AFTER DARK

Despite its modest size, Leiria has plenty of nightlife, both high-energy and laid-back. We usually begin with a promenade along **largo Cândido dos Reis,** which is lined with small tascas and bodegas. If you're looking for something more substantial, try the well-upholstered **Eurosol Bar,** in the Hotel Eurosol, rua Dom José Alves Correia da Silva (☎ 244/82-22-01). It presents live music every Wednesday and Saturday at around 9pm. A somewhat more countercultural crowd gathers at the **Galeria Bar,** Quinto do São António 43 (☎ 244/81-52-93). In a setting lined with unusual art, you can drink or flirt (or both) to your heart's content. Finally, look for one of the most diverse crowds in town at the **Yellow Bar,** rua João Pereira 103 (☎ 244/82-70-82).

2 Figueira da Foz

80 miles S of Porto, 125 miles N of Lisbon, 25 miles W of Coimbra

North of Cascais and Estoril, at the mouth of the Mondego River, Figueira da Foz is the best-known and oldest resort on Iberia's Atlantic coast. Its name means "Fig Tree at the Mouth of the River," but how it got that name is long forgotten. Aside from its climate (city leaders claim that the sun shines 2,772 hours annually, an average of more than 7½ hours a day), the resort's most outstanding feature is the golden-sand beach that stretches for more than 2 miles.

ESSENTIALS
ARRIVING
BY TRAIN   Trains arrive at largo da Estação (☎ **233/42-83-16**), near the bridge. Thirteen trains per day arrive from Coimbra (see below). The cost of the 1-hour trip is 300$ ($1.70) one way. Eight trains per day make the 3-hour trip from Lisbon. A one-way ticket costs 1,250$ ($7).

BY BUS   The bus station is the **Terminal Rodoviária,** largo Luís de Camões (☎ **233/42-30-95**). Four buses a day arrive from Lisbon; the trip takes 3½ hours and costs 1,200$ ($6.70) one way.

BY CAR   From Leiria (see above), continue north along Route 109.

VISITOR INFORMATION
The **Figueira da Foz Tourist Office** is on avenida do 25 de Abril (☎ **233/40-28-20**).

EXPLORING THE TOWN   Most visitors don't come to Figueira to look at museums, but the ✪ **Casa do Paço,** largo Prof. Vitar Guerra 4 (☎ **233/42-21-59**), is exceptional. It contains one of the world's greatest collections of Delft tiles, numbering almost 7,000; most depict warriors with gaudy plumage (some blowing trumpets). The puce-and-blue tiles are detailed and subtly executed. The *casa* was once the palace of Conde Bispo de Coimbra, Dom João de Melo, who came here in the last century when royalty frequented Figueira. It's at the head office of the Associação Comerciale e Industriale, a minute's walk from the post office and esplanade. The museum is open Monday to Friday from 9:30am to 12:30pm and 2 to 5pm. Admission is free.

Two miles north of Figueira da Foz, bypassed by new construction and sitting placidly on a ridge near the sea, is **Buarcos,** a fishing village far removed from casinos and overpopulated beaches. From its central square to its stone seawalls, it remains unspoiled.

OUTDOOR ACTIVITIES   Figueira da Foz is on a wide, sandy **beach,** on a site first occupied by the Lusitanians. In July and August the beach is usually packed body to body. Those who don't like sand and surf can swim in a **pool** sandwiched between the Grande Hotel da Figueira and the Estalagem da Piscina on the main esplanade.

You can also trek into the **Serra da Boa Viagem,** a range of hills whose summit is a favorite vantage point for photographers and sightseers. **Bullfights** are popular in season; the old-style bullring operates from mid-July to September.

Near Figueira da Foz, the **Quiaios Lakes** are ideal for sailing and windsurfing. (For information, contact the tourist office in Figueira da Foz.) Another good center for windsurfing is the bay at **Buarcos,** adjoining Figueira da Foz. You can rent most windsurfing equipment at kiosks right on the beaches.

SHOPPING   If you're looking for handcrafts, head for **Shangrira,** rua Dr. Calado (no phone), or **Chafariz,** rua do Estendal (☎ **233/42-06-86**). They carry terra-cotta, glazed porcelain, and some carved wood, leather work, and incised or burnished copper and brass. Looking for examples of the filigree, in gold or silver, for which Portugal is famous? Try the **Ourivesaria Ouro Nobre,** rua Dom Luís I (☎ **233/ 42-39-52**), for one of the town's most appealing selections.

WHERE TO STAY
Mercure Figueira da Foz. Av. do 25 de Abril, 3080 Figueira da Foz. ☎ **233/42-21-46.** Fax 233/42-24-20. 102 units. A/C MINIBAR TV TEL. 19,000$ ($106.40) double; 45,000$ ($252) suite. Rates include continental breakfast and parking. AE, DC, MC, V. Parking 650$ ($3.65).

Renovated in 1995, this 1950s-era hotel, on the seafront promenade overlooking the ocean, is the leading choice in town. It's popular with tour groups. Guests have free access to the adjoining Olympic-size saltwater pool. The hotel's interior is a world of marble and glass, more like that of a big-city hotel than a resort. A few of the midsize rooms on the sea have glass-enclosed balconies; most have open balconies, and all have firm beds. There's also a rather antiseptic restaurant and a game room. The hotel is open all year, though it's sleepy here in January.

WHERE TO DINE

Restaurante Tubarão. Av. do 25 de Abril. ☎ **233/42-34-45.** Main courses 1,000$–2,500$ ($5.60–$14). No credit cards. Daily 8am–4am. PORTUGUESE.

People come here for the food, not the decor. You dine in a large room filled with cloth-covered tables and cooled by revolving ceiling fans. However, you do get a sweeping view of the beach across the esplanade. Some of the tables spill onto the sidewalk, yet because of pedestrian traffic, they're often empty. A cafe in an adjoining room serves drinks throughout the day and night. Flavor, rather than culinary refinement, characterizes the menu. A battery of hurried waiters will serve you specialties like *gambas a la plancha* (grilled shrimp), grilled codfish, shellfish-flavored rice, seafood soup, and a variety of crab, lobster, and shrimp, priced by weight. The menu is heavy on heavy regional dishes.

FIGUEIRA DA FOZ AFTER DARK

Built in 1886, the **Grande Casino Peninsular,** rua Dr. Calado 1 (☎ **233/42-20-41**), features shows, dancing, a nightclub, and gambling salons. Games of chance include blackjack, American and continental roulette, and an old continental game known as French table (played with three dice). Admission, including one drink, is 1,500$ ($8.40) per person; expect to pay 900$ ($5.05) and up for beverages. An à la carte meal averages 4,000$ ($22.40); the food is standard nightclub chow. The casino show begins at 11pm, and the club is open daily 3pm to 3am.

You'll find many evocative, peaceful, or sleepy bars on travesso São Lourenço. One of the most appealing is the **Bar Dom Copo,** travesso São Lourenço (☎ **233/42-68-14**). Live music—presented four nights a week according to an oft-changing schedule—adds to the place's reputation as one of the most consistently popular bars in town. If you want to go dancing, four good discos await: **Disco Parlamento,** avenida de Tavarede (☎ **233/42-01-68**); **Pessidonio,** Condados Tavarede (☎ **233/43-56-37**); **Jet Set,** esplanade Dr. Silva Guimarães (☎ **233/42-00-00**); and perhaps the busiest and most amusing, **Bergantim,** rua Dr. António Lopez Guimarães (☎ **233/42-38-85**). They don't get animated until after 10:30pm. Admission is around 1,000$ ($5.60), including the first drink.

3 Coimbra

73 miles S of Porto, 123 miles N of Lisbon

Coimbra, known as Portugal's most romantic city, was the inspiration for the popular song "April in Portugal." On the weather-washed right bank of the muddy Mondego, Coimbra is also the educational center of the country. Dinis I originally founded its university at Lisbon in 1290. Over the years, the university moved back and forth between Lisbon and Coimbra, but in 1537 it settled here for good. Many of the country's leaders were educated here, none more notable than Dr. António Salazar, dictator from 1932 to 1968. Coimbra is at its best when the university is in session. Students still wear black capes; their briefcases bear colored ribbons denoting the school they attend. Yellow, for example, stands for medicine.

The city of medieval churches is also filled with youthful energy. Noisy cafeterias, raucous bars, and such events as crew races lend a certain joie de vivre to the cityscape.

The students of Coimbra band together in "republics" that usually rent cramped buildings in the old quarter, some up many flights of winding stairs. The republic isn't very democratic, run as it is on a strict seniority basis. A typical evening's bill of fare in a republic is likely to include grilled sardines, bread, and a glass of wine.

ESSENTIALS
ARRIVING

BY TRAIN   Coimbra has two train stations: **Estação Coimbra-A,** largo das Ámeias (☎ **239/83-49-98**), and **Estação Coimbra-B** (☎ **239/83-35-25**), 3 miles west of central Coimbra. Coimbra-B station is mainly for trains coming from cities outside the region, but regional trains serve both stations. Frequent shuttles connect the two. The bus ride takes 5 minutes and costs 190$ ($1.05). At least 14 trains per day make the 3-hour run north from Lisbon. It costs 1,310$ ($7.35) one way. From Figueira da Foz, there's one train per hour. The trip takes 1 hour and costs 270$ ($1.50) one way.

BY BUS   The **bus station** is on avenida Fernão de Magalhães (☎ **239/85-52-70**). Sixteen buses a day arrive from Lisbon, after a 3-hour trip that costs 1,300$ ($7.30) one way. Five buses per day make the 6-hour trip from Porto (see chapter 11). The one-way fare is 1,160$ ($6.50).

BY CAR   From Lisbon, take the express highway A1 north. The journey takes less than 2 hours, if there isn't too much traffic.

VISITOR INFORMATION

The **Coimbra Tourist Office** is on largo da Portagem (☎ **239/85-59-30**).

WHAT TO SEE & DO IN COIMBRA
EXPLORING THE TOWN

Coimbra's charms and mysteries unfold as you walk up rua Ferreira Borges, under the Gothic **Arco de Almedina** with its coat of arms. From that point, you can continue up the steep street, past antique shops, to the old quarter.

Across from the National Museum is the **Sé Nova (New Cathedral),** largo da Sé Nova, which has a cold 17th-century neoclassic interior. Admission is free. It's open Tuesday to Friday 9am to 12:30pm and 2 to 5:30pm. More interesting is the **Sé Velha (Old Cathedral),** largo da Sé Velha (☎ **239/82-52-73**), founded in 1170. Staunch as a fortress, the crenellated cathedral enjoys associations with St. Anthony of Padua. You enter by passing under a Romanesque portal. Usually a student is here, willing to show you (for a tip) the precincts, including the restored cloister. The pride of this monument is the gilded Flemish retable over the main altar, with a crucifix on top. To the left of the altar is a 16th-century chapel, designed by a French artist, that contains the tomb of one of the bishops of Coimbra. Admission to the old cathedral is free, to the cloisters 150$ (85¢). The Sé Velha is open Monday to Saturday from 10am to 6pm.

Velha Universidade. Largo de Dom Dinis. ☎ **239/85-98-00.** Admission to Sala dos Capelos, Museu de Arte Sacra, and Biblioteca 500$ ($2.80). Daily 9:30am–12:30pm and 2–5:30pm.

The focal point for most visitors is the University of Coimbra, established here in 1537 on orders of João III. Among its alumni are Luís Vas de Camões (the country's greatest poet, author of the national epic, *Os Lusíadas*), St. Anthony of Padua (also the patron saint of Lisbon), and the late Portuguese dictator Dr. Salazar, once a professor of economics.

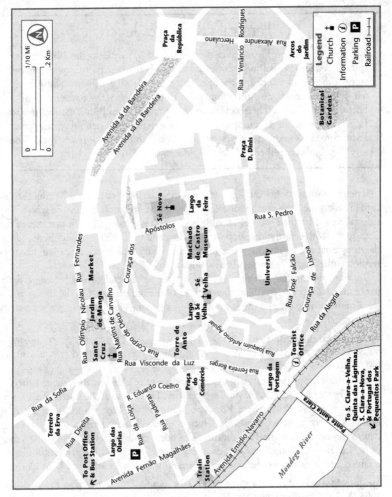

Legend
Church
Information (i)
Parking P
Railroad

Praça da República

Rua Alexandre Herculano

Rua Venâncio Rodrigues

Arcos do Jardim

Botanical Gardens

Avenida Sá da Bandeira

Praça D. Dinis

Sé Nova

Largo da Feira

Apóstolos

Rua S. Pedro

Machado de Castro Museum

Couraça dos

Rua Olímpio Nicolau Rui Fernandes

Market

Jardim de Manga

Santa Cruz

Sé Velha

University

Rua José Falcão

Couraça de Lisboa

Rua Martins de Carvalho

Rua Corpo de Deus

Largo da Sé Velha

Torre de Anto

Rua da Alegria

Rua Visconde da Luz

Rua Joaquim António Aguiar

Tourist Office (i)

R. Eduardo Coelho

Praça do Comércio

Rua Ferrera Borges

Largo da Portagem

Rua da Sofia

Rua da Loiça

Rua Padeiras

Ponte Santa Clara

To S. Clara-a-Velha, Quinta das Lágrimas, S. Clara-a-Nova, & Portugal dos Pequenitos Park

Terreiro da Erva

Rua Direita

Largo das Olarias

To Post Office & Bus Station

Avenida Fernão Magalhães

Train Station

Avenida Emídio Navarro

Mondego River

Ignore the cold statuary and architecture on largo de Dom Dinis and pass under the 17th-century **Porta Pérrea** into the inner core. The steps on the right take you along a cloistered arcade, **Via Latina,** to the **Sala dos Capelos,** the site of graduation ceremonies. You enter a world with a twisted rope ceiling, a portrait gallery of Portuguese kings, red-damask walls, and the inevitable *azulejos* (tiles). Afterward you can visit the **University Chapel,** decorated with an 18th-century organ, 16th-century candelabra, a painted ceiling, 17th-century tiles, and a fine Manueline portal.

The architectural gem of the entire town is the **Biblioteca Geral da Universidade (University Library),** also at largo de Dom Dinis. Established between 1716 and 1723 and donated by João V, the library shelters more than a million volumes. The interior consists of a trio of high-ceilinged salons walled by two-story tiers of lacquer-decorated bookshelves. The pale jade and sedate lemon marble inlaid floors complement the baroque decorations of gilded wood. Chinese-style patterns have been painted on emerald, red, and gold lacquer work. The library tables are ebony and lustrous rosewood, imported from the former Portuguese colonies in India and Brazil.

Portugal's Romeo & Juliet

Coimbra's reputation for romance derives at least in part from the 14th-century story of Pedro the Cruel and Inês de Castro. The Portuguese poet Camões told the story of the crown prince and the Spanish beauty, his wife's lady-in-waiting. They fell in love at what's now the Quinta das Lágrimas, where Inês was living on a fateful night in 1355. Three noblemen acting on orders of Pedro's father, Afonso IV, slit her throat in the quinta's garden. In the Igreja e Mosteiro da Santa Cruz, Pedro forced his courtiers to pay homage to her corpse and kiss her hand. The lovers are buried together in Alcobaça's Mosteiro de Santa Maria (see chapter 7).

The three-dimensional ceilings and zooming telescopic effect of the room's structure focus on the large portrait of João V, set against imitation curtains in wood. The side galleries, with their walls of valuable books in law, theology, and humanities of the 16th to the 18th century; the supporting pillars; and the intricate impedimenta all are dazzling, even noble. You may want to save the library for last; after viewing this masterpiece, other sights in town pale by comparison.

To wind down after leaving the library, walk to the end of the belvedere for a panoramic view of the river and the rooftops of the old quarter. On the square you'll see a statue of João III and the famous curfew-signaling clock of Coimbra, known as *cabra* (goat).

✪ **Museu Machado de Castro.** Largo Dr. José Rodrigues. ☎ **239/82-37-27.** Admission 500$ ($2.80), free for children under 12 accompanied by an adult. Tues–Sun 9am–5:30pm. Bus: 1.

A short walk from the university square leads you to this museum named for the greatest Portuguese sculptor of the 18th century. This is one of the finest museums in northern Portugal. Built over a Roman building as the Paço Episcopal in 1592, it houses a collection of ecclesiastical sculpture, especially polychrome, much of which dates from the 14th to the 18th century. The other exhibits include vestments, a relic of St. Isabella, paintings, antiques, coaches, silver chalices, old jewelry, embroideries, retables, and 16th-century ceramic representations of the Apostles and Jesus Christ.

Igreja e Mosteiro da Santa Cruz. Praça do 8 de Maio. ☎ **239/82-29-41.** Admission 200$ ($1.10). Daily 9am–noon and 2–5pm.

This former monastery was founded in the late 12th century during the reign of Afonso Henríques, Portugal's first king. Its original Romanesque style gave way to Manueline restorers in 1507. This is where the story of Pedro the Cruel and Inês de Castro reached its climax (see box, "Portugal's Romeo & Juliet"). Tiles decorate the lower part of the walls inside. Groined in the profuse Manueline manner, the interior houses the Gothic sarcophagi of Afonso Henríques, his feet resting on a lion, and of his son, Sancho I. The pulpit is one of the achievements of the Renaissance in Portugal, carved by João de Ruão in the 16th century. The choir stalls preserve, in carved configurations, the symbolism, mythology, and historic import of Portuguese exploration. With its twisted columns and 13th-century tombs, the two-tiered Gothic-Manueline cloister is impressive. The facade is decorated like an architectural birthday cake, topped with finials and crosses.

NEARBY ATTRACTIONS

Convento de Santa Clara-a-Velha. Rua de Baixo. Free admission. Daily 8:30am–6:30pm. Walk across the Santa Clara Bridge and turn left down the cobblestone rua de Baixo.

On the silt-laden banks of the Mondego stand the gutted, flooded, crumbling remains of the 14th-century Gothic (Old) Convent of St. Clara. This church housed the body of Coimbra's patron saint, Isabella, before her remains were transferred to the New Convent (St. Clara-a-Nova) higher up on the hill. Rising out of the in-rushing river, the Roman arches are reflected in the canals. You can walk through the upper part only—the river has already reclaimed the floor.

Convento de Santa Clara-a-Nova. Rua Santa Isabel. ☎ **239/44-16-74.** Admission 100$ (55¢). Daily 8:30am–6:30pm.

Commanding a view of Coimbra's right bank, the New Convent of St. Clara contains the tomb of St. Isabella. Built during the reign of João IV, it's an incongruous blend of church and military garrison. The church is noted for a rich baroque interior and Renaissance cloister. In the rear, behind a grille, is the original tomb of the saint (usually closed except on special occasions). In 1677, when her body was moved here from the Convent of St. Clara-a-Velha (above), her remains were said to have been well preserved, though she had died in 1336. Instead of regal robes, she preferred to be buried in the simplest habit of the order of the Poor Clares. At the main altar is the silver tomb (a sacristan will light it for you), which the ecclesiastical hierarchy considered more appropriate after her canonization.

Portugal dos Pequenitos. Jardim do Portugal dos Pequenitos. ☎ **239/44-12-25.** Admission 1,000$ ($5.60) adults, 500$ ($2.80) children. Daily Apr–Sept 9am–8pm; Oct–Mar 10am–6pm.

For children, this mixture of miniature houses—"Portugal for the Little Ones"—from every province of the country is Coimbra's main attraction. You get there by crossing Ponte de Santa Clara and heading out rua António Agusto Gonçalves. You'll feel like Gulliver strolling through a Lilliputian world. The re-creations include palaces, an Indian temple, a Brazilian pavilion (with photos of gauchos), a windmill, a castle, and the 16th-century House of Diamonds from Lisbon.

Quinta das Lágrimas. Rua António Agusto Gonçalves. ☎ **239/44-16-15.** Admission 150$ (85¢). Daily 9am–7pm.

The legendary poet Camões told the story of the "Garden of Tears." Inês de Castro, mistress of Pedro the Cruel, and their three illegitimate children lived in "sweet Mondego's solitary groves. (See box, "Portugal's Romeo & Juliet.") Although the gardens have been the property of the Osorio Cabral family since the 18th century, romantics from many countries visit them. The house has been turned into a deluxe hotel (see "Where to Stay," below), and you can wander through the greenery to the spring fountain, known as the Fonte dos Amores. On Camões's "black night obscure" in 1355, assassins hired by her lover's father killed Inês. Pedro returned to find her in a pool of blood.

OUTDOOR ACTIVITIES

There are tennis courts at the university stadium and at the **Club Tênis de Coimbra,** avenida Urbano Durate, Quinta da Estrela (☎ **239/40-34-69**). All are open to the public. For horseback riding or excursions in the Beiras, contact **Centre Hippique de Coimbra,** Mata do Choupal (☎ **239/83-76-95**), open daily 10am to 1pm and 3 to 7pm. A 3-hour excursion along country trails costs 2,000$ ($11.20) per person.

For swimming, head for the trio of pools at the **Piscina Municipal,** rua Dom Manuel I (☎ **239/70-16-05**). Take bus no. 5 from the center. Open in July and August daily from 10am to 1pm and 2 to 7pm, it charges 250$ ($1.40) admission.

SHOPPING

Many of Coimbra's most interesting shops lie near the Sé Velha, on the narrow streets radiating from **rua de Quebra Costas.** Because of its steep inclines, its name ("the street that will break your back") seems apt. Look for lots of outlets selling products manufactured in the surrounding region. The best bookstore, with a number of English editions, is **Livraria Bertrand,** largo da Portagem 9 (☎ **239/82-30-14**), a block from the tourist office.

Even the city's tourist authorities usually recommend short excursions into the suburbs and outlying villages for anyone seriously interested in shopping. Possibilities include the villages of **Lousa,** 13 miles east, and **Penacova,** 13 miles north, where unpretentious kiosks and stands beside the roads sell handwoven baskets and ceramics.

A better destination is **Condeixa,** 10½ miles south; its shops are better stocked, and the staff members are familiar with foreigners who don't speak Portuguese. To reach the village, take EN1 and follow signs toward Lisboa. Condeixa is home to nine independent ceramics factories, source of most residents' income. The most appealing are **Ceramica Berardos,** Barreira, EN1, Condeixia (☎ **239/94-13-31**); **Filceramica,** Avenal, Condeixa (☎ **239/94-18-38**); and **Keramus,** Zona Industrial, Condeixa (☎ **239/94-27-45**). The merchants will usually agree (for a fee) to insure and ship your purchases. Because of the expense, it's usually a lot easier just to buy an extra (hard-sided) suitcase, wrap your porcelain carefully, and haul it back with you on the plane.

WHERE TO STAY

Note that the **Pousada de Santa Cristina** (see "An Excursion to the Roman Town of Conimbriga," below) is nearby.

EXPENSIVE

✪ **Quinta das Lágrimas.** Rua António Agusto Gonçalves, Santa Clara, 3000 Coimbra. ☎ **239/44-16-15.** Fax 239/44-16-95. www.supernet.pt/hotelagrimas. E-mail: lagrima@relaischateaux.fr. 39 units. A/C MINIBAR TV TEL. 22,000$ ($123.20) double; from 57,500$ ($322) suite. Rates include breakfast. AE, DC, MC, V. Free parking.

The most luxurious place to stay in all the Beiras, the "Estate of Tears" gets its name from the story of Dom Pedro and Inês de Castro (see box, "Portugal's Romeo & Juliet"). Inês was murdered on the quinta's grounds, and her tears, it's said, were transformed into a pure, fresh stream of water. The red color of the rocks is said to be her blood.

The duke of Wellington, the emperor of Brazil, and various kings of Portugal once occupied these rooms. They're now a hotel of great modern comfort that maintains the romanticism of its past. The midsize to spacious guest rooms are often sumptuous but not overly decorated, and everything is in traditional Portuguese style. You can find ample retreats in the drawing rooms and among the centenarian exotic trees, lovely fountains, and well-maintained gardens and lawns.

Dining: In an elegant setting, the quinta serves some of the city's finest cuisine. Some dishes are based on ancient recipes that have been revived.

Amenities: Room service, laundry and dry cleaning, swimming pool, tennis facilities.

MODERATE

Hotel Astoria. Av. Emídio Navarro 21, 3000 Coimbra. ☎ **239/822-055.** Fax 239/822-057. www.almeidahotels.com. 64 units. A/C TV TEL. 14,000$–17,000$ ($78.40–$95.20) double. Rates include breakfast. AE, DC, MC, V.

When it was built in 1927, the domed, triangular Astoria was the most glamorous hotel in Coimbra. It played host to Portugal's famous and infamous before falling into neglect and decay. It reopened in a streamlined and somewhat simplified format in 1990. The comfortable but not overly plush hotel retains a faded grandeur. Its cupolas and wrought-iron balcony balustrades rise from a pie-shaped wedge of land in the city's congested heart. The guest rooms, as befits a hotel of this age, vary greatly in size, but all are comfortably furnished with smoothly running plumbing and excellent beds. Five units are air-conditioned, but they're usually reserved in advance. On the premises is an old-world restaurant, the Amphytryon, a favorite of local business-people at lunch, plus a pleasant bar. Room service is available daily 8am to 5pm.

✪ **Tivoli Coimbra.** Rua João Machado 4–5, 3000 Coimbra. ☎ **239/826-934.** Fax 239/826-827. 100 units. A/C MINIBAR TV TEL. 19,500$ ($109.20) double; 27,500$ ($154) suite. Rates include breakfast. AE, DC, MC, V. Free parking.

On a hillside above Coimbra's northern outskirts, a 15-minute walk from the town center, this is a favorite stop for bus tours. Built in 1991, it's a member of one of Portugal's most respected chains, the Tivoli Group, whose hotels in Sintra and Lisbon are among the finest in their four- and five-star categories. The midsize rooms are conservatively modern (too much so for some tastes) and filled with electronic gadgets such as bedside controls. There are safes and hair dryers in all rooms. Some have city views. The hotel has room service, baby-sitting, laundry service, and a concierge. There's a small garden behind the hotel, an indoor pool, and a health club with a sauna and Jacuzzi. The dignified Porta Férrea serves well-prepared Portuguese and continental cuisine daily from 12:30 to 3pm and 7:30 to 10pm. There's also a bar with a well-trained staff.

INEXPENSIVE

Hotel Bragança. Largo das Ámeias 10, 3000 Coimbra. ☎ **239/822-171.** Fax 239/836-135. www.maisturismo.pt/braganca.html. 83 units. A/C TV TEL. 12,000$ ($67.20) double; 17,000$ ($95.20) suite. Rates include breakfast. AE, MC, V. Free parking.

This bandbox hotel next to the train station should be considered only if you arrive late at night by rail, and other, better hotels are full (as is likely in warm weather). Primarily catering to businesspeople, it does a thriving trade in summer. The rooms vary in size—a few open onto balconies overlooking the main road; others are airless and often hot. The furnishings are utterly basic and recall the 1950s. Portuguese meals are served.

Hotel Dom Luís. Quinta da Verzea, 3000 Coimbra. ☎ **239/80-21-20.** Fax 239/44-51-96. www.bestwestern.com/pt. E-mail: hotel.d.luis@mail.telepac.pt. 100 units. A/C MINIBAR TV TEL. 14,200$ ($79.50) double; 20,000$ ($112) suite. Rates include breakfast. AE, DC, MC, V. Free parking.

Built in 1989, this is one of the most stylish hotels in the Coimbra area. About half a mile south of the city, it lies on the road to Lisbon. The comfortable, well-maintained guest rooms, though a bit small, offer good beds. The hotel has a pleasing modern design, brown-marble floors, and a restaurant that serves Portuguese and international food.

Hotel Domus. Rua Adelina Veiga 62, 3000 Coimbra. ☎ **239/828-584.** Fax 239/838-818. 19 units. TV TEL. 5,500$–8,500$ ($30.80–$47.60) double; 12,000$ ($67.20) suite. Rates include breakfast. AE, MC, V. Free parking on street.

The Domus lies above an appliance store on a narrow commercial street. Machine-made golden-brown tiles cover its 1970s facade, and its rectangular windows are trimmed with slabs of marble. The reception desk is at the top of a flight of stairs, a floor above ground level. Rooms are usually large and well maintained. Many have contrasting patterns of carpeting and wallpaper, creating a haphazardly functional but cozy family atmosphere. A stereo system plays in the TV lounge, which doubles as the breakfast room.

Hotel International. Av. Emídio Navarro 4, 3000 Coimbra. ☎ **239/825-503.** 20 units, 16 with shower only. 5,000$ ($28) double without bathroom, 5,500$ ($30.80) double with shower only. No credit cards. Limited free parking on street.

The International is very simple, unabashedly Portuguese in its mentality and decor. It occupies a once-grand 1840s building whose interior has been updated over the years. The building became a hotel in 1949, and the aura of that era lingers. Members of the family that owns the property staff the insignificant lobby; English is definitely not their second tongue. After registering, you climb a series of steep staircases to rooms that are often tiny, with furniture that's merely old, as opposed to antique. Yet at busy times, finding any room is a welcome relief. Ten rooms have phones. Naturally, the doubles with private showers go quickly. No room, however, has a private toilet. Breakfast is not served.

Hotel Oslo. Av. Fernão de Magalhães 25, 3000 Coimbra. ☎ **239/829-071.** Fax 239/820-614. 36 units. A/C TV TEL. 12,000$ ($67.20) double; 18,000$ ($100.80) suite. Rates include breakfast. AE, DC, MC, V. Free parking.

The Oslo, on one of the busiest streets in town, was built during the 1960s craze for Scandinavian design and decor. In 1993 it underwent a complete overhaul and upgrade. The small rooms are conservatively modern, unpretentious, simple, and equipped with firm mattresses. Because of traffic noise, ask for a room at the rear, especially if you're a light sleeper. Laundry service is provided, and there's a bar.

WHERE TO DINE
MODERATE

Dom Pedro. Av. Emídio Navarro 58. ☎ **239/829-108.** Reservations recommended. Main courses 1,600$–2,800$ ($8.95–$15.70). AE, DC, MC, V. Tues–Sun noon–3:30pm; daily 7–10:30pm. PORTUGUESE/CONTINENTAL.

Dom Pedro is across from the bank of the river, near a congested part of town. After negotiating a vaulted hall, you'll find yourself in an attractive room with tables grouped around a splashing fountain. In winter a corner fireplace throws welcome heat; in summer the thick walls and terra-cotta floor provide a kind of air-conditioning. Full Portuguese and continental meals might include codfish Dom Pedro, grilled squid, pepper steak, or pork cutlet Milanese. The food is basic; as our Portuguese host informed us at the end of the meal, "I didn't promise you a rose garden—only dinner."

O Alfredo. Av. João das Regras 32. ☎ **239/44-15-22.** Main courses 1,000$–2,200$ ($5.60–$12.30). MC, V. Daily noon–3pm and 7–11pm. PORTUGUESE.

O Alfredo lies on the less populated side of the river, on the street that funnels into the Santa Clara Bridge. The unobtrusive pink-fronted place looks more like a snack bar than a formal restaurant. The ambience is pleasant, albeit simple. Full Portuguese meals might feature pork Alentejo style, shellfish paella, an array of shellfish, Portuguese-style stew, several types of clam dishes, roast goat, and regional varieties of fish and meat. Although the wine is often better than the food, this is nonetheless a satisfying choice.

Piscinas. Rua Dom Manuel I. ☎ **239/71-70-13.** Reservations recommended. Main courses 1,600$–2,200$ ($8.95–$12.30). AE, DC, MC, V. Tues–Sun noon–3pm; daily 7–10pm. Closed Aug 1–15. Bus: 7 or 20. PORTUGUESE/CONTINENTAL.

The best restaurant in Coimbra (which isn't saying a lot) is hard to reach. It's best to go by taxi, though parking is easily available. On the eastern side of town, Piscinas ("swimming pools") adjoins a complex of sports and recreational facilities that include the municipal soccer stadium and public pools. Avoid it before and after soccer games and other sporting events, when it's especially packed. The air-conditioned eatery, which overlooks two swimming pools, combines regional food with large portions and a complete lack of pretension. The chefs take advantage of first-rate regional produce, and handle it extremely well. You might begin with shellfish soup or escargots. Main-dish specialties include beef Piscinas, grilled sole, pepper steak, pork piri-piri (with hot peppers), and fondue bourguignonne. Recorded music plays softly.

INEXPENSIVE

Café Nicola. Rua Ferreira Borges 35. ☎ **239/822-061.** Main courses 950$–1,500$ ($5.30–$8.40). MC, V. Mon–Sat noon–3pm and 7–10pm. PORTUGUESE.

Café Nicola is a plain but modern little restaurant over an old-fashioned delicatessen and pastry shop. It's Spartan inside—even the flowers are usually wilted. Students gather here for strong coffee. The food is good but simple; the fish and meat platters are usually large enough for two. A nourishing bowl of the soup of the day begins most meals. After that, you can order fillet of fish, roast chicken, chicken cutlets, or veal croquettes.

✪ **Café Santa Cruz.** Praça do 8 de Maio. ☎ **239/833-617.** Sandwiches 300$ ($1.70); coffee 80$ (45¢). No credit cards. Summer Mon–Sat 8am–2am; winter Mon–Sat 8am–midnight. Closed Sept 25–Oct 8. Bus: 3 or 4. SANDWICHES.

This is the most famous coffeehouse in Coimbra, perhaps in the whole of northern Portugal. In a former auxiliary chapel of the cathedral, it has a high ceiling supported by flamboyant stone ribbing and vaulting of fitted stone. The paneled waiters' station boasts a marble top handsome enough to serve as an altar. A favorite gathering place by day or night, it has a casual mood; cigarette butts are tossed on the floor. Scores of students and professors come here to read the newspaper. There's no bar to stand at, so everyone takes a seat on an intricately tooled leather chair at one of the marble-topped hexagonal tables. If you order cognac, the shot will overflow the glass, but most patrons ask for a glass of coffee with milk.

COIMBRA AFTER DARK

The city's large student population guarantees an active, sometimes raucous, nightlife. You'll find the bars around the Sé Velha and its square, largo da Sé Velha, packed with students, professors, and locals, who drink, gossip, and discuss academic priorities. Our favorite experience is hopping randomly from bar to bar. If you want a definite address, consider the **Diligência Bar,** rua Nova (☎ **239/82-76-67**), where folks drink and flirt early in the evening, then listen to the local fado diva's performances beginning at 10 or 10:30pm. A more Americanized option is the **Dixie Bar,** rua Joaquim António d'Agiar 6 (☎ **239/83-21-92**), where live jazz by local performers sometimes evokes New Orleans.

The town's discos rock at least 5 nights a week (and sometimes 7, depending on how many students are in town). The glamour and desirability of the three discos we recommend below increase or decrease every season based on the whims of the dance-aholic public. Depending on your mood and who's there at the time of your visit, the three most worthwhile are **Via Latina,** rua Almeida Garrett 1 (☎ **239/83-30-34**); **Joan Raton,** av. Afonso Henríques 43 (☎ **239/40-40-47**); and **States,** praça Machado Asses 22 (☎ **239/82-70-67**). Each becomes animated after 10:30pm and often stays open until around 3am or, on Friday and Saturday, to dawn.

Student celebrations in Coimbra include the **Queima das Fitas** (Burning of the Ribbons), a graduation ritual during the first or second week of May. Then loosely organized *serenatas* (troupes of students who re-create the music and aura of the troubadours of the Middle Ages) sing and wander through Coimbra's streets at unannounced intervals. It's impossible to predict when and where you're likely to find these spontaneous reminders of yesteryear.

AN EXCURSION TO THE ROMAN TOWN OF CONIMBRIGA

One of Europe's great Roman archaeological finds, ✪ **Conimbriga,** is 10 miles southwest of Coimbra. If you don't have a car, you can take a bus from Coimbra to Condeixa, about a mile from Conimbriga. The bus, Avic Mondego, leaves Coimbra at 9am and returns at 1 and 6pm. From Condeixa, you reach Conimbriga by walking or hiring a taxi in the village.

The site of a Celtic settlement established in the Iron Age, the village was occupied by the Romans in the late 1st century A.D. From then until the 5th century, the town knew a peaceful life. The site lay near a Roman camp but never served as a military outpost, though it was on a Roman road connecting Lisbon (Roman Olisipo) and Braga (Roman Braçara Augusta).

You can walk from the small **Museu Monográfico** along the Roman road to enter the ruins. The museum contains artifacts from the ruins, including a bust of Augustus Caesar that originally stood in the town's Augustan temple. The **House of Cantaber** is a large residence, and in its remains you can trace the life of the Romans in Conimbriga. The house was occupied until intruders seized the family of Cantaber. The invaders also effectively put an end to the town in the mid–5th century.

Another point of interest is the **House of the Fountains,** constructed before the 4th century, when it was partially destroyed by the building of the town wall. Much of the house has been excavated, and you can see remains of early Roman architecture as it was carried out in the provinces.

Roman mosaics in almost perfect condition have been unearthed in area diggings. The designs are triangular, octagonal, and circular; executed in blood red, mustard, gray, sienna, and yellow, the motifs include beasts from North Africa and delicately wrought hunting scenes. In one of the houses you can see mosaics with mythological themes. The diggings attest to the ingenuity of Roman design. Columns form peristyles around reflecting pools, and the remains of fountains stand in courtyards. There are ruins of temples, a forum, patrician houses, water conduits, and drains. Feeding the town's public and private bathrooms were special heating and steam installations with elaborate piping systems. The town even had its own aqueduct.

The ruins are open daily from 9am to 8pm (until 6pm in winter). The museum is open Tuesday to Sunday from 10am to 6pm. Admission is 400$ ($2.25) for adults, free for children under 14. For more information, call ☎ **239/94-11-77.**

WHERE TO STAY & DINE

✪ **Pousada de Santa Cristina.** Condeixa-a-Nova, 3150 Coimbra. ☎ **239/94-40-25.** Fax 239/94-30-97. www.pousadas.pt. 45 units. A/C TV TEL. 24,600$ ($137.75) double. Rates include breakfast. AE, DC, MC, V. Free parking.

One of Portugal's finest pousadas, this place opened in 1993 as a modern four-story hotel whose design was vaguely inspired by a 19th-century palace. It replaced a gone-to-seed mansion, and many of that building's embellishments, including moldings, were used in the reconstruction. Other furnishings were imported from the site of a tragic fire at the Palácio de Sotomaior, near Lisbon. The guest rooms are generally

Serra de Estrêla National Park

Portugal's largest national park, Serra de Estrêla, is one of the country's most popular rest and recreation areas. From January to May the great granite serra is a winter-sports center. In summer, campers, trout fishers, and mountain climbers replace the skiers.

Until the late 1800s the land was almost completely isolated from the rest of Portugal. It was known mainly to local hunters and shepherds. It's the home of the *cão de sena* ("dog of the mountain"), a tough species of canine bred for its shepherding skill. The area is still a major sheep-raising district, and is filled with wild animals, including boars, badgers, and packs of roving, often hungry, wolves. Traditional iron collars with long, sharp spikes protect the sheep dogs' throats from the wolves' teeth. In one of the strangest symbiotic acts in the natural world, many of the dogs survive by sucking ewes' milk.

Roads link the region's major points of interest in the mountain range. One major auto route (N339) runs between Covilhã and Seia via the scenic mountain hamlet of **Torre,** the highest point in Portugal (6,500 ft.). Torre has been developed into a resort and boasts two ski lifts, but the facilities don't compare with those found in Austria, Switzerland, and parts of France. If you're driving, expect sheer drop-offs and hair-raising curves and turns as panoramic views of the **Zêzere Valley** unfold.

The best trout fishing in the park is in the Zêzere Valley, where the river drains one of the deepest glacial gorges in Europe. Fishers also try their luck in the lakes of **Loriga** and **Comprida.**

The ideal time for hiking is spring, when wildflowers bloom. Well-marked trails cut through the park, meandering along the sloping terrain. Several official campsites are also in the park. The **Covilhã Tourist Office,** praça do Município (☎ **275/31-95-60**), can supply you with maps and information.

The easiest way to reach the park is from Coimbra. Take N17 east and follow signs.

---

spacious, light, and sunny. The furnishings are tasteful, with firm mattresses and well-chosen fabrics and carpeting.

If you're visiting the ruins nearby for the day, you may want to stop in for a meal of regional specialties. The fixed-price lunch or dinner is 3,650$ ($20.45). A tennis court, a pool, and a luxuriant garden add to the pousada's allure. Many guests visiting Coimbra, 9½ miles away, prefer to stay here.

4 Buçaco

17½ miles N of Coimbra, 144 miles N of Lisbon, 2 miles SE of Luso

The rich, tranquil beauty of Buçaco's forests was initially discovered by a humble order of barefoot Carmelites, following the dictates of seclusion prescribed by their founder. In 1628 they founded a monastery at Buçaco and built it with materials from the surrounding hills. Around the forest they erected a wall to isolate themselves further and to keep women out.

The friars had a special love for plants and trees, and each year they cultivated the natural foliage and planted specimens sent to them from distant orders. Buçaco had always been a riot of growth: ferns, pines, cork, eucalyptus, and pink and blue clusters of hydrangea. The friars introduced such exotic flora as the monkey puzzle, a tall Chilean pine with branches so convoluted that monkeys who climb in it become confused. The pride of the forest, however, remains its stately cypresses and cedars.

ESSENTIALS
ARRIVING
BY BUS   Buçaco is best explored by car. However, if you're depending on public transportation, you can visit the forest on a day trip from Coimbra. Buses from Coimbra to Viseu detour from Luso through the forest and stop at the Palace Hotel do Buçaco. Five buses per day (three on Sunday) make the 1-hour trip; a one-way ticket is 440$ ($2.45). For **information** and schedules, call ☎ **239/82-78-81.**

BY CAR   From Coimbra, head northeast along Route 110 to the town of Penacova at the foot of the Serra do Buçaco. From there, continue north, following signposts along a small secondary road.

VISITOR INFORMATION
The nearest tourist office is at Luso (see the following section).

EXPLORING THE AREA
The forest created by the order of Carmelite monks who settled here in 1628 has been maintained through the ages. Such was the beauty of the preserve that a papal bull, issued in 1643, threatened excommunication to anyone who destroyed a tree. Though the monastery was abolished in 1834, the forest survived. Filled with natural spring waters, the earth bubbles with many cool fountains, the best known of which is **Fonte Fria** (cold fountain).

The Buçaco forest was the battleground where Wellington defeated the Napoleonic legions under Marshal André Massena. The Iron Duke slept in a simple cloister cell after the battle. A small **Museu da Guerra Peninsular** (Museum of the Peninsular War), about half a mile from the Palace Hotel (☎ **231/93-93-10**), reconstructs much of the drama of this turning point in the Napoleonic invasion of Iberia. The small museum collection consists of engravings, plus a few guns. It's open Tuesday to Sunday, 10am to 5:30pm June 15 to September 15, 10am to 4pm in the off-season. Admission is 200$ ($1.10).

In the early 20th century a great deal of the Carmelite monastery was torn down to make way for the royal hunting lodge and palace of Carlos I and his wife, Amélia. He hardly had time to enjoy it before he was assassinated in 1908. The Italian architect Luigi Manini masterminded the neo-Manueline structure of parapets, buttresses, armillary spheres, galleries with flamboyant arches, towers, and turrets. After the fall of the Braganças and the transformation of the palace into a hotel, wealthy tourists took their afternoon tea by the pools underneath the trellis hung with blossoming wisteria.

One of the best ways to savor Buçaco is to drive the 1,800 feet up to **Cruz Alta** (high cross), through the forests and past hermitages. The view from the summit is among the best in Portugal.

WHERE TO STAY & DINE
✪ **Palace Hotel do Buçaco.** Mata do Buçaco, Buçaco, 3050 Mealhada. ☎ **231/93-01-01.** Fax 231/93-05-09. E-mail: almeida.hotelip.pt. 64 units. A/C TV TEL. 29,000$–34,500$ ($162.40–$193.20) double; 60,000$–150,000$ ($336–$840) suite. Rates include continental breakfast and parking. AE, DC, MC, V.

Once a vacation retreat for Portuguese monarchs, this is one of the most mythical buildings in the country. In one of Iberia's most famous farewells, the deposed Amélia passed from the earth after her final visit to Buçaco in 1945. The government had permitted the ailing queen a sentimental journey to all the places where she had reigned before her husband and son were assassinated in 1908. In 1910 the Swiss-born head of the kitchen, the former king's cook, persuaded the government to let him run the palace as a hotel.

The palace is an architectural fantasy, ringed with gardens and exotic trees imported from the far corners of the Portuguese empire. The designer borrowed heavily from everywhere: the Jerónimos Monastery in Belém, the Doge's Palace in Venice, and the Graustark Castles of Bavaria. One of Europe's most grandiose smaller palaces, it's in the center of a 250-acre forest.

Despite the wear and tear caused by thousands of guests, the structure is still intact and impressive. Especially notable is the grand staircase with ornate marble balustrades, 15-foot-wide bronze torchières, and walls of blue-and-white tiles depicting important scenes from Portuguese history. Each richly furnished drawing room and salon is a potpourri of whimsical architecture.

The most spectacular accommodation is the queen's suite, which has a private parlor, dressing room, sumptuous marble bathroom, and dining room. In 1992 many of the guest rooms were upgraded and restored, but they retain their dignified, conservative decor.

Dining/Diversions: The high-ceilinged dining room serves lunch and dinner. There's also a bar.

Amenities: 24-hour room service, laundry, concierge.

5 Luso

19½ miles N of Coimbra, 143 miles N of Lisbon, 5 miles SE of Cúria

Luso, a little spa town on the northwestern side of the Buçaco mountain, boasts a mild climate and thermal waters for both drinking and bathing. The radioactive and hypotonic water is low in mineral content. It is said to have great efficacy in the treatment of kidney ailments, alimentary complaints, circulatory problems, and respiratory tract or skin allergies.

Besides the health-oriented aspects of the spa, it's a resort area that shares many of its facilities with Buçaco, 2 miles away. During the spa season, festivities and sports events are held at the casino, nightclub, and tennis courts, as well as on the lake and at the two pools, one of which is heated. Thermal spa enthusiasts flock here from June to October.

ESSENTIALS
ARRIVING

BY TRAIN   From Coimbra, line 110 extends west. There's daily service to Luso. The one-way fare is 450$ ($2.50).

BY BUS   Five buses a day run to Luso from Coimbra, a 1-hour trip. Beginning at 7:45am, departures are about every 2½ hours. The one-way cost is 425$ ($2.40). For **information** and schedules, call ☎ 239/82-70-81.

BY CAR   From Coimbra, head north along the Lisbon-Porto motorway, the most important highway in the country, until you come to the signposted turnoff for Luso. Head east for another 3½ miles.

VISITOR INFORMATION

The **Luso Tourist Office** is on rua Emídio Navarro (☎ **231/93-91-33**).

WHERE TO STAY

Grande Hotel das Termas. Rua dos Banhos, Luso, 3050 Mealhada. ☎ **231/93-04-50.** Fax 231/93-03-50. 143 units. A/C MINIBAR TV TEL. 13,000$–15,800$ ($72.80–$88.50) double; 40,000$ ($224) suite. Rates include continental breakfast. AE, DC, MC, V. Free parking.

With a backdrop of rolling forests, the vanilla-colored Grande Hotel, built in 1945, nestles in a valley amid abundant foliage. It's a sprawling place adjacent to the spa, offering comfortable, well-proportioned rooms with matching furnishings; some open onto private terraces with views of the tree-covered valley. About 80 rooms are air-conditioned.

Guests praise the thermal spa facilities here. You can swim in a 150-foot Olympic-size pool, lounge and sunbathe on the surrounding grassy terrace, or relax under the weeping willows and bougainvillea arbor. There are hard tennis courts.

The mural-decorated dining room overlooking the pool serves large portions of regional and international cuisine. Try a bottle of full-bodied Messias and wine from nearby Mealhada.

✪ **Vila Duparchy.** Luso, 3050 Mealhada. ☎ **231/93-07-90.** Fax 231/930-307. 6 units (some with tub only, some with shower only). 10,000$–14,500$ ($56–$81.20) double. Rates include breakfast. AE, MC, V. Free parking.

A quarter of a mile from the center of Luso, this 21-acre working horse farm is across the highway to Mealhada from the town's only gas station. Conceived in the 19th century as a farmhouse, it was named after the French-born engineer who designed and built the town's rail station. He lived here during the late 19th century before selling it to the present owner's forebears. Today, under Oscar and Maria Santos, the place has some of the most appealing accommodations in the region. Rooms vary in shape and size; all are exceedingly comfortable, with fine bed linens and firm mattresses. The superbly kept bathrooms contain fluffy towels and deluxe toiletries. The Santos family's main business is rearing and training horses; if you're qualified, you can usually arrange to go horseback riding during your stay. Evening meals can be prepared if you notify your hosts in advance. They're served in the family's dining room and cost around 3,500$ ($19.60) per person. Guests have the use of a trio of downstairs sitting rooms, where TVs and phones are available. There is also a swimming pool.

WHERE TO DINE

Restaurant O Cesteiro. Rua Dr. Lúcio Pais Abranches. ☎ **231/93-93-60.** Main courses 1,000$–1,600$ ($5.60–$8.95). AE, MC, V. Daily noon–3pm and 7–10pm. PORTUGUESE.

This unpretentious restaurant is near the train station, about a 5-minute walk from the center. It's on the road leading out of town toward Mealhada. A simple sign and plain brown tiles cover the facade of the spacious room. Inside is a popular bar that does a brisk business with local artisans and farmers. The fare is likely to include duck stew, roast goat, roast suckling pig with saffron sauce, and an array of fish dishes, including cod. The food is decently prepared and fresh. On weekends, motoring Portuguese families fill the tables.

6 Cúria

7 miles NW of Luso, 16 miles NW of Buçaco, 142 miles N of Lisbon, 12 miles N of Coimbra

Cúria, in the foothills of the Serra de Estrêla, forms a well-known tourist triangle with Luso and Buçaco. Its spa has long been a draw for people seeking the curative properties of the medicinal waters, which are slightly saline and contain calcium sulfates and sodium and magnesium bicarbonates. In addition, the town has tennis courts, swimming pools, roller-skating rinks, a lake for boating, cinemas, and teahouses. The season for taking the waters is April to October; June sees the beginning of the largest influx.

In the Bairrada wine-growing district, Cúria offers the fine wines of the region. The famous local cuisine includes roast suckling pig, roast kid, and sweets.

ESSENTIALS
ARRIVING

BY BUS   Several buses run daily between the train station at Luso (see the preceding section) and the spa at Cúria. One-way tickets cost 425$ ($2.40).

BY CAR   From Coimbra, head north along N1.

VISITOR INFORMATION

The **Cúria Tourist Office** is on largo da Rotunda (☎ **031-51-22-48**).

WHERE TO STAY & DINE

✪ **Grande Hotel de Cúria.** 3780 Anadia. ☎ **231/51-57-20.** Fax 231/51-53-17. E-mail: gcuria@mail.telepac.pt. 84 units. A/C MINIBAR TV TEL. 12,500$–20,000$ ($70–$112) double; 31,500$ ($176.40) suite. Rates include breakfast. AE, DC, MC, V. Free parking.

The Grande Hotel was an elegant hideaway for many of Europe's crowned heads after it opened in the 1880s, but then it saw years of neglect. Following massive renovations by Portugal's Belver Hotel Group, it reopened in 1990. The most prominent structure in town, with a lavish art nouveau facade, the hotel reigns as the finest in the region. Decorative touches in the public rooms include marble floors and lavish upholstery and carpets. There's a carefully trained staff. The midsize to spacious guest rooms come in two styles: art deco nostalgic and conservative modern.

The food is upscale and well prepared. It's served in rooms of varying sizes, depending on how crowded the hotel is. The hotel has a concierge, room service (7am to 11:30pm), and massage. The health club offers a gymnasium, massage, Jacuzzis, and two pools.

The hotel is a few steps west of the center of the village, less than half a mile from the railway station.

Hotel das Termas. Cúria, 3780 Tamingos. ☎ **231/51-21-85.** Fax 231/51-58-38. 57 units. A/C TV TEL. 12,000$–18,000$ ($67.20–$100.80) double; 17,000$–25,000$ ($95.20–$140) suite. Rates include breakfast. AE, DC, MC, V. Free parking.

You approach Hotel das Termas on a curving road through a parklike setting with lacy shade trees. The guest rooms have a homelike feeling, with lots of floral chintz, wooden beds, and walls of wardrobe space. The hotel has a British colonial atmosphere, with lots of brass and wicker. It offers facilities for health and relaxation, including a free-form pool encircled with orange trees and tables. In the park a rustic wooden bridge leads over a lake to walks and tennis courts. The dining hall, with parquet floors and a brick fireplace, feels like a tavern, especially when it's filled with guests. The hotel even has bicycles so you can explore the countryside.

Palace Hotel de Cúria. Cúria, 3780 Tamingos. ☎ **231/51-21-31.** Fax 231/51-55-31. 114 units. TV TEL. 17,000$ ($95.20) double. Rates include breakfast. AE, DC, MC, V. Closed Nov–Mar. Free parking.

Opened in 1926, the four-story Palace Hotel is an elegant accommodation on 15 acres of gardens. Four female faces, almost outlandishly oversize, gaze over the gardens and parasols in front. Though it isn't the most famous hotel in Portugal, the Palace is one of the most prestigious, having received in recent years both the president and the prime minister. Parts of the movie *The Buster Keaton Story* were filmed here.

Between the twin towers of the hotel's Italianate facade lie well-furnished guest rooms, many quite spacious. The hotel's 60-by-107-foot pool is one of the largest in the land. Guests have access to the town's spa facilities, which lie a short walk away. There are two tennis courts, billiards, a playground for children, and miniature golf. There's also a miniature zoo, with exotic birds. Room service and laundry are available.

The bright, airy dining room serves excellent Portuguese and international cuisine. Whenever possible, it incorporates garden-fresh produce, much of it from the Beiras.

Pensão Lourenço. Cúria, 3780 Anadia. ☎ **231/51-22-14.** 38 units. 6,000$ ($33.60) double. Rates include breakfast. No credit cards. Closed Oct–May. Free parking on street.

Throughout the spa, a series of signs points motorists to this simple inn, which you'll find in a tree-lined hollow away from the town center. It occupies a pair of buildings on either side of a narrow road. One of the buildings contains a ground-floor cafe whose tables and patrons sometimes spill into the road. Guest rooms are small, with time-worn but still comfortable furnishings. Most of the guests are elderly; many are pensioners who come to Cúria season after season. They form a closely knit community of shared interests and needs.

7 Aveiro

35 miles N of Coimbra, 42 miles S of Porto

Myriad canals spanned by low-arched bridges crisscross Aveiro. At the mouth of the Vouga River, it's cut off from the sea by a long sandbar that protects clusters of islets. The architecture is almost Flemish, a good foil for a setting of low willow-reed flatlands, salt marshes, spray-misted dunes, and rice paddies.

On the lagoon, brightly painted swan-necked boats traverse the waters. Called *barcos moliceiros,* the flat-bottomed vessels carry fishers who harvest seaweed used for fertilizer. They're ever on the lookout for eels, a regional specialty, which they catch in the shoals studded with lotus and water lilies. Outside the town are extensive salt pits, lined with fog-white pyramids of drying salt.

ESSENTIALS
ARRIVING

BY TRAIN   The **rail station** is at largo da Estação (☎ **234/42-44-85**). At least 20 trains per day make the 30-minute run from Porto (see chapter 11). The fare is 370$ ($2.05) one way. Some 22 trains arrive daily from Coimbra; the trip takes an hour and costs 450$ ($2.50) one way. There are five trains per day from Viseu. The 4-hour trip costs 890$ ($5) one way. And 20 trains per day arrive from Lisbon; it's a 5-hour trip, and the one-way fare is 1,610$ ($9).

BY BUS   The nearest Rodoviária (national express bus company) station is at Águeda, 12 miles from Aveiro. Buses connect Águeda with the train station at Aveiro. For **information** and schedules, call ☎ **234/42-37-47.**

BY CAR   Continue north along A1 from Coimbra to the junction with N235, which leads west to Aveiro.

VISITOR INFORMATION

The **Aveiro Tourist Office** is at rua João Mendonça 8 (☎ **234/42-36-80**).

EXPLORING THE AREA   The town is quite congested, and many readers have expressed disappointment with it. They cite the incessant whine of Vespas as well as the relatively stagnant, foul-smelling canal water. Others, however, find it worth the journey.

The lagoons and many secret pools that dot the landscape around Aveiro make for a fine **boat excursion.** Inquire at the tourist office (see above).

Convento de Jesús, praça do Milenário (☎ **234/42-32-97**), is hailed as the finest example of the baroque style in Portugal. The Infanta Santa Joana, sister of João II and daughter of Afonso V, took the veil here in 1472. Her tomb, an inlaid rectangle of marble quarried in Italy, attracts many pilgrims. Its delicate pale pinks and roses lend it the air of a cherub-topped confection.

The convent, owned by the state and now called the **Museu de Aveiro,** displays a lock of the saint's hair, her belt and rosary, and a complete pictorial study of her life. A portrait of her, painted in intonaco, is exceptional. What's most noteworthy about the convent is its carved gilt work, lustrous in the chapel, despite the dust.

In this setting is an assortment of 15th-century paintings, royal portraits of Carlos I and Manuel II (the last two Bragança kings), antique ceramics, and 16th-, 17th-, and 18th-century sculpture. There are also some well-preserved 18th- and 19th-century coaches and carriages. After viewing all this, you can walk through the cloisters, which have Doric columns. The museum is open Tuesday to Sunday from 10am to 5pm. Admission is 300$ ($1.70) for adults, free for children under 15.

On rua Santa Joana Princesa is the 15th-century **Igreja de São Domingo,** with blue-and-gold altarpieces and egg-shaped windows flanking the upper nave. The facade, in Gothic-Manueline style, is decorated with four flame finials. To the right (facing) is a bell tower.

After a meal of stewed eels and a bottle of hearty Bairrada wine, you might wish to explore some of the settlements along the lagoon. In **Ilhavo,** 3 miles south of Aveiro, you can stop at the **Museu do Mar,** rua Vasco da Gama (☎ **234/32-17-97**). The unpretentious gallery offers an insight into the lives of people who live with the sea. It displays seascape paintings, boating paraphernalia, fishing equipment, ship models, and other exhibits. The museum is open Wednesday to Saturday 9am to 12:30pm, Tuesday to Sunday 2 to 5:30pm. Admission is 200$ ($1.10).

From Ilhavo, you can drive 1 mile south to **Vista Alegre,** the famed village of the porcelain works. Britain's Elizabeth II and Spain's Juan Carlos have commissioned pieces of Vista Alegre porcelain. On a branch of the Aveiro estuary, the village is the site of an open market held on the 13th of every month, a tradition dating from the late 1600s.

The **Vista Alegre Museum,** Fábrica Vista Alegre (☎ **234/32-53-65**), records the history of porcelain, starting in 1824 when the factory was founded here. It's open Tuesday to Sunday from 9am to 12:30pm and 2 to 4:30pm. Admission is free.

OUTDOOR ACTIVITIES   In the Rota da Luz area near Aveiro, you can go **windsurfing** in many places, including Ria de Aveiro and Pateira de Fermentelos. The long stretches of sand and the formation of waves also provide ideal conditions for **surfing;** particularly good Rota da Luz **beaches** are Esmoriz, Cortegaça, Furadouro, Torreira, São Jacinto, Barra, Costa-Nova, and Vagueira. The whole stretch of the Ria estuary is ideal for **waterskiing,** and many rivers, notably the Pateira and the Ria, are suited for **canoeing** and **rowing.**

There's good **fishing** along the Rota da Luz. The tourist office (see above) provides helpful information. The local waterways contain carp, lampreys, and barbels, along with gray mullet, bass, and eels. The best places for trout are the rivers Paiva, Arda, Antuà, Caima, Alfusqueiro, and Águada.

Horseback riders head for the **Escola Equestre de Aveiro,** Quinta Chão Agra, Vilarinho (☎ **234/91-21-08**), 4 miles north of Aveiro on N109. It offers trekking rides across the wetlands around Aveiro. The cost is 5,000$ ($28) per rider for 2 hours. Call for reservations and more information.

Many visitors to the area like to go **biking,** particularly along the traffic-free route between Aveiro and Ovar, the most ideal terrain. You can rent bikes next to the tourist office on rua João Mendonça (☎ **234/42-00-80**).

SHOPPING You'll find handcrafts and the sophisticated porcelain manufactured in the village of Vista Alegre, 4 miles south. To visit the **Vista Alegre factory outlet** (☎ **234/32-53-65**), follow the signs from the town center. Free visits to the manufacturing facilities are conducted Tuesday to Sunday from 9am to 12:30pm and 2 to 4:30pm. The factory outlet is open Tuesday to Sunday from 9am to 12:30pm and 2 to 7pm.

In the city center, a **Vista Alegre outlet,** with a choice but slightly less extensive inventory, is on rua Dr. Nascimento Leitão (☎ **234/32-53-65**), opposite the Imperial Hotel. Another outfit with worthwhile inventories of porcelain and pottery imported directly from a nearby factory is **O Buraco** (☎ **234/31-24-73**). Its downtown outlets are in the Centro Comercial Oita and on praça do Mercado.

One of the town's most visible and best-stocked shopping venues is the main boulevard bisecting the town, **avenida Dr. Lourenço Peixenho.** The shops here sell virtually everything a local resident might need to pursue the good life in the Portuguese and international style.

WHERE TO STAY

Arcada Hotel. Rua Viana do Castelo 4, 3800 Aveiro. ☎ **234/423-001.** Fax 234/421-886. 49 units. TV TEL. 8,350$–9,900$ ($46.75–$55.45) double; 13,300$ ($74.50) suite. Rates include breakfast. AE, DC, MC, V. Free parking.

The family owned Arcada enjoys an enviable central position, with a view of the traffic in the canal out front. In summer, white pyramids of drying salt on the flats are visible from the guest rooms. The modernized hotel retains its classic beige-and-white facade and its rooftop decorated with ornate finials. The hotel occupies the second, third, and fourth floors of the old building. Many of the midsize guest rooms open onto balconies, and each has central heating. Some are in the traditional Portuguese style; others evoke 1950s international style, with blond furnishings. Some rooms can be noisy. Breakfast is the only meal served. There's a hotel bar.

Hotel Afonso V. Rua Dr. Manuel das Neves 65, 3800 Aveiro. ☎ **234/425-191.** Fax 234/381-111. 80 units. A/C MINIBAR TV TEL. 12,600$ ($70.55) double; 17,000$ ($95.20) suite. Rates include breakfast. AE, MC, V. Parking 400$ ($2.25).

This is the best place in town, though many people prefer the Imperial (below). If you're driving, small but well-placed signs will direct you to the hotel, in a residential, tree-lined neighborhood. Small sea-green tiles line the facade. A recent enlargement and renovation turned the original core into a contemporary structure. The midsize guest rooms, which have firm mattresses, are comfortably furnished but uninspired. The hotel has an English-style pub and two restaurants (see "Where to Dine," below).

Hotel Imperial. Rua Dr. Nascimento Leitão, 3800 Aveiro. ☎ **234/422-141.** Fax 234/424-148. 103 units. A/C MINIBAR TV TEL. 12,700$ ($71.10) double; 16,100$ ($90.15) suite. Rates include breakfast. AE, DC, MC, V. Free parking.

Unexceptional but efficient and modern, the Imperial is often cited as the best hotel in town by those who prefer it over the Afonso V (see above). It attracts local young people, who gravitate to the lounge for drinks and TV watching, or to the airy dining

room (which is also a favorite with tour groups). Many of the small, neutrally decorated guest rooms and all of the lounges overlook the Ria de Aveiro and the garden of
the Aveiro museum, the old convent. From the summer terrace, a view sweeps over
the arid expanse of the district's salt pans. All rooms have individual central heating.
They're furnished in contemporary style, with many built-in features and firm beds.

Hotel João Padeiro. Rua da República 13, Cacia, 3800 Aveiro. ☎ **234/91-13-26.** Fax
234/91-27-51. 26 units. TV TEL. 8,800$ ($49.30) double; 10,500$ ($58.80) suite for 2. Rates
include breakfast. AE, DC, MC, V. Free parking.

Beside the highway, 4½ miles from Aveiro, João Padeiro is a sienna-colored building
concealing an elegant hotel. It was an unpretentious village cafe until the Simões
family transformed it more than a decade ago. You enter a velvet-covered reception
area filled with family antiques. Each unit is unique, and most contain an antique
four-poster; all boast exuberantly flowered wallpaper, coved ceilings, and hand-
crocheted bedspreads. Laundry and room service are offered.

  Meals are served in a blue-and-white dining room, with massive Portuguese chests,
leather-upholstered chairs, and fresh flowers. Specialties may include shellfish
omelette, house-style fillet of sole, goat cooked in wine, fried eels, and lobster curry;
try the walnut tart for dessert. Meals cost 1,200$ to 6,000$ ($6.70 to $33.60). The
restaurant is open daily from 12:30 to 3pm and 7:30 to 10pm; closed December 25.

✪ Paloma Blanca. Rua Luís Gomes de Carvalho 23, 3800 Aveiro. ☎ **234/38-19-92.** Fax
234/38-18-44. 48 units. TV TEL. 10,650$–14,200$ ($59.65–$79.50) double. Rates include
breakfast. AE, DC, MC, V. Parking 600$ ($3.35).

Paloma Blanca occupies a Moorish-style building that was once an aristocratic private
villa. An iron fence encloses the front courtyard, where trees, vines, and hand-painted
gold-and-white tiles surround a fountain. The best rooms look out over the third-floor
loggia onto a goldfish-filled basin in the garden. You'll find this well-preserved house
(known in Portuguese as an *antiga moradia senhorial*) on a busy downtown street
leading into the city from Porto. Most of the large guest rooms are old-fashioned;
about half are air-conditioned. Breakfast is the only meal served.

WHERE TO DINE

A Cozinha do Rei. In the Hotel Afonso V, rua Dr. Manuel das Neves 66. ☎ **234/42-68-02.**
Regular main courses 1,400$–2,600$ ($7.85–$14.55); seafood main courses 3,000$–10,000$
($16.80–$56). MC, V. Daily noon–midnight. PORTUGUESE/INTERNATIONAL.

A Cozinha do Rei is in the best hotel in town (see "Where to Stay," above). On the
left as you enter, the formal restaurant serves regional and international meals in a
modernized sun-washed room. You can order fresh fish with confidence. The veggies,
however, tend to be bland. Service is among the best in town.

Restaurante Centenário. Largo do Mercado 9–10. ☎ **234/42-27-98.** Main courses
1,600$–3,200$ ($8.95–$17.90). MC, V. Daily 9am–midnight. PORTUGUESE.

Centenário stands at the side of Aveiro's version of Les Halles. From the front door
you can see the teeming covered market; laborers often stream up to the elongated
bar after unloading produce early in the morning. At the napery-covered table, fine
food is served. The high-ceilinged, modern room contains lots of polished wood and
has a large window opening onto the street. The restaurant is also called "A Casa da
Sopa do Mar," and that shellfish-laden soup is the house specialty. In addition to a
steaming bowl, you can order grilled pork or veal, fried or grilled sole, codfish *brasa*,
and an array of other good-tasting specials. This isn't gourmet fare, but it's good and
satisfying.

WHERE TO STAY & DINE NEARBY

Pousada da Ria. Bico do Muranzel, 3870 Torreira-Murtosa. ☎ **234/83-83-32.** Fax 234/83-83-33. 19 units. TV TEL. 22,500$ ($126) double. Rates include breakfast. AE, DC, MC, V. Free parking.

The government operates this pousada, about 18½ miles from Aveiro on a promontory surrounded by water on three sides. Between the sea and the lagoon, it's a contemporary building that makes good use of glass and has rows of balconies on its second floor. You can reach it by boat from Aveiro (passengers only) or by taking a long drive via Murtosa and Torreira. A waterside terrace opens onto views of fishing craft. The inn is popular with vacationing Portuguese families. The compact guest rooms are furnished with built-in pieces, including firm beds.

If you're stopping for a meal, the cost is 3,650$ ($20.45). The chef's specialty is *caldeirada a Ria,* savory fish stew. Not surprisingly, the best dishes use the abundant local seafood. A sunny Sunday is likely to be bedlam here; otherwise, it's a peaceful haven.

Pousada de Santo António. Serem, Mourisca de Vouga, 3750 Agueda. ☎ **234/52-32-30.** Fax 234/52-31-92. 12 units. MINIBAR TV TEL. 16,000$–17,500$ ($89.60–$98) double. Rates include breakfast. AE, DC, MC, V. Free parking.

On a rise above the Vouga River stands the Santo António, a large villa near the main Lisbon-Porto highway. The pousada is about 30 miles north of Coimbra and 48 miles south of Porto. The Caramulo and Talhada mountains loom in the background. One of the first government-run pousadas, it was built in 1942 with a design inspired by the farmhouses of the region's wealthy landowners. The surrounding meadowlands and river valley are lush, filling the dining room and living room windows with vibrant colors.

The pousada is decorated like a warm provincial inn. High headboards on the country-style beds and patterned stone floors create an air of simple comfort in the immaculate, but rather small, guest rooms. Laundry and room service are available. The outdoor pool and tennis courts are inviting attractions.

Meals are served daily from 12:30 to 3pm and 7:30 to 10pm. At dinner, you can begin with *caldeirada* or *caldo verde;* if they're available, be sure to request the veal or *bacalhau* (codfish), followed by the fruits of the valley. Meals cost 2,500$ to 4,000$ ($14 to $22.40).

AVEIRO AFTER DARK

The core of the city's nightlife is the **Canal de São Roque,** near the Mercado de Peixe in the town center. Here you'll find a trio of 18th-century stone-sided salt warehouses. They've been transformed into attractive, richly folkloric bars that draw enthusiastically loyal local patrons. Two are the **Eugência Bar** (☎ 234/42-80-82) and the **Estrondo Bar** (☎ 234/38-33-66). A slight variation is **Cal Ponente** (☎ 234/38-26-74), which functions from 7 to 10pm as a well-managed restaurant, then from 10:30pm to around 4am as a venue for live concerts. Expect to hear lots of Brazilian samba and rock—everything except fado. Cal Ponente is one of the few eateries in town with views that encompass both the lagoon and the town's age-old salt pans.

Fado is the order of business, at least on Saturday night, at **Centenário,** largo do Mercado 9–10, at praça do Mercado (☎ 234/42-27-98; see "Where to Dine," above). The owner, who doubles as the chef most other nights, is the featured singer every Saturday. If you want to go dancing, head for the town's most appealing disco, **Disco Oito Graus Oeste** (Eight Degrees West), Canal do Paraiso (☎ 234/42-27-98).

8 Caramulo

50 miles NE of Coimbra, 174 miles N of Lisbon

Set against a background of mimosa and heather-laden mountains, this tiny resort between Aveiro and Viseu is a good place from which to view the surrounding country. About 2 miles north of town, at the end of a dirt road to the left, is a watch-tower that affords a panoramic view of the Serra do Caramulo.

ESSENTIALS
ARRIVING

There's no train service to Caramulo.

BY BUS   From Lisbon, you must go to Tondela, then make connections into Cara-mulo. You can also go from Lisbon to Viseu (see the following section), ride the bus to Caramulo, though you'll have to allow at least 5 hours. You can also take the train from Lisbon to Coimbra (see section 3 in this chapter), a bus to Tondela, and another bus to Caramulo.

BY CAR   The village is usually approached from Viseu (see the following section). Follow N2 south for some 15 miles to Tondela, then take a right onto N230 and follow signs for Caramulo for about another 12 miles.

VISITOR INFORMATION

The **Caramulo Tourist Office** is on estrada Principal do Caramulo (☎ **232/86-14-37**).

EXPLORING THE AREA

From the tip of the mountain, about 4½ miles from town at **Caramulinho,** you can see for miles. The panoramic sweep includes the Lapa, Estrela, Lousa, and Buçaco ranges; the serras da Gralheira and do Montemura, and the coastal plain. To reach the best viewing place on the 3,500-foot-high peak, take avenida Abel de Lacerda from Caramulo west to N230-3, then go about half a mile on foot. Another panoramic vista spreads out from the summit of **Cabeça da Neve,** off the same road you'd take to go to Caramulinho.

   The **Museu do Caramulo** (☎ **232/86-12-70**) houses at least 60 veteran and vin-tage cars, including a 1905 four-cylinder De Dion–Bouton, a 1909 Fiat, an 1899 Peu-geot, a 1902 Oldsmobile, a 1911 Rolls-Royce, and a 1902 Darracq. The cars have been restored to perfect condition. A few early bicycles, one dating to 1865, and motorcycles are on exhibit. The museum also contains Portuguese and foreign paint-ings and art, by such diverse artists as Dalí, Picasso, and Grão Vasco. Admission is 800$ ($4.50) for adults, 400$ ($2.25) for children. The museum is open daily from 10am to 1pm and 2 to 6pm.

WHERE TO STAY & DINE

Pousada de São Jerónimo. 3475 Caramulo. ☎ **232/86-12-91.** Fax 232/86-16-40. 12 units. A/C TV TEL. 22,500$ ($126) double. Rates include continental breakfast and parking. AE, DC, MC, V.

High as an eagle's nest, São Jerónimo is near the crest of a mountain ridge. The well-designed inn resembles a spread-out chalet. You ascend to the reception, living, and dining rooms; one salon flows into another. In winter, guests sit by the copper-hooded fireplace. Beyond the wooden grille is a pleasant dining room, with a window wall that overlooks the hills.

The guest rooms are small but attractive, with Portuguese antiques and reproductions. Wide windows open onto private balconies. Laundry service and baby-sitting are offered. The pousada also has a private park, a pool, and a playground. If you enjoy fishing, the Agueda and Criz Rivers teem with trout and achigas, a local barbel. From here, you can follow the Besteiros valley, and from its terraces you can see the impressive Estrela mountains, 48 miles away.

In the dining room, you sit on hand-carved provincial chairs and sample country-style cooking that ranges from pork to goat to codfish to octopus. If you're just dropping in, a table d'hôte lunch or dinner (by candlelight) goes for 4,000$ ($22.40). Food is served daily from 12:30 to 3pm and 7:30 to 10pm.

9 Viseu

60 miles E of Aveiro, 57 miles NE of Coimbra, 181 miles NE of Lisbon

The capital of Beira Alta, Viseu is a thriving provincial capital. It's also a city of art treasures, palaces, and churches. Its local hero is an ancient Lusitanian rebel leader, Viriatus. At the entrance of Viseu is the Cova de Viriato, where the rebel, a combination Spartacus and Robin Hood, made his camp and plotted the moves that turned back the Roman tide.

Some of the country's most gifted artisans ply their timeless trades in and around Viseu. Where racks creak and looms hum, the busy weaver women create the unique quilts and carpets of Vil de Moinhos. Local artisans of Molelos produce the region's provincial pottery, and women with nimble fingers embroider feather-fine bone lace.

ESSENTIALS
ARRIVING
BY TRAIN   The nearest rail station is at Nelas, about 15 miles south. For train **information,** call ☎ 21/888-40-25. Buses run from Nelas to Viseu; the fare is 335$ ($1.90). The fare from Lisbon to Nelas is 1,400$ ($7.85).

BY BUS   Five Rodoviária buses per day make the 2-hour trip from Coimbra. Five buses per day come from Lisbon, a 5-hour run. For **information,** call ☎ 239/85-52-70.

BY CAR   Viseu lies near the center of the modern expressway, IP-5, which cuts across Portugal. IP-5 hooks up with the Lisbon-Porto motorway. Coming from Spain, motorists enter Portugal at the Vilar Formoso Customs station, then head west to Viseu.

VISITOR INFORMATION
The **Viseu Tourist Board** is on avenida Gulbenkian (☎ 232/42-09-50).

EXPLORING THE TOWN
Viseu offers much to see and explore at random. Wander the cubistic network of overlapping tiled rooftops, entwining narrow alleys, and encroaching macadam streets. If your time is limited, head at once to **largo da Sé,** the showplace of Viseu. Here, on one of the most harmonious squares in Portugal, you'll find the town's two most important buildings.

Sé (Cathedral). Largo da Sé. ☎ **232/422-2984.** Free admission. Daily 9am–noon and 2–6:30pm.

The severe Renaissance facade of this cathedral evokes a fortress. Two lofty bell towers, unadorned stone up to the balustraded summit with crowning cupolas, are visible from almost any point in or around town. The second-story windows—two rectangular and one oval—are latticed and symmetrically surrounded by niches containing religious statuary.

On your right, you'll first find the two-story Renaissance cloister, adorned with classic pillars and arcades faced with tiles. The cathedral interior is essentially Gothic but infused with Manueline and baroque decorations. Plain, slender Romanesque columns line the nave, supporting the vaulted Manueline ceiling, with nautically roped groining. The basic color scheme inside plays brilliant gilding against muted gold stone. The emphasis is on the Roman arched chancel, climaxed by an elegantly carved retable above the main altar. The chancel makes ingenious use of color counterpoint, with copper, green gold, and brownish yellow complementing the gilt work. The ceiling continues in the sacristy.

Museu de Grão Vasco. Largo da Sé. ☎ **232/422-049.** Admission 250$ ($1.40), free for children under 15. Tues–Sun 10am–12:30pm and 2–5pm.

This museum, next door to the cathedral, was named after the 16th-century painter, also known as Vasco Fernandes. The Portuguese master's major works are on display; especially notable is *La Pontecôte*, in which lancelike tongues of fire hurtle toward the saints, some devout, others apathetic.

SHOPPING

Viseu has many handcrafts shops. The most obvious shopping area is **rua Direita,** the main street, where you'll find merchants purveying pottery, wrought iron, and wood carvings. The most comprehensive stock is at the **Casa de Ribiera,** Camera Municipal de Viseu, praça da República (☎ **232/42-35-01**), which carries selections from many of the region's best artisans.

WHERE TO STAY

Grão Vasco. Rua Gaspar Barreiros, 3500 Viseu. ☎ **232/42-35-11.** Fax 232/42-64-44. 110 units. A/C TV TEL. 14,000$ ($78.40) double; 20,000$ ($112) suite. Rates include breakfast. AE, DC, MC, V. Free parking.

In the heart of town, near praça da República, Grão Vasco sits amid gardens and parks. It's built like a motel; the guest-room balconies overlook an oval pool. After days of driving in the lodging-poor environs, you'll find it a pleasure to check in here. The decor is colorful and contemporary, and the guest rooms are decorated with reproductions of Portuguese traditional furnishings. Most are large, and all have firm mattresses. The dining room, with its baronial stone fireplace, features good Portuguese cuisine. If you're just dropping in, you can have lunch or dinner à la carte. Meals are served on a terrace in summer.

Hotel Avenida. Av. Alberto Sampaio 1, 3500 Viseu. ☎ **232/42-34-32.** Fax 232/435-643. www.turism.net/avenida. 29 units. TEL. 9,800$ ($54.90) double. Rates include breakfast. AE, DC, MC, V. Free parking.

Avenida is a personalized small hotel right off Rossio, the town's main plaza. It's the domain of the personable Mario Abrantes da Motto Veiga, who has combined his collection of African and Chinese antiques with pieces of fine old Portuguese furniture. The small guest rooms vary in size and character. For example, Room 210B boasts a high-coved bed and an old refectory table and chair; an adjoining chamber has a wooden spindle bed and a marble-topped chest. Portuguese meals in the plain family style dining room are well prepared and generous.

Hotel Montebelo. Urbanização Quinta do Bosque, 3510 Viseu. ☎ **232/420-000.** Fax 232/415-400. 100 units. A/C MINIBAR TV TEL. 15,000$ ($84) double; 17,500$–50,000$ ($98–$280) suite. Rates include breakfast. AE, DC, MC, V. Free parking.

This independent hotel is the best and newest in town, with an enviable reputation based on the attentiveness of its multilingual staff. Less than a quarter mile from the town center, on a rise providing a panorama over the countryside, it stands in a pleasant garden. The four floors, in an L-shaped design, incorporate hundreds of large windows. The midsize rooms are traditionally and comfortably furnished, and maintenance is state of the art. The basement contains a health club with Jacuzzis, a sauna, and an indoor pool; a restaurant; and two bars. Room service is available from 7am to midnight.

✪ **Quinta de São Caetano.** Rua Possa dos Feiticeiras 38, 3500 Viseu. ☎ **232/42-39-84.** Fax 232/42-17-61. E-mail: bfe0089@mail.telepac.pt. 6 units. A/C. 12,000$ ($67.20) double. Rates include breakfast. V. Free parking.

Half a mile north of the center of Viseu, this is one of the most renowned properties in the region. Built in the 17th century, with a chapel dating from 1638, it was the home for many years of the viscountess of St. Caetano. It was also the setting of the novel *Eugénia e Silvina,* by the prominent contemporary Portuguese novelist Agustina Bessa Luís.

Members of the Vieira de Matos family run the severely dignified hotel. On the premises is a pool, a garden with mature trees (including a century-old Atlantic cedar), and a greenhouse where flowers grow. Dark-grained, sometimes antique furnishings fill the thick-walled rooms. Guest rooms, in various sizes and shapes, are traditionally furnished, with excellent beds. Breakfast usually is the only meal served. With prior notice, lunch and dinner can be prepared for groups. There's a billiard table on the premises, and horseback riding can be arranged with the owner of a nearby stable.

WHERE TO DINE

✪ **Cortiço.** Rua de Augusto Helário. ☎ **232/42-38-53.** Main courses 1,000$–2,500$ ($5.60–$14). AE, DC, MC, V. Daily noon–3pm and 7–11pm. PORTUGUESE.

In the oldest part of Viseu's historic core, close to the cathedral and upstairs from the Museo de Grão Vasco, this is the most appealing restaurant in town. A team of articulate, English-speaking locals prepares winning versions of time-tested dishes. You can select from several tasty versions of codfish, roasted breast of duck, stewed or roasted partridge (when available), and rack of rabbit simmered in red wine. One of the most prized dishes is octopus, grilled or fried, with herbs and lemon. Many diners consider it the best in the region. The wines, from throughout Portugal, are reasonably priced.

VISEU AFTER DARK

Many thrill-seekers head away from Viseu for their nightlife. The local establishments draw the children of local farmers and livestock breeders. Among the best of the lot is the **Disco Metropolis,** in the hamlet of Bodiosa (☎ **232/97-25-50**), about 3½ miles east of Viseu. Follow signs pointing to São Pedro do Sousa. Farther along the same road, 15 miles east of Viseu, you'll come to the **Disco Picados,** in the hamlet of São Pedro de Sousa (☎ **232/72-39-59**). On EN2, 4½ miles north of Viseu, you'll find **The Day After,** Camp Viseu (☎ **232/45-06-45**).

Porto & Environs

11

Porto (Oporto in English) is Portugal's second-largest city and its capital of port wine. The 15th-century residence of the royal family, the city is rich in the legacy of the past—art treasures, medieval cathedrals, famous museums, a fine library, and other attractions. Many old noble homes trace their beginnings to the activities of the court, events leading to Portugal's Golden Age of Discovery and other milestones.

The port wine is brought to lodges at Vila Nova de Gaia, across the river from Porto, where it's blended, aged, and processed. In the past it was transported on flat-bottomed boats called *barcos rabelos*. With their long rudders and flapping sails, these boats with tails skirted down the Douro like swallows. Nowadays they've nearly given way to the train and even the unglamorous truck.

The city, which is undergoing a major renovation and sprucing up, has never looked better. Some of its streets look as if they haven't changed since the Middle Ages. Porto's labyrinth of steep streets, with their decorative *azulejos* (tiles) and wrought-iron balconies, often filled with potted flowers, is reason enough to visit the city.

Especially rewarding is the Barredo section, a UNESCO World Heritage Site. Architect Fernando Namora, a Porto citizen, is supervising the restoration of this old-fashioned district. The sectors of Miragaia and Ribeira are also being restored.

The city also boasts a lively arts and cultural scene. The Serralves Foundation, one of the country's most dramatic cultural centers, often sponsors events. Many art galleries are sprouting up in the hilly Miragaia district, near the river. Poetry readings, art exhibits, and even live jazz and rock concerts characterize Porto today.

An underrated stretch of coastal resorts and fishing villages lies between Porto and the southern reaches of the Minho district. The Atlantic waters, however, are likely to be on the chilly side, even in July and August. In recent years the resorts have grown tremendously; they're known more to European vacationers than to Americans, who still prefer the Algarve. Porto and the coast to its north and south are among the most rewarding places to visit in Portugal.

Flying from Lisbon is the speediest way to Porto, though the express train or motorway takes only 3½ hours. Once in Porto, the transportation hub of the area, you can explore the coastal towns by bus or car.

Many visitors come here not only to see Porto but also to take cruises along the Rio Douro of port-wine fame. Some trips are short, taking in only the famous bridges of Porto and some nearby fishing villages; mini-cruises last 1 or 2 days, with food and lodging provided on board. Cruise prices vary widely, beginning at 1,500$ ($8.40) for a 50-minute cruise of Porto and going up to 14,500$ to 35,000$ ($81.20 to $196) per person for trips of 1 to 2 days. Of course, summer is the best time to take these cruises, but they operate year-round, with greatly curtailed service in winter. Many prefer to take the cruises in early fall, at harvest time.

One of the most reliable cruise companies is **Endouro,** rua da Reboleira 49, Porto (☎ 22/332-42-36). The tourist office in Porto (see "Essentials" in section 1, below) provides information about an array of lesser-known companies offering cruises.

Exploring the Region by Car

Day 1   While based in Porto, consider a drive along its coast. The immediate area, with its industrial sites, particularly those around the port of Leixões, is best bypassed. The scenery improves considerably at **Vila do Conde,** 17 miles north, at the mouth of the Avenue. Here, if the weather's right, you might spend time at the beach and perhaps visit the **Mosteiro de Santa Clara** on the north bank of the Ave.

Continuing north for 2½ miles, you reach **Póvoa do Varzim,** noted for its long beach and high-rise hotels, where you might stop for a lunch of regional food. **Belo Horizonte,** rua Tenente Valadim 63 (☎ 252/62-47-87), serves moderately priced fish and seafood dishes, mostly to Portuguese families. The same type of fare is available at **Estrela do Mor,** rua Caetano de Oliveira 144 (☎ 252/68-49-75), which hasn't much in the way of decor but serves heaping platters of fish, often accompanied by rice. It lies 20 yards from the seafront.

If you have the time and inclination, you can continue north from Porto for 29 miles to **Ofir** and **Fão,** twin resorts where you'll find a number of restaurants and hotels, along with a good beach. You can spend the night or return to Porto. If you're planning to drive on to the Minho, you might want to stay here so you don't have to backtrack.

Day 2   Route N109 south of Porto takes you to **Espinho,** 11 miles away. Here you can enjoy a day at the beach and take advantage of the resort's leisure facilities and shopping. You can return to Porto for the night.

1 Porto

195 miles N of Lisbon, 189 miles S of La Coruña, Spain, 366 miles W of Madrid, Spain

Porto (known also as "the Port") gave its name not only to port wine but also to Portugal and its language. The name derives from the Roman settlement of Portus Cale. The Douro, which comes from "Rio do Ouro" (River of Gold), has always been Porto's lifeblood. The city perches on a rocky gorge that the Douro cut out of a great stone mass. According to the writer Ann Bridge, "The whole thing looks like a singularly dangerous spider's web flung across space."

Porto's most interesting quarter is the Alfândega. The steep, narrow streets and balconied houses evoke Lisbon's Alfama, though the quarter has its own distinctive character. The Alfândega preserves the timeless quality of many of the old buildings and cobbled *ruas* lining the riverbank.

Many visitors write off Porto as an industrial city with some spectacular bridges, but there's much to enjoy here. As the provincial capital and university seat, Porto has its own artistic treasures. The city beats with a sense of industriousness—it's not surprising that Henry the Navigator was born here in the late 14th century.

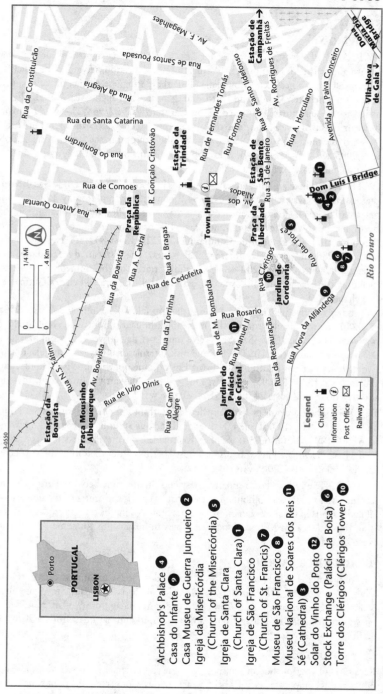

Porto

PORTUGAL
Porto
LISBON

Archbishop's Palace ④
Casa do Infante ⑨
Casa Museu de Guerra Junqueiro ②
Igreja da Misericórdia
(Church of the Misericórdia) ⑤
Igreja de Santa Clara
(Church of Santa Clara) ①
Igreja de São Francisco
(Church of St. Francis) ⑦
Museu de São Francisco ⑧
Museu Nacional de Soares dos Reis ⑪
Sé (Cathedral) ③
Solar do Vinho do Porto ⑫
Stock Exchange (Palácio da Bolsa) ⑥
Torre dos Clérigos (Clérigos Tower) ⑩

Legend
✝■ Church
ⓘ Information
⊠ Post Office
┼┼ Railway

ESSENTIALS

ARRIVING

BY PLANE   Porto stretches along the last 3 miles on the right bank of the river Douro and is the hub of northern Portugal's communication network. The quickest and easiest way to get there is by plane. TAP, the Portuguese airline, provides quick connections between Lisbon and Porto, and there are daily flights year-round. Flights arrive at the **Aeroporto Francisco de Sá Carneiro** (☎ 22/948-21-41). The main office of **TAP** is at praça Mouzinho de Albuquerque 105 (☎ **22/948-22-91**) in Porto.

A taxi, the most convenient way to get from the airport into the center, costs 2,500$ to 3,000$ ($14 to $16.80). Bus nos. 56 and 87 run between the airport and the center; a one-way ticket is 150$ (85¢).

BY TRAIN   There are three main rail stations in Porto. The **Estação de São Bento,** praça Almeida Garrett (☎ 22/200-10-54), is in the city center, only a block from praça da Liberdade. Trains from here serve the Douro Valley and destinations in the north, including Viana do Castelo and Braga. East of the center, but connected to São Bento by rail, is the **Estação de Campanhã** (☎ 22/536-41-41). It serves the south, including Lisbon, as well as international routes. The **Estação da Trindade,** rua Alferes Malheiro (☎ **22/200-48-33**), handles traffic in the immediate environs, including the beach resort of Póvoa do Varzim and the historic old city of Guimarães (see chapter 12).

Five trains arrive per day from Lisbon; the trip takes 4½ hours and costs 1,950$ ($10.90) one way. Twelve trains a day make the 2-hour trip from Viana do Castelo; a one-way ticket costs 650$ ($3.65). Twelve trains per day arrive from Coimbra; it's a 2½-hour trip and costs 910$ ($5.10) one way. International travelers can take one of two daily trains from Madrid to Porto via Entroncamento; trip time is 12 hours, and the cost is 9,100$ ($50.95) one way. One train per day arrives from Paris; the trip takes 27 hours and costs 24,000$ ($134.40) one way.

BY BUS   There are at least five daily departures from Lisbon. The trip takes 5 hours and costs 1,900$ ($10.65) one way. It ends at the **bus station,** rua Alexandre Herculano 366 (☎ **22/200-69-54**). Service is provided by the national bus company, Rodoviária Nacional. There are also 10 buses per day from Coimbra; the trip takes 1½ hours and costs 1,200$ ($6.70) one way.

BY CAR   The Lisbon-Porto superhighway cuts driving time between Portugal's two leading cities to just over 3 hours. For motorists, Porto is the center of the universe— all major roads in the north fan out from here. From Spain, the nearest border crossing is at Tuy–Valença do Minho. After that, you can head south for some 78 miles to Porto on N13.

VISITOR INFORMATION

One of the most helpful tourist offices in Portugal is the **Porto Tourist Board,** rua do Clube Fenianos 25 (☎ **22/205-27-40**). The office is open July to September, Monday to Friday from 9am to 7pm, Saturday and Sunday from 9:30am to 4:30pm; off-season, Monday to Friday from 9am to 5:30pm and Saturday from 9:30am to 4:30pm.

CITY LAYOUT

Regardless of your method of transport, you'll need to acquaint yourself with the geography of this complicated city. Its **bridges** are famous. Connecting the right bank to the port-wine center of **Vila Nova de Gaia** and the lands south is the **Ponte de Dona Maria Pía** (Dona Maria Pía Bridge), an architectural feat of Alexandre-Gustave Eiffel (of Paris tower fame). Another bridge spanning the Douro is the **Ponte de Dom Luís I** (Dom

Luís I Bridge). An iron bridge of two roadways, it was completed in 1886 by Teófilo Seyrig, a Belgian engineer inspired by Eiffel. Another bridge, the **Ponte da Arrábida,** which opened in 1963, is bright and contemporary. Totally Portuguese in concept and execution, it's one of the largest single-span reinforced-concrete arches in Europe, representing the work of Edgar Cardoso.

The heart of Porto is **avenida dos Aliados,** a wide *paseo* with a parklike center where families used to go for a stroll. It's bounded on the south by **praça General Humberto Delgado.** Two major shopping streets lie on either side of **praça da Liberdade: rua Clérigos** and **rua do 31 de Janeiro.** Rua Clérigos leads to the landmark **Torre dos Clérigos,** which some consider the symbol of Porto.

GETTING AROUND

Porto is well serviced by a network of **buses, trolleys, and trams;** tickets begin at 160$ (90¢). If you plan extensive touring in the area, a Passe Turístico is a good deal. It includes 4 days of transportation for 1,600$ ($8.95). Tobacco shops and kiosks around town sell the pass.

Taxis are available 24 hours a day. Call ☎ **22/52-80-61** for radio taxis, or hail one on the street or at a taxi stand.

Fast Facts: Porto

American Express   The representative in Porto is **Top Tours,** rua Alferes Malheiro 96 (☎ **22/208-27-85**). It's open Monday to Friday 9am to 12:30pm and 2:30 to 6:30pm.

Banks   Most banks and currency-exchange offices are open Monday to Friday 8:30 to 11:45am and 1 to 2:45pm. Two central ones are the **Banco Espírito Santo & Comercial de Lisboa,** av. dos Aliados 45 (☎ **22/332-00-31**), and the **Banco Pinto & Sotto Mayor,** praça da Liberdade 26 (☎ **22/332-15-56**).

Consulates   The United States and Canada don't maintain consulates in the north. There's a **British Consulate** at av. da Boavista 3072 (☎ **22/618-47-89**).

Drugstores   Porto has many pharmacies. A centrally located one is the **Farmácia Central do Porto,** rua do 31 de Janeiro 203 (☎ **22/200-16-84**). Otherwise, phone ☎ **118** for the location of a 24-hour pharmacy (these change from day to day). If you don't speak Portuguese, ask someone at your hotel to call for you.

Emergencies   Emergency numbers include **police** (☎ **112** or **22/208-18-33**), **fire** (☎ **22/508-41-21**), **Red Cross** (☎ **22/606-68-72**), and **Hospital de Santo António,** rua Prof. Vicente José de Carvalho (☎ **22/200-73-54**).

Post Office   The **main post office** is at praça General Humberto Delgado (☎ **22/208-02-51**), near the tourist office. It sells stamps Monday to Friday from 9am to 10pm. You can send telegrams and faxes during those hours.

Telephone   It's possible to place long-distance calls at the post office (see above). Otherwise, go to the **phone office,** praça da Liberdade 62. It's open daily from 8am to 11:30pm. By placing your calls at these public institutions, you avoid hotel surcharges, which can be as much as 40%.

EXPLORING THE CITY

Seeing the sights of Porto requires some legwork, but your discoveries will compensate you for the effort. The tourist office suggests that you take at least 3 days to explore Porto, but most visitors spend only a day.

For those on a short schedule, the most famous things to do are visiting a wine lodge at Vila Nova de Gaia; taking in the panorama from the Torre dos Clérigos, with its view of the Douro; visiting the Sé (cathedral); strolling through the most important museum, the Museu Nacional de Soares dos Reis; walking through Ribeira, the old quarter (best seen on market days); and, if time remains, seeing the Church of St. Francis, with its stunning baroque interior.

THE TOP ATTRACTIONS
Churches

Sé (Cathedral). Terreiro da Sé. ☎ **22/205-90-28.** Admission to Sé free; to cloister, 200$ ($1.10). Daily 9am–noon and 3–5:30pm. Bus: 15.

The cathedral grew and changed with the city—that is, until about the 18th century. Founded by a medieval queen and designed in a foreboding, basically Romanesque style, it's now a monument to changing architectural tastes. Part of the twin towers, the rose window, the naves, and the vestry are elements of the original 13th-century structure. The austere Gothic cloister was added at the end of the 14th century and later decorated with tiles depicting events from the Song of Solomon. Opening off the cloister is the Chapel of St. Vincent, built in the late 16th century.

The main chapel was erected in the 17th century, and in 1736 the baroque architect Niccolò Nasoni of Italy added the north facade and its attractive loggia. The monumental altar is flanked by twisted columns, the nave by fading frescoes. In the small baroque Chapel of the Holy Sacrament (to the left of the main altar) is an altarpiece fashioned entirely of silver. The work is so elaborate that the whole piece gives the illusion of constant movement.

Igreja de Santa Clara. Largo do 1 de Dezembro. ☎ **22/205-48-37.** Free admission. Mon–Fri 9:30–11:30am and 3–6pm, Sun 9:30am–12:30pm. Tram: 1. Bus: 15, 20, or 35.

Completed in 1416, the interior of the Church of St. Clara was transformed by impassioned 17th-century artists, masters of woodwork and gilding. Nearly every square inch is covered with angels, saints, cherubs, and patterned designs in an architectural melange of rococo and baroque, one of the most exceptional examples in Portugal. The clerestory windows permit the sun to flood in, making a golden crown of the upper regions. In deliberate contrast, the building's facade is squat and plain. If the keeper of the keys takes a liking to you, he'll lead you on a behind-the-scenes tour of the precincts. In the Tribute Room, for example, you'll see a devil carved on the choir stalls.

Igreja de São Francisco. Praça do Infante Dom Henríque. ☎ **22/200-64-93.** Admission (including church and museum) 500$ ($2.80). Mar–Oct daily 9am–5:30pm; Nov–Feb Mon–Sat 9am–5:30pm. Bus: 23, 49, or 88.

The Gothic Church of St. Francis, reached by steps leading up from the waterfront, was built between 1383 and 1410. In the 17th and 18th centuries it underwent extensive rococo dressing. The vault pillars and columns are lined with gilded woodwork: cherubs, rose garlands, fruit cornucopia, and frenzied animals, entwined and dripping with gold. Many of the wide-ribbed Gothic arches are made of marble resembling the Italian forest-green serpentine variety. Soaring overhead, the marble seems to fade and blend mysteriously with the gray granite columns and floors.

The Romanesque rosette dominates the facade, whose square portal is flanked by double twisted columns. Above the columns, a profusely ornamented niche contains a simple white statue of the patron saint. In the rose window, 12 mullions emanate from the central circle in apostolic symbolism, ending in a swaglike stone fringe. The steps spill fanlike into the square, along the base of the curved walls. Nearby, through a separate entrance, is the Museu de São Francisco (see below).

Museums

Casa Museu de Guerra Junqueiro. Rua de Dom Hugo 32. ☎ **22/205-36-44.** Admission 150$ (85¢), free for children under 10. Tues–Sun 10am–noon and 2–5pm. Bus: 15.

The famous Portuguese poet Guerra Junqueiro lived here between 1850 and 1923. The Italian architect Niccolò Nasoni (1691–1773) built the house. The room arrangements preserve Junqueiro's private art collection and memorabilia. The collection includes Georgian and Portuguese silver; Flemish chests; Italian, Oriental, Spanish, and Portuguese ceramics; and ecclesiastical wood and stone carvings.

Museu de São Francisco. Rua da Bolsa 44. ☎ **22/200-64-93.** Admission (including church and museum) 500$ ($2.80), free for children. Mar–Oct daily 9am–5:30pm; Nov–Feb Mon–Sat 9am–5:30pm. Tram: 1. Bus: 23, 49, or 88.

The sacristan at the Museum of St. Francis estimates that 30,000 human skulls have been interred in the cellars. He may be exaggerating, but this dank building was once the burial ground for rich and poor. Nowadays it's a catacomb unique in Portugal. A section of it looks like an antique shop. There are also paintings, including one of St. Francis of Assisi worshiping Christ on the Cross. Curios include some of the first paper money printed in Portugal, and an 18th-century ambulance that was really a sedan chair. The Sala de Sessões, built in rich baroque style, is now a meeting hall with a Louis XIV table and João V chairs. Wherever you go in the room, the painted eyes of framed bishops follow you.

Museu Nacional de Soares dos Reis. Rua de Dom Manuel II 56. ☎ **22/399-37-70.** Admission 350$ ($1.95), free for under 10. Tues–Sun 10am–noon and 2–6pm. Bus: 3, 6, 20, 35, 37, or 41.

Created in 1833 by order of Dom Pedro IV, the Soares dos Reis National Museum was called the Museu Português when it opened in 1840. A hundred years later it was declared a national museum and dedicated to Soares dos Reis (1847–89), the noted sculptor from Porto whose remarkable works include *Desterrado* and *Flor Agreste*. Portraits and allegorical figures can be seen in the same gallery.

In the foreign painters collection, you'll find Dutch, Flemish, Italian, and French works, including two portraits by François Clouet (1522–72), and landscapes by Jean Pillement (1727–1808). The most representative and unified display is that of the Portuguese 19th-century painters, particularly from the Porto School. Henríque Pousão (1859–87) and Silva Porto (1850–93) are represented by fine naturalistic work. Also on display are decorative arts—ceramics, glassware, gold and silver work, furniture, and other objects.

Fundação de Serralves (Museu Nacional de Arte Moderna). Rua Don Joàn de Castro. ☎ **22/618-00-57.** Admission 800$ ($4.50). Tues–Wed, Fri–Sun 10am–7pm; Thurs 10am–10pm. Bus: 3, 19, 21, 35, or 78.

Run by the Gulbenkian Foundation in Lisbon, the National Museum of Modern Art is an outpost of culture in western Porto. It occupies a new building in a 44-acre park next to the sherbet-pink art deco mansion where the collection was formerly displayed. Pritzker Prize–winning Álvaro Siza, a native son, designed the stark granite-and-stucco new structure. The building is Porto's finest example of 1930s art nouveau. The museum exhibits the work of an exemplary coterie of contemporary Portuguese painters, designers, and sculptures. Exhibits change constantly, but there's always something interesting. The descriptions of the works are in Portuguese, but you can ask to see an English-language video on the artists. It's also worth the time to wander through the sculptured gardens, along with their fountains. There's even old farmland tumbling down toward the Douro.

MORE ATTRACTIONS

Casa do Infante. Rua do Infante Dom Henríque. ☎ **22/205-60-25.** Free admission. Mon–Fri 9am–5pm. Tram: 1. Bus: 1, 15, 57, or 91.

Tradition has it that Porto's fabled hometown boy, Prince Henry the Navigator, was born in this house—now appropriately called the House of the Prince—which dates from the 1300s. In the 1800s the building was used as a customs house. Today it contains a Museu Histórico with documents, manuscripts, and various artifacts relating to the history of Porto.

Torre dos Clérigos. Rua dos Clérigos. ☎ **22/200-17-29.** Admission to tower 200$ ($1.10); to church, free. Tower Thurs–Tues 10am–7pm. Church Mon–Sat 10am–noon, 2–5pm; Sun 10am–1pm. Bus: 15.

West of praça da Liberdade, follow rua dos Clérigos to the Clérigos Tower, which the Italian architect Niccolò Nasoni designed in 1754. The tower's six floors rise to a height of some 250 feet, which makes it one of the tallest structures in the north of Portugal. You can climb 225 steps to the top of the belfry, where you'll be rewarded with one of the city's finest views, of Porto and the river Douro. The Italianate baroque Igreja dos Clérigos, at the same site, was also built by Nasoni and predates the tower.

TOURING THE PORT-WINE LODGES

The port-wine lodges lie across the river from Porto at **Vila Nova de Gaia.** Like the sherry makers at Jerez de la Frontera, Spain, these places are hospitable, and run free tours for visitors. Take bus no. 57 or 91 to reach the lodges.

Taylor's. Rua do Choupelo. ☎ **22/371-99-99.** Mon–Fri 10am–6pm.

The cellars of Taylor's are the most interesting in Porto. The firm is the last of the original English port companies to remain family owned. Tours here are less formal than those at the other wine lodges, and the atmosphere is less modernized. Known for its carefully selected grapes, Taylor's produces vintage ports, single Quinta wines, and even a rare 40-year-old tawny port. You'll be served a glass of wine on the terrace, which has a view of the city and the river.

Porto Sandeman. Largo Miguel Bombarda 3. ☎ **22/374-05-33.** Apr–Oct daily 10:30am–5:45pm; Nov–Mar Mon–Fri 9:30am–12:30pm and 2–5pm.

The most famous port-wine center is Porto Sandeman, owned by Seagram's of Canada. In a former 16th-century convent, Sandeman was established in 1790 by George Sandeman of Scotland. The House of Sandeman also operates a unique museum that traces the history of port wine and of the company. You can purchase Sandeman products on the premises.

Ferreira. Av. Diogo Leite 70. ☎ **22/375-20-66.** Mid-Apr to mid-Oct Mon–Fri 9am–noon and 2–5pm, Sat 9:30am–noon; mid-Oct to mid-Apr Mon–Fri 9am–noon and 2–5pm.

The legendary Ferreira is one of the biggest wine lodges. Dating from the early 1800s, it was launched by Dona António Adelaide Ferreira. From a modest beginning, with only a handful of vineyards, her company rose in power and influence, gobbling up wine estate after wine estate. At its apex, its holdings stretched all the way to the border with Spain, making its owner the richest woman in the nation. The fabled entrepreneur (known as Ferreirinha, or "Little Ferreira") nearly drowned in the Douro in 1861, but her voluminous petticoat kept her buoyant. (Her companion, an Englishman named baron de Forrester, who did not wear petticoats, wasn't as lucky.)

Port: One for the Road

I must have one at eleven,
It's a duty that must be done.
If I don't have one at eleven,
I must have eleven at one.

—Anonymous

Portugal's most famous wine is rich, fortified port, named for the old city of Porto. Even experts disagree about when the first port wine was made. One story is that the first port reached England in the early 1600s—perhaps by accident. Two sons of a Liverpool wine merchant on their way home from Porto were said to have added brandy to a wine they had liked in the Douro, hoping to fortify it for the long, bumpy trip back. They may unknowingly have created the first port.

Port has played a role in English history. Local port-wine producers jokingly suggest that the American Revolution would never have been fought were it not for the three bottles of vintage port that the English rulers drank every night in front of their thirsty American subjects.

Port wine can come only from the rugged mountainous terrain of the Upper Douro. The grape-growing region, running along the Douro, is only some 20 to 40 miles wide. The cultivation of the grape is strictly regulated. It's said that the best grapes grow where nothing else will. The ideal time to visit the region is autumn, during the age-old ritual of grape gathering. Centuries-old songs and the music of the pipe and drum often accompany the nightlong treading of the grapes, still done by foot in some places.

Vintage port isn't ready for drinking until it's 10 years old, and many connoisseurs prefer port that has been aged for 20 years, when it develops a tawny color. In our opinion, the best 20-year-old port is Ferreira. In recent years, white ports have become more popular. Try Taylor, Cockburn, or Sandeman as an apéritif, but only if it's chilled.

Crusted port, unlike vintage, doesn't have to be created from a single year or vintage, but might be made from wine gathered over three harvests. It spends a long time in wood to help its maturation. Wood ports, on the other hand, are blended wines created from several harvests and matured in casks until ready for drinking.

Caves Porto Cálem. Av. Diogo Leite 26. ☎ **22/374-66-60.** May–Sept daily 10am–6pm; Oct–Apr Mon–Sat 10am–6pm.

Founded in 1959 by the Cálem family, this wine production company was taken over by the Sojevinus Corporation in 1998. Its tour is much less formal than one at Sandeman, next door. The cellars are much newer than those at the more established firms, but the port is almost as good.

Caves Ramos Pinto. Av. Ramos Pinto 380. ☎ **22/370-70-00.** June–Sept Mon–Fri 10am–6pm, Sat 10am–1pm; Oct–May Mon–Fri 9am–1pm and 2–5pm.

Created in 1880 by Adriano Ramos Pinto, this company remained in the same family until its sale in 1991 to Louis Roederer, the champagne company. On a tour of the cellars, you'll learn about the illustrious founder and the history of port.

Walking Tour—The Heart of Porto

Start: Terreiro da Sé.
Finish: Estação de São Bento.
Time: 2½ hours.
Best Times: Any day between 10am and 4pm.
Worst Times: Monday to Friday from 8 to 10am and 4 to 6pm, because of heavy traffic.

The only suitable way to explore the heart of the inner city is on foot. Nearly all the major monuments are in the old part of town, and the major sights are close together. The streets are often narrow and sometimes confusing to the first-time visitor; even armed with a good map, you're likely to get lost from time to time. Long accustomed to entertaining foreigners, the people of Porto are generally friendly and hospitable, and will point you in the right direction.

Begin your tour in the heart of the old town, at:

1. **Terreiro da Sé,** a square dominated by the Sé, founded as a fortress church in the 12th century and greatly altered in the 1600s and 1700s. Square domed towers flank the main facade. "Cathedral Square" is also bordered by an 18th-century former episcopal palace, now municipal offices. Noted for its granite-cased doors and windows, it contains an exceptional stairway. Also on the square is a Manueline-style pillory and a statue of Vimara Peres, the warrior of Afonso III of León, who captured ancient Portucale in 868 A.D.

To the rear of the cathedral is one of Porto's most charming and *típico* streets:

2. **Rua de Dom Hugo.** If you continue along this street, you'll pass the Chapel of Our Lady of Truths. It's invariably closed, but you can peek through the grille at the gilded rococo altar, with a statue of the Virgin at the center. Along this same street at no. 32 stands the:

3. **Casa Museu de Guerra Junqueiro,** a white mansion—now a museum—that was the home of the poet Guerra Junqueiro (1850–1923). The Italian architect Niccolò Nasoni designed this mansion.

Rua de Dom Hugo, a narrow street, curves around the eastern side of the Sé. Continue along it until you come to some steep steps. These were carved through remaining sections of the town walls that existed in the Middle Ages. This brings you into one of the most colorful, and poverty-stricken, sections of Porto, the:

4. **Ribeira district.** The back streets of this decaying neighborhood, now under restoration, do have a certain charm. The area abounds with arcaded markets, churches, museums, monuments, and once-elegant buildings.

Regardless of which alley you take, everything eventually merges onto the:

5. **Cais da Ribeira,** the quayside section of the Ribeira district, opening onto the Douro. Locals come here for the low-cost *tascas* (taverns) and seafood restaurants, which were constructed into the street-level arcade of the old buildings.

☕ **TAKE A BREAK** If you're walking around at midday, stop for lunch at the **Taverna do Bêbodos,** Cais da Ribeira 24 (☎ **22/205-35-65**), which has been serving locals since 1876. A dining room upstairs opens onto views of the Douro. You might happily settle for a glass of the local wine from a cask balanced on the bar.

The center of the district is:

6. **Praça da Ribeira,** where locals sit in the sun telling tall tales. From here, visitors can take in the port-wine lodges across the Douro at Vila Nova de Gaia.

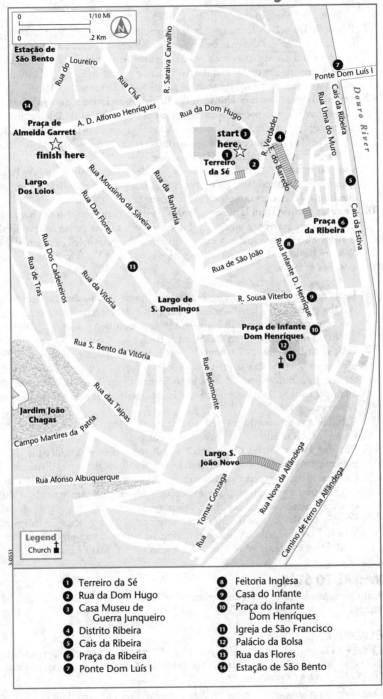

Walking Tour—Porto

Legend
Church ✝

1. Terreiro da Sé
2. Rua da Dom Hugo
3. Casa Museu de Guerra Junqueiro
4. Distrito Ribeira
5. Cais da Ribeira
6. Praça da Ribeira
7. Ponte Dom Luís I
8. Feitoria Inglesa
9. Casa do Infante
10. Praça do Infante Dom Henríques
11. Igreja de São Francisco
12. Palácio da Bolsa
13. Rua das Flores
14. Estação de São Bento

Now head north to the:

7. **Ponte de Dom Luís I,** the middle of the trio of bridges over the river Douro. The iron bridge was designed by Seyrig, a collaborator of Eiffel, in 1886. It has an upper and a lower span, both of which funnel traffic to Vila Nova de Gaia.

After viewing the bridge and the river, retrace your steps to praça da Ribeira. At the west side of the square, walk up rua de São João to the:

8. **Feitoria Inglesa (Factory House of the British Association),** the headquarters of the Port Wine Shippers' Association. One of the most fabled buildings in the Ribeira district, it stands where rua do Infante Dom Henríque crosses rua de São João. The "factory" was designed by the British consul John Whitehead in 1786.

Follow rua do Infante Dom Henríque to the:

9. **Casa do Infante,** at the corner of rua da Alfândega. Porto-born Henry the Navigator, who launched Portugal on the Age of Discovery, reputedly was born in this house. Follow rua do Infante Dom Henríque to:

10. **Praça de Infante Dom Henríque,** named after Henry the Navigator. A statue of Prince Henry graces the square. At this square, you can visit a big covered food market, where tripe is sold in great quantities. Although shunned by much of the Western world (except by Florentines), tripe is said to be the favorite food of the denizens of Porto.

The highlight of this square is the:

11. **Igreja de São Francisco,** originally a Gothic church. Its adjacent museum once was the property of a Franciscan monastery. This church boasts the most lavish, spectacular church interior in Porto—and the competition is keen.

Behind the church, facing the square, is Porto's:

12. **Palácio da Bolsa (Stock Exchange).** It takes up a great deal of the site of what used to be a Franciscan monastery. It's known for an oval Arab Room whose stained glass and arabesques are said to imitate the style of the Alhambra in Granada, built by the Moors. The Stock Exchange stands at rua da Bolsa and rua Ferreira Borges.

Follow rua Ferreira Borges west, veering north to largo de São Domingos. At the top of this square, continue northwest along:

13. **Rua das Flores (Street of Flowers),** which some visitors consider the most romantic street in Porto. It's long been known for the quality of its silversmiths, but what makes the street so architecturally striking is its wrought-iron balconies.

This street eventually opens onto praça de Almeida Garrett, named for the famed Portuguese writer. On this square is the:

14. **Estação de São Bento,** the most central of Porto's railway stations. Its grand main hall is decorated with large tiles tracing the history of transportation in Portugal. From this terminal you can catch a train to your next destination.

WHERE TO STAY

Porto provides the most interesting selection of superior accommodations north of Lisbon.

EXPENSIVE

✪ **Casa do Marechal.** Av. da Boavista 2674 Porto. ☎ **22/610-47-02.** Fax 22/610-32-41. 5 units. A/C MINIBAR TV TEL. 25,000$–30,000$ ($140–$168) double. Rates include breakfast. AE, DC, MC, V. Free parking. Closed Aug.

One of the most atmospheric hotels in Portugal is this little charmer. Built in 1935, it remained a private residence until its conversion in 1990 into a gem of a small hotel.

In a new section of Porto, near the modern art museum, the hotel is beautifully, even elegantly, furnished. Guest rooms are modern in comfort but traditional in style, with excellent mattresses and state-of-the-art plumbing. The hotel does not offer room service.

Dining/Diversions: The classic restaurant serves refined cuisine in the traditional Portuguese style. There is also a fashionable bar.

Amenities: Laundry, concierge.

Hotel Dom Henríque. Rua Guedes de Azevedo 179, 4000 Porto. ☎ **22/340-16-16.** Fax 22/340-16-00. www.hotel-dom-henrique.pt. E-mail: reserv@hotel-dom-henrique.pt. 114 units. A/C MINIBAR TV TEL. 21,000$–28,000$ ($117.60–$156.80) double; from 31,000$ ($173.60) suite. Rates include buffet breakfast. AE, DC, MC, V Parking 1,300$ ($7.30) nearby. Bus: 29 or 59.

Though designed for business travelers, Dom Henríque is equally accommodating to visitors. In the city center, the recently restored hotel is in a 22-story tower. Executive suites are available. While it's generally a moderately priced hotel, this place has some extralarge, amenity-filled rooms that fall into the "expensive" category. Rooms are equipped with videos, firm mattresses, and hair dryers; they look a little dated, though. Two floors are reserved for nonsmokers.

Dining: The 17th-floor bar, Anrrique, affords panoramic views. The cuisine in the ground-floor restaurant is often refreshingly imaginative. Meals are served daily from 12:30 to 2pm and 7:30 to 10:30pm. Also on the ground floor is a coffee shop, Tábula, open daily from 7am to 3pm and 7 to 11:30pm.

Amenities: Laundry, room service, baby-sitting, concierge.

Hotel Mercure Batalha. Porto Praça da Batalha 116, 4049 Porto. ☎ **22/200-05-71.** Fax 22/200-24-68. 158 units. A/C TV TEL. 18,000$–20,000$ ($100.80–$112) double; 21,000$–23,000$ ($117.60–$128.80) suite. Rates include breakfast. AE, MC, V. Parking 1,500$ ($8.40). Bus: 35, 37, or 38.

Opposite the National Theater, the Batalha reopened in 1992 following a complete renovation. Popular with international port-wine buyers, it's about a 10-minute walk from the river and the commercial center. In one of the more colorful sections of the old town, it combines the traditions of yesterday with the modern comforts of today, and is a bargain in its category.

The lobby sets the tone, with old paintings, antique furniture, pillars, and cushioned seating. The guest rooms are also traditional; while not grand, they're tastefully decorated, with coordinated fabrics, French windows, comfortable beds, and tiled bathrooms. About half a dozen can accommodate travelers with disabilities. In spite of soundproofing, traffic noise is audible from some front rooms.

Dining/Diversions: A restaurant, Burgo, serves regional and continental specialties, some toned down for foreign palates. The bar is a busy before-dinner rendezvous.

Amenities: Laundry, room service, concierge.

✪ **Infante de Sagres.** Praça Filippa de Lancastre 62, 4000 Porto. ☎ **22/339-85-00.** Fax 22/339-85-99. 74 units. A/C MINIBAR TV TEL. 24,500$–28,000$ ($137.20–$156.80) double; 50,000$ ($280) suite. Rates include breakfast. AE, DC, MC, V. Parking free on street; garage 1,600$ ($8.95) per hour. Bus: 35, 37, or 38.

The most traditional choice in town is the plush Infante de Sagres, last refurbished in 1991. The hotel sits beside a monumental square flanked by the town hall and Porto's showplace, avenida dos Aliados. Its rich, handcrafted ornamentation convinces most visitors that it dates from the 19th century, but it was built in 1951 by a wealthy textile manufacturer. Its imposing mass of carved paneling, stained glass, and wrought iron was assembled solely to house the businessman's powerful clients during their trips to Porto.

The hotel has been host to the rich and famous, including Princess Anne and Prince Philip, the president of Portugal, and many of his cabinet ministers. The hotel maintains one of the highest ratios of employees to guests (1.3 employees per room) in Porto and offers excellent service. A parasol- and plant-dotted sun terrace occupies a central courtyard. The spacious guest rooms contain large marble-trimmed bathrooms and elegant furniture, including excellent beds.

Dining/Diversions: The high-ceilinged dining room, Dona Filippa, serves formal breakfast, lunch, and dinner in an old-world setting. There's a bar on the premises.

Amenities: Laundry, room service, concierge. The helpful staff can make arrangements with nearby facilities if you wish to play tennis, swim, or go horseback riding.

Le Méridien Park Atlantic Porto. Av. da Boavista 1466, 4100 Porto. ☎ **22/607-25-00.** Fax 22/600-20-31. www.portugalvirtual.pt/meridien.porto/. E-mail: meridien.porto@mail.telepac.pt. 239 units. A/C MINIBAR TV TEL. 29,000$–32,000$ ($162.40–$179.20) double; from 65,000$ ($364) suite. Rates include breakfast. AE, DC, MC, V. Parking 150$ (85¢) per hour. Bus: 3 or 78.

One of the most dramatically modern hotels in town, the Méridien has three vertical rows of bay windows along its 13-floor concrete shell. The hotel, about 2 miles from the heart of the city, is owned by Air France and is a favorite of conventioneers. Though in the same price bracket, it's too big to offer the personalized service of Infante de Sagres. The well-furnished midsize guest rooms have in-house video movies. Two floors are smoke-free.

Dining/Diversions: There's a restaurant, Les Terrasses (see "Where to Dine," below). The basement-level disco is open Thursday to Saturday from 10:30pm to 4am; the 6,500$ ($36.40) drink minimum applies to nonguests only.

Amenities: 24-hour room service, laundry, baby-sitting, massages, hairdresser, business center.

Porto Palacio Hotel. Av. da Boavista 1269, 4150 Porto. ☎ **22/608-66-00.** Fax 22/609-14-67. E-mail: pto.palaciohotel@mail.telepac.pt. 262 units. A/C MINIBAR TV TEL. Mon–Thurs 22,500$ ($126) double; from 50,000$ ($280) suite. Fri–Sun 20,000$ ($112) double; from 50,000$ ($280) suite. AE, DC, MC, V. Parking 80$ (45¢). Tram: 2. Bus: Boavista 78.

Opened with a flourish in 1986, this 23-floor tower is one of Porto's most stylish and desirable modern hotels. In the Boavista section, a short distance from the city's commercial center, it rises across from its major competitor, the Méridien. Set back from a busy street, its exterior has bands of stone and reflecting bronze glass. Each good-sized guest room has a hair dryer, firm mattress, and video movies.

Dining/Diversions: The premier restaurant, Madruga, serves mainly regional fare, with some international choices. A businessperson's lunch is offered Monday to Friday from 12:30 to 3pm. Dinner is served from 7:30 to 11pm. The lobby's Nautilus Bar, which has nightly piano music, is open daily from 8am to 2am.

Amenities: Laundry and valet, baby-sitting, beauty parlor, hairdresser, 24-hour room service, heated pool, squash court, health club.

MODERATE

Hotel Ipanema Porto. Rua do Campo Alegre 156, 4100 Porto. ☎ **22/606-80-61.** Fax 22/606-33-39. E-mail: ipanema.porto@mail.infos.pt. 150 units. A/C MINIBAR TV TEL. 16,600$ ($92.95) double; 27,500$ ($154) suite. Rates include breakfast. AE, DC, MC, V. Free parking.

The Ipanema (don't confuse it with the five-star Ipanema Park Hotel) is one of the best four-star hotels in the north of Portugal. A sleek modern structure, it's a prominent feature of the city's skyline, with elongated rows of smoked glass that are visible from the highway to Lisbon. In fact, one of the place's assets is that it's easy to find. Exit the highway at the signs indicating the direction of Porto and you'll find it on a cobblestone road leading to the town center, about a mile away. The handsomely furnished midsize guest rooms have cedar accents and views of Porto.

The Restaurant Rios is especially popular on Sunday, when a brunch buffet is served. The menu features Portuguese regional dishes and international specialties, including some spicy favorites from Brazil. An attractive, dimly lit bar looks over a plant-filled atrium. The hotel has room service, laundry and valet, and a concierge.

INEXPENSIVE

Albergaria Miradouro. Rua da Alegria 598, 4000 Porto. ☎ **22/537-07-17.** Fax 22/537-02-06. E-mail: alb.miradouro@teleweb.pt. 30 units. A/C MINIBAR TV TEL. 10,000$–13,000$ ($56–$72.80) double. Rates include breakfast. AE, DC, MC, V. Free parking. Bus: 20, 21, 29 or 59.

Resembling an eagle's nest, Albergaria Miradouro is a slim 13-floor skyscraper built atop a hill outside the main part of the city. The Miradouro offers rooms with great vistas—you can watch ships laden with port making their way to the open sea. The corner guest rooms are preferable; two walls have wardrobes and chests (with a built-in pair of beds), and the other walls are glass. Every unit has a vestibule, luggage storage, a valet stand, desks, and a sitting room. A 1950s aura pervades. The small-scale public rooms are tasteful. The lower bar is decorated with wall tiles from Japan and Portugal. The walls of the upper bar open onto a view. The Restaurante Portucale, which serves international cuisine, is the best in town.

Castelo de Santa Catarina. Rua de Santa Catarina 1347, 4000 Porto. ☎ **22/509-55-99.** Fax 22/550-66-13. 25 units. TV TEL. 10,000$ ($56) double; 12,000$ ($67.20) suite. Rates include breakfast. AE, DC, MC, V. Free parking. Bus: 20, 49, or 53.

A former residential showplace, this hotel lies behind a high wall in a commercial neighborhood about a mile from the center. In the 1920s a Brazilian military officer returned to his native Porto determined to build the most flamboyant villa in town. He created a sprawling compound with greenhouses, terraced gardens, a chapel, and a sumptuous main house. A crescent of servants' quarters circles the other buildings. Today the tile-covered exterior walls almost give an encapsulated history of Portugal.

After ringing the bell, you'll be ushered down a labyrinthine series of halls and narrow stairways. To get to your room, you'll pass through opulent but disorganized sitting rooms and ballrooms, illuminated with chandeliers. Each of the small guest rooms contains carved antique furniture, often of rosewood. The plumbing fixtures are designed with a florid art nouveau flair. Laundry and baby-sitting are offered, but breakfast is the only meal served.

Holiday Inn Garden Court Hotel. Praça da Batalha 127–130, 4000 Porto. ☎ **800/465-43-29** in the U.S., or 22/339-23-00. Fax 22/200-60-09. www.maisturismo.pt/hinngaco.html. E-mail: reseruas.higep@grupo-continental.com. 118 units. A/C MINIBAR TV TEL. 12,500$ ($70) double. Rates include breakfast. Parking 900$ ($5.05). Bus: Any route to Estação de São Bento.

In the heart of the city, this new hotel lies in the Barredo section, which UNESCO recently declared a historic heritage site. The hotel is severely modern. The streamlined, functional guest rooms have excellent mattresses, new plumbing, hair dryers, and deluxe toiletries. Some units are suitable for travelers with disabilities, and other accommodations are reserved for nonsmokers. Businesspeople often gather in the lobby bar. The hotel offers laundry and limited room service. A group favorite, the hotel is part of the Continental Group, though run by Holiday Inn.

Hotel Castor. Rua das Doze Casas 17, 4000 Porto. ☎ **22/537-00-14.** Fax 22/536-60-76. 63 units. A/C MINIBAR TV TEL. 12,400$–14,400$ ($69.45–$80.65) double. Rates include breakfast. AE, DC, MC, V. Bus: 20.

This white-walled hotel lies in a relatively quiet neighborhood in a section of town rarely visited by foreigners. Known for its pleasant staff and antique furnishings, the Castor boasts a comfortably contemporary interior. Its English-style pub has a large-screen TV with European channels. The conservatively decorated guest rooms contain firm mattresses and good plumbing; many units are small. Laundry, baby-sitting, and room service are available.

Residencial Rex. Praça da República 117, 4050 Porto. ☎ **22/200-45-48.** Fax 22/208-38-82. 21 units. A/C TV TEL. 8,500$ ($47.60) double. Rates include breakfast. AE, MC, V. Bus: 7, 71, or 72.

The facade of this place fits in gracefully with its location on one of Porto's most beautiful squares. Its design, inspired by art nouveau, features sea-green tiles, cast-iron embellishments, and Roman-style window treatments. It was built by a Portuguese aristocrat around 1845 and transformed into a boarding house and pensão in 1925. The present family owners have been here since 1980. A majestic marble staircase leads from the street into the reception area. The lobby and small guest rooms are crowned with ornately molded plaster ceilings, and much of the furniture is antique. The bathrooms have been modernized. There's a tiny bar in the TV lounge at the back of the ground floor, but no restaurant. The iron gates enclosing an adjacent driveway swing open on request to allow you to park.

WHERE TO DINE

When Prince Henry the Navigator was rounding up the cattle in the Douro Valley to feed his men aboard the legendary caravels, he shipped out the juicy steaks and left the tripe behind. The people of Porto responded bravely and began inventing recipes using tripe. To this day they carry the appellation "tripe eaters," and it has become their favorite dish. To sample this specialty, the adventurous can order *tripas à moda do Porto* (tripe stewed with spicy sausage and string beans).

EXPENSIVE

✪ **Aquário Marisqueiro.** Rua Rodrigues Sampaio 179. ☎ **22/200-22-31.** Reservations recommended. Main courses 2,000$–5,000$ ($11.20–$28); fixed-price menu 2,900$ ($16.25). MC, V. Mon–Sat noon–10pm. Bus: 7, 77, or 79. PORTUGUESE.

In business for more than half a century, Aquário Marisqueiro is one of the finest seafood restaurants in Porto. One of two restaurants connected by a central kitchen, it's within sight of the city hall and close to the Infante de Sagres hotel. Seafood reigns supreme at this "aquarium." Soup made by boiling the shells of *mariscos* is a good starter. Main course options include cod, sole, and trout with ham. An excellent dish is clams Spanish style, but the house specialty is *açorda* (a traditional bread-and-egg dish) of shellfish.

✪ **Churrascão do Mar.** Rua João Grave 134. ☎ **22/609-63-82.** Reservations required. Main courses 3,500$–9,000$ ($19.60–$50.40). AE, DC, MC, V. Mon–Sat noon–3pm and 7–11pm. Closed Aug. Bus: 3 or 78. BRAZILIAN.

Porto's most elegant restaurant is housed in what locals call an *antiga moradia senhorial* (antique manor house), built in 1897 and beautifully restored to its belle epoque glory. The setting and elegance alone might justify a dinner here—and the cuisine matches the setting. Under the direction of owner Manuel Rocha, some of the town's finest chefs turn out excellent cuisine from South America. The staff seems determined not to let anyone leave unsatisfied. The best items are grilled fish and grilled seafood. Grilled meats are also superb. Everything is served with Brazilian spices or mild sauces to enhance the flavor, not destroy it. Service is in one of four rooms, all of which are quite charming.

Les Terrasses. In Le Méridien Park Atlantic Porto, av. da Boavista 1466. ☎ **22/600-25-00.** Reservations required. Main courses 2,600$–3,100$ ($14.55–$17.35); fisher's buffet (Fri–Sat night) 4,200$ ($23.50). AE, DC, MC, V. Daily 7–10:30am, 12:30–3pm, and 7:30–10:30pm. Bus: 3 or 78. PORTUGUESE.

Les Terrasses advertises itself as a restaurant/brasserie, but its uniformed maître d' and plush gardenlike decor give it the aura of a formal dining room. Located off the lobby of Le Méridien (see above), it lies nearly 3 miles from the city center. You can dine on a wooden terrace, but most guests prefer the air-conditioned interior because of the traffic noise. Tables sit in semiprivate alcoves. Buffet lunches are featured Sunday to Friday. The salad bar at lunch is loaded with smoked salmon, smoked swordfish, and other delectable offerings. Seafood buffet dinners, on Friday and Saturday, feature lots of expensive shellfish dishes—one of the most elaborate such spreads in the north of Portugal. The wine steward can suggest a reasonably priced Portuguese vintage.

✪ **Restaurante Portucale.** In the Albergaria Miradouro, rua da Alegria 598. ☎ **22/537-07-17.** Reservations required. Main courses 2,000$–6,000$ ($11.20–$33.60). AE, DC, MC, V. Daily 12:30–2:30pm and 7:30–11pm. Bus: 20, 21, 29, or 59. INTERNATIONAL/PORTUGUESE.

The Portucale, the best restaurant in town, perches on the rooftop of Albergaria Miradouro, outside the heart of the city. Seemingly the highest point in town, it offers wide views of the river, boats, and rooftops. Despite the views, the restaurant is fairly intimate; its tables are set with fine silver, china, and flowers. The chefs display a magic combination of inventiveness and solid technique. Specialties of the house include *bacalhau à marinheiro* (dried codfish), *cabrito à serrana* (kid in wine sauce), smoked swordfish, wild boar with clams and coriander, grilled breast of duck, roast sea bass, and homemade cakes. This is a good place to try the fabled tripe of Porto, especially with white beans and baked rice.

MODERATE

A Brasileira. Rua do Bomjardim 116. ☎ **22/200-71-46.** Main courses 1,000$–2,000$ ($5.60–$11.20). AE, DC, MC, V. Mon–Sat 12:30–10:30pm. PORTUGUESE/COFFEEHOUSE.

Uphill from the Estação de São Bento, the city's public transportation hub, A Brasileira is an art deco coffeehouse that serves as Porto's social center. It's also a first-class restaurant. Start with cream of shellfish soup, followed by such main dishes as roast chicken, grilled trout, or veal liver; finish with chocolate mousse. Savory specialties include *bolinhos de bacalhau* (codfish) and roast pork with beans and vegetables.

Garrafão. Rua António Nobre 53, Leça da Palmeira. ☎ **22/995-17-35.** Reservations recommended. Main courses 1,800$–2,600$ ($10.10–$14.55). AE, DC, MC, V. Mon–Sat noon–5pm and 7pm–midnight. PORTUGUESE/SEAFOOD.

A traditional restaurant in the suburbs, Garrafão overlooks Praia Boa Nova. Although it's standard fare made according to time-tested recipes, the cuisine is quite good. The kitchen staff deftly handles the fresh ingredients. The wine cellar, which contains a large selection of the best Portuguese wines, is another draw. À la carte Portuguese specialties include shrimp omelette, shellfish soup, grilled sole, veal dishes, and caramel custard. Prices of the seafood specialties vary according to the season.

Restaurante Escondidinho. Rua Passos Manuel 144. ☎ **22/200-10-79.** Reservations recommended. Main courses 2,850$–3,650$ ($15.95–$20.45). MC, V. Mon–Sat noon–3pm and 7–10pm. PORTUGUESE.

Near the transportation hub of the Estação de São Bento, the Escondidinho ("hidden" or "masked") is a 75-year-old regional tavern, popular with port-wine merchants and English visitors. The intimate 31-table dining area contains time-blackened beams and timbers, a baronial stone fireplace, and a collection of antique Portuguese ceramics. The chairs, with intricate carving and brass studs, are just right for a cardinal—or at least a friar. The waiters serve with old-world charm and will candidly tell you the day's best dishes. The restaurant serves excellent steaks, but most people come here for fresh seafood. Working with turbot, sole, hake, sea bass, shellfish, and anything else that's fresh, the chef creates well-seasoned grills, skewers, and other excellent dishes. Shellfish soup and charcoal-broiled sardines are always good choices. Specialties include hake in Madeira sauce and chateaubriand for two. For dessert, try a kirsch omelette or orange pudding.

Restaurante Tripeiro. Rua Passos Manuel 195. ☎ **22/200-58-86.** Main courses 1,500$–2,600$ ($8.40–$14.55). AE, DC, MC, V. Mon–Sat noon–3pm and 7–10:30pm. Bus: 35. PORTUGUESE.

Since 1942 this restaurant's textured stucco walls and elaborately crafted wooden ceiling have offered a cool, dark retreat from the glaring sunlight. It's a no-frills eatery with efficient waiters. The traditional cooking aims to please, and succeeds. You can enjoy *vinho verde* (green wine), which is ideal with the specialty, *tripas à moda do Porto* (tripe). If you're not up to tripe, you might order codfish, beef, or shellfish. Though most prices are reasonable, shellfish is priced daily by the kilo—dishes can cost to 6,000$ ($33.60) for a platter.

INEXPENSIVE

Abadia. Rua do Ateneu Comercial do Porto 22. ☎ **22/200-87-57.** Main courses 950$–1,600$ ($5.30–$8.95). AE, MC, V. Daily noon–2:30am. PORTUGUESE.

This large restaurant stands on a short street with a patio entrance and an open-air mezzanine. It's straightforward, with a hardworking staff, and serves generous portions in a style that hasn't changed since the place was founded (and nobody here can remember or knows when that was). The cook specializes in such fresh fish dishes as codfish Abadia and codfish Gomes de Sá. He also offers tripe stew Porto, savory fried pork, and succulent roast goat. Soups are hearty and full of flavor. English is definitely not spoken.

✪ **Taverna dos Bêbobos.** Cais de Ribeira 21–25. ☎ **22/205-35-65.** Reservations required. Main courses 1,750$–3,500$ ($9.80–$19.60). MC, V. Tues–Sun noon–3pm and 7–11:30pm. Bus: 15. PORTUGUESE.

Taverna dos Bêbobos ("Tavern of Drunks"), on the riverside dock, is the oldest (founded 1876) and smallest restaurant in Porto. The ground floor has a service bar with every sort of knickknack on its little tables. A narrow, open staircase leads to an intimate dining room with a corner stone fireplace and a coved ceiling. The portions are large enough to be shared. To begin your typically Portuguese meal, you might order a hearty bowl of *caldo verde* or a plate of grilled sardines. For a main course, we'd suggest trout with ham, codfish with béchamel sauce, or pork prepared Alentejana style (with savory clam sauce). All these dishes show flair and technique. Seafood rice and any of a number of grilled fish are also popular. Because of the small number of tables, it's necessary to have someone at your hotel call and make a reservation for you.

SHOPPING

Much of Porto's commercial space consists of shops that appeal mainly to residents, and, except for their curiosity value, only rarely to international visitors. In recent years many of these have clustered in shopping malls. The newest and most elegant are the **Centro Comercial Peninsular,** praça do Bom Sucesso, and the particularly charming **Centro Comercial Via Caterina.** It's in the pedestrian zone of the city's most vital shopping street, **rua de Santa Catarina,** at the corner of rua Fernandes

❷ Did You Know?

- The favorite local dish in Porto is tripe (the stomach of an ox, sheep, or goat).
- Afonso Henríques, the founder of the new kingdom in the 12th century, gave it the name of his homeland: Portucalia.
- Port wine is said to be the result of a "climatic" accident—warm weather produced too-sweet grapes, and the resulting wine had to be fortified with brandy.
- A 16th-century convent now holds about 200 million liters of Sandeman port in bottles and oak barrels.
- The 1832 siege of Porto during the "War of Two Brothers," as it was called, forced hungry residents to eat cats and dogs.
- In the mid-1700s a drunken mob set fire to port-wine offices—it was called the *revolta dos borrachos* (drunkards' revolt). Twenty-five men were hanged.
- Porto's most famous son was Prince Henry the Navigator, born to a Portuguese king and an English queen in the 1300s.
- Porto became one of the first towns in Iberia to kick out the Moors.
- At the marriage of the daughter of the king of León and Castile to Henry of Burgundy, Porto was included in her dowry.
- A local maxim shows the city's sense of distinctiveness: "Coimbra sings, Braga prays, Lisbon shows off, and Porto works."

Tomar. The storefronts inside duplicate the facades you'd probably see in a folkloric village of northern Portugal.

If you're looking for the designer wares of noteworthy clothiers from France, Italy, and Spain, these malls will have them. Other shopping malls have a sometimes-uneven distribution of upscale and workaday shops. They include the **Centro Comercial da Foz,** rua Eugênio de Castro, which is adjacent to the sea and especially pleasant in midsummer, and the **Centro Comercial Aviz,** avenida da Boavista, rather inconveniently located in the middle of the city's largest concentration of automobile dealerships. The big, centrally located **Centro Comercial Brasília** is on praça Mouzinho de Albuquerque; and the particularly large **Centro Comercial Cidade do Porto,** rua do Bom Sucesso, contains shops interspersed with restaurants, bars, movie theaters, and cafes.

Open-air markets supplement the malls. The most charming sell caged birds (**Bird Fair Cidade do Porto,** rua da Madeira, Sunday 7:30am to 1pm), potted plants (**Plant Market,** praça da Liberdade, April to October, Sunday 8am to 5pm), and coins and medallions (**Numismatics Fair,** praça Dom João I, Sunday 7:30am to 1pm). If **flea markets** appeal to you, head for **praça da Batalha** every day from 9am to 5:30pm.

For a glimpse of local fruits, vegetables, and meats, head for the **Mercado de Porto Bolão,** where hundreds of merchants sell food, flowers, spices, and kitchen equipment from the city's most famous open-air market. It sprawls for several blocks beside rua de Santa Catarina.

Porto boasts some of the finest gold- and silversmiths in Portugal. You'll find dozens of shops, especially along **rua das Flores.**

Pedro A. Baptista, rua das Flores 235 (☎ **22/200-51-42**), is an outstanding shop. It offers an unusual collection of antique and new jewelry (often based on traditional designs), plus several upper floors of decorator items. The owner buys rare and beautiful antique jewelry that he "offers first to his wife." In the ground-floor jewelry section, you'll find intricate, delicate filigree pins, brooches, pillboxes, and bracelets, in both solid gold (19.2 karats) and gold-plated silver. There's also an exquisite silver collection, including elaborately decorated tea services.

Other leading jewelers are **David Rosas, Lda.,** av. da Boavista 1471 (☎ 22/606-84-64); and **Elysée Joias,** praça Mouzinho de Albuquerque 113 (☎ 22/600-06-63). Branches of the well-recommended chain outfit **Rosior Manuel Rosas, Lda.,** are in the Centro Comercial da Foz (☎ 22/617-23-76) and the Centro Comercial Cidade do Porto (☎ 22/600-15-20). The company maintains a third branch at rua Eugênio de Castro 263 (☎ 22/606-81-34).

Cutting-edge home furnishings are sold at **Sátira Design,** rua Felizardo Lima 39 (☎ 22/610-72-28), and the three branches of **Móvel 4**—rua de Camões 19 (☎ 22/208-48-84), rua de Santa Catarina 1002 (☎ 22/202-63-40), and rua Dom Manuel II 196 (☎ 22/609-88-89), the largest.

For leather, go to **Haity,** rua de Santa Catarina 247 (☎ 22/205-96-30). At **Casa dos Linhos,** rua de Fernandes Tomás 660 (☎ 22/200-00-44), you'll find linen and embroideries. A particularly beautiful bookstore that stocks titles in Portuguese, English, Spanish, and French is the **Livraria Lello & Irmão,** rua das Carmelitas 144 (☎ 22/201-80-70). And if you're looking for any of the standard international perfumes, as well as more esoteric brands available for the most part only in Iberia, head for **Perfumaria Castilho,** rua de Sá da Bandeira 80 (☎ 22/205-78-55).

To stock up on traditional Portuguese handcrafts, begin at the **Regional Center of Traditional Arts (CRAT),** rua de Reboleira 33–37 (☎ 22/332-02-01). In an aristocratic 18th-century town house, it sells the best handcrafts from artisans throughout the country's northern tier. Lively competitors in the handcrafts trade include the following: **Casa do Coração de Jesús,** rua Mouzinho da Silveira 302 (☎ 22/200-32-17); **Casa Lima,** rua de Sá da Bandeira 83 (☎ 22/200-52-32); **Casa Margaridense,** travessa de Cedofeita 20A (☎ 22/200-11-78); and the **Boutique Perry Sampaio,** rua do Campo Alegre 713 (☎ 22/600-82-85).

One of the finest names in Portuguese porcelain is **Vista Alegre,** rua Cândido dos Reis 18 (☎ 22/600-91-26). It carries a variety of items and can arrange shipping. Prices vary greatly, depending on the handwork involved, how many colors are used, and whether a piece is decorated in gold.

A final note: Porto is fostering a new generation of galleries devoted to modern art by local painters and sculptors. The city boasts at least 30, the most interesting of which are the **Galeria Fluxos,** rua do Rosário 125 (☎ 22/201-10-74); the **Galeria Labirinto,** rua de Nossa Senhora de Fátima 334 (☎ 22/606-36-65); and the **Galeria Atlântica,** rua Galerie de Paris 67–71 (☎ 22/200-08-40).

PORTO AFTER DARK

There's no better way to begin your evening than by visiting the **Solar do Vinho do Porto,** rua de Entre Quintas 220 (☎ 22/609-47-49). The Port Wine Institute, a government body that controls the quality of the wine and authorizes its export, maintains the Romantic Museum of Quinta da Maceirinha. You can taste different types of port Monday to Saturday from 2pm to midnight. Drinks begin at 200$ ($1.10). From the old building, you'll also have a view of the Douro.

Porto isn't as vital a center for fado music as Lisbon, so few clubs promote the art form. The most appealing is **Mal Cozinhado,** rua do Outeirinho 13 (☎ 22/208-13-19). The name translates as "badly cooked." Five singers and musicians (three women, two men) perform folkloric guitar music and the evocative, nostalgic lyrics that go with it. They perform in 6-hour stints to an enthusiastic crowd Monday to

Espinho **7**
Fão **2**
Matosinhos **4**
Ofir **1**
Porto **5**
Vila do Conde **3**
Vila Nova de Gaia **6**

Saturday beginning at 9:30pm. À la carte dinners, priced at around 4,500$ ($25.20) per person, are served beginning at 8:30pm. After the music begins, most people opt just to drink, paying an initial 2,000$ ($11.20), which includes the first two drinks. After that, beer costs 1,000$ ($5.60) a bottle.

Many night owls simply walk through the commercial district, along streets radiating from rua de Santa Catarina, and stop at any appealing tavern or cafe. If you're looking to dance, try the **Discoteca Indústria,** in the Centro Comercial da Foz, av. do Brasil 843 (☎ **22/617-68-06**); or the well-recommended **Discoteque Anekibobó,** rua Fonte Tarina 36 (☎ **22/332-46-19**). Both have stripped-down interiors that cater to a crowd of artists, writers (and their readers), architects, and other well-behaved, cosmopolitan patrons. Open Friday and Saturday 10:30pm to 4am.

A nocturnal hangout near the river that includes a restaurant, a battery of snooker tables, and an active dance floor is the **Discoteca Twins,** rua Passeio Alegre 1000 (☎ **22/618-57-40**).

Via Rápida, rua Manuel Pinto Azevedo (☎ **22/606-85-62**), is a modern pub where recorded music plays softly enough to permit conversation. More intimate, but occasionally sleepy, is **Padaria,** rua Mártires da Liberdade 212–218 (☎ **22/208-83-84**). If you're looking for a sophisticated and mellow cocktail bar where people in their 50s won't feel hopelessly out of place, head for the **Bar Hiva-oa,** rua da Boavista 251 (☎ **22/617-96-63**). And if you're still a college student or want to re-create the life you led when you were, head for a bar catering to student raucousness. Three good ones are the **Bar Meia Cave,** praça da Ribeira 6 (☎ **22/332-32-14**); **Cosa Nostra,** rua São João 76 (☎ **22/208-66-72**); and the **Bar Taberna 2000,** rua Eugênio de Castro 228 (☎ **22/606-63-50**).

If you're gay and want to drink, dance, and flirt in a particularly friendly environment, drop into the **Discoteca Swing,** rua Júlio Dinis 766 (☎ **22/609-00-19**), near Parque Itália.

Of the dozens of cafes lining the streets of Porto, which is the most historic and beautiful? Our favorite is the lush art nouveau **Majestic Café Concerto,** rua de Santa Catarina 112 (☎ **22/200-38-87**). It occasionally stages concerts by small-scale jazz or chamber orchestras, and music drifts around you as you sip your beer, wine, scotch, or coffee.

2　Espinho

11 miles S of Porto, 191 miles N of Lisbon

Espinho is a popular resort on the Costa Verde. It offers many activities for growing crowds of vacationers. The town has a range of shops, restaurants, hotels, and campsites in the pine woods near the sandy beach. Sports enthusiasts will find tennis courts, a bullfighting ring, and an 18-hole golf course.

ESSENTIALS
ARRIVING

BY TRAIN　From Porto, trains depart from the Estação de São Bento about every hour during the day. Trip time is 20 minutes. A one-way ticket to Porto-Espinho costs 200$ ($1.10).

BY BUS　Buses depart about once an hour from Porto's **Garage Atlântico,** rua Alexandre Herculano, near praça de Batalha (☎ **22/200-75-44**). Trip time is 30 minutes. A one-way ticket to Porto-Espinho costs 250$ ($1.40).

BY CAR　From Porto, head south along IC-1.

VISITOR INFORMATION

The **Espinho Tourist Office** is at Ángulo das Ruas 6 (☎ **22/73-40-911**).

RELAXING IN ESPINHO

DAYTIME ACTIVITIES   Sports-related activities in Espinho tend to revolve around the beach. At least four **beaches** are within an easy walk from the town center. Closest, and most crowded, is **Praia Baia;** most distant (though only a quarter mile east of the center) and least crowded is **Praia do Costa Verde.** Between the two stretch the beige-colored sands of **Praia Azula** and **Praia Pop,** both of which boast clean sun-bathing areas and access to not particularly dangerous surf. If you prefer calmer waters, head for the town's largest swimming-pool complex, **Solar Atlântico,** adjacent to Praia Baia (☎ **22/734-01-52**). Fed with sea water, it has separate pools for diving and swimming, hundreds of devoted aficionados (only some of whom actually swim), and lots of options for voyeuristic intrigue. Open from mid-May to September.

Grass and hard tennis courts, soccer fields, and volleyball courts are in the **Nave Municipal,** rua 33 (☎ **22/731-00-59**). The cluster of outdoor playing fields on the eastern outskirts of town opened in 1996.

The **Oporto Golf Club** is on rua do Golf (☎ **22/734-20-08**), about 1½ miles south of Espinho.

SHOPPING   The three most interesting products produced in the surrounding region are carved-wood models of Portuguese fishing boats, painted bright colors; woven baskets; and dolls in regional dress whose bodies are carved from wood or fashioned from clay. Some shops operate only seasonally. Many sell items like suntan oil, sunglasses, and cheap souvenirs. The town's main shopping street is **rua 19.** If you're looking for authentic handcrafts, head for **Casa Ramos,** rua 23 (☎ **22/734-00-24**).

If you happen to be in town on a Monday, Espinho is home to one of the largest outdoor markets in the region. Known as the **Feira de Espinho,** it takes place every Monday from 7am to 8pm along the entire length of rua 24. Look for carloads of produce, meats, and foodstuffs, plus some clothing and other objects you expect in a flea market.

WHERE TO STAY & DINE

Hotel Praiagolfe. Rua 6, 4500 Espinho. ☎ **22/733-10-00.** Fax 22/733-10-01. E-mail: pgolfe@mail.telepac.pt. 139 units. A/C TV TEL. 17,000$–21,000$ ($95.20–$117.60) double; 26,000$ ($145.60) suite. Rates include continental or buffet breakfast and parking. AE, DC, MC, V.

Espinho's accommodations are a generally unimpressive lot. The best place to stay is the Praiagolfe, a totally renovated hotel offering many modern comforts. Many units were redecorated in 1996, and all are midsize and comfortable, with excellent mattresses and smoothly functioning plumbing. The streamlined hotel overlooks the sea, about 165 feet from the railway station. The two restaurants serve fixed-price lunches and dinners of regional cuisine for 2,950$ ($16.50) and up. The hotel offers an indoor pool, a squash court, and a health club. Tennis courts and golf courses are nearby. In summer the place is almost always booked, so reservations are imperative.

WHERE TO STAY & DINE NEARBY

Hotel Solverde/Granja. Estrada Nacional 109, 4405 Valadares. ☎ **22/731-31-62.** Fax 22/731-32-00. www.soleverde.pt. E-mail: hotel.soleverde@mail.telepac.pt. 174 units. A/C MINIBAR TV TEL. 24,000$–30,000$ ($134.40–$168) double; 50,000$–70,000$ ($280–$392) suite. Rates include continental breakfast and parking. AE, DC, MC, V.

Solverde/Granja is one of the most luxurious hotels in the north. Opened in 1989, it stands on the beach of Granja, about 10 miles south of Porto, less than a mile north of Espinho, and about 20 miles from the Porto airport. The rates are among the lowest in Portugal for a five-star hotel. The generally spacious guest rooms are well furnished, with excellent mattresses and roomy bathrooms that contain hair dryers. The hotel has a grill and restaurant, a coffee shop, several bars, a disco, a health club, three saltwater pools (one indoors), four tennis courts, and a heliport.

ESPINHO AFTER DARK

If you want to gamble, you're in luck. The big gray **Casino Solverde,** rua 19 no. 85, 4500 Espinho (☎ 22/733-55-00), offers roulette, French banque, baccarat, and slot machines. Open all year, it has a restaurant and nightclub in addition to the gaming tables. Admission is free for bingo and slot machines; to gain access to the gaming tables, you must show proper ID (such as a passport). The nightclub stages international cabaret. Dinner and the show costs 5,000$ ($28), without drinks; the show alone is 2,500$ ($14), which includes one drink. The casino is open daily from 3pm to 3am.

Espinho doesn't have any conventional discos. The town does have eight or nine bars where somebody might actually get up and dance to recorded music, which includes healthy doses of Brazilian samba and whatever happens to be prevalent in London and Lisbon. If you're into nighttime prowling, head to the beachfront near the southern perimeter of the historic center and take your pick. None have a listed phone number, and each has a character that varies according to who's in town. Our favorites are **Bombar,** rua 2; **Foradores,** rua 62; and the **Bar Mix,** rua 21.

3 Vila do Conde

17 miles N of Porto, 212 miles N of Lisbon, 26 miles S of Viana do Castelo, 26 miles S of Póvoa do Varzim

At the mouth of the river Ave, the charming little town of Vila do Conde has been discovered by summer vacationers who seek out its fortress-guarded sandy beaches and rocky reefs. Along the wharves, you may still see piles of rough hand-hewn timbers used in the building of the sardine fleet. **Shipbuilding** is a traditional industry here, and a few wooden-hulled vessels are still made, some for the local fishing fleet and others for use on the cod banks of Newfoundland.

The women of the town have long engaged in the making of **lace** using a shuttle, a craft handed down from generation to generation. So revered is this activity that the Feast of St. John, celebrated from June 14 to 24, features processions by the lace makers (*rendilheiras*) and the *mordomas* (women who manage the cottage-industry homes). The latter wear magnificent chains and other ornaments of gold. Lace makers parade through the narrow 16th-century streets of the town. The famous hand-knit and hand-embroidered fishers' sweaters are also made here. The making of sweets (there's a famous confectionery that uses convent recipes) is another local occupation; sweets provide part of the rich local cuisine.

ESSENTIALS
ARRIVING

BY TRAIN   From Porto, trains head north for Vila do Conde from the Estação da Trindade several times a day. Passengers arrive in the center of the resort.

BY BUS   Buses leave Porto from the Autoviação do Minho, praça Filippa de Lancastre (☎ 22/200-61-21). Three or four buses a day make the 30-minute trip.

BY CAR   From Porto, head north along IC-1.

VISITOR INFORMATION

The **Vila do Conde Tourist Office** is at rua do 25 de Abril 103 (☎ **252/24-84-73**).

EXPLORING THE RESORT

BEACHES OF VILA DO CONDE   Both of the resort's beaches, **Praia do Forno** and **Praia da Senhora da Guia,** combine fine-textured white sand with smaller crowds—often much smaller—than at equivalent beaches on the Algarve or near Lisbon. A handful of kiosks and shops sell suntan lotion, sunglasses, and beachwear, but overall, you'll have more privacy than you might have feared. Both are within about a 3-minute walk from the resort's commercial center.

CHURCHES   Sitting fortresslike on a hill, the large, squat **Igreja de Santa Clara (Convent of St. Clare),** on the north bank of Rio Ave (☎ **252/63-10-16**), was founded in the 14th century. The present monastery was built in the 1700s, accompanied by construction of a 999-arch aqueduct to bring water from nearby Póvoa do Varzim. Part of the water conduit is still visible.

In the upper rooms you can see relics and paintings collected through the centuries by the Poor Clares. The building is now a charity home. Simplicity and opulence play against each other in a combination of Gothic and Romanesque styles. The plain altar of its church offers contrast to the gilded stalls behind the communion grilles and the ornately decorated ceilings. A side chapel contains 14th-century sarcophagi. One is the elaborately carved tomb of Dom Afonso Sanche, founder of the convent; the feet of his effigy rest on a lion. Also here are the tomb of his wife, Dona Teresa Martins, topped by a figure dressed in the habit of a Franciscan Tertiary nun, and those of two of their children. The convent is open daily from 8:30am to noon and 2 to 7pm. Admission is free.

The 16th-century parish church, **Igreja Matriz** (☎ **252/63-13-27**), is also worth seeing. It stands in the center of town near the market. Another national monument is the **pillory,** opening onto praça Vasco da Gama. Built from 1538 to 1540, it consists of a graceful column, slightly twisted, which recalls many creations from the Manueline art style.

LACE MAKING   Visitors are welcomed free at the **Museu Escola de Rendas,** the lace-making school on rua de São Bento (☎ **252/24-84-70**). Here you can purchase the finest examples of lace for which the town is known. Vila do Conde guards its lace-making and pastry-making traditions with fierce pride. The Rendas school is devoted to perpetuating the traditions of Portuguese lace making, and it's one of the largest technical schools in the country. Some students enroll as early as age 4, and tend to have completed their technical training before they turn 15. A handful of the matriarchs, now in their 70s, associated with the school remember its importance in their town when they were young girls. You can buy most of the lace made in the school at its on-site boutique. A nearby annex, **Centro de Artesanato,** avenida Dr. João Canavarro (☎ **252/64-67-53**), also stocks lace curtains and tablecloths, doilies, and trim. Most of the lace you'll see here is white, designed according to traditional patterns established long ago. In recent years, however, some limited experiments have been conducted using colored, especially pastel, thread. The Museu Escola de Rendas is open Monday to Friday from 10am to noon and 2 to 7pm.

PASTRIES & SWEETS   During the 18th and 19th centuries, the nuns of Vila do Conde developed recipes for pastries and sweets that their detractors claimed were thinly masked substitutes for their yearnings for love and affection. Examples of the sweets they invented are still sold in almost every cafe and about a dozen pastry shops in the village. The best known of these pastries are *papo de anjo* (angel's belly) and *doce* *de feijão* (bean sweets). The ones seemingly best appreciated by modern-day palates are the *Jesuitas* (Jesuits), concocted from lavish amounts of eggs, flour, and sugar. You'll see dozens of outlets for these confections. One of the most appealing is the **Pastelaria Santa Clara,** rua do 5 de Outubro (no phone).

WHERE TO STAY

Estalagem do Brasão. Av. Dr. João Canavarro, 4480 Vila do Conde. ☎ **252/64-20-16.** Fax 252/64-20-28. 30 units. A/C MINIBAR TV TEL. 9,700$–14,200$ ($54.30–$79.50) double; 14,400$–17,900$ ($80.65–$100.25) suite. Rates include buffet breakfast and parking. AE, DC, MC, V.

Estalagem do Brasão, in the center of the village, is styled like a gracious pousada. Its compact guest rooms are of contemporary design, with built-in headboards, comfortable armchairs, and firm beds. If you stay for more than 3 days in high season, the staff will deduct 1,500$ ($8.40) per day. There's a combination bar and disco.

WHERE TO DINE

Pioneiro. Av. Manuel Barros. ☎ **22/63-29-12.** Reservations required. Main courses 1,800$–2,000$ ($10.10–$11.20). AE, DC, MC, V. Tues–Sun noon–3pm and 7–10pm. Closed Sept 15–30. REGIONAL PORTUGUESE.

Pioneiro is one of the best and largest of the numerous beachfront restaurants. Offering a panoramic view of the water, it can seat up to 265 and specializes in excellent regional fare and fresh shellfish. The latter, depending on daily market prices, can be quite expensive. However, most dishes are reasonably priced. The chef also prepares golden-brown roast kid and regional tripe Porto style.

4 Ofir & Fão

29 miles N of Porto, 226 miles N of Lisbon, 22 miles W of Braga

Once you pass through the pine forests of Ofir, you gaze down on a long white-sand spit dotted with windswept dunes and hear the sharp cries of seagulls. Ofir offers the best beach resort between Porto and Viana do Castelo. The beach is dramatic at any time of the year, but is exceptional during summer. The White Horse Rocks, according to legend, were formed when fiery steeds from the royal stock of King Solomon were wrecked on the beach.

While Ofir's hotels offer every convenience in a secluded setting, the nearest shops and more local color are at Fão, 1 to 2 miles inland on an estuary of the Cávado River. Framed by mountain ridges in the background and a river valley, the village, which dates from Roman times, is the sleepy gateway to Ofir. The *sargaceiros* ("gatherers of sargasso"), with their stout fustian tunics, rake the offshore breakers for the seaweed used in making fertilizer. On the quays you can lunch on sardines off smoking braziers. At the end of the day, counteract your overdose of sunshine with a mellow glass of port wine.

ESSENTIALS

ARRIVING

BY TRAIN   There's no direct rail service to Fão or Ofir. Passengers go to Póvoa do Varzim, 9 miles south, and continue by bus.

BY BUS   From Porto, buses depart from **Autoviação do Minho,** Praceto Regulo Maguana (☎ 253/200-61-21). Three or four buses per day service the area. Trip time is 65 minutes.

BY CAR   From Póvoa do Varzim, continue north along Route 30.

VISITOR INFORMATION

The nearest tourist office is the **Esposende Tourist Bureau,** avenida Arantes de Oliveira, Esposende (☎ **253/96-13-54**). Esposende lies on the opposite bank of the Rio Cávado Estuary from Ofir and Fão.

WHERE TO STAY & DINE

Estalagem Parque do Rio. Apdo. 1, Ofir, 4740 Esposende. ☎ **253/98-15-21.** Fax 253/98-15-24. www.parquedorio.pt. 36 units. A/C TV TEL. 8,600$–14,850$ ($48.15–$83.15) double or suite. Rates include continental breakfast. AE, V. Restaurant closed Nov–Mar. Free parking.

This first-class modern inn on the Cávado River is in a pine-covered garden 5 minutes from the main beach. It has two excellent garden pools with surrounding lawns. The small guest rooms are well designed, with private balconies and firm beds. The resort, planned for those who stay for more than a day, offers a full range of activities. In the beamed dining room, a snug wood-paneled bar sits against a stone wall. Regional meals are served from noon to 3pm and 8 to 9:30pm. The set menu costs 2,650$ ($14.85) per person. There are several lounges, including a TV lounge.

Hotel Ofir. Av. Raul de Sousa Martins, Ofir, 4740 Esposende. ☎ **253/989-800.** Fax 253/981-871. 200 units. A/C TV TEL. 15,000$ ($84) double; 24,000$ ($134.40) suite. Rates include buffet breakfast. AE, DC, MC, V. Free parking.

This hotel is on a par with resort developments on the Algarve. It consists of three sections. The older central core contains guest rooms furnished in traditional Portuguese fashion with reproductions of regional furniture; the adjoining wings are modern. One section is quite luxurious, built motel style right along the dunes, with a row of white tents and a pure-sand beach in full view of the second-floor balconies. There are well-styled public rooms, but the principal focus is on the wide oceanfront terrace, where guests sunbathe. The restaurant serves Portuguese cuisine. The set menu costs 3,000$ ($16.80), and à la carte options are served. Laundry service, baby-sitting, and room service are available.

The hotel is a resort unto itself, with a vast playground terrace, two pools (one for children), two tennis courts, and a flagstone terrace bordering soft green lawns. The hotel has a bowling alley as well, and is located near a golf course.

12 The Minho Region & Trás-os-Montes

The Minho, in the verdant northwest corner of Portugal, is almost a land unto itself. The region begins some 25 miles north of Porto and stretches to the frontier of Galicia, in northwest Spain. In fact, Minho and Galicia and their people are strikingly similar. The regions share a Celtic background.

Granite plateaus undulate across the countryside, broken by the green valleys of the Minho, Ave, Cávado, and Lima rivers. For centuries the region's bountiful granite quarries have been emptied to build everything from the great church facades in Braga and Guimarães to the humblest village cottages. Green pastures contrast sharply with forests filled with cedars and chestnuts.

The small size of the district and the proximity of the towns make it easy to hop from hamlet to hamlet and from pousada to pousada. Even the biggest towns—Viana do Castelo, Guimarães, and Braga— are provincial in nature. You'll sometimes see wooden carts in the streets, drawn by pairs of dappled and chocolate-brown oxen. These noble beasts are depicted on the pottery and ceramics for which the Minho (especially Viana do Castelo) is known.

Religious *festas* are occasions that bring people out into the streets for days of merrymaking and celebrations, including folk songs, dances, and displays of traditional costumes. The women often wear woolen skirts and festively decorated aprons with floral or geometric designs. Their bodices are pinned with golden filigree and draped with layers of heart- or cross-shaped pendants.

The Minho was the cradle of Portuguese independence. From here, Afonso Henrîques, the first king, made his plans to capture the south from the Moors. Battlemented castles along the frontier are reminders of the region's former hostilities with Spain, and fortresses still loom above the coastal villages.

Porto (see chapter 11) is the air gateway to the Minho. A car is the best way to see the north if you have only a short time; if you depend on public transportation, you can visit some of the major centers by bus and rail.

The far northeast province of Portugal is a wild, rugged land—Trás-os-Montes, or "beyond the mountains." Extending from south of the Upper Douro at Lamego, the province stretches north to Spain. Vila Real is its capital. Rocky crests and deep valleys break up the high plateau, between the mountain ranges of Marão and Gerês. Most of the population lives in the valleys, usually in houses constructed from shale or granite. Much of the plateau is arid land, but swift rivers and their tributaries supply ample water, and some of the valleys have fertile farmland. The Tãmega River Valley is known for the thermal springs found there as far back as Roman days.

This land is rich in history and tradition, offering the visitor a new world to discover, from pre-Roman castles to prehistoric dolmens and cromlechs to pillories and interesting old churches. The inhabitants are of Celtic descent, and most speak a dialect of Galician.

You can reach Trás-os-Montes by train from Porto. Service is to Régua, not far from Lamego, which serves as a gateway into the province in the Pais do Vinho, where grapes from vineyards on the terraced hills provide the wines that are credited to Porto. Lamego is actually in the province of Beira Alta. You can drive through this land of splendid savagery, but don't expect superhighways.

Exploring the Region by Car

Day 1   Spend the day exploring the attractions of **Guimarães,** 30 miles northeast of Porto. Spend the night at one of the two pousadas.

Day 2   Head toward Braga on N101; 5 miles outside Guimarães, turn right at the signposted Caldas das Taipas. This will take you to **Citania de Briteiros,** the ruins of a Celtic hill settlement believed to date from around 300 B.C. It's thought to have been one of the final Celtic forts holding out against the Roman invasion of Portugal. Walls and cellars of some 150 huts have been excavated.

Get back on the main road and drive 9 miles north to **Braga.** Explore its attractions in the afternoon and spend the night.

Day 3   From Braga, take N103 due west to the little market town of **Barcelos,** where you can spend the morning wandering and shopping. If it isn't market day, head instead for the Centro Artesanato. From Barcelos, N103 leads northwest to **Viana do Castelo,** where you can explore the town and spend the night.

Day 4   While based in Viana do Castelo, you can explore the northern Minho region. N13 continues north along the coast past several small villages, often with good stretches of sand. They include the small resorts of **Vila Praia de Âncora** and **Moledo.** At the town of **Caminha,** you reach the Rio Minho and the frontier with once-hostile Spain.

At **Vila Nova de Cerveira,** 7½ miles up the river, you can stop for lunch at the **Pousada Dom Diniz,** praça da Liberdade, 4920 Vila Nova de Cerveira (☎ 251/70-81-20). It occupies the remains of an ancient fortress close to the Minho River. To reach the hotel, go up the hill from the main square of the village. The history of this government-owned hotel dates from 1321, when Dom Diniz granted the castle its charter. Parts of the original interior have been incorporated into the pousada. You can enjoy a regional lunch or dinner for 3,650$ ($20.45). The rooms are in crenellated ramparts entered through a massive arched gate. Doubles are 16,500$ ($92.40).

After lunch, continue another 9 miles northeast, following the signposts into **Valença do Minho,** the major crossing point into Spain. The town has perfectly preserved walls, initially constructed to guard against invasion. From Valença, N101 continues for another 10 miles to **Monção,** a once-fortified border river town with the ruins of a castle from the 1300s.

South of Monção, N101 takes you through the valley of the Rio Vez to **Arcos de Valdevez,** 22 miles away. This is a little river town where you might want to stretch your legs before heading 3 miles south to **Rio Lima,** site of one of Portugal's most beautiful rivers. Continue south on N203, stopping at **Ponte da Barça,** with its 10-arched bridge from the 15th century, and **Ponte de Lima,** 11 miles down the road. Viana do Castelo lies 14 miles west of Ponte de Lima; you may want to return for a final night's stopover.

If you have 2 more days, you can explore Trás-os-Montes.

Day 5   From Porto, head due east on the express highway, A4, toward Amarante. Once at Amarante, continue east along N15 into Vila Real, where you can spend the night.

Day 6   In the morning, take E82 northeast to the remote northeastern city of Bragança. Spend the night.

1 Guimarães

30 miles NE of Porto, 43 miles SW of Viana do Castelo, 226 miles N of Lisbon

The cradle of Portugal, Guimarães suffers from a near embarrassment of riches. At the foot of a range of *serras,* this first capital of Portugal has preserved a medieval atmosphere in its core. The city was the birthplace of Afonso Henrîques, the first king of Portugal and son of a French nobleman, Henri de Bourgogne, and his wife, Teresa, daughter of the king of León and Castile. For her dowry, Teresa brought the county of Portucale, whose name eventually became Portugal. Portucale consisted of the land between the Minho and the Douro, taking in what is now the city of Porto. Teresa and Henri chose Guimarães as their court, and Afonso Henrîques was born here. The year was 1109 or thereabouts—historians aren't sure.

After Henri died 2 years later, Teresa became regent for the baby king. She soon fell into disfavor with her subjects for having an affair with a count from Galicia and developing strong ties with her native Spain. As a young man, Afonso revolted against the regent's forces outside Guimarães in 1128. A major victory for Afonso came in 1139, when he routed the Moors near Santarém. He broke from León and Castile and proclaimed himself king of Portucale. In 1143 Spain recognized the newly emerged kingdom.

Guimarães had another famous son, Gil Vicente (1470?–1536?). Founder of the Portuguese theater, he's often referred to as the "Shakespeare of Portugal." Although trained as a goldsmith, Vicente entertained the courts of both João II and Manuel I with his farces and tragicomedies. He also penned religious dramas.

Today Guimarães is a busy little town with an eye toward commerce, especially in weaving, tanning, and kitchenware and cutlery manufacturing. It's also known for its craft industries, especially pottery, silver- and goldsmithing, and embroidery.

ESSENTIALS
ARRIVING
BY TRAIN   Fifteen trains daily make the 2-hour run between Porto and Guimarães; the one-way cost is 500$ ($2.80). Call ☎ **251/41-23-51** for schedules.

BY BUS   Guimarães is easily accessible from Braga (see section 2 in this chapter); buses make the 1-hour trip frequently during the day. A one-way bus ticket from Braga to Guimarães is 365$ ($2.05). For **information,** call ☎ **253/41-26-46.**

BY CAR   Drive northwest from Porto on N105-2 and N105.

VISITOR INFORMATION
The **Guimarães Tourist Office** is at av. da Resistência ao Fascismo 83 (☎ **253/51-51-23**).

The Minho Region

Vigo **SPAIN**

Valença · Monção
N202 · Melgaço

Riba de Mouro

Sierra do Suajo

Rio Coura · Vila Nova de Cerveira
N101

Caminha
Moledo do Minho

Vila Praia de Âncora

Lindosa

N203 · Soajo

Rio Lima · Ponte da Barca

Ponte de Lima

N203 · **Sierra do Barroso**

Rio Homem

⑤ Viana do Castelo

Arcos de Valdevez

Gerêz

N103

Rio Cávado · Vieira do Minho

Mar

Cerdeirinhas

Póvoa de Lanhoso

Barcelos ③

⑨ Braga

Arosa

④ Esposende

Vila Nova de Famalicão

Cabeceiras de Basto

E01 N13

Guimarães ①

Fafe

N14

COSTA VERDE

Póvoa de Varzim

Vila do Conde

Caldas de Vizela

Celorico de Basto

N101

Atlantic Ocean

E82

Porto ○

N15

3-0553

The Minho Region

PORTUGAL

LISBON ★

Barcelos ③
Braga ②
Esposende ④
Guimarães ①
Viana do Castelo ⑤

| 0 | | | 10 Mi |
| 0 | | 10 Km | |

N

WHAT TO SEE & DO
EXPLORING THE TOWN

If you'd like to step into the Middle Ages for an hour or two, stroll down **rua de Santa Maria.** It has remained essentially unchanged for centuries, except that nowadays you're likely to hear blaring music—in English, no less. Proud town houses, once the residences of the nobility, stand beside humble dwellings. The hand-carved balconies, aged by the years, are most often garnished with iron lanterns (not to mention laundry).

At the end you'll come on a charming square in the heart of the old town, **largo da Oliveira** (Olive Tree Square). Seek out the odd chapelette in front of a church. Composed of four ogival arches, it's said to mark the spot where, in the 6th century, Wamba was asked to give up the simple toil of working his fields to become the king of the Goths. Thrusting his olive stick into the tilled soil, he declared that he would accept only if his stick sprouted leaves. So it did, and so he did—or so goes the tale.

Dominating the skyline is the 10th-century **Castle of Guimarães,** rua Dona Teresa de Noronha, where Afonso Henrîques, Portugal's first king, was born. High-pitched crenels top the strategically placed square towers and the looming keep. The view is panoramic. For more information, contact the staff at the Paço dos Duques (☎ 253/41-22-73). Almost in the shadow of the castle is the squat, rectangular 12th-century Romanesque **Igreja de São Miguel de Castelo,** where the liberator of Portugal, Afonso Henrîques, was baptized. Nearby is a heroic statue of the mustachioed, armor-clad Afonso, head helmeted, sword and shield in hand. The church keeps irregular hours; the castle (no phone) is open Tuesday to Sunday from 9am to 7pm. Admission is free unless you visit the panoramic tower, Torre Demanage, which costs 100$ (55¢).

Paço dos Duques de Bragança. Av. do Conde Dom Henrîque. ☎ **253/41-22-73.** Admission 400$ ($2.25), free for children under 15. Daily 9am–7pm.

From the keep of the castle you can see the four-winged Palace of the Dukes of Bragança. Constructed in the 15th century, it has been heavily restored. Many critics have dismissed the rebuilt structure with contempt. If you're not a purist, however, you may find a guided tour interesting.

Perched on the slope of a hill, the palace possesses an assortment of treasures. The portraits include one of Catherine of Bragança, who married Charles II of England, "the merrie monarch" and lover of Nell Gwynne. There are copies of the large Pastrana tapestries depicting scenes from the Portuguese wars in North Africa, scabbards and helmets in the armor room, Persian hangings, Indian urns, ceramics, and Chinese porcelains. The chapel opens onto the throne chairs of the duke and duchess. Nearby are the double-tiered cloisters.

Igreja de São Francisco. Largo de São Francisco. ☎ **253/51-25-07.** Free admission. Tues–Sun 9am–noon and 3–4:30pm.

The Church of St. Francis contains by far the most dramatic church interior in town. Entered through a Gothic portal, the spacious interior is faced with Delft blue and white *azulejos* (tiles). In the transept to the right of the main altar is a meticulously detailed miniature re-creation of the living room of a church prelate, from the burgundy-colored cardinal's chapeau resting on a wall sconce to the miniature dog and cat. On the second altar to the right is a polychrome tree of life that represents 12 crowned kings and the Virgin, with her hands clasped and her feet resting on the heads of three cherubs.

Museu de Alberto Sampaio. Rua Alfredo Guimarães. ☎ **253/41-24-65.** Admission 250$ ($1.40), free for children under 15. Tues–Sun 10am–12:30pm and 2–5:30pm. Closed holidays.

The Alberto Sampaio Museum is in the Romanesque cloister and the buildings of the old monastery of the Collegiate Church of Our Lady of the Olive Branch. Besides a large silver collection, it displays the tunic worn by João I at the battle of Aljubarrota, which decided Portugal's fate. There are priestly garments as well as paintings, ceramics, and medieval sculpture. A fresco illustrates a gloating Salome, rapturous over the severed head of John the Baptist. In one of the rooms are pieces from a baroque chapel, with enormous wood-carved angels bearing torches.

SHOPPING

In the town's historic core, two streets are particularly noteworthy. The one acknowledged by art historians as the most beautiful is the narrow medieval **rua de Santa Maria.** Here you'll find some outlets for handcrafts and souvenirs like ceramics, wood carvings, handmade lace, and embroidered linen. More geared to the needs of residents is the main commercial thoroughfare, **rua Gil Vicente.** For handcrafts, the best-stocked shop in town is **Artesanato de Guimarães,** rua Paio Galvão (☎ 253/ 51-52-50). Loosely affiliated with the municipal government, it functions as a showplace for the works of dozens of artisans from throughout the region, with an emphasis on textiles, wood carvings, ceramics, and metalwork.

WHERE TO STAY

Fundador Hotel. Av. Dom Afonso Henrîques 740, 4800 Guimarães. ☎ **253/51-37-81.** Fax 253/51-37-86. 63 units. A/C MINIBAR TV TEL. 13,000$ ($72.80) double. Rates include breakfast. AE, DC, MC, V. Free parking.

This central hotel offers comfortable but small guest rooms in the city's only high-rise. Though the pousadas are preferable, the Fundador is a decent place to spend the night. Rooms have piped-in music and firm beds. The hotel isn't stylish, but it's functional and well kept, and boasts fine service. The penthouse bar serves snacks.

Pousada de Nossa Santa Maria da Oliveira. Rua de Santa Maria, 4800 Guimarães. ☎ **253/51-41-57.** Fax 253/51-42-04. 16 units. A/C TV TEL. 24,600$ ($137.75) double; 30,500$ ($170.80) suite. Rates include breakfast. AE, DC, MC, V. Free parking.

The ambience at the second pousada in town differs from the atmosphere at the Santa Marinha da Costa, which is bigger and livelier. This establishment was created when a handful of 16th-century stone town houses were combined into a single rambling hotel. Many of their original features have been preserved. The pousada has a loyal clientele, a location on one of Portugal's most beautiful medieval squares, and a distinctive country-inn flavor. The street is so narrow that you'll have to park (free) in a well-marked lot about 100 feet away.

The front rooms are of good size, but those on the side tend to be smaller. The accommodations contain twin beds with firm mattresses, regional fabrics, and rug-covered tile floors. This place exudes intimate warmth, heightened by the wooden ceilings, tavern bar, and fireplace in the restaurant, whose windows look out over the square. Laundry, baby-sitting, and room service are available.

Regional fare is served daily from 12:30 to 3:30pm and 7:30 to 10pm. Specialties include a special beef à la pousada, fondue for two, and beef or veal flambé.

✪ **Pousada de Santa Marinha da Costa.** Costa, 4800 Guimarães. ☎ **253/51-44-53.** Fax 253/51-44-59. 51 units. A/C MINIBAR TV TEL. 31,000$ ($173.60) double; 51,000$ ($285.60) suite. Rates include breakfast. AE, DC, MC, V. Free parking.

With foundations dating from the 12th century, this restored pousada is one of the most impressive in Portugal. It was built in 1154 as an Augustinian convent by Teresa, mother of Afonso Henrîques. It gained a baroque facade in the 18th century, when the soaring interior halls and spouting fountains were installed. The ornate Manueline church that occupies part of the building still offers mass on Sunday, but the sprawling ex-convent was never outfitted as stylishly as you'll see it today. The property lies at the end of a winding road about 1¼ miles north of the town center on N101-2. Signs indicate the direction.

Take the time to explore both the upper halls and the gardens. One of the best rooms is a beautifully furnished large salon. At the end of one of the soaring halls, a fountain bubbles beneath an intricate wooden ceiling, surrounded by an open arcade that encompasses a view of the faraway mountains.

The guest rooms are a pleasing pastiche of old stonework, modern plasterwork, regional fabrics, and Portuguese lithographs. About half are in a relatively modern wing attached to the medieval core. The modern units, decorated in traditional Portuguese style, are air-conditioned; the original rooms aren't. The hotel is a popular venue for conferences. Room service and laundry are available.

Three restaurants serve unimaginative meals daily from 12:30 to 3pm and 7:30 to 10pm. A sunken bar serves drinks near the anteroom of the vaulted dining room.

WHERE TO DINE

Most people dine at one of the two pousadas (see "Where to Stay," above). The Pousada de Nossa Santa Maria da Oliveira has better food if you're interested in regional dishes.

El Rei. Praça de São Tiago 20. ☎ **253/41-90-96.** Main courses 1,150$–2,500$ ($6.45–$14); tourist menu 2,450$ ($13.70). AE, DC, MC, V. Mon–Sat noon–3pm and 7–11pm. MINHO.

In an enviable position in the heart of the medieval sector, this little restaurant opens onto the rear of the former town hall and the Pousada de Nossa Santa Maria da Oliveira. The patrons are mostly locals, joined by occasional foreigners. It offers good fish and tender meat dishes, including pork and codfish, plus country-fresh vegetables. Try hake fillets or house-style steak. Service is efficient, albeit sometimes rushed.

Mirapenha. Estrada de Fafe. ☎ **253/51-65-32.** Main courses 1,200$–1,800$ ($6.70–$10.10). No credit cards. Daily noon–2pm and 7–9pm. PORTUGUESE.

This typical restaurant lies half a mile (a reasonably priced taxi ride) from the center. It serves fine local food; specialties include *bacalhau* (codfish) cooked with olive oil and fresh vegetables, and *bife* (steak) flavored with garlic and braised in red wine. Other tasty regional dishes are available.

GUIMARÃES AFTER DARK

There are a lot of folkloric-looking taverns in the city center, many on such thoroughfares as **rua Gil Vicente** and **rua de Santa Maria.** For dancing and insights into what the new hipsters of northern Portugal are doing, head about 3 miles east. On the opposite side of the mountain that looms above the town center, you'll find the **Penha Club** (☎ 253/51-44-60). It doesn't have a formal address, but it's signposted from the town center. Its leading competitors include our favorite, **Seculo XIX,** localidade da Universidade (☎ 253/41-88-99), a replica of a century-old tavern, with lots of paneling and the kind of music that attracts every fun-loving person in town, regardless of age. More closely geared to a younger crowd is the deliberately trendy **Discoteca Tras-Tras,** rua Gil Vicente (☎ 253/41-69-85).

2 Braga

31 miles N of Porto, 228 miles N of Lisbon

Nearly everywhere you look in Braga there's a church, a palace, a garden, or a fountain. Known to the Romans as Bracara Augusta, the town has resounded to the footsteps of other conquerors, including the Suevi, the Visigoths, and the Moors. For centuries it has been an archiepiscopal seat and pilgrimage site; the Visigoths are said to have renounced their heresies here. Although aware of its rich history, the capital of Minho is very much a city of today. Its historic core with its cathedral lies at the center, but the periphery bustles with commerce and industry, including a lot of manufacturing—brick making, soap making, textiles, smelting, engineering, and leather goods.

Politically, Braga is Portugal's most conservative city. In 1926 a coup here paved the way for Salazar to begin his long dictatorship. Paradoxically, Braga is a hot place at night, primarily because of its young people. In fact, its lively streets and pedestrian thoroughfares have earned it a reputation for being "Lisbon in miniature."

Braga is also a religious capital. It stages the country's most impressive observances of Holy Week (*Semana Santa*). Torchlit processions of hooded participants, eerily evocative of the KKK, parade by. Sleepy Braga is gone forever. Today 65,000 residents live with noisy streets, increasing numbers of ugly and uninspired apartment blocks, and traffic congestion on streets that not long ago contained a few cars and maybe a donkey or two.

ESSENTIALS
ARRIVING

BY TRAIN   The **train station** is on largo da Estação (☎ 253/27-85-52). Some 13 trains per day arrive from Porto after a 1½-hour trip. It costs 520$ ($2.90) one way. From Coimbra, 12 trains a day make the 4-hour trip. A one-way ticket costs 1,150$ ($6.45). Eleven trains a day arrive from Viana do Castelo. The trip takes 2 hours and costs 490$ ($2.75) one way.

BY BUS   The **bus station** is at Central de Camionagem (☎ 253/61-60-80), a few blocks north of the heart of town. Buses arrive every 30 minutes from Porto; the trip takes 1½ hours and costs 900$ ($5.05) one way. From Guimarães there are six buses per day; the trip takes an hour and costs 520$ ($2.90). From Lisbon, four daily buses make the 8½-hour trip. The fare is 2,200$ ($12.30) one way.

BY CAR   From Guimarães (see the preceding section), head northwest along N101.

VISITOR INFORMATION

The **Braga Tourist Office** is at av. da Liberdade 1 (☎ 253/26-25-50).

WHAT TO SEE & DO
EXPLORING THE TOWN

Sé (Cathedral). Sé Primaz. ☎ **253/26-33-17.** Admission to Cathedral free; to museum and treasury 300$ ($1.70), free for children under 10. Daily 8:30am–6:30pm.

Inside the town, interest focuses on the Sé, which was built in the 12th century by Henri de Bourgogne and Dona Teresa. After he died, she was chased out of town because of an illicit love affair, but in death Henri and Teresa were reunited in their tombs in the Chapel of Kings.

The Sé has undergone decorative and architectural changes. The north triple-arched facade is austere and dominating, with a large stone-laced Roman arch flanked by two smaller Gothic ones. What appear to be the skeletons of cupolas top the facade's dual bell towers, which flank a lofty rooftop niche containing a larger-than-life statue of the *Virgin and Child*. Under a carved baldachin in the apse is a statue of Our Lady of the Milk—that is, the Virgin breast-feeding the infant Jesus. The statue is in the Manueline style but somehow pious and restrained.

Inside, you might think you've entered one of the darkest citadels of Christendom. If you can see them, the decorations, particularly a pair of huge 18th-century gilded organs, are profuse. In the 1330 Capela da Glória is the sarcophagus of Archbishop Dom Gonçalo Pereira, with an unctuous expression on his face. It was carved by order of the prelate.

You can visit the **Treasury of the Cathedral** and the **Museum of Sacred Art,** an upstairs repository of Braga's most precious works of art. On display are elaborately carved choir stalls from the 18th century, embroidered vestments from the 16th to the 18th century, and a 14th-century statue of the Virgin and a Gothic chalice from the same period. An 18th-century silver-and-gilt monstrance adorned with diamonds is by Dom Gaspar de Bragança. In the cloister is a pietà.

Museu dos Biscainhos. Rua dos Biscainhos. ☎ **253/61-11-49.** Admission 400$ ($2.25), free for children under 15. Tues–Sun 10am–12:15pm and 2–5:30pm. Closed holidays.

This museum is in Biscainhos Palace, a building from the 17th and 18th centuries that for about 300 years has served as the house of a noble family. The original gardens are still here. The museum has painted and ornamented ceilings and walls with panels of figurative and neoclassic tiles. Its exhibition rooms contain collections of Portuguese furniture and pottery, glassware, silverware, textiles, and Portuguese, Oriental, and Dutch Delft porcelain.

✪ **Bom Jesús do Monte.** N103-3, 3 miles southeast of Braga. ☎ **253/67-66-36.** Free admission. Daily 8am–8pm.

Bom Jesús do Monte is a hilltop pilgrimage site; it's reached on foot, on a funicular (the ride costs 100$/55¢), or by car along a tree-lined roadway. The baroque granite double staircase dating from the 18th century may look daunting, but if it's any consolation, pilgrims often climb it on their knees. Less elaborate than the stairway of Remédios at Lamego, the stairs at Bom Jesús (Good Jesus) are equally impressive. On the numerous landings are gardens, grottoes, small chapels, sculptures, and allegorical stone figures set in fountains.

CAMPING & PONY TREKKING

The **Parque Nacional da Peneda-Gerês,** named after the two mountains it encompasses, sprawls across Minho and Trás-os-Montes. Established in 1971, it's one of the best places for hiking in Portugal. The Lima River, running north-south, bisects the reserve. In the south the Cávado marks the border. Although the park has a limited infrastructure, and walking maps and signposted paths almost don't exist, organized tours offer both pony trekking and camping. For **park information,** call ☎ 253/20-34-80. The best tours of the park are offered by **Avic Tours,** rua Gabriel Pereira de Castro, Braga (☎ 253/27-03-02).

SHOPPING

The town's best outlet for gifts and handmade souvenirs is in the **tourist office** (see "Essentials," above). You'll find an impressive array of appealingly textured linens, pottery and ceramics, and wood carvings that evoke the values and traditions of northern Portugal.

Nearby is a textile factory that transforms flax into linens; the factory outlet boasts a rich stock of houseware linens, some of them of heirloom quality. Head 2½ miles north of the city, following signs to Prado. In the hamlet of Sanpaio Merelim, you'll find the factories of **Edgar Duarte Abreu,** Sanpaio Merelim (☎ 253/62-11-92).

WHERE TO STAY

Hotel João XXI. Av. João XXI 849, 4700 Braga. ☎ **253/61-66-30.** Fax 253/61-66-31. 28 units. TV TEL. 7,500$–10,000$ ($42–$56) double. Rates include breakfast. AE, DC, MC, V. Limited free parking on street.

This is a good second-class hotel. On a tree-shaded avenue leading to Bom Jesús do Monte, it stands opposite Braga's leading first-class hotel. The midsize guest rooms have warm modern decor, with the accent on neatness and efficiency; the singles have double beds. Each unit comes with a firm mattress. The entry to this modern little place is a salute to the 19th century. The tiny street-floor reception room is decorated à la Louis XVI. The social center is the living room–lounge, which has well-selected furnishings and an open fireplace. At the sixth-floor restaurant you can order breakfast or dinner.

Hotel Turismo de Braga. Praçeta João XXI, av. da Liberdade, 4700 Braga. ☎ **253/61-22-00.** Fax 253/61-22-11. 128 units. A/C TV TEL. 14,000$ ($78.40) double; 20,000$ ($112) suite. Rates include breakfast. AE, DC, MC, V. Parking 800$ ($4.50).

The best hotel in a town of bad hotels, Turismo de Braga is in a sprawling 11-story 1950s building fronted with flowering gardens and a parking lot. The entrance lies beneath an arcade that shelters some cafes. The hotel offers uninspired quiet and comfort. The two-story lobby lies below a spacious wood-paneled lounge bar and restaurant. Each midsize guest room contains a spacious balcony opening onto traffic; the walls are covered with blue-and-white tiles. Furnishings are standardized and a bit worn, but still comfortable, and the beds are firm. The hotel has a rooftop pool and an eighth-floor snack bar. It stands on a busy corner of traffic arteries, outside the most densely populated section of Braga.

AT BOM JESÚS DO MONTE

✪ **Castelo do Bom Jesús.** Bom Jesús do Monte, 4710 Braga. ☎ **253/67-65-66.** Fax 253/67-76-91. www.castello.bom.jesus.com. E-mail: charmhotels@mail.telepac.pt. 13 units. A/C TV TEL. 12,000$–16,800$ ($67.20–$94.10) double; 30,000$ ($168) suite. Rates include breakfast. AE, DC, MC, V. Free parking.

This 18th-century manor–turned–luxury hotel is the area's best choice. The windows open onto views of Braga, and a well-landscaped private park and a large lake with islets, ancestral trees, and tropical flora surround the building. The rooms have great charm; the rooftop unit is the most desirable. They're individually decorated in 18th-century traditional style, with swagged draperies, color-coordinated bedspreads and furnishings, and tasteful accessories. The nuptial chamber was a favorite of Dom Carlos, former king of Portugal, who installed his mistress, an actress, here.

Live music is presented on weekends, and the hotel has a bar as well as a pool. A few yards from the main building is a regional cellar that schedules vintage wine-tasting events on some evenings. Breakfast is served in the Oval Dining Room, frescoed by various artists. With advance notice, lunch or dinner can be served. The staff can arrange rowboat rentals, tennis, and horseback riding.

Hotel do Parque. Bom Jesús, Tenões, 4710 Braga. ☎ **253/67-65-48.** Fax 253/67-66-79. 49 units. A/C MINIBAR TV TEL. 16,500$ ($92.40) double; 24,000$ ($134.40) suite. Rates include breakfast. AE, DC, MC, V. Free parking.

Originally a turn-of-the-century villa, the Parque offers comfortably furnished but small rooms. They have modern amenities, such as firm mattresses. The decor is traditional, the grounds well maintained. At dinner, the hotel serves cuisine of the Minho and of France. There's a bar, and a spacious sitting room with an open fireplace.

EAST OF BRAGA

Casa de Requeixo. Frades, 4830 Póvoa de Lanhoso. ☎ **253/63-11-12.** Fax 253/63-64-99. 103 units. 10,000$ ($56) double. Rates include continental breakfast. No credit cards. Free parking. From the national highway N103 from Braga to Chaves, exit at the "16km" signposted stop in the village of Frades. From Braga, take a bus marked VENDAS NOVAS or CHAVES.

The area's most romantic place to stay is at Frades, near Póvoa de Lanhoso, 12½ miles east of Braga. Casa de Requeixo is a massive, elegant stone mansion from the 16th and 17th centuries. Dr. Manuel Artur Norton has beautifully furnished the guest rooms, each with a large living room, dining room, and kitchen. The *quinta* (manor house) combines old-fashioned charm with modern-day comfort in a bucolic setting. While based here, you can explore the area, including the Minho and Peneda-Gerês national parks.

Guests who don't cook in can dine nearby; the Restaurante Victor and the Restaurante Gaucho serve typical Portuguese meals, including wine from local vineyards. The casa serves after-dinner coffee and port.

WHERE TO DINE

O Alexandre. Campo das Hortas 10. ☎ **253/61-40-03.** Reservations recommended. Main courses 1,800$–2,600$ ($10.10–$14.55). DC, MC, V. Daily noon–3:30pm and 7–11pm. PORTUGUESE.

Since the 1970s this small eatery has attracted patrons from all walks of city life—from the mayor to the highest church official. It seems busiest at lunch, when businesspeople book most of the tables. Regional wines accompany most meals. There's an à la carte menu, but always ask about the daily specials. Portions are generous, and the cooking is rich. Roast *cabrito* (kid) is in season in June; the year-round favorite is *bacalhau* (dried salt cod), prepared in an infinite number of ways.

O Inácio. Campo das Hortas 4. ☎ **253/61-32-35.** Reservations recommended. Main courses 2,000$–3,200$ ($11.20–$17.90). AE, DC, MC, V. Wed–Mon noon–3:30pm and 7–10:30pm. Closed Sept. REGIONAL PORTUGUESE.

An old stone structure, O Inácio is the most popular restaurant in town. It has thrived at this spot since the 1930s. Its rugged walls and hand-hewn beams from the 1700s lie outside the town gate, the Arco da Porta Nova. The owner has a well-stocked wine cellar and, in our opinion, serves the best cuisine in Braga.

In the colder months a fire burns in an open hearth. The rustic decor features regional pottery and oxen yokes. The host, on the rare day that he's in a good mood, will tell you the day's Portuguese specialties. They usually include *bacalhau à Inácio* (codfish), *papas de sarrabulho* (a regional stew served in winter only), and *bife na cacarola* (pot roast). Roast kid is featured occasionally. Most fish dishes, which are fresh, are good alternatives. The dessert surprise is a rum omelette soufflé.

BRAGA AFTER DARK

There aren't any discos and there isn't a lot to do after dark. You'll probably remain in the bar of your hotel or head for one of three tried and true bars, favorites of many generations of locals. They lie almost adjacent to one another, near the corner of avenida Central and praça da República: the **Bar Barbieri** (☎ 253/61-43-81), the **Café Vianna** (☎ 253/26-23-36), and the **Café Astoria** (☎ 253/27-39-44). They serve coffee, wine, and whisky in a setting redolent of local gossip and intrigue.

3 Barcelos

14 miles W of Braga, 227 miles N of Lisbon

Barcelos is a sprawling river town that rests on a plateau ringed by green hills. Wrought-iron street lanterns glimmer late in the evening, long after the market in the open square of Campo da República has closed down.

The town doesn't feature any single major attraction, but it does have a famous symbol: the rooster. Although it was cooked and about to be served as the main course in a magistrate's dinner, the legend goes, the rooster crowed ecstatically to prove the innocence of a pilgrim wrongfully accused of theft.

ESSENTIALS

ARRIVING

BY TRAIN   The **station** is on avenida Alcaides de Faria (☎ 253/81-12-43). Thirteen trains a day arrive from Braga; the trip takes 1¼ hours and costs 170$ (95¢). Fifteen trains a day make the 1-hour trip from Viana do Castelo.

BY BUS   The **station** is on avenida Dr. Sidónio Pais (☎ **253/81-43-10**). Ten buses a day arrive from Braga. It's a 30-minute trip that costs 295$ ($1.65).

BY CAR   From Braga, follow N103 due west.

VISITOR INFORMATION

The **Barcelos Tourist Office** is at Torre da Porta Nova (☎ **253/81-18-82**).

EXPLORING THE TOWN   Try to visit Barcelos on Thursday, when the **market** (8am to 4pm) takes over the **campo da República,** almost 450 yards square with a fountain at the center. You'll see local handcrafts—rugs, dyed pillows stuffed with chicken feathers, chandeliers, crochet work, pottery, and hand-painted earthenware cockerels, Portugal's most characteristic souvenirs and often a symbol of the country.

The worship of the **Barcelos rooster** derives from a legend concerning a Gallego who was sentenced to hang despite his protestations of innocence. In a last-hour appeal to the judge, who was having dinner, the condemned man made a bold statement: If his protestations of innocence were true, the roasted rooster on the magistrate's plate would get up and crow. Suddenly, a glorious scarlet-plumed cockerel rose from the plate, crowing loud and long. The man was acquitted.

Opening onto the tree-studded main square are some of the finest buildings in Barcelos. The 18th-century **Igreja de Nossa Senhora do Terço** resembles a palace more than a church, with a central-niche facade topped by finials and a cross. The tile work around the baroque altar depicts scenes of monks at labor and a moving rendition of the Last Supper. Also fronting the *campo* is the **Hospital da Misericórdia,** a long, formal 17th-century building behind a spiked fence.

Of more interest is the small, octagonal **Igreja do Bom Jesús da Cruz,** with a tile-faced cupola. An upper balustrade, punctuated by large stone finials and a latticed round window about the square portal, contrasts with the austerity of the walls. The interior is more sumptuous, with crystal, marble, and gilt. There are no set hours for visits, though generally one can enter daily from 9am to 4pm. Don't count on always finding someone to admit you, however.

Overlooking the swirling Cávado River are the ruins of the 1786 **Palace of the Braganças.** The original palace site, as well as the town of Barcelos itself, was bestowed on Nuno Álvares by João I as a gift in gratitude for his bravery in the 1385 battle at Aljubarrota.

On the facade is a representation of the palace, re-created in splendor. You can wander through the ruins, which have been turned into an archaeological museum, filled with sarcophagi, heralded shields, and an 18th-century tile fountain. The **Museu Arqueológico** (no phone) is open daily 10am to noon and 2 to 6pm. Admission is free. The **Museu Regional de Cerâmica** (☎ 253/82-47-41) underneath the palace encapsulates the evolution of that handcraft (look for the blood-red ceramic oxen with lyre-shaped horns). Enter on rua Conego Joaquim Gaiolas. It is open Tuesday to Sunday 9am to 12:30pm and 2:30 to 5:30pm. Admission is 270$ ($1.50).

The shadow from the high palace chimney stretches across the old pillory in the courtyard below. The structure even exceeds in height the bell tower of the adjoining **Igreja Matriz** (parish church). Fronting the river, the Gothic church contains a baroque altar and an interior whose sides are faced with multicolored tiles. The altar is an array of cherubs, grapes, gold leaf, and birds.

SHOPPING   The unique ✪ **Centro do Artesanato de Barcelos,** Torre de Porta Nova (☎ **253/81-18-82**), is a gem tucked away in this provincial town. It displays some of the best regional handcrafts at the best prices we've encountered in the north. The center has an age-old stone tower that rises opposite the Church of São da Cruz. A wide display of goods is for sale on its street level and upper floor.

One outstanding collection is worth the trip to Barcelos. It consists of witty, sophisticated ceramics from the heirs of Rosa Ramalho, who was known as the Grandma Moses of Portuguese ceramics. Some of these figures show the influence of Picasso. Ms. Ramalho created figures depicting eerie people. For example, she put the heads of wolves on nuns and gave goats six legs—all in muted forest green or butterscotch brown. In addition, there's a good selection of the ceramic red-combed Barcelos cockerels, with many variations on the traditional motif in red and black. Local wares include black ceramic candlesticks, earthenware bowls used for *caldo verde,* hand-knitted pillows, handmade rugs in bold stripes, and hand-loomed bedspreads.

If this place doesn't have what you're looking for, head for **largo do Dom António Barroso,** where a handful of other souvenir and handcrafts shops sell the products of local artisans.

WHERE TO STAY

Quinta de Santa Combra. Lugar de Crujães, 4750 Varzea (Barcelos). ☎ and fax **253/83-45-40.** 6 units. TV TEL. 10,500$ ($58.80) double. Rates include breakfast. AE. Free parking.

In a little town without many places to stay, this 18th-century manor house comes as a welcome relief. Three miles from Barcelos on the road to Famalicão, it offers the best bed-and-breakfast in the area. The quinta is decorated in rustic but grand style, with spindle beds (with good mattresses) placed against stone walls on tile floors. Accommodations vary in shape and size. In the heart of Minho, this is grand country living—a true taste of Portugal, unlike the few dreary pensions in the area. The manor was converted into a small country inn in 1993.

WHERE TO DINE

Dom António. Rua Dom António Barroso 87. ☎ **253/81-22-85.** Main courses 650$–2,500$ ($3.65–$14); tourist menu 1,500$ ($8.40). AE, MC, V. Daily 9am–midnight. PORTUGUESE.

This local favorite opened in the mid-1980s on the street level of an old town house in the town's historic heart. It has a rustic interior and a polite staff. The restaurant features hearty soups, *bacalhau Dom António* (a popular house specialty concocted from codfish, onions, and potatoes), superb shellfish rice, grilled salmon, grilled steaks, and grilled pork chops.

Pensão Bagoeira. Av. Sidónio Pais 495. ☎ **253/81-12-36.** Reservations required for Thurs lunch. Main courses 950$–2,450$ ($5.30–$13.70). AE, DC, MC, V. Daily 8:30am–10:30pm. PORTUGUESE.

This is the most charming restaurant in town. You'll find oceans of local color, simple food of a type that hasn't changed in decades, and a staff that's virtually guaranteed to not speak a syllable of English. The setting boasts masses of fresh flowers, hand-wrought iron chandeliers, and wood with a patina that's older than many staff members (most of whom have been here since the days of Salazar). Try *feijoada,* the national dish of northern Portugal, redolent with beans and beef, and fresh vegetable soup, made with the finest produce. The chef also specializes in freshly caught fish, which he grills to perfection. Chicken with rice is a local favorite, but stewed pork with pig's blood is too much for most tastes.

BARCELOS AFTER DARK

Save your raucous nightclubbing for bigger cities like Lisbon or Porto and reconcile yourself to quieter nocturnal diversions. Our favorite watering hole is the **Café Conciliu,** rua dos Duques de Bragança (☎ **253/81-19-75**).

4 Esposende

12½ miles S of Viana do Castelo, 30 miles N of Porto, 228 miles N of Lisbon

Esposende is a beach resort town where Atlantic breezes sweep the pines and sand dunes, and cows graze in nearby pastures. The surrounding countryside is no longer unspoiled—though you'll still see an occasional ox cart in the street, the area has been extensively developed, and a wide new road runs along the seafront. Men and women in fustian clothes and broad-brimmed hats work the vineyards in the foothills. The beach, lining both sides of the Cávado estuary, is large and fine. Small fishing vessels plod along the river carrying anglers to the bass upstream. Recent archaeological digs have revealed the remains of a Roman city and necropolis, but that doesn't seem to have disturbed Esposende in the least.

ESSENTIALS
ARRIVING
Train service from Porto to Esposende is expected to be suspended soon.

BY BUS   The trip from Porto to Esposende takes about an hour and costs 630$ ($3.55) one way. Call ☎ **253/96-23-69** for schedules.

BY CAR   From Porto, take IC-1 north.

VISITOR INFORMATION
The **Esposende Tourist Office** is on avenida Arantes de Oliveira (☎ **253/970-00-00**).

WHERE TO STAY
Estalagem Zende. Estrada Nacional 13, 4740 Esposende. ☎ **253/96-46-64.** Fax 253/96-50-18. 25 units. A/C TV TEL. 6,500$–13,000$ ($36.40–$72.80) double; 18,000$–22,000$ ($100.80–$123.20) suite. Rates include breakfast. AE, DC, MC, V. Free parking.

Rated a luxury inn by the government, Estalagem Zende lies on the main road to Viana do Castelo, right outside Esposende. One-third of the well-maintained, midsize guest rooms have minibars. Furnishings are worn but comfortable, with good beds. The hotel offers a solarium, and laundry and room service are available. The inn has a cocktail bar; the restaurant, Martins, serves some of the best food in Esposende (see "Where to Dine," below). In winter a fire blazes on the hearth.

Hotel Suave Mar. Av. Eng. Arantes e Oliveira, 4740 Esposende. ☎ **253/96-54-45.** Fax 253/96-52-49. 79 units. A/C TV TEL. 8,500$–16,000$ ($47.60–$89.60) double; 12,000$–21,000$ ($67.20–$117.60) junior suite; 15,000$–25,000$ ($84–$140) suite. Rates include breakfast. AE, DC, MC, V. Free parking.

A semimodern hotel on the river, Suave Mar attracts frugal travelers who don't want to pay for the first-class accommodations at neighboring Ofir and Fão (see chapter 11). The midsize rooms are pleasant and comfortable, with firm beds.

The food is among the best in the resort. The restaurant, which is open to nonguests, serves Portuguese and Brazilian cuisine, a nod to the 20 years the owners spent in Brazil. Meals are served daily from 12:30 to 3pm and 7:30 to 10pm.

WHERE TO DINE
For the finest dining, consider the restaurants of the hotels we recommend.

Restaurant Martins. In the Estalagem Zende, Estrada Nacional 13. ☎ **253/96-46-64.** Main courses 1,300$–2,200$ ($7.30–$12.30). AE, DC, MC, V. Daily noon–3pm and 7–10:30pm. PORTUGUESE.

In the heart of Esposende, this large, bustling restaurant specializes in Portuguese seafood, often grilled lightly and seasoned with local garlic and herbs. Other choices include roast goat, smoked salmon, grilled fillets of sole, shellfish rice, and several preparations of codfish. Prices are reasonable. The regional produce and fresh seafood keep this traditional restaurant packed with devotees. "It's reliable and it's classic," one satisfied diner told us. "That's why I keep coming back."

5 Viana do Castelo

44 miles N of Porto, 241 miles N of Lisbon, 15½ miles N of Esposende

Viana do Castelo, between an estuary of the Lima River and a base of rolling hills, is the most folkloric city in northern Portugal. An occasional ox cart with wooden wheels clacking along the stone streets enhances the atmosphere. Boatmen can be seen near the waterfront, offering to sell visitors a slow cruise along the riverbanks. After years of decline, Viana today is bustling and prosperous, once again a major center of deep-sea fishing. It's also the site of industries like pyrotechnics, wood manufacturing, ceramics, and boat building.

For the best view, scale the Monte de Santa Luzia, reached by a funicular ride or, if you have a car, along a twisting road. From the Hotel de Santa Luzia at the summit, a great view unfolds, including Alexandre-Gustave Eiffel's bridge over the Lima.

Viana do Castelo is noted for its pottery and regional handcrafts; you can buy many of them at the Friday market. It's even better known for its regional dress, best seen at the annual Festa de Nossa Senhora de Agonia (Our Lady of Agony), which takes place the Friday, Saturday, and Sunday nearest August 20. The women wear strident orange, scarlet, and Prussian blue, and layers of golden necklaces with heart- and cross-shaped pendants.

ESSENTIALS
ARRIVING
BY TRAIN The **station** is on avenida dos Combatentes da Grande Guerra (☎ 258/82-13-15 for information). Eight trains per day arrive from Porto; the trip takes 2½ hours and costs 800$ ($4.50) one way.

BY BUS   The **station,** Central de Camionagem (☎ 258/82-50-47), is at the eastern edge of the city. Buses arrive every hour from Porto; the 2½-hour trip costs 950$ ($5.30) one way. There are four buses daily from Lisbon. It's a 6-hour trip, and a one-way ticket costs 2,450$ ($13.70). From Braga, eight buses a day make the 1½-hour trip; the fare is 620$ ($3.45) one way.

BY CAR   From Porto or Esposende, continue north along IC-1.

Visitor Information

The **Viana do Castelo Tourist Office** is on rua do Hospital Velho (☎ 258/82-26-20).

EXPLORING THE TOWN   The town center is **praça da República,** one of Portugal's most handsome squares. At its heart is the much-photographed 16th-century **Chafariz Fountain,** with water spewing from the mouths of its figures. The most impressive building on the square is the dour, squat three-story **Igreja da Misericórdia.** The lower level is an arcade of five austere Roman arches, and the two upper levels are ponderous Renaissance balconies. A rooftop crucifix crowns the structure. Each level's four supporting pillars are primitive caryatid-like figures. The church fronts rua da Bandeira and adjoins the former charity hospice, Hospital da Misericórdia. It contains pictorial tiles made in 1714, ornate baroque altars, a painted ceiling, and wood carvings.

The other building dominating the square is the 1502 **Paço do Concelho** (the former town hall), constructed over an arcade made up of three wide, low Gothic arches. The crenel-topped facade displays a royal coat of arms and wrought-iron balcony windows above each arch.

The best views of both turf and surf are from the ramparts of the **Castelo de São Tiago da Berra,** reached by following rua General Luîs do Rego. In 1589 Philip I of Spain ordered that the walls of the castelo be built—this is the reason "do Castelo" was added to Viana's name. It's open Tuesday to Sunday from 9am to 12:30pm and 2 to 5:30pm. Call ☎ 258/82-02-70 for more information.

To enjoy the other great view, take an elevator or funicular rail behind the train station. The funicular delivers you to the contemporary **Basilica of Santa Luzia** (☎ 258/82-31-73), a domed structure with panoramic views in all directions. A staircase at the side of the basilica leads to the pinnacle of the dome and its panoramic sweep of the "Green Coast." Santa Luzia, estrada de Santa Luzia, is open daily from 8am to 7pm. Access to the dome costs 120$ (65¢). The funicular operates every half hour daily from 10am to 7pm. It costs 120$ (65¢).

SHOPPING   The artifacts you'll find here tend to be earthier, more rustic, and less influenced by fads than what's usually available closer to Lisbon. In addition to the ceramics and wood carvings that are widely available in other regions, look for linens and embroideries, sometimes in bewitchingly subtle patterns. The main shopping streets, **rua Manuel Espergueira** and **rua da Bandeira,** contain shops selling virtually everything you'd need to dress yourself or accessorize a house.

If you're looking for handcrafts, try **Casa Sandra,** largo João Tomás da Costa (☎ 258/82-21-55). It carries fine linens and embroideries in all possible degrees of intricacy. The oldest and biggest store in town is **Casa Fontinha,** largo João Tomás da Costa (☎ 258/82-22-31). Smaller, dustier, and confusingly arranged is **A Tenda,** rua do Hospital Velho (☎ 258/82-28-13). Three more worthwhile choices are **Arte Regional,** avenida dos Combatentes da Grande Guerra (☎ 258/82-90-45); **O Traje,** rua Aurora do Lima (☎ 258/82-54-46); and **Arte Minho,** rua de São Pedro 21–23 (☎ 258/82-10-52).

WHERE TO STAY

Hotel do Parque. Praça da Galiza, 4900 Viana do Castelo. ☎ **258/82-86-05.** Fax 258/82-86-12. 124 units. A/C TV TEL. 18,500$–25,000$ ($103.60–$140) double; 35,000$ ($196) suite. Rates include breakfast. AE, DC, MC, V. Free parking.

This four-star hotel, at the base of the bridge crossing the Lima River on the edge of town, is the best in town. It feels like a small resort, with lounges overlooking two pools (one reserved for children). The main floor has a lounge and an interior winter garden. The midsize guest rooms are quite contemporary, with built-in furnishings, firm beds, piped-in music, and balconies.

Hotel Viana Sol. Largo Vasco da Gama, 4900 Viana do Castelo. ☎ **258/82-89-95.** Fax 258/82-89-97. 66 units. TV TEL. 13,500$ ($75.60) double. Rates include breakfast. AE, DC, MC, V. Limited free parking on street.

Behind a dignified granite-and-stucco facade, near a commemorative column and fountain in the town center, this well-designed hotel is 3 blocks south of praça da República. In contrast to its elegantly severe exterior, its spacious public rooms are sheathed with white marble, capped with mirrored ceilings, and illuminated with a three-tiered atrium. The lobby bar is near a pagoda-shaped fountain. The small to midsize guest rooms are sparsely furnished, and most don't have views. Nonetheless, they offer comfortable beds. There's no restaurant, but many are located nearby. The hotel has a pool, a health club, tennis courts, and squash courts.

✪ **Pousada do Monte de Santa Luzia.** Monte de Santa Luzia, 4900 Viana do Castelo. ☎ **258/82-88-89.** Fax 258/82-88-92. www.pousadas.pt. E-mail: enatur@mail.telepac.pt. 48 units. A/C MINIBAR TV TEL. 19,500$ ($109.20) double; 25,000$–38,000$ ($140–$212.80) suite. Rates include breakfast. AE, DC, MC, V. Free parking.

Some 3½ miles from the center, the government-owned Santa Luzia sits on a wooded hillside high above the most congested part of the city. It's just behind the illuminated dome of the neo-Byzantine Basilica of Santa Luzia. Built in 1895, the hotel has neo-classical details and granite balconies, giving it the appearance of a royal palace, especially when it's floodlit at night. Winding cobblestone roads run through a forest to the entrance. At the summit, you'll find the area's best view of the city and river.

Guest rooms are spacious, and some bathrooms have Jacuzzis. The high-ceilinged public rooms gained art deco sheen when the hotel was completely renovated in the '90s. It boasts long expanses of glistening marble, stylish Jazz Age accessories, a comfortable bar and restaurant, and enormous, echoing halls. The dining room serves excellent meals daily from 12:30 to 3pm and 7:30 to 10pm. One of the gardens contains an outdoor pool.

Residencial Viana Mar. Av. dos Combatentes da Grande Guerra 215, 4900 Viana do Castelo. ☎ and fax **258/82-89-62.** 36 units, 16 with bathroom. TV TEL. 5,000$ ($28) double without bathroom; 7,000$ ($39.20) double with bathroom. Rates include breakfast. AE, DC, MC, V. Free parking.

Viana Mar is on the main commercial thoroughfare, behind a granite facade whose severity is relieved by colorful awnings. Near the nondescript reception area lies a sunken bar. Each small guest room has basic furnishings, but comfortable beds, and all the doubles contain a private bathroom. A few rooms are in two nearby but dull annexes. Breakfast is the only meal served.

WHERE TO STAY NEARBY

The most romantic places to stay in and around Viana do Castelo are the antique quintas. In these restored manor houses, you can stay with the Portuguese aristocracy. You can make reservations through **Turismo de Habitação,** praça da República,

4990 Ponte de Lima (☎ 258/74-28-27; fax 258/74-14-44). Payment is made by check sent directly to the owners, with 50% prepayment required when your reservation is made. A minimum stay of 2 nights is required, and reservations must be made at least 3 days before arrival.

The Viana do Castelo area has some of the most elaborate and stylized quintas in Portugal. A random sampling follows.

Casa de Rodas. 4950 Monção. ☎ **251/65-21-05**. 10 units. 14,000$ ($78.40) double. Rates include breakfast. No credit cards. Free parking.

Constructed in typical quinta style with a red-tile roof and stucco walls, this hotel is between a wooded area and a farm that grows grapes for consumption in Santiago de Compostela. It's about half a mile from Monção, which is known for its *termas* (spa) treatments for rheumatism and respiratory ailments. Monção is 43 miles northeast of Viana do Castelo.

The house, now owned by Maria Luisa Távora, was built in the 16th century, destroyed by fire in 1658 during Portugal's battle for independence, and reconstructed soon after. Guest rooms come in a variety of shapes and sizes, but all are well maintained and traditionally furnished, with firm mattresses. There is a swimming pool on the grounds. The location along the border of Spain allows for day trips to the Spanish cities of Vigo and Santiago de Compostela, as well as the beach, about a 30-minute drive away.

Convento Val de Pereiras. Lugar Val de Pereiras, 4990 Arcozelo, Ponte de Lima. ☎ **258/74-21-61**. Fax 258/74-20-47. 9 units. TEL. 13,500$ ($75.60) double; 18,000$ ($100.80) suite. Rates include breakfast. No credit cards. Free parking.

The 37-acre site this hotel occupies has been famous since the Middle Ages for its freshwater springs. According to legend, they were blessed by St. Francis of Assisi, who performed many miracles here on his way to Santiago de Compostela. In 1316 a stone-sided building on the site functioned as a monastery. Some 200 years later the monks were evicted, and a community of Franciscan nuns controlled the premises for another 300 years. Around 1890 everything except one of the towers of the original monastery was demolished, and a new Minho-style monastery, similar in design to a large manor house, was erected. It lies less than a mile from Ponte de Lima, across the Douro from the town center.

Today the dignified building functions as a hotel, with a large pool, vineyards producing *vinho verde,* two tennis courts, and comfortable furnishings in the roomy guest rooms. Horseback riding can be arranged at a neighboring farm for around 1,800$ ($10.10) per hour.

WHERE TO DINE

A Ceia. Rua do Raio 331. ☎ **258/26-39-32**. Reservations recommended Sat–Sun. Main courses 900$–2,300$ ($5.05–$12.90). AE, MC, V. Tues–Sun noon–3pm and 7–10pm. PORTUGUESE.

Just about everyone in Viana do Castelo has dined at this artfully rustic restaurant, which occupies a prime position in the heart of town. You enter through a prominent bar area, where you'll be tempted to linger with the many regulars who appreciate their wine and only rarely seem to want to rush in to dinner. Portions are generous, and the food is flavored in traditional and time-tested (but not particularly innovative) ways. It seems universally popular among the extended families who sometimes conduct their once-a-week powwows at long connected tables. Menu items include steaming bowls of bean-and-meat stew, tripe, roast pork with clams, succulent roast goat, veal and beef dishes, and steaming bowls of such soups as *caldo verde.*

A Village Off the Beaten Path

Upriver 132 miles from Viana do Castelo is **Ponte de Lima,** which is exactly what one hopes a Portuguese village will be like. Spread lazily along the tree-lined banks of the Lima River, it's named for the Roman bridge with 27 arches spanning the water. Jagged ramparts surround Ponte de Lima, and massive towers, narrow winding streets, and fortified doors decorate the houses.

The drive along the north side of the river takes you through grape arbors, pastoral villages, and forests of cedar, pine, and chestnut. Red-cheeked locals stand silhouetted against moss-green stone walls as they interrupt their toil in the cabbage fields to watch you pass by. We've never recommended cabbages as a sightseeing attraction, but they're here. Jade green and monstrous, they grow to wild heights of 6 feet. They're most often used to make caldo verde, the fabled regional soup.

The town, founded on the site of a Celtic settlement, was developed by the Romans, who named it Forum Limicorum. It was important for both river trade and river defense. Thick stone walls enclose the town, guarding the bridge across the Lima. Part of the Roman bridge is still in use. It has buttressed extension, made under King Dom Pedro in 1355 because of changes in the river's course. Sometimes you'll see women wringing out their clothes along the riverbanks. At certain times of year the Lima is likely to be dry, but when it's full, anglers often catch trout.

The Roman wall has been partially destroyed to make room for roads, but you can walk along the top of what's left. An 18th-century fountain graces the town's main square, and houses of that era are still occupied. Ruins of ramparts from the Middle Ages and a solitary keep can be seen, opposite the old bridge. Go up the stone steps of the keep to visit the **Biblioteca Pública Municipal,** founded in the early 18th century. Its archives are rich in historic documents.

Two churches at right angles to each other, **São Francisco** and **São António,** have been secularized. They now contain museum treasures and artwork,

Alambique. Rua Manuel Espergueira 86. ☎ **258/841-364.** Main courses 850$–1,600$ ($4.75–$8.95); tourist menu 1,800$ ($10.10). AE, DC, MC, V. Wed–Mon noon–3pm and 7–10pm. MINHO.

You enter this typical Portuguese restaurant through a large wine vat. Inside you'll find many of the specialties for which the cooks of northern Portugal are known, including codfish Antiga Viana, *churrasco de porco* (pork), *cabrito* (goat), tripe Porto style, and lampreys bordelaise. One of the chef's most memorable dishes is *feijoada a transmontana* (bean-and-meat stew). To begin, you can order *sopa a alentejana* or *sopa do mar.* Such food may be too authentic for those who grew up on the Big Mac, though.

Os 3 Potes. Beco dos Fornos 7–9. ☎ **258/82-52-50.** Reservations recommended in summer. Main courses 1,800$–3,000$ ($10.10–$16.80). AE, DC, MC, V. Tues–Sun noon–1pm and 7–10:30pm. From praça da República, take rua de Sacadura Cabral. PORTUGUESE/ INTERNATIONAL.

Os 3 Potes, off praça da República, was an old bakery before its conversion into one of the best regional restaurants in Viana do Castelo. The atmosphere is rustic. On Friday and Saturday from June to September, folk dancing is featured and the place takes on a touristy feel. Have someone at your hotel call for a reservation. We especially handsome wood carving. Of particular interest in São Francisco is a strange image of St. George astride a saddle on a wooden trestle. The museum is open Wednesday to Monday from 10am to noon and 2 to 5:30pm.

The Ponte de Lima **market,** held on alternate Mondays, is known throughout Portugal. The sellers show up in regional costumes. On the north side of the bridge is the cattle market where oxen and steers are sold. A little bag nestling between the horns of the animals contains a "magic potion" said to ward off the evil eye. Below the bridge is a place reserved for eating alfresco delights like roast sardines accompanied by glasses of *vinho verde.* Taking the riverside walk, you can survey the stalls of various craftspeople, including cobblers, carpenters, and goldsmiths.

In recent years Ponte de Lima has opened a collection of beautiful antique properties, ranging from farms to manor houses. Staying in one of these treasures is reason enough to go. There are about 60 such properties in the region. Information about them is available through **Turismo de Habitação,** 4990 Ponte de Lima (☎ **258/74-16-72;** fax 258/74-14-44).

Another stellar property is the **Paço de Calheiros,** Calheiros, 4990 Ponte de Lima (☎ **258/94-71-64;** fax 258/94-72-94). Perched on a hill overlooking the town, it's the best-known *solar* (country villa) in Ponte. The nine doubles cost 15,500$ to 18,500$ ($86.80 to $103.60); five suites in converted stables go for 30,350$ to 32,000$ ($169.95 to $179.20). Breakfast and parking are included. A splendid dinner can be arranged on request. The solar has lush gardens and a pool.

Back in Ponte de Lima, you can dine at **Encanada,** praça Municipal (☎ **258/94-11-89**), which serves the best regional cookery. Opening onto an esplanade near the Lima River, it offers a panoramic view of the beautiful countryside. Try the special fried pork or homemade fish cakes. Eels with rice is a local specialty, but available only in winter. Meals are served Friday to Wednesday from noon to 3pm and 7 to 10pm; prices start at 2,000$ ($11.20).

recommend caldo verde to begin, followed by such main dishes as codfish 3 Potes, lampreys (eels), or fondue bourguignonne. The restaurant is somewhat hard to find, but worth the search.

Túnel. Rua dos Manjovos 9 (off av. dos Combatentes da Grande Guerra). ☎ **258/82-21-88.** Main courses 950$–1,800$ ($5.30–$10.10); tourist menu 1,800$ ($10.10). No credit cards. Daily 11:30am–2pm and 7–10pm. Closed Oct 20–Nov 30. REGIONAL PORTUGUESE.

Túnel is a good bet for regional cuisine. The quality of the food seems to vary from day to day. When they're available, you can order especially delectable quail or roast kid. The fresh fish dishes are usually the best, however. You might begin with a rich vegetable soup, made with fresh produce. The dining room is on the second floor, and you pass through a simple snack bar at ground level.

Viana's. Rua Frei Bartolomeu Martas. ☎ **258/82-47-97.** Reservations recommended. Main courses 1,200$–2,000$ ($6.70–$11.20). MC, V. Wed–Mon 12:30–3pm and 7:30–10pm. PORTUGUESE.

Since 1991, this well-managed restaurant has thrived. The keys are its generous portions, kindly staff, and flavorful dishes created from sometimes unappetizing-looking species of fish. In a historic-looking room that's close to the sea, you'll dine on fresh meat and locally caught fish. Codfish is everybody's justifiable favorite, but you can also order succulent cuts of meat braised (or grilled) according to your taste.

VIANA DO CASTELO AFTER DARK

You won't lack for bars and cafes that serve alcohol and refreshments. If you're interested in music and energy, consider a visit to the town's two most popular discos: **Cybar,** Praia do Cabedelo (☎ **258/33-28-52**), 2½ miles east of the town center; and its less popular neighbor, the **Foz Café,** Praia do Cabedelo (☎ **258/33-28-52**). About a mile north of the town center (follow signs pointing to Valença) is the **Disco-Bar Teatros,** rua de Monserrate (☎ **258/82-12-00**).

6 Vila Real

248 miles NE of Lisbon, 70 miles W of Porto

The capital of Trás-os-Montes is a lively little town built on a hilly plateau in the foothills of the Serra do Marão. Bridges across the ravines link some parts of town. Gorges cut by the Corgo and Cabril rivers, which flow together here, are visible from a terrace high above, where a castle once stood. The lookout is reached in a direct line from the cemetery. From this vicinity, you can also see houses overhanging the ravine of the Corgo.

You can spend a worthy 2 hours or so wandering through Vila Real's historic core and enjoy a glass of port in one of the cafes, which brim with youth. The main sights and buildings of interest are along the avenida Carvalho Araújo.

The agricultural town makes a good base for many beautiful trips into the area, including the Parque Nacional do Alvão to the northwest, with its waterfalls, flower-filled valleys, and ravines. The tourist office provides maps and suggests places to visit. To drive to the park, follow the IP-4 west for 6 miles, turning onto N304 heading for Mondim de Bastro and Campeã. This stretch will take you through some of the most scenic areas of Trás-os-Montes—once you've passed through the dreary modern suburbs of Vila Real, which are in marked contrast to the mellow historic core.

ESSENTIALS
ARRIVING
BY TRAIN Vila Real has awkward rail connections. The trip from Porto takes longer than the bus ride and requires a transfer at the town of Régua. There are five trains a day from Porto via Régua. It's a 4½ hour journey, and costs 980$ ($5.50) one way. For **information,** call ☎ **259/32-21-93.**

BY BUS Buses from Porto take only 2 hours. There are three runs a day, and the one-way fare is 900$ ($5.05). Four buses a day make the 7½-hour trip from Lisbon. The cost is 2,420$ ($13.55) one way. For **information** and schedules, call ☎ **259/32-32-34.**

BY CAR From Porto, continue east along the express route, A4, following signs to Amarante, where you continue east along N15 into Vila Real.

VISITOR INFORMATION
The **tourist office** is at av. Carvalho Araújo 94 (☎ **259/32-28-19**).

EXPLORING THE TOWN You won't be dazzled by "must-see" monuments, although the historic core as a whole makes for an interesting walk. Vila Real is called a Royal Town because it contains many formerly aristocratic houses dating from the 16th to the 18th centuries. It's fun to poke your nose down the tiny offshoot streets, hoping to make discoveries. The main monuments are concentrated in and around avenida Carvalho Araújo.

Chief among these is the **Cathedral (Sé) of Sao Domingos** on the main square of avenida Carvalho Araújo. It is open only for masses, daily at 7:30am and 6pm. There's no admission fee. The Gothic building contains a high altar with gold reredos, but if it's closed when you visit, you will not have missed a great deal. The place is a bit stodgy and the interior a little too simplistic for our tastes.

Much more charming is the **Capela Nova** (New Chapel), sometimes called the Capel dos Clérigos (Chapel of the Clergy) by the locals. It is the finest baroque monument in Vila Real. The Italian architecture may have been the work of Niccolò Nasoni, the 18th-century master. It has a floral facade. The chapel lies 2 blocks east of the cathedral, between rua Direita and rua 31 de Janeiro. It is open daily from 10am to noon and 2 to 6pm. Admission is free.

Farther north is **St. Peter's Church** (Igreja São Pedro), at largo de São Pedro, just off the main street. From 1528, though much altered over the ages, this church has an intriguing interior, with much baroque gilt carving and a chancel adorned with colorful tiles. Its main attraction, and reason enough for visit, is the coffered ceiling of carved and gilded wood. It is open daily from 8am to 8pm. Admission is free.

The **Town Hall,** or Camera Municipal, avenida Carvalho Araújo (☎ 259/30-81-00), also merits a look. It has an Italian Renaissance–style stone staircase constructed in the early 1800s. In front is a lantern pillory. It is open Monday to Friday 9am to 5:30pm. Admission is free.

Although it's not open to the public, you can stop to admire the **Casa de Diogo Cão,** avenida Carvalho Araújo 19. This is the reputed birthplace of the navigator who discovered the Congo River in 1482. The exterior of the house was altered, and it is now 16th-century Renaissance style. Although the explorer visited the legendary King Manicongo, and the powerful monarch reportedly was baptized as a Christian, little is know about Cão. Dom João II concealed all records in the Torre de Tombo in Lisbon to keep the discoveries from the Castilians. The earthquake of 1755 destroyed the archives.

The most interesting attraction lies not in Vila Real but 2½ miles east of the city, on the N322 highway signposted to Sabrosa. The grapes of the original Mateus rosé wine were grown in vineyards here.

✪ **Solar de Mateus** is a perfect example of baroque architecture, with a stunning facade preceded by a "mirror" of water. This is the building pictured on the Mateus wine label. Dating from the first half of the 18th century, the main section of the manor house has a stunning balustraded staircase and a high emblazoned pediment surrounded by allegorical statues. Sacheverell Sitwell called it "the most typical and the most fantastic country home in Portugal." The twin wings of the manor advance "lobster-like," in Sitwell's words.

An ornamental stone balustrade guards the main courtyard, and lovely pinnacles crown the roof cornices. The architect is unknown, although some authorities claim it was the work of Niccolò Nasoni, who may have designed the Capela Nova (see above).

The manor house and the gardens are open for tours. The house contains heavy silk hangings, high wooden ceilings, paintings of bucolic scenes, and a tiny museum. You'll see vestments, Sèvres vases, and an 1817 edition of the Portuguese classic, *The Lusiads,* printed in Paris. The gardens are among the most beautiful in Europe, with a tunnel of cypress trees shading the path.

From March to September the site is open daily from 9am to 7pm; off-season, daily 10am to 1pm and 2 to 5pm. A full guided tour costs 1,000$ ($5.60) per person. It's 600$ ($3.35) just to tour the gardens.

SHOPPING   If you happen to be in Vila Real on June 28 and 29, you can purchase some of the region's fine black pottery, which is sold at St. Peter's Fair. At other times, you can find the pottery, made in the surrounding countryside, at little shops throughout the historic district. Many visitors also come here to buy sparkling rosé wine directly from Solar de Mateus (see above).

WHERE TO STAY

Albergaria Cabanelas. Rua Dom Pedro de Castro, 5000 Vila Real. ☎ **259/32-31-53.** Fax 259/32-30-28. 29 units. A/C MINIBAR TV TEL. 7,500$–9,000$ ($42–$50.40) double. Rates include breakfast. AE, DC, MC, V. Free parking.

This 2-decade-old hotel sits in the center of the city, facing the marketplace. It is the second-best choice in town, but don't get your hopes up. Although well maintained and kept, it is simplicity itself. Beds are comfortable, with firm mattresses, but rooms are small.

Breakfast is the only meal served, but the hotel has a snack bar. Restaurants are nearby. Room service is available from breakfast until 11pm, and there's laundry service and a concierge.

Hotel Miracorgo. Av. 1 de Maio 78, 5000 Vila Real. ☎ **259/32-50-01.** Fax 259/32-50-06. 166 units. A/C MINIBAR TV TEL. 11,500$ ($64.40) double; 15,800$ ($88.50) suite. Rates include breakfast. AE, DC, MC, V. Free parking.

This is the city's best choice for lodgings. It's in the commercial section, popular with businesspeople, but has an impersonal aura. The hotel spreads across two buildings— one 5 floors, one 12 floors. It is 2 decades old, and was renovated in the mid-1990s. The sterile quality recedes somewhat when you enter the midsize accommodations, most of which open onto views of a scenic valley. All are comfortably furnished, with good mattresses and excellent plumbing.

The Miracorgo has a pub, a disco, two bars, laundry, and a concierge—more facilities than any other hotel in town. There's even an indoor swimming pool. The restaurant serves consistently good international and Trás-os-Montes cuisine, using the finest local products when available.

WHERE TO DINE

O Aldeão. Rua Dom Pedro de Castro 70. ☎ **259/247-94.** Reservations recommended. Main courses 1,000$–5,000$ ($5.60–$28). AE, V. Mon–Sat 8am–3pm and 7pm–2am. TRÁS-OS-MONTES.

In the historic center of town, this popular local eatery draws devotees with reasonably priced food and savory local cuisine. If you have only one day in Trás-os-Montes, pop in here. Dig into such regional fare as *feijoada branca á transmontana,* a robust stew made with white beans and a selection of meat products. If that isn't regional enough for you, try the city's best platter of tripe. For the faint of heart, other more recognizable platters are served, including some of the most tender and succulent grilled meats in the city. The house steak is laden with so many garnishes that you might not want to order an appetizer if you expect to finish it.

O Espadeiro. Av. Almeida Lucena. ☎ **259/32-23-02.** Reservations recommended. Main courses 2,000$–4,000$ ($11.20–$22.40). AE, MC, V. Thurs–Tues 9am–11pm. Closed Sept. TRÁS-OS-MONTES.

This is the finest independent restaurant in Vila Real. You climb a flight of stairs to the modern, rustically decorated restaurant, which has a large sunny terrace and a bar with a panoramic view. The chefs are rightly proud of their region and its foodstuffs. A delectable specialty is trout stuffed with Parma-style ham. Seafood rice is a savory offering, and if you are leery of the meat by-products used in the local bean stew (*fei-joada*), you can always opt for baked ham instead. Some dishes—including stewed tripe and roast kid—are very regional and not for the unadventurous palate. The dining room with the fireplace is where everybody wants to dine in winter. The name, which means "the swordsman," honors a brave transmontano warrior, Lourenço Viegas.

7 Bragança

86 miles NE of Vila Real, 324 miles NE of Lisbon

The medieval town of Bragança (Braganza, in English) was under the aegis of the House of Bragança, which ruled Portugal from 1640 until its overthrow early in the 20th century. During those years the heir to the throne of Portugal bore the title duke of Bragança. On a hilltop, a long, fortified wall surrounds Bragança, the best-preserved medieval town in Portugal. It overlooks the modern town in the northeastern reaches of the country on a rise of ground in the Serra da Nogueira, some 2,000 feet above sea level.

ESSENTIALS
ARRIVING

BY TRAIN   There is no direct train service. The nearest station is in the town of Mirandela, which is connected by bus to Bragança. For **information** and schedules, call ☎ 21/888-40-25.

BY BUS   Rodonorte (☎ 273/30-01-83) runs five buses a day from Porto via Mirandela. The trip takes 5 hours and costs 1,440$ ($8.05) one way. The same company runs three buses a day to Lisbon. The journey takes 8 hours and costs 2,680$ ($15) one way.

BY CAR   From Vila Real, continue northeast on E82.

VISITOR INFORMATION

The **tourist office** is at avenida Cidade de Zamora (☎ 273/38-12-73).

EXPLORING THE TOWN   Bragança lies at the edge of the Montesinho Natural Park, one of the wildest regions on the continent. Although the climate is harsh, the area's stretches of moorland have a raw beauty. The natural park encompasses medieval villages, oak forests, towering mountains, and wild animals such as boars and wolves. Golden eagles sometimes fly over. We are especially drawn to the region in the spring, when white almond blossoms cover the valleys like snow. The fierce heat of summer and the cold winds sweeping across the plain in winter may lead you to seek out balmier climes.

A walled citadel, or castle, on a hilltop crowns the town of Bragança. The Upper Town grew up around this brooding old castle. In a small public garden within the citadel stands a **Gothic pillory.** A medieval shaft has been driven through the stone effigy of a boar, which has a depression carved in its snout. The boar is believed to date from the Iron Age, and it's possible that it was used in ancient pagan rituals.

A **Cidadela** (sometimes called O Castelo) dates from the 12th century. Dom João I reconstructed it in the 14th century. The heyday of this castle came under the fiefdom of the Dukes of Bragança, the ruling family of Portugal from 1640 until the monarchy collapsed in 1910. The Upper Town was also a major silk center in the 1400s—in part because of a prosperous Jewish merchant community. The Inquisition dispersed most of the merchants. The citadel's tall, square keep, Torre de Menagem, today contains the **Museu Militar** (☎ 273/32-23-78). The military museum's displays range from medieval suits of armor to a World War I machine gun used in trench warfare. Unusual exhibits are collections of African art, some from Angola, gathered by Portuguese soldiers on duty. The museum is open daily from 9am to noon and 2 to 5pm. Admission is 250$ ($1.40), free for children under 10.

Beside the castle you can look at the **Torre da Princesa** or Princess Tower. Here the fourth duke of Bragança imprisoned his wife, Dona Leonor. She was said to be so beautiful that he didn't want other men to look at her. However, when he moved his court to Lisbon, he murdered her.

Also part of the castle complex in the Upper Town, the **Domus Municipalis,** or Town Hall—built over a cistern—dates from the 12th century. It is one of the few remaining Romanesque civic buildings in the country. The interior is a cavernous room lit by little round arches. It's open Friday to Wednesday 10am to noon and 2 to 5pm. Admission is free.

A final building of note is the 16th-century **Igreja da Santa Maria,** or St. Mary's Church (☎ 273/32-23-78). The interior is distinguished by a barrel-vaulted painted ceiling from the 18th century. The painting depicts the Assumption of the Virgin in many colors. Salomonic (twisted) columns frame the front door. Hours are Friday to Wednesday 9am to 12:30pm and 2 to 5pm.

The citadel and Upper Town are the reasons to go to Bragança. If time remains, you can also explore the Lower Town, with its major boulevard and (in the summer) sidewalk cafes.

The **Museu do Abade de Baçal,** rua do Consilheiro Abilio Beca 27 (☎ 273/33-15-95), occupies a former bishop's palace. A local priest, Francisco Manuel Alves (1865–1947), created this bizarre assemblage. He collected everything from Iron Age depictions of pigs to ancient tombstones. He also collected antiques, ceramics, folkloric costumes, old coins, regional paintings, silver, archaeological artifacts—virtually anything that caught his eye, including church plates and vestments. The museum is open Tuesday to Sunday 10am to 5pm. Admission is 200$ ($1.10).

If time is short, you can skip the **Cathedral,** or Sé, largo da Sé (☎ 273/30-01-40), in the center of the city. The lackluster structure, originally the Church of São João da Baptista, is not up to the standards of many of Portugal's other cathedrals. The cathedral dates from the 16th century and shows both Renaissance and baroque architectural influences. It is open daily from 9am to 6pm. Admission is free.

After exploring Bragança, head for the ✪ **Parque Natural de Montesinho.** Pick up a map at the tourist office (see above). This forbidding but beautiful land of towering mountains and high plateaus stretches northwest and northeast of Bragança. Here you'll discover some of the most rugged—certainly the wildest—land in the country. It is still home to the roving wolf, wild boar, and the elusive fox, among other animals. In the little villages you'll see as you drive through the vast land, life is lived nearly the way it was a century ago, although modern intrusions have occurred.

At least until the outbreak of World War II, many pre-Christian rituals were still practiced here. The area stretches over 290 square miles. In all, less than 9,000 people live in fewer than 100 villages. This is one of the best places in Portugal for trekking along well-worn mountain paths, most of which date from the fall of the Visigothic empire. Sometimes you can spot an endangered bird such as the black stork. Because trails are unmarked, the tourist office provides brochures, useful maps, and advice.

SHOPPING   Head for the shops around **largo da Sé** (sometimes called Praça da Sé), the cathedral precinct, for local handcrafts. You'll find locally produced copper and leather goods, plus woven fabrics. The shops also carry ceramics from the surrounding area. Many similar shops also lie within the walls of the citadel.

WHERE TO STAY

Classis. Av. João da Cruz 102, 5300 Bragança. ☎ **273/33-16-31.** Fax 273/234-58. 20 units. A/C MINIBAR TV TEL. 7,500$–9,000$ ($42–$50.40) double. Rates include breakfast. AE, DC, MC, V. Limited free parking on street.

This is the town's second-best choice, although its accommodations fall far short of the more luxurious ones in the pousada. (The pousada might be fully booked in the summer, usually with travelers from Spain.) You'll still sleep well here. The midsize guest rooms are comfortably maintained and furnished, with fine mattresses. The hotel is convenient to the train and bus stations. Breakfast is the only meal served. Several restaurants are a short walk away. The hotel has limited room service, laundry, and a concierge.

✪ Pousada de São Bartolomeu. Estrada de Turismo, 5300 Bragança. ☎ **273/331-493.** Fax 273/323-453. www.pousadas.pt. 28 units. A/C MINIBAR TV TEL. 16,300$–24,600$ ($91.30–$137.75) double. Rates include breakfast. AE, DC, MC, V. Free parking.

Built in 1959 and modernized since, this is the best accommodation in the area. It's on the heights of the Serra da Nogueira, with a panoramic view of the 12th-century castle of Bragança. The fairly spacious guest rooms were upgraded in 1996. They're well furnished and maintained, with private balconies and firm beds.

The pousada makes an ideal stop for travelers entering the country from Spain at Alcanices-Quintanilha, about a 30-minute drive away. This view at night is the most spectacular in Bragança, taking in the crenellated fortifications of the old city. Guests enjoy the rustically decorated public rooms, especially the one with an open fireplace. The international and regional cuisine is the best in the area. The hotel has room service, laundry, and a swimming pool (summer only).

Residencia Santa Isabel. Rua Alexandre Herculano 67, 5300 Bragança. ☎ **273/33-14-27.** Fax 273/32-69-37. 14 units. TV TEL. 7,500$ ($42) double. Rates include breakfast. No credit cards.

The best budget-conscious choice in town is this small-scale hotel, set among a handful of stores and businesses in the center of town. View it as a stop for the night, and don't expect too much of the Portuguese-speaking staff. The guest rooms are well scrubbed but simply furnished, with worn but comfortable mattresses. Rooms tend to be small. Breakfast is the only meal served, but there are several restaurants nearby. In the basement are the breakfast room and a bar. Guests can watch TV in a public room near the street-level reception desk.

WHERE TO DINE

La Em Casa. Rua Marquês de Pombal 7. ☎ **273/32-21-11.** Reservations required. Main courses 1,500$–2,500$ ($8.40–$14). AE, DC, MC, V. Daily noon–3pm and 7–11:30pm. TRÁS-OS-MONTES.

With pine-paneled walls and a rustic atmosphere, this modern, airy restaurant is one of the town's most consistently reliable. In the center of the city, it attracts the rare foreign visitor but has a devoted local following. Diners are drawn by the kitchen's deft handling of local produce. The rack or leg of lamb is aromatic and tender, and veal is served in the typical style of the province, grilled with potatoes and flavored with a sauce made with fresh garlic and vinegar. Octopus also appears on the menu, coated in egg batter and sautéed golden brown. Fresh seafood shipments arrive daily. Sometimes fado performances are staged here.

✪ Solar Bragançano. Praça da Sé (largo da Sé). ☎ **273/32-38-75.** Reservations recommended. Main courses 2,500$–4,000$ ($14–$22.40). Fixed-price menu 1,680$ ($9.40). AE, DC, MC, V. Daily 11am–3pm and 6–11pm. TRÁS-OS-MONTES.

In a 3-century-old house on the main square of town, this old-fashioned restaurant is our all-time favorite in the area. It serves the best, most flavorful regional dishes. You'll get a true taste of Trás-os-Montes here, and will likely have a good time, too. The tiled stairway leads to a formal dining room decorated in a typical style, with handwoven regional rugs, chandeliers, and wood ceilings. You can also dine in an inside garden. Host Antonio Vesiderio's local specialties include game dishes in autumn—perhaps pheasant with chestnuts or hare with rice. Spicy game sausages are another exciting choice, as is white Montesinho kid, perfectly roasted. Veal steak with wine sauce is available year-round. You might conclude your meal with regional goat cheese. Discerning locals do, and we always follow their example.

Madeira 13

The island of Madeira, 530 miles southwest of Portugal, is the mountain peak of a volcanic mass. Its craggy spires and precipices of umber-dark basalt end with a sheer drop into the blue water. The surrounding sea is so deep that large sperm whales often come near the shore.

The summit of the undersea mountain is at Madeira's center, where Pico Ruivo, often snowcapped, rises to an altitude of 6,105 feet above sea level. From that point the rocky ribs and ravines of the island project, running to the coast. If you stand on the sea-swept balcony of Cabo Girão, one of the world's highest ocean cliffs (1,933 feet above the sea), you'll understand the island's Eden-like quality. The Portuguese national poet Luís Vaz de Camões said it lies "at the end of the world."

Madeira, now an autonomous archipelago, is only 35 miles long and about 13 miles across at its widest point. It has nearly 100 miles of coastline but no beaches. In its volcanic soil, plants and flowers blaze like creations from Gaugin's Tahitian palette. With jacaranda, masses of bougainvillea, orchids, geraniums, whortleberry, prickly pear, poinsettias, cannas, frangipani, birds of paradise, and wisteria, the land is a botanical garden. Custard apples, avocados, mangoes, and bananas grow profusely. Fragrances such as vanilla and wild fennel mingle with sea breezes and pervade the ravines, sweeping down the rocky headlands.

In 1419, João Gonçalves Zarco and Tristão Vaz Teixeira, captains under Henry the Navigator, discovered Madeira while exploring the African coastline, some 350 miles east. Because it was densely covered with impenetrable virgin forests, they named it Madeira ("wood"). Soon it was set afire to clear it for habitation. The conflagration is said to have lasted 7 years, until all but a small northern section was reduced to ashes.

The hillsides are so richly cultivated today that you'd never know there had been a fire. Many of the groves and vineyards, protected by buffers of sugarcane, grow on stone-wall ledges that spill almost into the sea. The farmers plant so close to the cliff's edge that they must have at least a dash of goat's blood in them. A complex network of *levadas* (water channels) irrigates the terraced mountain slopes. There are approximately 1,330 miles of levadas, including about 25 miles of tunnels. The levadas were originally constructed of stone by slaves and convicts, and are most often 1 to 2 feet wide and deep. They carry water from mountain springs.

About 25 miles northeast, **Porto Santo** is the only other inhabited island in the Madeira archipelago. *Réalités* magazine called it "another world, arid, desolate and waterless." Unlike Madeira, Porto Santo has beaches and has built several hotels.

Madeira is a destination unto itself. Many Britons fly here directly, avoiding Portugal altogether. Most North Americans, however, tie in a visit to Madeira with trips to Lisbon. It isn't really suited for a day trip from Lisbon, though some visitors try to achieve that frantic goal. It deserves a minimum of 3 days, if you can afford that much. Madeira is an extremely popular destination in both summer and winter, and the limited number of planes flying here may not have seats at the last minute, so book well in advance.

Cruise ships sometimes anchor here, but there's no regular passenger boat service to Madeira from the mainland. That means you'll have to fly. Many charter flights link Funchal with the capitals of Europe, though the regular route is from Lisbon to Funchal on TAP Air Portugal (see "Arriving" under "Essentials," later in this chapter, for more details).

1 Essentials

ARRIVING

The quickest and most convenient way to reach Madeira from Lisbon is on a 90-minute **TAP** flight. The plane stops at the Madeira airport, then goes on to Porto Santo. There are six flights daily. If you're booking a TAP flight from, say, New York to Lisbon, you can have the side trip to Madeira included at no extra cost if you have a regular (not an excursion) ticket.

In addition, TAP has four direct flights daily from London to Funchal. Trip time is 4 hours.

In Madeira, planes arrive at **Aeroporto de Santa Catarina** (☎ **291/52-49-41**), east of Funchal at Santa Cruz. The ride into the town center takes about 35 minutes.

You don't need to go to the airport to reconfirm your ticket. TAP has an office in Funchal at av. das Comunidades Madeirenses 8–10 (☎ **291/23-92-90**). It's open daily 9am to 6pm.

British Airways, with local offices at rua São Francisco 8 (☎ **291/52-48-64**), flies nonstop to Funchal several times a week from London. For more information, call ☎ **800/247-9297** in the U.S., or 0345/22-111 in Britain.

Taxis wait to take airline passengers anywhere they want to go on the island. If you're going to Funchal, you can take a **bus** from the airport. Buses also run from Funchal to the airport. Departures are from avenida do Mar in Funchal, and service in both directions operates daily from 7am to 11pm.

VISITOR INFORMATION

An English-speaking staff runs the desk at the **Madeira Tourist Office,** av. Arriaga 18 (☎ **291/22-90-57**), in Funchal. It's open Monday to Friday 9am to 8pm, Saturday and Sunday 9am to 6pm. The office distributes maps of the island, and the staff will, if asked, make suggestions about the best ways to explore the beautiful landscape. You can also inquire about ferry connections to the neighboring island of Porto Santo.

ISLAND LAYOUT

The capital of Madeira, **Funchal** (pop. 100,000) is the focal point of the island and the gateway to outlying villages. When Zarco landed in 1419, the sweet odor of wild fennel led him to name it after the aromatic herb (*funcho* in Portuguese). Today, the southern coastal city of hillside villas and narrow winding streets is the island's garden spot. Its numerous estates, including the former residence of Zarco, the Quinta das Cruzes, are among the most exotic in Europe.

Madeira

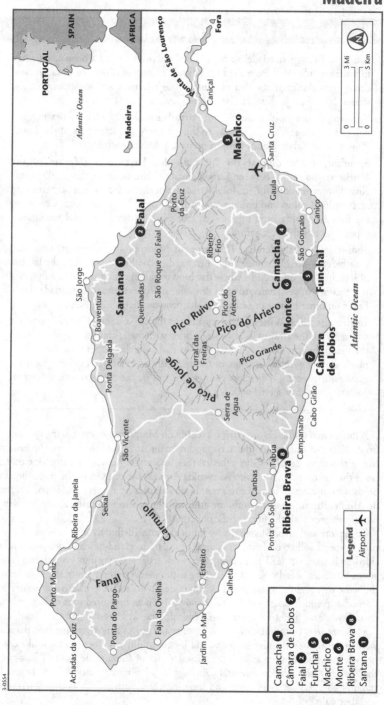

Legend
✈ Airport

Camacha ④
Câmara de Lobos ⑦
Faial ②
Funchal ⑤
Machico ③
Monte ⑥
Ribeira Brava ⑧
Santana ①

3-0554

361

⭐ Frommer's Favorite Madeira Experiences

Riding a Toboggan. Madeira's most fabled activity is taking a *carro de cesto* ride in a wicker-sided sled from the high-altitude suburb of Monte to Funchal. Two drivers run alongside the sled to control it as it careers across slippery cobblestones. It's a great joyride that lasts 20 minutes.

Escaping to the Golden Beaches of Porto Santo. Madeira has no beaches, but you can escape at least for the day to this relatively forgotten part of the world. Pirates of the Atlantic once romped on its 4 miles of beaches.

Spending a Morning at the Mercado dos Lavradores (Market of the Workers). Go early—between 7 and 8am at the latest—to see this market come alive. Flower vendors, fishers, local terrace farmers, and frugal shoppers create an array of local colors and produce not seen anywhere else in Madeira. Check out the fish, everything from tuna to eel, that you'll be served in local restaurants. Open Monday through Saturday.

Shopping for Handcrafts. The wares of Madeira—wine, wicker ware, and embroidery—are but some of the merchandise lavishly displayed in the bazaars of Funchal. You can spend a whole day browsing, bargaining, and just wandering this treasure trove. There are good deals on tooled leather and handmade shoes. Prices on other items can be high, so sharpen your bargaining skills.

Tasting the Local Wines. Go to any *taverna* (tavern) on the island and acquaint yourself with the array of local wines fortified with grape brandy. Before you leave the island, be sure select your favorite—perhaps the driest (Sercial), the golden-hued, slightly sweeter Verdelho, or the decidedly sweet Bual, a dessert wine that's good with cheese. Or perhaps your choice will be the sweetest—rich, fragrant Malmsey, which is served with dessert.

A long, often traffic-clogged street, **avenida do Mar,** runs east-west along the waterfront. North of this is **avenida Arriaga,** the "main street" of Funchal. At the eastern end of this thoroughfare is the cathedral (Sé), and at the western end is a large traffic circle that surrounds a fountain. As avenida Arriaga, site of most of the major hotels, heads west, it changes its name to **avenida do Infante.** As it runs east, it becomes **rua do Aljube.** Running north-south, the other important street, **avenida Zarco,** links the waterfront area with the heart of the old city.

To explore and savor Madeira, adventurous visitors (definitely not the queasy) with time to spend will go on foot across some of the trails. Hand-hewn stones and gravel-sided embankments lead you along precipitous ledges, down into lush ravines, and across flowering meadows. These dizzying paths are everywhere, from the hillsides of the wine-rich region of Estreito de Câmara de Lobos to the wicker-work center of Camacha. A much easier way to go, of course, is on an organized tour or local buses, though you may prefer to risk the hazardous driving on hairpin curves.

Heading west from Funchal, you'll pass banana groves almost spilling into the sea, women doing their laundry on rocks, and homes so tiny that they're almost like dollhouses. Less than 6 miles away is the coastal village of **Câmara de Lobos** ("Room of the Wolves"), the subject of several paintings by Sir Winston Churchill. A sheltered, tranquil cove, it's set amid rocks and towering cliffs, with hillside cottages, terraces, and date palms.

The road north from the village through the vineyards leads to **Estreito de Câmara de Lobos,** the heart of the wine-growing region that produces Madeira. The men who

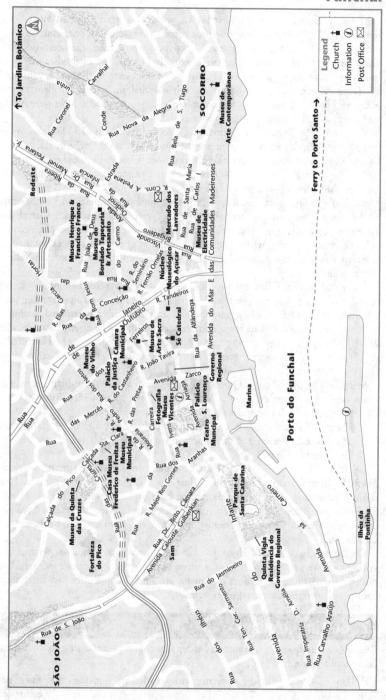

Funchal

Legend
+ Church
ⓘ Information
⊠ Post Office

Ferry to Porto Santo →

↑ To Jardim Botânico

SÃO JOÃO

Rua de S. João

Calçada do Pico

Fortaleza do Pico

Museu da Quinta das Cruzes

Casa Museu Frederico de Freitas

Museu Municipal

Calçada Sta. Clara

Rua das Cruzes

Rua dos Netos

Rua das Mercês

Rua Major Reis Gomes

Rua

Rua da Mouraria

Rua do Carmo

Museu do Vinho

Palácio da Justiça

Câmara Municipal

R. do Castanheiro

Avenida Zarco

Avenida Arriaga

Museu Fotografia Vicentes

Palácio S. Lourenço

Teatro Municipal

Avenida

Carreira

R. das Pretas

R. de S. Pedro

Rua das Aranhas

Rua dos Aranhas

Rua Dr. Brito Câmara

Avenida Calouste Gulbenkian

Sam

Parque de Santa Catarina

Quinta Vigia Residência do Governo Regional

Infante

Carmelo

Governo Regional

Avenida do Mar E das Comunidades Madeirenses

Marina

Porto do Funchal

ⓘ

Ilhéu da Pontinha

Rua do Jasmineiro

Rua Ten. Cor. Sarmento

Rua Imperatriz D. Amélia

Avenida

Rua Carvalho Araújo

Ilhéus

dos

Sá

Museu do Bordado Tapeçaria & Artesanato

Museu Henrique & Francisco Franco

Rua da Ribeira de S. Manuel Pestana Jr.

Rodeste

Horas

Garça

das

Rua Elias

Rua da

Rua Bom Jesus

Conceição

Rua João de Deus

Rua do Seminário

Anadia

Rua Dr. Infância da

Estrada

A. Pestana

Visconde do Carmo

Núcleo Museulógico do Açúcar

R. Fernão Ornela

de

de Janeiro

Outubro

Museu de Arte Sacra

Ferreiros

R. Tandeiros

R. João Tavira

Sé Catedral

Rua da Alfândega

Cons.

⊠

Rua de Santa Maria

Rua de Carlos I

Rua da Bela de S. Tiago

Rua Nova da Alegria

Conde

Cunha

Carvalhal

Rua Coronel

Mercado dos Lavradores

Museu de Electricidade

SOCORRO

Museu de Arte Contemporânea

cultivate the ribbonlike terraces wear brown stocking caps with tasseled tops. Along the way you'll spot women sitting on mossy stone steps doing Madeira embroidery.

Scaling a hill studded with pine and eucalyptus, you'll reach the ocean-side cliff **Cabo Girão.** It's the second-loftiest promontory in Europe, and a belvedere overlooks the sea and the saffron-colored rocks. Close by, you can see how the land is cultivated in Madeira, one terrace seemingly no larger than a small throw rug. (Incidentally, the islanders' blond hair doesn't come from a bottle; the straw-colored locks were inherited from early Flemish settlers sent to the island.)

Try to return to Funchal by veering off the coastal road, past São Martinho to the belvedere at **Pico dos Parcelos.** In one of the most idyllic spots on the island, you can see the ocean, mountains, orange and banana groves, bougainvillea, and poinsettias, as well as the capital. The sound—whether roosters crowing, babies crying in faraway huts, or goats bleating—carries for miles.

By heading north from Funchal, you can visit some outstanding spots in the heart of the island. Pass through Santo António, and you'll eventually reach **Curral das Freiras,** a petite village huddled around an old monastery at the bottom of an extinct volcanic crater. The site, whose name means "Corral of the Nuns," was originally a secluded convent that protected the good sisters from sea-weary, woman-hungry mariners and pirates.

If you go north in a different direction, one destination is **Santana.** Many visitors have described it as something out of Disney's *Fantasia.* Picture an alpine setting with waterfalls, cobblestone streets, green meadows sprinkled with multicolored blossoms, thatched cottages, swarms of roses, and plunging ravines. The novelist Paul Bowles wrote: "It is as if a 19th-century painter with a taste for the baroque had invented a countryside to suit his own personal fantasy. It is the sort of picture that used to adorn the grocer's calendar."

Southwest of the village is **Queimadas,** the site of a 3,000-foot-high rest house. From here, many people make the 3-hour trek to the apex of **Pico Ruivo** (Purple Peak), the highest point on the island, 6,105 feet above sea level.

Southeast of Santana, roads lead to **Faial,** a colorful hamlet with tiny A-frame huts. The road descends in a series of sharp turns into a deep ravine. The lush terraces here are built for cows to graze.

In the east, about 18 miles from Funchal (a short drive from the airport) is historic **Machico.** Its much-visited **Igreja do Senhor dos Milagres** dates from the mid–15th century. According to legend, the church was built over the tombs of the star-crossed English lovers Robert Machim and Anna d'Arfet. Try to view the village from the belvedere of **Camoé Pequeno.** A nearby 300-foot-long grotto is said to be the deepest on Madeira.

On the way back from Machico, you can detour inland to **Camacha,** perched in a setting of flowers and orchards. It's the island center of the wickerwork industry. You can shop here (though the stores in Funchal are amply supplied) or just watch local craftspeople making chairs and other items.

2 Getting Around

Remember that distances are short on Madeira, but allow plenty of time to cover them because of the winding roads.

BY BUS The cheapest way of getting around Madeira (provided that you're not rushed) is by bus. One of the island's best-kept secrets is that you can make excursions on local buses at a fraction of the cost the tour companies charge. Local buses go all over the island. A typical fare in town is 250$ ($1.40); rides in the countryside can cost 700$ ($3.90). Sometimes only one bus a day runs to the most distant points.

Most buses depart from the large park at the eastern part of the Funchal waterfront bordering avenida do Mar. Buses to Camacha or Camiço leave from a little square at the eastern sector of rua da Alfândega, which runs parallel to avenida do Mar near the marketplace.

BY TAXI   The going taxi rate is about 15,000$ ($84) per day. Always negotiate and agree on the rate in advance. Three or four passengers can divide the cost. Most taxis are Peugeots or Mercedes, so you'll ride in relative safety and not have to cope with the nightmarish roads. If you're in Funchal and want a taxi to a hotel in the area, you'll usually find a line of them across from the tourist office along avenida Arriaga. Many taxi drivers speak English.

BY CAR   Unless you're a skilled driver used to narrow roads, reckless drivers, and hairpin turns, we don't recommend that you rent a car on the island. If you need to, most hotels can make arrangements for car rentals.

Avis (☎ 800/331-2112 in the U.S.) has offices at the Aeroporto de Santa Catarina in Santa Cruz (☎ 291/52-43-92), and in Funchal at largo António Nobre 164 (☎ 291/76-45-46). **Hertz** (☎ 800/654-3001 in the U.S.) has a branch in Funchal at estrada Monumental 284 (☎ 291/76-44-10). **Budget Rent-a-Car** (☎ 800/472-3325 in the U.S.) has outlets at the airport (☎ 291/52-46-61) and in Funchal at estrada Monumental 239 (☎ 291/76-65-18).

Fast Facts: Madeira

American Express   The representative on Madeira is **Top Tours Travel Agency,** rua Brigadero Coseiro (☎ 291/74-26-28), in Funchal. It's open Monday to Friday 9:30am to 1pm and 2:30 to 6:30pm.

Area Code   The country code for Portugal is **351,** the area code for Madeira **091.**

Business Hours   **Shops** are usually open Monday to Friday 9am to 1pm and 3 to 7pm, Saturday from 9am to 1pm. They're closed Sunday. **Municipal buildings** are open Monday to Friday 9am to 12:30pm and 2 to 5:30pm.

Consulates   The Consulate of the **United States** is on avenida Luís de Camões, Block D, Apt. B (☎ 291/74-34-29), off avenida do Infante. The Consulate of the **United Kingdom** is at avenida Zarco 2 (☎ 291/22-12-21).

Dentist   A good English-speaking dentist, **John de Sousa,** has an office in the Marina Forum Building, avenida Arriaga (☎ 291/23-12-77), in Funchal.

Doctor   A good English-speaking doctor is **Francis Zino,** in the Edifício Jasmineiro, rua do Jasmineiro (☎ 291/74-22-27), in Funchal.

Drugstores   Drugstores (chemists) are open Monday to Saturday 10am to 1pm and 3 to 7pm. The rotation emergency and night service schedule are posted on the door of all drugstores. Sunday has a special schedule, too. A reliable, centrally located chemist is **Farmácia Honorato,** rua da Carreira 62 (☎ 291/20-38-80). Dial ☎ **118** to locate a pharmacy that's open.

Emergencies   Call ☎ **115** for a general **emergency,** ☎ 291/22-20-22 for the **police,** ☎ 291/74-11-15 for the **Red Cross,** and ☎ 291/74-40-78 for a **hospital** emergency.

Hairdressers   Many hotels maintain beauty salons and barbershops. A consistently reliable bet for both men and women is **Correia,** avenida Arriaga 30, 2nd Floor D (☎ **291/23-16-33**), in Funchal.

Hospital   The island's largest hospital is the **Hospital Distrital do Funchal,** Cruz de Carvalho (☎ **291/70-56-00**).

Laundry/Dry Cleaning   Try **Lavandaria Donini,** rua das Pretas (☎ **291/22-44-06**), Funchal. Clothing can be laundered or dry-cleaned in 1 or 2 days. It's open Monday to Friday 9am to 7pm.

Lost Property   Check at the island's main **police station** on rua João de Deus in Funchal (☎ **291/22-20-22**).

Luggage   There are no storage facilities other than those provided as a goodwill gesture by your hotel. Ask the receptionist or concierge.

Newspapers/Magazines   The island stocks a good selection of such English-language publications as *Newsweek, Time,* and the *International Herald Tribune,* as well as periodicals in French, German, and Spanish. Especially useful is a locally produced English-language publication, the *Madeira Island Bulletin,* distributed free at the tourist office and in many of the island's more visible hotels.

Police   Dial ☎ **291/22-20-22.**

Post Office   If you've had your mail sent *poste restante* (general delivery), you can pick it up at the **Zarco Post Office,** avenida Zarco, 9000 Funchal (☎ **291/23-21-31**), near the tourist office. Bring your passport to identify yourself. You can also place long-distance phone calls (without steep hotel surcharges) and send telegrams, faxes, and telexes. The office is open Monday to Friday 8:30am to 8pm, Saturday 9am to 12:30pm.

Other post offices offering the same services are **Calouste Gulbenkian,** avenida Calouste Gulbenkian (open Monday to Friday 9am to 12:30pm and 2:30 to 6:30pm), near the Monument of the Infante Dom Henríque; **Monumental,** on estrada Monumental, near the Lido swimming pool (Monday to Friday 9am to 7pm); and **Mercado,** rua do Arcipreste, near the Municipal Market (Monday to Friday 9am to 6:30pm). Signs in the center that read *CORREIOS* point the way to the nearest post office.

Rest Rooms   The airport, hotels, and some museums have public rest rooms. However, there are not enough public toilets. Locals often use cafes or taverns, though in theory these facilities are reserved for customers.

Safety   In terms of crime statistics, Madeira is safer than mainland Portugal, especially Lisbon. However, as in any area that attracts tourists, there is a criminal element that preys on visitors. Protect your valuables, as you would at any resort. Pickpockets and purse-snatchers are the major villains.

Taxes   Madeira imposes no special taxes, other than the value-added tax (VAT) on all goods and services purchased in Portugal. Refer to "Fast Facts: Portugal" in chapter 2 for more information.

Weather   Call ☎ **291/22-15-86.**

3 Where to Stay

In summer, when every other European oceanfront resort charges its highest rates, Madeira used to experience its low season. That's no longer the case, and Madeira now enjoys year-round popularity. In fact, it has become hard to get a plane seat in the peak summer season without reservations made way in advance. August is still not the most desirable month, however, because of the *capacete,* a shroud of mist that often envelops the island. Remember that Madeira is an African island, and it's hot, hot, and hotter for those from cooler climates. If you're visiting in the summer, air-conditioning might be vital to you—unless you're at a retreat in the mountains.

Madeira's hotels, among the best in Portugal, range from some of the finest deluxe accommodations in Europe to attractively priced old-fashioned *quintas* (manor houses) for budget travelers. Chances are that you won't be staying in the heart of Funchal but on the outskirts, where many of the best hotels are. For those who want to be in the heart of the action (and not be dependent on transportation), we have a few suggestions, all of which are reasonably priced. The most expensive hotels, with pools and resort amenities, are on the outskirts. Heavy traffic fills the center of Funchal most of the day, so hotels there tend to be noisy. Nevertheless, for shopping and the widest selection of restaurants, Funchal is a magnet.

VERY EXPENSIVE

Cliff Bay Resort Hotel. Estrada Monumental 147, 9000 Funchal, Madeira. ☎ **291/70-77-00.** Fax 291/76-25-25. www.cliffbay.com. E-mail: info@cliffbay.com. 201 units. A/C MINIBAR TV TEL. 33,000$–69,000$ ($184.80–$386.40) double; from 82,000$ ($459.20) suite. AE, DC, MC, V. Free parking.

One of the island's top lodgings, rivaled and surpassed only by Reid's, this nine-story hotel is dramatically located. It sits on a craggy bluff towering over wave-lashed rocks a mile west of the center. A group favorite, the deluxe hotel stands on the site of a former banana plantation. All but a dozen or so rooms have great exposure to ocean or harbor panoramas. Most accommodations contain queen-size beds with firm mattresses. Units are generally spacious, with such amenities as safes, sitting areas, and roomy marble bathrooms with deluxe toiletries, tub-shower combos, thick towels, and hair dryers.

Dining/Diversions: The restaurants, from the Rose Garden to Il Gallo d'Oro to the Blue Lagoon, are among the finest on the island, again surpassed only by the options at Reid's. They feature Portuguese and international cuisine. There are also three bars.

Amenities: Two pools (one indoor, one outdoor), concierge, laundry, 24-hour room service, health club, sauna, games room, children's activities program, beauty therapy, massages. Golf can be arranged.

Hotel Savoy. Av. do Infante, 9006 Funchal, Madeira. ☎ **291/22-20-31.** Fax 291/22-31-03. www.madinfo.pthotelsavoy. E-mail: savoy@mail.telephc.pt. 350 units. A/C MINIBAR TV TEL. 65,000$ ($364) double; from 85,000$ ($476) suite. Rates include breakfast. AE, DC, MC, V. Free parking. Bus: 1, 2, 3, 4, 13, or 35.

The Savoy is one of the leading five-star hotels not only in Madeira but in Portugal. Long known for its overstated lushness and often-garish theatricality, it stands at the edge of Funchal. A Swiss-trained hotelier founded it at the turn of the century, and over the years it has grown extraordinarily. The hotel is superbly situated, opening onto the ocean and the Bay of Funchal. With its vast public facilities, it captures a peculiar kind of Madeira *dolce vita.*

Each guest room has a balcony. The most expensive doubles are twins with sea views. The rooms have standard built-in older furniture, such as king or twin beds with firm mattresses, and small bathrooms with hair dryers, dual basins, and tub-shower baths. Faced with escalating popularity, each generation of management has introduced enlargements and improvements.

Dining/Diversions: Options include the Copulla restaurant and the Librerie coffee shop. You can also have lunch by the pool. For deluxe dining, try the elegant

Fleur-de-Lys, a grill room with a panoramic view (see "Where to Dine," later in this chapter). There are two bars.

Amenities: Room service, baby-sitting, laundry, two seawater pools (one heated), tennis courts, health center, minigolf, shopping arcade, hairdressers for men and women.

✪ **Reid's Palace.** Estrada Monumental 139, 9000 Funchal, Madeira. ☎ **800/223-6800** in the U.S., or 291/71-71-71. Fax 291/71-71-77. www.orient-expresshotels.com. 184 units. A/C MINIBAR TV TEL. 58,000$–75,000$ ($324.80–$420) standard double, 68,000$–90,000$ ($380.80–$504) superior double, 74,000$–95,000$ ($414.40–$532) deluxe double; 102,000$–144,000$ ($571.20–$806.40) junior suite, 139,000$–195,000$ ($778.40–$1,092) superior suite, 161,000$–216,000$ ($901.60–$1,209.60) executive suite, 191,000$–320,000$ ($1,069.60–$1,792) presidential suite. Rates include breakfast. AE, DC, MC, V. Free parking. Bus: 5 or 6.

The legendary place to stay in Funchal is Reid's, founded in 1891 by William Reid, a young Scotsman. It's now owned by the Orient Express. Its position is "smashing," as the British say, along the coastal road at the edge of Funchal, on 10 acres of terraced gardens that descend the hillside to the rocky shores. The English who frequent the hotel in large numbers (Sir Winston Churchill stayed here) spend their days strolling the walks lined with hydrangeas, geraniums, gardenias, banana trees, ferns, and white yuccas.

The main drawing rooms are refreshingly decorated in sea colors and tropical prints. The spacious guest rooms are conservative in the finest sense, with well-chosen furnishings (antiques or reproductions), plenty of storage space, sitting areas, and desks. The bathrooms have marble or tile walls and floors, plus hair dryers, robes, and luxurious toiletries.

Dining: The Tea Terrace, which has a panoramic view, serves afternoon tea. The Garden Restaurant, overlooking the pools, and the poolside buffet serve breakfast. In the dignified main dining room, the inevitable and very English silver trolley holds roast beef. The gourmet restaurant, Les Faunes (see "Where to Dine," later in this chapter), is on the sixth floor in the garden wing. The less formal Villa Cliff serves typical Portuguese cuisine.

Amenities: 24-hour room service, shoe shining, laundry, hairdresser, three saltwater pools, garden park, tennis courts.

EXPENSIVE

Casino Park Hotel. Rua Imperatriz Dona Amélia, 9000 Funchal, Madeira. ☎ **291/23-31-11.** Fax 291/23-20-76. www.pestana.com. E-mail: g.pestana@mail.telepac.pt. 334 units. A/C MINIBAR TV TEL. 22,000$–62,000$ ($123.20–$347.20) double; 32,000$–75,000$ ($179.20–$420) suite. Rates include buffet breakfast. AE, DC, MC, V. Free parking. Bus: 2, 12, or 16.

The Casino Park is a 7-minute walk from the town center, nestled in a subtropical garden overlooking the harbor. Designed by Oscar Niemeyer—one of the architects of Brasília, Brazil—the gray-concrete main building is low (only five stories) and undulating. The complex consists of the hotel and conference center and a casino.

The small to midsize guest rooms have balconies with panoramic views over the harbor and town. They're tastefully decorated in bright, sunny colors. Most rooms have twin beds, and all have first-class mattresses. Bathrooms have combined tubs and showers, dual basins, bidets, and hair dryers. Safes are provided for a fee. There are two comfortable lounge areas on each floor.

Dining: The luxurious dining room overlooks the port and town of Funchal, and the international Grill Room has an extensive wine cellar. There's a coffee shop adjacent to the pool.

⊕ Family-Friendly Hotels

Girassol *(see page 370)*   On the outskirts of Funchal, this is a family favorite. It not only offers reasonable rates but also has a pool set aside for children. Most doubles are actually suites.

Hotel Santa Isabel *(see page 371)*   Guests here enjoy the facilities of the deluxe Savoy without paying its steep rates. Next door to the Savoy, it's a satellite of the luxury hotel. There's a 50% discount for children 2 to 11 who stay in their parents' room.

Quinta da Penha de França *(see page 371)*   This large old manor house has charm and grace. Kids enjoy its snack bar, gardens, and pool.

Amenities: 24-hour room service, baby-sitting, laundry, shopping arcade. Tennis courts, pools, saunas, billiards, health club. Special facilities, including shallow pool, for children. The staff arranges fishing, sailing, and golf excursions.

Eden Mar. Rua do Gorgulho 2, 9000 Funchal, Madeira. ☎ **291/76-22-21.** Fax 291/76-19-66. www.edenmar.com. E-mail: edenmar@mail.telepac.pt. 146 units. A/C TV TEL. 22,000$–35,000$ ($123.20–$196) double. Extra bed 8,500$ ($47.60). AE, DC, MC, V. Free parking.

Last renovated in 1998, this decade-old hotel rises six floors up from the swimming complex (the Lido). Though often booked by tour groups from England, it is still suitable for the individual traveler, especially families that like its rooms with kitchenettes. The midsize to spacious guest rooms open onto views of the sea. Decorated in lively flowery prints, they have first-rate mattresses and excellent tiled bathrooms.

Dining/Diversions: The restaurant serves international and Portuguese cuisine. There is a bar indoors and another by the pool.

Amenities: Outdoor pool with children's corner, heated indoor pool, health club, sauna, sun terrace, library and card room, laundry, concierge, room service (breakfast only).

Madeira Carlton Hotel. Largo António Nobre, 9007 Funchal, Madeira. ☎ **291/23-10-31.** Fax 291/22-33-77. www.pestana.com. E-mail: mch@pestana.org. 369 units. A/C MINIBAR TV TEL. 27,000$–38,000$ ($151.20–$212.80) double; 52,000$ ($291.20) suite. Rates include breakfast. AE, DC, MC, V. Free parking.

The Madeira Carlton Hotel is a luxurious 18-story structure near the casino, with direct access to the sea. The hotel lies on a promontory overlooking Funchal Bay in the fashionable Vale-Verde Garden district, next to the landmark Reid's Palace. All the spacious accommodations, many furnished in provincial style, have private balconies and first-rate mattresses. The least expensive rates are for the standard mountain view, the more expensive for deluxe sea-view rooms. The oceanfront exposure (to the south) means the pool terraces and seaside guest-room balconies and patios receive dawn-to-dusk sunlight. Bathrooms are a bit cramped but contain dual basins, tub-shower combos, and hair dryers.

Dining/Diversions: The three restaurants serve fine cuisine, if only to tour groups at times. The Atlantico, open Thursday to Saturday nights, features a show with dinner for 7,300$ ($40.90) per person. Os Arcos has an international and regional menu, and the Taverna Grill serves succulent meats. The bar-pub serves drinks, pastas, and pizzas. There's disco action at O Farol on Friday and Saturday nights.

Amenities: Three pools, tennis court, 24-hour room service, health club, game room, solarium, sauna, laundry, concierge.

✪ **Madeira Palácio.** Estrada Monumental 265, 9000 Funchal, Madeira. ☎ **291/70-27-02.** Fax 291/70-27-03. www.madinfo.pt/hotel/m.palacio/. E-mail: mpalacio@mail.telepac.pt. 253 units. A/C MINIBAR TV TEL. 31,000$–39,000$ ($173.60–$218.40) double; 54,000$ ($302.40) suite. Rates include breakfast. AE, DC, MC, V. Free parking. Bus: 5 or 6.

Madeira Palácio is a luxurious, contemporary hotel on the seaside route to Câmara de Lobos, about 2 miles from the center of Funchal. It's perched on a cliff over the sea, with a view of Madeira's famous high cliff, Cabo Girão, looming in the distance. Guest rooms are well appointed and generally spacious. They have built-in furniture, excellent beds, color TVs with video systems, and balconies. Bathrooms have combined tubs and showers, plus vanity areas, dual basins, hair dryers, robes, and even a phone. Rooms opening onto the mountains are less desirable than those facing the sea. The star-shaped hotel consists of three wings. The decor in the public salons and guest rooms incorporates local woods, native construction materials, and Madeiran fabrics.

Dining/Diversions: The main restaurant is Cristóvão Colombo, with a menu of local and international dishes; Le Terrace serves regional dishes. The gourmet restaurant, Vicerei, offers international cuisine. There's a piano bar and an outdoor snack bar.

Amenities: 24-hour room service, laundry, baby-sitting, heated pool, tennis courts, shopping arcade with hairdresser and sauna, table tennis. Water sports can be arranged.

✪ **Quinta da Bela Vista.** Caminho do Avista Navios 4, 9000 Funchal, Madeira. ☎ **291/76-41-44.** Fax 291/76-50-90. E-mail: qbvista@mail.telepac.pt. 67 units. A/C TV TEL. 23,600$–30,500$ ($132.15–$170.80) double; from 50,000$ ($280) suite. Rates include breakfast. AE, DC, MC, V. Free parking.

The core of this hotel, in the hills above Funchal, was built around 1840 as a private villa. Its owner, a local surgeon, has added two outlying annexes in the Portuguese colonial style. The complex is now a five-star hotel, with four suites, a salon, a library, and the main restaurant in the original villa. A verdant garden surrounds the annexes, which hold comfortable guest rooms. Rooms are slightly larger in the newer annex, constructed in 1991. Furnishings include high-quality mahogany reproductions and a scattering of English and Portuguese antiques. Spindle headboards crown first-rate mattresses. The bathrooms have combined showers and tubs, deluxe toiletries, and hair dryers.

Dining/Diversions: A well-staffed formal restaurant, Casa Mãe, is in the original villa. The more relaxed Avistas Navios offers sweeping views and regional and international cuisine. There's a pleasant bar by the pool, and one in each restaurant.

Amenities: Concierge, room service, valet and laundry, baby-sitting, free taxi service to Funchal five times daily, tennis courts, sauna, Jacuzzi, health club and gym, heated outdoor pool, garden.

MODERATE

Girassol. Estrada Monumental 256, 9000 Funchal, Madeira. ☎ **291/76-40-51.** Fax 291/76-54-41. 133 units. TV TEL. 18,000$–22,000$ ($100.80–$123.20) double; 30,000$ ($168) suite. Rates include breakfast. AE, DC, MC, V. Free parking. Bus: 1, 3, 5 or 6.

Girassol offers immaculate accommodations at reasonable rates. It's on the outskirts of Funchal, overlooking the Tourist Club, where guests are allowed access to the sea for a small charge. Most double rooms are actually suites, consisting of a bedroom, bathroom, small sitting room, and veranda. Each unit has a terrace or balcony overlooking the garden, the mountains, or the sea.

The hotel sets aside one of its two pools for children. There's a solarium on the 12th floor, a concierge, and room service. On the street level are a bar and lounge and a hairdresser. The dining room, which serves regional and international cuisine, has sea views and, at dinner, live music.

Hotel do Carmo. Travessa do Rego 10, 9000 Funchal, Madeira. ☎ **291/22-90-01.** Fax 291/22-39-19. 80 units. MINIBAR TV TEL. 14,000$ ($78.40) double; 18,400$ ($103.05) triple. Rates include breakfast. AE, DC, MC, V. Parking 1,000$ ($5.60). Bus: 1, 2, 4, 5, 6, 8, 9, or 10.

Carmo provides modern accommodations in the center of Funchal, a 5-minute walk from the cathedral. It's laid out in a cellular honeycomb fashion; most guest rooms open onto balconies overlooking the busy street scene below. Rates for rooms with and without balconies are the same. Guests gather at the L-shaped rooftop pool, which affords a good view of the harbor. Created by the Fernandes family, the hotel was designed for thrifty guests who want to be near the heart of the city. The rooms are simple, with contemporary but well-used furnishings and good beds. Meals are served in a spacious dining room. A little lounge opens onto an inner patio and a bar. The hotel has a sauna and solarium, laundry, baby-sitting, and 24-hour room service.

Hotel Santa Isabel. Av. do Infante, 9006 Funchal, Madeira. ☎ **291/22-31-11.** Fax 291/22-79-59. 69 units. MINIBAR TV TEL. 16,000$–19,500$ ($89.60–$109.20) double; 19,500$–39,000$ ($109.20–$218.40) suite. Children 2–11 half-price in parents' room. Rates include breakfast. AE, DC, MC, V. Free parking. Bus: 2, 4, 6, 12, or 16.

Adjacent to the Savoy and under the same management, this is a small hotel with a homelike feeling and a well-deserved reputation for service and comfort. In the center of the deluxe hotel belt, it has a rooftop terrace with a small pool and solarium, a snack bar, a cocktail bar, and a well-appointed lounge overlooking the gardens. There are two grades of accommodations: The more expensive face the sea, and the cheaper units open onto a garden and a mountain view. Some suites cost the same as doubles, and "early birds" book them quickly. Rooms are appealingly dowdy in an eccentrically English way. Color schemes are monochromatic, and the furniture is the kind of Nordic modern that was installed with fanfare in 1961 (the year the hotel opened) and hasn't been upgraded since. Overall, it's appealingly old-fashioned, and especially popular with travelers from the British Midlands. The value derives from the access guests have to the resort facilities at the nearby Savoy, including the pool and restaurants.

✪ **Quinta da Penha de França.** Rua da Penha de França 2, 9000 Funchal, Madeira. ☎ **291/22-90-87.** Fax 291/22-92-61. 76 units. MINIBAR TV TEL. 14,000$–17,900$ ($78.40–$100.25) double; 18,000$–21,000$ ($100.80–$117.60) suite. Rates include breakfast. AE, DC, MC, V. Free parking. Bus: 2, 12, or 16.

This gracious old manor house is now a guest house, with an annex containing 33 sea-view rooms, a balcony, and a terrace. Rooms in the older section are high-ceilinged testimonials to the building techniques of yesteryear. They have thick walls, casement windows, and a scattering of old-fashioned furniture, including some family antiques. Rooms in the modern annex, completed late in 1999, are more contemporary, blending traditional country-house designs with solid craftsmanship and fine hardwoods. Like a family home, the *quinta* is chock-full of antiques, paintings, and silver. Near the Savoy, it stands in a garden on a ledge almost hanging over the harbor. It's a short walk from the center of the bazaars and is opposite an ancient chapel. The four-story *antiga casa* is bone white, with dark-green shutters and small-panel windows overlooking the ocean. Across the front terrace is a good-sized pool with white iron garden chairs arranged for lounging. A restaurant in the annex serves lunch daily, and the main restaurant in the manor house offers lunch daily and dinner nightly until 10:30pm.

Quinta do Sol. Rua Dr. Pita 6, 9000 Funchal, Madeira. ☎ **291/76-41-51.** Fax 291/76-62-87. www.madinfo.pt/hotel/quintasol. E-mail: qsol@mailmadinfo.pt. 151 units. A/C TV TEL.

14,900$–23,500$ ($83.45–$131.60) double; 30,000$–40,000$ ($168–$224) suite. Rates include buffet breakfast. AE, DC, MC, V. Free parking. Bus: 2, 12, or 16.

The four-star Quinta do Sol is among the best in its category on Madeira. In an attractive setting, it offers well-furnished guest rooms; some have their own balconies, and 30 contain minibars. Rooms are sun-flooded affairs with big windows and contemporary furniture; some have balconies with views of the sea. However, units without balconies are both larger and less expensive. The hotel has a number of resort-type facilities, including a pool, lounges, and a rooftop solarium. The bar-restaurant, Charola, offers Portuguese and international food and wine.

INEXPENSIVE

Albergaria Catedral. Rua do Aljube 13, 9000 Funchal, Madeira. ☎ **291/23-00-91.** Fax 291/23-19-80. 25 units. TV TEL. 6,600$–7,800$ ($36.95–$43.70) double. Rates include breakfast. AE, DC, MC, V. Bus: 1, 2, 4, 5, 6, 8, 9, or 10.

This is a good, budget-conscious choice if you want to be amid the commercial bustle of the center of town. Don't judge it by its narrow, dark entrance, across the street from the cathedral. Climb a flight of stairs to a slick "moderno" reception area and proceed to one of the cozy, comfortable guest rooms. They occupy five floors of a six-story building, and the quieter ones in the rear don't have much of a view. In front, eight of the units have balconies that open onto the street noise. The sunniest and most pleasant rooms occupy the two uppermost floors. Don't expect luxury—rooms are simple and somewhat Spartan, with serviceable but somewhat battered furniture.

Estrelícia. Caminho Velho da Ajuda, 9000 Funchal, Madeira. ☎ **291/76-51-31.** Fax 291/76-10-44. E-mail: opio54@mail.telepac.pt. 148 units. MINIBAR TV TEL. 13,600$ ($76.15) double. AE, DC, MC, V. Free parking.

A 5-minute drive from the center of town, this 20-year-old hotel was renovated in summer 1999 and is now better than ever. It's contained in the upper floors of a high-rise building constructed up a hill from the main hotel drag. The location is a bit inconvenient, so rates seem low considering the quality of the rooms. Most units are midsize. All are well appointed, with excellent mattresses, durable modern furniture, and a view of the sea. The hotel minibus runs to the center of Funchal several times a day. On the premises are a dance club, a tennis court, a saltwater pool, two bars, and a restaurant that serves Portuguese and international cuisine.

Hotel Madeira. Rua Ivens 21, 9009 Funchal, Madeira. ☎ **291/23-00-71.** Fax 291/22-90-71. 53 units. TV TEL. 12,300$ ($68.90) double; 14,000$ ($78.40) suite. Rates include breakfast. AE, DC, MC, V. Limited free on-street parking.

This five-story hotel sits in the center of Funchal, behind the park in a tranquil part of town. The rooftop pool has an extraordinary panoramic view of the town, mountains, and sea, and there's a solarium area with a bar and snack services. The small to midsize guest rooms surround a plant-filled atrium. One of the nicest features is the sheltered sun windows attached to each unit. Some rooms have balconies, and about 10 are air-conditioned. All are comfortably furnished, with worn but durable furniture and firm mattresses. Only breakfast is served; limited room service is available until 6pm.

Hotel Windsor. Rua das Hortas 4C, 9000 Funchal, Madeira. ☎ **291/23-30-81.** Fax 291/23-30-80. 67 units. MINIBAR TV TEL. 12,000$ ($67.20) double. Rates include breakfast. No credit cards. Free parking. Bus: 1, 12, or 16.

Opened with fanfare in 1987, this is one of the most stylish hotels in Funchal. The four-star hotel consists of two buildings connected by an aerial passage above a sun-flooded enclosed courtyard. The marble-sheathed lobby is laden with plants, wicker chairs, and art deco accessories. Because of the hotel's proximity to the buildings in the town center, few guest rooms have views. They're not particularly large, but they are comfortable and nicely decorated, with wall-to-wall carpeting and wooden furniture. The hotel has a cafe-bar designed to resemble a Jazz Age nightclub. The free parking garage is almost a necessity in this crowded commercial neighborhood. Also popular is a cramped but convivial rooftop pool with an outdoor bar. The Windsor Restaurant serves Madeiran cuisine, with fixed-price lunches and dinners. Local swordfish is a specialty.

ON THE OUTSKIRTS
EXPENSIVE

Estalagem Casa Velha do Palheiro. Palheiro Golf, Sao Conçalo, 9050 Funchal, Madeira. ☎ **291/794-901.** Fax 291/794-925. www.casa-velha.com. E-mail: casa.velha@mail.eunet. pt. 25 units. TV TEL. 32,000$–60,000$ ($179.20–$336) double. Rates include breakfast. AE, DC, MC, V. Free parking.

This unique inn, which appeals to golfers, was constructed in 1804 as a hunting lodge for the first Count of Carvalhal. In 1996, it was restored to become Madeira's first five-star country house hotel, a type of accommodation more common in England. The hotel adjoins the par-71 championship Palheiro golf course, about a 15-minute drive from Funchal. It is the only hotel in Madeira on a golf course. Rooms vary in shape and size, but all are richly furnished in an old-fashioned but comfortable way, with first-class mattresses and modern plumbing.

Dining/Diversions: The restaurant and bar serves quality international and Portuguese cuisine; there is also an elegant bar.

Amenities: Room service (until midnight), laundry, concierge, swimming pool, tennis court.

MODERATE

Quintinha São João. Rua da Levada de São João, 9000 Funchal, Madeira. ☎ **291/74-09-20.** Fax 291/74-09-28. E-mail: quintinhasj@mail.telepac.pt. 41 units. A/C MINIBAR TV TEL. 10,750$–16,750$ ($60.20–$93.80) double; from 17,000$ ($95.20) suite. Rates include breakfast. Half-board 4,000$ ($22.40). AE, DC, MC, V. Free parking.

Dating from 1900, this quinta is one of the best preserved in the Funchal area, surrounded by age-old trees and graced with classic architecture. Once an elegant private residence, it has been tastefully converted into a family inn. Most of the good-sized, standard guest rooms contain twins; some suites are available. All are handsomely decorated, often with traditional embroidery and Madeiran handiwork covering the beds. Old-style furnishings and antiques appear throughout, but modern amenities include a safe, hair dryer, and robes. The restaurant, A Morgadinha, is in a restored building adjoining the inn. It offers a variety of regional and international dishes, and features Goan specialties. The terrace bar, Vasco da Gama, overlooks the Bay of Funchal. The hotel also has an open-air swimming pool on the second floor, plus a tennis court.

4 Where to Dine

Many guests dine at their hotels, but perhaps you'll be able to sneak away for a regional meal at one of the places below. All are in Funchal. The list begins with the pick of the hotel restaurants.

EXPENSIVE

Chez Oscar/Restaurante Panorámico. In the Casino Park Hotel, av. do Infante. ☎ **291/23-31-11.** Reservations required. Chez Oscar main courses 2,150$–6,000$ ($12.05–$33.60). Panorámico fixed-price menus 7,800$ ($43.70). AE, DC, MC, V. Chez Oscar Tues–Sat 7:30–11pm. Panorámico Sun–Thurs 7:30–9:30pm. Bus: 2, 12, or 16. INTERNATIONAL.

The smaller and more elegant of the Casino Park Hotel's restaurants is Chez Oscar, housed in a large dark-bronze modern room that opens onto a flowering terrace. Pin lighting, candles, and a polite uniformed staff add to the glamorous ambience. The Panorámico is larger and somewhat less personal, but offers a cabaret performance on Sunday night. Both restaurants emphasize fresh ingredients. Chez Oscar's specialties include an array of flambéed dishes prepared table side. The food, more exotic and experimental than at the Panorámico—for example, grilled swordfish with sautéed pumpkin and basil-flavored marinara sauce. Dishes in either restaurant might include pork piccata, mixed grill of locally caught fish, roast lamb with thyme flowers, shell-fish in saffron-flavored sauce, or chateaubriand for two.

✪ **Fleur-de-Lys.** In the Hotel Savoy, av. do Infante. ☎ **291/22-20-31.** Reservations required. Main courses 2,500$–4,500$ ($14–$25.20). AE, DC, MC, V. Daily 7–11pm. Bus: 2, 12, or 16. FRENCH.

Its most devoted admirers claim that this restaurant serves the finest food on Madeira. We would rank it near the top. It's certainly scenic, with a panoramic view of the twinkling lights of Funchal. The eclectic decor includes antique reproductions and Oriental carpets. You can observe the activity in an open-grill kitchen. Reservations are important, and even with them you sometimes have a long wait. Meals are likely to include such well-prepared dishes as fresh lobster with mushrooms, shrimp in Pernod sauce, flavorful steak in peppercorn sauce, and veal medallions flavored with Calvados.

✪ **Les Faunes.** In Reid's Palace, estrada Monumental 139. ☎ **291/76-30-01.** Reservations required. Jacket and tie required for men. Main courses 2,900$–4,200$ ($16.25–$23.50). AE, DC, MC, V. Daily 7:30–10:30pm. Closed May–Oct. Bus: 5 or 6. FRENCH.

Try to dine at least once at Les Faunes, the island's finest restaurant. It takes its name from the series of Picasso lithographs decorating the walls. Live piano music accompanies your meal. True to English tradition, winter guests often dress for dinner, the men in sedate black tie.

The chef offers a variety of French specialties and some typical Portuguese dishes. The skilled kitchen staff transforms fresh ingredients into platters of haute cuisine quality. To begin, you can try everything from Portuguese soup to the chef's own smoked fish. Favorite entrees are *caldeirada* (fish stew) and lobster (grilled or poached). The chef's special pride is swordfish with banana. You can select from the dessert cart or ask for a hot soufflé, preferably made of passion fruit or strawberries.

✪ **Quinta Palmeira.** Av. do Infante 5. ☎ **291/22-18-14.** Reservations required. Main courses 2,000$–5,000$ ($11.20–$28). AE, DC, MC, V. Daily 11:30am–midnight. POR-TUGUESE/INTERNATIONAL.

The best and most elegant restaurant in Madeira is in a beautiful country home dating from 1735. Near the Hotel Savoy, it attracts diners with the most sophisticated palates. In fair weather, a table on the spacious veranda is the most desirable on the island. Manuel Jose da Sousa, the owner, insists on only the finest ingredients and the most talented chefs. They concoct palate-pleasing cuisine, including such dishes as tender, perfectly seasoned grilled fillet of beef on toast with Roquefort, or served with Madeira wine. Among the fish selections, curried shrimp is a delight, and sautéed swordfish or salmon goes perfectly with lemon and butter sauce. Some meat dishes have real island flair when they appear with regional fruit such as bananas or passion fruit. For a refreshing change of pace, opt for homemade avocado ice cream.

Restaurant Caravela. Av. do Mar 15, 3rd floor. ☎ **291/22-84-64.** Main courses 2,600$–8,000$ ($14.55–$44.80). AE, DC, MC, V. Daily noon–3pm and 6:30–11pm. Bus: 2 or 12. PORTUGUESE/INTERNATIONAL.

ⓘ Family-Friendly Restaurants

Casa da Carochinha (Lady Bird) *(see page 375)*   Facing the Centenary Gardens, this has long been a favorite with English families. They come for the familiar fare, including roast beef with Yorkshire pudding.

O Patio Jardim Tropicale *(see page 376)*   This is another family choice in the heart of Funchal. Located in an inner courtyard, it's a snug haven. The menu always has something to appeal to kids, including juicy roast chicken.

This modern restaurant on the waterfront overlooks the arriving and departing cruise ships. You can dine on a glass-enclosed terrace with an open fireplace or in the inner room. Unpretentious and proud of its Portuguese fare, the restaurant features Caravela fish but also turns out international dishes, such as chateaubriand flambé. The finest regional dish is *espetada*, skewered meat flavored with garlic and bay leaves and served only as a special request. Afternoon tea (2 to 5pm) includes open-faced Danish smorgasbord sandwiches.

MODERATE

Casa dos Reis. Rua Imperatriz Dom Amélia 101. ☎ **291/22-51-82.** Reservations required. Main courses 1,200$–3,800$ ($6.70–$21.30). AE, MC, V. Daily 7–10:30pm. Bus: 5 or 6. FRENCH/PORTUGUESE.

Casa dos Reis, in an appealing neighborhood downhill from the Madeira Carlton Hotel, is elegant and tranquil, with polished mahogany armchairs, brass chandeliers, and the aura of an aristocratic private club. Avoid the snack bar one flight above street level and head for a table in the more formal dining room. Meals include the chef's special fish soup, grilled scabbard fish, chateaubriand, rack of lamb with fines herbes, and fish fricassée with prawns. The fare will not dazzle, but the kitchen is dedicated to local ingredients, and the down-home tastes please most diners, many of whom are local residents.

Casa Madeirense. Estrada Monumental 153. ☎ **291/76-67-00.** Reservations recommended. Main courses 2,000$–5,000$ ($11.20–$28). AE, MC, V. Mon–Sat 1–3pm and 6:30–10:30pm. Closed Aug. PORTUGUESE/INTERNATIONAL.

In a former private home, this restaurant often draws diners from the nearby Reid's Palace. The owner, Filipe Gouveia, extends a hearty welcome and is delighted when guests enjoy his elegant regional decor of *azulejos* (tiles) and hand-painted murals. The lively bar evokes a thatched-roof house in the village of Santana. Fresh fish and shellfish dominate the menu, and are never better than in *cataplana de marisco* (savory shellfish stew). Tuna steak is grilled to perfection, and you can also enjoy tender, perfectly seasoned peppercorn steak or chateaubriand.

INEXPENSIVE

Casa da Carochinha (Lady Bird). Rua de São Francisco 2A. ☎ **291/22-36-95.** Reservations recommended for dinner. Main courses 950$–1,900$ ($5.30–$10.65). AE, DC, MC, V. Tues–Sat noon–3pm and 6–10pm. Tea Tues–Sat 3–5pm. Bus: 2, 12, or 16. MADEIRAN/ENGLISH.

Casa da Carochinha, a favorite retreat for British visitors, faces the Centenary Gardens, near the tourist office. This is the only place on Madeira where the chef doesn't use garlic. Specialties include coq au vin (chicken cooked in wine), beef Stroganoff, roast beef with Yorkshire pudding, and duck with orange sauce. The cuisine is refined but hardly imaginative. You've had better versions of all these dishes, but the food is still satisfying and filling. A staff member places a flag from the diner's country on the spotless white Nottingham lace tablecloth.

Dos Combatentes. Rua Ivens 1. ☎ **291/22-13-88.** Main courses 900$–1,500$ ($5.05–$8.40). AE, DC, MC, V. Mon–Sat 11:45am–3pm and 6:30–10:30pm. Bus: 2, 12, or 16. MADEIRAN.

Dos Combatentes is a good choice for regional food; it's a favorite with Funchal's professionals. At the top of the Municipal Gardens, this simple restaurant serves well-prepared dishes, including rabbit stew, roast chicken, stewed squid, and swordfish with bananas. Most dinners begin with a bowl of the soup of the day. Portions are ample, and two vegetables and a green salad come with the main dish. Desserts are likely to be simple—caramel custard, chocolate mousse, fresh fruit. The waiters are efficient, but not adept in English.

O Celeiro. Rua dos Aranhas 22. ☎ **291/23-06-22.** Reservations recommended. Main courses 1,400$–3,500$ ($7.85–$19.60). AE, DC, MC, V. Mon–Sat noon–2:30pm; daily 6–10:30pm. MADEIRAN.

This rustic-style restaurant serves some of the most authentic and best regional dishes in the capital. The setting evokes an old island farmhouse, and the cooks are known for their homey flavors. O Celeiro attracts visitors and business people with reasonable prices and big helpings of delectable fare. Freshly caught swordfish is cooked with bananas, a longtime island favorite. Tuna steak is marinated in wine and garlic sauce and served with fresh mushrooms. Our longtime favorite is cataplana de marisco, a kettle of seafood stew that tastes different every time we sample it. You might also opt for a tender steak in peppercorn sauce. With *espetada,* or skewered beef on a spit, you'll want crusty bread for soaking up the juices.

O Espadarte. Estrada da Boa Nova 5. ☎ **291/22-80-65.** Reservations recommended for dinner. Main courses 1,200$–1,800$ ($6.70–$10.10). AE, DC, MC, V. Tues–Sun noon–3pm and 6–10:30pm. Bus: 2 or 12. INTERNATIONAL/REGIONAL MADEIRAN.

O Espadarte is an unpretentious restaurant in a drab concrete building perched between a steep road and the mountains, about a mile east of Funchal on the road to the airport. It's owned and operated by a team of Portuguese entrepreneurs who have spent time in many other parts of the world. Guests dine at long trestle tables. Portuguese specialties include grilled swordfish, pepper steak, beef on a skewer, and grilled pork cutlets. Expect big portions of good-tasting Madeiran cookery. In honor of its namesake, the restaurant prepares its own smoked swordfish, the most delectable appetizer you can order. On nights devoted to folklore and fado, the place becomes very touristy.

O Patio Jardim Tropicale. Av. Zarco 21. ☎ **291/22-73-76.** Main courses 950$–1,600$ ($5.30–$8.95). AE, DC, MC, V. Mon–Sat noon–3pm and 7–10pm. Bus: 2, 12, or 16. PORTUGUESE.

In the center of town, O Patio Jardim Tropicale is in the inner courtyard of a complex of commercial buildings, and its entrance near a newspaper kiosk is easy to miss. The restaurant is a welcome refuge from the noise and traffic outside. You can sip coffee at an iron table in the atrium, but many local shopkeepers head for the pleasant restaurant every day. One of the best lunch bargains in Funchal is a heaping platter of the dish of the day, usually roast chicken or stewed codfish with onions. Meals, served on well-scrubbed wooden tables, might include house-style beef or squid, or tuna steak with potatoes, followed by pineapple flambé. This is not the lightest fare on Madeira, but it can be satisfying and definitely filling, especially on a windy, rainy day.

Pizzaria Xaramba. Rua Portão São Tiago 11. ☎ **291/22-97-85.** Reservations not accepted. Main courses 850$–1,900$ ($4.75–$10.65). No credit cards. Daily 6pm–4am. PIZZA/PASTA.

The dining bargain of Funchal, and a magnet for young islanders, this pizza joint lies in the old town. It serves the best pizza in town and an array of succulent pastas, and does so long after other Funchal restaurants have closed for the night. You can watch as the cooks prepare your pie, or opt for such rib-sticking fare as lasagna and ravioli Bolognese.

WHERE TO DINE NEARBY

✪ **A Seta.** Estrada do Livramento 80, Monte. ☎ **291/74-36-43.** Reservations recommended. Main courses 1,400$–1,800$ ($7.85–$10.10). AE, DC, MC, V. Thurs–Tues noon–3pm and 6–11pm. MADEIRAN.

A Seta ("the arrow") specializes in supreme regional cuisine. It's almost midway between Funchal and Monte, 2½ miles from either along winding roads. The mountainside restaurant, a favorite with tour groups, is a tavern where you can order inexpensive, tasty meals. The rustic decor incorporates burned-wood trim, walls covered with pine cones, and crude pine tables. An inner dining room adjoins the open kitchen with a charcoal spit and oven.

First, a plate of homemade coarse brown bread still warm from the oven arrives at your place. Above each table is a hook with a long skewer of charcoal-broiled meat attached. You slip off chunks while mopping up juices with the crusty bread. There are three specialties: beef, chicken, and grilled dry codfish. Seasoned with olive oil, herbs, garlic, and bay leaves, these concoctions are called *espetadas*. Fried potatoes are always done well here (ask for some hot sauce).

Aquário. Seixal, Porto Moniz. ☎ **291/85-43-96.** Main courses 1,300$–2,500$ ($7.30–$14). MC, V. Daily noon–10pm. MADEIRAN.

Aquário is a waterfront fish restaurant too often ignored by visitors who flock to the other dining spots in Porto Moniz. It serves some of the tastiest fresh fish on the island. The kitchen turns out simple fare, but its cooking often outshines that of the deluxe hotels. To begin, you get a heaping basket of homemade bread and a carafe of the local wine. We recommend the grilled fish of the day, served with three vegetables. The soups are hearty, the helpings generous.

5 Exploring Madeira

PRINCIPAL ATTRACTIONS

Funchal's stately, beautiful **praça do Município (Municipal Square)** is a study in light and dark; its plaza is paved with hundreds of black and white lava half-moons. The whitewashed buildings surrounding it have black-stone trim and ocher-tile roofs. On the south side of the square is a former archbishopric now devoted to a museum of religious art. Rising to the east is the Câmara Municipal (city hall), once the 18th-century palace of Count Carvalhal. It's noted for its distinctive palace tower rising over the surrounding rooftops.

Sé (Cathedral). Rua do Aljube. ☎ **291/22-81-55.** Free admission; donation suggested. Mon–Sat 7am–1pm and 4–7pm, Sun 8am–8:30pm.

The most intriguing of Funchal's churches is the rustic 15th-century Sé, with its Moorish carved cedar ceiling, stone floors, gothic arches, stained-glass windows, and baroque altars. The cathedral is at the junction of four busy streets in the historic heart of town. The most visible of these is rua do Aljube. Note that open hours are subject to change depending on church activities.

Museu da Quinta das Cruzes. Calçada do Pico 1. ☎ **291/74-13-82.** Admission 300$ ($1.70). Tues–Sat 10am–12:30pm and 2:30–5:30pm, Sun 10am–1pm.

This museum is the former residence of João Gonçalves Zarco, who discovered Madeira. The surrounding park is of botanical interest and contains a noteworthy collection of orchids. The museum houses many fine examples of English furniture and China-trade porcelains brought to Madeira by expatriate Englishmen in the 18th century. You'll see rare Indo-Portuguese cabinets and the unique chests, native to Madeira, fashioned from *caixas de açúcar* (sugar boxes, dating from the 17th century). Also worth noting is a superb collection of antique Portuguese silver.

Museu Municipal do Funchal. Rua da Mouraria 31. ☎ **291/22-97-61.** Admission 270$ ($1.50), free for children under 12. Tues–Fri 10am–6pm, Sat–Sun noon–6pm.

The Municipal Museum displays land and aquatic animal life of the archipelago. Specimens include moray eels, eagle rays, scorpion fish, sea cucumbers, sea zephyrs, sharpnosed puffers, and loggerhead turtles. Also on display are many of the beautifully plumed birds seen around Madeira. Access is by private car or taxi; no buses are allowed.

Museu de Arte Sacra. Rua do Bispo 21. ☎ **291/22-89-00.** Admission 450$ ($2.50). Tues–Sat 10am–12:30pm and 2:30–6pm, Sun 10am–1pm.

The Museum of Sacred Art occupies an old bishop's house in the center of town. Many of its exhibitions came from island churches, some of which are no longer standing. Its most interesting collections are a series of paintings from the Portuguese and Flemish schools of the 15th and 16th centuries. The paintings are on wood (often oak); an outstanding example is the 1518 *Adoration of the Magi*. A rich merchant commissioned it and paid for it with sugar. A triptych depicts St. Philip and St. James, and there's an exceptional painting called *Descent from the Cross.* Ivory sculpture, gold and silver plate, and gilded wood ornamentations round out the collection.

Jardim Botânico. Caminho do Meio. ☎ **291/200-20-85.** Admission 300$ ($1.70), children under 14 100$ (55¢). Daily 9am–5:30pm. Bus: 29, 30, or 31.

On the road to Camacha, about 2½ miles from Funchal, this botanical garden is one of the best in Portugal, with faraway views of the bay. Opened by the government in 1960 on the grounds of the old Quinta do Bom Sucesso plantation, the garden includes virtually every tree or plant growing on Madeira. Some of the subtropical plants were imported from around the world, including anthuriums and birds-of-paradise from Africa and South America. A heather tree, discovered near Curral das Freiras, is said to be 10 million years old. The gardens open onto panoramic views of Funchal and its port.

IN THE ENVIRONS

Immediately east of Funchal, the ✪ **Quinta do Palheiro Ferreiro** is a beautiful spot for a stroll. The mansion is the private property of the Blandy wine family, former owners of Reid's Palace. The 30-acre estate, with some 3,000 plant species, is like a pleasure garden. The camellia blooms that burst into full flower from Christmas until early spring are reason enough to visit. You'll also see many rare flowers (often from Africa) and exotic trees.

The estate is open Monday to Friday 9:30am to 12:30pm. Admission is 1,000$ ($5.60). Permission must be granted for picnics. Bus no. 36 from Funchal runs here. By car, drive 3 miles northeast of Funchal, following the N101 toward the airport. Fork left onto N102 and follow signposts toward Camacha until you see the turn-off to the quinta.

One of the island's great belvederes lies at ✪ **Eira do Serrado,** about 8 miles northwest of Funchal at Pico de Barcelos. This 3,385-foot lookout point tops the sawtooth of the crater of the island's most awesome volcano. As at Vesuvius, you can look down into the crater depths and out at terraced farms and the village of Curral das Freiras (see below). You can take a half-hour trek around Pico do Serrado to the belvedere point, where you'll be rewarded with one of the most stunning views in Portugal. Leave Funchal on Rua Dr. João Brito Camara, which leads to a new road signposted to Pico dos Barcelos.

After taking in the view, leave Pico dos Barcelos on N107, which is signposted to the stunningly situated village of **Curral das Freiras,** 4 miles north of Eira do Serrado. The name means "Corral of the Nuns." In olden days, the sisters of the Convento de Santa Clara retreated here for safety when pirates attacked. The whitewashed village, reached by way of two tunnels through the mountains, stands at the foot of a panoramic circle of extinct volcanoes. You can visit a small church on the main square and have coffee at a cafe. Allow about 2 hours to make the 22-mile circuit of Eira do Serrado and Curral das Freiras.

WINE, MARKETS & FESTIVALS

MADEIRA WINE   Funchal is the center of Madeira's **wine industry.** Grapes have grown in the region since the early 15th century, when Henry the Navigator introduced vines and sugarcane to the slopes. In Funchal, the must (fresh wine) from black and white grapes is used to make Bual, Sercial, and Malmsey. It's cultivated for its bittersweet tang; women used to scent their handkerchiefs with it. The wine growers still transport the foot-pressed must in goatskin bottles over the rough terrain by *borracheiros.* It undergoes pasteurization in its blending.

Madeira Wine Company, av. Arriaga 28 (☎ **291/74-01-00**), a well-stocked wine shop next to the tourist office, is one of the island's most potent unofficial ambassadors of goodwill. Proud of its traditions, it offers samples from the diverse stock, which covers virtually every vintage produced on the island for the past 35 years. The former convent dates from 1790. It contains murals depicting the wine pressing (by foot) and harvesting processes, which proceed according to traditions established hundreds of years ago. You can savor the slightly burnt sweetness in a setting of old wine kegs and time-mellowed chairs and tables made from kegs. Admission is free; it's open Monday to Friday 9am to 7pm, Saturday 9am to 1pm. Guided tours, conducted at 10:30am and 3:30pm, cost 500$ ($2.80).

Napoléon passed this way on his journey into exile on St. Helena in 1815. Bottles from a vintage year were given to him, but the former emperor died before he could sample them.

MARKETS   The Workers' Market, **Mercado dos Lavradores,** at Avenida Zarco and Hospital Velho, is in full swing Monday to Saturday from 7am to 8pm. It is liveliest in the morning. Flower vendors, dressed in typical Madeiran garb of corselets, leather boots, and striped skirts, will generally let you photograph them, especially if you ask them and buy some flowers. The market is filled with stalls selling island baskets, crafts, fruits, and vegetables.

In the **bazaars,** you can purchase needlepoint tapestries, Madeiran wines, laces, and embroidery on Swiss organdy or Irish linen, as well as local craft items like goat-skin boots and Camacha basketry of water willows. The **City Market,** at praça do Comércio on Saturday, is a study in color, offering everything from yams to papaws.

A FESTIVAL   The most exciting (and most crowded) time to visit Funchal is during the **End of the Year Festival,** December 30 to January 1. Fireworks light up the bay, and the mountains in the background form an amphitheater. Floodlit cruise ships anchor in the harbor to the delight of passengers who revel until dawn.

ORGANIZED TOURS

If you don't care to venture out on your own, you can take one of the many organized bus tours that cruise through the valleys and along the coast. Participants can be picked up at their hotels in Funchal or at the tourist office. Those staying at hotels outside Funchal usually pay a small surcharge to be picked up. For more information, contact the tourist office (see "Essentials," earlier in this chapter) or **Inter-Visa Tours,** av. Arriaga 30, 3rd floor (☎ **291/22-83-44**), in Funchal.

The most popular excursion is a **full-day island tour** that incorporates virtually every accessible point on Madeira, including the island's remote northwestern tip, Porto Moniz, and the lovely harbor of Câmara de Lobos, a few miles west of Funchal. The full-day tour, offered daily, is 8,000$ ($46.40) per person, including lunch.

A less-strenuous **half-day volcano-and-toboggan tour** is 4,500$ ($25.20) per person; it departs twice a week, usually on Monday and Friday. Another possibility, usually offered Wednesday morning for 4,500$ ($25.20), is **visiting the wickerworks at Camacha.** Thousands of pieces of locally crafted work, from small baskets to entire groupings of furniture, are on sale. On Friday night there's a **dinner featuring folklore and fado,** which costs 6,000$ ($33.60).

6 Sports & Outdoor Activities

The pleasant climate invites visitors to enjoy outdoor activities, even if they consist mainly of strolling through Funchal and along park pathways and country lanes. Visiting Victorians (some of the men looking like Mr. Pickwick) were carried around the islands in hammocks slung on poles supported by two husky bearers. Nowadays a more popular means of transport is hiring a bullock-pulled sledge on avenida do Mar, near the pier.

DEEP-SEA FISHING This is a popular sport on Madeira. The catch is mainly longtail tuna, blue marlin, swordfish, and several varieties of shark. Most boat rentals are moderately priced. The tourist office (see "Essentials," earlier in this chapter) will supply information about boat rentals and rates.

GOLF The island maintains two 18-hole courses, both open to the public and accustomed to foreigners. The easier and better established is the **Campo de Golfe de Madeira,** in the hamlet of Santo da Serra (☎ **291/55-23-45**), on the island's northeastern side, about 15 miles from Funchal. Greens fees are 6,000$ ($33.60) for 18 holes. On rocky, steep terrain that some golfers find annoying is the **Pelero Golf Course,** in the hamlet of Sítio do Balançal São Gonçalo, 9050 Funchal (☎ **291/79-21-16**), about 3 miles north of Funchal. It charges 9,900$ to 11,700$ ($55.45 to $65.50) for 18 holes. Clubs and carts are for rent, and local caddies are available. At both courses there's a clubhouse with a bar and restaurant, and both are abundantly accented with mimosas, pines, and eucalyptus trees.

SWIMMING Madeira doesn't have beaches. You can use the facilities of the **Lido Swimming Pool Complex (Complexo Balnear do Lido),** rua do Gorgulho (☎ **291/76-22-17**), which has an Olympic-size pool and a spacious pool for children. It's open daily in summer 8:30am to 7pm, off-season 9am to 6pm. Adults pay 250$ ($1.40). Children under 10 are free with parents; otherwise, they pay 110$ (60¢) to use the pool. Visitors who want to use the upper deck after 3pm can buy a special ticket for 110$ (60¢). You can rent sun beds and umbrellas for 280$ ($1.55). The complex has a cafe, a restaurant, an ice-cream parlor, bars, and a water-sports headquarters. To get there, drive out estrada Monumental from Funchal, and take the marked turnoff onto rua do Gorgulho. By public transit, take bus no. 6.

○ **TOBOGGAN RIDES**   By far the most entertaining rides on the island are on toboggans. The toboggan, a wide wicker basket with wooden runners, was the main means of transport in Monte from 1849 to 1942. The nearly 2-mile ride from Monte to Funchal down slippery-smooth cobblestones takes 20 minutes. Two expert guides in straw hats direct and sometimes propel the toboggan, manipulating the ropes like nimble-footed seamen. You may need to fortify yourself with a glass or two of Madeiran wine before taking the plunge. At Terreiro da Luta, at a height of 2,875 feet, you'll enjoy a panoramic view of Funchal. Here also are monuments to Zarco and Our Lady of Peace.

Before you begin your descent, visit the **Church of Nossa Senhora do Monte,** which contains the iron tomb of the last of the Hapsburgs, Emperor Charles, who died of pneumonia on Madeira in 1922. From a belvedere nearby, you can look down on the whole of Funchal.

You can take a taxi to Monte, 4 miles northeast of Funchal. More popular with locals are buses no. 20 and 21, painted *bright* yellow. They depart from Funchal every 30 minutes. Toboggan rides from Monte (the highest point) to Funchal cost 2,600$ ($14.55) per passenger. For more information, contact **Carreiros dos Montes** (☎ **291/78-39-19**).

WATER SPORTS   The activities desks of several major hotels, including the **Hotel Savoy** and **Reid's Palace** (see "Where to Stay," earlier in this chapter), arrange water sports for guests and nonguests. They'll set up waterskiing, windsurfing, and rental of boats or sailing dinghies. If you want to go snorkeling or scuba diving, check with the **Madeira Carlton Hotel,** largo António Nobre (☎ **291/23-95-00**).

7 Shopping

Crafts are rather expensive on the island, but collectors may want to seek out exquisite Madeira embroidery or needlework. Check to see that the merchandise has a lead seal attached to it, certifying that it was made on Madeira and not imported. The businesses listed in this section are in Funchal.

At the factory **Patricio & Gouveia,** rua do Visconde de Anadia 33 (☎ **291/22-29-28**), you can see employees making stencil patterns on embroidery and checking for quality. The actual embroidery is done in private homes. **Bordados de Madeira,** rua do Visconde de Anadia 44 (☎ **291/22-31-41**), carries an outstanding selection of completed embroidery.

A German family introduced needlepoint and tapestry making to Madeira at the turn of the century. It's been a tradition ever since. You can visit the needlepoint and tapestry factory of **Kiekeben Tapestries,** rua da Carreira 194 (☎ **291/22-20-73**), or its shop, **Bazar Maria Kiekeben,** av. do Infante 2 (same phone).

Camacha Wickerworks. Av. Arriaga. ☎ **291/92-21-14.**

This is a showcase for the wickerwork for which Madeirans have long been noted. Most of the products—everything from giraffes to sofas—were made in the village of Camacha, about 6 miles from Funchal. The store arranges shipment of items too large to carry home.

○ **Casa do Turista.** Rua do Conselheiro José Silvestre Ribeiro 2. ☎ **291/22-49-07.**

Near the waterfront in Funchal, this is the best place on the island for Madeira handcrafts. It has a policy of clearly labeled "firm" prices—there's no haggling here, as there is in many of the bazaars. The Tourist House is in an old *quinta* once inhabited by a distinguished local family. Its elegant rooms are a natural setting for the beautiful handmade items.

On the patio, with a fountain and semitropical greenery, is a miniature village, with small-scale typical rooms furnished in the local style. The merchandise includes handmade embroideries in linen or cotton (the fabric is often imported from Switzerland and Ireland), tapestries, wickerwork, Portuguese pottery and ceramics, Madeiran wines, fruit, and flowers. You'll find all types of embroidery and appliqués, as well as "shadow work," the prices determined by the number of stitches.

Casa Oliveira. Rua da Alfândega 11. ☎ **291/22-93-40.**

There's an embroidery factory on the premises of this shop. The store is primarily a retail outlet for one of the largest embroidery concerns in town. It turns out everything from delicate negligees to elegant "heirloom" tablecloths.

Lino and Araujo Ltd. Rua das Murcas 15. ☎ **291/22-07-36.**

The specialty here is hand-embroidered and -knitted goods. Many non-Portuguese residents of Madeira frequent the shop.

Madeira Superbia. Rua do Carmo 27. ☎ **291/22-40-23.**

This shop, known for its fine embroidery, also specializes in tapestries.

8 Madeira After Dark

The restaurants **O Espadarte** and **A Seta** are *tavernas* (taverns) where you can sample the local wine. See section 4, "Where to Dine."

The glittering **Entertainment Complex at the Casino Park Hotel,** avenida do Infante, Funchal (☎ **291/23-31-11**), is the most obvious entertainment venue for first-time visitors. The complex offers an array of options. Foremost is a **casino,** the only one on Madeira, which offers roulette, French banque, craps, blackjack, and slot machines. To be admitted, you must present a passport or other form of identification and pay a 500$ ($2.80) government tax. The casino is open Sunday to Thursday 8pm to 3am, Friday and Saturday 4pm to 4am.

Nearby is a dance club, **Copacabana,** that's liveliest after 11pm Wednesday to Saturday; it charges a cover (including one drink) of 1,000$ ($5.60). On Sunday at 9pm, the hotel offers a Las Vegas–style **cabaret show.** For the show only, there's a minimum bar tab of 2,500$ ($14) per person; dinner, two drinks, and a view of the show costs 7,800$ ($43.70). In addition, the complex contains bars, kiosks, and boutiques.

Options outside the casino complex are limited, though some hotels present dinner shows. Funchal isn't the best place in Portugal to hear fado, but you can hear the music at **Marcelino Pão y Vinho,** travessa da Torre 22A (☎ **291/23-08-34**). Fadistas perform nightly from 9:30pm to 2am. Nearby, you can hear fado and Brazilian music at **Arsênios,** rua de Santa Maria 169 (☎ **291/22-40-07**), which serves dinners from 3,800$ ($21.30). Open daily 6pm to midnight.

The **Teatro Municipal Baltazar Diaz,** avenida Arriaga (☎ **291/23-35-69**), in the center of Funchal, presents plays (in Portuguese only) and occasional classical concerts. The tourist office has information, and tickets can be purchased at the box office.

There's limited disco action, notably at **Vespas,** avenida Sá Carneiro 7 (☎ **291/23-48-00**), a warehouselike club near the docks. This postmodern disco attracts a young crowd. If you're over 35, you might head for the spacious **O Farol,** largo António Nobre (☎ **291/23-95-00**), in the Madeira Carlton Hotel. It features modern dance music and hits from the 1970s and '80s.

Prince Albert, rua da Imperatriz Dona Amélia (☎ **291/23-57-93**), is a Victorian pub complete with plush cut-velvet walls, tufted banquettes, and English pub memorabilia. Next to the Savoy, it serves English spirits and oversized mugs of beer at the curved bar and at tables under Edwardian fringed lamps. Open daily noon to 11pm.

9 Exploring the Island

The attractions of Madeira hardly end in Funchal. The capital can be a launching pad for exploring the island's mountainous interior and lush coastlines.

WESTERN MADEIRA   If time is limited, head for the western part of Madeira, where you'll find panoramic coastlines, dramatic waterfalls, and cliffs towering over the ocean. For those on tight schedules, highlights include Câmara de Lobos, Pico do Arieiro, Ribeiro Frio, and the mountainous village of Santana.

To plunge into your adventure, leave Funchal on the coastal road, N101, heading west for 12 miles to the village of Câmara de Lobos, so beloved by Sir Winston Churchill.

CÂMARA DE LOBOS

You approach the "Room of the Wolves" after passing terraces planted with bananas. The little fishing village of whitewashed red-tile-roofed cottages surrounds a cliff-sheltered harbor and rocky beach. If you come here around 7 or 8am, you can see fishers unloading their boats after a night at sea. There is nothing finer to do here than walk along the harbor taking in the view and perhaps deciding to follow Churchill's example and become a Sunday painter.

If you need a target for your sightseeing, head for **Henriques & Henriques Vinhos,** a winery at Sitio de Belém (☎ 291/94-15-51), in the heart of the village. It is open Monday to Friday 9am to 1pm and 2 to 5:30pm. Admission is free. You can tour the winery and buy wine.

The village makes a good spot for lunch. The best place is **Santo Antonio** (☎ 291/94-54-39), some 3 miles over Câmara de Lobos in the tiny village of Estreito. Near the little village church, owner Manuel Silvestro offers mostly grills, including golden chicken, cooked over an open hearth. A specialty is *espetada*, Madeira's most famous dish—delicately flavored skewered beef on a spit. Don't expect elegance—you dine at simple paper-covered tables on linoleum, and mop up juices with crusty bread. Santo Antonio is open daily from noon to midnight; main courses cost 11,000$ to 2,000$ ($5.60 to $11.20). MasterCard and Visa are accepted, and no reservations are needed.

If you don't want to make the trek up to Estreito, try the **Coral Bar,** Largo da Republica 3 (☎ 291/94-24-69), near the cathedral in Câmara de Lobos. The owner, Augustinho Ramos, secures the best of the day's catch for his Portuguese and international cuisine. His chefs turn out such dishes as the west coast's best *caldeirada* (fish stew), and swordfish grilled to perfection and topped with ham, cheese, and shrimp. Opt for a table on the rooftop terrace opening onto dramatic views of the fishing harbor itself and a backdrop of the cliffs of Cabo Girão. Hours are daily from noon to 11pm, and reservations are suggested. Main courses cost 1,500$ to 2,500$ ($8.40 to $14). American Express, Diners Club, MasterCard, and Visa are accepted.

Cabo Girão, whose cliffs you may have seen from Câmara de Lobos, lies 10 miles west of the village. To get there, take R214. The 1,900-foot headland is the second-highest promontory on earth. The panorama down the almost-sheer drop to the pounding ocean is thrilling. The terraced farms you'll see clinging to the cliff edges are cultivated entirely by hand, because the plots are too small for either animal or machine.

Continuing on the coast road west, you'll come to **Ribeira Brava,** which lies 9 miles west of Cabo Girão and 30 miles west of Funchal. Ribeira Brava means "wide river," and the little village was established at the river's mouth in 1440. You can walk along the shaded avenue bordering the beach. All that remains of the 17th-century fort, **Forte de São Bento,** is a tower that once protected the fishing village against pirates from the African coast. A little 16th-century church stands in the middle of the village.

From Ribeira Brava, head north along N104 into the center of the island, toward Serra de Agua.

SERRA DE AGUA

You traverse a sheer canyon to reach the little village of Serra de Agua, 4 miles north of Ribeira Brava. One of the best centers for exploring Madeira's lush interior, it's also the site of one of the island's best *pousadas* (government-sponsored mountain inns). Surrounded by abundant crops, jade-green fields, ferns, bamboo, weeping willows, and plenty of waterfalls, the village enjoys one of the loveliest settings in Madeira. Come here not for attractions but for pure scenic beauty. Mist and clouds often shroud the town.

For dining and lodging, seek out the **Pousada dos Vinháticos,** Estrada de São Vicente Serra de Agua, 9350 Ribeira Brava (☎ **291/95-23-44;** fax 291/95-25-40), near the top of a pass on the winding road to São Vicente. You can visit for a meal or spend the night. The solid stone pousada, a tavern-style building with a brick terrace, opened in 1940. The tasty food is hearty and unpretentious, often depending on the catch of the day. Specialties include *espetada* (a swordfish version), ox tongue with Madeira sauce, and local beef flavored with regional wines. Main courses cost 1,500$ to 2,000$ ($8.40 to $11.20); hours are daily from noon to 6pm and 7 to 10pm.

Most of the immaculate guest rooms are done in Portuguese modern style; a few contain antiques. All 20 have bathrooms and good views. The price of a double is 12,000$ ($67.20), including breakfast. American Express, Diners Club, MasterCard, and Visa are accepted, and parking is free.

From Serra de Agua, the route climbs to the 3,304-foot **Caminho de Encumeada,** or Encumeada Pass, 4 miles north of Serra de Agua. It's one of the island's best centers for hiking. A belvedere affords great panoramas over both sides of Madeira.

Following the route northwest of Boca de Encumeada, you reach the village of São Vicente, 9 miles northwest of Encumeada and 35 miles northwest of Funchal.

SÃO VICENTE

One of the best-known towns on the north coast lies where the São Vicente River meets the ocean. Again, you come here for the sweeping views, some of the most dramatic on the island. Part of the fun of going there is taking the one-lane north coast route. In a miraculous and costly feat of engineering, it was chiseled out of pure cliff face. It's a nightmare if you encounter one of the bloated tour buses taking this highway. You'll often have to back up, because the drivers rarely give way. Constructed in 1950, and nicknamed the "gold road," the drive offers views of water cascading down the slopes. Many locals have planted vineyards in this seemingly inhospitable terrain.

In such a remote outpost, an inn comes as a welcome relief. You'll find good food or lodging at **Estalagem do Mar,** Juncos, Fajã da Areia, 9240 São Vicente (☎ **291/84-01-01;** fax 291/84-99-19).

Most visitors pass through here only to dine on the excellent regional and international cuisine. Specialties include swordfish prepared in almost any style. Many versions of sea bass are served, and the meat dishes—especially perfectly grilled veal chop and beef filet in mushroom cream sauce—are also good. Main courses cost 2,500$ to 4,000$ ($14 to $22.40), with a set menu for 3,000$ ($16.80); it's open daily from noon to 3pm and 7 to 9:30pm. American Express, Diners Club, MasterCard, and Visa are accepted, and reservations are recommended.

If you decide to spend the night, the 91-room inn offers rather simply furnished accommodations opening onto views of the ocean. The inn has a provincial look, with flowery curtains and spreads. Rooms have modern tiled bathrooms, TVs, and phones. On the premises are an indoor and outdoor pool, a tennis room, Jacuzzi, sauna, gym, and games room. Limited room service is available. The three-floor hotel was built in the early 1990s and last renovated in 1998. A double costs 11,000$ ($61.60), a suite 16,000$ ($89.60), including breakfast. Parking is free.

From São Vicente you can continue west along N101 to the town of Porto Moniz, 10 miles away in one of the remotest parts of Madeira.

PORTO MONIZ

This portion of the "gold road" is one of the most difficult but dramatic drives in Portugal, requiring nerves of steel. The road is boldly cut into the side of a towering cliff that plunges vertically into the ocean below. Eventually you arrive at Porto Moniz, a fishing village of great charm built at the site of a sheltered anchorage shaped by a slender peninsula jutting out toward an islet, Ilhéu Mole. This is the only sheltered harbor on the north coast of Madeira. The spewing of lava eons ago formed the natural pools in the area.

Porto Moniz boasts no major sights other than the old village itself, with its fishermen's cottages and cobbled lanes. The adventure is surviving the trip. After you've come all this way, you'll welcome the offerings of the Residencial Orca (see below).

After leaving Porto Moniz, you can continue southwest along N101, going back along a winding road via Ribeira Brava and Câmara de Lobos until you finally make the full circuit back into Funchal.

For the best food and rooms in the area, head for **Residencial Orca,** Vila do Porto Moniz, Porto Moniz 9270 (☎ **291/85-00-00;** fax 291/85-11-19). The 12-room inn offers small, basic, comfortable rooms for 7,000$ to 8,000$ ($39.20 to $44.80), including breakfast and free parking. The most expensive rooms open onto a sea view and are well worth the extra money. Each unit has a TV and phone. Built in 1988, the inn is rustic, with white stucco walls and wood ceilings.

The inn serves excellent regional cuisine. Tasty options include swordfish in mushroom and cream sauce, and fillet of beef served with dates. We prefer fresh tuna steak breaded in corn flour, sautéed, and served with country cabbage and potatoes. Main courses cost 1,000$ to 3,000$ ($5.60 to $16.80). Food is served daily from noon to 5pm and 7 to 9:30pm. American Express, Diners Club, MasterCard, and Visa are accepted, and reservations are recommended.

SANTANA & CENTRAL MADEIRA   For a final look at Madeira, you can cut through the center of the island, heading north from Funchal. This route takes you to such scenic highlights as Pico do Arieiro and Santana. This is one of the finest parts of Madeira for mountain hiking.

PICO DO ARIEIRO

This village 22 miles north of Funchal evokes the island's volcanic nature better than any other place. When the 5,939-foot peak is not covered by clouds, the panoramas are stunning. Pico do Arieiro is the third-tallest mountain on the island. To reach it, follow Rua 31 de Janeiro out of Funchal, and take the N103 as it climbs to Monte. When you reach the pass at Poiso, some 6 miles north of Monte, hang a left and continue to follow the signposts into Pico do Arieiro.

Once at the ✪ *miradouro* or belvedere at Pico do Arieiro, you'll take in the Curral das Freiras crater, the crest of the Pico das Torrinhas, the Pico das Torres, and the Pico Ruivo. Pico Ruivo (6,105 feet) is the highest point on Madeira. To the northeast lie the famous Penha d'Aguia (eagle's rock), the Ponta de São Lourenço, and the Ribeira da Metade.

One of the island's most delightful *pousadas* (government inns) is at Pico do Arieiro. It's the **Pousada do Arieiro** (P.O. Box 478, Funchal), 9230 Santana (☎ **291/23-01-10;** fax 291/22-86-11). The 25-unit inn offers some of the finest lodgings and the best cuisine in the area. Built in 1989, the inn was last renovated in 1998. Its midsize rooms are comfortably furnished, with fine mattresses, TVs, and phones. Doubles cost 16,000$ ($89.60), or 22,000$ ($123.20) with half-board.

The view from the rustic dining room is reason enough to eat here, but the food is good, too. The international and regional dishes include everything from codfish in creamy onion and garlic sauce to rack of lamb flavored with rosemary and honey and served with sweet potatoes. Pepper steak is flambéed at table, and you can also order such classics as veal Marsala or marinated tuna steak sautéed with onions. Main courses cost 1,500$ to 3,200$ ($8.40 to $17.90), and hours are daily from noon to 3pm and 7 to 10:30pm; American Express, Diners Club, MasterCard, and Visa are accepted.

RIBEIRO FRIO

Instead of taking the left fork at Poiso (see above) and heading for Pico do Areiro, you can take the right fork to reach Ribeiro Frio, an enchanting spot 7 miles north of Poiso.

Ribeiro Frio ("cold river") is a little village in the Madeira Forest Park. It occupies a dramatic setting, with waterfalls, jagged peaks, and sleepy valleys. Levada do Furado irrigates the slopes.

One of the most dramatic walks in Portugal begins 40 minutes west of Ribeiro Frio. Follow signposts to the ✪ **Balcões,** which runs along Levada do Furado. It takes you on footpaths cut out of basalt rock until you reach the "balcony" or belvedere. The dizzying perch overlooks the jagged peaks of the Pico do Arieiro, Pico das Torres, and Pico Ruivo.

If the mountain air gives you an appetite, head for **Victor's Bar,** on N103 (☎ **291/57-58-98**), a chaletlike mountain restaurant known for afternoon tea and good regional food and wine. Trout from the area hatchery is a specialty. It's prepared in a variety of ways; we prefer it grilled golden brown. Victor Reinecke serves typical Madeiran cuisine, including lamb stew with potatoes, and swordfish with bananas. Main courses cost 1,500$ to 3,000$ ($8.40 to $16.80). The restaurant is open daily from 9am to 7pm; reservations are recommended. American Express, Diners Club, MasterCard, and Visa are accepted.

Follow N101 out of Ribeiro Frio, heading north toward the coast. In the village of Faial, you'll find the connecting route signposted west to the village of Santana.

SANTANA

Eleven miles northwest of Ribeiro Frio and 25 miles north of Funchal, Santana is the most famous village in Madeira, and certainly the prettiest. It is noted for its A-framed, thatched-roof cottages called *palheiros*. Painted in bright, often flamboyant colors, they are the most-photographed private residences on the island. On a coastal plateau, Santana lies at an altitude of 2,435 feet.

You can find food and lodging at one of the most frequented establishments on the north coast, **Quinta da Furão,** Achado do Gramacho, 9230 Santana (☎ **291/57-01-00;** fax 291/57-35-60). The 43-unit inn lies in a vineyard in a cliff-top setting that opens onto a panorama of the ocean. Most visitors stay just for the day to sample the cuisine, which is the finest on the north coast. The rustic dining room serves Madeiran, Portuguese, and international cuisine. Dishes include swordfish cooked with banana, grilled T-bone steak in garlic butter, and fillet of beef baked in a pastry case and served with Roquefort sauce. The goat cheese of the region is a delight. Main courses cost 3,000$ to 6,000$ ($16.80 to $33.60). Open hours are daily from noon to 3pm and 7 to 9:30pm.

The inn is also a delightful place to stay. The ample guest rooms are well furnished in regional style, with excellent mattresses, TVs, and phones. Some accommodations open onto sea views, and others face the mountains. The inn has a swimming pool, gym, Jacuzzi, and pub. Doubles with half-board cost 17,000$ to 28,500$ ($95.20 to $159.60), including breakfast. Parking is free. American Express, Diners Club, MasterCard, and Visa are accepted

10 Porto Santo

24 miles NE of Madeira

The second major island of the Madeira archipelago is Porto Santo, an arid landmass that presents a marked contrast to the lushness of the main island. It is 9 miles long and 3 miles wide, with a 4-mile strip of fine, sandy beach along the southern shore. The island is not as hilly as Madeira: Its highest elevation is about 1,670 feet above sea level, at **Pico do Facho.**

João Gonçalves Zarco and Tristão Vaz Teixiera, who discovered Madeira, landed on Porto Santo in 1418. They took refuge when a storm blew them off course, and named the island Porto Santo (Holy Port) to express gratitude for their survival. It was not until 1419 that they were in condition to sail on and make landfall on the main island. Prince Henry the Navigator gave Teixiera and Zarco authority to run Madeira, but he placed Porto Santo in the hands of Bartolomeu Perestrello. Perestrello reportedly brought in rabbits as a future food source, but instead, it is said, they ate everything in sight.

Christopher Columbus slept here. He married Isobel Moniz, Perestrello's daughter, before going on to Funchal to prepare for his sea exploration. The house in which he reputedly lived is in an alley in back of the little white church in the town of **Vila Baleira,** which is also called Porto Santo.

The island gets very dry in summer, which makes it popular with beachgoers but not good for crops. The foodstuffs grown on Porto Santo in the winter include grain, tomatoes, figs, and melons, as well as grapes from which a sweet white wine is made. Islanders who don't farm go fishing. A few remaining unusual windmills crown the low hills.

The water of Porto Santo supposedly has therapeutic value. It's a popular drink not only on the island but also in Madeira and Portugal. The water-bottling plants, fish canneries, and a lime kiln make up the island's industries.

ESSENTIALS
ARRIVING

BY PLANE   The flight from Madeira to the little Campo de Cima airport at Porto Santo takes only 15 minutes. (The views are spectacular.) Always reserve well in advance for July and August, when beach lovers descend en masse. Flights generally cost 7,677$ ($43) one way, 15,354$ ($86) round-trip. In peak season, count on eight flights per day; frequency diminishes off-season. For ticket reservations and information, call ☎ **291/98-21-46** or 291/52-40-11.

BY BOAT   Regularly scheduled ferry service connects Madeira and Porto Santo. The *Lobo Marinho* departs Funchal Harbor daily. Tickets cost 9,500$ ($53.20) round-trip if you return the same day. If you stay more than 1 night, a round-trip ticket costs 7,900$ ($44.25).

Saturday through Thursday, the ferry usually departs Madeira at 8am and arrives in Porto Santo at 10:30am. The departure from Madeira on Friday isn't until 6pm. Always check the schedules for return trips from Porto Santo, which vary. Tickets can be purchased at the *Lobo Marinho* office, rua da Praia, Funchal (☎ 291/21-03-00), Monday to Friday 9am to 12:30pm and 2:30 to 6pm. On weekends, you can buy a ticket at any travel agency in Funchal.

VISITOR INFORMATION

The tourist office is on Avenida Vieira de Castro (☎ 291/98-23-61) in Vila Baleira, the island's capital.

GETTING AROUND

Most visitors get around on foot or rely on a **taxi** (☎ 291/98-23-34) for excursions. Car rentals can be arranged at **Mainho**, in the Hotel Praia Dourada, Rua D. Estevão d'Alencastre (☎ 291/98-24-03).

EXPLORING THE ISLAND   Most visitors come here strictly for the wide beach of golden sand along the southern coast. It's ideal for swimming in unpolluted waters or for long strolls. If you tear yourself from the beach for a day, you will find some minor attractions. **Vila Baleira,** a sleepy town of whitewashed stucco houses, merits an hour of your time. You'll be following in the footsteps of Christopher Columbus as you make your way along its cobblestone streets.

Locals call the town "Vila," and it lies at the center of the 4-mile-long beach. Stop for a drink at the cafe on Largo de Pelourinho, the main square. Shaded by palm trees, it is the center of life on the island. To the right of the church on the square, follow a sign along the alley to the so-called **Casa de Cristovão Colombo,** Travessa de Sacristia (☎ 291/93-84-05). The explorer is said to have lived here in two rooms with his wife, Isobel Moniz. In an annex, you can view maps and engravings depicting major events in his life. The house is open Monday to Friday 9:30am to 5:30pm, Saturday 9:30am to noon. Admission is free.

Later you can follow Rua Infante Dom Henrique off Largo do Pelourinho to a **park** with a statue dedicated to Columbus. The beach surrounds the flower-filled park.

After seeing the town and its meager attractions, you can visit some of the island's scenic highlights. They include **Pico do Castelo,** north of Vila Baleira on a small and difficult road. It affords a perspective on the whole island and endless views of the sea. This is a favorite local picnic spot. You can pick up provisions at one of the little shops in Vila Baleira. The "castelo" in the name was a fortified castle that once stood here to guard Vila Baleira from attacks by pirates sailing off the coast of Africa. Only four cannons remain—islanders removed the rest of the castle's stone for building materials. The island government has planted pine trees to keep the air moist, but they never grow beyond 10 feet, so as not to obscure the view. From Pico do Castelo, you can follow signs to **Pico do Facho,** the tallest point on the island.

At the southwestern tip of the island, **Ponta da Calheta** is another scenic destination. To get there, take the road west out of Vila Baleira. It has a view of the little offshore island of Baixo, across a dangerous channel riddled with reefs. The beach is made of black basalt rocks, so you'll just want to take a photograph, not a swim.

Directly north lies another of the island's great lookout points, **Pico dos Flores.** Access is over a pothole-riddled dirt road. The cliffs here also have a panoramic view of the islet of Baixo, to your left. The tiny islet to your right is Ferro.

While in the southwestern part of the island, you can also follow the signs to **La Pedreira,** on the slopes of Pico de Ana Ferreira. The amazing basalt rock formation evokes organ pipes stretching toward the sky.

WHERE TO STAY

Porto Santo. Campo Baixo, 9400 Porto Santo. ☎ **291/98-23-81.** Fax 291/98-26-11. 94 units. A/C TV TEL. 18,600$–24,800$ ($104.15–$138.90) double. Rates include breakfast. AE, DC, MC, V. Free parking.

Right on the beach, a 15-minute walk from the center of town, this has been a leading hotel on the island since it opened in 1979. It contributed greatly to putting Porto Santo on the tourist map. Outside your window, you'll see a wide stretch of beach. The four-star hotel, renovated in 1996, is a mile from the town of Vila Baleira at Suloeste. It's a two-story building, decorated in contemporary style, in a garden setting with a swimming pool. The midsize rooms are standard, but well furnished with excellent mattresses. Make reservations far in advance if you plan to visit in August. There's a bar in the restaurant, which serves regional and international cuisine, plus another on the beach. In the summer, the lavish Wednesday night buffet, which costs 4,200$ ($23.50) per person, is the hottest ticket on the island. Room service is available until midnight, and the hotel has laundry service, a concierge, and tennis courts.

Praia Dourada. Rua D. Estevão d'Alencastre, 9400 Porto Santo. ☎ and fax **291/98-23-15.** E-mail: torrepraia@mail.telepac.pt. 100 units. TV TEL. 11,800$–13,500$ ($66.10–$75.60) double. Rates include breakfast. AE, DC, MC, V. Free parking on street.

The second-best hotel in Vila Baleira opened in 1980 and was last renovated in 1998. Its three floors contain fairly standard, motel-like rooms. Corridors are fairly dim, but rooms are light and airy. Although they're well furnished, with good mattresses, they lack any particular luster. Many units have private balconies. The hotel, about a 5-minute walk from a beach, attracts many frugal Madeirans in the summer. It has a saltwater outdoor poor. Breakfast is the only meal served; the bar does a thriving business with merchants and business travelers from Portugal. Laundry service is provided.

Residential Central. Rua Abel Magno Vasconcelos. ☎ **291/98-22-26.** Fax 291/98-34-60. 42 units. 6,000$–9,900$ ($33.60–$55.45) double; 7,500$–13,200$ ($42–$73.90) suite. Rates include breakfast. No credit cards. Limited free parking on street.

Built 4 decades ago, this was once about the only decent hotel in Porto Santo. Although the other accommodations we list have surpassed it, it remains a well-maintained and decent place to stay. In 1993 the inn, which sits in the center of town, expanded from a 12-room pension. It shows a bit of wear and tear, but the welcome and reception are friendly. The comfort level is high, although there is no air-conditioning. Many rooms have views over the town to the sea. In the summer, the hotel has a real family atmosphere; you'll find more businesspeople in the off-season. There's a sun terrace, a garden, and a bar; breakfast is the only meal served.

✪ **Torre Praia Suite Hotel.** Rua Goulart Medeiros, 9400 Porto Santo. ☎ **291/98-52-92.** Fax 291/98-24-87. E-mail: torrepraia@mail.telepac.pt. 65 units. A/C MINIBAR TV TEL. 17,000$–20,000$ ($95.20–$112) double; 25,000$–29,000$ ($140–$162.40) triple; 25,500$–32,000$ ($142.80–$179.20) suite. Rates include breakfast. AE, DC, MC, V. Free parking.

The island's premier hotel is on the outskirts of Vila Baleira, adjacent to its own beach. Opened in the summer of 1993 and rated four stars by the government, it offers a midsize to spacious guest rooms. Spread over three stories, they're well furnished, with excellent beds and state-of-the-art plumbing. All have hair dryers and safe-deposit boxes, and most have water views. Despite the name, the hotel has only three suites. The restaurant, constructed around an old watchtower, is one of the island's best. Its international and Portuguese dishes include fresh tuna steak, and breaded and sautéed swordfish. There is a bar with a great view on top of the hotel, plus another below, facing the sea and the on-site swimming pool. On the premises are a health club, a sauna, and a game room.

WHERE TO DINE

Most guests dine at their hotels, which are also open to nonguests (see above). Some little eateries around the island specialize in fresh fish.

A Gazela. Campo de Cima. ☎ **291/98-44-25.** Reservations recommended. Main courses 1,100$–2,000$ ($6.15–$11.20). AE, DC, MC, V. Daily noon–3pm and 7–11pm. PORTUGUESE/MADEIRAN.

We're not turned on by this modern restaurant's location near the little Campo de Cima Airport, but it's a local favorite because of its tasty regional food and low prices. Islanders flock here for weddings, anniversaries, and family reunions. Always look for the catch of the day, or try the classic Madeiran specialty, *espetada* (skewered and grilled beef), or excellent fresh grilled tuna with sautéed onions. Another specialty is beef loin à la Gazela (cooked with ham and cheese). The restaurant is less than a mile from the center of town and about a 10-minute walk from the Hotel Porto Santo.

Baiana. Rua Dr. Nuno S. Texeira. ☎ **291/98-46-49.** Reservations recommended. Main courses 1,250$–2,500$ ($7–$14). AE, DC, MC, V. Daily 10am–midnight. PORTUGUESE.

Near the town hall in the center of Vila Baleira, this is a regular rendezvous, popular with visitors and locals alike. In fair weather, guests select a table on the sidewalk, sometimes ordering drinks or sandwiches. Full regional meals are also available. Owner Jose Manuel Diaz presides over two rustic dining rooms. The tasty dishes include fillet of beef cooked at your table and served with a selection of sauces. Instead of beef, *espetada* comes with skewered squid and shrimp, delicately flavored and served with fresh lemon. Pork in wine and garlic marinade is another delectable offering.

Estrela do Norte. Sitio da Camacha. ☎ **291/98-34-00.** Reservations recommended. Main courses 1,200$–1,800$ ($6.70–$10.10). AE, DC, MC, V. Daily 11am–11pm. Closed Jan 15–Feb 15. MADEIRAN.

In a rustic setting, owner Ricardo Ferreira has opened this popular eatery on the north side of the island. It's about a 5-minute taxi ride from Vila Baleira and a mile from the airport. Seafood predominates, and the catch of the day is the way to go. Other regional dishes include pork marinated in wine and garlic. Like all the other island restaurants, Estrela do Norte specializes in *espetada* (skewered and grilled beef), served with potatoes and salad. The chef also features barbecues, but we consistently prefer fresh grilled tuna or swordfish.

Teodorico. Sera de Fora. ☎ **291/98-22-57.** Reservations recommended. Main courses 1,500$–2,000$ ($8.40–$11.20). No credit cards. Daily 7pm–midnight. MADEIRAN.

Our longtime island favorite, this restaurant occupies a former farmhouse. It has made its reputation on only one dish: *espetada* (skewered and grilled beef), which is tender and filled with flavor. The dish comes with fried potatoes, a salad, and perhaps some other fresh vegetables. Locals wash it down with a dry red wine that's made on the island and sop up the juices with hearty regional bread, *pão de caco*. The restaurant is in the hills, 1½ miles from the center, northeast of Vila Baleira. In fair weather you can dine outside (where the chairs are made from tree stumps). If it's cold, you can join the locals inside at a little table in a room warmed by an open fire.

Appendix: Portugal in Depth

Portugal, positioned at what was once thought to be the edge of the earth, has long been a seafaring nation. At the dawn of the Age of Exploration, mariners believed that two-headed, fork-tongued monsters as big as houses lurked across the Sea of Darkness, waiting to chew up a caravel and gulp its debris down their fire-lined throats.

In spite of these paralyzing fears, Portugal launched legendary caravels on explorations that changed the fundamental perceptions of humankind: Vasco da Gama sailed to India, Magellan circumnavigated the globe, Dias rounded the Cape of Good Hope. In time, Portuguese navigators explored two-thirds of the earth, opening the globe to trade and colonization and expanding the intellectual horizons of Western civilization for all time.

In spite of its former influence, Portugal still suffers from one of the most widespread misconceptions in European travel—that it's simply "another Spain," and a poorer version at that. Before its European political and economic integration in 1986, some dared to call it "the last foreign country of Europe."

1 Portugal Today

As tiny Portugal begins to move into a new century, a common question is, "Is there life after EXPO '98?" The fair brought representatives of some 130 countries to Lisbon. The world came to Portugal's doorstep, often for the first time. The visitors liked Portugal and wanted to see more, and many have returned in droves for a closer inspection.

Portugal today is a land in transition. It exhibits signs of the fever of national renewal, with a giant new bridge spanning the Tagus in Lisbon and its entry into the euro market.

The country is long past the quasi-fascism of the Salazar era and the leftist excesses (including revolution) that followed when the government fell in 1974. Portugal has moved forward since then, with a growth rate of 3.75% and an unemployment of 6.8%, better than Italy, France, or Spain.

An increasing trend toward revitalization has targeted the horribly inefficient state-run companies, including the national bus company. Banks and other financial institutions, newspapers, petroleum refineries, and food processors, among others, continue to fall into private hands.

This small country with its variety of climates and mixture of racial strains, is an assiduous copyist, mimic, and borrower. Any sizable Portuguese town looks like a superstitious bride's finery—something old, something new, something borrowed, and something blue.

—Mary McCarthy, February 1955 letter from Portugal,
in *On the Country* (1962)

Workers, however, continue to earn only about a third of the pay of their counterparts in the United Kingdom and France. There are dark sides. Life expectancy for men between the ages of 40 and 65 is among the worst in the European Union, roughly on the level of someone living in Mexico City. Nearly half of the people can barely read or do simple math, according to a literacy study. Some one-quarter of Portuguese households remain below the poverty level.

Portugal joined the European Union in 1986, instigating a major overhaul of the country. Fellow members of the European Union, along with investors in the United States and elsewhere, continue to pump money into Portugal, fueling industry and improving infrastructure. The use of that money is apparent in vastly improved railways, new highways, better schools, more sophisticated hospitals, and vastly upgraded port and airport facilities. Telecommunications and transport are improving, and greater numbers of young Portuguese are receiving on-the-job training to help them compete in the modern world, especially in the computer industry. Resort hotels continue to sprout around the country, and many old palaces are being reconditioned and opened to paying guests for the first time in their long histories.

Regrettably, however, all this refurbishing has led to Portugal's becoming quite expensive. Before the late 1990s, it was the unequivocal bargain vacation paradise of Western Europe. Now its hotels and restaurants are rapidly becoming as expensive as those elsewhere in Europe—though even in Lisbon the prices are nowhere near as staggering as those in London or Paris.

There's a general feeling of optimism in Portugal; people have more disposable income and high hopes for the new century. Lisbon's sidewalks are as crowded in the evening as Madrid's. Young Portuguese are much better tuned in to Europe than their parents were, and less willing to follow the dictates of the church and to conform to the restrictions of village life. The younger generation is as well versed in the electronic music coming out of London and Los Angeles as in *fado* repertoires, and more taken with French and Spanish films than with Portuguese lyric poetry. Still, as Portugal advances with determination into the 21st century, its people retain pride in their historic culture.

2 A Look at the Past

Dateline

- **210 B.C.** The Romans invade the peninsula, meeting fierce resistance from the Celtiberian people.
- **60 B.C.** During the reign of Julius Caesar, Portugal is fully

continues

PREHISTORIC PORTUGAL From about 8000 to 7000 B.C., tribes occupied the valley of the Tagus, stretching into Estremadura and Alentejo. Pottery and various artifacts attest to their presence. Neolithic people built hilltop forts that greeted the Celtic people around 700 to 600 B.C. Excavations have revealed important settlements in northern Portugal from this time.

It's believed that the Phoenicians, early traders, established a trading outpost at Lisbon around 900 B.C. In time, the Carthaginians recruited Celtic men to fight Rome's growing might.

THE ROMANS ARRIVE Starting in 210 B.C., the Romans colonized most of Iberia. They met great resistance from the Celtiberian people of the interior. The Lusitanian (ancient Portugal was known as Lusitania) leader Viriatus looms large in Portuguese history as a freedom fighter who held up the Roman advance; he died about 139 B.C. The Roman advance was unstoppable, however, and by the time of Julius Caesar, Portugal had been integrated into the Roman Empire. The Roman colonies included Olisipo (now Lisbon).

Christianity arrived in Portugal near the end of the 1st century A.D. By the 3rd century, bishoprics had been established at Lisbon, Braga, and elsewhere. Following the decline of the Roman Empire, invaders crossed the Pyrenees into Spain in 409 and eventually made their way to Portugal. The Visigothic Empire dominated the peninsula for some two centuries.

THE MOORS INVADE & RETREAT In 711 a force of Moors arrived in Iberia, and they quickly advanced to Portugal. They erected settlements in the south. The Christian Reconquest—known as the *Reconquista*—to seize the land from Moorish control is believed to have begun in 718.

In the 11th century, Ferdinand the Great, king of León and Castile, took much of northern Portugal from the Moors. Before his death in 1065, Ferdinand set about reorganizing his western territories into Portucale (now Portugal).

Portuguese, a Romance language, evolved mainly from a dialect spoken when Portugal was a province of the Spanish kingdom of León and Castile. The language developed separately from other Romance dialects.

PORTUGAL IS BORN Ferdinand handed over Portugal to his illegitimate daughter, Teresa. (At that time, the Moors still held the land south of the Tagus.) Unknowingly, the king of Spain had launched a course of events that was to lead to Portugal's development into a distinct nation.

integrated into the Roman Empire.

- **A.D. 409** Invaders from across the Pyrenees arrive, establishing a Visigothic empire that endures for some two centuries.
- **711** Moorish warriors arrive in Iberia and conquer Portugal within 7 years.
- **1065** Ferdinand, king of León and Castile, sets about reorganizing his western territories into what is now modern Portugal.
- **1143** Afonso Henríques is proclaimed first king of Portugal and begins to drive the Moors out of the Algarve.
- **1249** Afonso III completes the *Reconquista* of the Algarve, as Christians drive out the Moors.
- **1279–1325** Reign of Dinis, "The Poet King." Castile recognizes Portugal's borders.
- **1385** Battle of Aljubarrota; João de Avis defeats the Castilians and founds the House of Avis to rule Portugal.
- **1415** Henry the Navigator sets up a school of navigation in Sagres. Madeira is discovered in 1419, the Azores in 1427.
- **1488** Bartholomeu Dias rounds the Cape of Good Hope.
- **1498** Vasco da Gama rounds India's west coast, opening up trade between the West and the East.
- **1500** Brazil is discovered, the high-water mark of the reign of Manuel the Fortunate (1495–1521). Portugal's Golden Age begins.
- **1521** Portugal becomes the first of the great maritime world empires, dominating access to the Indian Ocean.
- **1521–57** Reign of João III, ushering in Jesuits and the Inquisition.
- **1578** João's son, Dom Sebastião, disappears in the

continues

battle of Morocco, leaving Portugal without an heir.

- **1581–1640** Philip II of Spain brings Hapsburg rule to Portugal.
- **1640** João IV, following a nationalist revolution, restores independence and launches the House of Bragança.
- **1755** A great earthquake destroys Lisbon and parts of Alentejo and the Algarve.
- **1822** Portugal declares Brazil independent.
- **1908** Carlos I, "The Painter King," and his son, the crown prince, are assassinated in Lisbon.
- **1910** The monarchy is ousted and the Portuguese Republic is established.
- **1916** Portugal enters World War I on the side of the Allies.
- **1926** The Republic collapses and a military dictatorship under Gomes da Costa is established.
- **1932–68** António de Oliveira Salazar keeps a tight hold on the government during his long reign as dictator. Portugal is officially neutral in World War II, but Salazar grants the Allies bases in the Azores.
- **1955** Portugal joins the United Nations.
- **1974** The April "flower revolution" topples the dictatorship; Portugal collapses into near anarchy.
- **1976–83** Sixteen provisional governments reign over a Portugal in chaos.
- **1986** Portugal joins the European Community. Mário Soáres is elected president.
- **1989** Privatization of state-owned companies begins.
- **1991** Soáres is reelected.
- **1992** Portugal holds the presidency of the European Union.

continues

Teresa was firmly bound in marriage to Henry, a count of Burgundy. Henry accepted his father-in-law's gift of Portugal as his wife's dowry, but upon the king's death, he coveted Spanish territory as well. His death cut short his dreams of expansion.

Following Henry's death, Teresa ruled Portugal; she cast a disdainful eye on, and an interfering nose into, her legitimate sister's kingdom in Spain. Teresa lost no time mourning Henry and took a Galician count, Fernão Peres, as her lover. Teresa's refusal to conceal her affair with Peres and stay out of everyone else's affairs led to open strife with León.

Teresa's son, Afonso Henríques, was incensed by his mother's actions. Their armies met at São Mamede in 1128. Teresa lost, and she and her lover were banished.

Afonso Henríques went on to become Portugal's founding father. In 1143, he was proclaimed its first king, and official recognition eventually came from the Vatican in 1178. Once his enemies in Spain were temporarily quieted, Afonso turned his eye toward the Moorish territory in the south of Portugal. Supported by crusaders from the north, the Portuguese conquered Santarém and Lisbon in 1147. Afonso died in 1185. His son and heir, Sancho I, continued his father's work of consolidating the new nation.

Successive generations waged war against the Moors until Afonso III, who ruled from 1248 to 1279, wrested the Algarve from Moorish control. The country's capital moved from Coimbra to Lisbon. After Portugal became independent in the 11th century, its borders expanded southward to the sea.

The Moors left a permanent impression on Portugal. The language called Mozarabic, spoken by Christians living as Moorish subjects, was integrated into the Portuguese dialect. The basic language of today, both oral and written, was later solidified and perfected in Lisbon and Coimbra.

Castile did not recognize Portugal's borders until the reign of Pedro Dinis (1279–1325). Known as "The Poet King" or "The Farmer King" (because of his interest in agriculture), he founded the university in Lisbon in about 1290; it later moved to Coimbra. Dinis married Isabella, a princess of Aragon. She was later canonized, but evidence indicates the vigorous young king (whose parents had a bigamous marriage) would have preferred a less saintly wife. Isabella was especially interested in the poor. Legend has it that she was once smuggling bread out of the palace to feed them when her husband spotted her and asked what she was concealing. When she showed him, the bread had miraculously turned into roses.

- 1995 Portugal is designated the cultural capital of Europe.
- 1998 Millions flock to Lisbon for EXPO '98, celebrating the heritage of the oceans.
- 1999 Portugal adopts the euro as its standard of currency.

Their son, Afonso IV, is remembered today for ordering the murder of his son Pedro's mistress. (See "Portugal's Romeo & Juliet," in chapter 10.) During Pedro's reign (1357–67), an influential representative body called the Cortes (an assembly of clergy, nobility, and commoners) began to gain ascendancy. The majority of the clergy, greedy for power, fought the sovereign's reform measures, which worked to ally the people more strongly with the crown. During the reign of Pedro's son, Ferdinand I (1367–73), Castilian forces invaded Portugal, Lisbon was besieged, and the dynasty faced demise.

In 1383, rather than submit to Spanish rule, the Portuguese people chose the illegitimate son of Pedro as regent. That established the house of Avis. João de Avis (reigned 1383–1433) secured Portuguese independence by defeating Castilian forces at Aljubarrota in 1385. His union with Philippa of Lancaster, the granddaughter of Edward III of England, produced a son who oversaw the emergence of Portugal as an empire—Prince Henry the Navigator.

HENRY BUILDS A MARITIME EMPIRE Henry's demand for geographical accuracy and his hunger for the East's legendary gold, ivory, slaves, and spices drove him to exploration. To promote Christianity, he joined the fabled Christian kingdom of Prester John to drive the Muslims out of North Africa. Facing him was a "Sea of Darkness," where ships supposedly melted in the equatorial regions, sea serpents flourished, and strange beasts sought to destroy any interloper.

To develop navigational and cartographic techniques, Henry established a community of scholars at Sagres, on the south coast of Portugal. He was responsible for the discovery of Madeira, the Azores, Cape Verde, Senegal, and Sierra Leone, and he provided the blueprint for continued exploration during the rest of the century. In 1482, Portuguese ships explored the mouth of the Congo, and in 1488 Bartholomeu Dias rounded the Cape of Good Hope. In 1497, Vasco da Gama reached Calicut (Kozhikode) on India's west coast, clearing the way for trade in spices, porcelain, silk, ivory, and slaves.

The Treaty of Tordesillas, negotiated by João II in 1494 for lands yet to be claimed in the western hemisphere, ensured Portugal's possession of Brazil, which the Portuguese didn't "discover" until 1500. Using the wealth of the whole empire, Manuel I ("The Fortunate"; reigned 1495–1521) inspired great monuments of art and architecture whose style now bears his name. His reign inspired Portugal's Golden Age. By 1521 the country had begun to tap into Brazil's natural resources and had broken Venice's spice-trade monopoly. As the first of the great maritime world empires, Portugal dominated access to the Indian Ocean.

João III (reigned 1521–57) ushered in the Jesuits and the Inquisition. His son, Sebastião, disappeared in battle in Morocco in 1578, leaving Portugal without an heir. Philip II of Spain claimed the Portuguese throne and began 60 years of Spanish domination. In the East, Dutch and English traders undermined Portugal's strength.

If there is one slice of Christendom, one portion of Europe which was made by the sea more than another, Portugal is that slice, that portion, that belt. Portugal was made by the Atlantic.

—Hilaire Belloc, *Places* (1942)

THE HOUSE OF BRAGANÇA   A nationalist revolution in 1640 brought a descendant of João I to the throne as João IV. That began the House of Bragança, which lasted into the 20th century, as well as a long series of revolutions and intrigues. João IV arranged an English alliance, arranging his daughter's marriage to Charles II. For her dowry, he "threw in" Bombay and Tangier. In 1668 Spain recognized Portugal's independence with the Treaty of Lisbon.

On All Saints' Day in 1755, a great earthquake destroyed virtually all of Lisbon. In 6 minutes, 15,000 people were killed, thousands of whom had been attending morning masses. The marquês de Pombal, adviser to King José (reigned 1750–77), later reconstructed Lisbon as a safer and more beautiful city. Pombal was an exponent of absolutism, and his expulsion of the Jesuits in 1759 earned him powerful enemies throughout Europe. He curbed the power of the Inquisition, and reorganized and expanded industry, agriculture, education, and the military. On the death of his patron, King José, he was exiled from court.

In 1793, Portugal joined a coalition with England and Spain against Napoléon. An insane queen, Maria I (reigned 1777–1816), and an exiled royal family facilitated an overthrow by a military junta. The Cortes was summoned, a constitution was drawn up, and Maria's son, João VI (reigned 1816–26), accepted the position of constitutional monarch in 1821. João's son, Pedro, declared independence for Brazil in 1822 and became a champion of liberalism in Portugal.

FROM REPUBLIC TO DICTATORSHIP   Between 1853 and 1908 republican movements assaulted the very existence of the monarchists. In 1908, Carlos I (reigned 1889–1908), "the painter king," and the crown prince were assassinated at praça do Comércio in Lisbon. Carlos's successor was overthrown in an outright revolution on October 5, 1910, ending the Portuguese monarchy and making the country a republic.

Instability was the watchword of the newly proclaimed republic, and revolutions and uprisings were a regular occurrence. Portugal's attempt to remain neutral in World War I failed when—influenced by its old ally, England—Portugal commandeered German ships in the Lisbon harbor. This action promptly brought a declaration of war from Germany, and Portugal entered World War I on the side of the Allies.

The republic's precarious foundations collapsed in 1926, when a military revolt established a dictatorship headed by Gomes da Costa. His successor, António de Carmona, remained president until 1951, but only as a figurehead. António de Oliveira Salazar became finance minister in 1928 and rescued the country from a morass of economic difficulties. He went on to become the first minister, acting as (but never officially becoming) head of state. He was declared premier of Portugal in 1932, and rewrote the Portuguese constitution along Fascist lines in 1933.

In World War II, Salazar asserted his country's neutrality, although he allowed British and American troops to establish bases in the Azores in 1943. After Carmona's death in 1951, Salazar became dictator, living more or less ascetically and suppressing all opposition. He worked in cooperation with his contemporary, the Spanish dictator Francisco Franco.

In 1955, Portugal joined the United Nations. Salazar suffered a stroke in 1968 and died in 1970. He is buried in the Panteão Nacional in Lisbon.

MODERN PORTUGAL WRESTLES WITH DEMOCRACY Dr. Marcelo Caetano replaced Salazar. Six years later, following discontent in the African colonies of Mozambique and Angola, revolution broke out. The dictatorship was overthrown on April 25, 1974, in a military coup dubbed the "flower revolution" because the soldiers wore red carnations instead of carrying guns. After the revolution, Portugal drifted into near anarchy. Finally, after several years of turmoil and the failures of 16 provisional governments from 1976 to 1983, a revised constitution came into force in the 1980s.

In 1976, Portugal loosened its grasp on its once-extensive territorial possessions. The Azores and Madeira gained partial autonomy, and Macau (which reverted to Chinese control in 1999) received broad autonomy. All the Portuguese territories in Africa—Angola, Cape Verde, Portuguese Guinea, Mozambique, and São Tome and Prîncipe (islands in the Gulf of Guinea)—became independent countries. Portugal also released the colony of East Timor, which Indonesia immediately seized.

From the time of the revolution until 1987, Portuguese governments rose and fell much too alarmingly for the country to maintain political stability. Moderates elected Gen. Ramalho Eanes as president in the wake of the revolution, and he was reelected in 1980. He brought the military under control, allaying fears of a right-wing coup to prevent a socialist takeover. However, Eanes appointed a socialist, Mário Soáres, prime minister three times.

In the 1985 elections the left-wing vote was divided three ways, and the Socialists lost their vanguard position to the Social Democratic Party. Their leader, Dr. Aníbal Cavaco Silva, was elected prime minister. In January 1986 Eanes was forced to resign the presidency. He was replaced by Soáres, the former Socialist prime minister, who became the first civilian president in 60 years.

Although his administration had its share of political scandal, President Soáres won a landslide victory in the January 1991 elections.

With the elections of 1995, constitutional limitations forced Soáres to step down. He was replaced by Jorge Sampaio, the former Socialist mayor of Lisbon. The Socialists currently remain a minority government, holding only 112 of 230 parliamentary seats.

In 1997, ugly headlines, perhaps prompted by the Nazi gold stories coming out of Switzerland, questioned Portugal's role in World War II. It was revealed that Portugal sold tungsten and other goods to Nazi Germany and profited greatly from its neutral status in the conflict. The German government paid with gold bullion looted from conquered countries and, it's suspected, from victims of the Holocaust.

The revelation of the Nazi gold has struck a sour note in Lisbon. After Switzerland, Portugal was the largest importer of the gold. Even though the country was officially neutral during the war, many government officials had Nazi sympathies. At the end of the war, the Allies demanded that Portugal return at least 44 tons of looted Nazi gold. Instead, Lisbon began to sell the bullion secretly through its colony in Macao. Much of this gold, sometimes marked with swastikas, went to China in the 1950s and 1960s.

Portugal took a major leap in 1999 it became part of the euro community, adapting a single currency along with other European nations such as Spain, Italy, Germany, and France.

We are starting to stop seeing ourselves as the really backward guy in Europe. We're not at the bottom any more. We don't see ourselves as a major player, but we're at the table and maybe we can provide the table where the players sit.
—Thomas Pereira, *The New York Times,* 1998)

3 Manuelino: Portugal's Unique Architectural Style

The style known as **Manueline or *Manuelino*** is unique to Portugal. It predominated between 1490 and 1520, and remains one of the most memorable art forms to have emerged from the country. It's named for Manuel I, who reigned from 1495 to 1521. When Dom Manuel I inaugurated the style, Manueline architecture was shockingly modern, a farsighted departure from the rigidity of medieval models. It originally decorated portals, porches, and interiors, mostly adorning old rather than new structures. The style marked a transition from the gothic to the Renaissance in Portugal.

Old-timers claimed that Manuelino, also called Atlantic Gothic, derived from the sea, although some modern-day observers see aspects of Salvador Dalí's surrealism in the striking juxtaposition of decorative themes from the farthest reaches of the Portuguese empire. Everything about Manueline art is a celebration of seafaring ways. In Manuelino works, Christian iconography combines with shells, ropes, branches of coral, heraldic coats of arms, religious symbols, and imaginative waterborne shapes, as well as with Moorish themes.

Many monuments throughout the country—notably the Monastery of Jerónimos in Belém, outside Lisbon—offer examples of this style. Others are in the Azores and Madeira. Sometimes Manuelino is combined with the famous tile panels, as in Sintra's National Palace. The first Manueline building in Portugal was the classic Church of Jesus at Setúbal, south of Lisbon. Large pillars in the interior twist in spirals to support a flamboyant ribbed ceiling.

Although it's mainly an architectural style, Manuelino affected other artistic fields as well. In sculpture, Manuelino was usually decorative. Employed over doorways, rose windows, balustrades, and lintels, it featured everything from a corncob to a stalk of cardoon. Manuelino also affected painting; brilliant gemlike colors characterize works influenced by the style. The best-known Manueline painter was Grão Vasco (also called Vasco Fernandes). His best-known works include several panels, now on exhibition in the Grão Vasco museum, that were originally intended for the Cathedral of Viseu. The most renowned of these panels are *Calvary* and *St. Peter,* both dating from 1530.

4 Portuguese Cuisine: Teeming with Seafood

In her *Invitation to Portugal,* Mary Jean Kempner got to the heart of the Portuguese diet: "The best Portuguese food is provincial, indigenous, eccentric, and proud—a reflection of the chauvinism of this complex people. It takes no sides, assumes no airs, makes no concessions or bows to Brillat-Savarin—and usually tastes wonderful."

DINING CUSTOMS & TAXES   Much Portuguese cooking is based on olive oil and the generous use of garlic. If you select anything prepared to order, you can request that it be *sem alho* (without garlic).

The Lady in the Tutti-Frutti Hat

She was called "The Brazilian Bombshell." In the 1940s, one critic labeled her Brazil's most famous export. But the great Carmen Miranda, the star of big Hollywood musicals in the 1940s and 1950s, was actually Portuguese. She was born Maria de Carmo Miranda da Cunha in 1909 in the little village of Marco de Cavavezes, in the north of Portugal.

Costumed garishly, with bowls of fruit perched on her head, she wriggled outrageously through kitschy numbers like "Tico Tico," in such 20th Century-Fox films as *Down Argentine Way* and *The Gang's All Here.* Although she appeared with a number of other stars, fans best remember her appearances with Cesar Romero and Alice Faye. Today, a whole new generation of young people is discovering the Latin bombshell as her old hits are revived on TV.

In 1911, she moved with her family to Rio de Janeiro, where in time she learned to make outrageous hats for wealthy customers. One of them asked her to sing at a party. With her sambas and tangos, she was an immediate hit. At age 19 she made her first record on the RCA Victor label. Called *Tai,* it sold a record-breaking (for the era) 35,000 copies. Her career was launched, eventually leading to 140 records and six films produced in Brazil.

The United States soon discovered her, and she was lured to Hollywood, where her career soared. By 1943, she (along with Barbara Stanwyck and Bing Crosby) was one of the highest-paid performers in the United States. Her act captured (and still does!) the fantasy of drag queens around the world. With her colored dresses, stylized bananas, turbans, outrageous platform shoes, dangling earrings, and shimmering dance steps, Carmen Miranda emerged as an ambassador of the Lusophone world like no star before or since.

Although a hit with American audiences, she did not always meet with approval in her native Latin world. Many Latin Americans objected to the stereotype she projected—that of an oversexed, vivacious, clownish cartoon of a Brazilian woman.

Regrettably, her career also degenerated into caricature. After a failed marriage and a severe bout of depression, she ended up making farcical appearances in the 1950s. She appeared on TV with Milton Berle, also dressed in Carmen Miranda drag. On August 5, 1955, she collapsed on the set of *The Jimmy Durante Show* and died of a heart attack shortly after.

Today, decades after her death, legions of impassioned fans keep alive the memory of the Portuguese-Brazilian legend. A biography, *Carmen Miranda,* by Cássio Emmanuel Barsante, was the result of 20 years of exhaustive research. A film was made of her life, *Bananas Is My Business.* Even the Film Forum in New York has honored her with retrospectives.

Coveted, adored, ridiculed, and eulogized, Carmen Miranda has been adopted as a Lusophone legend.

It's customary in most establishments to order soup (invariably a big bowl filled to the brim), followed by a fish and a meat course. Potatoes and rice are likely to accompany both the meat and the fish platters. In many restaurants, the chef features at least one *prato do dia*—a plate of the day. These dishes are prepared fresh that day and often are cheaper than the regular offerings.

Service is usually included in your restaurant bill, but it's customary to leave about 5% to 10% extra as a tip; 10% is usually de rigueur in first-class or deluxe restaurants. In addition, a 17$^{1}/_{2}$% IVA or value-added tax is added to restaurant bills, which means you'll be paying supplements on all your food and drink orders.

CUISINE *Couverts* are little appetizers, often brought to your table the moment you sit down. In many restaurants they are free; in others you will be charged extra. It's a good idea to ask your waiter about extra costs. Many restaurants charge for the bread and butter consumed and for the bits of cheese, country pâté, and olives that often go with them. In many places, the charge for these extras is per person. Remember: Not everything served at the beginning of the meal is free.

Another way to begin your repast is to select from *acepipes variados*, Portuguese hors d'oeuvres, which might include everything from swordfish to the inevitable olives and tuna. From the **soup** kitchen, the most popular selection is *caldo verde* ("green broth"). Made from cabbage, sausage, potatoes, and olive oil, it's common in the north. Another ubiquitous soup is *sopa alentejana,* simmered with garlic and bread, among other ingredients. Portuguese cooks wring every last morsel of nutrition from their fish, meat, and vegetables. The fishers make *sopa de mariscos* by boiling the shells of various shellfish, then richly flavoring the stock and lacing it with white wine.

The first main dish you're likely to encounter on any menu is **bacalhau,** or salted codfish, *o fiel amigo* (faithful friend) of the Portuguese. As you drive through fishing villages in the north, you'll see racks and racks of the fish drying in the sun. Bacalhau has literally saved thousands of Portuguese from starvation. Foreigners may not wax rhapsodic about bacalhau, although it's prepared in imaginative ways—reportedly one for every day of the year. Common ways of serving it include *bacalhau cozido* (boiled with such vegetables as carrots, cabbage, and spinach, then baked), *bacalhau* à *Bras* (fried in olive oil with onions and potatoes and flavored with garlic), *bacalhau* à *Gomes de Sá* (stewed with black olives, potatoes, and onions, then baked and topped with a sliced boiled egg), and *bacalhau no churrasco* (barbecued).

Aside from codfish, the classic national dish is **caldeirada,** the Portuguese version of bouillabaisse. Prepared at home, it's a pungent stew containing bits and pieces of the latest catch.

Next on the platter is the Portuguese **sardine,** which many gastronomes regard as elegant. Found off the Atlantic coasts of Iberia as well as France, these 6- to 8-inch long sardines also come from Setúbal. As you stroll through the alleys of the Alfama or pass along the main streets of small villages throughout Portugal, you'll sometimes see women kneeling in front of braziers on their front doorsteps and grilling the large sardines. Grilled, they're called *sardinhas assadas.*

Shellfish is one of the great delicacies of the Portuguese table. Its scarcity and the demand of foreign markets, however, have led to astronomical price tags. Visitors devour it and lament later when the bill is presented. The price of lobsters and crabs changes every day, depending on the market. On menus, you'll see the abbreviation *Preco V.,* meaning "variable price." When the waiter brings a shellfish dish to your table, always ask the price.

Many of these creatures from the deep, such as king-size crabs, are cooked and then displayed in restaurant windows. If you do decide to splurge, demand that you be served only fresh shellfish. You can be deceived, as can even the experts, but at least you'll have demanded that your fish be fresh and not left over from the previous day's window display.

When fresh, *santola* (crab) is a delicacy. It's often served stuffed (*santola recheada*), although this specialty may be too pungent for unaccustomed Western palates. *Amêijoas,* baby clams, are a reliable item. *Lagosta* is translated as lobster; in fact, it's a crayfish, best when served without adornment.

The variety of good-tasting, inexpensive **fish** includes *salmonette* (red mullet) from Setúbal, *robalo* (bass), *lenguado* (sole), and sweet-tasting *pescada* (hake). Less appealing to the average diner, but preferred by many discriminating palates, are *eiros* (eels), *polvo* (octopus), and *lampreas* (lampreys; a seasonal food in the northern Minho district).

Piri-piri is a sauce made of hot pepper from Angola. Jennings Parrott once wrote: "After tasting it you will understand why Angola wanted to get it out of the country." Unless you're extremely brave, consider ordering something else. Foreigners accustomed to hot, peppery food, however, might like it.

Porto residents are known as "**tripe** eaters." The local specialty is *dobrada,* tripe with beans, a favorite of workers. The *cozido á portuguesa* is another popular dish. This stew often features both beef and pork, along with fresh vegetables and sausages. The chief offering of the beer tavern is *bife na frigideira,* beef in mustard sauce, usually served piping hot in a brown ceramic dish with a fried egg on top. Thinly sliced *iscas* (calves' livers) are usually well prepared and sautéed with onion.

Portuguese **meat,** especially beef and veal, is less satisfying. The best meat in Portugal is *porco* (pork), usually tender and juicy. Especially good is *porco alentejano,* fried pork in a succulent sauce with baby clams, often cooked with herb-flavored onions and tomatoes. In the same province, *cabrito* (roast kid) is another treat, flavored with herbs and garlic. Chicken tends to be hit or miss, and is perhaps best when spit-roasted golden brown (*frango no espeto*). In season, game is good, especially *perdiz* (partridge) and *codorniz estufada* (pan-roasted quail).

Cheese (*queijo*) is usually eaten separately and not with fruit. The most common varieties of Portuguese cheese are made from sheep or goat's milk. A popular variety is *queijo da serra* (literally, cheese from the hills). Other well-liked cheeses are *queijo do Alentejo* and *queijo de Azeitao*. Many prefer *queijo Flamengo* (similar to Dutch Gouda).

Locked away in isolated convents and monasteries, Portuguese nuns and monks have created original sweet concoctions. Many of these **desserts** have been handed down over the years and are sold in little pastry shops throughout Portugal. In Lisbon, Porto, and a few other cities, you can visit a *salão de chá* (tea salon) at 4pm to sample these delicacies. Regrettably, too few restaurants feature regional desserts; many rely on caramel custard or fresh fruit.

The most typical dessert is *arroz doce,* cinnamon-flavored rice pudding. Flan, or caramel custard, appears on all menus. If you're in Portugal in summer, ask for a peach from Alcobaça. One of these juicy, succulent yellow fruits will spoil you forever for all other peaches. In a first-class restaurant, the waiter will go through an elaborate ritual of peeling it in front of you. Sintra is known for its strawberries, Setúbal for its orange groves, the Algarve for its almonds and figs, Elvas for its plums, the Azores for its pineapples, and Madeira for its passion fruit. Some people believe that if you eat too much of the latter, you'll go insane.

Portugal doesn't offer many egg dishes, except for omelettes. However, eggs are used extensively in many sweets. Although egg yolks cooked in sugar may not sound appealing, you may want to try some of the more original offerings. The best known are *ovos moles* (soft eggs sold in colorful barrels) that originate in Aveiro. From the same district capital comes *ovos de fio* (shirred eggs).

WINE   One of the joys of dining in Portugal is discovering the regional wines (see "The Best Wines" in chapter 1). With the exception of port and Madeira, they remain little known to much of the world.

Among the table wines, our personal favorites are from the mountainous wine district known as **Dão.** Its red wines are ruby colored, and their taste is often described as velvety; its white wines are light and delicate enough to accompany shellfish. From the sandy dunes of the **Colares** wine district, near Sintra, emerges a full-bodied wine made from Ramisco grapes. A Portuguese writer once noted that Colares wine has "a feminine complexion, but a virile energy."

The *vinhos verdes* (green wines) have many adherents. These light wines, low in alcohol content, come from the northwestern corner of Portugal, the **Minho** district. The wine is gaseous, because it's made from grapes that are not fully matured. Near Estoril, the **Carcavelos** district produces an esoteric wine commonly served as an apéritif or with dessert. As this wine mellows, its bouquet becomes more powerful. The **Bucelas** district, near Lisbon, makes a wine from the Arinto grape, among others. Its best-known wine is white, with a bit of an acid taste.

Port wine is produced on the arid slopes of the Douro. Only vineyards within this area are recognized as yielding genuine port. The wine is shipped from Portugal's second-largest city, Porto (Oporto, in English). Drunk in tulip-shaped glasses, port comes in many different colors and flavors. Pale dry port makes an ideal apéritif, and you can request it when you might normally order dry sherry. Ruby or tawny port is sweet or medium dry and usually drunk as an after-dessert liqueur. The most valuable ports are vintage and crusted. Crusted port does not mean vintage—rather, it takes its name from the decanting of its crust. Vintage port is the very best. In a decade, only 3 years may be declared vintage.

Port is blended to assure consistent taste. Matured in wooden casks, the wood ports are white, tawny, or ruby red. At first the wine is a deep ruby; it turns the color of straw as it ages.

Port wine "perpetuated and glorified the fame of Porto," as one citizen put it. The first foreigners won over by it were the English in the 17th century. More recently, however, the French have imported more of the wine than the British. The grapes are sometimes crushed by bare feet, but that shouldn't alarm you—the wine is purified before it's bottled.

Its greatest fame has passed, but **Madeira wine** remains popular. It was highly favored by the early American colonists. Made with grapes grown in volcanic soil, it's fortified with brandy.

The major types of Madeira are Sercial (dry, drunk as an apéritif), Malmsey (a dessert wine), and Boal (a heady wine used on many occasions, from a banquet following a hunt to a private tête-à-tête).

BEER   Beer (*cerveja*) is gaining new followers yearly. One of the best of the home brews is sold under the name Sagres, honoring the town in the Algarve that enjoyed associations with Henry the Navigator.

Index

FROMMER'S® COMPLETE TRAVEL GUIDES

Alaska
Amsterdam
Arizona
Atlanta
Australia
Austria
Bahamas
Barcelona, Madrid & Seville
Beijing
Belgium, Holland & Luxembourg
Bermuda
Boston
Budapest & the Best of Hungary
California
Canada
Cancún, Cozumel &
  the Yucatán
Cape Cod, Nantucket & Martha's Vineyard
Caribbean
Caribbean Cruises & Ports of Call
Caribbean Ports of Call
Carolinas & Georgia
Chicago
China
Colorado
Costa Rica
Denmark
Denver, Boulder & Colorado Springs
England
Europe
Florida
France
Germany
Greece
Greek Islands
Hawaii
Hong Kong
Honolulu, Waikiki & Oahu
Ireland
Israel
Italy
Jamaica & Barbados
Japan
Las Vegas
London
Los Angeles
Maryland & Delaware
Maui
Mexico
Miami & the Keys

Montana & Wyoming
Montréal & Québec City
Munich & the Bavarian Alps
Nashville & Memphis
Nepal
New England
New Mexico
New Orleans
New York City
Nova Scotia, New Brunswick &
  Prince Edward Island
Oregon
Paris
Philadelphia & the
  Amish Country
Portugal
Prague & the Best of the Czech Republic
Provence & the Riviera
Puerto Rico
Rome
San Antonio & Austin
San Diego
San Francisco
Santa Fe, Taos &
  Albuquerque
Scandinavia
Scotland
Seattle & Portland
Singapore & Malaysia
South Africa
Southeast Asia
South Pacific
Spain
Sweden
Switzerland
Thailand
Tokyo
Toronto
Tuscany & Umbria
USA
Utah
Vancouver & Victoria
Vermont, New Hampshire
  & Maine
Vienna & the Danube Valley
Virgin Islands
Virginia
Walt Disney World & Orlando
Washington, D.C.
Washington State

FROMMER'S® DOLLAR-A-DAY GUIDES

Australia from $50 a Day
California from $60 a Day
Caribbean from $70 a Day
England from $70 a Day
Europe from $60 a Day
Florida from $60 a Day

Hawaii from $70 a Day
Ireland from $50 a Day
Israel from $45 a Day
Italy from $70 a Day
London from $85 a Day
New York from $80 a Day

New Zealand from $50 a Day
Paris from $85 a Day
San Francisco from $60 a Day
Washington, D.C.,
  from $60 a Day

FROMMER'S® PORTABLE GUIDES

Acapulco, Ixtapa & Zihu-
  atanejo
Alaska Cruises & Ports of Call
Bahamas
Baja & Los Cabos
Berlin
California Wine Country
Charleston & Savannah
Chicago

Dublin
Hawaii: The Big Island
Las Vegas
London
Maine Coast
Maui
New Orleans
New York City
Paris

Puerto Vallarta, Manzanillo
  & Guadalajara
San Diego
San Francisco
Sydney
Tampa & St. Petersburg
Venice
Washington, D.C.

FROMMER'S® NATIONAL PARK GUIDES

Family Vacations in the
  National Parks
Grand Canyon

National Parks of the American West
Rocky Mountain

Yellowstone & Grand Teton
Yosemite & Sequoia/
  Kings Canyon
Zion & Bryce Canyon

FROMMER'S® GREAT OUTDOOR GUIDES

New England
Northern California

Southern California & Baja
Washington & Oregon

FROMMER'S® MEMORABLE WALKS

Chicago
London

New York
Paris

San Francisco
Washington D.C.

FROMMER'S® IRREVERENT GUIDES

Amsterdam
Boston
Chicago
Las Vegas

London
Los Angeles
Manhattan

New Orleans
Paris
San Francisco

Seattle & Portland
Vancouver
Walt Disney World
Washington, D.C.

FROMMER'S® BEST-LOVED DRIVING TOURS

America
Britain
California

Florida
France
Germany

Ireland
Italy
New England

Scotland
Spain
Western Europe

THE UNOFFICIAL GUIDES®

Bed & Breakfast in
New England
Bed & Breakfast in
the Northwest
Beyond Disney
Branson, Missouri
California with Kids
Chicago

Cruises
Disneyland
Florida with Kids
The Great Smoky &
Blue Ridge Moun-
tains
Inside Disney
Las Vegas

London
Miami & the Keys
Mini Las Vegas
Mini-Mickey
New Orleans
New York City
Paris
San Francisco

Skiing in the West
Walt Disney World
Walt Disney World
for Grown-ups
Walt Disney World
for Kids
Washington, D.C.

SPECIAL-INTEREST TITLES

Born to Shop: France
Born to Shop: Hong Kong
Born to Shop: Italy
Born to Shop: New York
Born to Shop: Paris
Frommer's Britain's Best Bike Rides
The Civil War Trust's Official Guide
to the Civil War Discovery Trail
Frommer's Caribbean Hideaways
Frommer's Europe's Greatest Driving Tours
Frommer's Food Lover's Companion to France
Frommer's Food Lover's Companion to Italy
Frommer's Gay & Lesbian Europe
Israel Past & Present
Monks' Guide to California

Monks' Guide to New York City
The Moon
New York City with Kids
Unforgettable Weekends
Outside Magazine's Guide
to Family Vacations
Places Rated Almanac
Retirement Places Rated
Road Atlas Britain
Road Atlas Europe
Washington, D.C., with Kids
Wonderful Weekends from Boston
Wonderful Weekends from New York City
Wonderful Weekends from San Francisco
Wonderful Weekends from Los Angeles

NOTES

NOTES